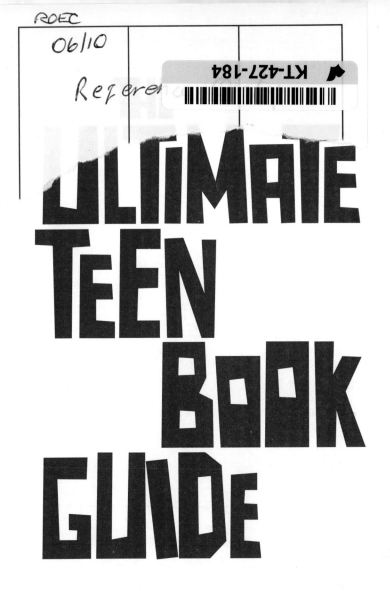

# ULTIMATE TEEN BOOK GUIDE

**Edited by Leonie Flynn,
Daniel Hahn & Susan Reuben**

A & C Black Publishers Ltd
36 Soho Square, London, W1D 3QY

www.acblack.com
www.ultimatebookguide.com

ISBN 978-1-4081-0437-8

A CIP catalogue for this book is available from the British Library.

This book is produced using paper that is made from wood grown in
managed, sustainable forests. It is natural, renewable and recyclable.
The logging and manufacturing processes conform to the
environmental regulations of the country of origin.

Printed and bound in Great Britain by the MPG Books Group.

# Contents

# Introduction
## by David Almond

Books. There they are lined up on shelves or stacked on a table. There they are wrapped in their jackets, lines of neat print on nicely bound pages. They look like such orderly, static things. Then you, the reader, come along. You open the book jacket, and it can be like opening the gates into an unknown city, or opening the lid on a treasure chest. You read the first word and you're off on a journey of exploration and discovery. When you find your own best books, which might be nothing like the best books for other readers, a kind of magic occurs. The language and the story and your own imagination blend and react and fizz with life and possibility. Sometimes it's like the book was written just for you, as if it's been waiting just for you, its perfect reader. It doesn't always happen, of course. Sometimes a book will fall flat for you. What's all the fuss about? you'll ask. But then you'll find another one that excites you, that speaks clearly to you, that sets up weird resonances in you. It goes on happening all through your life. It's happening to me now, this week, as I read Yukio Mishima's *The Sailor Who Fell from Grace with the Sea*. Why have I waited till now to read this wonderful book? Because I've been reading other books, of course.

Reading is a lifelong adventure. Mishima's is just the latest in a long line of books that have gripped me. Other recent highlights include Sarah Waters's hypnotic narratives, and the novels of Ha Jin. In my teenage years? Two out-of-print books: *The Grey Pilot* by Angus MacVicar that took me from my Tyneside home to flee through the Western Isles with Bonny Prince Charlie; and *The Adventures of Turkey* by Ray Harris that allowed me to share the adventures of a Huckleberry Finn-ish Australian lad. Then John Wyndham's marvellous *The Day of the Triffids* (UTBG 98) followed quickly by his *The Chrysalids* (UTBG 80), *The Midwich Cuckoos*, *The Kraken Wakes*, as I discovered the excitement of exploring an author's whole oeuvre for the first time. Next an astonishing book called *The Third Eye* by the ex-Tibetan monk T. Lobsang Rampa. For a time I felt that I was Lobsang in some weird way. Then he turned out to be a bloke from Essex. Did I care? Not at bit. His book had worked its magic on me. The 'hoax' was just another part of that magic. Then Hemingway came along. I remember pulling out a collection of his short stories from the library shelf, opening the book, and reading the first line of a story called 'A Clean, Well-Lighted Place', a story in which hardly anything seems to happen, but which set up resonances inside me that have never stopped. Then Stevie Smith's poems, and Sylvia Plath's, and Kafka, and so it went on and so it goes on.

The wonderful book that you're holding in your hands now is a kind of traveller's guide. It points you to many sidetracks and highlights and landmarks that other travellers have found worth visiting. Many of them will be as exciting to you as they were to the folk who recommend them. Others might not be. The world of books is almost limitless. As you travel, you'll hit upon your own best books, the books that have a particular fascination and excitement for you. You'll keep moving on, free to roam and explore and discover at will…

## On the second edition

It's wonderful to see this new updated edition of *The Ultimate Teen Book Guide*, and it's great that the book has been such a success. The last few years have been a time of real growth and development in the teenage book world. The 'teenage' and 'young adult' shelves in bookshops have lengthened and, like all good bookshelves, they contain a massive range: novels, short stories, poems, graphic novels, funny books, dark books, books that enlighten, books that disturb. Publishers have poured more resources into publishing and marketing books for the young. There are prizes targeted directly at books for teenagers – the Booktrust Teenage Prize in the UK, the Michael L. Printz Award in the USA. Of course, as this guide shows, teenage readers don't restrict themselves to books that are targeted simply at them. Good readers, like good books, evade easy classification. All this activity helps to blow apart the tired old pessimistic myths that 'kids don't read any more', that their minds have been stunned by screens and PlayStations and iPods, that they're the 'PlayStation generation'. Books matter as much as they ever did. There's a hunger for language and story. Writers for the young know that their readers respond with passion to the books they love and hate. It's great that the world at large is coming to recognise that teenagers form an engaged, informed and adventurous audience.

David Almond

# How to Use This Book

You'll find that the majority of this book is self-explanatory, and we hope you'll find it easy to use. But here's a bit of help just in case...

Most of *The Ultimate Teen Book Guide* is made up of book recommendations. Our team of contributors has recommended over 750 books for you, so there's bound to be stuff you'll like, whatever your tastes. The book recommendations are listed alphabetically by title, and they work like this:

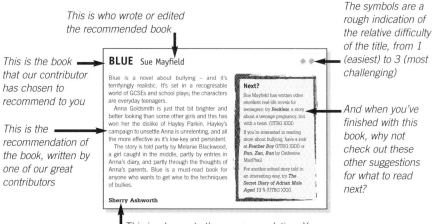

*This is who wrote or edited the recommended book*

*The symbols are a rough indication of the relative difficulty of the title, from 1 (easiest) to 3 (most challenging)*

*This is the book that our contributor has chosen to recommend to you*

*This is the recommendation of the book, written by one of our great contributors*

*And when you've finished with this book, why not check out these other suggestions for what to read next?*

**BLUE**  Sue Mayfield

Blue is a novel about bullying – and it's terrifyingly realistic. It's set in a recognisable world of GCSEs and school plays; the characters are everyday teenagers.

Anna Goldsmith is just that bit brighter and better looking than some other girls and this has won her the dislike of Hayley Parkin. Hayley's campaign to unsettle Anna is unrelenting, and all the more effective as it's low-key and persistent.

The story is told partly by Melanie Blackwood, a girl caught in the middle, partly by entries in Anna's diary, and partly through the thoughts of Anna's parents. Blue is a must-read book for anyone who wants to get wise to the techniques of bullies.

**Sherry Ashworth**

**Next?**

Sue Mayfield has written other excellent real-life novels for teenagers; try *Reckless*, a story about a teenage pregnancy, but with a twist. (UTBG XXX)

If you're interested in reading more about bullying, have a look at *Feather Boy* (UTBG XXX) or *Run, Zan, Run* by Catherine MacPhail.

For another school story told in an interesting way, try *The Secret Diary of Adrian Mole Aged 13 ¾* (UTBG XXX).

*This is who wrote the recommendation. You can find out more about them on pp. 454–465.*

The Next? box gives you ideas of what you might like to read once you've finished the recommended book. It might include other books by the same author, or books which are funny / exciting / inspiring / terrifying in the same way as the book you've just finished, or which deal with a similar subject in a different way. The letters UTBG mean the book to read next has a recommendation in *The Ultimate Teen Book Guide*, too, which you can find on the page indicated. For example, if you see...

For another powerful tale of fighting racial prejudice in the American South, read Harper Lee's classic *To Kill a Mockingbird*. (UTBG 398)

...then you can turn to p. 398 to read about *To Kill a Mockingbird* and decide whether it might be just the book for you.

There are also 13 short features on particular types of book – on fantasy, on historical fiction, on books about love and sex, on horror stories, on sci-fi, etc.

If you have a favourite genre of book, you'll find lots of good suggestions about what to read here. Or if you fancy trying something in a genre you don't know much about ('Hmm, I've never really read much fantasy…') the features will give you a good idea of where to start. You'll find a list of these features on p. 3.

The features are all written by experts in the field – usually people who write that kind of book themselves (Catherine Fisher on fantasy, Bali Rai on race, Kevin Brooks on stories about characters going off the rails, K.K. Beck on detective stories). If you want a short and snappy title to start off with – something not too challenging, that will grip you from the first line – Pete Johnson has some great suggestions for you on p. 448. And next to them you'll find lists of relevant titles, most of which you can read about elsewhere in *The Ultimate Teen Book Guide.*

Finally, you'll come across lists of winners of the biggest children's prizes going, and the editors' desert island dozen – the top twelve books in this guide that they would select if they had to make that very tough choice.

# About the Editors

**LEONIE FLYNN** lives and works in London. As librarian at a small prep school in St John's Wood she has ample opportunity to test books on willing minds and to disprove the theory that boys don't read. In her non-working hours she gardens on her roof terrace and peruses her ever-growing collection of cookery books. Sometimes she even reads for pleasure.

**DANIEL HAHN** has translated his fourth novel, published a literary guide to Britain and Ireland, and organised a national writing competition for secondary school students. Also this year he's written short biographies of the poets Shelley and Coleridge and judged the 2009 Booktrust Teenage Prize. He would have done much more had he not discovered Facebook. It's really a problem.

**SUSAN REUBEN** co-owns Baobab Editorial and Design Ltd (www.baobabltd.com), a company that carries out freelance work for children's publishers. She's also busy writing a children's book about food and religion, designed by her lovely friend and colleague, Sophie Pelham. Susan has a small son called Isaac and a baby called Emily, who drive her a bit crazy, but are very helpful when doing children's book research.

# 1066 AND ALL THAT
## W.C. Sellar and R.J. Yeatman

This wickedly funny skit on British history, written by a teacher and an ad man in 1930, is every bit as effective today. It's not just the puns on names, so bad they're positively brilliant (the Egberts, Ethelwulfs and Ethelbalds become Eggberd, Eggbreth and Eggfroth). It's not just the wry recognition that the grand old tales are mostly bunk, and the great old triumphs (a.k.a. the massacre of other civilisations) look a little different now. It's not even the fake test papers ('Why do you picture John of Gaunt as a rather emaciated grandee?'). No – it's the fact that truth really is stranger than fiction, and that this is the kind of 'nonsense' that actually makes more and more sense, the more you know about history.

**Sarah Gristwood**

### Next?
For the same offbeat humour, try *Down with Skool!* (UTBG 113). Or George Mikes's guide to being British, *How to Be an Alien*.

Watch *Blackadder* on TV, and read the scripts; they're hilarious, too.

John O'Farrell's *An Utterly Impartial History of Britain* is another slightly skewed look at history.

---

# THE 13½ LIVES OF CAPTAIN BLUEBEAR
## Walter Moers

### Next?
Someone else who writes extraordinary fantasy is Terry Pratchett; try *The Colour of Magic* and the rest of the books in the **Discworld** series. (UTBG 107)

*Life of Pi* is a strange story involving a lifeboat, a hyena, a monkey, a tiger and a boy. (UTBG 237)

Two lives encapsulated in one book? Try *Ethel and Ernest* by Raymond Briggs. (UTBG 123)

'People usually start life by being born. Not me, though.'

From the first page you are catapulted into a world that is just so refreshingly *different*: full of Hobgoblins, Minipirates, a headless Bollogg, a Bolloggless head, Nocturnomaths and many other weird and wonderful creatures (including, of course, blue bears).

This book covers Bluebear's adventures starting with his rescue from a dreaded whirlpool as a baby floating in a nutshell, through 12 eventful lives, to his final half-life 'at peace', and holds you entranced throughout.

Not only does this book cover many genres, from sci-fi to romance, but it also travels at such a fast-moving pace that you will sail through it like a jet-propelled sponge through a sea of information.

**Samuel Mortimer, age 11**

# 84 CHARING CROSS ROAD   Helene Hanff

*84 Charing Cross Road* is a collection of letters exchanged between down-to-earth New York writer Helene Hanff and London bookseller Frank Doel between 1949 and 1969. Miss Hanff, who had a passion for obscure and out-of-print books, initially wrote to Marks & Co, a bookshop at 84 Charing Cross Road, with a list of second-hand books she would like, if they could supply them, so long as they didn't cost more than $5 each. Mr Doel replied, saying that they had managed to find some of the items on her list and were sending them on, with an invoice.

Thus a wonderful correspondence and a 20-year association began. Rereading a few of the letters today I was captivated all over again – this is one of the most delightful books ever published.

**Michael Lawrence**

> **Next?**
> Helene Hanff's *The Duchess of Bloomsbury Street* is a sequel to *84 Charing Cross Road*. *Apple of My Eye* is about her native New York and *Q's Legacy* is about her education in English literature.
>
> Anne Fadiman's *Ex Libris* charts a lifelong love affair with books.
>
> Or for another feel-good story that's told in letters, try Mary Ann Shaffer's *The Guernsey Literary and Potato Peel Pie Society*.
>
> Or how about a detective story involving characters from other books? Try Jasper Fforde's *The Eyre Affair*. (UTBG 125)

# 87th PRECINCT series   Ed McBain

> **Next?**
> Start the series with *Cop Hater* or *The Mugger*.
>
> More detective stories? Try a British version with the **Inspector Morse** books, starting with *Last Bus to Woodstock* (UTBG 204), or the great Agatha Christie; try *Murder on the Orient Express*.
>
> One of the great classic detective writers is Dashiell Hammett; try *The Maltese Falcon*. (UTBG 253)

I wish I'd known Ed McBain's **87th Precinct** series of police procedural mysteries when I was a teenager. They're short and beautifully written with tight plots, sharp social detail and vivid characters. There are more than 50 of them, written over as many years. The quality dipped a little halfway through, but the late ones show him back on top form, which is unusual for a long-running series.

Each title is set in a fictionalised version of New York with multiple storylines and recurring characters like detectives Steve Carella, Meyer Meyer and Fat Ollie Weeks. They're carefully researched and shot through with world-weary attitude. Many crime writers have borrowed from McBain (as have loads of TV cop shows), but nobody did it better.

**David Belbin**

# ABARAT  Clive Barker

Candy Quackenbush lives in Chickentown, USA, the most boring place in the world. But Candy has a destiny. Fate is leading her to an extraordinary land: the Abarat, a great archipelago where each island sits at a different hour of the day. There she must fight the evil that is overtaking the islands, helped and hindered by a cast of bizarre allies and enemies.

Barker's imagination is astonishing, and he leaves most other writers in the dust. *Abarat* is a dizzying ride for children and adults alike. It is sometimes scary, sometimes funny, but always enthralling. If you thought fantasy was all about wizards and elves and fairies, read *Abarat* and find out what real fantasy feels like.

**Chris Wooding**

> **Next?**
> If you enjoyed this, read the sequels: *Abarat: Days of Magic, Nights of War* and *Abarat: Absolute Midnight.*
> Or look out for Henry Chancellor's *The Remarkable Adventures of Tom Scatterhorn.* The first book, *The Museum's Secret*, has Tom living in the most boring museum ever.
> Or for more creepiness, check out Neil Gaiman's *Coraline.* (UTBG 86)

# ABOUT A BOY  Nick Hornby

This should really be called *About Two Boys*: it tells of 36-year-old big-kid Will whose independent income means he doesn't have to work and he owns all the latest state-of-the-art gadgets; his main ambition is to sleep with as many women as possible, with no ties. Into this emotionally barren existence stumbles Marcus (12), a vegetarian hippy with the dress sense of a middle-aged geography teacher, thanks to his depressive mother. Bullied at school, he craves a father figure and imagines Will ideal for the role. Unfortunately, Will disagrees and resents this geeky kid impinging on his life. Somehow, though, their lives become intertwined, and each learns something important from the other: Will teaches Marcus about popular culture and how to be hip, and in turn learns from Marcus how to be grown-up. Witty, cynical and touching – seriously cool stuff!

**Catherine Robinson**

> **Next?**
> All Nick Hornby's books are worth reading. Try *High Fidelity* (UTBG 180) or *Fever Pitch* (UTBG 131). Or check out his book about the books he reads (and means to read, one day): *The Polysyllabic Spree*. Nick has also written specifically for teens: *Slam* (UTBG 367).
> *Man and Boy* by Tony Parsons also deals with a grown man facing up to his emotional responsibilities – sounds heavy, but it's oh so readable! (UTBG 254)

# THE ABSOLUTELY TRUE STORY OF A PART-TIME INDIAN   Sherman Alexie

**Next?**

Although this is the only book (so far!) by Alexie Sherman to be aimed directly at teen readers, you could try his others, all of which deal with life in or around the Spokane Indian Reservartion. You could start with **Reservation Blues**, about Thomas Builds-the-Fire and his efforts to start a band.

There's poverty, oppression and hope in Laure Halse Anderson's work. Try either **Speak**, about the aftermath of rape, or **Chains**.

Or for something else about Native Americans, try Tanya Landman's **Apache**. (UTBG 26)

Arnold Spirit lives on the Spokane Indian reservation with his alcoholic parents. The bright 14 year old has water on the brain, ten teeth too many, a lisp and a stutter. He's regularly beaten up by bullies and his family are so poor they often don't eat.

'Where is hope?' Arnold asks his teacher. 'Away from this sad, sad, sad reservation,' he is told.

And so, despite knowing he'll become an outcast in his own community, Arnold leaves to attend the rich white school miles away. His arrival is like a UFO landing.

This is the funniest, wisest book I've read in a long time. A complex story of identity. Truly beautiful.

**Jenny Downham**

# ACROSS THE NIGHTINGALE FLOOR
Lian Hearn

From its opening, in which a young boy wanders back from a carefree afternoon spent picking mushrooms to find a massacre going on in his village, this story grips the reader and refuses to let go until the very last word. It's an extraordinarily powerful and highly original fantasy packed with scenes of haunting beauty and horrifying violence.

In a world where warring clans vie for supremacy, while hidden strings are pulled by the mysterious Tribe, the boy Takeo must make a painful choice between power, love and revenge.

This is fantasy at its most sophisticated – but it's not for the squeamish.

**Brian Keaney**

**Next?**

Read the sequels: **Grass for His Pillow**, **Brilliance of the Moon** and **The Harsh Cry of the Heron**.

**Pagan's Crusade**, set at the time of the Crusades, is just as exciting – and gory! (UTBG 307)

For other books that delve into Japan and its history, try Chris Bradford's **Young Samurai** series, starting with **The Way of the Warrior**.

# THE ADVENTURES OF TOM SAWYER
## Mark Twain

**Next?**

Sequels? *Tom Sawyer Abroad* is a comic follow-up in which Tom, Huck and Jim go to Africa in a balloon. Or try *Tom Sawyer Detective*, an ingenious murder-mystery.

For something more challenging, try *Huckleberry Finn*. It's darker, tougher, but just about perfect. (UTBG 191)

Another journey afloat? Michael Morpurgo's *Alone on a Wide, Wide Sea*, or perhaps Yann Martel's ingenious *Life of Pi* (UTBG 237).

Mark Twain tells us early on that Tom Sawyer 'was not the model boy of the village. He knew the model boy very well, though, and loathed him', which tells us everything we need to know about his hero, a fast-talking boy who can even persuade his friends that painting a fence is fun. Destined always to disappoint his Aunt Polly, and never to live up to the standards of his half-brother Sid or his cousin Mary, he skips school to go swimming, fishing or to spend time with his friend Huckleberry Finn, son of the town drunkard. When Tom and Huck witness the aftermath of the murder of Horse Williams, their adventures suddenly become a lot less innocent.

The first of Twain's novels concerning these characters, this book captures exactly what it's like to be on the cusp of adulthood.

**Matt Thorne**

# AFTER THE FIRST DEATH  Robert Cormier

Terrorists have hijacked a school bus and are threatening to blow it up. Among them is Milo, a teenager who has known nothing but war and believes only in violence. Kate is the bus driver. Seventeen years old, she fears that she doesn't have the strength to look after the children suddenly in her charge. Unknown to both, the General in charge of the effort to resolve the crisis is sending his 15-year-old son to the terrorists as a show of good faith. All are, in their own ways, morally and politically innocent, and Cormier shows how innocence can have terrifying and deadly consequences.

Fifteen years after I first read it, *After the First Death* still has the power to make me gasp. Complex and multi-layered, it yields new meanings and fresh insights on every rereading.

**Graham Gardner**

**Next?**

All of Cormier's books are dark adventures in reading. Try *Heroes*. (UTBG 176)

Ian Bone's *The Song of an Innocent Bystander* is about a girl taken hostage. (UTBG 371)

*The Boys Who Saved the World* is a stunning look at how twisted school life can be, how we view terrorism and the power of belief. (UTBG 57)

# AIRBORN  Kenneth Oppel

**Next?**

There are two sequels: *Skybreaker*, in which Matt encounters a ghost ship and lost treasure and *Starclimber*, which takes Matt and Kate into space.

Or try the exciting *Mortal Engines*, which has cities on wheels and more airships! (UTBG 270)

Or for sailing ships, cutthroats and savages, try Paul Dowswell's *Powder Monkey*, Geraldine McCaughrean's *Plundering Paradise* or Elizabeth Laird's *Secrets of the Fearless*.

Matt Cruse is a cabin boy aboard the luxury airship, *Aurora*. Matt has called this airship home for three years. He has a good chance of being promoted to a junior sailmaker. That is, until a girl called Kate de Vries arrives on board. She is fired by a mysterious quest and they soon become good friends. However, one night, in the middle of the ocean, they are attacked by deadly Sky Pirates. The ship crash-lands on a strange island and Matt and Kate are thrown into adventures beyond imagining, and the mystery unfurls...

I loved this book. It was like a jigsaw, every page like a piece, fitting together to make a superb adventure that was full of humour.

**Edward Fry, age 12**

# AIRMAN  Eoin Colfer

Conor Broekhart is obsessed with flying. Not surprising for a boy who was born in a hot-air balloon. Set in the 19th century in an alternate reality in which the Irish Saltee Islands are a separate monarchy, this pacy adventure story follows Conor, a talented swordsman and budding aeronaut, as he becomes the victim of the treacherous Bonvilain, who covets the crown. Condemned to hard labour in the diamond mines on Little Saltee, and convinced that his parents and his beloved princess Isabella have turned their backs on him, Conor's spirit is almost broken. Almost. Will his survival instinct and his lifelong ambition to invent flying machines be enough to free him? Intrigue, romance, duels, a full cast of heroes and villains, not to mention lots of seemingly crazy inventions, are enough to keep anyone entertained. In one word – swashbuckling.

**Noga Applebaum**

**Next?**

No doubt one of the inspirations for *Airman* was Dumas's *The Count of Monte Cristo*. The classic tale of betrayal and revenge set in 19th-century France and Italy is one of the best-selling novels of all times.

Jules Verne, the father of science fiction, also wrote about new technological inventions. Try *Five Weeks in a Balloon*, about a group of explorers travelling across Africa.

Or for more classic swashbuckling: *The Prisoner of Zenda*. (UTBG 323)

# ALANNA, THE FIRST ADVENTURE
Tamora Pierce

**Next?**

This is the first part of the **Song of the Lioness** quartet. Alanna's quest to become a knight continues in **In the Hand of the Goddess**.

If you want a story where the heroine chooses to be a wizard, try **So You Want to Be a Wizard** by Diane Duane.

Alanna wants to be a knight, but is supposed to become a magician. Her twin brother Thom wants to be a magician, but is supposed to become a knight. So they decide to swap places. The only catch is that to become a knight Alanna has to pretend to be a boy. But keeping her true identity secret and dealing with the harsh routine of knightly training turn out to be the least of Alanna's problems – there's a conspiracy in the royal castle, and Alanna's friendship with Prince Jonathan is going to drag her into the middle of it! Alanna is one of the most likeable heroines you'll ever find in a story – good-hearted, adventurous, and brave.

**Benedict Jacka**

# AL CAPONE DOES MY SHIRTS
Gennifer Choldenko

Moose Flanagan's family move to Alcatraz where his dad is to be a guard of the infamous inmates at the famous prison there. Life is tough at first and his family are all so tied up with looking after the every need of his (probably autistic) sister that they've no time or energy left to give a thought to how Moose is settling in. Feeling angry, he goes out to find new friends and adventures of his own. This enjoyable and exciting insight into the imagined life and times of gangster Al Capone packs a huge emotional punch.

**Eileen Armstrong**

**Next?**

More Choldenko? There's a sequel, *Al Capone Shines My Shoes*, or try *Notes from a Liar and Her Dog*, which tells of a girl trying to come to terms with her adoption.

Theresa Breslin's *Prisoner in Alcatraz* offers another compelling insight into conditions in the infamous prison.

Other books bringing historical people and places to life include *Stratford Boys* by Jan Mark (playwright William Shakespeare), and *Fleshmarket* (surgeon Dr Knox) (UTBG 134).

# THE ALCHEMIST  Paulo Coelho

This is, on the face of it, a simple fable about Santiago, an Andalucian shepherd boy, and his search for treasure. But the more you read this wonderful story, the more you begin to see in its pages. The book describes Santiago's journey from Spain to Tangiers and on into the deserts of Egypt, where he meets the mysterious alchemist. With his mentor's help, Santiago begins to listen to The Soul Of The World and learns that the treasure he seeks is right under his nose.

This is a brilliant story that asks us to believe in our dreams and listen to our hearts. Coelho is a master storyteller and this is a masterful tale. Remember all that glitters is not gold and prepare to be enchanted. This novel really does live up to the hype.

**Bali Rai**

**Next?**

Paulo Coelho has written many other books about searching for meaning; try *The Pilgrimage*. Other stories to make you think? *Jonathan Livingston Seagull* (UTBG 216) or *Zen and the Art of Motorcycle Maintenance* by Robert M. Pirsig, which really does have something to do with both the things in its title.

For an accessible introduction to all things philosophical, try *Sophie's World*. (UTBG 372)

# THE ALCHEMIST'S APPRENTICE
## Kate Thompson

**Next?**

Go on to read more Kate Thompson – *The New Policeman* (UTBG 282) is a terrific exploration of Irish myth, or look out for *Annan Water*, a story of horses, love and growing up.

Or try Alan Garner's *The Owl Service* (which Kate Thompson herself has recommended on p. 306).

Or how about some Leon Garfield? Read *Smith* first.

Since his mother died, Jack has been apprenticed to a blacksmith. But – frankly – he's not very good at it. So one day, having crashed his master's cart, Jack decides to run away. He leaves London, heading south, and soon finds himself at the house of Jonathan Barnstable. Barnstable, it seems, is an alchemist, secretly working away at the mysteries of how to create gold...

And this Mr Barnstable – tall and extraordinary, with white hair and piercing blue eyes – invites Jack to be his apprentice. Under his guidance, Jack learns the secrets of the alchemist's art, and a lot more besides. But this is just the beginning of his adventure...

Full of 18th-century atmosphere, with a likeable hero in Jack and a fascinating character in the mysterious Barnstable, this is an enthralling read.

**Daniel Hahn**

# ALCHEMY  Margaret Mahy

Roland has it all – he's going out with the sexiest girl in the school, he's effortlessly clever, he's a natural leader. But then things start to go bizarrely awry – his teacher catches him shoplifting, and uses this knowledge to blackmail him into making friends with a girl in his class he normally wouldn't be seen dead talking to.

Then when Roland goes to the girl's house, he enters a disturbing world where nothing in the rooms ever changes, and there's a peculiar presence at the top of the stairs that definitely is not human.

*Alchemy* combines a seriously sinister story of the supernatural with all the normal concerns of a boy on the verge of adulthood – and the result is gripping, quite scary and life-affirming, too.

**Susan Reuben**

**Next?**
Another Margaret Mahy ghost story? Try *The Changeover* (UTBG 72). Or for a Mahy book set entirely in this world, try *Memory*.

Caroline Pitcher's *Mine* is also about a teenager encountering the supernatural. (UTBG 265)

For classic ghost stories, try those by Algernon Blackwood, or M.R. James (UTBG 153).

Another delicious romance set in a paranormal world is *Twilight*. (UTBG 411)

# THE ALCHEMYST: THE SECRETS OF THE IMMORTAL NICHOLAS FLAMEL
Michael Scott

**Next?**
Read the sequels: *The Magician, The Sorceress* and *The Necromancer*, with two more to come.

More engrossing fantasy? Try the **Bartimaeus** trilogy. (UTBG 21)

Dr Dee turns up in Livi Michael's *The Angel Stone* and also in the much tougher but wonderful *The House of Dr Dee* by Peter Ackroyd.

Nicholas Flamel and Dr John Dee were real people, and according to history they died a long time ago... But this book is set in the present day, and Flamel is alive and battling against the powers of the Elder Race of Gods and Goddesses who, assisted by an equally alive Dr Dee, are attempting to take over the world. He's also losing. His wife has been captured and Dee has stolen a book containing all Flamel's secrets. Cue two ordinary American kids. Except they're not ordinary after all...

This book is hard to categorise, not only because it skilfully blends the real and the imagined, but because it blurs the boundary between sci-fi and fantasy. The one certainty about it is that its author has spun a tale to hold the attention of even the most demanding reader.

**Ken Fisher**

# ALEX RIDER series   Anthony Horowitz

Alex Rider is certainly no ordinary teen. While most kids worry about spots and homework, Alex has a far bigger problem – how to save the world! At the mere age of 14 and after the mysterious death of his uncle, he is thrown into the dangerous world of espionage. He quickly learns the tricks of the trade and, armed with an array of amazing (and well-disguised) gadgets, he is sent on his first mission: to the lavish mansion of millionaire Herod Sayle.

If that whets your appetite, Alex's adventures don't stop there. They span over eight incredible books (to date), each more exciting and gripping than the last. The characters are unique and believable, the plots are inventive and the scrapes Alex gets himself into are absolutely brilliant. It's definitely recommendable to anyone with a thirst for espionage and mystery.

**Gareth Smith, age 14**

> **Next?**
> The **Alex Rider** books in sequence are: *Stormbreaker, Point Blanc, Skeleton Key, Eagle Strike, Scorpia, Ark Angel, Snakehead, Crocodile Tears*, with two more to come. Or try his paranormal series, **The Power of Five** (UTBG 327).
>
> Another teen with spies for parents can be found in Julia Golding's *Empty Quarter*.
>
> Look out for David Gilman's great series, **Danger Zone**. The first one is *The Devil's Breath* – no fancy gadgets, just great adventure. (UTBG 103)

# ALICE series   Susan Juby

As a big fan of novels featuring funny teen 'diarists', I was delighted to discover Susan Juby's **Alice** series. 16-year-old Alice MacLeod lives in tiny Smithers, British Colombia, where she has been home-schooled since the age of six, after having made the grave mistake of arriving at first grade dressed in a hobbit costume. When the first book in the series opens, Alice is going back to school hoping that this time she'll fit in. Alas, however, her hobbit days are still vividly remembered by her fellow Smithers teens, and Alice is not exactly welcomed with open arms. Between her thrift-shop wardrobe and her aspirations of becoming a novelist, Alice has no hope of ever going 'mainstream'!

Alice MacLeod is the Canadian answer to Sue Townsend's hilarious **Adrian Mole** series and, like Adrian, I hope she'll be around for a very long time.

**Meg Cabot**

> **Next?**
> The next books in the series are *I'm Alice (Beauty Queen?)*, *Miss Smithers*, *Alice MacLeod, Realist at Last, Alice in a Box* and *I'm Alice, I Think*.
>
> Try some of Meg Cabot's books – *Jinx*, about a girl who thinks she's bad luck, or *How to Be Popular*.
>
> Or, of course, try the very funny **Adrian Mole** series. (UTBG 347)

# ALL AMERICAN GIRL  Meg Cabot

Sam is an ordinary teenager who dresses in black and tries hard to be different. She has an extraordinary talent for drawing celebs, and loves music. She's also fallen for her perfect cheerleader older sister's boyfriend, Jack. Skiving her art class one day, Sam ends up saving the President's life outside a record shop, in a completely believable and inventive plot twist. Suddenly she is catapulted into fame and life in the spotlight as Teen Ambassador to the UN – which isn't as easy as it sounds. Luckily, the President's son David is on hand to help her out.

This is an exciting, action-packed rom-com with realistic and riveting Top Ten Lists of Everything separating the chapters, and a totally American flavour.

**David Gardner, age 16**

### Next?

There is a sequel: *All American Girl: Ready or Not*. All Cabot's books make ordinary characters take on extraordinary roles – a chaperone to a drop-dead-gorgeous star in *Teen Idol*, the heir to the throne in *The Princess Diaries* (UTBG 323), a ghosthunter in the **Mediator** series and a specially gifted crime solver in the **Missing** series.

*Jane Airhead* by Kaye Woodward is about *Jane Eyre* obsessed Charlotte and the trouble she gets into whilst trying to find a Mr Rochester for her mum.

Sophie McKenzie writes about life and love in the here and now – try *Six Steps to a Girl*.

## MICHAEL L. PRINZ AWARD WINNERS

*The Graveyard Book* by Neil Gaiman

*The White Darkness* by Geraldine McCaughrean

*American Born Chinese* by Gene Luen Yang

*Looking for Alaska* by John Green

*How I Live Now* by Meg Rosoff

*The First Part Last* by Angela Johnson

*Postcards From No Man's Land* by Aidan Chambers

*A Step From Heaven* by An Na

*Kit's Wildnerness* by David Almond

# ALL QUIET ON THE WESTERN FRONT

Erich Maria Remarque

**Next?**

For more fiction set during the First World War, try *Strange Meeting*, the story of an intense friendship set against the run-up to the fateful Somme offensive. (UTBG 380)

Robert Graves's *Goodbye to All That* is a riveting autobiography of life in the trenches.

For a female perspective on the war, see Vera Brittain's *Testament of Youth*.

First published in Germany in 1929, later banned by the Nazis, this is the classic anti-war novel. All the horrors of the trenches are here: the sheer terror of shellfire; rats; lice; hand-to-hand combat with sharpened spades; and how it feels to be trapped in a shell hole with a man you've just killed.

But it's as much about youth as it is about war. There's a lyrical quality to the quieter scenes, such as the visit to see a wounded comrade in hospital, melancholy trips home on leave, night swimming in a French river, and a brief romantic interlude with a local girl. The final chapter is as moving as it is cathartic: a fitting epitaph for a lost generation.

**Thomas Bloor**

# ALPHA FORCE series Chris Ryan

In *Rat Catcher*, the second in the **Alpha Force** series by Chris Ryan (a former member of the SAS) Alex, Li, Paula, Hex and Amber are undercover agents – the Alpha Squad. They are highly trained in martial arts, code breaking, computer hacking and many other skills. The team is on a mission in South America. They hear rumours about a man called the Rat Catcher who has been killing street kids in Ecuador, and decide to investigate. Are they sufficiently skilled to lead a successful operation? There are useful how-to-be-a-spy tips from Chris Ryan in the back of the book, and the gripping twists-and-turns narrative is always accompanied by a strong sense of realism.

**Next?**

The first **Alpha Force** story is *Survival*, or try Chris Ryan's other thrilling series, **Code Red**, starting with *Flash Flood*.

If you haven't read them already, get the **Alex Rider** books by Anthony Horowitz, starting with *Stormbreaker*. (UTBG 17)

Another set of great adventures is Robert Muchamore's **CHERUB** series, starting with *The Recruit*. (UTBG 73)

Or look out for Joe Craig's **Jimmy Coates** series, starting with *Killer*.

**Brenda Marshall**

# THE AMAZING ADVENTURES OF KAVALIER AND CLAY  Michael Chabon

Sammy Clay wakes one night to find that his cousin Joe Kavalier has escaped from Nazi-occupied Prague and has come to live in New York with him and his family. As the two cousins sit on the fire escape, smoking the remnants of a cigarette, Sammy realises that this cousin can help him achieve his dreams of fame and fortune. Joe is intrigued by Sammy's plan and hopes to make enough money to bring his family over to America, so the two create a partnership that will change their lives.

This is an enthralling read. The exciting plot, marvellous characters and exuberant writing make it impossible to put down. I immediately fell in love with the dashing, creative escape artist, Joe Kavalier. I often found myself becoming so absorbed in the book and its characters that I missed my subway stop...

**Next?**

More Michael Chabon? Start with *Wonder Boys* or *The Yiddish Policemen's Union*.

There are more superheroes than you ever imagined – some of them gay – in *Hero*. (UTBG 176)

If you haven't tried any of the recent graphic novels about superheroes, then the superb *Watchmen* by Alan Moore is a great place to start. (UTBG 426)

**Clio Contogenis, age 14**

# THE AMAZING MAURICE AND HIS EDUCATED RODENTS  Terry Pratchett

**Next?**

Terry Pratchett is one of the most prolific authors around. So, good news: there are LOTS of other **Discworld** books to read; try *The Colour of Magic* next. (UTBG 107)

For a fun-packed trip around our universe why not try *The Hitchhiker's Guide to the Galaxy*? (UTBG 182)

For different humour, try Philip Ridley's *Mighty Fizz Chilla*.

Smart, sharp, wickedly funny and very fast-moving sums up this, Terry Pratchett's first book for younger readers set in the fabulous Discworld universe. The story itself is loosely based on the traditional tale of 'The Pied Piper of Hamelin'. The Amazing Maurice of the title is a streetwise tomcat, always on the look-out for the perfect scam. He even has his own 'plague' of educated rats, who travel ahead to 'infest' a given town. Maurice then arrives with a 'stupid-looking kid' who plays a pipe, and the townspeople pay him to persuade the boy to charm the rats away. A nice little earner all round. It usually works like magic, but oh dear, not this time. Evil awaits...

**Chris d'Lacey**

# THE AMULET OF SAMARKAND
Jonathan Stroud

In a modern-day London controlled by magicians, Simon Lovelace is a master magician who possesses the fabled Amulet of Samarkand. Nathaniel is a young magician's apprentice with a rather precocious talent, who summons the querulous 5000-year-old Djinni, Bartimaeus, to relieve him of it. What starts out as a smallish act of revenge eventually leads to a largish web of intrigue, murder and rebellion. The plot is thrilling enough, but much of the story (including hilarious footnotes) is told by Bartimaeus himself in such a quirky and cranky fashion that it makes it very hard indeed to put down. In fact, I challenge you not to want to read straight through all three books (this is the first of a trilogy) without stopping.

**Chris d'Lacey**

**Next?**

The Golem's Eye and Ptolemy's Gate complete the **Bartimaeus** trilogy. Look out, too, for his latest, The Heroes of the Valley (UTBG 177), about a boy who one day plays a practical joke – one that seriously backfires and wakes an ancient blood feud.

Or take a sideways step into high fantasy with **Sabriel**. (UTBG 339)

More magicians? Try **The Alchemist** (UTBG 15) or Trudi Canavan's **Black Magician** trilogy (UTBG 45).

# THE ANARCHIST'S ANGEL  Gareth Thompson

It's not easy being Samson Ashburner. His real troubles started with a party game – a party game called Death in the Barley – that went horribly wrong, and left his face badly scarred. Now, years later, brooding and self-conscious, without friends and constantly battling with his mother (the T-shirts he wears to annoy her made me laugh), Samson spends most of his time sitting darkly in the wood, alone in his grandfather's old charcoal-burner's hut. Alone, that is, apart from 'Angel'. Maybe she will be his friend, and his ally in the fight against the developers who want to take his wood from him? But things are not that simple. Angel herself is a more complex character than Samson first imagined. An engaging story (and very pleasingly resolved, though I do wonder about that final chapter), well told with a couple of lovely strong characters at its heart.

**Daniel Hahn**

**Next?**

More Gareth Thompson: Great Harlequin Grim or Sunshine to the Sunless.

In Benjamin Zaphaniah's Face, Martin learns to deal with the consequences of a terrible accident that has left him badly scarred.

OK, Carl Hiaasen's books are nothing like this. But for a different take on the theme of struggling against the eco-threats of corporate development, try **Hoot**. (UTBG 186)

# ANGELA'S ASHES
## Frank McCourt

**Next?**

There are plenty of other Irish coming-of-age stories to get your teeth into. *Paddy Clarke Ha Ha Ha* is another book to make you laugh and cry. (UTBG 307)

Or try *Twenty Years A-Growing* by Maurice O'Sullivan, and *Reading in the Dark* by Seamus Deane. Or *The Glass Castle*, in which Jeanette Walls tells the story of her unique, terrifying and yet exhilarating childhood.

And look out for the next two volumes of Frank McCourt's memoir: *'Tis* and *Teacher Man*.

When Frank McCourt was four years old, his parents took him back from America to live in Ireland. You might think that the story of his childhood, from poverty in New York to absolute poverty in the back lanes of rain-sodden Limerick, would make for depressing reading. In fact, due to the beauty of the writing and the wry humour that worms its way through even the bleakest of scenarios, it's a wonderful, life-enhancing read. Although many of the characters in the book are not so lucky, Frank's is a story of survival of body and spirit against all the odds. A deeply moving, powerful and unforgettable book.

**Malachy Doyle**

# THE ANGEL COLLECTOR Bali Rai

This straightforward, gripping thriller sees Jit, a stubborn and determined boy with a high IQ, tormented by the disappearance of his friend Sophie at a music festival eight months previously. There are other suspicious factors in the mix, such as the presence at the festival of a strange cult, led by a man called Shining Moon, as well as the fact that other girls have disappeared. A serial killer could be on the loose, but the truth is more shocking than Jit can imagine.

The book delivers in terms of tension, but its main strength is the complex and well-drawn relationships between the different characters, particularly the developing friendship between Jit and Sophie's best mate, Jenna.

**Narinder Dhami**

**Next?**

There are some great books in which the creepiness of cults features: try Robert Swindells's *The Abomination*, Judy Waite's *Forbidden*, Celia Rees's *The Stone Testament* and Sarah Singleton's *The Amethyst Child*.

Bali Rai is always worth reading. Try something very modern – *The Crew*. Or look for his *City of Ghosts*, which ranges from the India of the Amritsar massacre to the Europe of the First World War.

There's another disappearance – and a shocking twist – in Bernard Ashley's taut thriller, *Solitaire*.

# THE ANGEL FACTORY  Terence Blacker

**Next?**

Try another Terence Blacker. *Boy2Girl* (UTBG 54) is about a boy who has to pretend to be a girl, and *ParentSwap* is about a boy so unhappy with his parents he's willing to try different ones – perfect ones. Or are they...?

Sophie McKenzie's *Girl, Missing* is about a girl who finds her parents might not be quite who they say they are. (UTBG 156)

Or try Catherine Forde's *Tug of War*, about a girl who has to choose between her real, but hopeless, mother, and the woman who nurtured her.

Everything is just a little bit too perfect for Thomas Wisdom – until he discovers his family's secret and knows that life will never be the same again. The repercussions of this discovery – which concerns his sister's and parents' true identities – go far beyond Thomas's own home. Soon, Thomas finds himself in terrible danger, with some big moral choices to make.

Terence Blacker is a great writer, and though this book has its limits – the ending seems a bit easy and the main character feels older than 12 – *The Angel Factory* is clever, sinister, and compelling, full of deft characterisation and slow-burning suspense.

**Sophie McKenzie**

# ANGUS, THONGS AND FULL-FRONTAL SNOGGING  Louise Rennison

I read this book when I was tired and fed up. I bought it at a station bookstall to read on the train. Three minutes later, the train was clattering out of London, and I was already smiling. Two hours later, when I arrived back home, I was grinning from ear to ear. It's about the daily life of Georgia Nicolson (a lovable teenage rogue), her cat Angus and the human males in her universe who offer much in the way of aggravation.

One of Georgia's many issues is: if she ever gets up close and personal with the boy of her dreams, how will she cope with the challenging business of snogging? Luckily for Georgia, there's a boy in the neighbourhood who's prepared to give girls private lessons in the sacred art. Sheer entertainment from cover to cover. Laughs guaranteed.

**Sue Limb**

**Next?**

Next in the series is *It's OK, I'm Wearing Really Big Knickers!*, and there are lots more after that.

Ros Asquith also writes about the perils of boys (and girls) in *Love, Fifteen* (UTBG 244) and *I Was a Teenage Worrier* (UTBG 209).

A slightly more serious take on the whole kissing thing happens in *The Serious Kiss*. (UTBG 354)

# ANIMAL FARM George Orwell

The animals at Manor Farm are unhappy with their lot: their drunken master is letting the farm go to ruin and they're all starving, so they stage a revolution to take over. To begin with everything seems rosy – the animals all work overtime, and everyone's belly is full of food. But it doesn't take long for the pigs to decide that because of their intelligence, they are superior to the stupid chickens and the workhorse, Boxer.

A simple animal story? Yes, but this is also an allegory of the Russian Revolution and the society it created. As the pigs famously say: 'All animals are equal, but some animals are more equal than others'. This is a rare kind of book that works as both a political satire and as a great read.

**Julia Bell**

> **Next?**
>
> Orwell will make you think about the world. Try the equally alarming political satire, *Nineteen Eighty-Four*. (UTBG 284)
>
> For a dystopian world that's real, try *One Day in the Life of Ivan Denisovich*. (UTBG 293)
>
> Sometimes it's easier to see something clearly by stepping aside from it. For instance, mice in a concentration camp. To some, the Holocaust may not seem a suitable subject for comics, but the allegory *Maus* proves them wrong. (UTBG 258)

# ANITA AND ME Meera Syal

Meena is nine and growing up fast. She lives with her Punjabi family in a small, otherwise all-white, mining village on the edge of Wolverhampton. She longs to be someone, to run with the pack and be accepted – not because of her colour, but because she wants to be seen as an equal among her peer group. She lies and steals – and idolises the feisty, brassy, blonde Anita, whom Meena's parents worry is leading her astray.

At first, despite their Indian dress, food and Diwali celebrations, Meena and her family seem to fit into the village. But in one searing moment the scales fall from her eyes when Sam Lowbridge, the Bad Boy of the village whom she has always secretly admired, sneers about 'darkies' and 'wogs'. Nothing will feel the same again.

**Jamila Gavin**

> **Next?**
>
> Another Meera Syal? Try *Life Isn't All Ha Ha Hee Hee*: three friends, three weddings, three stories.
>
> Nikita Lalwani's *Gifted* is the story of a young maths prodigy who is also Hindu and growing up in the United Kingdom.
>
> Randa Abdel-Fattah also writes about fitting in. Try *Ten Things I Hate About Me* and *Does My Head Look Big in This?* (UTBG 112)

# ANNA KARENINA  Leo Tolstoy

**Next?**

If this has given you a taste for huge, heart-rending novels, try Tolstoy's epic, *War and Peace* (UTBG 423), or *Dr Zhivago* (UTBG 115) by Boris Pasternak.

There's lots of doomed love from French novelists, too – try Gustave Flaubert's unbeatable *Madame Bovary*.

Or for something epic and English, try George Eliot's *Middlemarch*, a magnificent novel of Victorian society, featuring unforgettable characters.

I first read *Anna Karenina* when I was 13 and although it is a very long book with a complicated plot, I was transfixed by it. I think it is the best story about the different kinds of love between men and women that has ever been written – and when I was 13, this was a subject that fascinated me. Anna herself is a real, living woman, with a real woman's virtues and failings, and her life forms the main thread of the narrative. But through the other characters, the book also gives us a living picture of a society quite different from ours that miraculously becomes as real to us as our own.

**Nina Bawden**

# THE ANT COLONY  Jenny Valentine

This book is fantastic – I couldn't put it down. It is a contemporary novel about 15-year-old runaway, Sam, who hopes he can forget his past and disappear, somewhere in deepest London. There he meets ten-year-old Bohemia, his unlikely saviour. Bohemia has enough problems of her own, but despite Sam's attempts to remain 'alone', Bohemia makes it her business to get to know him.

What makes this story so special is the author's brilliant eye for choosing the perfect detail to help us really know the people and places, or feel the atmosphere. She draws you in and you cannot help but grow to love the quirky, flawed characters that inhabit 33 Georgiana Street. As the story of Sam and Bohemia unfolds, you discover the real secrets about their lives. The climax is superb. If you ever thought of running away from your troubles, you should read this book.

**Next?**

More Jenny Valentine? Try *Finding Violet Park* (UTBG 132) or *Broken Soup* (UTBG 63), though all her books are brilliant and very real.

There are a lot of books about people running away from something or someone – that 'someone' often being themselves. One fast-paced option is Julia Donaldson's *Running on the Cracks*.

In Kate Thompson's *Creature of the Night*, Bobby's mum is running away, taking her family with her, but is the country any safer than the city?

**Judi James**

# ANTHEM FOR DOOMED YOUTH
### edited by Jon Stallworthy

'Too terrible to remember, too important to forget', the poetry of the the First World War never fails to stir up a yearning outrage that such things happened, were allowed to happen. The 12 poets included here are both the chroniclers of war and its casualties.

Starting with Brooke's romantic idealism, progressing to Sassoon's savage, bitter railing, the book pays homage to less well-known poets, too, with biographies and portraits, photographs of the battlefields and reproductions of the manuscripts. But it has nothing of the 'school project' about it. It's a window on the senselessness and horror of war. And it bites at the heart like the rat in Rosenburg's 'Break of Day in the Trenches', scurrying through the mud to feast on the dead.

**Geraldine McCaughrean**

**Next?**

*Regeneration* is a fictional account of Sassoon and Owen's time at a hospital for the 'mentally unstable'. (UTBG 330)

One of the most famous war novels of recent years is *Birdsong*. (UTBG 44)

Field Marshall Lord Wavell assembled an anthology of all the poems he memorised over the course of his life – it's called *Other Men's Flowers*.

# APACHE Tanya Landman

**Next?**

More Tanya Landman? *Aztec: The Goldsmith's Daughter* is the thrilling tale of Itacate and her struggle to deny her destiny, or look out for her **Poppy Fields** mysteries.

*The Absolutely True Diary of a Part-Time Indian* by Sherman Alexie is about a boy taken from the Spokane Indian Reservation to go to an all-white school. (UTBG 11)

For another book that immerses you in a different culture while keeping you on-the-edge-of-the-seat thrilled, read Lian Hearn's *Across the Nightingale Floor*. (UTBG 11)

Siki is bereft when her younger brother is killed by Mexicans. Horrified by his brutal death, she vows to avenge his murder and forsakes her life as a woman of the Apache tribe for that of a warrior.

Siki's considerable courage and resourcefulness is called upon, as she attempts to prove herself to the men of her tribe, particularly the powerful, wise warrior, Golahka, with whom she feels a strong connection. As she pursues her brother's killers, Siki discovers things about herself and her family, which change her for ever.

This beautifully written story of Siki's journey from girl to woman and Apache warrior gives a fascinating portrayal of Native American life, which will stay with you long after reading.

**Rebecca Wilkie**

# APOCALYPSE Tim Bowler

When Kit and his family survive a dramatic boating accident, they are lucky to get washed up on a small island. Unfortunately it doesn't provide the sanctuary they need. The inhabitants are openly hostile and they soon realise their lives are in great danger. What is more disturbing is that Kit starts to notice the presence of a strange, naked man with a birthmark on his face, just like his. In his ensuing struggle to stay alive and make sense of what is happening around him, Kit finds himself dealing with far more than he'd bargained for.

If you enjoy books that are rich in atmosphere, with nail-biting plots, you will love *Apocalypse*. Tim Bowler has written a wonderful, haunting book that kept me on the edge of my seat as events careered towards its thrilling conclusion.

**Susila Baybars**

> **Next?**
>
> Tim Bowler's books are all edgy; try *Stormchasers*, about a boy trying to save his kidnapped sister, or *River Boy*. (UTBG 332)
>
> *Darkhenge* by Catherine Fisher is a tense adventure about the blurring of the real and the imagined.
>
> Or look for Lucy Christopher's *Stolen*, about a kidnapped girl struggling against her captor and the barren Australian desert.

# ARCHER'S GOON Diana Wynne Jones

> **Next?**
>
> Other titles by Diana Wynne Jones include *Howl's Moving Castle* (UTBG 191), *Fire and Hemlock* (UTBG 132), and *Eight Days of Luke*.
>
> Another book that is all about words is Frances Hardinge's *Fly by Night*. (UTBG 137)
>
> For a more serious magic book, read Michael Lawrence's **The Aldous Lexicon** trilogy, starting with *A Crack in the Line*, or try the wonderful stories in Neil Gaiman's *M Is for Magic* (UTBG266).

Archer sends his goon to collect the two thousand that Quentin Sykes owes him. Only the 'two thousand' are words, not money, and Sykes is an English lecturer and writer. His children, Howard and Anthea (known universally as Awful), become fascinated by the Goon and by what on earth their father is doing for Archer.

Gradually, we discover that the town in which the Sykes family live is governed by seven megalomaniac wizard siblings, two of whom are women. Archer is one of this family, but who is his goon and what has happened to the youngest brother, Venturus?

The complex plot gets weirder and weirder towards the end – only Diana Wynne Jones could carry this off!

**Mary Hoffman**

# ARE YOU DAVE GORMAN?
## Dave Gorman and Danny Wallace

Dave and Danny are flatmates who, with too much time on their hands and alcohol in their systems, set out to find 54 other people called Dave Gorman (that's one for every card in a pack including the jokers but not the card explaining the rules of bridge).

Danny's reluctance to get involved in this adventure is clear from the start and increases as his relationship with his girlfriend suffers and he and Dave clock up some 25,000 miles of travelling. In this great book, Dave's bizarre dedication to his ridiculous task is matched only by the bemusement of the other Dave Gormans he meets.

**Anthony Reuben**

### Next?

Dave Gorman's *Googlewhack Adventure* is different because Gorman spends the first half of it trying to avoid getting involved in another bet on the grounds that he's too old for that sort of thing and wants to write a novel instead.

*Frost on My Moustache* by Tim Moore is another hilarious tale of unheroic travelling. (UTBG 149)

Another random quest? Try Joseph O'Connor's *Sweet Liberty*, in which he tries to visit every 'Dublin' in America.

# ARE YOU EXPERIENCED?
## William Sutcliffe

### Next?

Paranoia among narrators kept William Sutcliffe going for three novels: try the extremely funny *New Boy* (UTBG 279), his first, or his look at family in *Whatever Makes You Happy*.

Alex Garland's *The Beach* is another captivating book of adventuring abroad. (UTBG 35)

There's more backpacking in *Lone in Luka* by Gill Harvey, which tells of a gap-year love affair, and try *I Is Someone Else* by Patrick Cooper.

When Dave and his girlfriend Liz can't manage to adjust their seatbacks on the flight to India, you know the holiday that follows won't all be plain sailing. (And this is only on the first page of the novel.) The ideals that they set out with prove not to be worth much, and the realities all too real for these cushy teens. Dave's naïve, deadpan narrative will have you shaking with laughter and wondering why any of us bother to get out of bed in the morning, let alone try anything ambitious like travelling around the world.

If you are contemplating travel in your gap year, read this book. If you simply feel your horizons need widening, read it, too. You'll realise you're not as inadequate as you thought.

**Jon Appleton**

# ARTEMIS FOWL    Eoin Colfer

**Next?**

The sequels are: *The Arctic Incident*, *The Eternity Code*, *The Opal Deception*, *The Lost Colony* and *The Time Paradox*.

*Faerie Wars* by Herbie Brennan is a more serious take on fairies.

Or for something else action packed, try Robert Muchamore's thrilling **CHERUB** series. (UTBG 73)

*Artemis Fowl* is one of those books that is able to combine magic, adventure and humour into one roller-coaster read. Artemis Fowl – a 12-year-old boy with a girl's name! – is on a quest to find fairy gold. He plans to kidnap Captain Holly Short of the LEPrecon unit and get the gold as ransom. But he doesn't realise what he's getting into… From Bio-bombs to tri-barrelled blasters, Artemis is in great danger.

You'll meet many interesting and hilarious characters: Mulch Diggums, a smelly dwarf on the run from the authorities; 20-foot trolls with the capacity to kill anything they think is edible; and one of my favourites, Artemis's bodyguard, Butler. Eoin Colfer keeps you spellbound and even manages to involve the reader in a bit of code breaking. Intrigued? Well, there is only one way to find out more… Read the book!

**Benjamin Cuffin-Munday, age 11**

# THE ASTONISHING LIFE OF OCTAVIAN NOTHING, TRAITOR TO THE NATION VOLUME ONE: THE POX PARTY    M.T. Anderson

This is a disturbing book set during the first days of the American Revolution. Octavian and his mother are African slaves owned by a group of free-thinking scientists and scholars. They are treated like royalty, but Octavian must weigh his food and faeces; in truth, he's just a scientific experiment to his owners. When a harsh new benefactor takes control, the experiment takes a dark turn, and Octavian's polite, well-reasoned narrative voice goes silent…

The history in the book is very accurate, but there are added twists that give it a fantasy flavour. Besides fascinating characters and a page-turning plot, the story is chock full of ideas about human rights, freedom and the fuzziness of right and wrong. It's not an easy read and it's long. Give it a chance, though, and you'll never forget it.

**Next?**

If it's the disturbing twists and provocative style you like, read more M.T. Anderson, especially *Feed* (UTBG 131) and *Thirsty*.

Another heartrending read? Daniel Keyes's *Flowers for Algernon*. (UTBG 136)

For another satire, try *Gulliver's Travels* by Jonathan Swift.

**Alicia Anderson**

# ATONEMENT   Ian McEwan

### Next?

None of Ian McEwan's books are easy reads, they're too unsettling for that, but you might want to try two others he's written: *The Cement Garden* (UTBG 71) and *On Chesil Beach*, which is a novella also on the theme of misunderstanding.

A hilarious take on someone seeing something they shouldn't have and misinterpreting it can be found in *Cold Comfort Farm*. (UTBG 83)

Another story about growing up, war and loss is Mary Lawson's *The Other Side of the Bridge*; read it and be prepared to cry.

I guess I started reading 'grown-up' fiction when I had gone through my own stack of books and the library was closed. I picked up something my mother had left on the coffee table and discovered a new world, complete with naughty bits. I was hooked.

*Atonement* is a novel I would have gobbled up back then. The story starts in 1935 when 13-year-old Briony witnesses a moment that she's not quite old enough to understand, between her older sister and a young man. Her interpretation of this moment leads us into a world of secrets, lies and unbearable damage. The book spans a lifetime and the ending is one you'll probably read at least twice.

**Sara Nickerson**

# AT SWIM-TWO-BIRDS   Flann O'Brien

I first read this as an undergraduate and even now it can reduce me to tears of mirth. The book is a brilliant farce, satire and send-up of different aspects of Irish life, including the Catholic Church and Celtic heroes... But it's also poking fun at literature, and in particular the novel. The narrator believes that stories should have several beginnings and endings and sets out to write such a book. The descriptions of lodging with his hideous uncle and his drunken friends are hilarious.

This book is full of crazy fantasy and characters such as the Pooka, the Good Fairy and Orlick Trellis. It's a sort of Celtic Goon humour. Not for the faint-hearted but very rewarding.

### Next?

Flann O'Brien's *The Poor Mouth* is another satire on Irish life.

Or read *The Crock of Gold* by James Stephens, another Celtic fantasy and satire.

Or if you're feeling especially adventurous, try *Finnegans Wake* by James Joyce, or his easier (and brilliant) *Portrait of the Artist as a Young Man*.

Or for another book that can make you cry from laughter, try Douglas Adams's *The Hitchhiker's Guide to the Galaxy* and its sequels. (UTBG 182)

**Anne Flaherty**

# AT THE SIGN OF THE SUGARED PLUM

## Mary Hooper

Summer 1665, and Hannah journeys to London to work in her sister's confectionery shop, The Sugared Plum. Plague threatens the city so she never receives the letter forbidding her visit, and once there, she cannot return. 'At home in Chertsey, life had been peaceful... Here, there was a bitter, heart-stopping danger in each day.' As more people die, the bustling city that first intoxicated Hannah becomes increasingly gruesome, and the sisters are forced into action to save just one life from the carnage.

It is the details – of clothes, smells, foods, plague symptoms (nasty!), mass burials – that bring this novel to life. Hannah's curious viewpoint really draws you into this absorbing historical story, and parts of her plague-ridden London are recognisable today.

**Helen Simmons**

### Next?

More Hannah? Read *Petals from the Ashes* or try a different heroine in Mary's **At the House of the Magician** trilogy.

If you like historical fiction, *No Shame, No Fear* by Ann Turnbull is well worth a read; set in the 17th century, it follows the fate of two lovers divided by religion. (UTBG 286)

*A Parcel of Patterns* by Jill Paton Walsh is another gripping novel about the plague, based on the true story of the village of Eyam, where villagers imposed quarantine on themselves to stop disease spreading.

## The Ultimate Teen Book List

## CARNEGIE MEDAL WINNERS

2009    **Bog Child** (p. 51)

2008    **Here Lies Arthur** (p. 175)

2007    **Just in Case** (p. 220)

2005    **Tamar** (p. 388)

2004    **Millions** (p. 264)

2003    **A Gathering Light** (p. 151)

2002    **Ruby Holler** (p. 337)

2001    **The Amazing Maurice ...** (p. 20)

2000    **The Other Side of Truth** (p. 302)

1999    **Postcards From No Man's Land** (p. 318)

# AUSLÄNDER  Paul Dowswell

I studied it, my eldest son is studying it and I bet you are, too. The rise of Hitler was so remarkable that no history curriculum can resist it. But Nazi Germany is a puzzle. Why didn't more of its citizens question Hitler's twisted philosophies?

*Ausländer* explains why. This gripping novel puts you in the shoes of Piotr Bruck, an orphan from Poland who is on the verge of being carted off to the sort of institution that believes in small rations and hard labour. But he is blond and tall, just like the propaganda posters that depict the perfect German teenager, and he is adopted by a family delighted by his Aryan looks. Oh, it is very seductive for a boy – even if he dislikes fascism – to feel he belongs. And so we comprehend how Hitler's madness could prevail. *Ausländer* is so fascinating and illuminating, it really ought to be compulsory reading.

**Alyson Rudd**

> **Next?**
> For another fictional insight into living in Nazi Germany, try *Daniel, Half Human* by David Chotjewitz.
>
> Or for something fast-paced, and also set during World War II, try Robert Muchamore's **CHERUB** prequel, *The Escape*.
>
> Or try Paul Dowswell's historical series about a boy in Nelson's navy: **The Adventures of Sam Witchall**.

# AUTOMATED ALICE  Jeff Noon

> **Next?**
> Another book that takes Alice as its starting point is Frank Beddor's *The Looking Glass Wars*. (UTBG 240)
>
> Jasper Fforde plays around with classic works of literature in *The Eyre Affair*. (UTBG 125)
>
> The disturbing *Feed* by M.T. Anderson shows a future world where everyone's brain is directly linked to the internet. (UTBG 131)
>
> And *Alice's Adventures in Wonderland* by Lewis Carroll is just as freaky!

In 1860, Alice, frustrated by being unable to complete a jigsaw, follows her aunt's riddle-ranting parrot into the workings of a clock, which transports them forward in time. One hundred and thirty years later Alice finds herself in a surreal world populated by all manner of the eccentric, electric and eclectic.

Accompanied by her now turbo-charged doll, Celia (an anagrammed, automated Alice), she stumbles upon the gruesome jigsaw murders for which they are framed by the sly Civil Serpents. Alice soon discovers that in order to return home she must retrieve the missing jigsaw pieces. But can Alice – both automated and alive – get home before the villains get them? A chaotically creative, ingeniously inventive psychedelic plot.

**Felicity-Rose Barrow, age 16**

# BAD ALICE  Jean Ure

Unusually for a teenage book, this cleverly crafted novel features characters younger than its likely readers. Duffy, staying with his grandmother, befriends Alice, the strange, withdrawn girl who hides in a burrow in a neighbouring garden. Duffy's grandmother can't speak highly enough of Alice's adoptive father, Norman, a key figure in the local church. But when Duffy reads Alice's poems – brilliant, darkly suggestive parodies of 'The Walrus and the Carpenter', 'Jabberwocky' and other *Alice in Wonderland* poems – he realises that the supposedly saintly Norman is mistreating her, and she urgently needs help.

Ingenious and thoroughly engrossing, *Bad Alice* involves the reader by making us feel the powerlessness of a child controlled by a persuasive adult.

**Linda Newbery**

## Next?

Jean Ure's teenage novels are many: *See You Thursday*, which begins the relationship between Marianne and a blind musician Abe, is highly recommended; *One Green Leaf*, *The Other Side of the Fence* and *Plague* are also outstanding.

Siobhan Dowd's wonderful novel, *A Swift Pure Cry*, is about a girl struggling with an alcoholic father, religion and the need for love. (UTBG 385)

## CLASSIC LOVE

*Pride and Prejudice* by Jane Austen

*Far From the Madding Crowd* by Thomas Hardy

*Wuthering Heights* by Emily Brontë

*Ivanhoe* by Walter Scott

*Jane Eyre* by Charlotte Brontë

*North and South* by Elizabeth Gaskell

# BALZAC AND THE LITTLE CHINESE SEAMSTRESS  Dai Sijie

This book should be full of anguish, but it's uplifting rather than tragic. It's about two Chinese students who, during China's Cultural Revolution, are forced to work as manual labourers in a remote and extremely primitive area. Their misery is relieved in the most unlikely way – by the discovery of a chest full of novels by Balzac. Such books were banned at the time so the students have to keep their treasure secret, but they can't help sharing the stories with the gorgeous little local seamstress, with whom they both fall in love. This novel is funny, sad, but never solemn, and it gave me an unforgettable picture of China during one of the greatest upheavals in its history.

**Elizabeth Laird**

> **Next?**
>
> Look out for *Once on a Moonless Night* and *Mr Muo's Travelling Coach*, also by Dai Sijie.
>
> If you want to read more about the appalling realities of life in 20th-century China, read *Wild Swans* by Jung Chang. (UTBG 439)
>
> *Tulku* is about love and friendship amidst the horrors of China's Boxer Rebellion. (UTBG 408)
>
> Try something by Balzac himself – *Cousin Bette* or maybe his *Selected Short Stories*.

---

# BARREL FEVER  David Sedaris

> **Next?**
>
> *Are You Dave Gorman?* (UTBG 28) by, um, Dave Gorman, is a wacky story of everyday madness, as is *Round Ireland with a Fridge* (yes, it is about exactly that) (UTBG 335).
>
> Bill Bryson can make the commonplace hilarious; try *Notes from a Small Island*. (UTBG 288)
>
> Or simply look for more Sedaris: *When You Are Engulfed in Flames* is just as acute and hilarious.

This is a collection of really funny short stories and essays in which David Sedaris accidentally swallows Mike Tyson's false teeth, finds squirrel tails in his fridge, and watches his dad hit his sister with a bag of frozen chicken wings after her boyfriend has accidentally set the sofa on fire. Yes, it's a book about normal life, in which the author makes us realise what a thoroughly weird species we are. In the final and funniest essay, 'The Santa Land Diaries', David becomes an elf called Crumpet, working at a big New York department store. There, along with 49 other elves, he poses for photos with children, telling them that Santa will burgle their houses if they don't behave. But be warned! This book is a bit rude (no, a lot rude actually!), something that is obviously guaranteed to put at least 95 per cent of teenagers off reading it. So that's a relief!

**Michael Cox**

# THE BEACH  Alex Garland

Imagine you're on holiday, backpacking somewhere exotic. You check into a cheap and crummy hotel. There you meet a man who calls himself Daffy (as in Duck), who tells you about a secret place he knows – a secluded beach, almost inaccessible, beautiful and unspoilt, where a young community lives in paradise. Sounds tempting, doesn't it?

So Richard decides to set off to find this heavenly spot, and when he does find it, well, it's just too good to be true. Too good, perhaps, to last…

Alex Garland's first novel was an instant bestseller and it was a worthy success – it's an enthralling tale, sometimes enchanting and sometimes very dark and savage. And the ending, well, many people didn't think it worked, but I thought it was amazing – read it and judge for yourself!

**Daniel Hahn**

**Next?**

Alex Garland's *The Tesseract* is more sophisticated than *The Beach* – a better book, though a harder one.

*Lord of the Flies* is the classic story of a paradise that quickly becomes a living hell. (UTBG 241)

More stories about backpacking? Try *Are You Experienced?* (UTBG 28) or John Harris's disturbing *The Backpacker*.

# BEAST  Ally Kennen

**Next?**

If you liked this, try *Finding Violet Park* by Jenny Valentine, which also has a strong male teen voice and a great story. (UTBG 132)

Anthony McGowan writes hard-hitting books about being a boy; try *The Knife That Killed Me* (UTBG 229) or the hilarious and rude *Henry Tumour* (UTBG 175).

Obviously you'll need to read more Ally Kennen; reach for *Berserk*, about out-of-control Chas, or the absolutely terrifying *Bedlam*, which is about the secrets hidden in an abandoned asylum.

Ally Kennen's *Beast* grabs you by the throat on page one and never lets you go. An exciting story with lots of unexpected twists and turns, its real strength is its central character.

Stephen has had a really tough life but he deals with everything that comes his way with humour and a complete lack of self pity. On top of that, he's spent years secretly looking after a strange and dangerous animal – a bizarre state of affairs that Kennen consistently manages to make both completely convincing and absolutely terrifying.

I loved Stephen's distinctive narrative voice and the way it carried me through his story – and I found myself caring desperately that he somehow found a way to deal with *all* the dangers in his world.

**Sophie McKenzie**

# BEAU GESTE P.C. Wren

At 13 I wanted desperately to join the French Foreign Legion. The newspapers said that legionnaires were the scum of the earth – but I knew differently. Beau Geste was the book responsible for my inside information and I read it over and over again.

When the fabulous Blue Water sapphire is stolen, suspicion immediately falls upon Michael Geste, who mysteriously disappears only hours after it vanishes. Protesting their brother's innocence, John and Digby Geste follow Michael into the French Foreign Legion in an attempt to solve the puzzle of the missing jewel.

What follows next is the most marvellous, heartbreaking adventure. They really don't write books like this any more and the world is poorer for that.

**Laura Hutchings**

> **Next?**
>
> A lot of people don't know that there are two sequels – *Beau Sabreur* and *Beau Ideal*.
>
> If you enjoy this kind of historical novel, try D.K. Broster's *The Flight of the Heron* or A.E. Mason's *The Four Feathers*.
>
> Or for another story involving a missing jewel, try Wilkie Collins's *The Moonstone*. (UTBG 269)

# BEAUTY Robin McKinley

> **Next?**
>
> More Robin McKinley? Try *Spindle's End*. (UTBG 373)
>
> Kate Petty and Caroline Castle's collection *Tales of Beauty and Cruelty* is based on old tales by Hans Christian Andersen.
>
> Patricia McKillip also delves into fairy tale to create magical worlds. Read *Winter Rose*, a dark story of love, murder and obsession.
>
> Shannon Hale spins her own take on Grimm in both *The Goose Girl* (UTBG 162) and *The Book of a Thousand Days*.
>
> Or try *The Tower Room*, part of the **Happy Ever After** series by Adèle Geras. The series retells the tales of 'Rapunzel', 'Sleeping Beauty' and 'Snow White'.

We all know the story of 'Beauty and the Beast': in order to save her father, Beauty, the unselfish heroine, goes to live in the house of the Beast, only to find her self-sacrifice eventually rewarded. So far, so fairy tale.

Robin McKinley's poetic retelling sticks close to the established story (though in this book Beauty's older sisters are very much more sympathetic than in the original tale) and the growth of Beauty's true love for the Beast is satisfying, as are her trials and suffering en route. (The luxury that surrounds her in the Beast's castle may help.) The story is focused on the heroine's crises and responses, and will be particularly enjoyed by readers like me with a taste for tales in which real life blends into fantasy.

**Margaret Mahy**

# THE BEET FIELDS Gary Paulsen

**Next?**

Gary Paulsen's *Hatchet* is also about a boy learning to survive, this time alone in the wilderness; there are sequels, too. (UTBG 172)

Or try Roddy Doyle's take on survival in *Wilderness*.

For more about the kind of life Paulsen is describing, try *Of Mice and Men* (UTBG 291) and *The Grapes of Wrath* by John Steinbeck, set about 20 years earlier.

A stranger tale of labouring outside? Try the magnificent *Holes* by Louis Sachar. (UTBG 184)

The boy – we never learn his name – runs away from an abusive home, leaving everything behind. It's time to grow up, fast. He takes the first job he finds, hoeing beets on the prairie farms of North Dakota, working in fields so vast they stretch from horizon to horizon. He moves on to driving a tractor, is robbed of his hard-earned wages by a corrupt cop and finally joins a carnival – a travelling fair. In one summer he becomes a man – first work, first wages, first woman – and learns a lot about people, from the illegal immigrant Mexican workers in the beet fields to the geeks and shills of the carnival. Short, punchy, easy to read, hard to forget.

**Jan Mark**

# BEFORE I DIE Jenny Downham

Tessa Scott is going to die. Everyone around her is hoping she might not. When you read this book you'll be hoping, too, but you'll be wrong. Tessa is dying and before she goes, she wants to live. She wants to have sex and take drugs and fall in love. She wants to cram everything into the short time she has left. And she just about does.

A brave book with a personality just like Tessa's – angry, frank, inquisitive, adventurous, joyful, perceptive, and deeply sad. Jenny Downham has a real eye for the beauty in everyday things. And the ending is so skilful – free of cliché, true to Tessa's voice and absolutely devastating.

**Jenny Valentine**

**Next?**

*Life on the Refrigerator Door* by Alice Kuipers is a delicate story, told in notes, about a mother, her daughter and the illness that stands between them.

In *Thirteen Reasons Why* by Jay Asher Clay receives a box of tapes – tapes that tell exactly why his classmate Hannah committed suicide.

*Things I Want My Daughter to Know* by Elizabeth Noble is about a woman dying from cancer and the important things she wants to tell each of her children.

*Before I Die* is a book that's more about living than dying – so is *Elsewhere*. It may be about a girl who is dead, but is far more about what it means to be alive. (UTBG 120)

# BEING Kevin Brooks

**Next?**

If you liked this, try *Lucas* (UTBG 249), *Black Rabbit Summer* (UTBG 46) or any other Kevin Brooks.

For a completely different take on identity issues, read Scott Westerfeld's exciting sci-fi series that begins with *Uglies*. (UTBG 412)

Melvin Burgess's *Sara's Face* is a taut thriller about identity, image and celebrity.

In Gareth Thompson's *The Anarchist's Angel*, scarred and bullied Samson meets someone who he thinks might be a friend. But is she? (UTBG 21)

Or for more existential exploration, try *Jacoby's Game* by Alison Prince.

'Who or what is Robert Smith?' is the question that runs like a spine through *Being* by Kevin Brooks.

Robert wakes in the middle of a routine operation to discover the people by his bed in a state of shock – whatever lies inside Robert is definitely not normal! But then, as Robert later asks himself, what *is* normal? *Being* is not for readers who demand a plot that delivers straightforward answers. Kevin Brooks – who always writes with punch and elegance – is far more interested in serving up philosophical questions about identity for his readers to ponder.

Dramatic, intriguing and suspenseful by turns, *Being* is a thought-provoking story that makes you question, as Robert does, what it is exactly that makes us human.

**Sophie McKenzie**

# THE BELGARIAD David Eddings

I read the five books of *The Belgariad* more times than I can recall when I was a teenager. I was a big fantasy fan, and these were some of the best fantasy books I'd ever read. The story of a young, seemingly ordinary boy, who gets swept away from his village and involved in a world of wizards and kings, it lacks the imaginative scope of Tolkien, but it's fun, exciting, intriguing fantasy in which the characters are as important as the quest and magical elements.

Easy to read and great to share, this was one of the most popular series of books at my school, appealing even to those who didn't read fantasy. Immerse yourself and enjoy!

**Darren Shan**

**Next?**

**The Belgariad** is a five-book epic. Start with *Pawn of Prophecy*. The **Mallorean** series is another epic by David Eddings.

*Sword of Shannara* by Terry Brooks and **The Magician** by Raymond E. Feist are epic fantasy stories that will keep you absorbed for hours.

There's more epic fantasy in Robin Hobb's **Farseer** trilogy. (UTBG 127)

# THE BELL  Iris Murdoch

## Next?

Another Iris Murdoch? All are fabulous. Try *Henry and Cato*, *The Sea, The Sea* or *The Unicorn*.

Murdoch's husband John Bayley wrote a tender portrait of their life together and her final years with Alzheimer's disease – *Iris*.

Another story set against summer heat and a turmoil of emotions is Ian McEwan's *Atonement*. (UTBG 30)

*Frost in May* and its sequels by Antonia White depict the claustrophobic world of a convent school. (UTBG 148)

I can't overemphasise the impact of reading *The Bell* aged 16. It kick-started a chain reaction and I did not stop reading Iris Murdoch until about ten books and a year later when I came up for air. Iris Murdoch is a must for anybody seriously interested in human relationships, beliefs, beauty, darkness and extraordinarily powerful writing.

Be prepared to enter into a world that is immediately riveting, disturbing and totally adult. Dora is the wife of a handsome, powerful, but brutal older man, Paul; she tries to leave him but finds she cannot. Instead, she joins him at a strange 'spiritual' community deep in the English countryside. Against a seething backdrop of summer heat, there is far more going on than meets the eye. Who is in love with whom? Who believes in what? And will they find the great bell that legend says has lain buried for years in the great lake?

**Rebecca Swift**

# THE BELL JAR  Sylvia Plath

Sylvia Plath is perhaps better known for her poetry and for being the wife of Ted Hughes, but her only novel, *The Bell Jar*, is undoubtedly one of the greatest of modern novels. It's about Esther Greenwood, a 19-year-old girl who suffers a mental breakdown. We watch her gradually becoming disconnected from the world around her while she's working in New York on a magazine, then witness her descent as she returns home to the Boston suburbs, and see her behaviour becoming increasingly erratic until she is finally admitted to a mental hospital.

As dark as *The Bell Jar* is, it's shot through with an unforgettable lyrical beauty. It's a demanding and harrowing read – a real classic.

## Next?

Susanna Kaysen spent time at the same psychiatric hospital as Sylvia Plath – read her story in *Girl, Interrupted*.

Tabitha Suzuma never flinches from the real – read *A Note of Madness*. (UTBG 288)

Or there's *Cut* by Patricia McCormick, about the treatment of a self-harmer in the US. (UTBG 93)

**Sherry Ashworth**

# FANTASY
## by Catherine Fisher

Fantasy is a wide field. Or if you like, a dark wood. Somewhere in its depths tangle ghost stories and sci-fi and legends and psychological archetypes. But all of them grew from the seeds of myth. Like many readers, I first ventured into fantasy through fairy tale, reading Japanese and Russian and Scandinavian versions of tales where girls defeat witches and third sons kill dragons; and then found they led to myth: to the wild and crazy tales of Wales and Ireland – you can find some of these in *The Mabinogion*

translated by Jones and Jones, or *Early Irish Myths and Sagas* translated by Jeffrey Gantz. In *The Tain*, Thomas Kinsella brilliantly retells the story of the hero Cu Chulain's lone stand against the armies of Connaught, which is epic fantasy of the best kind, up there with Homer; and in the wonderful translations of *Beowulf* we can confront the terrors of the monsters that crawl from the dark swamps of the Viking imagination. Most literary fantasy is a direct continuation of these themes. **The Lord of the Rings** trilogy (UTBG 242) and *The Silmarillion* are steeped in Tolkien's enormous knowledge of Norse languages and stories; they are wonderful, sweeping tales full of adventure and cosmic questions. Along with C.S. Lewis (especially perhaps his sci-fi trilogy *Out of the Silent Planet*, *Perelandra* and *That Hideous Strength*), it was Tolkien who founded the modern genre, though

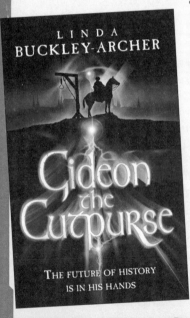

### SLIPPING THROUGH TIME

*Gideon the Cutpurse* by Linda Buckley-Archer

*Follow Me Down* by Julie Hearn

*The Sterkarm Handshake* by Susan Price

*A Wrinkle in Time* by Madeleine L'Engle

*A Traveller in Time* by Alison Uttley

**Time Runners** series by Justin Richards

*The Time Traveler's Wife* by Audrey Niffenegger

'Charming, seductive and completely enthralling...'
EOIN COLFER

KATE THOMPSON

The NEW POLICEMAN

Winner of the
Whitbread Children's Book Award

## MORE WORLDS THAN ONE

*Stravaganza* by Mary Hoffman

*Salem Brownstone* by John Harris Dunning

**The Aldous Lexicon** trilogy by Michael Lawrence

*The Dark Lord of Derkholm* by Diana Wynne Jones

**His Dark Materials** trilogy by Philip Pullman

*The New Policeman* by Kate Thompson

**The Divide** trilogy by Elizabeth Kay

**Chrestomanci** series by Diana Wynne Jones

he himself was influenced by early writers like William Morris (try *The Well at the World's End*), and Lewis loved George MacDonald's books. Writing a little before them was William Hope Hodgson, whose bizarre mixes of sci-fi and fantasy are now cult classics. Look out for *The House on the Borderland* and the amazing *Night Land*, which is sometimes so bad it's unreadable, and yet its nightmare landscapes are breathtakingly brilliant.

A contemporary of Tolkien's was E.R. Edison, mostly known now for *The Worm Ouroboros*. If you're not afraid of flamboyant costumes, endless names, fantastic swordplay and a very mannered style, you might love this. I do, though it's not for everyone.

A writer who built his own creations on these and other foundations was Mervyn Peake, whose superb **Gormenghast** trilogy (UTBG 163) has to be on anyone's list of great imaginative achievements. The endless corridors, halls and towers of Gormenghast castle are mirrored throughout later films and trilogies, album covers and comics. In children's fiction in the 1960s fantasy really took off, too, especially in the books of Susan Cooper and the brilliantly gifted Alan Garner, whose style grew more clipped and taut with each novel, culminating in two of the best young-adult books ever, *The Owl Service* (UTBG 306), with its terrifying loop of relived Celtic myth, and *Red Shift* (UTBG 329), a complex triple-time story that really moves up a gear into an almost unbearable intensity. Garner's later books have been for adults, but I'd recommend his most recent, *Thursbitch*.

Fantasy these days is immensely popular. Look out for *Mythago Wood* and its sequels by the admirable Robert Holdstock, or the wonderful, teeming **Majipoor** chronicles of Robert Silverberg. And then, in other parts of the wood, there's Philip Pullman, Terry Pratchett, Tanith Lee, Diana Wynne Jones and many others – all excellent. Keep exploring.

# BELOVED Toni Morrison ✱ ✱ ✱

*Beloved* is the story of Sethe, a woman haunted by a terrible decision she took, back in her past – to slit the throat of her baby girl rather than give her up to slavery.

This deeply powerful novel taps veins of history, folkloric tradition and memory. In often beautiful prose, Morrison conjures up pain and suffering, guilt and torment, love and sacrifice. This author is at her best when writing about feelings, about yearnings and about the human spirit. And *Beloved* is full of these ingredients. It's a huge-hearted, tragic story that tugs constantly at your emotions.

**Neil Arksey**

### Next?

Other great novels by African-American women writers include Alice Walker's **The Color Purple** (UTBG 84) and Maya Angelou's **I Know Why the Caged Bird Sings** (UTBG 198).

Toni Morrison's other books are all good too. Try **The Bluest Eye** or **Jazz**.

Another writer who makes you understand the most powerful of emotions is Gabriel García Márquez; try **Love in the Time of Cholera** (UTBG 248) or **One Hundred Years of Solitude** (UTBG 296).

# THE BIG SLEEP Raymond Chandler ✱ ✱

### Next?

How about some spies? Try the **James Bond** books, starting with **Casino Royale**. (UTBG 211)

All the other Raymond Chandler's are must-reads. Try **The Long Goodbye**, **Farewell, My Lovely** and **The Lady in the Lake** first.

More hard-boiled detective novels? Read Dashiell Hammett, starting with **The Maltese Falcon** (UTBG 253) or **The Glass Key**. Both Chandler and Hammett had most of their books made into great films!

*The Big Sleep* tells the story of the quick-thinking, fast-talking American private eye, Philip Marlowe. He becomes involved in the affairs of the Sternwood family after he's asked by the old dying General Sternwood to deal with the blackmail of his younger daughter, Carmen.

Philip Marlowe is cool, smooth and everything an American private eye should be. The girls seem to like him, too – both the Sternwood daughters fall for his charms early on in the book.

This is a fantastic story filled with memorable description and laden with twists and great one-liners: 'She looked as if she'd been poured into the dress and someone forgot to say whoa'. 'It was a blonde. A blonde to make a bishop kick a hole in a stained-glass window'. 'He looked as inconspicuous as a tarantula on a slice of angel cake'.

**Raffaella Barker**

# BILGEWATER Jane Gardam

Marigold Green is the daughter of Bill, the headmaster of a boys' boarding school in Yorkshire, and her nickname, Bilgewater, is a corruption of 'Bill's daughter'. She perceives herself as ugly and awkward and, because she is also motherless, is well aware that she is searching for love and friendship. When Grace Gathering arrives at the school, everything changes. Grace and Marigold were friends in their early childhood and Grace, with her cloud of wondrous hair, appears almost like an angel in the austere surroundings of the school.

The story is told in the first person by Marigold, and Gardam's sure touch brings every character to life. Because the novel begins with the narrator being interviewed for a place at Cambridge, we know that Marigold has achieved some academic success... But at what cost? And will she fulfil her potential? A marvellously rich and elegantly written book.

**Adèle Geras**

**Next?**

Libba Bray's *A Great and Terrible Beauty* is about a girl sent home from India to attend a boarding school. She is lonely, unhappy and after a while realises she's being watched...

Or for another tense look at school life try Joanne Harris's *Gentlemen and Players*. Or the very different *Chocolat* (UTBG 77), about what it takes to fit in.

# BINDI BABES
## Narinder Dhami

**Next?**

Read the sequels: next is *Bollywood Babes*, then *Bhangra Babes* and *Superstar Babes* follow on.

The **Mates, Dates...** series by Cathy Hopkins is about three friends, boys, parents and everything girly. (UTBG 257)

Or what about something a little tougher about being Asian in Britain today? Try the series of linked short stories in *Dominoes* by Bali Rai.

Amber (Ambajit), Jazz (Jasvinder) and Geena are sisters. They live with their dad as their mum is dead. They have a pretty cool life, they're popular, even the teachers like them and the only things they hate are people pitying them, or trying to control their lives. After all, everything's fine, isn't it? They have great clothes, fun friends, lots of freedom and, best of all, each other. But then their bossy, interfering unmarried aunt comes over from India and the fun can't last. She makes them go to bed early and won't let them eat junk food. What's to be done? Hmm, how about an arranged marriage? Matchmaking begins and, well, things get complicated – and very funny. This is an easy read, but it's oh so much fun.

**Leonie Flynn**

# BIRDSONG Sebastian Faulks

*Birdsong* is one of the most powerful novels I've ever read. It's a love story, and a deeply moving one at that, and it's also a story about discovering the past, but first and foremost it's a story of war. Stephen Wraysford falls in love with a French woman, loses

her, and is sent back to France as a lieutenant in the early stages of the First World War. The horrors of that war – the endless mud, the unspeakable waste of life, the heroism, the despair – can rarely have been as clearly conveyed. This is an unforgettable book and I urge you to read it.

**Malachy Doyle**

### Next?

How about a first-hand perspective on the First World War? *Memoirs of an Infantry Officer* by Siegfried Sassoon is incomparable. (UTBG 261)

For a good historian's overview try any of Lyn MacDonald's books. *Somme* and *1915: The Death of Hope* are particularly good.

You could also try another gripping Sebastian Faulks: *Charlotte Grey*, which is set during World War II.

# THE BIRDS ON THE TREES
## Nina Bawden

### Next?

Try *The Fifth Child* by Doris Lessing, in which four contented siblings struggle with the family's latest addition.

Another Nina Bawden? Try *Circles of Deceit*, a story of fidelity and forgery.

A boy who has similar problems with life is the hero of *Wounded Bird of Paradise* by Mary Essinger; or try Susan Hill's disturbing *I'm the King of the Castle* (UTBG 201).

If you are interested in the dark and complex things that go on behind the polite, bright surface of everyday life, Nina Bawden is the writer for you. She writes grippingly about what ordinary families suffer in an everyday kind of way. In *The Birds on the Trees* you will meet Toby, who is different. Adored by his younger sister, Lucy, he bemuses his parents and others around him. Does Toby have a 'problem', or doesn't he? Is he ill in some way, or just a normal, rebellious, intelligent boy? Intensity, emotion, darkness and light are perfectly communicated, making you think about how a good book is actually written – as well as about the particular delicate, uneasy world that this one is trying to explore.

**Rebecca Swift**

# BITTER FRUIT Brian Keaney

**Next?**

Try Brian Keaney's *Family Secrets*, about a girl who has never met her father, or his most recent book, *Jacob's Ladder*, a powerfully original take on families, dealing with bereavement and death itself. Or maybe the very different *Falling for Joshua*, about a girl with a secret.

There aren't many authors who can write about death without getting overly sentimental or horribly depressing; look out for Gabrielle Zevin's startling *Elsewhere* (UTBG 120), but be warned – it couldn't be less like *Bitter Fruit*! – and Tabitha Suzuma's disturbing *From Where I Stand*.

We all say things we regret – we lose our temper with our friends, our siblings, our parents, then patch things up the next day. But just imagine if you never saw them again, if the next day they died, suddenly. 'I hate you!' Rebecca shouts at her father – and these will be the last words she says to him.

*Bitter Fruit* is the stunning story of Rebecca's grief and guilt, and how she struggles to cope with them. She will learn to rebuild her life and her friendships, but it's not easy. Keaney pulls no punches – his book is tough and clear-sighted; though moving, it's never over-sentimental, and the writing's fantastic, too.

**Daniel Hahn**

# The BLACK MAGICIAN trilogy
## Trudi Canavan

In Imardin, magicians of the Guild gather yearly for the Purge of vagrants, miscreants and street urchins from the city. As the gathered mob is herded, an angry young slum girl called Sonea throws a stone with all her might. To the surprise of everyone present, the stone breaks the shield of the magicians and knocks one unconscious. As the situation develops, the Guild's worst fear is realised. A desperate race starts to find Sonea before her uncontrolled power obliterates her and the whole city. Filled with magic and conspiracy, this is one trilogy that cannot be missed.

**Next?**

The trilogy comprises: *The Magician's Guild*, *The Novice* and *The High Lord*. And look out for more Trudi Canavan with *Priestess of the White*, the first in the **Age of the Five** series and *The Ambassador's Mission*, which starts the **Traitor Spy** trilogy.

Tamora Pierce's **Song of the Lioness** quartet is about a girl's quest to become a knight. (UTBG 14)

*Dream Merchant* by Isobel Hoving is a magnificent fantasy.

Terry Brooks's *Sword of Shannara* starts another great epic fantasy series.

**Gary Chow, age 17**

# BLACK RABBIT SUMMER   Kevin Brooks

**Next?**

More Kevin Brooks? *Candy* (UTBG 66) is just as hard-hitting or try the controversial *Killing God*.

B.R. Collins's *The Traitor Game* is about what happens when secrets are betrayed. (UTBG 402)

Tabitha Suzuma's *From Where I Stand* is about a boy looking for justice after his mother is murdered.

Unrelentingly grim, gritty and gripping, this is a cleverly crafted crime novel which lets the reader into the shadowy world of a group of five friends who meet up post-GCSEs 'for old time's sake'. Drink and drugs blur their memories so no one can quite remember how one of their group dies and another, the loner, becomes prime suspect with the police. Except that Pete can't believe his friend could have done it, and sets out to prove his innocence. Countless 'issues' jostle for page space, but it perfectly reflects teenage emotional turmoil and insecurities as friendships shift, and the future in the real adult world looks ever more uncertain and scary.

Characteristically, Brooks tells it like it is and never passes judgment on his characters, crediting his readers with enough intelligence to do that for themselves. This is one book you're unlikely to forget in a hurry.

**Eileen Armstrong**

# BLAME MY BRAIN
## Nicola Morgan

So, you like to sleep late, you get cranky with parents / teachers / whoever, you want to try everything that adults tell you that you shouldn't and you sometimes think that life is pretty pointless. Well, guess what – you're normal! Even scientists think so.

This book is all about you. Well, actually it's about your brain and all the changes it's going through. If you ever wanted to know why you do certain stuff – read this. It's funny, cool and amazingly interesting (as well as being great ammunition the next time someone moans about you). With polls, quizzes, sections on drugs, alcohol, depression, eating disorders, sex, gender, hormones and self-harm, this books tells life like it is, and is something every teen – and parent – should read.

**Leonie Flynn**

**Next?**

Nicola Morgan writes brilliant fiction, too – try *Mondays Are Red* (UTBG 268) or *Sleepwalking*, about a future world where ideas are forbidden and emotions regulated.

She also has more books about how to cope with being you; try *The Leaving Home Survival Guide*.

Or for a male perspective, Matt Whyman's *Unzipped: A Toolkit for Life*.

# BLANKETS Craig Thompson

**Next?**

*Goodbye Chunky Rice*, also by Craig Thompson, deals with the close friendship between two unlikely animals.

More graphic novels? Try the deeply unsettling **Salem Brownstone** by John Harris Dunning. And if you want to know more about this kind of book, look out for Paul Gravett's **Graphic Novels: Stories to Change Your Life.**

*A Portrait of the Artist as a Young Man* by James Joyce shows the way an artist develops, falls in love, and comes to terms with his past. (UTBG 317)

Growing up is never easy. Especially if you live in a fundamentalist Christian household, your younger brother wets the bed you share and you secretly want to be an artist in a world where art is considered the work of the devil. Well, there's always winter Church camp. Except that only the rich kids can afford ski passes and Craig, the hero of this stunningly drawn 'illustrated novel', hasn't even got enough money for a day one. Then he falls in love for the first time, with the fascinating Raina, and everything changes. But his troubles are only just beginning. Craig Thompson takes us on a moving journey of discovery: about love, friendship, and the importance of a good blanket.

**Ariel Kahn**

# BLOOD RED HORSE K.M. Grant

I never was a fan of horse books, being more of a puppy / kitten girl myself. I read *Blood Red Horse* because it was a historical novel about medieval England and the Crusades, but I wound up falling for the horse. Oh, I liked the people: the young crusaders, Gavin and Will, their beloved Ellie, who had to stay behind, and the Muslim boy, Kamil, an enemy who becomes an ally and a friend. Theirs is a story of adventure, of the futility and horror of war, of the importance of friendship, loyalty, courage, and love. They and the other characters are realistically and respectfully drawn, so I didn't have to choose sides but could understand their conflicts and cheer for all of them. And I did – but most of all for the magical horse, the blood-red Hosanna, who inspired people by his example to be more than they thought they could be. And, in his honour, I plan to read another horse book soon.

**Next?**

The next books in the **de Granville** trilogy are **Green Jasper** and **Blaze of Silver**.

If you like the bloodier side of history, try Adèle Geras's **Troy** (UTBG 405), a retelling of Homer's *Iliad* (UTBG 199).

Julie Hearn's **The Merrybegot** is set in 1645, when accusations of witchcraft could lead to death. (UTBG 261)

**Karen Cushman**

# BLOOD RED, SNOW WHITE  Marcus Sedgwick

**Next?**

More Marcus Sedgwick? Try the violent, fascinating *My Swordhand Is Singing*. (UTBG 275)

More Russians? Try Eva Ibbotson's *The Secret Countess*, about a girl exiled from Russia at the time of the revolution. Or try Esther Hautzig's real-life *The Endless Steppe: Growing Up in Siberia*.

If you're in the mood for something complex, try Jonathan Safran Foer's *Everything Is Illuminated*.

Russian fairy tale and historical events collide in this account of *Swallows and Amazons* author Arthur Ransome and his adventures in revolutionary Russia.

Leaving his unhappy marriage behind in England, Ransome moves to Russia for a job as a journalist for the *Daily News*. Little does he realise a bloody revolution will soon erupt before his eyes. Called on by the British to spy upon the Bolsheviks, Ransome finds his loyalties torn when he falls in love with Trotsky's secretary and is forced to make some difficult decisions.

You don't need to have previous knowledge of Ransome or the Russian Revolution to enjoy this compelling tale, set against a backdrop of Rasputin, the Romanovs and Lenin; with Ransome, a troubled Englishman amidst them all.

**Rebecca Wilkie**

# THE BLOOD STONE  Jamila Gavin

This is the tale of Filippo Veroneo, born in Venice in the 14th century, who journeys in search of his father, missing since just before his birth. He travels from Venice to Afghanistan, carrying a ransom – the invaluable jewel, the Ocean of the Moon – sewn into his head for safe-keeping. Love, loyalty, betrayal and cruelty are fundamental to Filippo's world, and there is risk on every page. This great epic is fabulous and atmospheric and gives us tastes of worlds long since gone, including that of the great Moghul court in Agra, home of the Taj Mahal. It is a huge adventure, a compelling journey, as rich and desirable as the jewel that is its title.

**Wendy Cooling**

**Next?**

Jamila Gavin's *Coram Boy* tells the story of two boys, one a rescued slave, the other the illegitimate son of the heir to a great estate and how their lives collide. (UTBG 87)

Another journey of challenge, adventure and survival, Marcus Sedgwick's *Blood Red, Snow White* mixes a real story with Russian fairy tale. (UTBG 48)

Or for something else set in magical Venice, Cornelia Funke's *The Thief Lord* (UTBG 393) or Michelle Lovric's *The Undrowned Child*.

# BLOODTIDE   Melvin Burgess

※ ※ ※

This extraordinary book. This extraordinary, extraordinary book. For more than a year after reading it I was still preoccupied by its images and characters.

*Bloodtide* is a retelling of an old Norse myth, the 'Volsunga Saga', set in a future London where normal society has broken down into two fiercely rival gangs, the Volsons and the Conors. The book is about their struggle for power but, as in all the old myths, Fate plays a part, the gods pick their favourites, and a 14-year-old girl and her brothers are left to pick up the pieces of it all.

I'm not going to pretend for a minute that *Bloodtide* is a book for everyone. It is deeply violent in places – so much so that at one point I put the book down (and then picked it up again – I had to pick it up again). It is magnificently well written, but it is brutal. If you want a story that will grip your heart, take you to places other books have never taken you, and leave you changed, then take a deep breath and let *Bloodtide* eat its way into your soul.

**Cliff McNish**

**Next?**

Try the sequel, *Bloodsong*, or another of Melvin's searing novels, such as **Junk** (UTBG 218), which is about drug abuse.

Robert Cormier is another author who doesn't pull any punches; try **Heroes**. (UTBG 176)

Or for something else that's woven from Norse myth (and is even more violent than **Bloodtide**!), try Neil Gaiman's **American Gods**.

# BLOOD TIES   Sophie McKenzie

※ ※

**Next?**

More Sophie McKenzie? Try *The Set Up*.

For more stories on identity and genetics, try Alison Allen-Gray's **Unique** (UTBG 414), about Dominic and the life he leads when he finds out he is a clone of his dead older brother. Or **Being** (UTBG 38) by Kevin Brooks.

Tabitha Suzuma's **Without Looking Back** is about a boy who finds he's been kidnapped by his own father.

Theo has never known who his dad is and the only link he has to him is a photograph given to him by his mother. Denied any other information about his past and hounded by a bodyguard, Theo tries to discover his true identity.

As his search continues, his life and the life of new friend Rachel start to unravel before their eyes. Rachel and Theo have never met but are inexplicably linked by a fire bomb at a genetic research clinic a long time ago. What follows is a search for understanding and identity in a world of experiments and lies, where no one can be trusted, and everything that Theo and Rachel have believed to be true is challenged.

**Adam Lancaster**

# BLUE  Sue Mayfield

*Blue* is a novel about bullying – and it's terrifyingly realistic. It's set in a recognisable world of GCSEs and school plays; the characters are everyday teenagers.

Anna Goldsmith is just that bit brighter and better looking than some other girls and this has won her the dislike of Hayley Parkin. Hayley's campaign to unsettle Anna is unrelenting, and all the more effective as it's low-key and persistent.

The story is told partly by Melanie Blackwood, a girl caught in the middle, partly by entries in Anna's diary, and partly through the thoughts of Anna's parents. *Blue* is a must-read book for anyone who wants to get wise to the techniques of bullies.

**Sherry Ashworth**

### Next?

Sue Mayfield has written other excellent real-life novels for teenagers; try *Reckless*, a story about a teenage pregnancy, but with a twist.

If you're interested in reading more about bullying, have a look at *Feather Boy* (UTBG 130) or *Run, Zan, Run* by Catherine MacPhail.

In Kate Cann's *Escape*, Rowan needs to get away from her bullying parents. Will her gap year solve her problems? (UTBG 122)

# BLUE MOON  Julia Green

### Next?

There's a sequel, *Baby Blue*, which you must read to find out what happens to Mia next.

Other novels about teenage pregnancy include *Dear Nobody* (UTBG 101) and the terrifying *Roxy's Baby* (UTBG 336).

Sarah Dessen's *Someone Like You* looks at two girls having to come to terms with sex, love, parents and pregnancy.

Mia is only 15, and her mother left her when she was a small child. *Blue Moon* tells the story of what happens when Mia discovers she is pregnant – her disbelief, her denial, the trauma of letting her father know, and all the decisions that have to be made after that point. The novel is realistic and sensitively told. The ending is utterly convincing. Not only do you journey with Mia through the most difficult months of her life, but also discover how the ripples caused by a pregnancy travel much further than you might expect – it's not just Mia, but her family, her boyfriend, her friends and even some strangers on a barge who are caught up in this compelling drama.

**Sherry Ashworth**

# THE BODY IN THE LIBRARY Agatha Christie

I think this is my favourite Miss Marple story. In it, Agatha Christie takes a conventional detective-story opening (body in library) and adds layer upon layer of intrigue, with twists and red herrings. Just enough to make you feel marvellously clever and smug for working out whodunnit all on your own, and then marvellously stupid when it turns out that you got it altogether wrong, and of course Miss Marple has got it right.

She's a lovely old thing, Miss Marple; apparently quite harmless (meaning that suspects routinely let down their guard in her presence), but at the same time harbouring no happy, optimistic faith in human nature whatsoever. She is a delightful, prim old cynic. And in this story, as in them all, she shines.

**Daniel Hahn**

### Next?

Definitely more Miss Marple – *The 4:50 from Paddington* is another favourite of mine.

Dorothy L. Sayers wrote classy murder mysteries. My favourite is *Murder Must Advertise*, but they're all worth a read. (UTBG 243)

For another series of books from the same time as Agatha Christie's mysteries, with classy country houses aplenty, try the **Jeeves** stories. (UTBG 214)

# BOG CHILD Siobhan Dowd

### Next?

Siobhan Dowd's *A Swift Pure Cry* (UTBG 385). Or her poignant *Solace of the Road* (UTBG 371).

Anthony McGowan writes complex, intriguing books. Try *Hellbent*.

Anne Cassidy's *Forget Me Not* is about a kidnapped child and the difficult choice that sometimes sits between truth and lies.

We are in Ireland in 1981, at the height of the Troubles. Teenage Fergus and his uncle Tally are stealing peat from a plot right on the border between North and South, when they find the body of a child – not, as they first assume, a victim of the conflict, but a girl who died 2,000 years ago. The girl is a human sacrifice, and her story, told in the first person, neatly counterpoints Fergus's contemporary entanglement in terrorism. His brother is on hunger strike in the Maze, and he himself smuggles packages, which may contain explosives, over the border.

Dowd eschews easy answers to complex problems, and the book is dark to its core, but there is hope at the end, seen literally by the dying girl as a silver light. The writing is not quite as perfect as it was in *A Swift Pure Cry*, and I suspect that Dowd would have given it a final polish had her own tragically early death not intervened. Nevertheless, her prose still caries a powerful poetic charge.

**Anthony McGowan**

# BONJOUR TRISTESSE Françoise Sagan

Cécile is a precocious 17 year old who lives a hedonistic life in the French Riviera with her father, Raymond. The pair drive fast cars, pursue love affairs and sunbathe. But when Raymond decides to marry Anne, Cécile is filled with jealousy and indignation, terrified that her amoral pleasures will be curtailed. She cooks up a plan to prevent the marriage, with unexpectedly tragic consequences.

*Bonjour Tristesse* was Sagan's first novel, written at the age of 18, when having failed her exams at the Sorbonne she decided to write instead. It is brief, deceptively simple and utterly compulsive.

**Francesca Lewis**

### Next?

*A Summer Bird-Cage* by Margaret Drabble or *The Rachel Papers* (UTBG 325) by Martin Amis. (Both also first novels, incidentally.)

Other books that take place in the summer and convey the season's heat, moral ambiguity and subsequent loss of innocence (or at least acquisition of knowledge) are *The Cement Garden* (UTBG 71) and *The Greengage Summer* (UTBG 167).

Find another feisty, French female narrator in Colette's **Claudine** stories, beginning with *Claudine at School*. (UTBG 81)

# THE BOOK THIEF Markus Zusak

### Next?

For a different viewpoint on the Holocaust, try Lois Lowry's classic, *Number the Stars*, or Bette Greene's *Summer of My German Soldier*.

For more by Markus Zusak, pick up *I Am the Messenger*, though it's different in topic and tone

The Jews have been persecuted throughout Christian history. Alice Hoffman's *Incantation* takes you back to 16th-century Spain. (UTBG 202)

When I learned that the narrator of this book was Death, I knew I had to read it. How intriguing it would be to be led around Nazi Germany by the one thing I fear most.

Death was fascinated by Liesel. She was so young, yet so mature, calm and collected. He had stolen her brother from her at a young age, but she managed to carry on with her life. After her mum left her, she was forced to move in with the Hubermans on Himmel Street. She liked her dad. He taught her to read and played the accordion for her. Life was looking pretty good. Then the bombings came and everything changed. She was forced into a life of stealing, fighting for every meal and living each day knowing it may be her last. The only things helping her through the hard times were the books. How did she get the books, you ask? You will have to read this amazing story full of courage, fear, and accomplishment to find out.

**Haley Fletcher, age 17**

# BORN CONFUSED Tanuja Desai Hidier

## Next?

You might also like Bali Rai's novels; try *(Un)arranged Marriage* (UTBG 413). Or read his feature on race in young adult literature on pp. 416–417 for more ideas.

Or for a poetic look at life in Kerala, try Arundhati Roy's *The God of Small Things*.

There's a healthy dose of reality in Vikas Swarup's *Q&A* – it was filmed as *Slumdog Millionaire*.

Or try Pratima Mitchell's *Indian Summer*, in which a British-Asian girl visits her mother's family in India, and uncovers secrets that could change her life.

*Born Confused* is a big, technicolour novel, swirling with the music, smells and images of two continents. Dimple's 17th birthday present from best friend Gwyn is a fake ID. But for Dimple, identity is complicated: she's an ABCD – American Born Confused Desi. Should she date a 'suitable – Indian – boy' or follow Gwyn, dating American college boys? And when the 'suitable boy' isn't the loser she'd thought and Gwyn embraces Indian-ness to snare him – then what?

Dimple discovers 'you have to get lost to get found': in getting lost, she comes to understand more about her parents' history, about India and about friendship. I love Dimple's unsureness, her devotion to her camera and her sound heart, in this funny / sad quest for belonging.

**Helen Simmons**

# THE BOWER BIRD Ann Kelley

Gussie needs a heart and lung transplant, but really wishes only to be a healthy pink. I admit to not warming to Gussie, while admiring her: she's a strange know-it-all with thoughts that veer from child to adult in an unorthodox and yet arguably realistic way. But then Gussie is neither one thing nor another: neither child nor adult, neither fully alive nor yet dead.

I admired this book for its rule-breaking nature (like Gussie's) and for the author's ability to make me care (as Gussie does) far more about whether her missing library books are discovered than whether she dies. Of course I care, underneath, but, like Gussie, the reader does not get to wallow.

**Nicola Morgan**

## Next?

Gussie's story begins in *The Burying Beetle* and is completed in *Inchworm*. In 1985, the author's son died after a heart and lung transplant. His story inspired the **Gussie** books.

For a beautiful book about a teenager dying – told in her own voice – read Jenny Downham's *Before I Die*. (UTBG 37)

Helen Dunmore's *Ingo* is set in Cornwall and lyrically describes its land and seascapes. (UTBG 203)

# BOY2GIRL  Terence Blacker

**Next?**

For a boy and girl switching bodies, try Michael Lawrence's **The Aldous Lexicon** trilogy. (UTBG 41)

More Terence Blacker? Try *The Angel Factory*, about a seemingly perfect world that is actually dark and treacherous. (UTBG 23)

Pete Johnson's *Faking It* is about a boy pretending a gorgeous girl in a photo is his girlfriend. What happens when the real girl turns up? (UTBG 126)

In most stories involving the theme 'distant orphan cousin arrives', the cousin is often a wimp or a nerd. But Sam Lopez, who comes to live with his English cousin Matthew, is smelly, rude and full of brassy confidence. And he also has a certain glamour: he is from California, after all.

Matthew and his mates impose an amazing initiation test on Sam. He has to attend school dressed as a girl. Astonishingly, he is very convincing… But I'll leave you to discover the delicious sequence of events.

'This book will make you laugh – or your money back,' it says on the cover. But this is not an easy way to make a fast buck, unfortunately. To avoid laughing at Terence Blacker's book, you'd have to be clinically dead.

**Sue Limb**

# THE BOY IN THE BURNING HOUSE
## Tim Wynne-Jones

Jim Hawkins is just beginning to get over the disappearance of his dad, now presumed dead. So when wild Ruth Rose appears with her crazy theories about what happened to him, accusing Father Fisher, the beyond-reproach local priest, Jim doesn't want to know. But he can't ignore a niggling doubt – what if Ruth Rose is right? Their urgent investigation takes them back to the events of a generation earlier, when a wayward local boy died in a fire no one has yet been able to explain…

Consistently engaging and beautifully crafted, *The Boy in the Burning House* is a real read-in-one-sitting book.

**Daniel Hahn**

**Next?**

Another Tim Wynne-Jones? *A Thief in the House of Memory* is about family secrets and visions that turn into nightmares.

Another book in which the past comes back in unsettling ways is Robert Westall's **The Watch House**. (UTBG 426)

Or for another exciting American adventure, read Mark Twain's *Huckleberry Finn*. (UTBG 191)

Or try the classic **Treasure Island** for a great adventure starring another Jim Hawkins! (UTBG 402)

# THE BOY IN THE STRIPED PYJAMAS
## John Boyne

This book is about innocence and naivety existing in the midst of horror and despair. It's a book that changes the way you think, and is one to read best when you know nothing about it! So that presents a real problem for someone trying to recommend the book. Oh, but there's a film, too! And you've probably seen that, but you really need to read the book first, and if you've seen the film you need to try and forget it and read this without remembering all the things the film told you. I promise you it'll be worth it, because this book is unlike anything else, and if you can read it with a child's innocence, it is absolutely one of the most horrifying stories ever written – a Grimm, and grim, fairy tale for the 21st century.

**Leonie Flynn**

'A small wonder of a book' GUARDIAN

# The Boy
# in the
# Striped
# Pyjamas

## JOHN BOYNE

### Next?

Try the stories of the Brothers Grimm or Perrault and be amazed at how different they are from how you remember. Look out, too, for a collection of familiar and unfamiliar stories – Angela Carter's **Book of Fairy Tales**.

Something else just as shocking? Michael Morpurgo's **Private Peaceful**. (UTBG 324)

Or try the wonderful, amazing and terrifying **The Book Thief** by Marcus Zusak. (UTBG 52)

## PRISON – PAST, PRESENT AND FUTURE

*Furnace: Lockdown* by Alexander Gordon Smith

*Guantanamo Boy* by Anna Perera

*Incarceron* by Catherine Fisher

*Papillon* by Henri Charrière

*The Colditz Story* by P.R. Reid

*The Prison Runner* by Deborah Ellis

*Inside the Cage* by Matt Whyman

# BOY KILLS MAN   Matt Whyman

Based not on a true story exactly, but on the genuine existence of child assassins in modern-day Colombia, *Boy Kills Man* is a short, powerful book that thrills, but also emotionally engages, the reader.

The book follows the life of Shorty, a young teenage boy who gets sucked into the underworld of life in the city: a world where the drug lords use children to kill their rivals, since a loophole in Colombian law means they are exempt from prosecution for murder. Desperate for money, but more desperate to prove himself to his peers and his family, Shorty quickly finds himself in way over his head.

This is a book with a troubling ending and no easy answers, but that is its power – it is unashamedly honest and brutal, and at the same time does not sensationalise its material.

**Marcus Sedgwick**

> **Next?**
>
> Matt Whyman's *The Wild* is about two brothers growing up in Kazakhstan. Bringing in mental illness, destitution and the nuclear arms race, this is a powerful, unsettling story.
>
> The hero of *Vernon God Little* is accused of perpetrating a school massacre. (UTBG 419)
>
> For another sort of child killer, read Anne Cassidy's gripping, distressing *Looking for JJ.* (UTBG 240)

# BOY MEETS BOY   David Levithan

Paul doesn't have a problem being gay – he's lived with the knowledge since his kindergarten teacher declared it. Loads of his friends are gay, too. But that doesn't make forming new relationships easy. Especially when the ex who dumps him wants him back and Noah, his new beau, finds out. Keeping old friendships alive is just as hard – everyone around Paul is freaking, it seems, and pretty soon he's freaking himself. It's time to get a grip and get the guy he wants. But there's so much more to this wonderfully funny book than that. Sometimes the characters seem over the top but everything about this book is true to life.

**Jon Appleton**

> **Next?**
>
> It's not easy to find a similar book, but try Paul Magrs's *Strange Boy* (UTBG 380) or Will Davis's witty and shocking account of growing up gay: *My Side of the Story*.
>
> David Levithan also writes with Rachel Cohn; look out for *Naomi and Ely's No Kiss List*, in which the fact that Ely turns out to be gay puts a crimp in his and Naomi's childhood wish to get married and have kids; or *Nick and Norah's Infinite Playlist*.
>
> Or what about a gay superhero? Read Perry Moore's fabulous, unique *Hero*. (UTBG 176)
>
> Or try *Thinking Straight* by Robin Reardon, about a boy sent to be 'reprogrammed' out of his homosexuality.

# BOY SOLDIER   Andy McNab and Robert Rigby

If there's anyone who knows about the thrills and perils of the SAS, it's Andy McNab. And now he's drawn on his own experience to co-author this nail-bitingly exciting story of Danny Watts and his quest for his grandfather Fergus (a disgraced former SAS officer). As you read of the dangers that Danny and Fergus face together, you'll quickly learn the SAS jargon and techniques, and that'll help this extraordinary tale feel real and immediate. (Which in turn will make it even more exciting, and more nerve-wracking, as the dangers Danny faces will seem pretty real and immediate, too!)

It's fast-paced, smart and engaging; and best of all, Andy McNab and Robert Rigby have written three sequels!

**Daniel Hahn**

> ### Next?
>
> The sequels are: *Payback*, *Avenger* and *Meltdown*.
>
> Read about the teenagers training to be secret agents in A.J. Butcher's **Spy High** series. (UTBG 374)
>
> Or for the greatest super-spy of all – James Bond in his teenage years – start with *SilverFin*. (UTBG 362)
>
> For another extraordinary reconciliation between grandson and wayward grandfather – but treated as differently as you can imagine – read David Grossman's beautiful and witty *The Zigzag Kid*. (UTBG 453)

# THE BOYS WHO SAVED THE WORLD
## Sam Mills

> ### Next?
>
> Sam Mills also wrote the complex, thrilling *A Nicer Way to Die*.
>
> For a very different perspective on terrorism, read Matt Whyman's *Inside the Cage*.
>
> For more dark power play within a sinister school group, read Graham Gardner's *Inventing Elliott*. (UTBG 206)
>
> Or try Sarah Wray's *The Trap*, about a boy who is sent to summer camp. He thinks it will be a trip of a lifetime, but it turns out to be less like fun and more like horror.

Jon is a member of the Brotherhood, a group set up at school by Jeremiah, who runs it as though it were his own private religion. Jeremiah is charismatic, clever, manipulative, and it's no wonder the others willingly follow him. But what happens when his ideas turn to kidnapping, and maybe worse? Is Jeremiah responding to a real threat, or just playing power games? One thing is for sure – it can't end well…

A dark and thrilling story about a society's greatest fears, about extremism and intolerance, and above all about the seductions of power, *The Boys Who Saved the World* is a gripping and thought-provoking read.

**Daniel Hahn**

# BRAT FARRAR  Josephine Tey

You get two books for the price of one with *Brat Farrar*, and it's this unique combination that makes it the best mystery story that I've ever read.

The premise is simple: Patrick Ashby, heir to a considerable fortune, disappears when he is 13. For eight years his family believe he committed suicide but then, just weeks before his twin's coming-of-age, Patrick turns up again. Everyone is happy to see him and accepts that he is who he says he is – everyone except his supplanted twin, Simon.

What really happened to Patrick is, of course, the mystery, but this book also serves as a time machine. When you read it, you are transported back to the 1940s and a way of life that has vanished for ever.

**Laura Hutchings**

> **Next?**
>
> More Josephine Tey?
> Try *The Franchise Affair*,
> about a girl accusing two
> old ladies of kidnap, and
> *The Daughter of Time*,
> in which a convalescing
> detective tries to solve the
> mystery of the princes in
> the Tower.
>
> For modern mysteries set
> in the world of horses, Dick
> Francis's thrillers are top.
> Try *Reflex* or *Whip Hand*
> (UTBG 434) to start with.

# BRAVE NEW WORLD  Aldous Huxley

> **Next?**
>
> For some other angles
> on dystopian futures, try
> *Nineteen Eighty-Four*
> (UTBG 284) and the
> satirical *Animal Farm*
> (UTBG 24).
>
> If you liked the dark sci-fi
> edge to the book, try
> *Fahrenheit 451* (UTBG
> 126) or *The Day of the
> Triffids* (UTBG 98).
>
> Meg Rosoff's *How I Live
> Now* is a harrowing novel
> about how life could be
> after the world is changed
> by war. (UTBG 190)

Published in 1932, *Brave New World* creates an imaginary world many years in the future, a seeming paradise where everything is perfect, where illness and poverty have been defeated and where, theoretically, everyone is happy. But of course, they are not.

Huxley depicts his world in a terrifying and convincing way; here, intense social engineering succeeds only at the expense of some fundamental human traits, and the ideas of family, love and freedom all suffer at the hands of the State. In place of natural happiness, joy is instead derived from promiscuous but meaningless sex, from consuming material goods, from watching certain state-controlled sports and from indulgence in a pleasure drug. If that sounds like Huxley was writing about our own age, then people who see his book as prophetic are vindicated, but there is more to this enjoyable and disturbing science-fiction novel than simple prophecy.

**Marcus Sedgwick**

# THE BREADWINNER  Deborah Ellis

Four days after her father's arrest, food runs out for Parvana's family. Though Taliban rule absolutely forbids women to leave the house alone, Parvana has no option but to take the risk, disguising herself as a boy and dodging the deadly landmines in an attempt to save her family from starvation.

Using the imagined life story of a young Afghan teenager, Ellis clearly conveys the brutality and fear of Taliban rule, and brings the human stories behind the headlines to life in a way that is far more hard-hitting and emotionally striking than any TV news report. A brave, timely and topical book – continued in the equally eye-opening *Parvana's Journey*, in which Parvana flees across war-torn Afghanistan in search of her father.

**Eileen Armstrong**

> **Next?**
>
> As well as *Parvana's Journey* there's another sequel, *Mud City*, which takes up the story of one of Parvana's friends.
>
> Ellis's *The Heaven Shop* tells the story of AIDS-stricken families in Malawi through the eyes of one young girl. Or try her books set in Bolivia, *The Prison Runner* and *Beyond the Barricade*. They're also based on appalling real-life events.
>
> Maya Angelou's *I Know Why the Caged Bird Sings* is also about repression. (UTBG 198)

# BREAKFAST AT TIFFANY'S
## Truman Capote

> **Next?**
>
> You'll find another seductive and amoral heroine in François Sagan's *Bonjour Tristesse*; but beware, you may find it a more shocking read. (UTBG 52)
>
> The eponymous heroine of *Zuleika Dobson* by Max Beerbohm is another young woman finding her place in the world.
>
> One of the greatest barbed wits of the 20th century belonged to an American woman called Dorothy Parker. Read her work in *The Collected Dorothy Parker*.

Holly Golighty is a Carrie Bradshaw in waiting. Today she would write a column about her adventures in the captivating city of New York, meeting her equally successful friends for brunch and buying herself presents at Tiffany's. Half a century ago, young women who wanted to reinvent themselves needed to do it through men. Capote's short novel is less frothy than the Audrey Hepburn film. Holly's barbed wit barely masks her insecurity; her casual racism and shallowness is jarring to a modern reader. But it's hard not to become smitten with her as the narrator does, and even when you fall out of love with her, you still wish her well.

**Geraldine Brennan**

# BREAKTIME Aidan Chambers

**Next?**

The sequence continues with *Dance on My Grave* (UTBG 94), *Now I Know*, *The Toll Bridge* (UTBG 399), *Postcards from No Man's Land* (UTBG 318) and *This Is All*.

When characters keep diaries and records in fiction, all kinds of unexpected things are revealed. Jan Mark's *The Hillingdon Fox* is one of my all-time favourites.

Or try Jean Ure's *Get a Life*, about a boy who discovers secrets about his brother's sexuality.

This is the first in a ground-breaking sequence of six novels by Aidan Chambers, all of which look at physical and emotional experiences – and how we understand and talk about them. All that sounds pretty heavy, but Chambers introduces lots of jokes and playfulness that remind us that experiences are only as real as the language we use to describe them. Several things happen in this book over the course of the holiday period that Ditto is recording – he's been dared to keep a record by his schoolmate Morgan – culminating in, for Ditto, the ultimate experience: his first sexual encounter, with a girl called Helen. Or is it?

When it was first published, this book caused a stir for its explicit description of sex; it remains a bold and thought-provoking read today.

**Jon Appleton**

# BREATHE: A GHOST STORY Cliff McNish

Jack and his mother, Sarah, are struggling to come to terms with the death of Jack's father. They move into a new house; what they don't know is that four children already live there, 'still wearing the clothes they had died in'. Jack, sensitized by bereavement and illness, feels their misery and pain and longs to help them. He also becomes aware of the malevolent presence of the Ghost Mother, who feeds on the children's souls and keeps them away from the peace they should have found after their deaths. The living Jack is forced to battle the dead Ghost Mother for the children's souls and his own survival.

If you like ghost stories, or films like *The Sixth Sense* and *The Others*, you'll love *Breathe* – it will scare you witless!

**Antonia Honeywell**

**Next?**

Cliff McNish writes atmospheric and unsettling stories; try *Angel* next.

There's more terrifying malignity in Kate Cann's *Leaving Poppy*. (UTBG 234)

Or try some scary short stories: *Uncle Montague's Tales of Terror* (UTBG 413) or *Tales of Mystery and Imagination* by Edgar Allen Poe (UTBG 387).

Sonia Hartnett's *The Ghost's Child* spins a dfferent sort of ghostly tale.

# BRIDESHEAD REVISITED

## Evelyn Waugh

**Next?**

*The Great Gatsby* by F. Scott Fitzgerald is also a classic tale of glittering wealth, love, unhappiness and loneliness. (UTBG 166)

Another novel with a pre-war setting which deals with changing attitudes towards class is E.M. Forster's *Howard's End*.

For those on a Waugh path (!), try *Decline and Fall* or *Vile Bodies* – both very different, dark satires.

Oh man! Describing why I like *Brideshead* in 120 words is a bit like trying to sum up *The Bible* in one sentence. Saying it's about a doomed aristocratic Catholic family isn't, methinks, going to make you want to rush out and buy it. But it's about so much more – it's a great love story; it's a heartrending tale of loss and rejection; it's a great sweeping narrative that takes in pre-war Oxford, Venice, Paris and Morocco and a large cast of brilliantly drawn characters; it deals with religion and morality, guilt, repression and pain; it's dark, complex, powerful, evocative, poetic, compelling, sumptuous, passionate, moving, at times extremely funny, and ultimately tragic. In short, it's a masterpiece and I totally love it!

**Catherine Robinson**

# BRIDGET JONES'S DIARY

## Helen Fielding

Bridget is in her thirties and worried. Although she has a good job, a home of her own and many good friends, she is single and, more than anything, she wants a boyfriend. But the men in her life seem to be too standoffish or too untrustworthy to fit the bill. Her family teases her for being alone and she worries endlessly about how much she weighs, drinks and smokes. Only her closest friends can make her see that life is not so bad after all.

Written as a diary, this sweet and very funny book takes us through a year of Bridget's life, as she searches for love, happiness and the perfect diet while dodging unsuitable men, annoying parents and the dreaded 'smug marrieds'.

**Marianne Taylor**

**Next?**

Read the sequel, *Bridget Jones: the Edge of Reason*.

*Does My Bum Look Big in This?* is another light-hearted tale of the struggles of a singleton. (UTBG 111)

Of course the original Mr Darcy features in Jane Austen's *Pride and Prejudice*. (UTBG 320)

Another female with body-image issues is Virginia in Carolyn Macker's *Earth, My Butt and Other Big Round Things*. (UTBG 118)

# BRIDGE TO TERABITHIA  Katherine Paterson

Jess doesn't really have any friends until new girl Leslie comes to his rural school. Leslie is rich and lives in a big house and her parents don't even own a television. Like Jess, Leslie is an outsider. Together they create a magical kingdom – Terabithia – down by the creek; as King and Queen of Terabithia they can make a world just as they want it to be. Life is perfect ... until tragedy strikes.

A moving and insightful book about friendship, death and creativity.

**Ann Jungman**

**Next?**

Read *Anne of Green Gables* (and sequels) by L.M. Montgomery; set on Prince Edward Island, Canada, the stories show how close rural family life can be, as does Karen Wallace's *Raspberries on the Yangtze* (UTBG 326).

Or try Frances Hodgson Burnett's *The Secret Garden*, in which a lonely boy and girl find redemption in a magical place.

*Walk Two Moons* by Sharon Creech is a stunning American story about coming to terms with tragedy. (UTBG 422)

# BRIGHTON ROCK  Graham Greene

**Next?**

Graham Greene's short stories are wonderfully various, as are his novels; try *Our Man in Havana*. (UTBG 302)

The **Maigret** books (UTBG 252), featuring the bumbling inspector, have a cast of crooks and seedy thugs and a similar feel to *Brighton Rock*.

For another story of murder with a powerful setting, this time pre-war London, try *Hangover Square* by Patrick Hamilton. (UTBG 170)

Over 40 years ago the first page of *Brighton Rock* made me want to be a writer. It's an opening to die for ... and somebody does. Graham Greene's story walks out of Brighton station and straight off the page; it intrigues and appals you, and then goes on haunting the streets of your imagination for the rest of your life. Its characters, their desperate lives, the busy seafront and dark alleys of the dangerous town where Good and Evil are in relentless pursuit of one another stay with you for ever. Because, like all the very best books, *Brighton Rock* lives on long after you've turned the last page. Join the crowd on the promenade and you'll see what I mean.

**Michael Cronin**

# BROKEN SOUP Jenny Valentine

**Next?**

Read Jenny Valentine's *Finding Violet Park*, another compelling portrait of broken family life. (UTBG 132)

In *Lucas*, Kevin Brooks paints the bleak East Anglian coast in the same true colours with which Valentine draws Camden Town. (UTBG 249)

Or try Julia Donaldson's thriller, about a boy who runs away from home: *Running on the Cracks*.

I don't come across them often. You know, those books that, when you open them up, you get that tingling, butterflies-in-the-stomach moment, and you know, instantly, that they're going to change your life in some small way.

*Broken Soup* is one of those books. Like the discarded photo negative that is the catalyst for change and revelation, it altered the way I look at things.

Jenny Valentine's second foray into contemporary family life, the book follows 15-year-old Rowan as she tries to navigate London, and the maze of her parents' failed marriage, her father's absence, and her mother's depression.

On face value a tale about grief, relationship break-up and responsibility, *Broken Soup* is full of hope, of romance and freedom.

**Joanna Nadin**

# THE BROMELIAD trilogy Terry Pratchett

For the Nomes in the Store there is no day and night, no sun and rain. All these things are just old myths – just like 'the Outside'. However, all that changes when a group of Nomes from the Outside arrive…

In *Truckers*, the Nomes capture a truck, and escape in it before their home, the Store, is demolished. In *Diggers*, the Nomes try to survive in the Quarry – but this becomes a nightmare, especially when the humans intervene… In *Wings*, three Nomes try to get to America to find a spacecraft to take them home, using the Thing (a microcomputer) as a guide.

This gripping fantasy adventure is full of humour, misunderstanding and deeper meaning, too – strongly recommended!

**Samuel Mortimer, age 11**

**Next?**

More Pratchett of course. Try the **Johnny Maxwell** series, beginning with *Only You Can Save Mankind*; or one of his **Discworld** books, try *Monstrous Regiment* (UTBG 107) first.

For another fantasy that'll make you laugh, read Paul Stewart and Chris Riddell's *Muddle Earth*; or the **Edge Chronicles**, beginning with *Beyond the Deepwoods* (UTBG 119).

Or for more confusion involving a spacecraft, try Andrew Norris's *Aquila*.

# BROTHERS  Ted van Lieshout

**Next?**

Paul Magrs's *Strange Boy* is set in the north-east of England and deals with sexuality. (UTBG 380)

If you're interested in the treatment of bereavement in *Brothers*, try Brian Keaney's *Bitter Fruit*. (UTBG 45)

*Skin* by A.M. Vrettos is about a boy learning his sister's dark secrets.

Warning – this is an immensely moving novel. It begins when teenage Luke finds his younger brother Marius's diary – Marius died six months ago. Luke is reluctant at first to start reading it, but begins to write his own diary in it, in which he struggles with his feelings about losing his brother and his growing knowledge that he's gay. When he finally starts to read Marius's entries, he discovers exactly what it is he and his brother had in common and why their relationship will always be meaningful. This is a novel about the big stuff – sexuality, bereavement – but this Dutch author writes with a real lightness of touch. The book will draw you in from the start.

**Sherry Ashworth**

# THE BUDDHA OF SUBURBIA
## Hanif Kureishi

Karim Amir lives in the South London suburbs with his English mother and Indian father. Restless and easily bored, he's desperate to escape and experience life. The book follows his escapades through 1970s London, where he finds himself mixing with every social circle, from the punk scene to the theatre world.

Karim ends up in many of the positions we all find ourselves in (and some we almost certainly don't). The unexpected ways in which he deals with these situations are hilarious, yet at the same time painfully honest and genuinely moving. Karim's narrative has a wonderfully fresh and self-mocking tone – however great his dilemmas are he's never going to take life too seriously. But this isn't a book to read if you're easily offended (or if you're looking for a real insight into Eastern philosophy!).

**Katie Jennings**

**Next?**

More Kureishi? Try *Something to Tell You*, which is about a man looking back on the violence and mistakes of his youth in the 1970s.

If you want to know more about how teenage boys think, read *The Rachel Papers* by Martin Amis. (UTBG 325)

*Generation X* by Douglas Coupland has more pop culture. (UTBG 151)

Alan Warner is brilliant, too; try *Morvern Callar*, about a girl's search for her identity in Ibiza, or *The Sopranos*, a funny story of bad girls on a school choir trip.

# CALLING A DEAD MAN  Gillian Cross

A sick man with no memory awakes in a snowy Siberian wood. All he knows is that something has happened that is too terrible to recall. Meanwhile, far away, a family obliterates every trace of an adored son; a gangster organisation senses a threat to its security; and a bereft lover sets out into the unknown with only the slenderest of hopes to support her.

*Calling a Dead Man* takes place after the fall of Communism, when criminal organisations, the Mafiya, are moving in to make as much profit as possible in the resulting power vacuum. We see a frozen world of small, valiant people, some acting with extraordinary generosity and heroism in the face of death, cruelty and relentless poverty.

This is an amazing book, not just for being a taut thriller in an exotic setting, but for describing huge emotions in a barren landscape, and portraying the Siberian people with insight and compassion.

**Sally Prue**

> **Next?**
>
> Gillian Cross has written another thriller about a criminal organisation in *Tightrope*. Look out, too, for Anne Fine's story of courage and endurance, *The Road of Bones* (UTBG 332).
>
> A brilliant thriller set around the cold war is John le Carré's *The Spy Who Came in from the Cold*. (UTBG 374)
>
> A true story of Russia, Communism and Siberia is *One Day in the Life of Ivan Denisovich* by Alexander Solzhenitsyn. (UTBG 293)

# THE CALL OF THE WILD  Jack London

> **Next?**
>
> Jack London wrote amazingly about animals; try another classic, *White Fang*.
>
> *Roll of Thunder, Hear My Cry* by Mildred D. Taylor is about humans being cruel to humans. (UTBG 333)
>
> There are some wonderful books about animals and humans where sometimes you simply end up loathing being human – try Michael Morpurgo's *Born to Run* or Anna Sewell's classic, *Black Beauty*.
>
> Another book that's set in the wild American landscape is J. Fenimore Cooper's *Last of the Mohicans*.

This is a book about appalling animal cruelty. Buck is kidnapped from his home and taken to the wild north of Canada. Beaten, clubbed and whipped until he obeys, he is harnessed to a sledge with eight other dogs and forced to pull his new owners and their belongings across rock and snow in their search for gold. He learns to fight for his place in the pack, to survive the cruelty of man, dog and nature, and eventually finds a new pride in himself. But things get worse and worse for Buck, until it seems that a happy ending is impossible – or is it?

**Leonie Flynn**

# CANDY   Kevin Brooks

Kevin Brooks pushes his characters into situations you hope will never happen to you: extreme situations, but ones you will believe in absolutely. Candy is a beautiful girl, trapped in heroin addiction and prostitution – and Joe Beck, bass guitarist and genuine good guy, falls madly in love with her. Iggy, Candy's utterly terrifying pimp / drug dealer, is not happy, and when Iggy is not happy, violence is inevitable.

This is a story about lack of control, whether because of drugs, or love, or pure chance, or because of the adults who run the world that teenagers have to live in. Lock your door when you read this dark, dangerous and utterly gripping book – you will not want to be interrupted.

**Nicola Morgan**

> **Next?**
>
> Kevin Brooks's other books – they're all amazing.
>
> *Skarrs* (UTBG 364) deals with similar issues and is just as hard hitting. Or try *Dirty Work* by Julia Bell, in which a young girl is forced into prostitution.
>
> Melvin Burgess never shrinks away from being hard-hitting, and his *Nicholas Dane* is no exception. Read it, be shocked, then remember that in real life it all happens…
>
> London Zoo, one of the settings for *Candy*, also features in another, quite different, book – Russell Hoban's *Turtle Diary*. (UTBG 410)

# CANNERY ROW / SWEET THURSDAY
## John Steinbeck

> **Next?**
>
> John Steinbeck's most famous books are *The Grapes of Wrath* and *Of Mice and Men* (UTBG 291), but you might like to try some more of his lesser-known stuff. My favourites are *The Wayward Bus* and *Travels with Charley*.
>
> Another writer who deals in misfits is Flannery O'Connor. Try *A Good Man Is Hard to Find*.
>
> Jenny Valentine's *The Ant Colony* is about a group of misfits who all live together. (UTBG 25)

These two short books make up a beautifully written portrait of a group of people living on the margins of society. Set in a rundown Californian fishing town in the 1940s, both are based around a community of characters who exist on the edges of life – idlers, tramps, low-lifes, wasters.

There isn't much of a plot in these novels – the stories are more like a jigsaw of relationships and events – but the characters are so fascinating, and the writing so hypnotically good, that they don't need a plot.

Although both books can be read independently, the characters are first introduced in *Cannery Row*, so it's probably a good idea to start there.

**Kevin Brooks**

# CAN YOU KEEP A SECRET?
Sandra Glover

The last thing on earth Karen wants is to hang out with compulsive liar Zoe, let alone hear the appalling secret that she's pregnant. When a baby is found abandoned nearby some months later, Zoe 'confesses' that her secret was an attention-seeking lie – or was it? The reader, like Karen, struggles to separate fact from fiction. But the secret meant more to Karen than Zoe realises, for Karen herself was found abandoned and adopted as a baby and must now face up to her own secret past.

Glover is one of the most versatile writers around and this is one of her most intricate, involving, read-it-in-one-sitting books.

**Eileen Armstrong**

**Next?**

Sandra Glover's books challenge you to make up your own mind. Try *Somewhere Else*, about a girl who may or may not be who everyone thinks, or *Dangerously Close*, about love and abuse, or *Spiked*, about a girl abducted after her drink is spiked at a post-GCSE party.

In Chris Lynch's *Inexcusable*, Keir is a good boy – or is he? How will he defend himself against accusations of rape? (UTBG 202)

# CARWASH
Lesley Howarth

I really enjoyed this story about a group of teenagers in a village in Cornwall and the events of one hot summer that leave everyone changed in some way. It's funny, and real, and convincing in every detail. I love the way the story is narrated by different characters: it starts with Luke who runs his own car-washing business in the village, and then moves to Sylvie Bickle ('Bix') who spends most of her time up a tree watching what everyone else is up to. Her sister Liv also plays a central role in the story, as does Luke's brother Danny. Liv likes writing and is on the lookout for material for her stories, but the most dramatic and significant thing is actually happening to her…

You really get to know these characters and live that summer along with them… Brilliant!

**Julia Green**

**Next?**

Try other novels by the same author: *Ultraviolet* (UTBG 412) is set in a world trying to recreate itself after nuclear war; *Drive* is about a boy pulled towards crime.

Or try Julia Green's beautifully written, unforgetable *Breathing Underwater*, about a girl returning to the place where her brother died.

Or read *LBD: It's a Girl Thing* by Grace Dent, it's a light, funny, perceptive look at teenage life. (UTBG 233)

# CATALYST  Laurie Halse Anderson

## Next?

More by the same author? Try *Speak*, another painfully honest look at growing up, fitting in and social pressure.

For another emotional and intelligent ride through adolescence, try *The Moth Diaries* by Rachel Klein. (UTBG 270)

*What the Birds See* by Sonya Hartnett is a painfully wonderful book with a similar feel, though it's less direct and raw. (UTBG 432)

*You Don't Know Me* by David Klass is about a boy pushed to the edge by his stepfather. (UTBG 452)

Kate is brilliant and seems in control of everything; everyone expects her to succeed. The fact that she seems to have taken her dead mother's place so effortlessly makes everyone believe that she is fine. But inside, she is losing control, and carries unbearable burdens. When a truly shocking event occurs, will this tip her over the edge or save her?

If this is one of the most painful books I have ever read, why am I recommending it? Perhaps because it captures so perfectly some of the pain of growing up. Parents should read it, too – then they'll think twice before putting their sons and daughters under the intense pressure that Kate Malone faces.

**Nicola Morgan**

# CATCH-22
## Joseph Heller

When I was a teenager, reading *Catch-22* by Joseph Heller changed the way I thought about life, and it changed the way I thought about books. It made me see, for the first time, that war is a kind of insanity. And it made me realise that a book could be funny and intensely serious at the same time.

The book's anti-hero, Yossarian, is an American fighter pilot stationed in Italy during World War II, desperate to be excused from flying more missions and to escape the madness of a situation where every kind of military double-think and capitalist excess seems to thrive. The book has fantastic comic energy and builds towards a triumphant surprise ending.

**Jonathan Coe**

## Next?

Yossarian and friends reappear in *Closing Time*, where this time the enemy is death itself.

A scathing look at the contemporary world, particularly America, is *Dude, Where's My Country?* by Michael Moore.

Jonathan Coe's own novel, *What a Carve Up!*, is great satire and a stark black comedy about murder (and other things).

Read our feature on cult books on pp. 280–281 for more books that will change the way you think and view life.

# THE CATCHER IN THE RYE
## J.D. Salinger

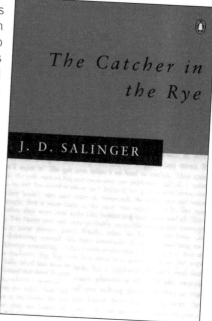

After being thrown out of his fourth expensive boarding school, Holden Caulfield puts time on hold and spends two disastrous days in New York before facing his parents. Heading for a mental and physical breakdown, his favourite word is 'phony', which describes just about everyone he meets and anything he doesn't like; and yet he desperately wants to fit in somewhere, have friends, figure out his future. The people he most admires are children like his little sister. He imagines himself being a 'catcher', someone who can get between them and danger, always haunted by the memory of his brother who died young, the one he couldn't save.

All teen novels are descended from this one, and yet it isn't a teen novel, just a book about one unhappy 16 year old, and millions have identified with him.

**Jan Mark**

### Next?

Another 16 year old who deals with a crisis rather differently is the hero of *The Beet Fields*. (UTBG 37)

*Billy Liar* by Keith Waterhouse is an account of a teenager in northern England getting himself into every kind of trouble and trying to blag his way out of it.

For more Salinger try *For Esmé – with Love and Squalor*, his collection of short stories about youth and childhood. (UTBG 138)

Meg Rosoff's *Just in Case* is a more modern take on a boy growing up. (UTBG 220)

I was 19 and not enjoying my first year at university when I first met Holden Caulfield, the 16-year-old protagonist of *The Catcher in the Rye*. Holden is having a bad time, too – we soon discover he is about to flunk out of yet another school, and doesn't know what to do with his life. So he sets out for a weekend in New York before going home to his parents.

Holden is trapped between childhood and maturity, desperate to grow up but afraid of it, too, and disgusted by the 'phony' way adults behave. He is also the original teen and one of the great characters of literature. His story is both funny and very moving. Most of us have a Holden Caulfield moment at some time – and I know he helped me with mine.

**Tony Bradman**

# CAT'S CRADLE  Kurt Vonnegut

This story is told by a man who is planning a book about the day the first atomic bomb was dropped on Japan. In the course of his researches he meets Newt Hoenikker, son of Dr Felix Hoenikker, 'father of the bomb', which leads him to a small Caribbean island where he comes into contact with a brand-new religion, falls in love, and becomes president. He also learns about Ice-9, a substance created by Dr Hoenikker which, when brought into contact with water, instantly freezes it and spreads – endlessly.

Kurt Vonnegut is one of the easiest writers to read, and often one of the funniest, but he also puts a very individual spin on the most serious subjects. Everyone should give Vonnegut a try. Even if you don't like the way he writes, you'll have to admit he's an original.

**Michael Lawrence**

### Next?

For a look at what the world might be like before and after The Bomb, read Raymond Briggs's graphic novel, **When the Wind Blows**. (UTBG 434)

The spine-chilling **Why Weeps the Brogan?** is set in a world that has been destroyed. (UTBG 437)

More Vonnegut? He lived through the bombing of Dresden and wrote about it in **Slaughterhouse 5** (UTBG 368). There's also **Breakfast of Champions** and many more. All weird and brain expanding.

# CAT'S EYE
## Margaret Atwood

### Next?

If you enjoyed the theme of art and what it says about life, read **To the Lighthouse** by Virginia Woolf.

If the theme of bullying and its effects interested you, try **I'm the King of the Castle** (UTBG 201) by Susan Hill, Heather Morrall's **The Echo Glass** or B.R. Collins's **The Traitor Game** (UTBG 402).

If it's the adult's view of the child they once were that you enjoyed, try **The Go-Between** by L.P. Hartley. (UTBG 159)

As a successful artist, Elaine Risley returns to Toronto where she grew up, for an exhibition. Elaine's paintings have been inspired by her own experiences, and the truths she splashes on her canvases aren't ones that her former friends are ready for. In order to move on with her adult life, Elaine is forced to confront her past and to relive the bullying she endured at the hands of her fascinating and manipulative friend Cordelia.

*Cat's Eye* is a brilliant and absorbing novel about art, about the nature of time, about friendship, and about how the child you were will always be a part of the adult you become.

**Antonia Honeywell**

# CAUGHT IN THE CROSSFIRE
## Alan Gibbons

**Next?**

Try another of Alan's novels, such as *The Edge* or *The Defender*. Or look for his terrifying time slip, *Scared to Death*.

Joan Lingard's **Across the Barricades** series, starting with *The Twelfth Day of July*, is also set amidst religious conflict. (UTBG 410)

*Ruby Tanya* by Robert Swindells is a thriller that mixes racism, asylum seekers and prejudice.

*Little Brother* by Cory Doctorow is the story of one boy's rebellion – against everyhting.

The Patriotic League, an extreme right-wing racist party, wants to claim white Britain back, and the events of September 11th give them the perfect excuse to stir up trouble in the north of England. Caught in the crossfire of mounting violence are six teenagers: two Irish lads looking for trouble; a Muslim brother and sister; and Mike and Liam, brothers taking different sides, one of whom is heading for a terrible fate.

Alan Gibbons is a brilliant writer, and this book is typically fast-paced, compulsive and frighteningly relevant. As one teenager wrote recently about it: 'It was just so sensitive, emotional and real... I will never be able to forget this book'.

**Cliff McNish**

# THE CEMENT GARDEN   Ian McEwan

As a teenager, I was not a reader. I had always been a TV and computer games kid. Then, aged 16, I was given Ian McEwan's *The Cement Garden*. I was gripped, and I still remember the feeling of staying up late into the night, in my own private pool of bedside light, reading and reading, unable to contemplate sleep until I had got to the end of the book. From that moment on, I was transformed from a TV watcher into a reader, and possibly even into a writer.

The story is dark, gory, twisted, funny, and contains sex, bad language, masturbation, gender-bending and the improvised burial of parents. It's a sort of *Lord of the Flies* of the family, with a suburban house standing in for the desert island. Your English teacher could get into serious trouble for giving you this kind of book...

**William Sutcliffe**

**Next?**

Read *Lord of the Flies* itself and see what you think. (UTBG 241)

Ian McEwan is an amazing writer; read all his books, especially *Enduring Love*, about the destructiveness of obsession.

Sadie Jones's *The Outcast* is another claustrophobic novel about twisted love and appalling families.

# CENTURY
## Sarah Singleton

**Next?**

For a very different take on living for ever read Natalie Babbitt's *Tuck Everlasting*.

And for more books about slipping between points in time, try both Daphne Du Maurier's *The House on the Strand* and Michael Lawrence's trilogy, **The Aldous Lexicon**.

If you liked Sarah Singleton's very distinctive writing style and want more, then try *The Poison Garden* (UTBG 317) or *Sacrifice*, which weaves madness, magic and a generations-old curse.

If you like mystery stories, with a bit of horror thrown in for good measure, then this is the book for you. Two sisters, Mercy and Charity, live what is virtually the same day over and over again, trapped in a house called Century. It's always winter and it's always dark. Their father is a distant, frightening figure who is in perpetual mourning for his wife. Then, one day, Mercy wakes to find a snowdrop on her pillow and everything starts to change.

The book follows Mercy as she unravels the mystery of her mother's death and her own imprisonment and it contains some genuinely chilling moments. Not one for the fainthearted!

**Laura Hutchings**

# THE CHANGEOVER   Margaret Mahy

Apart from the fact that she sometimes has 'premonitions' and suspects that Sorensen Carlisle, a senior boy whom she secretly fancies, might be a witch, Laura Chant is an ordinary 14 year old. She does well at school and helps her divorcee mum to look after her little brother, Jacko. Then one day a vile man called Carmody Braque brands his evil image on the back of Jacko's hand and from that moment the toddler starts to shrivel and fade. Braque is feeding like a vampire on Jacko's youth. In desperation, Laura turns to Sorensen Carlisle for help and discovers that to defeat Carmody Braque she herself must become a witch, too. Sorensen is a terrific character, dangerous and sexy, yet curiously vulnerable, and Laura (along with many readers!) finds herself falling for his enigmatic charms. Mahy makes the extraordinary utterly believable in this supernatural romance.

**Kathryn Ross**

**Next?**

What about a graphic novel about a Wiccan girl falling in love? *Skim* by Mariko Tamaki and Jillian Tamaki. (UTBG 366)

In Catherine MacPhail's chilling *Another Me*, a young girl's life is taken over by someone her own age; someone who looks just like her…

Scott Westerfeld manages to create a brilliantly tense atmosphere in his **Midnighters** series.

# CHERUB series Robert Muchamore

This thriller is a cross between Anthony Horowitz's **Alex Rider** books and the violent Luc Besson film *Nikita*. A 12-year-old yobbo on the verge of becoming a delinquent is 'recruited' by a special branch of the British Secret Service. He undergoes brutal training and at the end of it is sent on his first mission.

The story is never predictable, there are no clear-cut goodies or baddies and it's sometimes violent and crude. But all this just adds to the 'real feel'. If your librarian has sent you off to borrow a book and you can't bear to read a story about elves or princesses or spoiled rich kids who never go to the toilet, try this. You won't regret it.

**Caroline Lawrence**

## Next?

*The Recruit* is first in the **CHERUB** series. Sequels are *Class A*, *Maximum Security*, *The Killing*, etc. There's also a new series which explores Cherub's World War II origins: **Henderson's Boys**. Start with *The Escape*.

Look out for Mark Walden's **H.I.V.E.** series – it's about a school for villains.

*Boy Soldier* (UTBG 57) by Andy McNab has a great deal of real detail about military life – the author was in the SAS, as was Chris Ryan, author of the **Alpha Force** books (UTBG 19).

There's more non-stop action in Andrew Klavan's *The Last Thing I Remember*.

# CHICKEN DANCE Jacques Couvillon

## Next?

For another heartfelt story with a boy protagonist, try *Freak the Mighty* by Rodman Philbrick. (UTBG 147)

A similarly written tale, *The Curious Incident of the Dog in the Night-Time* by Mark Haddon, should not be missed. (UTBG 92)

Another writer who manages to make the zany seem quite normal is Frank Cottrell Boyce; try *Millions* (UTBG 264) or *Cosmic*.

Set in a Louisiana town populated by chicken farmers, this is the story of Don, a smart, sensitive boy who has a knack for going unnoticed, even by his own parents. He can't seem to shake the curiosity he feels when he finds his birth certificate and realises it actually says 'Stanley'. Suddenly things in his life don't add up, and he's determined to get to the bottom of it all.

The book is a slice of life that most people could only imagine. Full of kooky characters and even crazier situations, it is both hysterical and touching. Best of all is Don, whose quirks and anxieties are entirely endearing. The scenes in which he dances to KC and the Sunshine Band or he reads out loud to chickens are priceless, and when the big mystery surrounding his family's past allows Don to show his true colours, you will love him even more.

**Mary Kate Castellani**

# PINK LIT
## by Cathy Hopkins

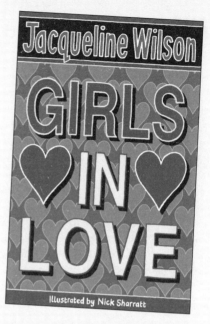

In the current marketing trend (or obsession) to brand and pigeon-hole, pink lit has emerged as the 10–16-year-old equivalent of adult chick lit. The books are recognisable by their bright-coloured 'girlie' covers. Pink lit is frothy and humorous, with a twist of escapism, whilst also managing to deal with serious(-ish) contemporary teenage girl preoccupations: chiefly, relationships (especially with the opposite sex), maddening or embarrassing parents, school life and friends, and questions such as 'How do boys tick?', 'Where do I fit in?' or 'Where is my life heading?'

These books have become incredibly popular because the characters and situations are instantly recognisable and easy to identify with. They are realistic enough, but not threateningly over-gritty or grim. There is romance without sexually transmitted diseases; embarrassing parents without extreme poverty or distressing abuse. Pink lit books are light and easy reading. They have a wide appeal, being read voraciously by literate teen bookworms, by boys (in secret), who want to get a handle on what goes on in girls' minds and by many who claim normally not to read anything more than the cornflake packet.

Pink lit is often dismissed by critics as trivial or facile, probably because of its light-hearted approach. But I think the reviewers miss the point. As well as providing a bit of welcome leisurely escapism, pink lit also provides a chance to explore some of the problems that beset teenagers at an often wretched and difficult time in their lives.

I've written two series that fit into the pink-lit genre: **Mates, Dates...** (UTBG 257),

which is set in North London, and **Truth, Dare...**, set in Cornwall. There is the usual mix of romance, family, school life, and questions such as 'Is there a God?' or 'What am I going to do with my life?' But the main thread that runs through these books is the importance and affirmation of friendship. My publisher has coined a sub-genre, calling them 'friend lit'.

I find my writing very rewarding for two reasons in particular. It is great to know that my stories are popular not just in the UK, but all over the world: the two series have been sold in 21 countries. And I love to get emails from my readers. The most gratifying thing for me is to hear how I have turned someone on to reading. This sort of message is fairly typical: 'I hated reading, but then I picked up your books and it was like reading about my own life'. Score.

# A CHILD CALLED 'IT'  Dave Pelzer

This is a true story. As a child, Dave Pelzer was brutally beaten, emotionally tortured and starved by his unpredictable, unstable, alcoholic mother, while his fireman father, who had 'broad shoulders and forearms that would make any muscle man proud', did nothing but watch. No longer considered a son but a slave, no longer a boy but an 'it', he slept in an old army cot in the basement, dressed in smelly rags, and when he was allowed the luxury of food it was scraps from the dogs' bowls.

What singled Dave out from his two brothers? Perhaps it was that his voice just carried farther than others. He had to learn to play his mother's games – every humiliation a victory as it meant he had survived yet another day.

Told from the child's point of view, this is a heartbreaking yet heart-warming tale of courageous endurance, of one child's dream of finding a family to love and care for him, to call him their son.

**Elena Gregoriou**

### Next?

Read the sequels: *The Lost Boy* and *A Man Named Dave*.

Dave's brother Richard B. Pelzer has written his own account of their childhood in *A Brother's Journey*.

Other writers have been brave enough to tell of their own terrible childhoods. Augusten Burroughs survived life with an alcoholic father; read his memoir *Running with Scissors*.

Or for the fictional account of the aftermath of brutality try *The Lovely Bones* by Alice Sebold. (UTBG 248)

# CHILD X  Lee Weatherly

### Next?

More Lee Weatherly? Try *Missing Abby*, about a girl whose friend goes missing, or *Kat Got Your Tongue*, about a girl who loses her memory.

Jules performs in a stage version of *Northern Lights* – so read the first part of Pullman's **His Dark Materials** trilogy. (UTBG 181)

For another girl finding strength to cope with adversity, read *Lola Rose*. (UTBG 238)

When Jules's dad leaves home, things are bad enough. He takes all his possessions, but leaves behind his favourite photo of Jules. Why? What has she done? And why are the newspapers suddenly hounding Jules and her mother? Why are they all trying to get pictures?

As she uncovers the long-buried secret that has torn her world apart, Jules is forced to question everything she has taken for granted about herself and the people closest to her. Lee Weatherly really helps us feel what Jules is going through – one of the worst nightmares of any child's life.

**Yvonne Coppard**

# CHINESE CINDERELLA Adeline Yen Mah

This isn't a fairy story; it's a true story, an autobiography. When Adeline was born in China, she was named Jun-ling. Shortly afterwards her mother died, and baby Adeline was blamed. Her family thought her unlucky, and wished she had been the one who'd died. All of them, especially her stepmother, treated her with contempt. Her 'fairy godmother', an aunt who loved her, protected her as much as she could, but that wasn't much. Despite all the ill-treatment, Adeline's story is inspiring. She doesn't fight back – sometimes you wish she would – but she doesn't give up, either, and now she's a doctor and businesswoman and writer, free of her cruel family. If you like learning about different lives and different cultures, you'll love this.

**Julia Jarman**

## Next?

There is a sequel: *Chinese Cinderella and the Secret Dragon Society*. These books tell of her childhood; if you want to know what happened next, read *Falling Leaves*, written for adults.

If you find yourself interested in Chinese traditions, read Yen Mah's *Watching the Tree*.

Or for a record of the dark days in Holland when being Jewish was a crime, read Anne Frank's *The Diary of a Young Girl*. (UTBG 106)

# CHOCOLAT Joanne Harris

Life in the tiny French village of Lansquenet-sous-Tannes is turned upside down when two strangers arrive, and almost overnight open a shop selling the most delicious chocolates imaginable. At first, many of the villagers are suspicious of the glamorous Vianne and her little girl Anouk, but they soon realise that the newcomers have a knack for finding out people's problems and working out solutions to them, and generally making life better. Only the village priest remains unfriendly – he doesn't trust Vianne or her seductive chocolates and thinks she may be a witch.

*Chocolat* is a lovely, richly detailed story, full of enchanting characters, magical moments and, above all, mouth-watering chocolate!

**Marianne Taylor**

## Next?

The sequel – *The Lollipop Shoes*. Then maybe Harris's *Blackberry Wine*, which has magical realism and more gloriously sensuous description.

For another story where food plays an important role, try *Like Water for Chocolate* by Laura Esquivel.

For another story of a stranger, try *Lucas* by Kevin Brooks. (UTBG 249)

Food and seduction? In Anthony Capella's *The Food of Love*, Tommaso pretends to be a chef in order to seduce Laura, but it's really his friend Bruno who's doing all the cooking...

# THE CHOCOLATE WAR   Robert Cormier

Archie Costello is the mastermind behind the Vigils, the secret society that rules Trinity High School, forcing boys to undertake Assignments such as booby-trapping classrooms and baiting teachers. Leon is the corrupt priest who plans to be Headmaster of Trinity. He ignores the Vigils unless they get in his way – or can be of use to him. Jerry is the new boy at Trinity, wanting nothing more than a quiet life, until the Vigils select him for an Assignment and he decides to rebel. When his rebellion threatens both Archie's and Leon's authority, Jerry discovers that he is powerless in the face of the forces they bring down on him.

This is a book like no other: savage, violent, but with moments of strange beauty. Why is it called *The Chocolate War*? Read it and find out.

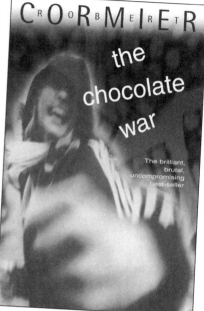

CORMIER
the chocolate war

The brilliant, brutal, uncompromising best-seller

**Graham Gardner**

## Next?

If you like dangerous, uncompromising novels, you'll enjoy Robert Cormier's other books, such as *I Am the Cheese* (UTBG 194) and the deeply disturbing *Heroes* (UTBG 176).

Or try Kevin Brooks's (in my opinion most brilliant) book, *Candy*. (UTBG 66)

Or for a really biting read, Catherine Forde's *Skarrs*. (UTBG 364)

S.E. Hinton's *The Outsiders* is another no-holds-barred story of the strengths and weaknesses of gangs and groups. (UTBG 305)

For me, *The Chocolate War* is the perfect example of teenage fiction. Actually, it's a perfect example of fiction. It was published in 1974, after being rejected by seven publishers as too dark, too complicated, too downbeat, too violent. It's set in a Catholic boys' high school, which Cormier called a 'metaphor for the world', a school riddled with corruption, bullying, and rigid systems that depend on frightened obedience. On another level, the book is about what happens when a boy refuses to sell chocolates for the annual chocolate sale. And continues to refuse. The book is shot through with scenes that leave you reeling with questions; questions like 'Is this what humans can do to each other?' Read a newspaper and you'll have to say 'yes'.

**Nicola Morgan**

# CHRISTINE   Stephen King

Stephen King writes the best horror stories, and *Christine* is the most enjoyable of his early books. Arnie Cunningham is a bit of a nerd, but his friend Dennis finds him more interesting than their cooler classmates. Christine is a classic car, a '58 Plymouth Fury that 17-year-old Arnie buys for $250 from a weird old man called Roland D. LeBay. From the moment Arnie buys Christine, Dennis senses something malevolent about her; a suspicion only confirmed when LeBay's brother tells Dennis that LeBay's daughter died, and his wife committed suicide, in the car. As Arnie becomes increasingly obsessed with Christine, Dennis realises his friend's love for the car is going to lead to death and destruction, but he's powerless to stop it.

**Matt Thorne**

> **Next?**
>
> *Carrie*, King's first novel, follows the torment of teenager Carrie White.
>
> *The Shining*, King's most literary novel, is a tale of madness, isolation and writer's block.
>
> James Herbert and Clive Barker are both British writers of the most chilling horror stories, but they have quite different approaches. If you like being scared witless, try them both – Barker's *The Books of Blood* and Herbert's *The Fog*, for starters.

# A CHRISTMAS CAROL
## Charles Dickens

> **Next?**
>
> *The Bible*, if only for Luke 2 and Matthew 2 – the origins of the Christmas story.
>
> *Oliver Twist*, the story of another great Dickensian creation: Fagin, and his gang of boys.
>
> Or what about the story of a ragged young pickpocket in the back streets of 18th-century London: *Smith* by Leon Garfield?
>
> Or try a quirky look at London (and its rubbish) with China Miéville's *Un Lun Dun* (UTBG 414) or the strange *Neverware* by Neil Gaiman.

It is Christmas Eve. Bitterly cold. Snow underfoot. Ebenezer Scrooge, a hard-hearted old miser, makes his way home through the narrow, gas-lit streets of London. What does he think of the season of goodwill? 'Christmas! Bah! Humbug!'

But Scrooge was not always such a bitter skinflint. As a boy he was good-hearted. What happened to change him? That night four ghosts visit his cold, bare house and he is taken on a journey to Christmases past, present and future. Scrooge is terrified...

This is a wonderful story, well-nigh perfect, and worthy of its place as (after *The Bible*) the best-known Christmas story in the world.

**Alan Temperley**

# THE CHRYSALIDS John Wyndham

## Next?

Even if you're not a sci-fi buff, you'll find that John Wyndham writes great stories; try *The Midwich Cuckoos* (UTBG 263) or *The Day of the Triffids* (UTBG 98).

There are other books that wonder what life would be like 'after'. Try Jeanne DuPrau's *City of Ember*, *The Declaration* by Gemma Malley, or *Shade's Children* by Garth Nix.

Or read Rhiannon Lassiter's **Hex** trilogy, about the next generation of humans. (UTBG 177)

The world has changed. Many generations after Tribulation (a cataclysmic nuclear war), young David Strorm lives in Waknuk, a farming settlement in Labrador. Life is basic, with horses and oil lamps. Nearby is the Fringe, a wilderness where mutants live. Beyond that lie the Badlands, earth blasted and turned to glass. Waknuk is ruled by a stern religion. Mutant animals are offences to God and ritually slaughtered. Human mutants are Blasphemies and driven out. But though visibly normal, David, son of the fiercely righteous Joseph Strorm, is himself a Blasphemy; he can talk to other children, miles off, in his thoughts.

This is a terrific, fast-moving story, packed with ideas. I loved it as a teenager and I love it now.

**Alan Temperley**

# CIDER WITH ROSIE
Laurie Lee

Laurie Lee paints a vivid and fascinating portrait of growing up in an English countryside that has disappeared. With a poor but close-knit family as his backdrop, Laurie uncovers people and places around him that are brimming over with intrigue and delight.

His honest prose and evocative imagery stimulate each of the reader's senses as he takes you on a journey from his first experiences of school, through a murder in the locality, to the alluring and powerful Rosie.

Above all, *Cider with Rosie's* true magic lies in the way it captures a snapshot of a young boy's life where the possibilities are unlimited and the future is for the taking.

## Next?

Laurie Lee's life adventures continue in *As I Walked Out One Midsummer Morning* and *A Moment of War*.

*The Secret Life of Bees* by Sue Monk Kidd is very different, but just as warm and just as full of hope. (UTBG 351)

Or try *Pool Boy* by Michael Simmons, in which a boy from an affluent family is suddenly forced to face the harsh realities of living 'on the other side of the tracks'.

Something else about growing up in the country? Try Alison Uttley's *A Country Child*.

**Jonny Zucker**

# CLAUDINE AT SCHOOL Colette

Claudine is an attractive, headstrong and precocious adolescent who lives with her unworldly father in the village of Montigny. This, the first novel in Colette's **Claudine** series, is about her mischievous and disruptive behaviour at school. Claudine is bright enough to cruise by on little work, so devotes much energy to battling with her formidable headmistress for the amorous attention of the pretty, golden-eyed classroom assistant Aimée. This witty novel is packed with flirting, bullying and the petty horrors of taking exams.

**Francesca Lewis**

### Next?

*Claudine Married* is the next one in the series followed by *Claudine in Paris* and *Claudine and Annie*. And look out for Colette's story of *Gigi* (UTBG 315), a girl destined to be a courtesan.

In *The Prime of Miss Jean Brodie*, Muriel Spark breathes life into a band of schoolgirls and their teacher. (UTBG 321)

If you're a sybarite who enjoys Colette's descriptions of beautiful clothes and objects, try *The Picture of Dorian Gray* by Oscar Wilde, about a man who doesn't seem to get older. (UTBG 311)

# CLAY David Almond

### Next?

For a classic tale of learning to animate lifeless matter, read Mary Shelley's *Frankenstein*. (UTBG 141)

Or for a rather less alarming tale of a boy's relationship with a great, inexplicable giant: Ted Hughes's *The Iron Man*.

If you fancy another David Almond, try *Jackdaw Summer* (UTBG 209) or *Kit's Wilderness* (UTBG 228).

For a story of two people locked in a power struggle that just gets darker and darker, read Susan Hill's *I'm the King of the Castle*. (UTBG 201)

Stephen Rose, an odd boy with a tragic past, has just arrived at Felling. Stephen Rose, who forms stunning, life-like figures in clay. Local boy Davie soon learns just how remarkable Stephen Rose is; but is his gift a force for good, or for evil?

As always, David Almond paints a world we seem to recognise; but as we read on we realise that we recognise it only in part, we see only its surface. For around us there are always things that we don't see or understand – things hidden in shadows, spirits of the past, powers we can't explain. Throughout his books, these inexplicable things emerge in ways that are sometimes beautiful, sometimes terrifying, but always haunting.

This is a book of secret magic, of faith and doubt, of death and life (no less). And it's one of Almond's best, I think. And if you knew how highly I rate all his work, you'd know just what praise that is.

**Daniel Hahn**

# A CLOCKWORK ORANGE Anthony Burgess ✹✹✹

I was coerced into reading this story of tolchocking ultraviolence and rape by my 16-year-old son. I thought my feminist soul would hate it. Wrong. It's Burgess's extraordinary achievement to make you empathise with his appalling hero, Alex. Using Nadsat, a brilliant invented language that borrows from Slavic, Burgess contrives to make you into one of Alex's 'droogs'. It's a big book, dangerous, one that grapples with choice and morality. All the more extraordinary for that fact that Burgess wrote it after an attack on his wife which resulted in her miscarrying their child. He might have written it from the perspective of the victim, but instead he writes as the aggressor.

I horrorshow wish I'd read it as a teenager.

**Nicky Singer**

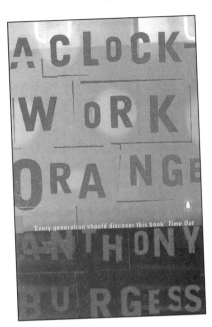

'Every generation should discover this book' *Time Out*

## THE FUTURE IS DARK: DYSTOPIA

*Unwind* by Neal Shusterman

*Nineteen Eight-Four* by George Orwell

*Brave New World* by Aldous Huxley

*The Knife of Never Letting Go* by Patrick Ness

*The Hunger Games* by Suzanne Collins

*Incarceron* by Catherine Fisher

*Fahrenheit 451* by Ray Bradbury

*The Handmaid's Tale* by Margaret Atwood

*How I Live Now* by Meg Rosoff

**Next?**

If you like the macabre and bizarre, enter the world of 16-year-old Frank in Iain Banks's *The Wasp Factory*. (UTBG 425)

More disturbingly dystopian futures? Try William Gibson's *Neuromancer* or Scott Westerfeld's *Uglies* (UTBG 412).

Another group of antisocial friends appear in *Trainspotting* by Irvine Welsh. (UTBG 401)

Want to know more about cult books? Read the feature on pp. 280–281.

# COLD COMFORT FARM  Stella Gibbons

**Next?**

Try one of the types of novel that Stella Gibbons is satirising, like Mary Webb's *Precious Bane*.

Or another comic novel, such as *Miss Pettigrew Lives for a Day* by Winifred Watson. Timid Miss Pettigrew goes to work for a nightclub singer and learns to enjoy life.

Sophie Kinsella's frothy *The Undomestic Goddess* takes another sophisticated urbanite and drops her into the depths of the country.

Stella Gibbons's first novel, *Cold Comfort Farm*, published in 1932, remains fresh, relevant and witty today.

Flora Poste, 20, newly orphaned, with no property and only £100 a year, has to decide which relatives to live with. She plumps for the Starkadders on their farm in Howling, Sussex. There she finds an extraordinary collection of individuals, locked into age-old family feuds, stirring lumpy porridge and washing dishes with a thorn stick. At their centre sits Aunt Ada Doom, malevolent, brooding and implacable, haunted by the 'something nasty in the woodshed' she saw as a child and refusing to leave her room.

Flora is determined to create order out of chaos, to inject sanity into the madness, in a novel that is sheer delight from beginning to end.

**Valerie Mendes**

# THE COLDITZ STORY  P.R. Reid

Colditz Castle was the German maximum-security prison for Allied prisoners of war captured in World War II. The castle was built on a vertical cliff, the guards outnumbered the prisoners at all times, and barbed wire and floodlights were everywhere. Colditz was supposed to be inescapable. But the English, Dutch, French, and Polish POWs were undaunted. Out of stolen material, they created tools, disguises, electrical systems and tunnelling equipment; from outside the castle they smuggled in maps, money, civilian clothes and even radio sets in preparation for escape.

I love this book because of how amazingly resourceful the prisoners are: starting from nothing they manage to get the better of their captors not once, but dozens of times.

**Benedict Jacka**

**Next?**

P.R. Reid wrote a sequel, *The Latter Days at Colditz*. Or look out for *Colditz: The German Story* by Reinhold Eggers, who was a security officer there.

*The Great Escape* is another very good World War II escape story, written by Paul Brickhill, who also wrote *The Dam Busters*, the story of the RAF's bouncing bombs.

A classic story of escape and revenge is Alexandre Dumas's *The Count of Monte Cristo*.

# THE COLOR PURPLE  Alice Walker

**Next?**

Tashi (from *The Color Purple*) gets her own story told in *Possessing the Secret of Joy* – another dark and heart-wrenching story.

Or try reading Grace Nichols's poetry, which manages to be sharp and funny while dealing with issues such as oppression, slavery and self-image: check out *The Fat Black Woman's Poems*.

Another classic African-American novel is *Beloved*. (UTBG 42)

This unforgettable tale about Celie, a black woman growing up and living in the American South, must have touched more lives than any other book I know.

Raped by the man she believes to be her father, Celie twice falls pregnant and each time has to give up her child for adoption. This awfulness is just the beginning of a long journey through suffering so heartbreaking that on more than one occasion the reader is left wondering how Celie can possibly carry on. But carry on she does. Inspired and loved by the stunning *femme fatale* blues singer Shug Avery, Celie realises for the first time that she doesn't have to put up with the appalling treatment meted out to her by men. And so her life begins to change.

Walker's story is deeply intimate, and her characters so complex, well rounded and deftly drawn you feel they could walk right off the page.

**Neil Arksey**

# COMING UP FOR AIR  George Orwell

World War II is imminent. People are fearful but – for now – still going about their daily lives. George Bowling, a middle-aged insurance salesman with a wife and two children, is one such. As the story opens, George is about to set off into town to collect his new false teeth. Later, walking along a busy street (rather pleased with his brand-new smile), his mind is suddenly full of his childhood home in the country, and a longing to see it again. To go back there, away from the hustle and bustle of the city and the threat of war, would be like coming up for air, he thinks. So without a word to his wife, he visits the country town he knew as a boy. What he finds when he gets there, and what he learns about himself and the world he lives in, make up the bulk of this excellent novel.

**Michael Lawrence**

**Next?**

More George Orwell: *Nineteen Eighty-Four* (UTBG 284) or *Animal Farm* (UTBG 24).

H.E. Bates writes lyrically on both the countryside and war; try *The Darling Buds of May* or *Fair Stood the Wind for France*.

H.G. Wells's *The History of Mr Polly* is about an ordinary man just trying to cope with life.

# COMPLETE SHORT STORIES J.G. Ballard ✳✳✳

**Next?**

J.G. Ballard is the author of many novels; try *Empire of the Sun* (UTBG 120), based on his childhood in a Japanese internment camp; or *Hello America*, about a band of future explorers returning to a United States abandoned after catastrophic climate change.

Ray Bradbury is another astonishing writer of short stories. Try *The Illustrated Man*, which influenced many later writers. (UTBG 200)

Deranged aviators haunt the overgrown runways and gantries of an abandoned Cape Canaveral; the body of a drowned giant washes up on a beach; inhabitants of perfect suburbs succumb to strange psychological states; and in the skies above the desert resort of Vermilion Sands, airborne sculptors carve the clouds into portraits of an insane heiress...

J.G. Ballard's compelling stories balance on a knife-edge between science fiction and surrealism. Some deliver a nightmarish twist; others, almost plotless, return obsessively to the same dream-like landscapes – abandoned testing grounds, empty swimming pools, mysterious deserts. No one else writes like Mr Ballard, and beneath his luminous, metallic prose lie wry humour and a profound humanity. Once read, never forgotten.

**Philip Reeve**

# CONFESSIONS OF A TEENAGE DRAMA QUEEN  Dyan Sheldon ✳

For Lola, the whole world is a stage and she's the star of the show. Funny, daft, infuriating, kind, totally over the top, Lola (whose real name is Mary) tells the story of her new life after her parents separate and she and her twin sisters are moved to New Jersey and a new school.

Wearing clothes to match her mood (velvet capes are the least of it) Lola makes friends with Ella and seriously annoys the most popular girl in the school by winning the coveted lead role in the school play. Then her favourite band, Sidartha, breaks up and the story spins back to New York as Lola and Ella meet rock gods and more police than should ever be strictly necessary. Fun? You bet.

**Next?**

The sequels: *My Perfect Life*, which tells more about Ella and Lola, this time from Ella's point of view, and *Confessions of a Hollywood Star*.

Cathy Cassidy has a similar warm touch with teen angst; read *Driftwood* or *Lucky Star* (UTBG 250).

Or try Fiona Dunbar's **Lulu Baker** trilogy, starting with *The Truth Cookie*.

**Leonie Flynn**

# CONSIDER PHLEBAS Iain M. Banks

Horza is a hero, except he's fighting for the wrong side. Which side is that? The one that's losing, of course. From the opening scenes where Horza faces a death that seems impossible to get out of, through a series of complex, terrifying and brutal adventures, this novel drags you through it, your hand over your eyes, half afraid that something awful will happen any minute. And most often it does.

This is a universe where spaceships are sentient and where aliens are truly alien. Bringing in issues of faith, tolerance and morality, it still manages to be one of the most exciting books I've read. There are some writers whose imaginations seem too huge to belong to one person, and Iain M. Banks is just such a writer.

**Leonie Flynn**

> ### Next?
> *Consider Phlebas* is part of a sequence of novels about the Culture, Banks's invented universe. Try *Use of Weapons* or *Excession* next.
>
> Just to prove his genius, Banks also writes contemporary novels. Look for books under the name Iain Banks (the 'M' is only used for his sci-fi). Try *Complicity* first.
>
> Someone else with as vivid an imagination is Michael Marshall Smith; try *Only Forward*. (UTBG 296)

# CORALINE Neil Gaiman

Coraline lives in just part of a big old house with her mum and dad and a clutch of eccentric neighbours. One day when she's bored, she opens a door she's never opened before and goes into a parallel universe. It's much more exciting in there! The food is delicious, her bedroom captivating, the toys magical – and there are a new Mum and Dad who love her very much and want her to stay. At first it all seems very cosy, but then stranger and stranger things start to happen.

Neil Gaiman writes in a matter-of-fact, non-sensational way, and this only serves to enhance the strange and haunting quality of his tale... I can still see the deeply creepy 'other mother' with her shiny, black-button eyes...

**Mary Hooper**

> ### Next?
> More Neil Gaiman: *M Is for Magic* is a collection of brilliant and inventive short stories.
>
> Something with a similar feel? Try *Tom's Midnight Garden* by Philippa Pearce.
>
> Robert Westall writes disturbing, scary stories – read *The Scarecrows* and try and work out what's real and what's imagined. (UTBG 342)
>
> Or try the scary, brilliant book that blends magic, circus, marionettes and atmospheric Prague: Joanne Owen's *The Puppet Master*.

# CORAM BOY  Jamila Gavin

Captain Thomas Coram was a philanthropist who opened a hospital for abandoned children in the mid-18th century. This book tells the tale of Otis Gardiner, who purported to collect children for Coram's hospital, but actually murdered them, neglected them or sold them as slaves.

The sordid story of Gardiner and his simpleton son is set alongside the tale of a young woman who falls in love with an aristocrat and then, sadly, comes to need Gardiner's services. It's a densely embroidered story contrasting rich and poor and city and countryside, and is crammed with detail.

This is real edge-of-the-seat stuff, the plot carefully woven and the characters fascinating, and I defy you to finish it without a tear in your eye.

**Mary Hooper**

### Next?

There are many great stories set around this period in history – try Leon Garfield's **Black Jack**, Linda Buckley-Archer's **Gideon the Cutpurse** (UTBG 153) or **Sovay** by Celia Rees.

For something about slavery, try Rosemary Sutcliff's **The Outcast**, set in the ancient world, or two set in America – Gary Paulsen's **Nightjohn** and **The Astonishing Life of Octavian Nothing** (UTBG 29) by M.T. Anderson. They're very different, but each pack a strong emotional punch.

# CORBENIC  Catherine Fisher

### Next?

Try more Catherine Fisher. **Darkhenge** is a mystery about a boy trying to save his sister, or look out for **Incarceron**, the first in a trilogy about a boy growing up in a huge prison.

For more Arthurian legends try **Arthur: The Seeing Stone**. (UTBG 352)

Want something scary? Try Margaret Mahy's book about change, romance and danger: **The Changeover**. (UTBG 72)

For another book about escaping a tough real world through fantasy, read **Jake's Tower**. (UTBG 210)

Since he was six, Cal has spent a miserable childhood in Bangor with his mother who is schizophrenic and an alcoholic. He is offered a new life with his uncle Trevor in Chepstow and tries to leave the past behind. On the way he falls asleep on the train and gets off at the wrong station, Corbenic, where he is directed to the Castle Hotel.

He finds himself at the castle of the Fisher King, and from then the novel intertwines the Arthurian myth of the Grail and Cal's own journey to find self-knowledge and peace of mind. It's an exciting and moving story with a contemporary theme, a sense of place, the mystery of legend and strong characterisation.

**Brenda Marshall**

# COUNTING STARS David Almond

This is an autobiographical collection of short stories about the childhood of my favourite author. Many of the stories in here were written before any of Almond's novels were published, so reading *Counting Stars* feels like peering into the author's heart and soul to learn what makes him tick.

I love the way Almond writes. He never wastes a word, only tells you about things that matter, and from the first page of this book you know the centre of his universe is family, living and dead. Sisters. Brother. Mam. Dad. It's hard to write about how much you love and cherish and miss people without being schmaltzy and sentimental, but Almond does this brilliantly throughout *Counting Stars*. It's a wonderful book about the important things in life: love, loss, childhood... But so is everything Almond writes.

**Catherine Forde**

# THE BEST DAYS OF YOUR LIFE?

*The Traitor Game* by B.R. Collins

*A Great and Terrible Beauty* by Libba Bray

*The Knife That Killed Me* by Anthony McGowan

*Teacher's Dead* by Benjamin Zephaniah

*New Boy* by William Sutcliffe

*Picnic at Hanging Rock* by Joan Lindsay

The **Egerton Hall** trilogy by Adèle Geras

*Inventing Elliot* by Graham Gardner

*The Boys Who Saved the World* by Sam Mills

**Next?**

Now go away and read all of David Almond's other books. You'll find some of them listed on p. 469.

If you liked the childhood reality that these stories are based on, try Laurie Lee's memoir **Cider with Rosie**. (UTBG 80)

Or read another author's autobiography, such as Michael Lawrence's **Milking the Novelty**.

Or more short stories? Try **Minor Miracles** by Will Eisner or **Across the Wall** by Garth Nix.

# CRAZY Benjamin Lebert

**Next?**

*The Old Man and the Sea* – if you've read *Crazy*, you'll know why. (UTBG 21)

Pete Hautman's *Invisible*, about unlikely friendships and not fitting in.

Troy reads Stephen King's terrifying *Misery*; but I reckon you should try King's *The Body* instead. Like *Crazy* it's about the bonds of friendship, and a tale of discovery.

Benjamin is 16 and starting at a new school – his fifth. He keeps failing maths, and he's not very good at German; he's 'different', too, partially paralysed down his left side, and finds it hard to fit in. But this time Benjamin settles quickly into a group: Janosch (the ringleader), Fat Felix and Skinny Felix, Florian a.k.a. Girl, and silent Troy. Benjamin fits right in. After all, none of his new friends are really 'normal' either – and anyway, who is?

*Crazy* is engagingly told, about a few months in the lives of the group – they get drunk, get laid and get on each other's nerves. They talk for hours about profound things, and they complain about school food, teachers, rules – in fact, school in general; but you know they'll miss it when the time comes to leave. And when the book ends you'll be sorry to leave them, too.

**Daniel Hahn**

# CRIME AND PUNISHMENT
## Fyodor Dostoyevsky

Don't be scared off by the weighty title and this novel's reputation as a Great Work of Russian Literature; this is a gripping read right from the start – a psychological / crime thriller as unputdownable as any bestseller.

Raskolnikov is an intelligent, proud and embittered young man, living in poverty in St Petersburg. To escape his desperate situation, he plans a robbery and murder. His intended victim is a vile old pawnbroker, whom he feels society will be better off without. He rationalises the murder to himself and is confident that he will be able to get away with it. The reality of the deed is very different...

The inner world of Raskolnikov is at the heart of the story. Dostoyevsky takes us deep into the nightmare of Raskolnikov's conscience as he confronts the horror of what he's done.

**Next?**

For a gripping tale of murder and guilt, there's nothing better than Shakespeare's *Macbeth*.

For something shorter by Dostoyevsky, but still full of atmosphere and energy, try his *The Gambler*.

For high drama, this time in France, try Émile Zola's *Thérèse Raquin*. (UTBG 392)

Or read the extraordinary tale of an extraordinary man, *Perfume*. (UTBG 310)

**Katie Jennings**

# THE CRY OF THE ICEMARK  Stuart Hill

If you like fantasies on an epic scale, with desperate battles against invincible armies, you can't go wrong with *The Cry of the Icemark*. Thirrin Freer Strong-in-the-Arm Lindenshield, Wildcat of the North, Monarch of the Icemark, earns every one of her titles before she has been queen for a year. At the start of the book she's eager for battle with the mighty Polypontian army bent on conquering the world; by its end, she's a seasoned warrior, bloodied and battle-scarred, understanding loss and pain as well as the euphoria of victory. She's also become an astute politician, holding together an unlikely alliance of Greek-style archers and lancers, vampires and werewolves, gigantic white leopards and her own army of the Icemark.

**Gill Vickery**

> **Next?**
>
> The sequels: *Blade of Fire* and *Last Battle of the Icemark*.
>
> For other battle-filled books, try Adèle Geras's *Troy* (UTBG 405), her magnificent account of the fall of the legendary city; or *Warrior Girl* (UTBG 424) by Pauline Chandler, a reworking of the true story of Jeanne, the teenage girl who led France against the English in medieval times.
>
> For other Norse-based epics full of battles and really good names, try *Sea of Trolls* (UTBG 345) by Nancy Farmer or Joanne Harris's *Runemarks* (UTBG 338).

# THE CRYSTAL CAVE  Mary Stewart

> **Next?**
>
> The series continues with *The Hollow Hills* and *The Last Enchantment*.
>
> *The Mists of Avalon* by Marion Zimmer Bradley is the Arthurian legend told by the women involved. There are sequels, too.
>
> Catherine Jinks's own **Pagan** books recreate the past with just as much relish. (UTBG 307)
>
> Or you could have a go at the original – Thomas Malory's *Le Morte d'Arthur*.

Meet the historical Merlin – or the closest you'll ever get to him! He's not so much a magician as a seer, and his gift is more of a burden than a blessing. A thinker surrounded by fighters, and an illegitimate outcast to boot, he's condemned to a life of rejection and isolation. Yet he battles on single-handedly to ensure that his nephew, Arthur, is born and raised to fulfil the prophecies that plague poor Merlin like a recurring headache.

These fabulous novels are not only drenched in utterly convincing detail about post-Roman Britain and the Gaelic culture, but also introduce one of the wisest, loneliest, most convincing heroes you'll ever encounter. Even readers who aren't fantasy fans will enjoy them.

**Catherine Jinks**

# CUE FOR TREASON  Geoffrey Trease

This was my all-time favourite book when I was a child. It's a swashbuckling historical novel set in Tudor times. It has everything – spies, actors, escapes over mountains, treason, and even romance. Real historical characters have walk-on parts. You'll meet Queen Elizabeth I, Shakespeare and Sir Walter Raleigh, among others. Through it all, like a silken weave, are wonderful descriptions of the countryside of England in the days before industrial cities and roaring motorways scarred the landscape; a time when the air was clear, and Kensington was a village miles away from London.

**Elizabeth Laird**

> **Next?**
>
> There are some brilliant historical novels out there. Try *King of Shadows* by Susan Cooper, almost anything by Cynthia Harnett or Rosemary Sutcliff, or the fantastic Jill Paton Walsh's *The Dolphin Crossing*; and, of course, Baroness Orczy's *The Scarlet Pimpernel* (UTBG 343).
>
> For more exciting adventure, look out for Julia Golding's **Cat Royal** series.
>
> Leon Garfield has written many wonderful stories set in the past. Try *Jack Holborn*, about a search for an African diamond.

# THE CUP OF THE WORLD / THE WIDOW AND THE KING  John Dickinson

> **Next?**
>
> For a recreation of the real Middle Ages, try Kevin Crossley-Holland's **Arthur** trilogy; set in the 13th century, it begins with *Arthur: The Seeing Stone*. (UTBG 352)
>
> The *Sterkarm Handshake* (UTBG 376) and *A Sterkarm Kiss* by Susan Price combine sci-fi with the violent history of the Scottish border country.
>
> *The Princess Bride* by William Goldman is a mad, exhilarating fairy tale for adults (and anyone else), set in a time that never was or could have been. (UTBG 322)

Phaedra runs away from a dynastic marriage to join the man who has wooed her by means of 'undercraft'. Other people mistakenly call this witchcraft, and there is a fearful price to pay for practising it. Everything else in these two wonderful novels is entirely human as the players in a power game struggle for control over whole kingdoms, over other people or simply over their own lives, never knowing that someone else is manipulating their every move. Phaedra, discovering how she has been used, learns to play the game herself; and her son, as he grows up, finally brings it all to a conclusion. Set in an imaginary but intensely real medieval country, the story is just as relevant to the times we live in.

**Jan Mark**

# THE CURIOUS INCIDENT OF THE DOG IN THE NIGHT-TIME
## Mark Haddon

The most amazing thing about a good book is that it can take you inside the mind of a completely different person. Mark Haddon does exactly that in this utterly gripping mystery story. The main character of the book is a 14-year-old autistic boy whose 'voice' rang utterly true to me. Christopher loves the mysteries of Sherlock Holmes, because he often has to rely on clues to know how the people around him are feeling. When he discovers a murdered dog on his neighbour's lawn, he decides to solve the mystery using the deductive methods of his idol.

**Caroline Lawrence**

### Next?

Try other stories of people who see the world in a different way, like those collected by Oliver Sacks in *The Man Who Mistook His Wife for a Hat*.

Or try Virginia Euwer Wolff's *Probably Still Nick Swanson*, about a 16-year-old boy who is learning disabled, and the struggles he has with life.

To find out where Christopher gets his methods – and where Haddon got his title – read the **Sherlock Holmes** stories. (UTBG 359)

*Al Capone Does My Shirts* charts life growing up with an autistic sister on Alcatraz at the time of Al Capone. (UTBG 14)

It's always great to read exciting books about magic and faraway lands filled with mystical creatures, but every now and then a great book comes along which despite the absence of all things fantastical still has the power to amaze you. This is one of them. It follows teenager Christopher Boone as he grows up with a condition called Asperger's; we are introduced to his strange world and how he copes within it. You see, Christopher is brilliant at maths but can't understand simple human emotions such as fear and confusion. One night Christopher finds his neighbour's dog Wellington brutally murdered in the garden, and so begins his quest to find the killer.

Despite dealing with some serious issues, this story is told in a light and witty style, and as it progresses the characters really feel alive.

**Gareth Smith, age 14**

# CUT  Patricia McCormick

**Next?**

Novels about teenagers suffering breakdowns? Try *A Note of Madness* (UTBG 288) by Tabitha Suzuma or *The Bell Jar* (UTBG 39) by Sylvia Plath, both complex and challenging – but worth it!

*Disconnected* by Sherry Ashworth is about a girl who suffers burn-out and stops working at school. (UTBG 106)

Or look out for *Sold* by Patricia McCormick – this time she deals with the appalling subject of Nepalese girls being sold into slavery.

*Love, Aubrey* by Suzanne LeFleur is about love, loss, grief and healing. It might just break your heart.

*Cut* is a sensitive treatment of the subject of self-harm. The heroine, Callie, who tells the story, has been cutting herself and is admitted to Sea Pines – or Sick Minds as she calls it. Callie used to be a keen runner until her obsession led her to withdraw from the world completely, to the point where she chooses not to talk anymore – not even to the people who are trying to help her. But as she gets to know the other girls at Sick Minds – anorexics, drug addicts, other self-harmers – she begins to come out of her self-imposed isolation. Reading about Callie's struggle to want to get better is moving, absorbing – and realistic, too.

**Sherry Ashworth**

# DAISY MILLER  Henry James

Winterbourne is a good-natured but rather idle young American man, with not much to do with his life but drift from one European town to another, visiting friends and enjoying 'Society'. But at Vevey he meets Daisy Miller, and he is quite changed.

He's never met anyone like Daisy. She's both so smart and so naïve, totally innocent and yet an incorrigible flirt. And she's tremendously pretty. Winterbourne can't stop thinking about her. I think Henry James is one of the greatest of all novelists, and *Daisy Miller* is just the way to meet him first. This is only the slimmest of novels – a novella, really – but in the hundred or so pages, James creates a portrait of a character (and a society she can't help being at odds with) that is perfectly poised and thoroughly enchanting.

**Daniel Hahn**

**Next?**

For another Henry James, this time with more substance, move on to his *Turn of the Screw*. (UTBG 409)

For more turn-of-the-century innocent young ladies travelling around Europe, try E.M. Forster – *A Room with a View* (UTBG 335) or *Where Angels Fear to Tread*. After James's prose you'll find him an easy read!

Or for another dark sort of love story, read *Ethan Frome* by James's close friend, Edith Wharton. (UTBG 122)

# DANCE ON MY GRAVE
## Aidan Chambers

**Next?**

This is one of Aidan Chambers's six novels for teenagers called the **Dance** sequence. If you liked it, try *Postcards from No Man's Land* next. (UTBG 318)

*Johnny My Friend* by Peter Pohl is admittedly a little hard to find, but if you come across a copy – grab it! It's a beautifully written novel about a relationship revolving around a dark secret.

For a quite different story of teen sexuality, read David Levithan's lovely, warm and engaging *Boy Meets Boy*. (UTBG 56)

In my opinion, this is the best novel from one of the most provocative authors writing for teenagers today. 16-year-old Hal Robinson is caught 'interfering' with the grave of the recently deceased Barry Gorman. In his own words, and with the aid of extracts from diaries, newspaper clippings and even homework essays, Hal unravels the sweet-sour roller coaster of events leading to his peculiar behaviour and subsequent arrest. This story of an unforgettable summer, packed with lust, obsession and death, is told in a remarkably clever and unusual way. Chambers writes it like it is, and his characters are real and raw. This book will challenge your ideas about love, life, sex and literature...

**Noga Applebaum**

# DANDELION WINE
## Ray Bradbury

Ray Bradbury is a master of short stories. Whether they're about ghosts, Martians, his childhood, Mexico, Ireland, or a thousand other subjects, he can tell a great story using a minimum of words. For this book, he wove several tales together to create arguably his best novel. It's the tale of a young boy and his adventures one magical, mysterious summer. Funny, scary, but above all *warm*, this is a book that leaves you with a smile on your face, a book that you're truly sorry to put down. Bradbury has been one of my biggest influences, and if you read this book, then one of mine, you'll find shades of the master in just about everything I write.

**Darren Shan**

**Next?**

Try some of Bradbury's sci-fi, such as the dark, brutal stories in *The Martian Chronicles* or *Fahrenheit 451* (UTBG 126).

Or the short-story collections of Clive Barker, the *Books of Blood*, which are just as scary and gory as they sound.

Or something by Darren Shan – the horrifically gruesome *Lord Loss* (UTBG 241) or *Cirque du Freak* in which the hero's name is ... Darren Shan!

# THE DARK BENEATH Alan Gibbons

## Next?

Anything by Alan Gibbons is worth a read. Try the fast-paced thriller *Blood Pressure*, or *The Edge*, which is about racism, bullying and abuse or *Caught in the Crossfire* (UTBG 71).

*Inside the Cage* by Matt Whyman is a brutal book about a boy wrongly convicted of terrorism.

*Fugitives* by Alex Shearer is about a prank that goes seriously wrong.

Or try something by Bali Rai. Most of his novels are about fitting (and not fitting) in, like *(Un)arranged Marriage* (UTBG 413) and *City of Ghosts*.

Issue novels, when they're done well, are worth their weight in gold. Authors who get them right are worth even more. Alan Gibbons is one such author. Imogen is 16 and, having finished school, she is looking forward to summer. But when her path crosses those of three very different refugees, things start to go wrong.

This is a very dark, tension-packed read, with strong characters. You are drawn in from the first page and the story never lets you go. Prepare to think differently about what a refugee actually is, as the author takes you on an often-harrowing journey beneath the fabric of normality. A brilliant book by a brilliant author.

**Bali Rai**

# THE DARK GROUND Gillian Cross

Gillian Cross's novels always grip you in a stranglehold from the very first page. Her writing is compelling, direct and thought provoking. This extraordinary book is no exception. Part thriller, part fable, it made me look at the world in a totally different way.

Robert regains consciousness, after what he supposes is a plane crash, to find himself alone in thick jungle. There is no sign of his family or any other survivors. For some days he struggles to stay alive. And then he becomes aware that someone – or some*thing* – is watching him...

I daren't write more for fear of giving away the original and ambitious idea behind this novel. All I can say is *read it*!

**Patricia Elliott**

## Next?

This is the first of a trilogy entitled **The Lost**, and you'll need to read the sequels, *The Black Room* and *The Nightmare Game*.

*Calling A Dead Man* (UTBG 65) is another gripping thriller by Gillian Cross, or you could try the creepiness of *Wolf*.

William Golding's great classic, *Lord of the Flies* (UTBG 241), also shows human behaviour under extreme conditions, as does Tim Bowler's chilling *Apocalypse* (UTBG 27), or Alex Garland's *The Beach* (UTBG 35)

# THE DARK IS RISING sequence
## Susan Cooper

**Next?**

The full order is *Over Sea, Under Stone*, *The Dark Is Rising*, *Greenwitch*, *The Grey King* and *Silver on the Tree*.

Try Alan Garner's brilliant *The Owl Service* (UTBG 306), or Mary Stewart's **Merlin** books, beginning with *The Crystal Cave* (UTBG 90).

*The Various* by Steve Augarde is a sprawling magical fantasy. Or try Catherine Fisher's own books. Start with **The Book of the Crow** series or *The Glass Tower*, a collection of some of her short, intense and unsettling novels.

Moving from the fairly unsophisticated treasure hunt of *Over Sea, Under Stone* to the wonderful final battle under the midsummer tree in *Silver on the Tree*, this quintet of novels is a classic fantasy series. Cooper's books grow in depth and allusion as the reader journeys through them; they move from Cornwall to Wales, and the quest to possess the Grail becomes a cosmic war between the powers of light and darkness, fought through Celtic myth and the archetypes of the Arthurian legend. Cooper is good at atmosphere and brooding landscapes, and these books are a gripping read.

**Catherine Fisher**

# THE DARK LORD OF DERKHOLM
## Diana Wynne Jones

Where teenage Blade lives, they re-enact 'Dark Lord'-type fantasies for tourists from another world. This year, the Oracle puts Blade's father in charge. And suddenly everything turns dangerous. Why? For one thing, the wizards, the magic, the dragons, demons, griffins and flying pigs are all real; and Blade's father is the last wizard anyone would have chosen to run things. When Blade and his siblings get drafted in to help, they have to grow up rather quickly.

A very exciting book full of elegant magic, but also touching as the pressures and tensions act on Blade's family. Oh, and I should add: while Blade and his parents are human, his siblings have feathers and wings – they're griffins, and they're delightful!

**Rosemary Cass-Beggs**

**Next?**

There's a sequel, *The Year of the Griffin*, in which a griffin daughter and her classmates (accidentally) transform their shoddy university into a centre of excellence.

You should also look for Diana Wynne Jones's *Hexwood* (puzzling at first, but deeply satisfying).

And try Mercedes Lackey's **Valdemar** series, where the horses have strange powers! Start with *Take a Thief*, about a pickpocket chosen to become a Herald.

# DAUGHTERS OF JERUSALEM
## Charlotte Mendelson

The dysfunctional Lux family lives in Oxford. Victor Lux is a professor, desperate to win the prestigious annual Spenser lecture. His wife Jean is tempted by extramarital advances while their daughters, Eve and Phoebe, are locked in a vicious battle of mutual dislike. Eve is academic but can seemingly do nothing right; Phoebe, the wild, spoilt and needy one, is Jean's favourite, to Eve's increasing resentment. This simmering cauldron of dissatisfaction threatens to boil over in spectacular fashion when a predatory don, Victor's rival from way back, arrives in town and shows an unsavoury interest in the neglected Eve. Dramatic revenge-wreaking and revelations result. Mendelson is both erudite and accessible in this delicious black comedy of frustration in a rarefied setting.

**Francesca Lewis**

### Next?

Move on to Charlotte Mendelson's first novel, *Love in Idleness*, the witty story of newly graduated Anna Raine's struggle to cope with London life.

If novels set in academia appeal to you, try *Foreign Affairs* by Alison Lurie and *The Secret History* (UTBG 350) by Donna Tartt .

For more on sibling rivalry, try *A Summer Bird-Cage* by Margaret Drabble.

# THE DA VINCI CODE  Dan Brown

### Next?

*The Holy Blood and the Holy Grail* by Michel Baigent (et al) is a real-life investigation into the same mysteries.

More religious controversy? Nikos Kazantzakis's novel *Last Temptation* explores the 'did Jesus really die on the cross?' question.

*Fatherland* is a fast-paced thriller that will leave you gasping for breath! (UTBG 128)

This book was at the top of the bestseller lists for ages. Why? Well, the story imagines a truly astonishing secret that would challenge the very basis of the world's most deeply held Christian beliefs. This secret has been protected for centuries by a hidden society which is still active today. It's wildly controversial and stirs up ferocious, even murderous, passions...

This is a real page-turner, with an endless series of cliffhangers that catapult you through the book. It begins with a murder, and the body is weirdly arranged to resemble a famous drawing by Leonardo da Vinci. Perhaps da Vinci actually belonged to one of those secret societies. Maybe more of his paintings contain hidden signs and symbols, messages we must try to decode... I don't normally read thrillers, but this one's like a movie in your head: dark, mysterious and compelling.

**Sue Limb**

# THE DAY OF THE JACKAL
## Frederick Forsyth

In 1963, a young English assassin is hired by a secretive group to kill the French president at a public parade. This assassin's code name is The Jackal, and the account of his bid to stay ahead of the detective on his trail makes for gripping thriller writing. The book is hailed as a classic of the genre, and rightly so. The suspense never lets up, but the detail makes it so convincing. Often research can weigh a novel down, but here it fuels the story. Famously, Forsyth begins with a criminal masterclass on how to acquire a foolproof false identity. So long as you harbour no plans to follow in the footsteps of the story's anti-hero, you won't fail to be rewarded by this compelling read.

**Matt Whyman**

> **Next?**
>
> More Forsyth? Try *The Dogs of War*, about a group of mercenaries.
>
> *Jarhead: A Soldier's Story of Modern War* by Anthony Swofford is a true story and packed with military knowledge.
>
> Or for another nail-biting thriller, try Robert Ludlum's *The Bourne Identity* or Robert Harris's *Fatherland* (UTBG 128).

# THE DAY OF THE TRIFFIDS
## John Wyndham

> **Next?**
>
> More Wyndham? Try *The Kraken Wakes*, a story of global catastrophe and how humans deal with their possible extinction.
>
> *The War of the Worlds* is another classic sci-fi tale that's still just as effective as when it was first written. (UTBG 424)
>
> Or try another classic about humanity descending into barbarism: *The Death of Grass* by John Christopher. Or the bleak, violent classic *I Am Legend* (UTBG 194) by Richard Matheson.
>
> Or what about people fighting off other dangerous creatures? Try *Jurassic Park* by Michael Crichton. (UTBG 219)

A mysterious comet fills the sky with green shooting stars, and the next day everyone who has seen them is struck blind. William Masen is one of the few who can still see. Now he has to survive, but it won't be easy. There are triffids – walking poisonous plants – to deal with. And other humans, who want to rebuild the world their own way...

Nowadays there are a lot of 'post-apocalypse' books and movies, in which some disaster strikes the entire planet, leaving only a handful of people alive; but *The Day of the Triffids*, written more than 50 years ago, is the original and still the best. You'll worry about staring at shooting stars for years to come...

**Benedict Jacka**

# DAZ 4 ZOE  Robert Swindells

*Daz 4 Zoe* resembles a futuristic *Romeo and Juliet* in that its main characters are 'star-crossed lovers'. Yes, it's love at first sight, but how will Zoe and Daz manage to see each other? Zoe is a Subby (a member of the well-off suburban classes) and Daz a Chippy (living in poverty in the inner city), so they're forbidden to meet. But neither will be told what to do, and both face enormous risks in breaking the rules of this strictly divided society. The story is told alternately by Zoe and Daz, and you'll have to get used to Daz's unusual spelling (as he's had only very basic schooling, unlike middle-class Zoe), as well as learning new vocabulary. But it's well worth the effort to find out whether Swindells's lovers manage to defy the system and earn themselves a happier ending than Shakespeare's doomed teenagers.

**Linda Newbery**

### Next?

More love against the odds? Try Valérie Zenatti's *Message in a Bottle*, about an Israeli girl and a Palestinian boy. Or maybe Simone Elkeles's *Perfect Chemistry*, about a perfect cheerleading girl falling for Mexican gang member, Alejandro.

Or look out for more Robert Swindells; try *Brother in the Land*, which is a harrowing look at post-apocalyptic life, or *Stone Cold* (UTBG 377), about lives lived on the streets.

# DEAD FAMOUS  Ben Elton

### Next?

Ben Elton's novels all combine a gripping plot with a political or social agenda. Try *High Society*, about drug culture, or *Popcorn*, about movie violence. There's even one that's a bit *X Factor* – *Chart Throb*!

For a different take on how reality TV might evolve, try the deeply terrifying *The Hunger Games* by Suzanne Collins, in which kids have to literally fight for survival. (UTBG 192)

Or for something a little lighter, try *The Next Big Thing* by Johanna Edwards, about a girl who goes on a TV show to lose weight.

There's been a gruesome murder on 'Peeping Tom' – a (barely) disguised version of *Big Brother*. With scores of TV cameras in the house and the nation watching the contestants' every move, you would think this would be impossible – and yet no one knows who did it! This is a truly riveting modern-day detective story, and at the same time it's a fantastic pastiche of *Big Brother*, the characters beautifully parodied with their inane conversations and egocentricity.

Elton sends up the whole cult of reality TV whilst cleverly sucking you into its addictive world, almost as if you were watching one of the shows themselves. It's a must for all *Big Brother* lovers, and for all *Big Brother* haters.

**Susan Reuben**

# DEADKIDSONGS
## Toby Litt

At first, Andrew, Peter, Paul and Matthew seem just like the Famous Five (or rather, Four). They are Gang – not the Gang, just Gang – and they play war games in an English village, prizing Gang loyalty above everything. But the easy bit ends there. Real soldiers fight enemies, and for Gang, most of the adults around them are enemies. Gang wages a dark and brutal war that is far from being a game, especially as the only place that it makes sense is in Gang's head. *deadkidsongs* is a disturbing story about the horrific consequences of confusing fantasy and reality, and about how even adults only see what they want to see, no matter what terrible reality is staring them in the face.

**Antonia Honeywell**

TOBY LITT
deadkidsongs

'The most exciting new British novel I've read this year ... extraordinarily haunting'
John Preston, *Sunday Telegraph*

---

### Next?

Toby Litt likes to experiment with different styles and types of story, so you'll find each book quite different from the others. Try **Beatniks: An English Road Movie** or **Corpsing** next, and see what you think.

If you're fascinated by the bleak portrayal of human nature, try **Lord of the Flies** (UTBG 241) or **Heart of Darkness** (UTBG 174).

If you like the way Toby Litt writes about children, try **Cat's Eye** by Margaret Atwood. (UTBG 70)

If you want to read a novel about a real war, try **Regeneration** (UTBG 330) and its sequels by Pat Barker or **Birdsong** (UTBG 44) by Sebastian Faulks.

### SAYING IT WITH PICTURES

*Bone* by Jeff Smith

*Get a Life* by Philippe Dupey

*Batman: The Dark Knight Returns* by Frank Miller

*Palestine* by Joe Sacco

*Barefoot Gen: A Cartoon Story of Hiroshima* by Keiji Nakazawa

*Gemma Bovery* by Posy Simmonds

**The Sandman** series by Neil Gaiman

# DEAD NEGATIVE  Nick Manns

Nick Manns writes gripping and intelligent political thrillers, set in the deceptively normal worlds of home and school. Elliott is haunted by visions of his dead photographer father, who may have been killed for 'shooting the truth' in the Bosnian conflict. When two men from the Bosnian Embassy turn up to examine his father's photographs, claiming they are hunting down war criminals for their murder of Muslims, Elliott is not sure whether to trust them. At school, meanwhile, racist thugs are bullying his Sikh friend, Jaspreet.

Written in short, terse sentences, this powerful novel makes you think about the roots of racism here and abroad, and the courage required to stand up for what you believe to be right and true.

**Patricia Elliott**

### Next?

Linda Newbery's *Sisterland* and Bernard Ashley's *Little Soldier* both deal with different aspects of racism and the conflict it causes. Bali Rai's *The Last Taboo* deals with racism between the Black and Asian communities in the UK. Or try Suzanne Fisher Staples's *Storm* (UTBG 378).

And if you've enjoyed this, don't miss Nick Manns's thriller, *Fallout*, about a government nuclear cover-up.

For another boy on a quest to find his father, read Joan Lingard's *Tell the Moon to Come Out*.

# DEAR NOBODY
## Berlie Doherty

### Next?

Berlie Doherty is the author of many excellent novels for young adults; both *The Snake-Stone* and *Tough Luck* are very good.

Or what about teen pregnancy from the boy's perspective? Try *Slam* by Nick Hornby. (UTBG 367)

Or take a look at our feature on love, sex and relationships on pp. 178–179 for more suggestions.

*Dear Nobody* is a novel about a teenage pregnancy, but it's so much more than that.

Helen and Chris are in love, and when Helen falls pregnant, each of them wants to do the best they can, despite their fears. But will they stay together under the pressure? Their parents aren't much help. Both Helen and Chris come from homes where there are family secrets, and the unborn baby prompts the couple to explore their own pasts. The story is told partly by Chris, and partly through the letters Helen writes to her unborn baby, the 'Dear Nobody' of the title.

This is a very moving and lyrical account of what it means to inadvertently start a new life.

**Sherry Ashworth**

# DEATH AND THE PENGUIN
## Andrey Kurkov

**Next?**

*A Wild Sheep Chase* by Haruki Murakami is another bizarre animal / human tale; a fantastic, hilarious story that really is about chasing a sheep! (UTBG 438)

How about more Kurkov? Try *The General's Thumb*, which features a tortoise.

Something else truly surreal? Try Franz Kafka's superb novella, *Metamorphosis*.

Or perhaps the literary surrealism of Jasper Fforde's *The Eyre Affair*. (UTBG 125)

It may sound a bit odd and pretentious to recommend a bit of Ukrainian fiction. But who cares? This surreal black comedy is fantastic.

Viktor is a writer who lives in an apartment in Kiev. His flatmate is a penguin called Misha, who flip-flops round the apartment eating frozen fish. Viktor manages to get himself tangled up in a world of crime and intrigue. He has to keep a step ahead to stay alive.

Andrey Kurkov creates a surreal, deadpan world, in which it seems perfectly natural for a man and a penguin to be friends. It's a real disappointment when you finish the book and find that the real world is a lot more boring and down-to-earth...

**James Reynolds**

# DEEP SECRET  Berlie Doherty

*Deep Secret* is based on the flooding of a valley in the Peak District in the 1930s, to create Ladybower Reservoir. What would it be like to live in a village destined to be drowned? The inhabitants of Birchen are faced with the loss of all they know – their farmland, the graves of relatives in the churchyard, the magnificent Hall. But first there's tragedy when Grace, one of twins, slips and is drowned in the stream. Madeleine, her double, pretends she was the twin who died, and takes on Grace's identity; only blind Seth knows the truth.

Multiple viewpoints show us the effects of forthcoming change on a range of characters, all of them strongly individualised. This is a moving, memorable story with a wonderful evocation of time and place.

**Linda Newbery**

**Next?**

More Berlie Doherty: try *Dear Nobody* (UTBG 101) or *Abela: The Girl Who Saw Lions*, about two girls, one from Africa and one from Sheffield, or her mystery *A Beautiful Place for Murder*.

*Saskia's Journey* by Theresa Breslin and *A Pattern of Roses* by K.M. Peyton both combine past and present in intriguing ways.

*Exodus* by Julie Bertagna is a book about colossal change on a global level. (UTBG 124)

# DESIRE LINES  Jack Gantos

This is that rare thing, a novel without heroes, or indeed anyone you can really like; but it is not without the power to involve and to keep you reading. Walker is gutless, easily preyed upon, and in the end corrupted and treacherous. When a fundamentalist preacher comes to Walker's small Florida town, the preacher's boy, a bigoted zealot like his father, starts a rumour that Walker is gay in order to make him 'out' any 'ho-mo-sexuals' in his school. A bullying and vicious gang of boys also get hold of Walker and involve him in their delinquencies. Walker, caught between the devil and the deep, finally betrays two girls whom he's spied on in the woods making love.

Gantos is a powerful writer who is here challenging his readers' loyalty and integrity as much as the preacher's boy challenges Walker's.

**Lynne Reid Banks**

**Next?**

Jack Gantos has also written a memoir about his time in prison, *Hole in My Life* (UTBG 183). Or try his hilarious, shocking and very gothic novel, *The Love Curse of the Rumbaughs*.

Aidan Chambers's *Postcards from No Man's Land* is also about sexuality and the burden of making choices. (UTBG 318)

For a funny look at female sexuality, try Julie Burchill's *Sugar Rush*. (UTBG 384)

# THE DEVIL'S BREATH  David Gilman

**Next?**

The sequels, *Ice Claw*, about an X-treme sports challenge, and *Blood Sun*, in which Max takes on flesh-stripping piranhas.

M.G. Harris's **The Joshua Files** is another fast-paced, globetrotting adventure series – look for *Invisible City* and *Ice Shock*.

For something set in the English countryside but just as breathtaking, try Will Peterson's *Triskellion*. (UTBG 404)

Max Gordon is 15 and he wants to find his dad. Tom Gordon, a geologist, was investigating a billion-dollar hydroelectric dam scheme when he went missing.

Flying out to Namibia, Max journeys deep into the wilderness on an adrenalin-fuelled adventure in search of Skeleton Rock, the fortress headquarters of Shaka Chang, the evil businessman in charge of the dam. But the desert is a dangerous place. Max takes on trucks full of armed enemies, man-eating lions, and giant albino crocodiles. And once he gets to The Devil's Breath, a gigantic sinkhole that is the only way into the fortress, Max has to summon every ounce of courage and strength to stay alive.

This book is fast-paced and buzzing with action. By the end of it you'll be able to fly a plane, chop off a cobra's head and poison your own arrows.

**Ally Kennen**

# THE DEVIL'S KISS · Sarwat Chadda

Angels, demons, vampires, werewolves, the ten plagues of Egypt and maths homework – they're all here, layered up into a fantastic feast that you'll want to devour in one sitting. This is a smorgasbord of a book. Heaped on the basic bread of *girl hates over-strict dad* and *there are monsters in the dark* are tasty slices from Chadda's favourites; from *Buffy* (our heroine, Billi, is a fighting adept in training), Dan Brown (yes, there are the Knights Templar), King Arthur, *Hellblazer*, *Supernatural*, and from just about every religion that you study in school. Do you think that makes *The Devil's Kiss* sound like too much of a mouthful? Too much like something with nothing original to say? Well, you'd be wrong, because this is a brilliant book. Somehow Chadda has taken all those disparate elements, and created something totally original and completely involving. It's also fast-paced, intriguing and very real. So, seriously – stock up on snacks, turn off the mobile, curl up in a safe place and then start this book. It'll be worth it.

**Leonie Flynn**

> **Next?**
>
> *The Demon's Lexicon* by Sarah Rees Brennan is about two brothers fighting demons in London.
>
> If you like graphic novels, try some of the **Buffy the Vampire Slayer** tie-ins, such as *The Long Way Home*. Cliff McNish spins a completely different take on celestial beings in *Angel*. Or if you want something just as fast-paced and Gothic, try *Skulduggery Pleasant* by Derek Landy.

# THE DIAMOND GIRLS · Jacqueline Wilson

> **Next?**
>
> More Jacqueline Wilson? Try *Lola Rose* (UTBG 238), or *My Sister Jodie*, about the power-play between two sisters.
>
> Ann Brashares's *The Sisterhood of the Travelling Pants* is about a group of friends during one hot summer. (UTBG 364)
>
> Can you ever be too young to fall in love? And what if the boy you love has a deep secret? Read Jean Ure's *Love Is Forever*.

I love Jacqueline Wilson's books – she is one of my favourite authors because she deals with issues we can all relate to. In this book, we meet Dixie, her sisters – Jude, Martine and Rochelle – and Sue, their pregnant mum. Dixie is happy, but wishes they didn't live in a poky flat on an estate where no one has their own space. When her mum announces they are moving to a dream house with lots of bedrooms and a large garden, Dixie thinks her wish has come true.

But all is not as it seems – what is wrong with the new house and the baby? Mum has a secret – and Dixie is determined to find out what it is.

**Florence Eastoe, age 13**

# DIARY OF A CHAV  Grace Dent

Shiraz Bailey Wood is all about keeping it real. An Essex girl halfway through her final GCSE year, she lives in Thundersley Road with her mum, dad, Emo sister Cava-Sue, gross little bruv Murphy, and Penny, their morbidly obese Staffie. This is real life, complete with £5 buffets from Iceland and unwanted pregnancies, but it is also a very funny account of someone realising that they don't have to be limited by other people's expectations. By the end of her diary, Shiraz has met the love of her life, Wesley Barrington Bains II, and reunited her dysfunctional family on TV's *Fast-Track Family Feud*. But, before all that you have to start at the beginning, when it's Christmas Day and her nan's given Shiraz a new diary…

**Laura Hutchings**

**Next?**

Follow Shiraz Bailey Wood's further adventures as she does her A/S exams, moves to London to become (amongst other things) a Christmas elf, gets stranded in Ibiza and finally ends up as personal assistant to glamorous WAG, Tiffany Poole in: *Slinging the Bling*, *Too Cool for School*, *The Ibiza Diaries*, *The Fame Diaries* and *The Real Diaries*.

For other humorous accounts of life in diary form, try **Adrian Mole** (UTBG 347) or the equally hilarious *Big Woo: My Not-So-Secret Teenage Blog* by Susie Day.

# DIARY OF A NOBODY
## George and Weedon Grossmith

This surely must be the first comic diary: before the teen-angst diaries, before **The Princess Diaries** – before, even, **Adrian Mole**. Adrian, actually, has a lot in common with poor old Mr Pooter, the writer of this diary… Both are stoical, humourless, think highly of themselves and, hilariously, fail time and again to see themselves as others see them. Pooter is a social bumbler who desperately wants to rise in society but who inevitably slips on a piece of cabbage along the way. The language of the book is somewhat archaic, but this only adds to the delicious irony of it all.

It's wonderfully reassuring to think that the Victorians laughed at Pooter just as we laugh at him – we can't be so different from them then, can we?

**Mary Hooper**

**Next?**

For some more humour that has stood the test of time, try **Three Men in a Boat** by Jerome K. Jerome. (UTBG 395)

Or *The History of Mr Polly* by H.G. Wells, the story of another Everyman and his quest for happiness.

Or try the modern equivalent – *The Secret Diary of Adrian Mole Aged 13¾*. (UTBG 347)

# THE DIARY OF A YOUNG GIRL
Anne Frank

**Next?**

*Surviving Hitler* by Andrea Warren is a book about life in a concentration camp.

*Hitler's Canary* by Sandi Toksvig is based on a true story. Or try a novel about surviving the Nazis – *Saving Rafael* by Leslie Wilson, in which a girl finds her courage – and her love – tested in war-torn Berlin.

Another inspirational life story is *The Story of My Life* by Helen Keller.

Anne Frank, a Jewish girl living in Amsterdam, was 13 when she began her diary in June 1942. The city was under German occupation. With her family and friends, she hid in a secret annexe of a house. She was 15 when she made her last entry in the diary on 1 August 1944. On 4 August, the eight people in hiding were caught and sent to Auschwitz concentration camp; from there she and her sister Margot were sent to the Belsen camp, where they both died the following spring, a month before the camp was liberated. Telling us everything about her life, from her boredom and fear to her feelings about herself, boys and the future, Anne's remarkable diaries were found scattered all over the floor of the annexe after the police left. Luckily for us, as this is probably the most moving war diary ever written. Unmissable.

**James Riordan**

# DISCONNECTED  Sherry Ashworth

Sixth form can be a daunting experience for many students. The pressure to do well in exams that have such an enormous impact on your future can prove more than some people can handle. Catherine is one of these people. Always a straight-A student, she suddenly loses her way. Not sure what she wants to do with her life, and unable to deal with the high expectations of her parents and teachers, she simply gives up. Her grades plummet and she starts drinking heavily. Catherine relates her own journey towards self-discovery in an honest, realistic way, addressing each section of the book to one of the significant people in her life. A hard-hitting novel about things that they may not teach you in school.

**Noga Applebaum**

**Next?**

Another Sherry Ashworth? *Paralysed* deals with an accident and its aftermath.

Ally Kennen's books are hard-hitting, too – try *Beast*. (UTBG 35)

*The Catcher in the Rye* by J.D. Salinger is an amazing novel narrated by the unforgettable Holden Caulfield, a cynical, troubled teenager who has been expelled from school and has an opinion about everything. (UTBG 69)

# DISCWORLD: MONSTROUS REGIMENT
## Terry Pratchett

**Next?**

Terry Pratchett has fortunately written loads, including more **Discworld** books; read *The Colour of Magic* next, followed by *The Light Fantastic*, then head for later offerings such as *The Wyrd Sisters* and *The Fifth Elephant*.

Or try Robert Rankin for offbeat, mad humour – and wacky titles such as *The Hollow Chocolate Bunnies of the Apocalypse*.

Or for more really daft humour, try Spike Milligan's *Adolf Hitler: My Part in His Downfall*.

The old ballad 'Sweet Polly Oliver' is a splendidly sentimental tale, but by the time Pratchett has done with it, the result is blackly witty and scathing. It's also a thrilling read.

We meet Polly in the act of cutting off her long golden hair – she is signing up with the Borogravia army disguised as a boy. But as Polly soon learns, things in the army are not all they seem. Not being a patriot, the fact that her country is losing the war does not much bother her. Finding herself on the front line does, since no one expects her regiment to survive.

Pratchett delights in building tension then releasing it in *tour-de-force* action sequences. The motley regiment is full of startling characters, and the real revelations are saved up for the end.

**Geraldine McCaughrean**

# DIVIDED CITY  Theresa Breslin

May in Glasgow means the marching season and the start of the Orange Walks. Graham, a Protestant, is like any other boy, turning his back on the protests in favour of playing football with his Catholic friend Joe and following the fortunes of Rangers. Witnessing a racist attack on a Muslim asylum seeker draws both boys into the rivalries that are tearing their poverty-ridden society apart, pitting neighbour against neighbour and even friends and families against each other.

A bold and brave book about religious, racial, social and political bigotry that shows how sectarianism can be overcome. It can't help but make you see the world differently.

**Next?**

Breslin's **Remembrance** details the lives of five young people drawn into the horrors of the First World War.

Other stories tackling small-minded bigotry, sectarian tensions and politically provoked violence include Alan Gibbons's powerful *Caught in the Crossfire* (UTBG 71), Joan Lingard's **Kevin and Sadie** series, set in Northern Ireland, starting with *The Twelfth Day of July* and continuing with *Across the Barricades*, or her *Tell the Moon to Come Out*, which is set during the Spanish Civil War.

**Eileen Armstrong**

# DETECTIVE STORIES
## by K.K. Beck

There are many reasons to read detective novels. First of all, you are pretty much guaranteed that things will happen and the plot will move along. That's because, with very few exceptions, a crime has already been, or is about to be, committed and must be solved. So the characters cannot just sit around. They are forced into action, which makes for a plot-driven, engaging read. And, because the criminals are still at large, and presumably don't want to be caught, the detectives are often in jeopardy as they go about their work. This means that the reader can enjoy the suspense of knowing the characters are in danger. There's also something very satisfying about seeing a crime solved, getting everything properly sorted out, and making sure the guilty are exposed and presumably punished. If only justice always prevailed in real life! Plus, the reader can detect along with the characters. In classic, old-school detective fiction, the clues are usually arranged hiding in plain sight. The author's goal in these kinds of books is to get the reader to say 'Of course! Why didn't I see that?!' Agatha Christie is famous for these sorts of stories. In *The Secret Adversary*, two friends recently returned to London from the First World War start their own detective agency, trace a girl named Jane Finn who has disappeared with a packet of important government papers, and foil a plot to take over the world. Agatha Christie was also, of course, the creator of the great sleuths Miss Marple and Hercule Poirot.

There are all kinds of detectives, from amateurs, who accidentally stumble onto a crime, to hardened private eyes and police

THE NUMBER ONE BESTSELLER

IAN RANKIN

Knots & Crosses

AN INSPECTOR Rebus NOVEL

---

### DETECTIVES WITH AN ACCENT (Northern Eurocrime)

*Kurt Wallander Mysteries*
by Henning Mankell (Swedish)

*Borkman's Point* by Håkan Neser (Swedish)

*Arctic Chill* by Arnaldur Indridason (Icelandic)

*The Girl with the Dragon Tattoo*
by Stieg Larsson (Swedish)

*Last Rituals* by Yrsa Sigurdardottir (Icelandic)

*The Devil's Star* by Jo Nesbø (Norwegian)

*The Winter Queen* by Boris Akunin (Russian)

A PHILIP MARLOWE MYSTERY

RAYMOND CHANDLER

THE BIG SLEEP

INTRODUCTION BY
IAN RANKIN

detectives. Because detective stories often feature the same detective in multiple books, after a little dabbling in the field, it's easy to find the ones you know you'll enjoy. One of the first and best amateur detectives is Sherlock Holmes. *A Study in Scarlet* is the first Holmes mystery, but you needn't start there. Try *The Hound of the Baskervilles* or any of the 56 short stories (UTBG 359). There's a reason Holmes and his sidekick Dr Watson have lasted so long.

Detective novels can be hard-boiled – violent and action-packed tales of guns and gangsters. Think of Raymond Chandler's *The Big Sleep* (UTBG 42). They can be soft-boiled – gentle stories of pale corpses found neatly on the hearthrug in the vicarage in a quiet village – like Dorothy L. Sayers's **Lord Peter Wimsey** books (UTBG 243). Or anything in between.

Detective novels can also take the reader on interesting journeys to exotic settings and different time periods. Some were written long in the past (traditionally, experts date the beginning of the form to 1841 and Edgar Allan Poe's short story 'Murders in the Rue Morgue', featuring an eccentric Paris detective called Auguste Dupin), and many of those written more recently are set in historic periods; some of the best are Lindsey Davis's **Falco** stories (set in the year AD 79), which start with *The Silver Pigs*.

Many different sorts of books can fall under the banner of detective fiction. You could try *I'm Not Scared* (UTBG 201) by Niccolò Ammaniti, which is scary, gripping and beautifully written; or Mark Haddon's funny, moving, fascinating *The Curious Incident of the Dog in the Night-Time* (UTBG 92); or the deliciously creepy *Strangers on a Train* (UTBG 381) by Patricia Highsmith; or *The No. 1 Ladies' Detective Agency* (UTBG 285), the first book in Alexander McCall Smith's popular **Precious Ramotswe** series; or Lee Child's page-turner *Killing Floor*, which begins with drifter Jack Reacher suddenly being arrested for murder...

**DARKER DETECTIVES**

*52 Pick-Up* by Elmore Leonard

*The Maltese Falcon* by Dashiel Hammet

**Rebus** books by Ian Rankin

*Tourist Season* by Carl Hiaasen

**87th Precinct** series by Ed McBain

*One for the Money* by Janet Evanovich

# DIZZY Cathy Cassidy

Birthdays for Dizzy are extra special because each brings a gift from the ditzy mum who abandoned her as a baby to travel the world – a rainbow stripy hat, a ragdoll, a pink jewelled necklace, an exotic dreamcatcher. The best present of all comes on her 12th birthday, when her mum turns up in person to whisk her off for the summer into a very different life – on the road, under canvas and at festivals – meeting up with some colourful characters along the way, in places Dizzy has never even dreamed of. Suddenly she is forced to rethink her life with her dad and the values she's always accepted, and do some growing up of her own.

Not just another pink and girly book, this one is essential teen reading. Sparkling with warmth, humanity and hope, it will make you laugh and cry.

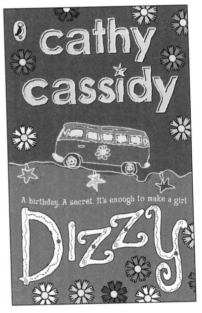

**Eileen Armstrong**

## Next?

More Cathy Cassidy is a must. A character from *Dizzy*, Mouse, appears in *Lucky Star* (UTBG 250). Then after that try *Driftwood* and *Ginger Snaps* (UTBG 154), though all her books are well worth reading.

Kate Cann is another writer who 'gets' teens – try *Leader of the Pack* (UTBG 234) or *Escape* (UTBG 122).

*Heaven Eyes* by David Almond and *You Can't Kiss It Better* by Diane Hendry are both excellent glimpses into the lives of looked-after children – while Hendry's is very realistic, Almond's has a more magical edge.

## CHILDHOODS YOU WOULDN'T WANT

*Angela's Ashes* by Frank McCourt

*The Glass Castle* by Jeannette Walls

*Once in a House on Fire* by Andrea Ashworth

*Chinese Cinderella* by Adeline Yen Mah

*Wild Swans* by Jung Chang

*The Hard Man of the Swings* by Jeanne Willis

*A Child Called 'It'* by Dave Pelzer

*Frost in May* by Antonia White

*This Boy's Life* by Tobias Wolff

# DO ANDROIDS DREAM OF ELECTRIC SHEEP? Philip K. Dick

When I was about ten or eleven I outgrew Nancy Drew and fell in love with science fiction. I discovered the sci-fi ABC: Asimov, Bradbury and Clarke, but it wasn't till I was over 30 that I discovered D – Philip K. Dick. This book was made into a brilliant film called *Blade Runner*. The book is quite different, though it is still about bounty hunter Rick Deckard, and set in a dystopian future. The thing I love most about Philip K. Dick is something I don't get excited about in any other author: his *ideas*. But be warned. He was a strange Californian who used to play with his daughters' Barbie dolls.

**Caroline Lawrence**

### Next?

Philip K. Dick's short story collection: *We Can Remember It for You Wholesale*. (UTBG 430)

And Caroline's ABC? Try one of each: Asimov's **Foundation** trilogy (UTBG 140), Bradbury's *Fahrenheit 451* (UTBG 126), and Clarke's *2001: A Space Odyssey*.

Or look at a collection of classics in *The Oxford Book of Science Fiction Stories*, edited by Tom Shippey.

# DOES MY BUM LOOK BIG IN THIS?
Arabella Weir

### Next?

*The Secret Dreamworld of a Shopaholic* is about life, the universe and shopping. Oh, and it's also very funny. (UTBG 350)

Or how about another Arabella Weir? Try *Onwards and Upwards*, the story of three 20-something friends.

If you're looking for another heroine who is completely likeable in spite of her (many) flaws, try *Rachel's Holiday*. (UTBG 325)

This is the diary of Jacqueline M. Pane, your average 30-something manic singleton who obsesses over every detail and scrutinises every possible meaning of every little word. Naturally, Jacqueline's life is dominated by food and tormented by exercise, and her love life is troubled. Her flat is small, but at least work is good; she is the Senior Conference Organiser for the Pellet Corporation, the largest computer and parts supplier in England (but does 'Senior' mean old? Hmm...). She can get irritating at times, but then you can't help liking her when she does something caring such as doing a big shop at Sainsbury's because she's heard the supermarket's profits are down!

Read this book for a chuckle, and for some great advice on leaving the room without anyone seeing the size of your bum!

**Elena Gregoriou**

# DOES MY HEAD LOOK BIG IN THIS?
## Randa Abdel-Fattah

Sixteen-year-old Amal has sleepless nights about all the usual teenage things – school, boys, parents, image, identity, shopping – but as an Australian-Palestinian-Muslim she's also got to contend with the consequences of deciding to wear a hijab full-time to demonstrate her religious belief. Although this is a book that is long overdue, it's so much more than just a worthwhile story. Amal's is an authentic and often very funny voice, which helps readers confirm their own identity and forces them to look beyond the headlines and the hype and enter fully into Amal's world.

**Eileen Armstrong**

### Next?

More Randa Abdel-Fattah: *Ten Things I Hate About Me* is about a Muslim girl who leads a double life; *Where the Streets Had a Name* is about a Palestinian girl determined to find a way to visit her grandmother's old house in Jerusalem.

*Palestine* by Joe Sacco is a graphic novel that tells the Palestinian story. While *Persepolis* (UTBG 142) tells of a girl in Iran.

*Shabanu: Daughter of the Wind* by Suzanne Fisher Staples is about a Muslim nomad girl and the traditional way of life that she slowly comes to question.

# DOING IT
## Melvin Burgess

### Next?

*Junk* (UTBG 218), also by Melvin Burgess, is about the treacherously easy slide into heroin addiction. Or try his twist on our fame-hungry and image-conscious culture: *Sara's Face*.

Another boy dealing with all the tribulations of adolescence is Junior, in Sherman Alexie's *The Absolutely True Diary of a Part-Time Indian*. (UTBG 11)

Or for a really devastating look at teen sex and sexuality, read *Boy Toy* by Barry Lyga.

This is a story about sex. The main characters (three 17-year-old boys and their girlfriends) spend 330 pages talking, fantasising, worrying, planning and thinking about sex. Oh, yes, and doing it. There's a lot of doing it. There are things in this book you wouldn't want your mother to read, and I wasn't sure I should be reading it myself. But this is Melvin Burgess writing, so you know he's going to be ruthlessly honest as well as laugh-out-loud funny, and that in the end he's going to burrow his way down to the truth. And when he does, the truth is wonderfully liberating.

It's an excellent book. Why not ask your parents to give it to you for Christmas? No, seriously. Go on, I dare you...

**Andrew Norriss**

# DOWN WITH SKOOL!
## Geoffrey Willans and Ronald Searle

**Next?**

There are sequels: *How to Be Topp*, *Whizz for Atomms and Back in the Jug Agane* (collected in one volume as **Molesworth**).

Harry Potter contains a dim reflection of it: in *How to Be Topp*, Molesworth writes a play called 'The Hogwarts'!

The same anarchic spirit can be found in *1066 and All That* by W.C. Sellar and R.J. Yeatman. (UTBG 8)

I know exactly where I was standing when my friend Eve first showed me this book. With its amazing cartoons and misspelled ramblings about a boys' boarding school, it was, and remains, one of the funniest reads ever.

Our hero Molesworth 1 (brother of Molesworth 2) leads us through the characters and manners of St Custard's in a private language, interspersed with blots. Why did Eve and I – two teenage girls at a London day school in the heart of the sixties – roar with laughter at a book published in a very different era: 1953 (the year we were born)? Because schools, and people, don't really change. In fact, with education becoming ever more earnest, I suspect that modern children may laugh even louder. We all love Molesworth. In fact, while we're reading, we *are* Molesworth. Very odd. But a work of pure genius nonetheless.

**Eleanor Updale**

# DRACULA   Bram Stoker

Bram Stoker wrote many novels and short stories, but he is best known for one extraordinary book, which if not actually originating a genre, has become the undisputed foundation of not just vampire fiction but the gothic in general. I won't waste time expounding the intricacies of the plot here, but simply implore you to forget almost any film version you may have seen (with the possible exception of 1922's *Nosferatu*) and delight in discovering the slow beauty of the original book. Quite adventurous stylistically for its time, it uses several different narratives that weave together to create a momentum that by the end of the book is simply unstoppable.

A true masterpiece.

**Marcus Sedgwick**

**Next?**

More Gothic fiction? Try *Carmilla* by Sheridan Le Fanu or Stevenson's *Dr Jekyll and Mr Hyde*. (UTBG 115)

Modern vampires abound; try the **Night World** series by L.J. Smith (UTBG 283), Stephanie Meyer's *Twilight* (UTBG 411) or Anne Rice's *Interview with the Vampire* (UTBG 205).

Or what about a Gothic parody, in Jane Austen's *Northanger Abbey*? (UTBG 286)

# The DRAGONS OF PERN series
## Anne McCaffrey

**Next?**

There are many books set in Pern, some written by Anne's son, Todd. But the best remain the first three: *Dragonflight*, *The White Dragon* and *Dragonquest*.

More dragons, this time in the age of sailing ships? Try Naomi Novak's wonderful melding of history and fantasy in the **Temeraire** series, starting with *Temeraire* itself.

Or try the **Black Magician** trilogy (UTBG 45) (dragonless fantasy), Robin Hobb's **Farseer** trilogy (heavily dragonsome fantasy) or Alison Goodman's *Eon*.

The first three books about the planet Pern tell the story of the huge, fire-breathing dragons who defend their world against the periodic fall of deadly spores from a neighbouring planet. But dragons cannot do this alone – riders have to guide them in battle. As soon as they hatch, the green, blue, brown and bronze dragonets bond with boys, and the golden queens with girls, to become their lifelong soulmates. Lessa, one of the Dragonriders, impresses Ramoth, the last surviving queen, and together they risk everything to save their planet. By the third book, Jaxom, the boy lord of Ruatha, accidentally impresses a small, unique white dragon with extraordinary abilities who is destined to help Pern in a way no one dreams possible.

**Gill Vickery**

# DRAMA QUEEN  Chloë Rayban

Jessica's life is crammed with people whose love lives need sorting out. Mum and Dad have split up, but the divorce hasn't come through yet so surely there's still hope. Best-friend Clare has fallen for the dweeby boy downstairs – but how to get them together? And most intriguing of all is a marriage proposal Jessica receives in the post by accident – but who's it from, and who was it really intended for? Fortunately she's thought of a fail-safe matchmaking formula so she'll know who's destined to belong together: for example, his perfect teeth but sticky-out ears = her long legs but bitten nails: match! Apply it each time and you can't go wrong ... can you?

**Susan Reuben**

**Next?**

For another story of teenage angst, but this time with an unexpected regal twist, try **The Princess Diaries**. (UTBG 323)

*11 o'clock Chocolate Cake* by Caroline Pitcher is about the life and loves of M. and the dramas that happen on the school bus.

In Susie Day's *Girl Meets Cake*, Heidi is a fangirl and a geek, her life dominated by her laptop and her TV. But when her online and real lives collide, things get interesting!

# DR JEKYLL AND MR HYDE
## Robert Louis Stevenson

**Next?**

Another story that looks at the truth – or not – of surface appearance, is Oscar Wilde's *The Picture of Dorian Gray*. (UTBG 311)

For a modern take on the Gothic horror genre, try *The Picador Book of the New Gothic*, edited by Patrick McGrath.

If you want another classic horror story, you must try Mary Shelley's *Frankenstein*. (UTBG 141)

This short novel by the author of *Treasure Island* is an altogether more sophisticated story, and drips with the darkness to be found in the best of his writing.

The story unfolds, piece by piece, of Dr Jekyll, a respectable London medical man, and Mr Hyde, an unsettling and plainly evil man who seems to have become an acquaintance of the doctor's, much to the horror of his friends. You may already know the secret of the connection between the two men, because this story became so famous that its title has become proverbial, but if you do not, then you are lucky enough to get to read this story as its Victorian audience would have done. To contemporary reviewers the book was weird and shocking, and I think it still is, as it speaks of the potentially horrific nature of humankind, as well as its more noble aspects.

**Marcus Sedgwick**

# DR ZHIVAGO   Boris Pasternak

Boris Pasternak was a poet and novelist who fell out with the Soviet dictator Stalin, so he was unable to publish any works in Russia after 1933. He had to have his greatest work smuggled abroad: *Dr Zhivago* was published in 1957 in Italy. This is a thrilling, if challenging, read, encompassing half a century of Russian history: from the excitement of revolution and civil war to the labour camps in which Zhivago's love is confined.

Whose side would you have been on? That is the question that the gentle, aristocratic doctor, Yuri Zhivago, has to answer about himself.

**Next?**

If you fancy reading more about the Russian Revolution, try Mikhail Sholokhov's *And Quiet Flows the Don*.

For an epic account of another country's revolution, this time China, try Jung Chang's *Wild Swans*. (UTBG 439)

There are other epic love stories: try the Australian setting of *The Thorn Birds* by Colleen McCullough, the American Civil War of Margaret Mitchell's *Gone with the Wind* (UTBG 161) or *Outlander* by Diana Gabaldon, in which Claire steps back in time and meets her destiny. (Real men wear kilts!)

**James Riordan**

# THE DUD AVOCADO   Elaine Dundy

'I am totally incomprehensible to everyone including myself...'

These are the words of Sally Jay Gorce – a heroine you will never forget. Sally has come as if on fire from a quiet upbringing in America to Paris, capital of Europe, romance and exploration. Once there, she positively flings herself into life.

*The Dud Avocado* is as original and funny as its title. From the first line, readers of this novel should hold onto their hats as Elaine Dundy takes you on a ride that is racy, sexy, risqué and hilarious. It's a rites-of-passage novel that is increasingly recognised as a classic of its time, and it's a joyous, intelligent, must-read romp from beginning to end. But be warned, this novel is definitely not for children.

**Rebecca Swift**

> ### Next?
>
> More Elaine Dundy? Try her autobiography, *Life Itself*.
>
> Or *Mariana* by Monica Dickens, about another girl encountering life and love.
>
> Another surprising and risqué modern classic is Hanif Kureishi's *The Buddha of Suburbia*. (UTBG 64)
>
> You might like Kathy Lette and Gabrielle Curley's account of growing up as surfer chicks in Australia, *Puberty Blues*.
>
> For more coming-of-age stories, read our feature on pp. 314–315.

# DUNE   Frank Herbert

> ### Next?
>
> Any of the **Dune** sequels – *Dune Messiah*, *Children of Dune*, *God Emperor of Dune*, *Heretics of Dune* and *Chapterhouse Dune*.
>
> Robert Heinlein's *Stranger in a Strange Land* is a classic science-fiction epic that calls into question both religious and political beliefs.
>
> Ursula Le Guin's *The Dispossessed* contrasts the stories of two planets, each with political and ecological problems to solve.

Dune is a desert planet inhabited by enormous sand-worms which produce a mind-altering substance called 'melange'. This and water are the most precious commodities. The story describes the battle for supremacy between the Atreides family and their enemies, most notably the fantastically spooky Bene Gesserit sisterhood, which is dedicated to harnessing the pure power of thought and so dispensing with science and technology. But it becomes clear that in the course of learning to control their environment and their own fateful vulnerability, the inhabitants cannot do without either technology or mysticism. If you love travelling in alien worlds, then this book is a must – a science-fiction epic of grandeur and complexity, realised in intricate detail.

**Livi Michael**

# DUSK  Susan Gates

Curtis is a lab assistant at a secret military research base. He feeds the overly aggressive rats, including the mutated General who is supposed to have human intelligence, although Curtis strongly doubts this. But there's one door he isn't allowed to enter. Behind this door is a creature who shrieks and cries, who eats microwave-defrosted mice and who can demand dinner in a little girl's voice. Behind this door is Dusk. Only once does Curtis dare to break the rules, but once is enough, because when the door is opened, things spiral beyond anyone's control. Dusk's terrifying existence is powerfully described as this fast-paced sci-fi novel explores the boundaries between human and animal and the ethics of genetic engineering.

**Noga Applebaum**

### Next?

*Eva* by Peter Dickinson also examines the relationship between humans and animals, through the eyes of a girl whose brain has been transplanted into a chimp's body.

*Bloodtide* is another novel looking at genetic hybrids, though it's much darker. (UTBG 49)

The ethics of cloning are explored in many books. Some suggestions to try are *House of the Scorpion* (UTBG 189), *Sharp North* (UTBG 358), *Unique* (UTBG 414) and Rune Michael's fast-paced *Genesis Alpha*.

# THE EAGLE OF THE NINTH  Rosemary Sutcliff

### Next?

More Rosemary Sutcliff? The other books in the **Roman** trilogy are *The Silver Branch* and *The Lantern Bearers*. She writes great tragic endings, too; try *The Mark of the Horse Lord* or the medieval-set *Knight's Fee*.

There are some great historical novels to devour: try *Ivanhoe* (UTBG 208) by Walter Scott or *The Flight of the Heron* by D.K Broster, set during the Jacobite uprising, or Simon Scarrow's **Roman Legion** series, starting with *Under the Eagle*.

This was one of my favourite books as I was growing up. Set in Britain during the last days of the Roman Empire, it's the story of a young Roman officer, Marcus, who sets out with his ex-gladiator slave, Esca, in search of his father's legion. Everyone knows the tale of the 'vanished' Ninth Legion, who marched into the mists one day and were never seen again. But the loss of their standard – the Eagle – means that the Ninth will always be cursed, and that the men who died to protect it – including Marcus's father – will never regain their honour. Posing as itinerant healers, Marcus and Esca travel north of Hadrian's Wall into unconquered, barbarian territory, to restore his father's reputation and to discover a dark and darkest secret...

**Joanne Harris**

# THE EARTH, MY BUTT AND OTHER BIG ROUND THINGS Carolyn Mackler

I confess: Carolyn Mackler is a close friend of mine. But our friendship does not preclude me from writing an unbiased rave of this book. You see, I wasn't her friend when I first read it. But after meeting heroine Virginia Shreves – follower of the Fat Girl Code of Conduct and self-proclaimed minus-three on the Popular to Dorky scale – I was determined to become friends with her creator. Anyone who writes an opening sentence like 'Froggy Welsh the Fourth is trying to get up my shirt' is a person I want to hang with.

But this novel isn't just for laughs. The best coming-of-age stories are both entertaining and true-to-life. Virginia copes with the insecurities and identity crises *all* teens suffer through – no matter where they fall on the Popular to Dorky scale. And when her family life gets messy in a very unexpected way, Virginia's resilience makes her a heroine worth looking up to. You may not be as lucky as I am to have befriended Carolyn, but getting to know Virginia Shreves is the next best thing.

**Megan McCafferty**

## SUPER-RICH & SUPER-BITCHY & SUPER-SEXY

**Gossip Girls series**
by Cecily Von Ziegesar

*Young, Loaded and Fabulous*
by Kate Kingsley

**The Clique** series by Lisi Harrison

**The Private** series by Kate Brian

**The Luxe** series by Anna Godberson

**Pretty Little Liars** series by Sara Shepard

**The A-List** series by Zoey Dean

*Prep* by Curtis Sittenfeld

### Next?

If you like Carolyn Mackler's writing, you shouldn't miss her other novels: try *Love and Other Four-Letter Words* and *Vegan Virgin Valentine* for starters.

Another book that explores an overweight narrator is Julia Bell's *Massive*, although it has a more serious tone. (UTBG 256)

*Keeping the Moon* by Sarah Dessen is another superbly drawn novel, with a protagonist who has shed her excess weight but not her negative self-image.

# THE ECLIPSE OF THE CENTURY
Jan Mark

**Next?**

Another Jan Mark? Try *Useful Idiots*, about a world where the seas have risen and what's left of civilisation is a dystopian nightmare. (UTBG 418)

Tim Lott's *Fearless* (UTBG 129) is set in a future world of extreme control. Or try *The Blue Hawk* by Peter Dickinson, about a world controlled by priests and a boy who commits sacrilege.

Keith's near-death experience brings him not to the gates of heaven but to Qantoum, a city in 'the armpit of Asia', which has been all but forgotten by the rest of the world. After his recovery, he makes his way there and finds himself taking part in an extraordinary drama that is destined to conclude 'beneath a black sun, at the end of a thousand years'.

A must-read for anyone of 14 and upwards who is interested in imaginative fiction. This book reaches parts of the mind that others don't.

Reading it is a bit like participating in a vivid dream and, as though the dream were your own, the characters and events will remain with you for a long, long time afterwards.

**Kate Thompson**

# The EDGE CHRONICLES
Paul Stewart and Chris Riddell

I found *Beyond the Deepwoods*, the first book of the **Edge Chronicles**, almost impossible to put down. It features a teenage boy named Twig. Twig is the son of a sky pirate – though he doesn't realise it. As a baby he was left on the outskirts of a woodtroll village, and is brought up by them. Being weak, he is bullied, and comes home with bumps and scars. Then, one day, his 'mother' finally tells him about his origins.

The book is about how Twig spends a year wandering the Deepwoods. Along the way he finds friendship, danger and fear. He also stumbles upon his father, Cloud Wolf, who then abandons him again and Twig finds the most feared creature in all the Deepwoods... I loved this intriguing and exciting book – and the detailed illustrations are amazing!

**Andrew Barakat, age 12**

**Next?**

This is the first of the **Edge Chronicles**, and you're in luck as there are ten books in all – read *Stormchaser* next, followed by *Midnight Over Sanctaphrax*.

Brian Jacques's **Redwall** series is just as fast and exciting. As is the **Warrior Cats** series by Erin Hunter.

Or try Bernard Cornwell's *Sharpe's Company* for adventuring in a real historical context. (UTBG 357)

# ELSEWHERE  Gabrielle Zevin

While crossing the road (and not looking both ways), Liz is hit by a car. She is now dead. *Elsewhere* is the story – in her words – of what happens next.

I can't count the number of stories I've read that have been narrated from beyond the grave. Dozens, probably. But this one is special. This is not like any book I've ever read. The world beyond death is so well imagined and so consistent it feels totally realistic – which is a strange thing to say about a book about the afterlife, I know... But that's how it is – the dream-like elements of the tale are blended with what feels like absolutely stone-cold reality and clarity; and throughout, Zevin's writing is impeccable.

*Elsewhere* is full of character and warmth; it's a book about death, but more than that it's about life. It's an uplifting story about how Liz lives hers, and about how to live yours, too.

**Daniel Hahn**

### Next?

Towards the end of *Elsewhere*, Owen reads to Liz from *Tuck Everlasting* by Natalie Babbitt, another beautiful tale of endless life.

A lyrical book about dying is *Before I Die* by Jenny Downham. (UTBG 37)

Or how about a series in which four dead teens try and solve their own murders? Look out for the **Beautiful Dead** series by Eden Maguire – *Jonas*, *Phoenix*, *Arizona* and *Summer*.

# EMPIRE OF THE SUN  J.G. Ballard

### Next?

Some of the most powerful books about war are memoirs such as Anne Frank's *The Diary of a Young Girl*. (UTBG 106)

For a fictional account of life under the Japanese occupation, read Martin Booth's *Music on the Bamboo Radio*.

*Mukiwa: A White Boy in Africa* by Peter Godwin is about growing up in Zimbabwe, then Rhodesia.

In 1942, at the age of 12, J.G. Ballard was interned in a Japanese prisoner-of-war camp in Shanghai. This powerful, moving novel is based on his own experiences, and gives us a real insight into the horrors of war. Jim, the 11-year-old narrator, is separated from his parents when the Japanese invade Shanghai, and spends weeks living alone until he is captured. Over the next four years, malnutrition, violence and death become everyday facts of life to Jim, whose survival instinct draws him into some sort of rapport with his Japanese guards whom, despite their cruelty, he admires for keeping the inmates secure from the chaos outside. Jim's incomprehension of war, plus his utter determination to survive and to be reunited with his parents, makes for an unforgettable piece of writing.

**Malachy Doyle**

# ENDER'S GAME  Orson Scott Card

Set in the medium-term future, a group of children and teenagers are being trained in Battle School to fight an extraterrestrial race of insect-like beings. Each child is specially chosen: they are the brightest in the world, and the most adaptable. Together, working in teams, the army commanders believe that they will come up with new ways of fighting that no adult could ever conceive. And they do. Or rather, Ender does. Ender Wiggin.

This is the story of his personal struggle, put under constant, relentless pressure, to become the next military commander. It is a brilliant book. Believable, full of thrilling battles, unusual aliens and well-crafted characters; but in the end what you remember is Ender. You'll grow to love Ender Wiggin.

**Cliff McNish**

**Next?**

You can go straight on to the sequels: *Speaker for the Dead*, *Xenocide*, *Children of the Mind*, *A War of Gifts* and *Ender in Exile*. **The Shadow Saga** tells the story from Ender's friend Bean's perspective. Start with *Ender's Shadow*.

For another great series about training to live and fight in space, try *Midshipman's Hope* by David Feintuch.

Or what about being a cadet on an airship? Try Kenneth Oppel's *Airborn*. (UTBG 13)

# ERAGON
## Christopher Paolini

**Next?**

If you enjoyed *Eragon*, the next books in the **Inheritance** cycle are *Eldest* and *Brisingr*, with a fourth to come.

For a marvellously realised world, and amazing battle scenes, read *The Cry of the Icemark* by Stuart Hill. (UTBG 90)

Another great series of dragon books (though very different) starts with Chris d'Lacey's *The Fire Within* and continues with *Icefire*, *Fire Star* and *The Fire Eternal*.

Or for more epic, oriental dragons, try Carole Wilkinson's magnificent *Dragonkeeper*.

*Eragon* is the first part of the **Inheritance Cycle**. It follows the tale of a boy, Eragon, who discovers a dragon's egg near his home. When strange figures come to look for the newly hatched dragon, his home is destroyed and he embarks on a quest to seek revenge and discover his heritage as a mythical dragonrider. Along the way he befriends Brom the storyteller, magical elves and the mysterious Murtagh.

*Eragon* is very fast-paced, without a single boring moment. It is well written, and emotions are wonderfully conveyed. Eragon's world of Alagaësia is so well described that it seems almost real.

**Eleanor Milnes-Smith, age 13**

# ESCAPE Kate Cann

### Next?

For more Kate Cann, this time about love, life and the paranormal, try *Leaving Poppy* (UTBG 234). Or maybe you want a sun-filled beach read? Try *Fiesta*, all about a holiday in Spain.

William Sutcliffe's *Are You Experienced?* is another story of travelling and sex. (UTBG 28)

Why not try a look at the way young sex and life decisions have been handled in the past? Look at *Georgy Girl* by Margaret Forster or *The L-Shaped Room* (UTBG 249) by Lynne Reid Banks.

Kate Cann writes about first love and early sexual relationships. Her great strength lies in handling all this without following the fashion of making it nasty or predatory. But she doesn't sanitise it, either, and you'll probably recognise the worries and preoccupations of her characters. This book follows a girl through her gap year – from the nightmare of nannying for a neurotic American mother, to the jealous torment of a romance on the road and at the beach. The main character, Rowan, finds her attitudes and plans reshaped by her experiences.

    *Escape* is packaged in quite a girly way, aimed by the publisher at the 'holiday reads' market, but it's way above the 'teen trash' level.

**Eleanor Updale**

# ETHAN FROME Edith Wharton

This little book is one of the saddest love stories you'll ever read. Ethan, a lonely farmer in 19th-century Massachusetts, has married his older cousin Zena for company. But she has quickly turned into a miserable, complaining hypochondriac.

    When a young woman, Mattie Silver, comes to live with them, Ethan finds himself fascinated by her energy and joyfulness. A kind, inarticulate man, he hardly admits to himself his real feelings for Mattie, as he walks her home from a dance through starlit snows. Chance allows them one night together in the isolated farmhouse.

    It's a passionate love story. We know from the outset it will end tragically, but the cruel twist will still take you by surprise.

**Jane Darcy**

### Next?

Read Wharton's *Summer* – she nicknamed it 'Hot Ethan'. Or her very different, but equally powerful, novel of repressed sexuality, *The Age of Innocence*.

Another excellent short novel set in 19th-century America is Henry James's *Washington Square*.

There are many wonderful, tragic love stories out there; try *Love Story* by Erich Segal, or Margaret Mitchell's *Gone with the Wind* (UTBG 161) (though you'll have to decide whether you think the end is tragic or not!).

# ETHEL AND ERNEST  Raymond Briggs

This is Raymond Briggs's beautiful, candid and moving illustrated account of his parents' married life. Ernest, a milkman, cheekily courts Ethel, a lady's maid. They marry in 1930, and stay together in the same house until they die within months of each other in 1971.

As well as a loving biography, the book is an illustrated social history of what used to be called The Respectable Working Class. During this middle span of the 20th century, the mangle in the back yard gives way to the laundrette, the bike gives way to the car, Hitler and Stalin come and go, ordinary people acquire telephones and television, the Welfare State is born. And so (with difficulty) is Raymond, who later horrifies his parents by going off to art school. ('That lot's all long hair, drink and nude women,' Ernest tells Ethel, wistfully.) There's nothing rose-tinted here. Briggs doesn't flinch from relating and drawing his parents' deaths, either, and it makes you gasp.

**Mal Peet**

### Next?

Search out all of Raymond Briggs's books, from the upsetting *When the Wind Blows* (UTBG 434) and the altogether gross *Fungus the Bogeyman*, to the pathos of *The Snowman*.

Berlie Doherty's *Granny Was a Buffer Girl* has more 'ordinary' family memories.

Another book that uses pictures to devastating effect is Keiji Nakazawa's *Barefoot Gen*, about the bombing of Hiroshima.

# AN EVIL CRADLING  Brian Keenan

### Next?

John McCarthy's *Some Other Rainbow* is an account of the same awful years.

Or try Brian Keenan's look at his own childhood, growing up in Belfast in *I'll Tell Me Ma*.

Another man who endured terrible times is Nelson Mandela. Read his story in *A Long Walk to Freedom*.

For a tale of lost youth, read Sebastian Faulks's *The Fatal Englishman*.

What do you do if it's 1985, you're a teacher from Belfast, and you want a change of scene? You probably don't move to Beirut, where the Lebanese civil war is raging.

Well, Brian Keenan did just that. And guess what happened? He got kidnapped. He spent the next four years as a hostage, kept in blindfold and chains, with no contact with the outside world.

*An Evil Cradling* is Keenan's story. It's about pain, fear and madness. But it's also about the friendship he makes with his fellow hostage, John McCarthy.

Keenan is an astounding, exhilarating writer. If you're ever going to be marooned on a desert island – take this book. It'll show you how to cope.

**James Reynolds**

# EXCHANGE Paul Magrs

**Next?**

For another Paul Magrs, read *Strange Boy* next. (UTBG 380)

Penelope Fitzgerald has written a short and beautiful – and sad! – story about a bookshop, called *The Bookshop*.

One of my favourite things about this book is the finely drawn relationship between grandson and grandparents; read about Daniel and his adopted 'grandmother' Laura, in *Lost and Found* (UTBG 243) or Kit and his grandfather in *Kit's Wilderness* (UTBG 228).

The Great Big Book Exchange is a wonderful place for a book lover like Simon. But the Great Big Book Exchange isn't like any normal bookshop. Simon knows this the moment he and his grandmother walk in it for the first time. What he doesn't know is that this place, and the people he meets here, will change his life. His grandmother will be reunited with an important someone from her distant childhood, and Simon himself will meet an extraordinary, bold, plain-speaking Goth girl called Kelly…

A story about keeping secrets, about the past and present, and about friendship and family, this is my favourite Paul Magrs book. Full of warmly drawn characters and with a gripping plot, it's beautifully done.

**Daniel Hahn**

# EXODUS Julie Bertagna

2099 – the ice caps have melted due to environmental damage and Britain is covered in water. Mara watches as the waters slowly rise around Wing, her island home, threatening to swallow everything she has ever known. Cooped up due to violent storms, Mara escapes into the Weave, a virtual-reality cyberspace now in ruins, as civilisation has disintegrated and communities have lost touch. A chance virtual encounter sends Mara's community on a treacherous journey to find shelter in New Mungo, a sky-city erected on the site of today's Glasgow. They are unaware of the cruel fate that awaits them there…

This fascinating, futuristic, sci-fi quest-adventure, inspired by the Glaswegian coat of arms, raises crucial questions about the consequences of the way we live our lives today.

**Noga Applebaum**

**Next?**

Read the stunning sequel, *Zenith*, or other Julie Bertagna; *The Opposite of Chocolate* is the story of a pregnant girl, a strange boy and one summer of life-changing decisions.

There's more environmental issues in Tim Winton's *Blueback: A Fable for All Ages*, about a boy and his mother's love for the sea.

*Bloodtide* is another great sci-fi novel inspired by a myth. (UTBG 49)

# EXPOSURE  Mal Peet

Mal Peet's *Exposure* is a meaty and enthralling resetting of the Othello story in the world of football, but Peet's far too good a storyteller for it to be merely that. South American footballer Otello has just signed a multi-million dollar transfer to change clubs, becoming the team's first prominent black player. He falls immediately in love with the white owner's daughter, Desmerelda, and they marry, instantly becoming a hot celebrity couple. But Otello's agent, Diego, isn't the friend he seems to be and tragedy is just around the corner.

Peet makes very few concessions to the young-adult genre, expecting – rightly – that his readers want a thumping good story first and foremost. A cracking read for adults and teens.

**Patrick Ness**

> **Next?**
>
> For more books featuring Paul Faustino, read *Keeper* (UTBG 222) and *The Penalty* (UTBG 309). For a different Mal Peet, read *Tamar* (UTBG 388).
>
> *Exposure* has many threads. For more about children living on the streets, try Elizabeth Laird's *The Garbage King* (UTBG 150); for another story that features football, try Neil Arksey's *Playing on the Edge*; and for another story that spins itself from something by Shakespeare, try Mirjam Pressler's *Shylock's Daughter*.

# THE EYRE AFFAIR  Jasper Fforde

When the publishers came to publicising this, Jasper Fforde's first book, they didn't spend their money on advertising. They just sent out free copies saying 'READ IT'. So how can I hope to describe it if they couldn't?

Well, if you're into literature, you'll get the joke. Picture 'grammarcites' that eat the punctuation out of sentences. Picture Heathcliff from *Wuthering Heights* meeting Miss Havisham from *Great Expectations* at an anger-management session. Picture Jane Eyre kidnapped out of *Jane Eyre*. Picture darning narrative loopholes. Picture critical analysis of *The Flopsy Bunnies*, quotes from nonexistent books, or Prose Portals that let fugitives hide out inside *Hamlet*. It's Douglas-Adams-meets-Pagemaster. It defies the laws of time, place, probability, boredom and sanity... Beyond all that, all I can say is: 'READ IT'.

**Geraldine McCaughrean**

> **Next?**
>
> How about a hard-boiled whodunnit set in the world of Nursery Rhymes? Sounds daft? Well, yes, but Jasper Fforde pulls it off brilliantly in his **Nursery Crime Adventures**.
>
> Look out for Neil Gaiman's short story collection *M Is for Magic*, for another take on fairy tales. (UTBG 266)
>
> Or try Douglas Adams – *The Hitchhiker's Guide to the Galaxy* is a great place to start. (UTBG 182)

# FAHRENHEIT 451 Ray Bradbury

This is the story of a world where books are forbidden, a world where free thought is firmly discouraged, where people feel closer to television characters than to their spouses or children or friends. It's a world where firemen like Guy Montag aren't employed to put out fires but to start them – to track down people who have secretly been hoarding books, and burn their houses down. All for the public good, of course.

This is no fantasy world, though, but our own, some years in the future. *Fahrenheit 451* takes a chilling look at where we might be going, and does so with imagination and momentum and often-brilliant writing. Bradbury has said that he always wrote 'at the top of my lungs' – and in this book you can't help but listen to his warning.

**Daniel Hahn**

> ### Next?
>
> Classic dystopian novels include *Brave New World* (UTBG 58) and *Nineteen Eighty-Four* (UTBG 284).
>
> Or try more recent takes on the same subject such as Scott Westerfeld's *Uglies* (UTBG 412) or the harrowing *The Road* by Cormac McCarthy.
>
> More Bradbury? Try his magical *Dandelion Wine*. (UTBG 94)
>
> Or read about the formative years of a real revolutionary hero: Che Guevara's *The Motorcycle Diaries*. (UTBG 271)

# FAKING IT Pete Johnson

Fifteen-year-old Will has plenty of friends who are girls, but no 'girlfriend', so in a desperate bid to improve his street cred he makes one up, with the help of his best friend, Barney. Basing his dream girl on his stepmum's drop-dead-gorgeous, aspiring-actress niece ensures his popularity explodes – but sooner or later she's going to have to put in an appearance or his cover will be blown.

The story's diary form makes Will seem like one of your friends and draws you in. Well-meaning, witty and woefully disaster prone, he's one of the best teenagers ever brought to life in a novel, by an author whose understanding of what makes teenagers tick is second to none. Just the book for when you need cheering up or to make you feel you're not alone!

**Eileen Armstrong**

> ### Next?
>
> More by Pete Johnson? Try *The Protectors* and *Avenger*, or the very funny *Cool Boffin*.
>
> Some other books which show boys'-eye views are *(Un)arranged Marriage* (UTBG 413) by Bali Rai, *Tangerine* by Edward Bloor and *Peeps* by Scott Westerfield.
>
> *The Edge* and *The Lost Boys' Appreciation Society* by Alan Gibbons show that boys can have feelings, too.
>
> Or try *How to Snog an Alien* by Graham Joyce.

# THE FALCONER'S KNOT   Mary Hoffman

### Next?

Mary Hoffman's **Stravaganza** series has power, intrigue and flying horses; start with *City of Masks*. (UTBG 381)

Medieval Ethiopia is the setting for Elizabeth E. Wein's *The Sunbird*, whose teenage hero spies for his emperor and pays a high price.

*The Medici Curse* by Matt Chamings takes up the theme of Renaissance painting, combining contemporary action with a story set in the Medici's Florence.

Silvano and Chiara are reluctant residents at a convent and friary who get caught up in a murder mystery. Silvano is suspected of at least one killing and must clear his name. Chiara is a feisty heroine forced to live amongst nuns because her brother cannot afford to keep her at home. The teenagers band together to try and find out who is behind the grisly deaths of the friars. Medieval Italy makes for an exotic backdrop, and there is a colourful cast of strong women and devious men. A lot of the plot centres around the methods used to mix the amazing colours found in medieval paintings, from gold to the rare and brilliant blue known as ultramarine. But there is more to the art of making pretty pictures than meets the eye, as Silvano and Chiara find out.

**Sarah Hilary**

# The FARSEER trilogy   Robin Hobb

Do you want books you can immerse yourself in? Where the created world is so perfect, so real, that you feel you are there, breathing the strange scents, walking in distant alleyways? Then look no further than these amazing books. Fitz is the bastard son of a prince. He grows up with nothing. Apprenticed to the king's master spy and assassin, Fitz can kill in hundreds of ways and is an adept spy. He also learns (sometimes painfully) about his own magics, the Skill that comes from his father, and the Wit, a forbidden and reviled beast-magic. With only two friends, a Wolf, Night-eyes, who he is Wit-bonded to, and the strange boy who is the king's fool, Fitz has to survive. He has to – for fate has plans for him. Plans that will lead him into desperate danger.

### Next?

This trilogy consists of: *Assassin's Apprentice*, *Royal Assassin* and *Assassin's Quest*. There are two more sequences, the **Tawny Man** trilogy, and the **Liveship Traders** trilogy, about the same characters.

Another epic that feels real is Frank Herbert's *Dune* and its sequels. (UTBG 116)

You only have to wander into a bookshop to find endless fat fantasy sagas; good authors to look for are David Gemmell, David Eddings, Raymond E. Feist, George R.R. Martin and J.V. Jones.

**Leonie Flynn**

# FAT BOY SWIM  Catherine Forde

A brilliant, gripping book about 'fatso' Jimmy Kelly. He's endlessly tormented and bullied because of his size, he's useless at PE, and school in general is a nightmare. But at home, in the kitchen, he can really shine and be himself, with his enviable talent for creating truly fantastic food.

Over the summer, however, things change for Jimmy in all sorts of ways. Being forced into serious swimming leads to self-discovery plus the unearthing of family secrets. There's the challenge of the Swimathon. And he gets together with Ellie. It's an absorbing tale with totally believable characters, and the turmoil of Jimmy's life is beautifully depicted. For anyone whose heart sinks at the thought of games lessons, the first chapter captures to perfection the horror of school football, while the descriptions of Jimmy's cooking will have you drooling and desperate to try some tablet, the Scottish version of fudge.

**Nick Sharratt**

### Next?

Another Forde? Look out for the thriller *Sugarcoated*, about a less-than-thin girl who witnesses an appalling beating and how her life changes afterwards.

*Dark Waters* by Catherine MacPhail is another gritty thriller set in Scotland.

*Girls Under Pressure* by Jacqueline Wilson tackles weight issues seen from a female perspective, as does *Massive* (UTBG 256).

The hero of *Kissing the Rain* is another boy bullied for being fat. (UTBG 226)

# FATHERLAND  Robert Harris

### Next?

Robert Harris has a talent for taking the past and making it real. Try *Pompeii* about the eruption of Vesuvius; or *Enigma*, about the code-breakers of Bletchley Park.

Someone else who writes terrific thrillers is Dan Brown; try *The Da Vinci Code*. (UTBG 97)

Or try a thriller set in 1930s Berlin: Philip Kerr's *Berlin Noir* is bleak, dark, violent and very exciting.

This is a rare thing; a thriller that makes you think. Set in 1964, in a world in which Germany won World War II and Hitler is still alive and celebrating his 75th birthday, it concerns Xavier March, a Berlin policeman who starts off investigating a murder and ends up uncovering a deep, dark secret that puts his life at risk.

Aside from the great plot, there's also all the detail of how life would be different: like if Edward and Mrs Simpson had become King and Queen of England. Written in a taut, spare style, this is a true thriller. You have to keep reading to find out what's going to happen – and if March will survive.

**Leonie Flynn**

# FAT KID RULES THE WORLD   K.L. Going

Sure, K.L. Going's first novel features one of the darkest and funniest narrators in contemporary young-adult fiction – the extravagantly fat, copiously perspiring 16-year-old Troy Billings. But it is his friendship with gutter punk Curt that makes this novel one of my all-time favourites. Troy is a marine's son; Curt seemingly no one's son. Troy is hugely fat; Curt 'looks like a blond ferret'. But really they're perfect for each other: Curt needs a drummer, and Troy needs something to hit.

Going writes about troubled guys in a way that isn't boring or didactic or false – and, in the end, *Fat Kid...* evokes the power of friendship and punk rock music brilliantly.

**John Green**

**Next?**

For more by K.L. Going, try *Saint Iggy* or *The Liberation of Gabriel King*.

*Freak the Mighty* (UTBG 147) by Rodman Philbrick and *When Zachary Beaver Came to Town* by Kimberly Willis Holt also look at unlikely friendships between very different teens.

There's more music in Drew Gummerson's hilarious, rude and fast-paced *Me and Mickie James*. (UTBG 259)

# FEARLESS   Tim Lott

**Next?**

More Tim Lott? Try his wonderful book about growing up, love, loss and depression: *The Scent of Dried Roses*.

For other well-imagined future prison worlds, try Catherine Fisher's *Incarceron* or Alexander Gordon Smith's *Furnace: Lockdown*.

Gemma Malley's *The Declaration* is set in a world where to have a child is a crime, and those who are born are Surplus – fated to a second-class existence.

My favourite books are ones that manage the nearly impossible trick of being willing to tell the complete truth about the world around me, while also taking me to far-off lands that aren't anything like my world at all. Tim Lott's excellent and tough *Fearless* takes you to a possible future, where freedom is extremely limited and you can end up in a prison-like 'school' just for being an orphan. The girls at the City Community Faith School don't even get their own names; they're stuck with numbers and letters and only the nicknames they give each other. But Little Fearless isn't like the other girls. She's brave and daring and knows that if only the world outside could see what the school was really like, then they'd tear down its walls... Wouldn't they?

Lott doesn't give any false hope in his story, but all that means is that the real hope, when it comes, is all the more precious. A tough little fable, this book, creating a world all of its own.

**Patrick Ness**

# FEATHER BOY   Nicky Singer

Robert Noble has a hard time at school; nicknamed Norbert Nobottle by his classmates, his chief tormentor is a boy called Niker, who is full of the casual self-confidence that Robert lacks.

But then Robert's life changes when he meets an old lady with a tragic past. She lost her son years back, when he fell out of the window of their flat. The old lady is dying, and at her request, Robert finds himself going back to the abandoned building where the disaster took place. This is the beginning of a journey that gives him a whole new sense of purpose – although ultimately he discovers that life does not always have simple answers.

**Susan Reuben**

## BEING DIFFERENT

*Midget* by Tim Bowler

*Face* by Benjamin Zephaniah

*Mondays Are Red* by Nicola Morgan

*The Curious Incident of the Dog in the Night-Time* by Mark Haddon

*Wheels* by Catherine MacPhail

*The Boy in the Dress* by David Walliams

*Paralysed* by Sherry Ashworth

*Freak the Mighty* by Rodman Philbrick

**Next?**

Another Nicky Singer? Try *Doll*, *The Innocent's Story* or *Knight Crew* (UTBG 230).

Other books about a journey of self-discovery are *The Shell House* (UTBG 358) and *Postcards from No Man's Land* (UTBG 318).

For other stories about bullying, try *Kissing the Rain* (UTBG 226) by Kevin Brooks, *Fat Boy Swim* (UTBG 128) by Catherine Forde or *Drowning Anna* by Sue Mayfield.

# FEED M.T. Anderson

**Next?**

Another M.T. Anderson? Try *Thirsty*, about a boy who gets very thirsty – for blood.

Or try Patrick Ness's stunning *The Knife of Never Letting Go*, about a world in which you can hear everyone's thoughts, and everyone can hear what you are thinking... (UTBG 229)

*Sleepwalking* by Nicola Morgan is about waking up to the reality of a controlled life.

Or what happens when your genetically modified perfect life starts to crumble? Try Nicky Singer's *GemX* and see.

Imagine a world in which everyone has a live internet feed hard-wired into their brains, and is online all the time. The teenage hero of *Feed*, Titus, has grown up barraged with advertising, information and email chat that all come into his head with the speed of mental telepathy. He's completely content until the day he meets Violet, an eccentric girl who wonders what it might be like to live without the Feed. Her questions awaken in Titus a curiosity and intellect he never knew he had. But they both discover, with tragic consequences, that it's not so easy to free themselves. The novel is both science fiction and contemporary satire; it's a technological and environmental cautionary tale; it's a moving love story. It's told with astonishing energy and inventiveness and is nothing short of a masterpiece.

**Kenneth Oppel**

# FEVER PITCH Nick Hornby

When this book came out, I thought it had been specifically written for me! It tracks one man's life as seen through the prism of Arsenal football club. Everything in his world is inexorably linked with the fortunes of his favourite team. For the football fan, it strikes a tremendously deep chord. For the non-football fan, it is a brilliant invitation inside the mind of an obsessive fan's allegiance to his club. It's funny, clever, thoughtful and fresh.

*Fever Pitch* started a stampede of books that plot people's lives in parallel with their most cherished cultural icons, be they sport, music, art, etc. But in my view it remains the original and best.

**Jonny Zucker**

**Next?**

More Nick Hornby? Try *A Long Way Down*, about suicide, or *High Fidelity* (UTBG 180).

For great football novels, try the superbly atmospheric, rainforest-based *Keeper* by Mal Peet. (UTBG 222)

Football players' memoirs include *David Beckham: My Side*, and *Off the Record* by Michael Owen. Both are very reader-friendly and each offers a fascinating look behind the scenes of today's world of football megastars.

# FINDING VIOLET PARK Jenny Valentine

### Next?

Jenny Valentine's **Broken Soup** is a second novel that, for once, meets all expectations, and exceeds them. (UTBG 63)

Or try something by Joanna Nadin. **Wonderland** is about a small-town girl with big dreams for a career in acting and one obsessive friend.

**Looking for Alaska** by John Green is another compelling coming-of-age story with an unlikely hero. Green's book is a tale of first love, and death, at an American boarding school.

Winner of the Guardian Children's Fiction Prize, and shortlisted for both the Carnegie Medal and Branford Boase Award, Valentine's debut is deserving of every shred of praise heaped upon it.

Tired and stoned, 15-year-old Lucas Swain stumbles upon the ashes of Violet Park in a mini-cab office in North London, and sets out to find out who abandoned her, and why. But was his discovery really a coincidence? As Lucas searches for Violet, he comes closer than ever to finding his own father.

Valentine has not only rendered a true portrait of North London; in Lucas she has created a hero who is both strange and recognisable.

As original and funny as Mark Haddon, with the bleak beauty of Kevin Brooks.

**Joanna Nadin**

# FIRE AND HEMLOCK
## Diana Wynne Jones

A photograph that 19-year-old student Polly has had since childhood now looks different from how she remembered: where are the horse and the figures that once ran among the burning cornfields? Fragments of long-suppressed memories begin to force themselves into Polly's consciousness and she realises that her recollection of the events of the past five years is false. The truth has something to do with an evil, ageless woman and a gifted musician, Tom Lynn, who was once the most important person in her life. How – and why – has she forgotten him? Polly searches for the truth in one of Diana Wynne Jones's most fiendishly complex plots.

### Next?

Another of Diana Wynne Jones's wonderful novels, where memory plays tricks and time is turned upside down, is **Hexwood**.

If you like books based on myths and legends, try Catherine Fisher's novels: **The Lammas Field**, based on the ballad of 'Thomas the Rhymer', or **Corbenic** (UTBG 87), based on the legend of the Holy Grail.

Sarah Singleton's **Century** is about two sisters who one day realise they have no recollection of their mother, or her death. (UTBG 72)

**Gill Vickery**

# THE FIRE-EATERS  David Almond

**Next?**

Try David Almond's *Clay*, about belief, friendship and evil. (UTBG 81)

You might also like *Thursday's Child* by Sonya Hartnett, another extraordinary and original writer. (UTBG 396)

Or what about another book that shows how hope can triumph over the darkest of circumstances? Try Elizabeth Laird's *Jake's Tower*. (UTBG 210)

This memorable story starts with Bobby's first encounter with the fire-eater, McNulty, on a particular Sunday in late summer 1962: 'It was like my heart stopped beating and the world stopped turning'. Bobby and his friends Ailsa (from a sea-coaling family), Daniel (newly moved to the area) and Joseph are living under the shadow of the Cuban missile crisis: World War III might start at any moment. The world is at the edge of the abyss. There are other scary things happening, too: Bobby's dad, a shipyard worker, is sick, and Bobby is starting secondary school.

Darkness, inhumanity and war threaten life, love and family throughout the story, and for me make this book seem particularly relevant now. As with Almond's other novels, the writing is beautifully honed and polished, and at the novel's heart, holding back the darkness, are strong, tender friendships and family bonds, and a sense that the world is truly an amazing place. Wonderful.

# FIRE FROM HEAVEN  Mary Renault

You think you have a dysfunctional family? Try Alexander's... His mum hates his dad (but is kind of kinky for snakes), his dad hates his mum and has loads of girlfriends (no, Mum does not approve). Oh, and Alexander? He has ambitions. BIG ambitions (they didn't call him The Great for nothing...).

This is a true story. It tells of Alexander in all his god-like, insane glory, and of his lovers – both male and female. If you've ever thought history boring, read this. For here a legend steps off the page and becomes human: flawed, imperfect, yet utterly wonderful. In fact, be careful, for you might fall in love. I did.

**Leonie Flynn**

**Next?**

There are two sequels; next is *The Persian Boy*, Alexander's story told by Bagoas, a Persian eunuch who becomes his lover. *Funeral Games* is the final part of the trilogy.

If you want to read a non-fiction account of Alexander the Great, try Robin Lane Fox's biography. Or Mary Renault's own book about him, *The Nature of Alexander*.

Or how about another great portrayal of history that makes it real? Try Steven Pressfield's *Gates of Fire*, about the Battle of Thermopylae.

# FIREWEED   Jill Paton Walsh

*Fireweed* was first published in 1969. Many Blitz novels have been published since, but this, losing none of its potency, is among the strongest. Fifteen-year-old Bill, on the run from evacuation in Wales, returns to London where he meets another refugee – Julie, whose parents suppose her to have sailed for Canada on the doomed ship *City of Benares*. Teaming up, the two eke out an existence on the streets of London, establishing a domesticity beyond their years when they settle in a cook's basement together with an abandoned child, Dickie. Disillusionment for Bill when he feels betrayed by Julie can't diminish, in hindsight, the intensity of their time together. Wonderful writing brings the dangers and uncertainties of the Blitz vividly to life.

**Linda Newbery**

### Next?

Another Jill Paton Walsh worth seeking out is *The Dolphin Crossing*, about the retreat from Dunkirk. Neither of these titles is easily found, but both books are well worth hunting down in libraries or second-hand shops.

Try the series by Judith Kerr that begins with *When Hitler Stole Pink Rabbit* and follows the story of Anna and her German family.

Or for another book about a wartime runaway, read Robert Westall's *The Kingdom by the Sea*. (UTBG 225)

# FLESHMARKET   Nicola Morgan

This novel transports you immediately – and shockingly – to the raw, rough Edinburgh of the 19th century, where the teenage protagonist (Robbie) is determined on a seemingly futile mission of revenge. As a small boy, he witnessed a brutal operation on his mother at the hands of a renowned surgeon, Dr Knox. Days afterwards, she died. Now Dr Knox has come into Robbie's life once more, and Robbie has to face some hard choices.

Dr Knox is a real historical character, as are the corpse-stealers Burke and Hare, with whose murderous work Robbie becomes involved. The writing is so vivid you can almost taste the reeking fog rising between the tenement buildings of the old city, while you suffer with Robbie and his younger sister in their struggle to survive deprivation and danger.

**Patricia Elliott**

### Next?

All of Nicola's books are great: try *The Highwayman's Footsteps* next. (UTBG 180)

Also set in Edinburgh, Robert Louis Stevenson's *Dr Jekyll and Mr Hyde* is a more difficult read. (UTBG 115)

Try, too, Julie Hearn's *Follow Me Down*, an extraordinary time-slip novel set in London. (UTBG 137)

More Edinburgh and murder? Alison Prince's *Oranges and Murder* or any of the **Rebus** books (UTBG 328).

# FLOODLAND  Marcus Sedgwick

**Next?**

More Marcus Sedgwick. Maybe *The Book of Dead Days* next, or the stunning *My Swordhand Is Singing* (UTBG 275).

Two other fascinating looks at the possible effects of global warming are Julie Bertagna's *Exodus* (UTBG 124) and Susan Gates's *Beyond the Billboard*.

Or try Garth Nix's *Shade's Children*, about a world run by despotic Overlords.

'Zoe ran. Harder than she had ever run in her life...'

For such a slim book, *Floodland* packs quite a punch. It's a story set in the not-too-distant future, when global warming has caused the waters to rise and cover large parts of England. Zoe has been stranded on Norwich – now an island, unhappy and inhospitable; her attempts to get away and find her parents land her on Eels Island, which is even worse – inhabited by wild children, all under the leadership of the sinister and violent Dooby, whom Zoe finds very frightening indeed. Her only friend on Eels Island is old William, and he's mad. Isn't he?

This is a story of bravery and resilience, a story about unusual friendships; it's sometimes very dark, but always beautiful, and it grips from the first line.

**Daniel Hahn**

# FLORA SEGUNDA OF CRACKPOT HALL
## Ysabeau Wilce

Flora Segunda is the youngest of the noble Fyrdraaca family, and the most miserable one by far. Ever since her mother banished their magickal butler Valefor, Flora has been burdened with responsibilities. She has to take care of a lively gang of dogs and her drunken father, and the mess they leave everywhere. It doesn't help that all 11,000 rooms of Crackpot Hall, once a grand mansion, are now constantly changing and shifting so that getting lost is easy. As her Catorcena ceremony approaches, Flora knows she must decide whether to follow her family's tradition and join the army, or attempt to fulfil her own ambition to become a ranger – a magickal spy. As she tries to restore her home to its former glory, Flora is caught in a series of adventures that involve traitorous butlers, dangerous magick, pirates, and one boy obsessed with hats.

**Next?**

More Flora? Try *Flora's Dare* next.

*Howl's Moving Castle* is another imaginative story, about a wizard, an old lady and a castle – none of which are what they seem. (UTBG 191)

Or try the hilarious, whimsical *The Name of This Book Is Secret* (UTBG 276) and its sequel, *If You're Reading This, It's Too Late*, by Pseudonymous Bosch.

**Noga Applebaum**

# FLOWERS FOR ALGERNON   Daniel Keyes

**Next?**

For another pitiful tale full of doctors and loners, try Ken Kesey's *One Flew Over the Cuckoo's Nest*. (UTBG 294)

Two more classics that showcase characters that are not quite the same as other people are Steinbeck's *Of Mice and Men* (UTBG 291) and Faulkner's *The Sound and the Fury*.

A less heartbreaking look at being different is Nigel Richardson's *The Wrong Hands*. (UTBG 447)

Charlie Gordon, a 37-year-old man, is mentally retarded. Charlie gets selected to participate in a scientific experiment that will attempt to enhance his intelligence. The novel, which is told in the form of Charlie's journal entries, tracks his progression from sub-human to super-human intelligence. His early, pre-experiment entries are riddled with bad grammar and are primitive in style. But as the experiment continues and Charlie gets smarter and smarter, his writing drastically improves. Eventually, Charlie's intelligence progresses to extraordinary levels. He can now speak 20 languages, whereas before the experiment he couldn't even master one. Things start to go downhill, however, when Algernon, a mouse who has undergone the same experiment as Charlie, begins to rapidly lose his enhanced intelligence. And then Algernon dies. Will Charlie suffer the same horrible fate? The only way to find out is to read this powerful page-turner.

**Jeremy Tramer, age 17**

# THE FLOWING QUEEN   Kai Meyer

Everyone says that Venice is a magical place, but in Kai Meyer's *The Flowing Queen* this is literally true. To read this book is to enter an alternative universe where the Egyptian Empire is intent on world domination. Only Venice, protected by the mysterious *Flowing Queen*, can stand against the Pharaoh and his armies. But now Venice is under attack – from enemies within.

This book has everything: orphans and pickpockets; mermaids and talking stone lions; evil councillors and ambassadors from Hell, all of it woven together in an intricate narrative that sweeps you away.

This is hardcore fantasy, and for those of you that enjoy this book, the great news is that there are more to follow.

**Laura Hutchings**

**Next?**

The sequels: *The Stone Light* and *The Glass World*. Or try Kai Meyer's **Waverunners** trilogy, which combines pirates, ghosts and a whole world under the waves.

If you enjoyed the Venetian setting, try *The Thief Lord*. (UTBG 393)

Or for an alternative world just as imaginative, try Debi Gliori's *Pure Dead Magic* and its sequels.

# FLY BY NIGHT  Frances Hardinge

This book is luminescent with words: it spins them, plays with them, laughs at – and with – them, juggles their meaning and has metaphors and similes to make you gasp (and groan). But around the fascination with words is a real, old-fashioned tale that starts with a young girl (Mosca Mye, named after a fly), and throws her immediately into cahoots with the charismatic yet dubious adventurer, Eponymous Clent. Mosca loves words, but her world is one where girls (especially poor ones) don't read, and where reading the 'wrong' books can bring imprisonment or even death. For their country is divided, both politically and religiously – and books are a tool used by both sides. There's byplay and banter, thrills, spills, escapes, drama, and a goose of immense moral fibre. OK … so the goose is a homicidal maniac, but don't let that put you off him – or the book!

**Leonie Flynn**

### Next?

Frances Hardinge's other books are just as good; try **Verdigris Deep** or **Gullstruck Island**, another historical-esque rip-roaring adventure with great heroines!

Another strong-willed heroine is Dido Twite; read about her in Joan Aiken's **Black Hearts in Battersea**.

Or try Leander Deeny's delightfully macabre and deliciously exciting **Hazel's Phantasmagoria**.

# FOLLOW ME DOWN  Julie Hearn

### Next?

For more graverobbers, try Nicola Morgan's **Fleshmarket** (UTBG 134) or Ann Rinaldi's fast-paced and dramatic **An Aquaintance with Darkness**.

Another sideways look at London happens in Charlie Fletcher's thrilling **Stone Heart**. (UTBG 377)

Or if you liked the way Julie Hearn writes, read her **The Merrybegot**, about witches and witch finders. (UTBG 261)

Or **I, Coriander** by Sally Gardner, about a girl straying from our world into that of the fairies. (UTBG 196)

It sounds like a classic story: Tom and his mum visit his gran in London and adventures happen. But … Tom's recently divorced mother has cancer, his gran is vicious-tongued and rarely seen without a drink in her hand, and neither woman really likes the other. To add to the miseries of Tom's life, he starts hearing voices. Voices that lead him down into the cellar … and back in time to a London where freaks are sold by the hour to the curious, and where he meets Astra, the mysterious Changeling Child.

In a story that weaves the past into the present, and blurs the real into the unreal, this stunning work is both horror and history, and makes you think about who exactly the real freaks are.

**Leonie Flynn**

# FORBIDDEN
Judy Waite

**Next?**

If you like this, you might also like other stories set in a cult: **Blinded by the Light** by Sherry Ashworth or **Leaving Fishers** by Margaret Peterson Haddix.

Judy Waite pulls no punches; try her **Game Girls**, about three girls who think prostitution might be an easy way to make money, or **Shopaholic**, about consumerism and theft.

Read a love story between two 'outsiders' in **Naked without a Hat**. (UTBG 275)

Elinor has grown up with The Chosen, following the True Cause. She is especially privileged, as she is destined to be the 'bride' of the cult leader when she reaches her 16th birthday. Elinor is happy to be a part of all that – until she happens to meet an 'outsider' boy. She begins to question what the cult is all about and what she really wants to do with her life. But when she thinks about making a break, Elinor discovers how little freedom she truly has. Can she, will she, break free? This tense and gripping story takes the reader through many a twist and turn to find out.

**Yvonne Coppard**

# FOR ESMÉ – WITH LOVE AND SQUALOR
J.D. Salinger

J.D. Salinger is best known for his classic (and only) novel *The Catcher in the Rye*, but he also wrote some other lesser-known stories which are just as good, if not better. *For Esmé – with Love and Squalor* is a collection of nine short stories, many of which deal with the relationships between children and adults, a theme that Salinger approaches like no other writer – he not only sees things from the children's point of view, but he takes us into their minds and their hearts and shows us the world through their eyes.

These are weirdly wonderful stories – 'A Perfect Day for Bananafish', 'Uncle Wiggily in Connecticut', 'Just Before the War with the Eskimos'. They're funny, sad, tragic, mad ... and every one is a perfect gem.

**Kevin Brooks**

**Next?**

*Raise High the Roof Beam, Carpenters and Seymour: an Introduction* and *Franny and Zooey* (UTBG 146), also by J.D. Salinger, are worth seeking out, as is, of course, the classic **The Catcher in the Rye** (UTBG 69) if you haven't read it yet.

*The Best Short Stories of Ring Lardner*. If you like short stories, particularly by American writers, this is a brilliant collection.

O. Henry writes very American, very wonderful, short stories; look out for his **Selected Stories**.

# FOREVER  Judy Blume

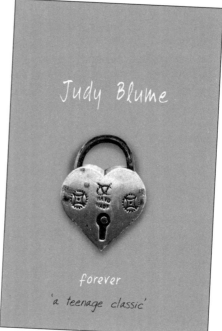

*Forever* follows the developing relationships of teenage couples and their interaction with the adult world. How do liberal parents deal with the reality of their teenage daughter's long-term and developing sexual relationship?

Until I read this book I thought nothing could shock me. First published in the 1970s, *Forever* talks more graphically about teenage sex than anything I've read that has been written since. Of course being shocked is not necessarily a bad thing. The book gives a very realistic insight into the workings of teenage relationships and answers questions young people cannot always ask their parents.

Well worth reading.

**Anna Posner, age 16**

Erica has insight. She knew Katherine liked Michael the moment they met at a New Year's Eve party. Katherine admits the fact to herself, which allows the attraction to develop. Eventually she is sure it is love and not childish infatuation. Michael feels it, too, and after a few failed attempts, they make love.

Their relationship becomes intense and exclusive. But with their future plans all figured out, the couple have to face up to the fact that their senior year at high school is coming to an end and they will be going to different universities. To make matters worse they both have summer jobs. They put their love to the test with a long separation. For Katherine it's a time to reflect and wonder if their love really is forever...

**Elena Gregoriou**

### Next?

More Judy Blume, of course: *Are You There, God? It's Me, Margaret* or *Tiger Eyes*.

For a more recent take on teenage sex, Melvin Burgess's *Doing It* (UTBG 112). Or Sarah Dessen's *Someone Like You*.

Other life-changing experiences happen in *Festival* by David Belbin and the **Megan** trilogy by Mary Hooper.

Or for more books on love and life, read Catherine Robinson's feature on pp. 178–179.

# THE FORTUNE TELLER  Alison Prince

If you are interested in clairvoyants, psychic powers, premonitions and horoscopes, this is a book for you. Mick lives with his sister and his mother. His father died in an accident and Mick tries to support his mother Cathie in her struggle to run a bed and breakfast business. Cathie visits a fortune-teller, who tells her Mick is going to die. Much of the story is about how Mick and those close to him deal with this premonition. Mick's sister moves out to live with her boyfriend. Cathie meets a new partner and Mick becomes increasingly isolated. The action takes place against the background of the Scottish coastline and a lighthouse, as Mick is compelled to question his destiny.

**Brenda Marshall**

### Next?

Another Alison Prince? Try *Three Blind Eyes*, a Dickensian mix of bleak history, creepy characters, gangs and mystery.

Peter Dickinson's *The Gift*: Davy Price has inherited the ability to see what others are thinking and learns his family are in danger.

Rachel Ward's *Numbers* is about a girl who, when she looks at someone, has a number pop into her head – the number is the date of that person's death.

Another Scottish author with her finger on the real teen pulse is Catherine Forde. Try *Fat Boy Swim*. (UTBG 128)

# The FOUNDATION trilogy  Isaac Asimov

### Next?

After completing the trilogy – *Foundation*, *Foundation and Empire* and *Second Foundation* – Asimov wrote more **Foundation** books. *Foundation's Edge* is next.

Asimov wrote some of the most brilliant sci-fi ever. Try *I, Robot*, which starts the excellent **Robot** series. (UTBG 207)

Philip K. Dick's *Do Androids Dream of Electric Sheep?* is full of amazing and original ideas. (UTBG 111)

Another epic series that spans time and space starts with *Dune* by Frank Herbert. (UTBG 116)

The human race has spread across the galaxy to occupy millions of worlds, all ruled from the metal-covered planet, Trantor. Only one man, Hari Seldon, realises that the Galactic Empire is in decline. Charting the fall of civilisation by means of the predictive science of Psychohistory, Seldon sets up two secret Foundations 'at opposite ends of the galaxy' to hold it together over the next thousand years.

In the course of the trilogy we meet buccaneering mayors, deep-space traders, merchant princes, thieves, mutants, emperors, scheming generals and a host of other colourful characters. Generations and crises come and go, centuries pass, with considerable excitement and a great many twists. The greatest of all sci-fi epics.

**Michael Lawrence**

# THE FOURTH HORSEMAN  Kate Thompson

This is genuinely scary; a dark, contemporary tale about terrorism, gene experiments and emotional betrayal, combined with chilling elements of Biblical mythology. The suspense builds slowly. Laurie and her brother gradually come to realise their own father might be the (misguided) villain of a story that deals with sweeping, chilling themes.

This book frightened me – and I was weaned on Stephen King. It worried me as well: I still can't quite shake the feeling that it could actually happen ... and perhaps happen soon. It's a great way to forget your own cares for a while. Beautifully crafted and intelligently written – two of its author's trademarks.

**Herbie Brennan**

### Next?

Try Kate Thompson's **Missing Link** trilogy starting with *Origins*. Or try her mythical, magical, hilarious *The New Policeman* (UTBG 282).

How about something by the terrifically scary Stephen King? *The Stand* is also about a future plague...

Or try Stephen Davies's African-set adventure, *Yellowcake*, about uranium, nuclear war and a cattle herder who becomes a spy.

There's another father who might accidentally destroy the world in the **Time Quake** trilogy by Linda Buckley-Archer. (UTBG 153)

# FRANKENSTEIN  Mary Shelley

### Next?

*Angelmonster* by Veronica Bennett tells the story of Mary Shelley's life and how her own experiences gave her the idea for writing **Frankenstein**.

For another experiment that goes wrong, read H.G. Wells's *The Invisible Man*.

Another classic horror story that's still appallingly scary is R.L. Stevenson's *Dr Jekyll and Mr Hyde*. (UTBG 115)

There's a wealth of wonderfully gothic stories in Angela Carter's collection, *The Bloody Chamber*.

If you think that Mary Shelley just played the dutiful wife to her famous poet husband, Percy Bysshe Shelley, think again...

*Frankenstein* started out as a challenge by the great Lord Byron to each of his guests at the Villa Diodati on Lake Geneva: 'Write a horror story'. So Mary sat down to write a book that would have more readers than those of all her poetic contemporaries; it turned out to be one of the most chilling stories ever written. Dr Frankenstein puts pieces of dead bodies together to assemble a creature that he brings to life. The monster escapes and roams the hills and villages around, wreaking havoc. But the monster also gains our sympathy, for within a misshapen body there is a lost soul that craves affection.

**James Riordan**

# GRAPHIC NOVELS
## by Mal Peet

I was in a branch of Waterstone's recently and asked where the graphic novels were. 'We don't keep them any more,' I was told, 'they just get stolen.' It's a small triumph for the form, I suppose, that it encourages reading among the thieving classes; but it's a shame that it gets harder to buy graphics just when it seems that they are beginning to win the struggle for serious critical recognition. Of course there are still diehards who dismiss graphic novels *en masse* as immature or flippant reading matter best suited to young readers reluctant to read 'proper' books.

It's true that there's a pretty leaky border

---

**SEEING THE WORLD DIFFERENTLY – TEN GRAPHIC NOVELS YOU OUGHT TO KNOW**

*Maus* by Art Spiegelman – the Holocaust re-imagined. Heartbreaking. (UTBG 258)

**Bone** by Jeff Smith – three cousins get lost in the pre-technological past. This is a series that actually gets better as it goes along.

**Castle Waiting** by Linda Medley – do you want a strong heroine with a dark secret, hilarious dialogue and a wonderfully original plot? Start with book one: *The Lucky Road*.

*Superman for All Seasons* by Jeph Loeb and Tim Sale – this is the story of how Clark Kent became Superman. A must for anyone interested in the origin of heroics.

*Persepolis* by Marjane Satrapi – her own story about growing up in Iran during the Islamic revolution. (UTBG 310)

*Fun Home* by Alison Bechdel – this graphic novel autobiography explores grief, death (Alison lives in a funeral home) and sexuality (via her own and her dead father's).

*Skim* by Mariko Tamaki and Jillian Tamaki – Skim angsts, endures school and home, falls in love, dabbles in Wicca, and slowly grows up. (UTBG 366)

**Barefoot Gen** by Keiji Nakazawa – a brilliant look at the aftermath of the bomb on Hiroshima.

*Jimmy Corrigan, the Smartest Kid on Earth* by Chris Ware – this is considered by some to be the best comic of recent years. (UTBG 215)

*Ghost World* by Daniel Clowes – two kids hang around their town after graduation. They're very cynical. That's it … but wow, is it so much more!

## ARE YOU OLD ENOUGH? SOME SERIOUSLY DARK MANGA

**Death Note** by Tsugumi Ohba and Takeshi Obata – a supernatural cat-and-mouse battle? A complex look at the nature of good and evil? A multi-stranded thriller? All these and more, **Death Note** is one of the most intriguing series around.

**Akira** by Katsuhiro Otomo – epic, convoluted, heartbreaking, this is set in post-apocalyptic Neo-Tokyo.

**Lone Wolf and Cub** by Kazuo Koike and Goseki Kojima – a samurai and his young son travel across feudal Japan. Beautiful, bleak, violent. Hugely popular, it has spawned six films, a TV series, four stage plays and more!

**Ghost in the Shell** by Shirow Masamune – a classic sci-fi epic, with one of the best strong female protagonists in Manga. Fantastically complex, start with *The Ghost in the Shell* and move on with *Man-Machine Interface*. There are various anime films and computer games, too.

**Vampire Knight** by Matsuri Hino – at Cross Academy humans attend the day classes and vampires attend the night classes. Yuki is the adopted daughter of the headmaster, and she is determined to protect the vampires and to enable them to co-exist peaceably with humans. Not everyone thinks the same way…

between 'comic books' and graphics, and that movie and TV spin-offs and fantasy books (often daringly and beautifully drawn) are predominant. Yet the term 'graphic novel' was coined in 1978 to describe Will Eisner's immensely serious *A Contract with God*, and some of the greatest graphics of the last 20 years have dealt with extremely sombre matters: the Holocaust in Art Spiegelman's two-volume *Maus* (UTBG 258) and Joe Klubert's *Yossel*; the Hiroshima bombing in Keji Nakazawa's **Barefoot Gen** books; nuclear war in Raymond Briggs's *When the Wind Blows* (UTBG 434); war and ethnic cleansing in Joe Sacco's *Palestine* and *The Fixer: A Story from Sarajevo*. Indeed, if there is a criticism to be made of the form generally, it would be that graphics tend not towards the lightweight and the comical, but towards the shadowy and the bleak. Even the good old escapist superhero genre has turned darkly ironic; see, for example, *Batman – The Dark Knight Returns* by Frank Miller, and *Watchmen* (UTBG 426) by Alan Moore and Dave Gibbons.

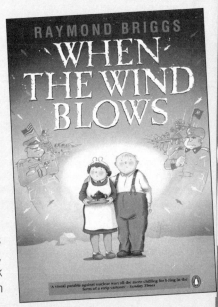

## NOT FOR THE FAINT OF HEART – SOME HARDCORE GRAPHIC NOVELS

**The Sandman** series by Neil Gaiman – start with *Preludes and Nocturnes* and just keep going. It is brilliant, innovative and utterly addictive. (UTBG 342)

*The Dark Knight Returns* by Frank Miller – in the 1980s, this one reinvented comics for a new generation. It's still a must-read.

**Fables** by Bill Willingham – Snow White's sister is missing and detective Big Bad Wolf has to solve the crime. Set in a parallel Manhatten, Fabletown, this is a place where storybook characters are real. Start with *Legends in Exile*.

**Queen and Country** by Greg Rucka – forget James Bond, this is the reality of spying; dark and gritty. Volume one is *Operation Broken Ground*.

*Watchmen* by Alan Moore and Dave Gibbons – set in an alternate reality, this is a bleak world where heroes (few of them truly 'super') exist but are feared and despised. Claustrophobic, atmospheric, literary, this is comic art of the highest order. (UTBG 426)

*The League of Extraordinary Gentlemen* by Alan Moore and Kevin O'Neill – pit a handful of Victorian literature's greatest adventurers against the powers of evil and you have this; a genius reworking of the superhero genre.

*All Star Superman* by Grant Morrison and Frank Quitely – this is a wild, brilliant spin on the Superman myth, written and illustrated by two of the genre's giants.

*We3* by Grant Morrison and Frank Quitely – this is a very adult take on *Homeward Bound* for the 21st century, which involves three test-subject animals searching for a place of safety. Savage, violent, deeply affecting – once read never to be forgotten.

*V for Vendetta* by Alan Moore – a bleak dystopia, a misunderstood terrorist and a young woman meet in this classic. (UTBG 420)

The fact is, though, that there are now as many genres of graphic as there are of mainstream prose fiction; and in one important respect the graphic is far more challenging and experimental than the prose novel. By combining text, art and the 'grammar' of movies and animation, graphic novelists have devised new, startling and complex narrative techniques that make interesting demands on the reader's verbal and visual literacy. Actually, strip cartoonists have always taken a subversive approach to logical narration; look at collections of Winsor McCay's weird and beautiful *Dreams of the Rarebit Fiend* and *Little Nemo*, and George Herriman's brilliant *Krazy Kat*, which date from the early years of the 20th century and were a major influence on the 'underground' comics of the

1960s and 70s. Contemporary graphic sci-fi / fantasy novelists, such as Bryan Talbot (*The Adventures of Luther Arkwright*) and Neil Gaiman (the extraordinary *Black Orchid*, illustrated by Dave McKean), as well as the ongoing **The Sandman** series (UTBG 342) make it a point of honour to offer few concessions to the reader, weaving together different time frames and points of view to create a 'parallel universes' style of narration which, in a prose novel, would deter all but the most sophisticated readers.

## SOMETHING FOR EVERYONE – TEN MANGA CLASSICS

**Fruits Basket** by Natsuki Takaya – an orphan girl is taken in by a family; a family who, when weak or embracing the opposite sex, turn into vengeful spirits of the Chinese zodiac. Funny, sweet and with just enough darkness to keep you gripped.

**Neon Genesis Evangelion** by Yoshiyuki Sadamoto – the Earth is under attack from alien machines when Shinji's long-absent father summons him. And it's not just for a family reunion…

**Dragon Ball Z** by Akira Toriyama – a massive series spun out of *Dragon Ball*, involving a monkey-tailed boy and a quest to find mystical objects that can summon dragons.

**Yu-Gi-Oh** by Kazuki Takahashi – trading cards, video games, toys, anime and manga. If you haven't come across any of these, where have you been?

**Marmalade Boy** by Wataru Yoshizumi – could you love a boy who was bitter and sweet at the same time? You can. But then so can lots of other people…

**Sailor Moon** by Naoko Takeuchi – ordinary girls by day, superheroes by night! This is one of the best shojo manga (manga written for, and about, girls) and it spawned an empire, including anime, toys and video games.

**Naruto** by Masashi Kishimoto – Naruto Uzumaki is a boy with a demon locked inside him. He's also a trainee Ninja… Cue a story full of great fights, deep characterisation and many, many volumes!

**Bleach** by Tite Kubo – Ichigo Kurosaki is a high-school kid who can talk to ghosts and who finds that ghosts are drawn to him; not just good ghosts, but 'Hollows' – ghosts who are ravenous for human souls.

**Captive Hearts** by Matsuri Hino – would you like a servant to do your every bidding? Yes? Well, Suzuka isn't so sure, even though Megumi is very, very cute! You see he's suffering from an ancient curse that forces him into this slavery. Together, can they find a way to free him?

**Buddha** by Osamu Tezuka – a religious epic that tells the story of Prince Siddhartha and his quest for enlightenment. If you think that sounds boring – don't be fooled!

# FRANNY AND ZOOEY

## J.D. Salinger

For some people, *The Catcher in the Rye* is the only important Salinger book. But his true masterpiece remains incomplete. Since the early 1950s, Salinger has been writing an epic narrative series about a New York family called the Glasses. 'Franny' and 'Zooey' are two of the stories from this sequence, with a sweet simplicity that makes them incredibly enjoyable to read. 'Franny' is a short story about a young female student who meets her boyfriend for dinner, and can't help disagreeing with everything he says; while 'Zooey' is a longer novella, narrated by Buddy Glass, who claims his family hate him writing about them but don't protest because they know he'd burst into tears. All the children in the Glass family are prodigies, appearing on a radio quiz show called 'It's a Wild Child', but when they grow up their problems drive them to depression and suicide.

**Matt Thorne**

---

**Next?**

*The Cheese Monkeys* by Chip Kidd, a novel about a year in art school, has some of Salinger's sarcastic humour.

*Studs Lonigan* by James T. Farrell tells of teenage dissatisfaction, but Studs is a harder character than Salinger's whimsical Glass siblings.

For other books about complex family life, and also the trials of growing up, try Colette's *Gigi* or Françoise Sagan's *Bonjour Tristesse* (UTBG 52).

---

## The Ultimate Teen Book List

### DANNY'S DESERT ISLAND SELECTION

**The Buddha of Suburbia**
(p. 64)

**Fly by Night**
(p. 137)

**Frost on My Moustache**
(p. 149)

**Great Expectations**
(p. 166)

**The Invention of Hugo Cabret**
(p. 206)

**Kit's Wilderness**
(p. 228)

**One Hundred Years of Solitude** (p. 296)

**The Outsiders**
(p. 305)

**A Prayer for Owen Meany**
(p. 318)

**Saffy's Angel**
(p. 340)

**Up on Cloud Nine**
(p. 415)

**The Vanishing of Katharina Linden**
(p. 419)

# FREAK THE MIGHTY   Rodman Philbrick

Even though he's six feet tall, Max Kane is scared of a lot of things. Kevin, a.k.a. Freak, is half Max's height and not scared of anything, not even the disease that might kill him. The summer before eighth grade they become Freak the Mighty – Freak is the brain, Max is the brawn.

The idea of a legendary creature made of two people may sound whimsical, but this is realistic fiction. Both Freak and Max have complex and challenging lives, and in the course of the book they each have to stare down their most terrifying enemies.

There's so much I love about this story – the strength and bravery, humour and friendship, and a page-turning plot. But what really makes it a favourite is Max's voice. It's self-effacing and heartbreaking, while also funny and real. Max claims (without exactly saying so) that he isn't lovable and doesn't have a future. Everything about his friendship with Freak tells you otherwise.

**Sara Zarr**

> **Next?**
>
> Other books that feature unlikely friendships are Pete Hautman's *Invisible*, Ron Koertge's *Stoner & Spaz*, and Ellen Wittlinger's *Hard Love*.
>
> There's a different look at being different in Robert Cormier's *The Chocolate War* (UTBG 78) and also in Benjamin Zephaniah's *Face*. Neither are easy reads but each, in its own way, is brilliant.

# FRENCHMAN'S CREEK   Daphne Du Maurier

> **Next?**
>
> There's more West-Country romance in R.D. Blackmore's classic, *Lorna Doone*; or for corsets and passion try *Wuthering Heights* (UTBG 447).
>
> Richard Hughes's *A High Wind in Jamaica* is a story of pirates, unsuitable obsession and adventure.

Romance was never quite as passionate or daring as in *Frenchman's Creek*. Prepare to fall in love right along with our heroine Dona; for never was there quite as elusive, romantic or swashbuckling a lover as the pirate known as 'the Frenchman'!

Dona is married, the mother of two, and about to turn 30. She had been the toast of London (of the men at least), but one day, she decides to leave it all and move to her husband's country estate in Cornwall, and her life changes for ever. All of Cornwall is desperately trying to capture a French pirate – but who would have thought that his hideout was right in the middle of Dona's estate? And what exactly happens after he offers her a place on his ship? Will Dona choose adventure and love, or stay faithful to her husband and children? You will find yourself holding your breath as the story unfolds...

**Candida Gray**

# FRIENDLY FIRE  Patrick Gale

Patrick Gale's recent novels coax you in gently until you find – quite soon – you are pulled into a heady, messy tangle of relationships. We enter *Friendly Fire*, which is set during a 1970's boarding-school adolescence, through the eyes of defensive, pragmatic Sophie, whose parents abandoned her and who's been brought up in a children's home. At the nearly all-male Tatham's School she immerses herself in the cold-but-steadfast world of academia, but she cannot evade the complex web of passions that the students spin around them. Her life becomes enriched in unexpected ways, but with that comes the power to threaten the happiness of those closest to her.

This book is aptly titled – friendly fire is one of the most dangerous situations of all.

**Jon Appleton**

**Next?**

Hooked? Try two other Gale novels that home in on the truth about childhood: *Rough Music* and *A Sweet Obscurity*.

There are two schools in Lauren Henderson's *Kiss Me, Kill Me*, which tells the story of Scarlett, who suddenly finds herself one of the 'it' girls. Life's great – until she kisses Dan and he dies.

Sometimes you can be too sensitive or too protective, as Sophie is. Tom's guilty of this, too, in Anne Fine's short, sharp *Round Behind the Ice-House*.

# FROST IN MAY  Antonia White

You think your school's tough on you? Read this book. Ten-year-old Nanda is sent to the Convent of the Five Wounds, a boarding school so pious that at night the girls drape their stockings over the rest of their clothes in the shape of a cross. Nanda tries hard to fit in, and this astonishing novel follows her progress until, at 14, disaster and expulsion strike.

Written for adults over 60 years ago, this autobiographical account of a fanatically Roman Catholic schooling will fascinate older readers who can, like Nanda, face a challenge. It also forcefully brings home just what 'faith schooling' can mean, how tightly it can grip, and how long-lasting the effects can be. A salutary eye-opener for today's teenager – and a classic.

**Anne Fine**

**Next?**

There are sequels: *The Lost Traveller*, *The Sugar House* and *Beyond the Glass*.

*Bilgewater* is about a girl at an all-boys' school. (UTBG 43)

Or try a book set in Nigeria and about family and the terrifying nature of religion: *Purple Hibiscus* by Chimamanda Ngozi Adichie.

Karen Armstrong has written an account of her life as a nun in *Through the Narrow Gate*.

Or try the classic *The Nun's Story* by Kathryn Hulme.

# FROST ON MY MOUSTACHE   Tim Moore

## Next?

For more crazy men doing heroic (or crazy) things, read *The Worst Journey in the World*. (UTBG 445)

Or try *Terra Incognita* for a woman's ice adventure. (UTBG 390)

Or less heroic, but as funny as Tim Moore: *Round Ireland with a Fridge*. (UTBG 335)

Or more Tim Moore? Try his hilarious *I Believe in Yesterday*, which is about his exploits with various historical re-enactment groups, or *Nul Points*, about the tragedy and farce behind the Eurovision Song Contest.

Once it gets started, this is one of the funniest books ever. A hundred and fifty years ago, fearless, swashbuckling Lord Dufferin went off on his derring-do travels, battling with icebergs and polar bears through Iceland and Norway. Modern-day author Tim Moore is a self-confessed 'girl's blouse', and, oozing with derring-don't, he sets off in his footsteps. As Tim watches himself fall so far short of the doughty Victorian in pluck and stamina on the demanding Arctic journey, he gets funnier and funnier. Skip chapter one first time round if you must and start, as does Tim, at 4.30 am in Grimsby, boarding a boat in a force-8 gale. ('Eat, like, 12 Mars bars,' suggests the taxi driver. 'So you'll have something to chuck up.')

**Anne Fine**

# FROZEN FIRE   Tim Bowler

Since her brother Josh disappeared, things haven't been the same for Dusty's family. Then her mother walks out, leaving just Dusty and her dad trying to cope alone. And it's not easy. But things get much harder – and a lot stranger – when Dusty starts receiving chilling phone calls from a boy who seems to know something important about her, perhaps something about Josh's whereabouts… And lately a figure has been seen walking in the snow up on the fells – could this be her mysterious caller?

In this extremely original novel, Tim Bowler mixes totally familiar reality with forces that are harder to explain, to create a gripping supernatural thriller that's sure to keep you up at night, wondering…

**Daniel Hahn**

## Next?

Tim has written a lot, but if you want something else by him that's thriller-like, try *Bloodchild*, about a boy waking with amnesia after a car crash and finding himself surrounded by hostile strangers, or *Storm Catchers*, about a kidnapping.

For another thrilling supernatural read in a snowy landscape – but a very different kind of writing – try Marcus Sedgwick's stunning *My Swordhand Is Singing*. (UTBG 275)

Sarwat Chadda's *The Devil's Kiss* is a first novel that rips you along at a breathless pace. (UTBG 104)

# THE GAME OF TRIUMPHS Laura Powell

Cat lives in Soho with her aunt Bel, a casino croupier. She's lived with Bel since her parents were killed in a car crash when she was three. Cat sees herself as tough and pretty cool – and when she stumbles across a group of people engaged in some kind of geeky role-playing game and taking it unbelievably seriously, she is both amused and condescending.

But not for long. It turns out that this game has a tendency to suck you into it whether you want to be involved or not – and when it sheds light on the way her parents died, Cat is suddenly as passionate a player of the Game as any of the people she used to laugh at.

Just as Cat thought she could never get interested in the fantasy world she had discovered, I didn't expect to get into this novel, because fantasy isn't usually my sort of thing. But we were both proved wrong.

**Susan Reuben**

**Next?**

You'll want to move straight on to the sequel, *The Lord of Misrule*.

*The Roar* by Emma Clayton is also about a sinister game. Or for a different kind of game playing, try *The Traitor Game* (UTBG 402) by B.R. Collins.

You might find yourself interested in Tarot cards; if so try Helen Dunwoodie's *The Tarot Reader's Daughter*.

# THE GARBAGE KING Elizabeth Laird

**Next?**

Elizabeth Laird makes no concessions – all her books are powerful and hard-hitting. Try *Jake's Tower* (UTBG 210), *Kiss the Dust* (UTBG 227) and *The Lost Riders*.

Another shocking book about living on the streets, this time in London: *Stone Cold* by Robert Swindells. (UTBG 377)

Linzi Glass's *The Year the Gypsies Came* is about friendship, trust, rape and apartheid in South Africa. (UTBG 451)

Elizabeth Laird has lived in Ethiopia and from her experience there has crafted this wonderfully true-feeling novel about rich-boy Dani who runs away from his father's ruthless plans for him, and finds himself living on the streets of Addis Ababa among the poorest of the poor. Anyone who has ever tried to imagine everything that makes life safe, happy and comfortable being stripped away, leaving them with nothing but hunger, dirt and danger, should read this book. Amid all the fear and squalor, however, Dani finds a new strength, and the true meaning of friendship, independence and solidarity. A superb and gripping read for anyone who is not afraid of plumbing the depths.

**Lynne Reid Banks**

# A GATHERING LIGHT
## Jennifer Donnelly

**Next?**

*Anne of Green Gables* by L.M. Montgomery shows the toughness of life on a farm and the warmth of small communities.

*Some Other War* by Linda Newbery gives a good picture of country life in England, shown from a working-class viewpoint.

Or try Jennifer Donnelly's epic *The Tea Rose*, set in late 19th-century London and New York.

There is more mystery and murder in Philip Pullman's *The Ruby in the Smoke*. (UTBG 341)

This wonderful book brilliantly intertwines fiction and reality. Set in a small New England resort town in 1906, it tells the story of Mattie and how her life interacts with that of drowned Grace Brown.

Mattie is torn between her duty to help her father run his farm and to look after her motherless siblings, and her desire to be a writer. When handsome Royal Loomis starts to show an interest, there is an extra reason for Mattie to turn her back on her dreams and stay put. She has in her possession the letters Grace wrote to her lover Chester, and these help Mattie resolve the dilemma about what to do with her own life.

Sympathetic, beautifully written and wonderfully constructed, this is an outstanding read.

**Ann Jungman**

# GENERATION X
## Douglas Coupland

Dag, Claire and Andy are good friends in their 20s who live in neighbouring bungalows in a quiet American town. Their jobs are dull, they have little money and they see the future as frightening, full of the threat of nuclear bombs and environmental catastrophe. So they escape from all of this by telling one another bizarre, beautiful stories about other worlds where things make more, or sometimes less, sense to them. This is a thoughtful book about friendship, human nature and trying to understand an uncertain world. It is a true 'cult novel' – its popularity spread by word of mouth. It is full of new and clever words and terms, like 'McJob' for a low-paid and unimportant job, which are explained in amusing side-notes to the main text.

**Marianne Taylor**

**Next?**

More Douglas Coupland? Try his *Shampoo Planet*.

*The Lawnmower Celebrity* by Ben Hatch is the sad, funny tale of a teenage boy trying to see the point of it all.

*The Beach* by Alex Garland is another book that started as a cult novel – then they made a film of it! (UTBG 35)

And read our feature on cult books on pp. 280–281.

# GEORGIE  Malachy Doyle

**Next?**

*Disconnected* is about a girl escaping life through the solace of alcohol. (UTBG 106)

*Who Is Jesse Flood?* is another great Malachy Doyle, about a boy coming to terms with life and himself. (UTBG 436)

For another tale of problematic children finding their place, read Sharon Creech's rather gentler *Ruby Holler*. (UTBG 337)

Georgie lives in a home for disturbed children. He has a terrible secret he won't talk about to anyone. He destroys anything given to him. He rejects anyone who attempts to win his trust.

Then he moves to a new home, where he meets Shannon and Tommo. Shannon is a girl with her own secrets. Tommo is a care worker who won't let Georgie push him away. Together, they help Georgie overcome the nightmares in his past and develop the courage to love again.

*Georgie* is no easy read. At times, it's so honest it's painful. It's also one of the most positive and uplifting books I've ever read. I'm still not sure about the last chapter, which doesn't quite ring true, but other than that, *Georgie* is utterly believable and totally compelling.

**Graham Gardner**

# GETTING RID OF KARENNA
## Helena Pielichaty

Suzanne gets a Saturday job in a hairdresser's and is horrified to discover that Karenna, the bully who made her life miserable in school, is the junior stylist there. All the old, humiliating memories come flooding back. At first Karenna doesn't even recognize Suzanne, but it soon becomes clear neither girl has changed much since they last met. Karenna resents Suzanne being there, butting in on the new life she has carved out for herself since school. Suzanne must overcome the humiliations of the past and find some way to stop Karenna haunting her future.

A real and convincing exploration of the bully-victim relationship.

**Yvonne Coppard**

**Next?**

More Helena? Try *Accidental Friends*, about how things change after a chance meeting.

Or Jacqueline Wilson's *Kiss*, about how even long-standing friendships can change.

Robert Cormier's *The Rag and Bone Shop* is about a bully whose victim turns on him. *Inventing Elliot* (UTBG 206) by Graham Gardner is also about bullying.

*Stargirl* by Jerry Spinelli is a book about what it takes to be popular. (UTBG 375)

# GHOST STORIES M.R. James

The living people in these stories are usually learned, respectable types; scholars, clergymen, amateur archaeologists, often nursing a guilty secret, poking about where they ought not to in burial mounds, tombs, churches, libraries. All their learning and respectability cannot protect them from what they disturb. These are not strictly speaking ghosts but crawling, slithering, soft dark things lit only by the occasional glint of sunlight on white bone, trailing cobwebs, mildew, damp musty smells, unspeakable rags of cloth and flesh, bluebottles and fog. You would not want any of them to touch you, but touch is what they do: touch and hang on. After a century, the writing may seem a little stately but the stories are thoroughly nasty.

**Jan Mark**

## Next?

Some of the best British ghost stories were written in the early 20th century. Look out for authors like Algernon Blackwood and E.F. Benson. Read Benson's *The Tale of an Empty House* or any of his short story collections. For something more recent, try Neil Gaiman's *The Graveyard Book* (UTBG 165).

Susan Hill's *The Woman in Black*, set at around the same time, is unusual – a ghost story that is a full-length novel. (UTBG 443)

A deeply unsettling ghost story can be found in Cliff McNish's *Breathe*. (UTBG 60)

# GIDEON THE CURPURSE Linda Buckley-Archer

An accident with an experimental anti-gravity machine flings Peter Schock and Kate Dyer back into the 18th century. In this world of highwaymen, gin cellars, thief takers, botched hangings and corsets, they are guided and helped by Gideon Seymour, a reformed cutpurse. Now if they can only recover the machine from the infamous criminal known as the Tar Man, they might be able to get home…

This is a wonderful chance to be dropped into another age, experiencing everything from the taste of milk just out of the udder to the crush of Newgate Gaol. The 18th-century characters are not simply modern people in fancy dress; they think, feel, speak and act in keeping with their time. Eventful, funny and full of fascinating detail.

**Frances Hardinge**

## Next?

The sequels, as you'll need to know What Happens Next: *The Tar Man* and *Time Quake*.

Celia Rees's *Sovay* is about a girl who takes to highway robbery in order to avenge her family – and to protect herself.

Frances Hardinge writes about the past, but layered with her own imagination; try the very different *Fly by Night*. (UTBG 137)

# GINGER SNAPS Cathy Cassidy

*Ginger Snaps* is a great story about being yourself – and finding friends who accept you as you are. On the face of it, Ginger appears to have it all – she's cool, pretty and, best of all, is great friends with the ultra-confident Shannon. But she also hides a dark secret – once, back in primary school, she was bullied, unpopular and alone.

When attractive, eccentric, sax-playing Sam starts at school, Ginger faces a terrible choice: go out with Sam and risk Shannon's disapproval, or stay safe inside a one-sided friendship? And what does friendship mean to Shannon anyway?

*Ginger Snaps* is Cathy Cassidy at her best – a fast-moving story with convincing characters, and powerful emotional dilemmas concerning love and loyalty.

**Sophie McKenzie**

> ### Next?
> If you liked this, you're bound to already be a Jacqueline Wilson fan, but in case you missed it, try *My Sister Jodie*.
>
> Luckily Cathy Cassidy has more titles to hunt out; try **Sundae Girl** or *Dizzy* (UTBG 110).
>
> Sarra Manning writes about teen life as it is; try the story of two girls, one boy in the **Diary of a Crush** series, starting with *French Kiss*. Or look for her **Fashionistas** series, about a group of girls trying to make it in the world of fashion.

# GIRL, 15, CHARMING BUT INSANE
## Sue Limb

> ### Next?
> Jess continues her adventures in *Girl (Nearly) 16: Absolute Torture*, *Girl 16: Pants on Fire* and *Girl 15: Flirting for England*.
>
> Tui Sutherland's **This Must Be Love** gives a classic Shakespearean tale a modern makeover, with witty results.
>
> **Cross Your Heart, Connie Pickles** is quality chick-lit for teens, too, penned by adult author Sabine Durrant; or try the hilarious **Diary of a Chav** by Grace Dent (UTBG 105).
>
> Or read Jacqueline Wilson's books for older readers, such as *Love Lessons*.

Limb's novel is a riotous take on Jane Austen's *Emma* and – like *Clueless* before it – is modern, snazzy and very up-to-date. Jess Jordan feels that by comparison to the blonde, beautiful, rich Flora she is hideous, poor and doomed. She spends her time being mesmerised by the fabulously handsome Ben Jones – who is so totally wrong for her.

Jess has been invited to do a stand-up routine at the school show, the one thing she knows she's good at. But the glamorous Flora and her vile band Poisonous Trash threaten to steal the show. Disaster strikes before Jess realises who the man of her dreams really is. It's classic stuff and laugh-out-loud funny.

**John McLay**

# GIRLFRIEND IN A COMA Douglas Coupland ✹✹✹

This is an immensely hard-hitting but also extraordinarily gripping novel, which starts with Karen, aged 17, losing her virginity to her boyfriend on a ski slope in Vancouver, Canada, and an hour later falling asleep at a house-wrecking party and falling into a coma. The book traces the effect of this and other events on the lives of her friends, who go from bright teenagers to embittered drug- and alcohol-dependent adults. A weird and wonderful read, encompassing drug-induced visions, talking ghosts and even the end of the world as we know it. Basically, and brilliantly, Coupland is telling us to take a long hard look at the way we live our lives, and to do something about it before it's too late.

**Malachy Doyle**

**Next?**

All Douglas Coupland's books are exciting, thought provoking and well worth a read. Try *Generation X* (UTBG 151) next or *All Families Are Psychotic*, about a family so outrageously awful that your own will suddenly seem too normal for words.

Also read Irvine Welsh's *Trainspotting* for a really hard look at the dark side of drugs. (UTBG 401)

And for a story from the other side of the coma, Alex Garland's *The Coma*.

# THE GIRL IN THE ATTIC ✹
## Valerie Mendes

**Next?**

*Green Fingers* by Paul May and *Zillah and Me* by Helen Dunmore are both gripping reads about moving house and making a new start.

*The Wish House* (UTBG 440) by Celia Rees centres on a house that harbours more sinister secrets, as does Linda Newbery's atmospheric, enthralling *Nevermore* (UTBG 279).

Or try Valerie Mendes's *The Drowning*, about a terrible accident that changes a girl's life.

Being dragged off to Cornwall for Christmas by his mum, then being told they're to move there permanently, isn't the best present in the world for 13-year-old Nathan.

Separated from his dad, missing his best friend Tom and his action-packed life in London leads to lots of strops and sulking and a determination never to settle in ... until the day he sees a girl painting in the attic of a house they're thinking of buying – a girl who turns out to have a dark family secret Nathan just has to discover.

Mixing mystery, love and contemporary Gothic horror, this is a spooky, spine-tingling thriller to read in one sitting.

**Eileen Armstrong**

# GIRL, MISSING Sophie McKenzie

Laura has always known she's adopted, but when internet research for a school project throws up the possibility that she's a missing child, suddenly she's no longer sure of anything. Was she kidnapped from an American family as a toddler? Has her life till now been a lie? And how deeply are her mum and dad involved in the conspiracy? Together with her best friend Jam, she travels to the States to uncover the truth about her past – but others are equally determined to ensure it stays buried.

This is a terrific page-turner – fast paced and thought provoking. McKenzie's main characters are realistically and engagingly flawed and Lauren's spiky relationship with her adoptive parents will feel uncomfortably familiar to many readers.

**Kathryn Ross**

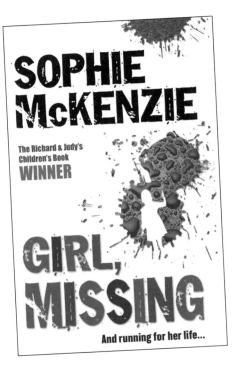

## SIBLINGS

*Round Behind the Ice-House*
by Anne Fine

*The Diamond Girls*
by Jacqueline Wilson

*Brothers* by Ted van Lieshout

*Ruby Holler* by Sharon Creech

*Reckless* by Sue Mayfield

*Saffy's Angel* by Hilary McKay

### Next?

Read more by Sophie McKenzie – *Blood Ties* is another chilling and action-packed thriller, raising issues of cloning and genetic engineering. (UTBG 49)

Anne Cassidy's *Missing Judy* explores what life is like for the family of a missing child. Kim is still racked with guilt because she lost her little sister in the park eight years ago. Then one day some new evidence turns up…

Self-discovery is also the theme of Jenny Valentine's funny, bittersweet *Finding Violet Park*. (UTBG 132)

# GIRLS IN LOVE Jacqueline Wilson

### Next?

*Girls Under Pressure, Girls Out Late* and *Girls in Tears* continue the series.

Louise Rennison's books tackle familiar problems: try *Angus, Thongs and Full-Frontal Snogging* for starters. (UTBG 23)

For more friends, families and the trials and tribulations of life in general, read Cathy Cassidy. Start with the funny, sassy *Ginger Snaps*. (UTBG 154)

This series of books is about three teenage girls who are going through the usual teenage problems. It's full of jealousy, tears, boys and family difficulties. The main character, Ellie, thinks she's fat and boring and is very insecure. Her two best friends are Magda (who is gorgeous and totally boy-mad) and Nadine (who is very cool and striking, though sometimes blunt and rude).

Jacqueline Wilson's books are light and gripping, and I felt I had a real connection with the characters. I would recommend this book to anyone who wants an easy, enjoyable read.

**Rachel Shaw, age 13**

# GIRL WITH A PEARL EARRING
## Tracy Chevalier

*Girl with a Pearl Earring* is narrated by servant-girl Griet, and simmers with her passion. Griet is a tile-maker's daughter, taken to be a maidservant to the great artist Vermeer. With her we are drawn into the Vermeer family house, a small world full of almost unbearable tensions. It is fraught with tensions over class and religion, servants vying for superiority over each other, and rivalries for the affection of a genius who cares only for his painting.

Griet reveals the process of painting as magically as she evokes the mood of the house and its people, and we sense that she herself might have been an artist, had she not been a girl, and of the servant class. I am not sure I like Griet, and I can never predict what she will do next. Yet her narrative is as spellbinding as Vermeer's portraits themselves. This is a dazzling book with erotic undercurrents. Look out for the ear-piercing scene.

**Caroline Pitcher**

### Next?

Deborah Moggach's *Tulip Fever* is like stepping into a Vermeer painting and sneaking behind the canvas into a world of betrayal.

*Lady Chatterley's Lover* by D.H. Lawrence tells the story of a lady and a gamekeeper (aristocratic totty seeks working-class rough). (UTBG 230)

Or try more Tracy Chevalier with *Burning Bright*, which features the poet, William Blake.

# GO AND COME BACK   Joan Abelove

**Next?**

*Shabanu: Daughter of the Wind* by Suzanne Fisher Staples is also about a girl on the brink of marriage, this time in the Pakistan desert.

*The Moorchild* by Eloise McGraw is fantasy, but it's also another look at our world through fresh eyes: the eyes of a half-fairy inserted into a human family.

For more outsiders trying to understand a different culture, read Robert Swindells's **Ruby Tanya** or Elizabeth Laird's **Kiss the Dust** (UTBG 227).

I know this book inside out – that's how many times I've read it. *Go and Come Back* changed me for ever.

Alicia is on the brink of marriage when two white women, anthropologists, arrive in her Peruvian village for a year's stay. To Alicia and the others in Poincushmana, the tall blonde woman is ugly and the short fat one beautiful. They're not even related to each other. They're friends, a word that doesn't exist in Isabo. The anthropologists ask a million questions and they're incredibly stingy.

Months pass. Alicia adopts a *nawa* (outsider) baby. The rains come and go. Army recruiters come and young men flee. The two white women learn the values of the village. You will, too. You'll see yourself and your life in a new way – and dental floss will never seem the same again!

**Gail Carson Levine**

# GO ASK ALICE   Anonymous

What happens when you're so desperate for acceptance that you'll do just about anything to get it?

This is the real diary of a 15-year-old girl whose name is never revealed. She feels like the odd one out in her well-off, over-achieving family; she's snubbed by the boy she adores; she has problems with her looks, and with the new school that she attends when she moves house. Then a spiked drink at a party changes her life; she plunges into the local drug scene, eventually running away from home and ending up in a psychiatric ward.

Though sad and scary, her story is so painfully honest, vivid and touching that it's hard to put down.

**Catherine Jinks**

**Next?**

*Streetkid in the City* by Delphine Jamet is another strikingly fresh, real-life account of a tough teenage life.

Or try **Junk** by Melvin Burgess. (UTBG 218)

Terri Paddock's **Come Clean** is the story of a girl who tries to use alcohol as a way of escaping her troubles.

Something equally shocking? Try **Tender Morsels** by Margo Lanagan.

# THE GO-BETWEEN L.P. Hartley

**Next?**

*Atonement* by Ian McEwan (UTBG 30) and *The Remains of the Day* by Kazuo Ishiguro are totally different books, but they do deal with similar subject matter – lost innocence.

Michael Frayn's **Spies** is set during World War II, about two boys convinced one of their mothers is a spy.

Or another L.P. Hartley? Try **The Shrimp and the Anemone**.

What a shame *The Go-Between* is a set text! I'm sure it puts some people off, thinking it's 'brainy'. Well, it isn't – but it *is* atmospheric, nostalgic and beautifully written. This tale of class, lust and lies binds you in and doesn't let you go. Set in a country house during the hottest summer on record, at the turn of the last century when men were gentlemen and nothing was ever the lady's fault, it's stuffed full of mystical symbolism and references to the ever-rising temperature that combine to make you just know something terrible is going to take place...

What does happen is the losing of childhood innocence in a way that affects Leo, the narrator, for the rest of his life. Poignant and ultra-descriptive, this book also happens to contain one of the most famous opening lines in English fiction: 'The past is a foreign country: they do things differently there...'

**Catherine Robinson**

# GOING FOR STONE Philip Gross

Nick runs away after his stepdad hits him. With no money, he lives in squats, sleeping when he can and trying to survive. Then he finds out about the living statues – people who stand in busy streets pretending to be made of stone or metal. Nick tries it himself and finds he's good. Very good. But someone is watching him...

Recruited into a school for statues, Nick meets the brilliant Antonin and the money-man, Dominic, who chooses the best students and sets them up for life. That's the promise. The reality might be something else...

Sharp, unsettling, utterly convincing, this book kept me awake until I'd got to the end. Philip Gross is a genius, creating real characters and a nail-bitingly taut story that'll have you gasping for breath.

**Leonie Flynn**

**Next?**

For other, very different, Philip Gross books try **The Lastling**, set in the remote reaches of Tibet or **The Storm Garden**, which starts with a boy confessing to having planted a bomb ... one that has exploded.

Another book about the problems of striving for perfection is **Disconnected**. (UTBG 106)

Or for something else about fitting in, try **The Passion Flower Massacre** by Nicola Morgan.

# GOLDKEEPER   Sally Prue

**Next?**

There are not enough really funny books around, but others to try are Alan Temperley's *Harry and the Wrinklies* and Kjartan Poskitt's *Urgum the Axeman*.

If you liked this book, you'll almost certainly enjoy Jonathan Stroud's *The Amulet of Samarkand*. (UTBG 21)

For fast-paced adventure, read Eoin Colfer's *Artemis Fowl* and its sequels. (UTBG 29)

For a magical story with an interesting twist on demons, try Sally Prue's first book, *Cold Tom*, or try her very different *Wheels of War*.

I'm not keen on the title of this book, but don't let that put you off, as the story itself is excellent: very funny indeed and packed with bizarre twists and turns. It spins the yarn of Sebastian, a surprise candidate for the job of high priest's apprentice in the temple of Ora, and his pet rat, Gerald. Not everyone is pleased when Sebastian actually gets the job, particularly a certain Mr Meeno (a gangster) and his nephew Horace (who was quite expecting to be chosen himself). The tale darkens as Sebastian and Gerald survive several nasty – and rather unusual – accidents. Is there a plot to get rid of them? Well, of course there is, but that's only the start of their problems...

**Chris d'Lacey**

# GONE   Michael Grant

What would you do if your teacher disappeared mid-sentence? No flash, no smoke, just gone, chalk dropping to the carpet. What would you do if every adult, everyone over 15, your parents included, disappeared and you had no idea why?

In a small town in southern California, Sam is trying to figure out what to do next. Cut off from the rest of the world, Perdido Beach has descended into chaos and violence. Bullies are roaming the streets in gangs and some people seem to be developing strange and terrifying powers.

Engrossing, taut, and addictive, *Gone* shows us the darker side of our own nature. You won't be able to put it down.

**Matthew Humpage**

**Next?**

Eventually, this will be a six-book series. Titles so far are *Hunger*, *Lies* and *Plague*.

For another gripping tale of impossible circumstances read *The Knife of Never Letting Go* by Patrick Ness. (UTBG 229)

For more wild, nightmarish communities in isolation, try John Wyndham's The *Midwich Cuckoos* or Golding's classic *Lord of the Flies* (UTBG 241).

Or try another book about a world with no responsible adults; Charlie Higson's *The Enemy*.

# GONE WITH THE WIND  Margaret Mitchell  ✹ ✹

At the beginning of this book, the heroine Scarlett O'Hara is 16. She is a wilful, flirtatious southern belle from a wealthy Irish-American family. But it is 1861 and Scarlett and her family are soon plunged into the violence and chaos of the American Civil War.

In five years Scarlett loses everything: her home, her family and two husbands. She eventually marries the dashing Captain Rhett Butler, a man as passionate and determined as she is. Her troubles have barely begun.

Scarlett does much to invite the reader's disapproval, but her indomitable spirit and her refusal to accept defeat in hopeless situations wins our admiration, and we crave her survival. The book is a thousand pages long but the protagonists are so lively, and the story so rich in events, it is hard to put down.

**Jenny Nimmo**

### Next?

There are sequels! Try *Scarlett* by Alexandra Ripley or Alice Randall's *The Wind Done Gone*, which tells the story from the slaves' point of view.

For another romance on an epic scale, try *Katherine* by Anya Seton. (UTBG 221)

Also set during the American Civil War, *Cold Mountain* by Charles Frazier is about a soldier's dangerous journey home to the woman he loves.

# GOODBYE TO ALL THAT  Robert Graves  ✹ ✹ ✹

### Next?

If this gives you a taste for Graves, try *I, Claudius* next.

Siegfried Sassoon not only wrote some of the best war poetry in existence, he also wrote excellent semi-autobiographical novels – look out for *Memoirs of an Infantry Officer*. (UTBG 261)

Or for a wonderful account of trying to give up being a hero and aiming to be ordinary, read T.E. Lawrence's *The Mint*.

This autobiography covers the first 33 years of poet and author Robert Graves's extraordinary life. He joins the army when he leaves school in 1914 and, for me, this is the best account of the trenches we have. The book, with its matter-of-fact and darkly humorous tone (it is often very funny), reminds me of the old men's stories I heard as a child of something that sounded just like hell. Robert Graves is the most independent-minded of soldiers, and his is an honest, though very personal, story that gives us a glimpse of Siegfried Sassoon, T.E. Lawrence (of Arabia) and Wilfred Owen.

There are lots of First World War novels about the unfairness and butchery of the trenches. Read this wonderful real-life book about a young man determined to be a good soldier, whilst refusing to accept anyone's principles but his own.

**Sally Prue**

# GOOD OMENS Terry Pratchett and Neil Gaiman ✳ ✳

**Next?**

If you haven't read Terry Pratchett's **Discworld** series then do so at once. (UTBG 107)

Neil Gaiman's imagination is elaborately wonderful, as are all his books. Try *Neverwhere*, about a world under London, or the eerie *The Wolves in the Walls*, a picture book that will make you shiver.

*Good Omens* is parodying Richmal Crompton's *Just William*; try it and see how. (UTBG 221)

Terry Pratchett's **Discworld** novels are fabulous. I didn't think he could get any better. Then he got together with Neil Gaiman, the incredibly dark writer of **The Sandman** comics, and the result was *Good Omens*. This book starts out much like the **William** books: small boy playing with his dog in a rural setting. Then it turns out that the little boy is the Antichrist, his dog is the hound of hell and Armageddon is approaching. The story also features a reliable prophet, an angel, a demon, the four horsemen of the apocalypse and the explanation of the satanic origins of the M25 motorway. It's undoubtedly the best book ever written.

**Anthony Reuben**

---

# THE GOOSE GIRL Shannon Hale ✳

Anidora-Kiladra Talianna Isilee, Crown Princess of Kilindree, spent the first years of her life listening to her aunt's incredible stories and learning the language of the birds. She feels a failure as a princess: only her father and her horse Falada accept her as she is. Her only friend is her maid ... or so she thinks.

When her father dies, Ani inherits the throne, and has to marry the prince of the neighbouring country in order to avoid a war. The plot twists and Ani becomes a goose girl. Falada plays a memorable role as Ani learns to understand herself before she can overcome her enemies. The book is a beautifully written tale of magic, excitement and courage.

**Brenda Marshall**

**Next?**

More Shannon Hale! The sequels to this are *Enna Burning* and *River Secrets* – but look out for another story inspired by Grimm, *The Book of a Thousand Days*.

*Fairy Tales* by the Brothers Grimm has an earlier version of 'The Goose Girl'.

*Beauty* by Robin McKinley is a retelling of the story of 'Beauty and the Beast'. (UTBG 36)

# The GORMENGHAST trilogy
## Mervyn Peake

The TV version of **Gormenghast** made me wonder why I'd so loved this book when I first read it. Then I realised TV had bypassed romance in favour of the grotesque. Titus Groan, with his lilac eyes, heir to a dust-clogged palace, vast but claustrophobic as a tomb – clambers his way out of it through the best piece of world-creation in all literature, to discover a whole other world, sunlit and vibrant.

The characters are monstrous but riveting. The rites and rituals that rule palace life are spectacularly zany. To break out of Gormenghast is to escape everything fusty, ancient, suffocating, dull, sterile and pointless... It's about being a teenage rebel, I suppose (though it never occurred to me then).

The trilogy grows stranger as it goes along. Mervyn Peake was a sick man, getting progressively more ill as he completed this massive masterpiece. By the time I reached *Titus Alone*, it was all getting a little too strange... But see what you think.

**Geraldine McCaughrean**

When I first read the **Gormenghast** trilogy by Mervyn Peake I had never come across anything like it in my life. Over 30 years later, I still haven't. How to describe it? It's fantasy in one sense, set in an imaginary time, in the endless, winding castle of Gormenghast and its numberless towers and passages and uncountable rooms and halls. But you search in vain for wizards and soldiers here. The characters are all unique – bizarre and distorted in one way, but incredibly real and human in others. They have more life in their little fingers than you'll find in all Tolkien's hordes. The prose is gothic and perfect, every sentence ending on exactly the right note. It's a unique invention.

**Melvin Burgess**

VINTAGE **PEAKE**

Gormenghast Trilogy

### Next?

World-building as complete as this is rare, as is the extraordinary depth of Peake's Gothic imagination. But do try Tolkien's **The Lord of the Rings** (UTBG 242) and see if you agree with Melvin's estimation of his and Peake's respective talents.

There are an awful lot of fantasy novels out there; maybe you could try something like *Lord Foul's Bane* by Stephen Donaldson.

Or the very different *American Gods* by Neil Gaiman.

And see our fantasy feature on pp. 40–41 for more ideas.

# GOSSIP GIRL series Cecily von Ziegesar

Welcome to the world of the Gossip Girl – privileged, catty, and irresistibly impossible to put down. With her long-running series, Cecily von Ziegesar has coined a new phrase in teen literature: the 'guilty-pleasure read'. She's also spawned a whole host of wannabe titles, but if you're really looking for a juicy read as delicious as gossip itself, look no further than the original.

In book one, you meet all the major players: popular Blair; her ex-best friend, Serena; Nate, the boy they're both fighting over; Dan, the sensitive, artistic type; and many others. In the Manhattan-élite world of the Gossip Girl, anything can happen – sex is consequence-free, alcohol flows no matter the age, and money is absolutely no object. It is a fun, fast-paced and utterly fantastical look at teenage life that, while it may not bear even a slight resemblance to your own life, will certainly entertain you from the beginning of the series to the end.

**Stacy Cantor**

### Next?

Or try the same author's **It Girl** series, starring one of the Gossip Girl's younger sisters.

There's more New York and more cattiness in Lisa Harrison's *The Clique*.

Or what about Sarah Dessen's *Just Listen*, for a slightly grittier take on teen relationships. (UTBG 220)

Or what about high society circa 1899? According to Anna Godbersen it was just as cut-throat! Read *Luxe*, *Rumours*, *Envy* and *Splendour* to see how.

# LE GRAND MEAULNES Alain-Fournier

### Next?

If you're hunting this down, remember it is also published as *The Lost Estate*. Sadly, Alain-Fournier died before writing any other books. But why not try *Claudine at School* (UTBG 81) by Colette, another French coming-of-age story.

As is the dark and adult *Bonjour Tristesse* by Françoise Sagan. (UTBG 52)

Read our feature about coming-of-age books on pp. 314–315.

A magical novel set in the dreamy hinterland between childhood and adulthood. Augustin Meaulnes, 17 and bursting with energy, if a bit rude, explodes into life at a small rural boarding school in France. Confiding only in his friend François, Meaulnes departs on a journey involving a house in the woods in the dead of night, enchanted revelries, scarlet waistcoats and vagabonding in Paris, all of which slip away from our hero as quickly as they present themselves.

In a blend of fantasy and reality, Alain-Fournier conjures a quest for the unobtainable, at the same time painting a memorable portrait of lost love, and lost youth. Marvellous.

**Sara Wheeler**

# THE GRAVEYARD BOOK   Neil Gaiman

**Next?**

Neil Gaiman's *Coraline* is another wonderfully imagined, dark tale. (UTBG 86)

For a quite different afterlife, read Gabrielle Zevin's *Elsewhere*. (UTBG 120)

And if you loved the Riddell pictures as I did, look into his **Edge Chronicles**, written by Paul Stewart (UTBG 119).

*The Graveyard Book* is more than just a book. It is a whole world – a small, wonderful world – that will entrance you for eight chapters, and which you will be very sorry to leave. It's set, as the title suggests, in a graveyard, where young Bod (short for 'Nobody') makes his home after his parents are murdered on page one. Here Bod finds himself a new family and new friends – most of them long dead – a set-up which allows Gaiman's macabre imagination to run fantastically wild. And along with the great characters and friendships there's a page-turner of a story (tender coming-of-age with bits of thriller, too…), some delightful humour, and as a bonus a set of typically superb illustrations by Chris Riddell. (Or Dave McKean, depending on your preferred edition.) And I kept wondering how he was going to pull off an adequate ending – but he manages something that's moving without being sentimental – a brilliant balancing act. It's impeccable, really. I rarely say this, but this is pretty nearly perfect.

**Daniel Hahn**

# THE GREAT BLUE YONDER   Alex Shearer

'You sometimes imagine it … being dead and how everyone will be so upset.' But when Harry dies – killed by a lorry – it's harder than he'd imagined. He's desperate to un-say his parting words to his sister: 'You'll be sorry when I'm dead'. Also to say goodbye to his friends, who aren't missing him as he'd envisaged. And someone called Bob Anderson has taken over his life! Slowly, he realises everyone has a different way of accepting his going – and that his arch-enemy Jelly Donkins actually liked him!

In turns funny, sad and hugely thought provoking, this book about being dead makes you think about how to live better – and reveals where ghosts go in the afternoons!

**Helen Simmons**

**Next?**

You may also like Alex Shearer's other books; each one is very different and they are all about unusual people and events. My favourite is **The Speed of the Dark**.

A book that packs a strong emotional punch, and looks at the aftermath of a terrible car crash, is Gayle Forman's **If I Stay**.

Or read **Elsewhere**, a book about death, or rather life after death. It's brilliantly original and beautifully written. (UTBG 120)

# GREAT EXPECTATIONS  Charles Dickens

**Next?**

A prolonged diet of Dickens can be a little bit rich, so have a break before you start your next meal, and then try the wonderful *Nicholas Nickleby*.

*The Moonstone* by Dickens's contemporary Wilkie Collins, is a mystery involving a missing jewel. (UTBG 269)

*Jack Maggs* by Peter Carey is the story of a convict returning from Australia to seek justice – and on the way he runs into a certain Mr Charles Dickens...

Pip starts off in life as a humble country boy. As we follow him through the years, we encounter escaped convicts, spooky graveyards, unrequited love, and of course the unforgettable Miss Havisham, languishing in her eerie, dust-filled house, still in her bridal gown from years before.

Reading Dickens is like watching the performance of a play given just for you. This was one of the first 'grown-up' books that ever made me cry – and laugh out loud, too. It frightened and delighted me. It made me realise that those were the things that good books did. It did all the things that Dickens, the consummate actor, the writer with boundless energy and more feelings sometimes than even his enormous heart could contain, loved to do and does better than anyone else.

P.S. Make sure you read the 'Cancelled Conclusion', the alternative ending Dickens discarded, and make up your own mind whether he was right.

**Michael Cronin**

# THE GREAT GATSBY  F. Scott Fitzgerald

A compact but engrossing read, *The Great Gatsby* propels you into a world of fast cars, fancy cocktails and the cool of 1920s America. Through the narrator, Nick Carraway, we meet an array of characters who epitomise the glamour, opulence and wealth of the Jazz Age. Everything revolves around Jay Gatsby and his legendary parties in rich and trendy West Egg. However, Gatsby soon discovers that he can't have it all. He thought his long-held love for Nick's cousin Daisy was mutual, but despite her feelings for him, she remains with her adulterous husband, Tom.

Fitzgerald immerses us in life in the fast lane, but the pace inevitably burns out and the decadence descends into a gripping and tragic climax...

**Next?**

More American literature – Salinger's *For Esmé – with Love and Squalor* (UTBG 138) or Hemingway's *A Moveable Feast*.

Also Truman Capote's *Breakfast at Tiffany's*. Not the same period, but something about the yearning strikes the same chords. (UTBG 59)

Or more F. Scott Fitzgerald: try *Tender Is the Night*.

**Melanie Palmer**

# THE GREAT RAILWAY BAZAAR  Paul Theroux

**Next?**

Move on to Theroux's *The Old Patagonian Express*.

Jenny Diski writes wry and well observed travelogues that often end up being as much about her as the country she's in. Try *Skating to Antarctica*.

Bill Bryson writes very, very funny books about his travels; the best is definitely the fabulous one about Britain – *Notes from a Small Island*. (UTBG 288)

Paul Theroux is the doyen of modern travel writing and to my mind this is his best book. A railway odyssey from London's Victoria station to the Trans-Siberian Express, with a cornucopia of journeys in between, including The Mandalay Express from Rangoon, a local Burmese train to Naung-Peng and, in Vietnam during the war, a rattling ride from Saigon to Bien Hoa. Purposeless travel for fun and adventure by a writer with a gift for luminous prose, as well as an eye for the telling detail and a robust sense of humour (not to mention irony). There is acerbic social comment, and plenty of serious stuff here, too.

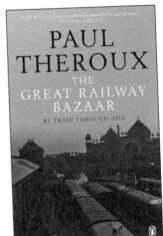

**Sara Wheeler**

# THE GREENGAGE SUMMER  Rumer Godden

Don't attempt to grow up without reading this book; it has old-fashioned charm, it has the delicious romance of summer, and first, unsuitable love; the struggle to cast off the shackles of family and the toppling, incredible sense of being able to follow your instincts even though they are confusing. Set in lush champagne country, the landscape echoes the action as summer shifts from dappled beauty into over-ripe stifling intensity and the children and adults inhabiting Les Oillets break boundaries and grow and change. It is a rites-of-passage novel every bit as lyrical as *Le Grand Meaulnes*.

**Raffaella Barker**

**Next?**

Another Rumer Godden? Try the intense novel of suppressed passion, *Black Narcissus*.

*Le Grand Meaulnes* by Alain-Fournier is a fabulous of coming-of-age story, too! (UTBG 164)

Or for another novel of sexual awakening, try L.P. Hartley's *The Go-Between*. (UTBG 159)

And don't miss our feature on books about coming of age on pp. 314–315.

# GULF  Robert Westall

War is a central theme of many of Westall's novels, including the classic *The Machine-Gunners*. In *Gulf*, however, he moves away from World War II, which forms the background of much of his fiction, and chooses a more contemporary conflict. He sets his story against the background of the first Gulf War in the early 1990s. Twelve-year-old Figgis is somehow linked to Latif, a boy caught up in the horror. Figgis's older brother Tom is forced to witness his younger brother's torment as he empathises with Latif's experiences. The whole family is affected by Figgis's troubles and Westall explores family relationships with a sure touch.

Great fiction has the ability to make us see through somebody else's eyes, walk in somebody else's shoes, feel the rhythms of somebody else's life and, in *Gulf*, Westall has produced a great piece of fiction.

**Alan Gibbons**

**Next?**

More Robert Westall? Try *The Machine-Gunners* (UTBG 251) or *Blitzcat* for very different looks at war.

Another two boys involved on different sides of another war? *Crusade* by Elizabeth Laird.

*All Quiet on the Western Front* is a classic fictional look at the First World War. (UTBG 19)

Or try Peter Dickinson's *AK*, about a coup in a fictional African country.

# GULLIVER  Martin Jenkins and Chris Riddell

**Next?**

More political satire? Try the fabulous *Vanity Fair* by William M. Thackeray.

Chris Riddell collaborated with Paul Stewart on *Muddle Earth* and *Beyond the Deepwoods* (UTBG 119). And you really have to read Jenkins and Riddell's retelling of Cervantes's classic, *Don Quixote*.

Why am I recommending that you read a picture-book retelling of a long 18th-century novel? In part because of the genius of the original, Jonathan Swift's brilliant satire *Gulliver's Travels*. Martin Jenkins's retelling inevitably loses a lot of the edge and detail of Swift's novel, but the story and the inventiveness and the satire are still there. But it's mainly for the pictures. Few people can do the things Chris Riddell can with a picture – he's part of a great tradition of English cartoonists who have a great eye for character and a wonderfully precise way with a pen that captures these figures – absurd and pompous or spiky and nasty – with great wit and imagination. The perfect illustrator for Swift, in fact. And of all his work, Riddell's *Gulliver* pictures are my favourites, feeding off Swift's ideas to produce a catalogue of figures that expose all our human follies and frailties for what they are.

**Daniel Hahn**

# HAMLET   William Shakespeare

The ghost of your father, the dead king, appears to you, demanding revenge for his murder by your uncle – the same uncle now wearing your father's crown and married to your mother. But is the ghost truly your father's spirit, or a devil in disguise, tempting you to commit the mortal sin? And while you try to decide this you are in danger, because your uncle is suspicious and is planning your death...

I hated Shakespeare at school. I couldn't understand the plays, and was convinced that no one really liked them. People just pretended they did, to seem intelligent. But I wasn't used to reading poetry, and one day realised that I was mentally putting a full stop at the end of each line, chopping the words up into nonsense. So I read 'To be or not to be –' while paying strict attention to the punctuation. A revelation! I was a depressed teenager, and it was as if Shakespeare had put my mood into words – 'How weary, stale, flat, and unprofitable / Seem to me all the uses of this world'.

I read the rest of the play and loved it. The drama, humour and magnificent poetry had been there all along – I'd just been blind to them. Give Bill a chance. He really did write the most amazing stuff.

**Susan Price**

'It has everything – intrigue, romance, politics, violence, revenge, jealousy, wit. It plays itself out on such a grand scale'
KENNETH BRANAGH

*William* SHAKESPEARE

### Next?

More Shakespeare, of course. *Romeo and Juliet* and *A Midsummer Night's Dream* are old favourites.

Or if you find reading plays hard, have you read his beautiful *Sonnets*? Or look out for the manga and comic versions of the plays.

Shakespeare is a character in Susan Cooper's *King of Shadows* and in Geoffrey Trease's *Cue for Treason* (UTBG 91).

*Dating Hamlet* by Lisa Fiedler tells the story from Ophelia's point of view.

# THE HANDMAID'S TALE Margaret Atwood ✸✸✸

**Next?**

If you like Margaret Atwood's style, look for her science-fiction tale, *Oryx and Crake*.

Another good mix of science fiction and feminism? Read Ursula Le Guin's *The Left Hand of Darkness*. (UTBG 235)

Or try a world where all women are being forced to have children – *The Year of Compulsory Childbirth* by Nigel Farringdon.

Or seek out Carrie Ryan's bleakly unsettling tale of truth, lies and zombies, *The Forest of Hands and Teeth*.

In some ways this book is really science fiction, but you'll find no spaceships or laser guns here. The story opens in a high-school gymnasium, converted into a dormitory and patrolled by 'aunts' armed with electric cattle prods. It is a frightening near-future scenario, where men have taken away women's independence by the simple method of cutting off their access to money.

The handmaid of the title is a young woman named Offred ('Of Fred'), whose job it is to have babies for Fred's infertile wife. She has no choice in this, because much of the population is infertile following a nuclear disaster. Right from the start we know this is going to be a sinister tale, and it becomes more chilling with every page.

**Katherine Roberts**

# HANGOVER SQUARE Patrick Hamilton ✸✸✸

This has to be one of the most grimly funny books of all time – grim because of Hamilton's evocation of a dark, seedy, miserably anxious London just before the outbreak of World War II.

George Harvey Bone is totally caught up in his volatile, ever-changing world, but things get infinitely worse when he pursues the thoroughly awful (but attractive) Netta. Watching Bone slide further and further into dissolute decay makes for compelling reading (and offers a useful warning!).

There's not much to enjoy in the milieu of Hamilton's novel, and yet we do care deeply about Bone and his plight in this gripping (sometimes melodramatic) book.

**Jon Appleton**

**Next?**

If you enjoyed this, look out for Hamilton's *Twenty Thousand Streets Under the Sky*, a novel sequence full of loss and vivid descriptions of pre-war London's underbelly.

Irvine Welsh's *Trainspotting* could be considered a modern-day version of this book. (UTBG 401)

William Boyd's *A Good Man in Africa* is another comedy – lighter in tone – about a man finding himself increasingly adrift in circumstances not entirely of his own making.

# HARD CASH  Kate Cann

**Next?**

There are two sequels: *Shacked Up* and *Speeding*. Kate Cann writes brilliantly about relationships, so try *Footloose*, about three girls going on holiday together and *Escape* (UTBG 122). Look out, too, for her supernatural romances; *Leaving Poppy* (UTBG 234) and *Possessing Rain*.

Another good contemporary teen read is *Carwash* by Lesley Howarth. (UTBG 67)

A series about bring very rich? Try the **Gossip Girl** series by Cecily Von Ziegesar, about a group of outrageous New York friends. (UTBG 164)

Richard Steele is a hard-up art student – and his life is blighted by his lack of cash. In this very funny, highly readable contemporary novel, the author takes a look at what happens when Rich makes some serious money from getting an ad agency interested in his drawings. Suddenly the girl he's been lusting after for ages actually seems interested in him, and he enters a world of trendy adult parties, posh restaurants and designer gear. But is selling his talent the same as selling out? And is Portia, the girl of his dreams, worth the trouble it takes to get her? With her customary light touch, Kate Cann answers these questions and creates a very believable hero in Rich.

**Sherry Ashworth**

# THE HARD MAN OF THE SWINGS
## Jeanne Willis

Young Mick goes through difficult, unsettled times as he's forced to leave his mother, stepfather and beloved little brother, and move in with a father he barely knows. And life with his father's family is complicated; they variously ignore him, scold him and lust after him. So it's no surprise that Mick soon starts getting into fights, and then his troubles get worse, much worse – though I mustn't tell you how...

This story, set in post World War II Britain, is remarkable, and the character of Mick is, too – he's totally realistic, he's positive, he's tough – you'll love him, and you'll worry about him. Oh, and the ending of the book – the last few lines – is amazing. It'll just blow you away.

**Daniel Hahn**

**Next?**

Jeanne Willis writes uncompromisingly. Look out for (my own favourite) *Naked without a Hat* (UTBG 275), *Shamanka* – which is a stunning look at the nature of magic and illusion – or *Rocket Science*.

For another story of a boy facing troubles and surviving, somehow, read Frank McCourt's *Angela's Ashes*; this one's true, but you'll really wish that it wasn't. (UTBG 22)

# HARRY POTTER series J.K. Rowling

We first meet Harry as a small baby; his parents are dead and the only family he's got left are his muggle (non-wizard) aunt and uncle, Petunia and Vernon Dursley. Harry has a painful upbringing; he is bullied by his cousin Dudley and forced to live in a dingy cupboard under the stairs.

During his time at Hogwarts School for Witchcraft and Wizardry, Harry develops from a young boy into an adolescent who seems to get moodier by the chapter! But he still has time to save the day, with the help of his loyal friends Ron Weasley and Hermione Granger.

J.K. Rowling has written a colourful masterpiece full of suspense, action and magic. Millions of people have read and loved these books, and I'm sure they'll continue to do so for decades!

**Olivia Armes, age 14**

> **Next?**
>
> In order they are: *Harry Potter and the Philosopher's Stone*; *HP and the Chamber of Secrets*; *HP and the Prisoner of Azkaban*; *HP and the Goblet of Fire*; *HP and the Order of the Phoenix*; *HP and the Half-Blood Prince*; *HP and the Deathly Hallows*.
>
> Another wizarding school? Try Ursula Le Guin's *A Wizard of Earthsea*. (UTBG 442)
>
> For a classic school story, try Anthony Buckeridge's **Jennings** series.

# HATCHET Gary Paulsen

> **Next?**
>
> There are sequels: *The Call*, *Winter* and *The Return*.
>
> Another great Paulsen is *The Beet Fields*, about a boy learning to survive on his own. (UTBG 37)
>
> Or look out for Roddy Doyle's *Wilderness*, about family, dogs and survival.
>
> Or Tim Wynne Jones's tougher book about a boy who escapes his bullying father by running away into the Canadian wilderness, *The Survival Game*.

Fourteen-year-old Brian is the sole survivor of a plane crash in the Canadian wilderness. Stranded hundreds of miles from civilisation, he must survive a harsh, unforgiving environment. All he has to help him are his wits and a small hatchet.

At first, Brian makes mistake after mistake – one of them almost fatal – as he attempts to build a shelter, find food, protect himself from wild animals and make fire. Then, slowly, he learns to look after himself. As his body and mind adapt to his new life, he undergoes a profound change in outlook and attitude.

*Hatchet* is a gripping story of survival against all odds – of a teenager from the city up against nature in the raw. It is also the story of a boy coming to a new understanding of himself, his abilities and the natural world.

**Graham Gardner**

# THE HAUNTING OF ALAIZABEL CRAY
Chris Wooding

**Next?**

Chris Wooding writes dark and atmospheric novels. Try *The Storm Thief* and *Poison*. Or look for *Malice*; it's half ordinary novel, half graphic novel!

Or read **The Wardstone Chronicles** by Joseph Delaney – Thomas Ward is the seventh son of a seventh son. In theory he can do battle with demons and spirits, but first he has to learn his trade...

Marcus Sedgwick writes wonderfully shaded, atmospheric books. Try *The Book of Dead Days*.

If you want a macabre, eerie story set in a vividly portrayed cityscape, full of action, with foulsome enemies and ghoulish creatures, then this is the book for you. Hideous things lurk within the labyrinth of the city's Old Quarter, and those who venture out at night are easy prey for the wolves and murderers that stalk the crooked streets, and for creatures far more deadly – the wych-kin. But evil disguised is the deadliest kind of all. Behind the façade of wealth and charity that surrounds the uppermost levels of society lies a terrifying pact with the wych-kin that threatens humankind's very existence. And the key to the conspiracy? The enigmatic Alaizabel Cray.

**Brenda Marshall**

# THE HEART IS A LONELY HUNTER
Carson McCullers

The Depression still grips McCullers' small town in the Deep South on the eve of World War II, with rumours of fascist activity drifting from Europe. A deaf-mute jeweller's-engraver called Singer takes the pulse of the segregated community through a year, as black and white townsfolk alike tell him their troubles. They are all lonely and desperate, but Singer is lonelier still since his one friend was incarcerated in an asylum – unsatisfactory though that friendship was, as his role of confidant only worked one way. This book is intensely sad, but rewarding for the depiction of human relationships and of people who fail to see that they already have what they need.

**Geraldine Brennan**

**Next?**

More by the same author? Try *The Ballad of the Sad Café and Other Stories*.

From 1940–1941, W.H. Auden, Benjamin Britten, Paul and Jane Bowles, Gypsy Rose Lee and Carson McCullers shared a house in Brooklyn. The story is told in Sherill Tippins's **February House**.

Julius Lester's **Guardian** is set in the turbulent Deep South of 1946.

For a different sort of cold-and-lonely: *The Great Gatsby* by F. Scott Fitzgerald. (UTBG 166)

# HEART OF DARKNESS  Joseph Conrad

Say Joseph Conrad to most people and this is the book that they will think of; between the covers of this slim novel lurks an unforgettable indictment of man.

The premise is simple: Marlowe (the narrator) is employed by a trading company to locate their most effective operative, who is living in the heart of the Congo. The journey that Marlowe undertakes, the man he finds at the end of his travels, and his dawning insight into himself, form the bulk of the narrative.

It's not an easy read, but when Frances Ford Coppola wanted to make a film about the horrors of the Vietnam War and the way in which it had corrupted good men, this was the book that he turned to.

**Laura Hutchings**

### Next?

*Lord Jim* has always been my favourite Conrad novel – not only is Marlowe again the narrator but it also shares the theme of a man discovering essential truths about himself.

If you want to know how this turn-of-the-19th-century novel could be adapted for 20th-century Hollywood, read Michael Herr's book *Dispatches*, and then watch *Apocalypse Now* to see how the two books were melded into a cinematic masterpiece.

# A HEARTBREAKING WORK OF STAGGERING GENIUS  Dave Eggers

### Next?

Dave Eggers's subsequent book, *You Shall Know Our Velocity*, is about a road trip.

The original crazy road trip with a friend is Jack Kerouac's *On the Road*. (UTBG 297)

*The Zigzag Kid* by David Grossman has a 13th birthday go terribly wrong, as the son of a famous detective is whisked away by his archenemy on a journey of discovery. (UTBG 453)

Written on pure joy and adrenaline, this autobiographical book more than lives up to its title, which pokes fun at the things reviewers write. This is all the more amazing considering its subject. The deaths of both parents leave Dave in charge of his younger brother, Toph. To help them deal with their grief, he gives Toph the most anarchic education possible, struggling with the demands of suddenly becoming a single teenage parent while also trying to run a magazine and have a love life.

A rip-roaring journey into the heart of modern America, dealing with heartbreak with a swagger, this may be the funniest book you ever read. With such a humble author, how could you miss it?

**Ariel Kahn**

# HENRY TUMOUR Anthony McGowan

**Next?**

Anthony McGowan is an adventurous and exhilarating writer; try something else of his, either *Hellbent* or *The Knife That Killed Me* (UTBG 229).

A less foul-mouthed look at terminal illness can be found in Jenny Downham's *Before I Die*. (UTBG 37)

Or how about another voice that lives inside a boy's head? Try *Freewill* by Chris Lynch.

This remarkable teenage novel tackles a subject still considered taboo. It deals with 'the big issues' – Why are we here? Why do we die? – with pathos, laugh-out-loud humour and a perfectly judged lightness of touch.

Hector, a geeky schoolboy, has a brain tumour, a character in his own right called Henry. While Hector is the unassuming product of his liberal background, Henry is more anarchic. Cunning, fearless and cool, he advises Hector how to beat the bullies and get the girl – though the stunner Henry selects is not the one Hector would choose for himself.

All the while, tension is mounting as the visit to the hospital for surgery approaches; surgery that will lead to the death of one or both protagonists. Hilarious, wise and totally unputdownable.

**Paul Stewart**

# HERE LIES ARTHUR Philip Reeve

How do heroes come to be heroes? What is the truth behind the legends we love? Where does history end and mythology begin? And what is the point of telling stories, anyway? In *Here Lies Arthur*, Philip Reeve turns his attention to one of the greatest heroes of them all, King Arthur. Gwyna, a feisty servant girl, escapes when her master's home is destroyed by soldiers. She is rescued by Merlin, who uses her to pull off the most significant practical joke in British history, then sends her to Arthur's court disguised as a boy. And that's just the beginning. This is a gripping page-turner of an adventure that shows true power lies not with the sword, but with the storyteller.

**Next?**

There's another complex look at the character of Arthur in T.H. White's, *The Once and Future King*. Or try Rosemary Sutcliff's *Sword at Sunset* or Bernard Cornwell's *The Winter King*, both of which are more realistic.

Philip Reeve is a stunning writer; look out for anything he's written, particularly *Mortal Engines* and its sequels. (UTBG 270)

Or for another story re-imagined, look for Robin McKinley's lush take on the 'Beauty and the Beast' fairy tale: *Beauty*. (UTBG 36)

**Antonia Honeywell**

# HERO   Perry Moore

**Next?**

There are more superheroes in Michael Chabon's *The Amazing Adventures of Kavalier and Clay*. (UTBG 20)

A book that deals warmly with growing up gay is David Levithan's *Boy Meets Boy*. (UTBG 56)

Or more superheroes? Try *Superpowers* by David J. Schwartz, in which a group of friends wake up one morning and find that overnight they've developed the most amazing superpowers.

There are some books that you enter almost as if you're living the story. For me, this is one of those books. Not that I'm that interested in superheroes (and this is about a world where superheroes are real, and everywhere) or that I'm a boy (and the central character here is definitely a boy), but somehow the world that Moore has created is so vivid and the characters so perfectly drawn, that none of that matters. What matters is Thom Creed, an average teen whose life is in turmoil. His dad's an ex-hero (he apparently did something un-heroic and is scorned by everyone) and Thom, well Thom's pretty sure he's gay. Oh, and he's inherited superpowers, too – if only he could master them.

This is a book about fitting in, about learning to be who you are, and about confronting pre-supposition and prejudice. But there's no preaching here, just a warm-hearted, funny, moving and completely believable story of one boy growing up different.

**Leonie Flynn**

# HEROES   Robert Cormier

Two men, both with medals for bravery, both survivors of World War II – but one comes home to Frenchtown to kill the other. Why?

Prompted by the 50th anniversary celebrations of D-Day, Cormier wrote this book to express his ideas about heroism. Larry and Francis are inextricably linked by their involvement with Nicole Renard, but guilt and the desire for revenge, rather than love, are the forces that really drive this narrative.

I've never read a Cormier novel that didn't make me think long and hard about the subject matter – and this book is no exception. Personally, I find it hard not to feel sorry for Francis, but you'll have to make up your own mind about him!

**Laura Hutchings**

**Next?**

More Cormier? Try *After the First Death*. (UTBG 12)

A series about surviving invasion in some future war is John Marsden's **Tomorrow** series, starting with *Tomorrow, When the War Began*.

Slightly more challenging war novels include *Strange Meeting* (UTBG 380) by Susan Hill and *All Quiet on the Western Front* (UTBG 19) by Erich Maria Remarque.

# HEROES OF THE VALLEY Jonathan Stroud

**Next?**

Like heroic tales? Try **The Lord of the Rings** by J.R.R. Tolkien. (UTBG 242)

Or for a stunning fantasy that reads like realism try the **Old Kingdom** series by Garth Nix, start with *Lirael*.

Or for more Jonathan Stroud, try his best-known series, the **Bartimaeus** trilogy, which begins with *The Amulet of Samarkand* (UTBG 21).

All his life Halli has grown up listening to old legends of the Valley – of the bloodthirsty Trows and the great heroes who sacrificed their lives to defeat them. Now Halli longs for an adventure of his own; but the Valley is a peaceful place, and his daydreaming antics are angering the farmers. His days are filled with boredom and chores until a practical joke ignites an old blood feud and thrusts him into a dangerous quest of his own – one that will challenge his vision of heroism and uncover the dark secret of the Valley.

Jonathan Stroud gives us an unusual, unforgettable hero in an adventure that questions the nature of heroes and the power that legends hold over our lives.

**Matthew Humpage**

# HEX Rhiannon Lassiter

Have you ever sat in front of a computer and really, really wanted to be able to just mesh with it – to make it do exactly what you want? Well, thanks to a mutant gene, that's what Raven can do. Trouble is, the government don't approve of Hexes, and if they found her, she'd be dead – or, worse, used as a lab-rat for experimentation. But Raven's clever and, with her brother, Wraith, she's hunting for their sister who's a prisoner somewhere in the city.

Set far into the future, this is totally credible sci-fi. But Raven, Wraith and the people they meet are all like you and me – just with cooler hardware and more amazing abilities!

**Leonie Flynn**

**Next?**

There are two sequels – *Hex: Shadows* and *Hex: Ghosts*. Or look out for Rhiannon Lassiter's terrifying ghost story, *Bad Blood*.

Or try her **Borderland** trilogy, about a group of friends who accidentally wreak havoc when they travel into a parallel universe; books two and three are about their efforts to put everything right.

For more utterly real sci-fi, try Diana Wynne Jones's *The Dark Lord of Derkholm*. (UTBG 96)

# LOVE, SEX AND RELATIONSHIPS –
## where it's all at
### by Catherine Robinson

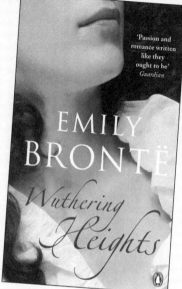

'Passion and romance written like they ought to be'
*Guardian*

EMILY BRONTË

*Wuthering Heights*

When I was growing up – when dinosaurs roamed the land – there were no books for teenagers. Strange, but true. For a keen reader, there was nothing to bridge the gap between kiddies' books and fiction for adults. Oh, sure, there were books which appealed, either because of their style or subject matter or both (some of which feature in this guide) but there was nothing specifically aimed at teens, which dealt with the complex yet oh-so-common issues and concerns that make up your average teenager's life.

If ever there is a time in your life when you could do with some reassurance that you're not alone, that whatever you're currently going through, there is, amazingly enough, somebody else out there who's been through exactly the same thing, it's when you're in your teenage years. (Fiction can be hugely comforting for this, in a way that all the self-help books in the world, for all their practical worthiness, simply cannot.) And what is the one topic that, almost without exception, unites us all? That begins to grab us at that age, and continues to be a subject of huge interest and enjoyment, concern and anxiety until we are old and grey? Yup, you've guessed (although the title of this essay may well have given you a bit of a clue) – I'm talking about lurve. Sex. Relationships. Whatever you want to call it, whatever your own particular experience, it's somehow enormously soothing to read a book that strikes a chord, that makes you break off in the middle of a sentence and stare into the middle distance and nod and think: 'Yes, that's *just* how it feels.' Which is not to say, of course, that this only happens in books with this subject matter, only that it is a genre that seems to me to be

---

### DOOMED LOVE

*Anna Karenina* by Leo Tolstoy

*Tess of the d'Urbervilles* by Thomas Hardy

*Thérèse Raquin* by Émile Zola

*Noughts and Crosses* by Malorie Blackman

*Wuthering Heights* by Emily Brontë

*Madame Bovary* by Gustave Flaubert

*The Romance of Tristan and Iseult* retold by Joseph Bédier

*The End of the Affair* by Graham Greene

particularly relevant to teenage readers.

Don't get me wrong – I don't want to make any naff claims that I write love 'n' relationship books 'to help people' (if I wanted to do that I'd have become a doctor, or a teacher, or something – if only I'd had the brains!). No – the main reason I'm that most curious of beasts, a Teen Author, is because I am blessed, or possibly cursed, with almost total recall of how it felt to be growing up amidst a sea of confusion, raging hormones and adults who just didn't understand what it was like to be me, and when I began to write, it just felt right to reflect some of those feelings in the kind of books I'd have grabbed off the shelves had they been around in my own teenage years.

Things have moved on a lot since then, of course – even since I started. Now, practically anything goes. I remember when Judy Blume's *Forever* (UTBG 139) first came out, to teachers' and librarians' apoplexy – it was the first teen book that dealt with the ins and outs (if you'll pardon the phrase) of sex in a realistic, wholly honest and, I have to say, ultimately unromantic way. Now the likes of Melvin Burgess have pushed the envelope just about as far as it can be pushed, and *Forever* seems pretty tame by comparison (though it's still a great read).

And good on them, I say. Why should teenagers be fobbed off with junior Mills & Boon that paints everything in a rosy glow? Let's tell it like it is, and let the readers decide! That's what I shall carry on doing, at any rate. Because, let's face it, it's all just so *fascinating*...!

MELVIN BURGESS
**Doing It**
*do you remember the first time?*

"Comically toe-curling ...
funny, honest and touching"
*Observer*

---

**FIRST LOVE (or first sex...)**

*Forever* by Judy Blume

*Escape* by Kate Cann

*I Capture the Castle* by Dodie Smith

*Crazy* by Benjamin Lebert

*Doing It* by Melvin Burgess

*How I Live Now* by Meg Rosoff

*Lost and Found* by Valerie Mendes

---

**EXPLORING SEXUALITY**

*The Toll Bridge* by Aidan Chambers

*Doing It* by Melvin Burgess

*Boy Meets Boy* by David Levithan

*Sugar Rush* by Julie Burchill

*Strange Boy* by Paul Magrs

*Oranges Are Not the Only Fruit* by Jeanette Winterson

# HIGH FIDELITY   Nick Hornby

A great read, this. It's about a guy who's trying to come to terms with having just been dumped by his girlfriend. When he's not thinking about sex, which he is almost constantly, he's thinking about music (he works in a second-hand record shop). It's about male obsessions and it's one of the funniest (and saddest, and truest) books I've ever read. If you're female and you want to find out why men are like they are, read it. If you're male, read it and find yourself laughing and cringing, all at the same time. It clues into the mind of just about every teenage boy I've ever known, except that our hero – and this is what makes it even funnier and even sadder – is actually 35 years old.

**Malachy Doyle**

### Next?

More Nick Hornby? Try *About a Boy* (UTBG 10) or the wonderful history of his own musical passions, *31 Songs*.

Or for more men refusing to grow up, read Tony Parsons's *Man and Boy*. (UTBG 254)

*Doing It* by Melvin Burgess is another hard-hitting novel about male obsession. (UTBG 112)

Or for another very funny look at young men, try *The Liar* by Stephen Fry. (UTBG 236)

# THE HIGHWAYMAN'S FOOTSTEPS
## Nicola Morgan

### Next?

Check out the Noyes poem – look particularly for the version illustrated by Charles Keeping.

More Nicola Morgan? Look for the gruesome *Fleshmarket* (UTBG 134) or the thought-provoking *Mondays Are Red*.

If you like realistic history in your novels, try Eleanor Updale's **Montmorency** series. (UTBG 268)

Inspired by Alfred Noyes's poem 'The Highwayman', this adventure is set in 18th-century England. William de Lacey, the son of a High Sheriff, has run away from home to escape his abusive father. Forced to live by his wits, he struggles with the moral conviction that it is wrong to steal, knowing that the alternative is starvation. Then he meets 14-year-old Bess, daughter of a highwayman and a female Robin Hood. Passionate and independent, spurred on by the memory of her parents' cruel fate, Bess conceals a young fugitive from the hated Redcoats and plans her vengeance.

This is a story of honour and bravery found in unexpected places; it deals with love, friendship and loyalty. There is plenty of derring-do and dramatic tension but it is also a novel of great subtlety: *The Highwayman's Footsteps* is as much about thoughts and feelings as it is about action. The story will grip you, and the vivid characters will keep you transfixed. Books don't get much better than this!

**Nikki Gamble**

# HIS DARK MATERIALS trilogy
## Philip Pullman

Philip Pullman manages to make you believe fantasy is real, in this series of three stunning books (*Northern Lights*, *The Subtle Knife* and *The Amber Spyglass*), and each one is better than the last.

A young girl, Lyra, is drawn into a fantastic adventure when her good friend Roger disappears under the most mysterious circumstances. She soon finds out that Mrs Coulter and her evil friends are after her, for some purpose she must discover for herself. An expedition to the North turns into a flight for her life. And now she's started, there's no way of turning back...

Be warned ... once you've started you won't want to be interrupted.

**Hattie Grylls, age 12**

---

### Next?

More Philip Pullman? Some of his best are the historical Sally Lockhart books, starting with **The Ruby in the Smoke**. (UTBG 341)

*The Speed of the Dark* by Alex Shearer is an atmospheric novel about sculptures that come to life – one of them is of a polar bear.

If you're interested in the debate on religion, try C.S. Lewis's *The Screwtape Letters*. (UTBG 344)

Or read **The Lord of the Rings** (UTBG 242) by J.R.R. Tolkien or **The Chronicles of Narnia** by C.S. Lewis for more classic fantasy.

---

If like me you're not a huge fan of fantasy, don't be put off reading this trilogy. Philip Pullman is one of the finest storytellers and once you've been sucked into the intriguing world of *Northern Lights* you'll not want to stop till you've read all three volumes.

Grounding his fictional world in the hauntingly familiar, Pullman weaves reality and imagination with a masterful touch. There are witches, angels, talking polar bears and other much stranger creatures. There is also Oxford and London. Canal boats and cowboys. Milton and cutting-edge science.

Since the publication of **His Dark Materials**, Pullman has famously attacked C.S. Lewis for the religious subtext of his **Narnia** stories. I, for one, read Lewis as a child and remained totally oblivious to any religious message. I have grown up to be a lying, cheating, gambler addicted to Turkish delight, a cannibal, and a devout non-believer to boot. If Lewis was out to Christianise young minds, he failed. Pullman, on the other hand, in his crusade against organised religion, stuffs his trilogy full of imaginary beings and figures from Christian mythology. Despite his intentions, I'd wager that Lyra's adventures will lead far more young readers to religion than **Narnia** ever did. Oh, the irony.

The **His Dark Materials** trilogy cannot be praised enough. Read it and marvel!

**Neil Arksey**

# THE HITCHHIKER'S GUIDE TO
# THE GALAXY Douglas Adams

*The Hitchhiker's Guide to the Galaxy* is the most mind-bogglingly brilliant comedy sci-fi series ever to come out of The Western Spiral Arm of the Galaxy. Packed with hilarious characters and insanely unlikely adventures, *The Hitchhiker's Guide...* propels the unprepared reader into a wormhole of mayhem, where having a guide to the inside of the wormhole simply makes the wormhole a more dangerous place to be. Among the aforementioned crazy characters are two-headed presidential pirates, planet-destroying bureaucrats, murderous beasts and a hapless human in his bathrobe. In chapter one, the Earth is destroyed and it's all downhill from there. 'What?' you say. 'The Earth is destroyed? How can it get any worse than that?' Well it does, a lot worse, but there's a chance that you may survive if you keep your towel close and can tell your waiter in six hundred languages how to make the perfect cup of tea. Good luck, human.

## Next?

The rest of Adams's 'trilogy', continuing with *The Restaurant at the End of the Universe*; *Life, the Universe and Everything*; *So Long, and Thanks for All the Fish* and *Mostly Harmless*. Or part six, written by Eoin Colfer, *And Another Thing....*

There's nothing really like *Hitchhiker...*, but you could try *Good Omens*, in which a devil and an angel conspire to prevent the apocalypse – from London. (UTBG 162)

Or anything by Philip K. Dick. Try *Do Androids Dream of Electric Sheep?*. (UTBG 111)

**Eoin Colfer**

Arthur Dent is an ordinary Earth bloke having a very bad day when his old mate Ford Prefect reveals he's not really an Earthling. Ford, it turns out, is a roving reporter from a distant planet, on Earth to compile an entry for a travel guide to the galaxy. But unfortunately that entry will now be redundant as planet Earth is about to be demolished...

It's a brilliant start to a hilarious book. *The Hitchhiker's Guide to the Galaxy* is a subversive and zany jaunt through space, poking fun along the way at all manner of familiar earthly institutions – science and science fiction, bureaucrats, alcohol, gadgets, geeks, jargon, philosophy and pomposity, to name but a few. The surreal universe Adams creates for his travellers is filled with the ridiculous and the absurd. The adventures of our two heroes are comic to the end.

Tragically, Adams died in his 40s; but thankfully he left us not just *The Hitchhiker's Guide...* but also the rest of the great 'trilogy of five' that it begins.

Do not leave the planet without it.

**Neil Arksey**

# THE HOBBIT   J.R.R. Tolkien

## Next?

**The Lord of the Rings** – Tolkien at his greatest. (UTBG 242)

Diana Wynne Jones creates complex worlds that seem as real as our own (and often weave in and out of ours, too). Try *The Merlin Conspiracy* or the fabulous **Chrestomanci** series, starting wtih *The Lives of Christopher Chant*.

*Eragon*, the first in the **Inheritance Cycle**, is another quest-with-a-dragon book. (UTBG 121)

Or try Lloyd Alexander's **Chronicles of Prydain**, starting with *The Book of Three*, and find out about Taran, the heroic pig keeper!

*The Hobbit* is a prelude to **The Lord of the Rings** trilogy. Since it was written in 1937, this classic tale has delighted generations of readers throughout the world. Bilbo Baggins is a friendly hobbit who is content with his quiet life. One day he receives some strange visitors: a wizard called Gandalf and a band of dwarves. He joins them on a dangerous and exciting quest to raid the treasure hoard of Smaug the dragon. At first Bilbo is nervous and uncertain. He worries about getting back home. As the journey progresses, he encounters elves, goblins and trolls and finds himself surprised by his own enthusiasm. Life will never be the same again.

**Brenda Marshall**

# HOLE IN MY LIFE   Jack Gantos

Jack Gantos is a normal kid; he's lazy, bored, constantly stoned and not really sure what he wants to do, though he kind of thinks he wants to write. Which means college. Which in America means money – something he doesn't have. Then, one day, a guy offers him a way to make ten grand. All he has to do is help sail a boat to New York, and not care that there is over 900 kg of hash hidden in the bows. Great? No way...

Caught and sent to prison, he does time surrounded by violence, rape and misery. Somehow though he still wants to write – and that need alone is what saves him. This is a true story that reads like a thriller – one full of brutality and steeped in drug culture. Read and be shocked – I promise it'll put you off smuggling for life.

**Leonie Flynn**

## Next?

Jack interprets his life through the books he reads. Try Jack Kerouac's **On the Road** (UTBG 297) for the road trip of a lifetime. Or *The House of the Dead* by Fyodor Dostoyevsky, which tells of the author's own imprisonment.

Or try another novel that spins around drugs – *House of the Scorpion* by Nancy Farmer. (UTBG 189)

Jack Gantos has also written the disturbing **Desire Lines**. (UTBG 103)

# HOLES   Louis Sachar

Stanley Yelnats IV is an 11-year-old boy wrongly accused of stealing a pair of trainers. Stanley serves his punishment at Camp Green Lake (where there is no lake), where in the unbearable heat he is made to dig holes: a five-feet x five-feet hole each day, starting at 4:30 every morning!

During breaks in the digging, the reader is introduced to such characters as Kissin' Kate Barlow, an avenging outlaw; Madame Zeroni, a gypsy fortune teller; and of course Stanley Yelnats, a palindrome in himself! It is Stanley's destiny to be the fourth generation to fall foul of Madame Zeroni's curse.

Will Stanley and his new-found friends unravel the mystery of Camp Green Lake and lift the terrible curse that has been laid upon his family?

louis sachar

"Unmistakably powerful"
Philip Pullman, The Guardian

**Benjamin Cuffin-Munday, age 11**

---

### Next?

More Sachar? *Small Steps* continues the story of Armpit and X-Ray a year after they've left Camp Green Lake. Or try *The Boy Who Lost His Face*, about a boy bowing to peer pressure, with dramatic consequences... And don't forget the slim-but-great *Stanley Yelnats' Survival Guide to Camp Green Lake*.

Or the darker, sadder, *Milkweed* by Jerry Spinelli. (UTBG 263)

Or *Millions* by Frank Cottrell Boyce, in which a lot of money comes into the hands of a boy obsessed by saints. (UTBG 264)

---

Set in America, this story starts with poor and luckless Stanley Yelnats being sent to Camp Green Lake, a correction facility for wayward boys. Upon arrival, he is told that his punishment will be to dig a hole five feet wide and five feet deep, every day in the scorching heat, for the next 18 months. Anything he finds must be handed over to the Warden, no questions asked. It all sounds straightforward, but is anything but...

Louis Sachar has woven the cleverest of plots around characters with fabulous names such as Armpit, Mr Sir and Kissin' Kate Barlow. In a nutshell, *Holes* is one of the best children's books I have ever read – and I've read a lot of them!

**Helena Pielichaty**

# HOMBRE   Elmore Leonard

I've always loved reading Westerns, and this is my all-time favourite. John Russell has lived with the Apaches since he was six years old, but now he's back in the white man's world. It's an ugly world – full of prejudice, greed and exploitation – but John Russell walks through it all with pride and silence. And when things begin to go wrong, he does what has to be done.

That's what this book is all about: doing what has to be done, regardless of the consequences. It's a thrilling read – tough and uncompromising – and when you get to the end, you'll wish that you could live your life like the man they called Hombre.

**Kevin Brooks**

### Next?

*Valdez Is Coming* is another Western by Elmore Leonard.

Some more fantastic Westerns (if you've never tried them, give them a go; they're better than you think!): *Shane* by Jack Schaffer; *Lonesome Dove* by Larry McMurtry, *True Grit* by Charles Portis and *Anything* by J.T. Edson.

Or what about Elmore Leonard writing crime? Try *52 Pick-Up*.

---

# HOMECOMING   Cynthia Voigt

### Next?

The sequence is known as the **Tillerman** series. It continues with *Dicey's Song, A Solitary Blue, The Runner, Sons from Afar* and *Seventeen Against the Dealer*.

*Johnnie's Blitz* by Bernard Ashley is the story of a wartime search for family. (UTBG 216)

*Journey to Jo'burg* by Beverley Naidoo is about two children travelling across South Africa to find their mother.

What would you do if your mother left you in charge of three younger siblings and just disappeared? Dicey does a great job. Having decided that the family should stay together, she avoids the police and sets off across America... When they discover that they have a grandmother in Maryland, they wonder whether maybe she will give them a home. Full of hope, they set off to find her. Will their gran take them in?

A wonderful picture of a family and the rich, complex web of American society, full of interesting and sympathetic characters and a really exciting plot. Dicey, James, Maybeth and Will make terrific travelling companions.

**Ann Jungman**

# HOOT  Carl Hiaasen

**Next?**

More Carl Hiaasen? Try *Flush*. Or move on to an adult Hiaasen – *Tourist Season* (UTBG 400) is a good place to start.

If you like Hiaasen's humorous, offbeat characters, try Jonathan Kebbe's *The Bottle-Top King*.

If you want to know the real story behind the fast-food industry, read *Fast Food Nation* by Eric Schlosser – it could put you off burgers for life! There's a kids' version of the same book: *Chew on This: Everything You Don't Want to Know About Fast Food*.

This is a conservation story with a difference. It carries a powerful eco-message, but it's hilariously funny, too, and packed with quirky characters and crazy situations. Roy Eberhardt has recently moved to Florida; he's bright, resourceful and used to being the new kid in town. Roy soon makes friends with Mullet Fingers – a boy who lives on the fringes of society – and his stepsister Beatrice, and he finds himself caught up in their campaign to save a colony of rare owls. The tiny birds live in burrows on land that's earmarked to be the site of yet another Mother Paula's All-American Pancake House. The three unlikely allies take up their cause against a corrupt adult establishment, in a lively story with plenty of suspense, wit and great good humour.

**Kathryn Ross**

# HOPE WAS HERE  Joan Bauer

A book to touch all the emotions, as the narrator, Hope, tells the story of her life – and her hopes. There's a gentle thread of humour throughout the book, centred in a sleepy Wisconsin town. Sixteen-year-old Hope works in the local diner with her wonderful-cooking aunt Addie and other great characters. She's soon caught up in the intricacies of small-town politics as she helps her sick boss campaign against the corrupt mayor standing for re-election. A joy to read as it swings between cooking, serving, eating and politics – there's a good deal of love interest, too, and moments of anxiety over Hope's unreliable mum.

**Wendy Cooling**

**Next?**

More Bauer? *Squashed* is an extraordinary story of first love – and of a girl who is determined to grow the biggest pumpkin in the world; *Rules of the Road* is about a drive from Chicago to Texas – though it's about the rules of life, really; and *Peeled* is about a girl trying to preserve her town's way of life.

Look for Joan O'Neill's books, always full of truth as well as telling strong family stories. Start with *Daisy Chain War*, the first of a quartet of books that follows the life of an Irish family.

Meg Rosoff's *How I Live Now* is another story told in a strong, distinctive voice that demands to be read. (UTBG 190)

# HORACE  Chris d'Lacey

**Next?**

More Chris d'Lacey? Try the dragon-themed stories that start with *The Fire Within*, or *Fly, Cherokee, Fly*, about courage, being bullied and finding yourself.

*Rhino Boy* by John Brindley tells the story of a school bully who wakes up one day to find a rhino horn on his head, and finds out for himself how his victims feel.

Jack Gantos's **Joey Pigza** books take a hilarious look at a boy who finds it difficult to fit in at school. Start with *Joey Pigza Swallowed the Key*.

Something just as funny? Try Sally Prue's *Goldkeeper*. (UTBG 160)

Joel is driven to distraction by his hard-up, always-arguing family and unfathomable first-ever girlfriend. Looking for something to draw for his art project, he comes across an old teddy bear in a skip at a charity shop. But this is no ordinary bear and it gets him into more trouble than it's worth; and as Joel discovers after an antique evaluation at school, it's worth an awful lot! Is the bear the answer to all Joel's problems?

Teddy bears, being arrested, ice cream, broken legs, unspeakably annoying family members... Seemingly random and ridiculous elements for a story, but d'Lacey weaves them all together into a hilariously funny and hugely readable tale we really believe in. It shouldn't work but it does!

**Eileen Armstrong**

# THE HOURS  Michael Cunningham

*The Hours* is an uplifting novel about death. Because it's about death, it's also about life – three lives. Virginia Woolf, in the 1920s, struggles against suicidal depression and writes her novel, *Mrs Dalloway*. In the 1940s, Mrs Brown, suffocated by domestic bliss, longs only for the time to read. And in the 1990s, Clarissa organises a party for Richard, who is dying of AIDS.

It's intriguing to discover the connections between the characters, and the story is fascinating. For me, though, the novel's beauty lies in the way the various protagonists discover the difference between the choices they would like to make for the sake of the people they love, and the choices they must make for themselves.

**Antonia Honeywell**

**Next?**

If you liked the lyrical, poetic writing, try Michael Cunningham's *Home at the End of the World*.

If you felt sympathy for Mrs Brown, try Alice Sebold's *The Lovely Bones* (UTBG 248) or *Mrs Dalloway* itself.

If you like the way the innermost thoughts of the characters form the story, try *Hotel World* by Ali Smith.

# THE HOUSE IN NORHAM GARDENS
## Penelope Lively

Penelope Lively's speciality, both in her books for adults and in those for children, is to describe how the past affects the present and how the people in the present deal with such things as memory and history. In this beautifully written and moving novel, Clare goes to live with two ageing aunts in the house of the title. The aunts are described so well that you feel you know them as intimately as Clare does, and if ever a book showed how powerful and intelligent old ladies can be, this is it.

Clare discovers an ancient woodcarving in the attic, and becomes involved with the people who made it long ago and those who brought it back to Oxford.

This is a ghost story of sorts, and a wonderful addition to the literature of growing up and finding out about who you are and how your life follows on from the lives of those who came before you.

**Adèle Geras**

> **Next?**
>
> More Penelope Lively? Try *Oleander, Jacaranda: A Childhood Perceived*, about her experience of growing up in Egypt, or **A House Unlocked**, the history of her family's house in Somerset.
>
> Another story about a house is Daphne Du Maurier's **House on the Strand**.
>
> Another book about the past, the future and how they depend on each other is **The Secret Life of Bees** by Sue Monk Kidd. (UTBG 351)

# THE HOUSE OF SLEEP   Jonathan Coe

> **Next?**
>
> Try some more Jonathan Coe: **What a Carve Up!** and **The Rotters' Club** are particularly good, though if you like this one, you should probably read them all!
>
> **Time for Bed** by David Baddiel is about one man's battle with insomnia. Or try the scary tale by Stephen King, **Insomnia**.
>
> **Life of Pi** by Yann Martel is a completely different, but equally quirky and entertaining read. (UTBG 237)

Sarah has an alarming tendency to fall asleep suddenly, with no warning, at any time of day. Terry swears that he hasn't slept at all for years, and spends his nights watching movies. And Gregory Dudden studies sleep as a science, gradually coming to see it as a disease that must be eradicated at all costs. A group of students are all linked by their obsession with sleep, and though they drift apart when they leave college, this same obsession brings them together again a decade later.

This very odd subject for a novel results in a read which is touching, gripping, sometimes shocking and occasionally properly, laugh-out-loud funny. I became a Jonathan Coe fan from practically the first page.

**Susan Reuben**

# HOUSE OF THE SCORPION Nancy Farmer ✻✻

Opium is a country that was once Mexico – and its only crop is field upon field of white opium poppies. Matteo grows up hidden away, but some secrets cannot be kept for ever, and one day the outside world comes crashing in and Matt's life changes dramatically. Whether caged as an animal or pampered as a pet, Matt finally realises that in order to survive, he has to escape. But if he leaves Opium, could worse things await him outside?

Thought provoking, brilliantly told, with characters you feel for and situations that leave you chewing your fingers in anxiety, this book is amazing. With drug culture gone crazy, cloning and slavery, this book is extreme, full of gory detail and packed with suspense. Will Matt survive? And when he finds out what is planned for him, will he even want to?

**Leonie Flynn**

### Next?

Nancy Farmer is amazing – read the very different *Sea of Trolls* next. (UTBG 345)

Another fast, gripping story, set in the future, where the hero battles for survival is *Leviathon* by Scott Westerfield.

For something else that explores the ethics of cloning, try *Unique* (UTBG 414) by Alison Allen-Gray, or *Taylor Five* (UTBG 389) by Ann Halam

# HOUSE OF THE SPIRITS Isabel Allende ✻✻✻

### Next?

More Allende: *City of Beasts* is an exciting adventure about 15-year-old Alexander, who joins his grandmother on a dangerous expedition deep into the heart of the Amazon rainforest; *Daughter of Fortune* has a more historic feel, charting the life of the unconventional Chilean Eliza, caught up in the gold rush.

Eva Ibbotson's *Journey to the River Sea* is an easier but equally riveting Amazonian adventure. (UTBG 217)

Clara, destined to become the larger-than-life mother figure, is a sparky and spirited girl, gifted with telepathic abilities, who delights in making objects move and predicting the future. Falling mute on the mysterious death of her beautiful sister, Clara speaks again only to tell of her imminent wedding to the husband she has foreseen, the dark and brooding Esteban, once her sister's fiancé. He builds her a magnificent house which becomes home to their children, grandchildren and an assortment of colourful characters from the neighbourhood. Allende's magical realism, poetic prose and vivid pictures of a country and its people are widely acclaimed, but her real achievement here is in making the reader feel as much a part of the Trueba family as they do of their own.

**Eileen Armstrong**

# HOW I LIVE NOW  Meg Rosoff

Teenage Daisy is sent to England to stay with her aunt, two male cousins and their little sister. The aunt goes abroad, leaving them 'home alone' on the farm. For a short while, Daisy lives in blissful limbo without adult rules, without anyone telling her she's too young for sex with cousin Edmond with whom she has a psychic bond nothing can break. Then a bomb goes off in London. Britain is under attack. And, as the enemy closes in, Daisy and her cousins are forced to survive in a terrifying world they no longer recognise.

*How I Live Now* has a brilliant plot, it's beautifully written, and is all the more scary since 9/11. (Damn, I wish I'd written it!)

**Jeanne Willis**

### Next?

*The Fire-Eaters*, set during the Cuban missile crisis, similarly shows both the wonder and fear that life holds. (UTBG 133)

*Apples* by Richard Milward tells of sex and enemies, but in the Britain of today.

Something with sort of the same feel (yet utterly, utterly different) is *I Capture the Castle*. (UTBG 195)

Or simply more Meg Rosoff: *What I Was* (UTBG 431), *Just in Case* (UTBG 220) and the very different, Gothic, *The Bride's Farewell*.

# HOW TO DISAPPEAR COMPLETELY AND NEVER BE FOUND  Sara Nickerson

### Next?

More stories in words and pictures? *The Invention of Hugo Cabret* (UTBG 206) by Brian Selznick or *Malice* by Chris Wooding, in which kids start disappearing, only to turn up within the pages of a comic.

A funny story with comic-style illustrations is Jeff Kinney's *The Diary of a Wimpy Kid*.

A 12-year-old girl's father drowns; her mother becomes a chain-smoking, chain-sleeping recluse and won't tell the girl anything about her father's death.

There's a constant atmosphere of menace in this riveting story, as the girl – Margaret – runs away to an island to investigate what happened to her father. His story becomes inextricably linked with a series of anonymous, hand-painted comic books that appear in the town library every day. And when the comic-book stories start to show Margaret herself in dire peril, she realises she has entered a far more dangerous world than she could have imagined.

Elements of the graphic novel are interspersed with this story, turning an excellent adventure yarn into something really original, and giving it a superbly spooky edge.

**Susan Reuben**

# HOWL'S MOVING CASTLE  Diana Wynne Jones

### Next?

There are two sequels, *Castle in the Air* and *House of Many Ways*. Then look for everything else Diana Wynne Jones has written. Try and watch the movie based on this book, too – it's an animation, and one of the best.

Other books with a similar flavour include Annie Dalton's *Out of the Ordinary* and Geraldine McCaughrean's *A Pack of Lies*.

Moving cities appear in Philip Reeve's dazzlingly imaginative *Mortal Engines*. (UTBG 270)

Sophie is the oldest of three sisters in a world where fairy-tale conventions hold sway, and she never expects to be the one who finds fortune. So she is not really surprised when the Witch of the Waste puts her under an age spell. For most of the book, Sophie becomes the aged crone of traditional stories, but it doesn't stop her being the heroine, and the only person who has any control over Wizard Howl.

It was a boy on a school visit who suggested that Jones could write a book about a moving castle, and she has interpreted the idea with characteristic quirkiness. The four doors of the castle each open on a different place, one of which is in Wales, where Howl becomes known as 'Howell', a local rugby player.

**Mary Hoffman**

# HUCKLEBERRY FINN  Mark Twain

Scared that his drunken father might pursue him for the money he discovered with Tom Sawyer, Huckleberry Finn signs his fortune over to Judge Thatcher; but this doesn't stop his dad from dragging him off to an old cabin and beating him every day. Huck escapes to Jackson's Island where he meets his friend Jim, a runaway slave. Leading the townspeople to believe Jim has murdered Huck for his money, the two of them set sail on the Mississippi, beginning a series of adventures that are far more elaborate, amusing and exciting than those in *The Adventures of Tom Sawyer*. Considered one of the best sequels ever, and a great novel in every respect, this is a must-read.

**Matt Thorne**

### Next?

*The Further Adventures of Huckleberry Finn* by Greg Matthews. Written in 1983, this sequel takes Twain's characters and uses them in a much darker Western that nevertheless manages the near-impossible task of capturing the spirit of Twain's original. One warning: it's much more adult.

For modern stories of the American West, read Annie Proulx's short-story collection, *Close Range*.

Or for other tales of the ills of slavery try Harriet Beecher Stowe's *Uncle Tom's Cabin* and Laurie Halse Anderson's *Chains*.

# THE HUNGER GAMES   Suzanne Collins

**Next?**

More Suzanne Collins? Try the sequel, *Catching Fire*, with one more to follow, or her **Underland Chronicles**.

What would it be like to know when people were going to die? Read Rachel Ward's *Numbers* and find out.

Try the best re-imagining of the Theseus story in Mary Renault's *The King Must Die*. (UBG 225)

Or for another game that has terrifying consequences: *The Game of Triumphs* by Laura Powell. (UTBG 150)

Katniss Everdeen lives in Panem, a country whose government deliberately keeps its citizens short of food and living in terrible poverty. Panem is the country that has risen from the ashes of the United States. Each of the 12 districts must send a boy and girl between the ages of 12 and 18 to participate in a reality television programme called *The Hunger Games*, in which the contestants fight to the death. Last one standing wins – and lives. When her sister is chosen as a contestant in the 74th games, Katniss takes her place, even though she knows it will mean almost certain death.

With its echoes of the Theseus myth, this book is like a five-star action movie – the adrenaline is non-stop.

**Elizabeth Reid**

# HUNTER'S HEART   Julia Green

Fourteen-year-old Simon Piper lives on the Cornish coast with his mum and little sister. They're new to the area. Across the road from Simon lives 16-year-old Leah who decides to manipulate him for her amusement. He is to be her 'summer project'. Told from alternate points of view, Leah and Simon reveal their frustrations with life in their own unique ways. Authentic teenage angst and wild emotions rage on every page and both Leah and Simon are powerfully portrayed. This book is about many things – love, jealousy, obsession and growing up – and is in the immensely likeable 'one of those summers where everything changed' formats that make it a delight to read.

**Next?**

*Blue Moon* is Julia Green's earlier novel about growing up – this time from a girl's point of view. (UTBG 50)

Other rites-of-passage summer stories can be found in **Carwash**. (UTBG 67) Or the graphic novel, *Skim* (UTBG 366) by Mariko and Jillian Tamaki.

John Green's *Looking for Alaska* is a tough but absorbing look at how an American college girl dominates the lives of some of her fellow students.

For lighter relief, but similar poignancy, try *Stargirl*. (UTBG 375)

**John McLay**

# I AM DAVID
## Anne Holm

David is a young prisoner. He is undernourished, has very little experience with 'people' and knows nothing of the big and dangerous world outside the camp. Late one night, the only friendly guard helps him escape. With few resources and only a little money, David goes in search of his family. He encounters many people, some friendly and some less friendly; all the while knowing that the enemy might catch up with him...

This story touched me in a way that is hard to describe. It brought me to tears at some points, both happy and sad. It's a book about one small boy's outlook on life, how he makes the most of having very little, and it's incredibly moving. Don't be surprised if you're reduced to tears while reading it, too.

**David Bard, age 12**

### Next?

Another boy trying to find a way home is the hero of Ian Serraillier's *The Silver Sword*.

Donna Jo Napoli's *Stones in Water* is about a group of Italian boys taken captive during the war and forced into being slave labourers far away from home.

Holocaust stories will make you weep. Read Jerry Spinelli's *Milkweed* (UTBG 263) and Morris Gelitzman's *Once* (UTBG 292) and its sequel, *Then*.

Or try the simply told yet horrifying *The Boy in the Striped Pyjamas* by John Boyne. (UTBG 55)

## The Ultimate Teen Book List
## GUARDIAN CHILDREN'S FICTION PRIZE WINNERS

# I AM LEGEND  Richard Matheson

**Next?**

More Matheson? Another high-concept adventure that led to countless movies is *The Incredible Shrinking Man*.

If you like psychological thrillers, try one of the earliest: *Caleb Williams* by William Godwin, in which a young man is pursued and persecuted by a remorseless enemy.

James's *The Turn of the Screw* is another tale in which the mind of the protagonist is as important as the supernatural menace. (UTBG 409)

Or for another original look at the future, try Cormac McCarthy's bleak masterpiece, *The Road*.

This book is every writer's dream: a brilliant idea beautifully executed. Robert Neville is the last man left alive on Earth. A virus has turned everyone else into vampires. Each night, creatures that were once his neighbours crowd around Robert's fortified house, baying for his blood. Each day he goes out into the ruined city, killing the undead and hunting desperately for a cure.

Spare, economical and hauntingly atmospheric, this novel mingles fantasy, science fiction and horror, but it is above all a psychological thriller, a study of a man alone. Many films and books have mimicked its concepts, but *I Am Legend* remains supreme because it follows its logic unerringly, right up to the breathtaking conclusion.

**Jonathan Stroud**

# I AM THE CHEESE
## Robert Cormier

Robert Cormier was a brilliant American writer – I deliberately haven't read all his books, because I would hate to feel there were no more left to read. I'm not really a risk taker but reading his books is the sort of risk taking I can cope with: you don't know what Cormier is going to do with you and his books take you to the edge of fear and emotion. This is definitely the most powerful one I've read. It's a simple story – Adam Farmer is on a journey, on his bike, delivering a package for his father. But all is not as it seems and the truth is clever, surprising and deeply moving. And as for the ending...

**Nicola Morgan**

**Next?**

Obviously, any Robert Cormier books. Try *The Chocolate War* (UTBG 78), *Fade*, about a boy who can make himself invisible or *Tenderness*, about a young serial killer.

And try *Malarkey* by Keith Gray, about a school where nothing is quite as it should be. (UTBG 253)

More risk taking? Try Graham Marks's look at life, fate, angels and really bad language, *How it Works* or *Omega Place*, about runaway Paul and a world under surveillance.

# I CAPTURE THE CASTLE Dodie Smith

'I write this sitting in the kitchen sink' is one of the most memorable opening lines in literature, and sets the tone for this beautiful, genuine and very funny novel.

Seventeen-year-old Cassandra and her brother and sister live with their writer father and bohemian stepmother in a half-ruined castle in 1930s England. Despairing of their poverty, Cassandra's sister Rose declares she'll do anything to escape – even marry one of the American Cotton brothers who own the nearby estate.

I love books that send me to worlds I want to live in, and I'd move to Cassandra's castle in a second if I could. But this is a book not just for those of us who secretly want to live in castles – it's about love, writing, families and the complicated process of growing up.

**Sally Nicholls**

### Next?

Nancy Mitford's *The Pursuit of Love* and *Love in a Cold Climate* (UTBG 245) are set against the same sort of background, and are both warm and humorous.

Or try something set during World War II (but written much more recently) that captures the life of one family: the **Cazalet Chronicles**, starting with *The Light Years*, by Elizabeth Jane Howard.

Another delightful read is to be found in Winifred Watson's *Miss Pettigrew Lives for a Day*.

This book sparkles and bubbles like vintage champagne. Generations of readers have loved it as teenagers, and gone on loving it throughout the years. It captivates from its very first line: 'I write this sitting in the kitchen sink.' Who could resist?

Seventeen-year-old Cassandra is practising her writing skills by keeping a diary. Through her eyes – sometimes naïve, sometimes knowing – we follow the lives of her eccentric family as they struggle to survive, in genteel poverty, amidst the ruins of an ancient castle. With the arrival of two brothers from America, love with all its complications enters Cassandra's life and nothing will ever be quite the same again. We share her awakening to the joys and pains of unrequited passion, right through to the unexpected ending.

Funny, romantic, witty, charming, *I Capture the Castle* is a total delight from beginning to end.

**Jean Ure**

# THE ICE ROAD   Jaap ter Haar

If you read Nicola Morgan's feature on pp. 348–349, you'll see that she defines good fiction as writing that 'can make you feel the cold'. This book does just that. Boris is living in Leningrad in 1942, during the city's appalling siege in which 700,000 people died. For 150 pages you'll be there, too. You will feel cold and hungry, just as Boris does, you will despair at the death and desolation that surrounds him, and you will be entranced, utterly elated at every little sign of hope. You will fear for the health of Boris's ailing mother, delight in the company of his best friend Nadia; and when a death comes it will hit you hard. But don't be put off if it sounds grim – you'll come away from this book sober, certainly, but Boris's generosity and courage will make you stronger too, and full of admiration and hope.

**Daniel Hahn**

### Next?

Mary Renault's *The Last of the Wine* is set around the siege of Athens during the Peloponnesian War, and is just as harrowing.

Or try something else cold and Russian – *One Day in the Life of Ivan Denisovich* (UTBG 293), or Slavomir Rawicz's *The Long Walk* (UTBG 239).

For another novel that tells of the Siege of Leningrad and the despair of war, read Helen Dunmore's *The Siege*.

# I, CORIANDER   Sally Gardner

### Next?

Other books that deal with the meeting of the human and the fairy world include Herbie Brennan's *Faerie Wars*, Michelle Harrison's *The Thirteen Treasures*, Eoin Colfer's *Artemis Fowl* (UTBG 29) and *Tithe* (UTBG 397) by Holly Black .

For classic historical novels, try anything by Rosemary Sutcliff; *The Eagle of the Ninth* is a great starting point. (UTBG 117)

For another Sally Gardner that blends historical fact with magical happenings, read *The Red Necklace*. (UTBG 329)

When she is 12, Coriander Hobie is locked in a chest and left to die. Her mother is dead and her father has fled abroad, leaving her at the mercy of a wicked stepmother and an evil preacher. Three years later, Coriander comes out of the same chest alive, having learnt of her fairy heritage and determined to defeat her mother's murderer. This is a story that succeeds in weaving two very different worlds together. The account of Cromwell's reign provides real insight into this period of history, whilst Coriander's adventures in her mother's world are pure fairy tale. Beautifully written and highly recommended, this book won the Nestlé Book Prize when it was first published.

**Laura Hutchings**

# IF ONLY THEY COULD TALK  James Herriot

James Herriot was a vet in the Yorkshire Dales, and this is the first collection of stories about the strange creatures (animal and human) he met. Look out for the psychotic pig, the sliding seat, the flying chickens, the wailing labrador, the story of the lightning strike, the great pig disaster, James's wonderfully inconsistent partner Siegfried, and his younger brother Tristan. Some of the stories are of triumph, some of failure, and others are just really, really embarrassing, but all are incredibly funny. If you like animals, you'll love this book. I guarantee it.

**Benedict Jacka**

## Next?

James Herriot wrote six more in the same series, of which the next is *It Shouldn't Happen to a Vet*.

Another very funny story about animals and people is *My Family and Other Animals* by Gerald Durrell. (UTBG 273)

And if you just want a pure animal story, without any humans around, you can't do better than *Watership Down*. (UTBG 427)

# IF YOU COME SOFTLY  Jacqueline Woodson

This love story has a touch of *Romeo and Juliet* about it, and it is gentle, heart-wrenching and unforgettable. The growing love between two 15 year olds – a black boy and a white girl – is threatened by prejudice, but never defeated by it. Ellie and Miah have a very special relationship, something apart from the rest of the world, so why can't the rest of the world see it like that? It takes an act of fate to change the story, and you will be aching for a happy ending. Although set in America, this is a universal tale that should appeal to young people everywhere.

**Wendy Cooling**

JACQUELINE WOODSON
*if you come softly*

## Next?

More Woodson? Try *Locomotion*, a novel in verse that tells the story of Lonnie, his life, his grief and how he survives it all.

Bali Rai's *Rani & Sukh* looks at the 'Romeo and Juliet' theme, too, but this time the lovers come from Indian families. (UTBG 326)

There's more love against the odds in Linzi Glass's *Ruby Red*, which is set in prejudice-torn South Africa.

*Star-Crossed* by Rachel Wing is about a school production of *Romeo and Juliet* that goes wrong.

# I KNOW WHY THE CAGED BIRD SINGS

## Maya Angelou

*I Know Why the Caged Bird Sings* is the autobiography of a young black girl struggling against the brutal racial discrimination of America in the 1930s and 1940s. But it's also the story of a woman finding herself in the experiences of her childhood and celebrating the people she loves, especially her beloved older brother and her fierce-but-brilliant grandmother. Even though she's caged by segregation and injustice, Maya still sings of hope and self-respect. Cruel things happen (and at times, this isn't the easiest book to read), but she never presents herself or her family as victims. This fascinating life story is blisteringly honest but never bitter, and that's what makes it so difficult to put down.

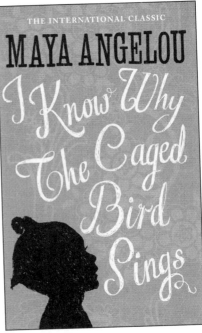

**Antonia Honeywell**

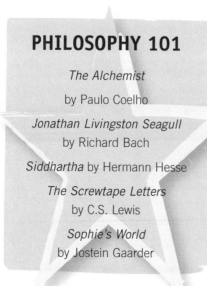

## PHILOSOPHY 101

*The Alchemist*
by Paulo Coelho

*Jonathan Livingston Seagull*
by Richard Bach

*Siddhartha* by Hermann Hesse

*The Screwtape Letters*
by C.S. Lewis

*Sophie's World*
by Jostein Gaarder

### Next?

Written in a way that has no strict chronography, the rest of the series comprises: *Gather Together in My Name*, *Singin' and Swingin' and Gettin' Merry Like Christmas*, *The Heart of a Woman*, *All God's Children Need Travelling Shoes* and *A Song Flung Up to Heaven*.

If you enjoyed reading about the experience of being a black American, try *The Color Purple*. (UTBG 84)

Or for a book that looks at the nature of slavery and prejudice, read M.T. Anderson's stunning *The Astonishing Life of Octavian Nothing*. (UTBG 29)

# THE ILIAD and THE ODYSSEY   Homer

*The Iliad*, generally thought to have been completed around 750 BC, is the story of a great war between the Greeks and the Trojans that broke out after Paris, son of King Priam of Troy, ran off with Helen, beautiful young wife of Menelaus, King of Sparta in Greece. The Greeks gathered a massive army and set sail in 'a thousand black ships' to lay siege to the city of Troy – a siege that lasted for ten full years. It's a story full of rivalry, jealousy, heroism and love, plus a fair whack of meddling from the dear old gods.

*The Odyssey* is the story of Odysseus, one of the Greek warriors of *The Iliad*, sailing home at the conclusion of the siege of Troy. But what a time he has getting there! The journey takes him a further decade to complete because so much happens on the way. Among other diversions, Odysseus and his crew are held captive by a one-eyed giant (the Cyclops), visit the land of the dead, and battle a man-eating sea monster and a ship-swallowing whirlpool. Odysseus also falls for the odd temptress, which slows him down a bit. What happens when he eventually makes it back is worth waiting for.

These two books are not always an easy read, but once you have read them, these heroes, adversaries and adventures will stay with you for life. (I mean that in a good way.)

**Michael Lawrence**

## Next?

Homer's books are available in many translations, some in verse, some in prose. There is a really accessible modern version by Robert Fagles.

Christopher Logue's *War Music* is a segment of the story retold in modern language and verse.

In Adèle Geras's *Troy*, the story of the siege is told from the point of view of the women involved. (UTBG 405)

# THE ILLUSTRATED MAN   Ray Bradbury

I've always been a fan of short stories, particularly when grouped together by a linking device. For me, this seems to give the reader the pleasure of a novel together with the unexpected twists and turns of a short-story collection. When I was a teenager, I discovered Ray Bradbury, one of the greatest science-fiction writers of the 20th century, and avidly read every book of his I could find. My favourite was *The Illustrated Man*, a collection of 18 stories told through the moving tattoos on a carnival performer's body, observed by his fascinated fireside companion while the tattooed man sleeps. Including tales of alien invasion, colonisation of Mars and ancient cities lying in wait for unwary visitors, each story contains a satisfying twist. My favourite is an expedition to the watery world of Venus, being hunted through the swamps by vengeful amphibians, but every story is compelling, right up to the surprise ending – a classic.

**Chris Riddell**

> **Next?**
>
> More Bradbury. Read *Dandelion Wine*, in which he links short stories into a novel about one's boy's summer. (UTBG 94)
>
> More dark and horrific short stories? Try Clive Barker's *Books of Blood*.
>
> Or for more science fiction, try John Wyndham's *The Midwich Cuckoos*. (UTBG 263)

# THE ILLUSTRATED MUM   Jacqueline Wilson

> **Next?**
>
> More Jacqueline Wilson? Try *The Diamond Girls*, about sisters fending for themselves while Mum has a baby – and what happens when Mum and the baby come home. (UTBG 104)
>
> Anne Fine also writes about families and friends in crisis; try *Up on Cloud Nine*. (UTBG 415)
>
> Rowan in Jenny Valentine's *Broken Soup* is also trying single-handedly to keep her family together. (UTBG 63)

Two sisters, Star and Dolphin, have a mother who is romantic, tattooed and clinically crazy. From the first page, this story exudes apprehension. It subsequently moves through a series of nightmarish domestic crises to a hopeful end, though that initial apprehension is not totally dismissed. Love will continue to strengthen the two young heroines as they sustain their deeply confused 'illustrated' mum, but we know their hard times are not over yet. The story is not only concerned with eccentric events, but also with the way in which vulnerable Star and Dol move towards maturity and strength.

This story somehow manages to deal with a frightening family situation without becoming too depressing; and like anything by Jacqueline Wilson, it is compulsive reading.

**Margaret Mahy**

# I'M NOT SCARED  Niccolò Ammaniti

It is the scorching summer of 1978. A hideous discovery in a ruined farmhouse deep in the Italian countryside tears nine-year-old Michele Amitrano's childhood apart in this dark, claustrophobic novel. The sense that something terrible is about to happen grips you from its opening sentence and keeps you turning the pages. (And in my case flicking them back to find the clues I'd missed first time round.)

So be warned: this story will haunt you. Guaranteed. It's a chiller, a thriller, a horror, and a heartbreaking study of the evil and cruelty that can lurk in the hearts of those you love and trust more than anyone. Oh, and like all the best stories, it's beautifully written and there is final redemption. But at what a price!

**Catherine Forde**

> **Next?**
>
> More Ammaniti? Try the tragedy and comedy of *Steal You Away*, which is about crime and punishment, or *The Crossroads*, about a boy whose father is planning to rob a bank.
>
> Sonya Hartnett's *Thursday's Child* is another claustrophobic novel. (UTBG 396)
>
> Robert Cormier writes about the dark side of human nature; try *The Chocolate War* (UTBG 78) or *I Am The Cheese* (UTBG 194).
>
> And read our detective stories feature on pp. 108–109.

# I'M THE KING OF THE CASTLE
## Susan Hill

> **Next?**
>
> Try Susan Hill's ghostly *The Woman in Black* for another terrifying read. (UTBG 443)
>
> Or try her poignant, lyrical look at the First World War, *Strange Meeting*.
>
> Or Henry James's perplexing and scary *The Turn of the Screw*. (UTBG 409)
>
> For other books about the power one young person can have over another, try Anne Fine's *The Tulip Touch* (UTBG 407) or Sue Mayfield's *Blue* (UTBG 50).

Six years after an unhappy marriage and his wife's death, Joseph Hooper advertises for a housekeeper. Into his life come Helena Kingshaw and her fatherless son, Charles. Hooper's son Edmund throws Charles a note: 'I didn't want you to come here.' The feeling is mutual.

What follows is a brilliant and disturbing story about – as Susan Hill says – 'cruelty and the power of evil … a victim and a tormentor … isolation and the lack of love'. As the balance of power shifts to and fro between Edmund and Charles, we begin to fear the worst. The ending is brutal and terrifying. Read the novel and be afraid. Be very afraid.

**Valerie Mendes**

# INCANTATION Alice Hoffman

**Next?**

Alice Hoffman is a wonderful writer. Some of her other young-adult books include **Green Angel**, which is a heartbreaking, lyrical look at despair and **The Foretelling**, about an Amazon girl growing up amidst a battle for survival.

A clash of western and tribal cultures is explored in Lloyd Jones's **Mister Pip**. (UTBG 267)

Or for another story about belief, try Ann Turnbull's **No Shame, No Fear**. (UTBG 286)

Don't be fooled by the cover – *Incantation* is no easy tale of spells and magic. It is a beautiful, harsh and uncompromising account of what it might have meant to be Jewish in the 1500s, when the Spanish Inquisition forced any religious non-conformity underground with horrific extremes of torture and execution. The heroine, Estrella, narrates her tale in a calm, lyrical voice, weaving the laws of her time with her domestic concerns and her first love so gently that you don't see the full significance of her story until the terror is upon you, by which time it's too late to do anything other than suffer with her. A challenging, profoundly moving novel with a significant and essential message.

**Antonia Honeywell**

# INEXCUSABLE Chris Lynch

Keir Sarafian doesn't like it when people he loves don't listen to him. He considers himself to be a good guy ... sort of. He likes it when people like him, and after a football accident, he gets the popular nickname of 'Killer'. Popularity clouds his views and, as his love for Gigi Boudakian intensifies, Keir's view of himself gets even more clouded. Keir loves her so much, he doesn't realise what he is doing, and doesn't want to take responsibility for his actions.

In this story, the chapters switch between the past and the future to keep the reader interested and intrigued – it works. Did Keir really do it? What really happened between him and Gigi? The book comes with its own set of twists and turns, and there's no map to show where it's going to take you next. *The way things look is definitely not the way they really are...*

**Rosa Mateo, age 17**

**Next?**

**Speak** by Laurie Halse Anderson should not be missed – it's a gritty read about the horrors of rape, from the victim's point of view.

For more by Chris Lynch, try **Sins of the Fathers**, a story about three best friends and the secrets of their parish's Catholic priests.

A rape is the catalyst for all that happens in Robert Cormier's **Heroes**. (UTBG 176)

# INGO  Helen Dunmore

**Next?**

There are more books about Ingo: *Tide Knot*, *The Deep* and *The Crossing of Ingo*.

Alice Hoffman's novella, *Aquamarine*, is about a mermaid, as are Alan Temperley's *Huntress of the Sea* and Angela McAllister's *The Tide Turner*.

Or look for the original Hans Andersen version of *The Little Mermaid* – it's not as cute as Disney made out!

There's a half-woman, half-mermaid heroine in *Sleeping with the Fishes* by Mary Janice Davidson.

Feisty Sapphire and her brother Conor live in Cornwall by the sea. Sapphire loves her cottage and her family, but the pull of the sea is very strong. And when her dad vanishes, one midsummer night, it is not long before Sapphire is drawn into Ingo, the wild and dangerous home of the Mer.

When reading this book, I let the phone ring and the dinner burn. It's gripping stuff, and Helen Dunmore's writing made me want to drive 50 miles to the sea, throw off my trainers, and plunge into the seaweed and surf. Once you get sucked into Ingo's currents, you'll be swept away in an exhilarating tale of adventure, mourning, love and friendship, until you're spat out, gasping for breath, onto the shore. But drinking all that salt water makes you thirst for more.

**Ally Kennen**

# INKHEART  Cornelia Funke

We all know the power of books and the power of storytelling. They can take us to different worlds, seeming to make them and their magic real. But for Mo, Meggie's father, this is a real gift – he really can make characters from stories appear and send people and things into other stories.

One night Mo's past catches up with him, when the shadowy and mysterious Dustfinger arrives to warn him about the evil Capricorn who is hunting him. Unbeknownst to Meggie, these are sinister characters that her father conjured up from the strange world of Inkheart long ago. As Meggie begins to discover more about her father, she realises a story doesn't always end when you close the book...

**Adam Lancaster**

**Next?**

To continue the story straight away, read the rest of the trilogy: *Inkspell* and *Inkdeath*. Then more Cornelia – *The Thief Lord* (UTBG 393) is brilliant.

Or how about reading *Endymion Spring* by Matthew Skelton? It's another great story about the power of books.

If books are the power in *Inkheart*, then paintings are the power in Mike Wilks's vivid *Mirrorscape*.

# INNOCENT BLOOD P.D. James

With all the confidence of her new freedom as an adult and aided by a new law passed by the government, 18-year-old Philippa Palfrey sets out to find the birth mother who gave her up for adoption as a small child. She discovers that her parents were the infamous Ductons, guilty of murdering a child. Philippa confidently thinks she can rebuild a life with her mother, who is due for release from jail – she even eschews older, established relationships in preparation. But is Philippa truly equipped to operate in a murky new world – and is she truly naïve enough to think she can 'own' her mother exclusively?

A brilliant thriller about innocence and guilt, from a master storyteller.

**Jon Appleton**

> ### Next?
>
> James is more famous for her Detective Dalgleish books – try the first, *Cover Her Face*.
>
> P.D. James has been called the Queen of Crime – but so has Ruth Rendell! Try Ruth's *A Sight for Sore Eyes* (UTBG 361) or *A Fatal Inversion* (Ruth writing as Barbara Vine) and decide for yourself.
>
> Another mystery in which no one is quite as they seem is Patricia Highsmith's chilling *The Talented Mr Ripley*. (UTBG 386)
>
> For more crime, turn to our detective stories feature on pp. 108–109.

# INSPECTOR MORSE series Colin Dexter

> ### Next?
>
> The **Morse** books start with *Last Bus to Woodstock* and end with *The Remorseful Day*, with eleven others in between.
>
> Arthur Conan Doyle's *The Hound of the Baskervilles* – Sherlock Holmes is one of the all-time great literary detectives. (UTBG 359)
>
> Agatha Christie's Miss Marple – try *The 4:50 from Paddington* or *The Body in the Library* (UTBG 51).
>
> Or a wonderful story that involves solving a crime, this one set in the past – *A Gathering Light*. (UTBG 151)

John Thaw's TV portrayal of Chief Inspector Morse has helped to popularise the novels of Colin Dexter. Morse is intelligent, well read, a lover of Wagner, a swiller of ale and solver of crossword puzzles. Together with his faithful partner, Sergeant Lewis, an honest egg-and-chip-loving Geordie, he unravels a succession of crimes based around Oxford. The books are well written with plenty of twists and red herrings. My favourite is *The Dead of Jericho*, in which the corpse discovered is Anne, one of Morse's ex-girlfriends. Apparently it is suicide, but Morse digs beneath the world of publishing and the bridge society in Oxford to get at the truth behind the tragedy. It is an intriguing page-turner.

**Brenda Marshall**

# INTERVIEW WITH THE VAMPIRE
## Anne Rice

In a dingy room a boy listens to a despairing vampire tell his story. While a tape spools on, he hears of centuries of life, of love and passion, of the enigmatic and captivating Lestat, the beautiful vampire child Claudia, and above all of Louis, the one cursed with hating his own life and its eternal craving for blood.

Lush, compelling, horribly beautiful, this macabre, gruesome and exquisite book is steeped in the erotic, the sensual and the perverse. Though there had been vampire books before it, and there have been many since, this is the one that started a cult and – for a while – made Anne Rice into the heroine of black-clad teens across the world.

**Leonie Flynn**

### Next?

The **Vampire Chronicles** continue with *The Vampire Lestat* and *The Queen of the Damned*, both of which are just as dark and engrossing. (The series goes on, but the later stories are not quite as good.)

Or try Holly Black's *Tithe* (UTBG 397) and *Valiant* for all-out sex, drugs and faeries.

Stephanie Meyer is undoubtedly Anne Rice's successor – read *Twilight*. (UTBG 411)

# INTO THIN AIR: A PERSONAL ACCOUNT OF THE MOUNT EVEREST DISASTER
## Jon Krakauer

When Jon Krakauer was offered the chance to write about Everest from Base Camp, he declined. Even though he didn't have the high-altitude experience needed, he didn't want to just stay behind while others climbed – he wanted to climb the mountain himself and fulfil a lifelong dream. But the harsh reality of the mountain and its extremes pushed his abilities to the limit and others to their deaths.

Krakauer's minute-by-minute first-person retelling of the 1996 Everest tragedy, when five of his fellow climbers died in a sudden storm, is a thrilling, roller-coaster adventure that puts you right there in the clouds. The fact that the story is true makes it all the more compelling and poignant.

**Charli Osborne**

### Next?

*The Perfect Storm* by Sebastian Junger is the tragic story of the men of the Andrea Gail, who are set upon by a collision of three storm systems.

*Alive: The Story of the Andes Survivors* by Piers Paul Reid is a horrific tale about the struggle to survive.

For more mountains, try Joe Simpson's *Touching the Void*. (UTBG 400)

# INVENTING ELLIOT   Graham Gardner

**Next?**

*Inventing Elliot* was inspired by Orwell's *Nineteen Eighty-Four*. So read that next. (UTBG 284)

Another boy who re-invents himself is the hero of *Just in Case*. (UTBG 220)

*Thirteen Reasons Why* by Jay Asher is about the very final consequences of other people's actions.

Maybe at the new school everything will be different. Nobody knows Elliot there; nobody knows anything about him – so he can be whoever he wants to be, right? Well, yes, but...

Scratch the surface and you'll see that Holminster High is really run not by the teachers but by a powerful and sinister group of older students called The Guardians. And The Guardians want Elliot. Joining them will allow him to belong, but to what exactly? The Guardians aren't a warm and friendly social club; they're cold and clever and manipulative. And they're used to getting what they want. Is Elliot strong enough to resist?

The first page will grab you, and then won't let go; Gardner keeps the momentum and tension up right to the thrilling closing sentence. It's a gripping, often terrifying, book – a great piece of spare and powerful writing.

**Daniel Hahn**

# THE INVENTION OF HUGO CABRET
## Brian Selznick

Want to read a 525-page book in a couple of hours? Want to read a book that's a lot like watching a movie? Look no further!

Hugo Cabret keeps all 27 clocks in the Paris train station running smoothly. He lives and works behind the walls, only entering the station to steal food or small mechanical parts from a toymaker's stall. He is obsessed with mending a small automaton, a man that will write something when it's fixed. Hugo is sure it will be a message from his dead father. Instead, it leads him to an early French silent film and its creator, Georges Méliès, who was supposed to be dead...

The cinematic presentation of the tale blends mystery, action, and plenty of visuals: the perfect combination for telling a story about silent film.

**Next?**

If you enjoyed the black-and-white illustrations, try *Monster Blood Tattoo* by D.M. Cornish.

For another mystery adventure with enigmatic clues, try *Chasing Vermeer* by Blue Balliet.

More Brian Selznick? Try *The Houdini Box*.

Or for another story told through words and pictures, try Chris Wooding's *Malice*.

**Alicia Anderson**

# I, ROBOT   Isaac Asimov

## Next?

You'll probably enjoy some of the other 'robot' books by Asimov. *The Rest of the Robots* is another collection of short stories, and the follow-up to *I, Robot*; *Bicentennial Man* was turned into a movie with Robin Williams.

*Robot Dreams* by Sarah Varon is a glorious, wordless graphic novel about an unusual friendship.

*Dot.Robot* by Jason Bradbury takes an up-to-the-minute look at what is possible with real science, now. It's also a fast-paced thriller!

And if you just like science fiction, well frankly you're spoilt for choice. Read our feature on pp. 246–247.

This is a collection of short stories by one of the masters of sci-fi – the man who invented the idea of robots as we know them today. Originally published in 'pulp' magazines in the 1940s, many of them take the form of an 'interview' with Susan Calvin, founder of US Robotics, who is looking back over the development of robots in her lifetime and discussing the problems the manufacturers faced along the way.

Asimov had a fantastic imagination and, although the language is a tad dated, these are truly great stories. One of them was recently used as the basis for a movie of the same name. They're immensely readable and filled with that sense of what it would be like to live in a world served by intelligent machines.

**Andrew Norriss**

# IS ANYBODY THERE?   Jean Ure

Would you like to have a mum who was a medium? That is, someone who could predict the future. Sounds fun, doesn't it? But what if you took after her and you were psychic, too? And what if your friends expected you to use your powers when you didn't want to?

Jean Ure's book starts off in the most compelling way, with the narrator Joanna telling how she did that one thing that everyone always tells you not to do: get into a car with someone you don't know. The tension goes on from here and you won't be able to read fast enough to find out what happens. A story of friendship, of growing up and something more besides…

**Mary Hooper**

## Next?

Another Jean Ure? Try *Sugar and Spice*. A new girl at school finally means that nerdy Ruth has a best friend, but what is she really like?

Another girl who is psychic and has to live with the consequences features in *When Lightning Strikes*, the first of Meg Cabot's **Missing** series.

Or try Marcus Sedgwick's *The Foreshadowing*, in which Sasha tries to use her psychic powers to save the lives of her brothers in the trenches.

# THE ISLAND  Armin Greder

### Next?

Pictures that have huge emotional impact fill Raymond Briggs's work; try the terrifyingly sad **When the Wind Blows**. (UTBG 434)

Michael Rosen and Quentin Blake's **The Sad Book** is a desolate look at loss and grief.

Or try something illustrated by Dave McKean. **The Wolves in the Wall** and **The Day I Swapped My Dad for Two Goldfish**, both written by Neil Gaiman, or look for his work with David Almond: **The Savage**.

A man, slight and naked, is washed up on the shores of a forbidding island. He's different, and the islanders don't know what to make of him. They won't give him work, they talk about him behind his back and slowly their suspicion turns to paranoia. The island closes in on itself; a fortress afraid of the rest of the world. And the stranger? Well, let's just say there are no happy endings here.

This is a picture book, but it's not for babies. It's for anyone old enough to think about the world around us and how we live in it. It's for anyone who has ever thought suspiciously of others – fleetingly or otherwise – for just being different. With very little text and scant use of colour, this story gets to the heart of bigotry and prejudice. It won't take you long to read, but it'll take you a long time to forget.

**Leonie Flynn**

# IVANHOE  Walter Scott

In an England torn apart by civil war, where Saxons battle Normans, Wilfred of Ivanhoe returns from the Crusades. Disinherited by his scheming father he battles for his name, his country, his life and his love, Rowena. From the deadly games of jousting, to witch trials, rescue and healing by the black-eyed, beautiful Jew, Rebecca, *Ivanhoe*'s story is fast, furious and compelling. And in Brian de Bois Gilbert it also has one of the best villains ever.

This is a story of hatred and conflict, of Christians, Jews, Muslims, families and kings. It is also about the healing power of compassion and the enduring strength of love. In weaving all the threads together, Scott spins a tale that has become a true legend.

**Leonie Flynn**

### Next?

Charles Dickens's *A Tale of Two Cities*, set at the time of the French Revolution, is also about love and hatred and is very exciting. (UTBG 386)

Alexandre Dumas was influenced by Walter Scott; try *The Three Musketeers* (though try and forget the films!) or the classic *The Man in the Iron Mask*.

Walter Scott wrote many books, mostly set in his native Scotland; try *The Pirate* or the wild adventure that is *Rob Roy*.

# I WAS A TEENAGE WORRIER  Ros Asquith

Letty Chubb is a 15-year-old Bridget Jones in the making and this is her compulsively readable, cringe-makingly realistic diary crammed full of really fascinating stuff about everything from food fads to families, school to spots, clothes to contraception. No problem is left unexplored and her sound factual advice is livened up by a riot of laugh-out-loud funny illustrations.

The original and still the best of the crop of teenage diaries, it's 'speling and gramar' mistake-ridden, which adds to the fun, making it the 'ultimate teenage handbook'. It's also the heartstring-tugging and hilarious story of Letty's love for Daniel and the trials and tribulations of life in the eccentric Chubb family. Definitely one to share with your friends again and again!

**Eileen Armstrong**

> **Next?**
>
> Sneak a look at Matt Whyman's *Unzipped*, which presents the boy facts in a stylishly packaged user's manual.
>
> How about the fictional *Girl, 15, Charming But Insane*? (UTBG 154)
>
> And to find out more about the changes going on in your head, read *Blame My Brain*. (UTBG 46)
>
> More diaries to make you laugh? Try **The Princess Diaries**. (UTBG 323)

# JACKDAW SUMMER
## David Almond

> **Next?**
>
> It's hard not to recommend David Almond, as all his books are amazing. Try *Skellig*. (UTBG 365)
>
> A book about dealing with the violence within oneself in a very different way is Sonia Hartnett's *Surrender*. (UTBG 385)
>
> There's violence, mystery and a terrifying secret in Tim Bowler's *Bloodchild*.
>
> Or what about when violence is forced upon you? Try Jane Mitchell's *Chalkline*, about a Kashmiri boy coerced into becoming a rebel soldier.

Liam Lynch lives in Northumberland; an empty, wild land where soldiers train and fighter jets roar, and Roman roads trace the lines of old wars. Into his life come strangers trailing new conflicts; a baby abandoned in an ancient farmhouse and Oliver, a Liberian refugee with a bloody history. Liam is fascinated and repelled by the violence he sees in others – but how much violence is there within himself?

David Almond's novels are sparse and evocative, and *Jackdaw Summer* is no exception. Powerfully and humanely written, it is a story about love and savagery and what we are capable of as human beings.

**Sally Nicholls**

# JAKE'S TOWER Elizabeth Laird

Jake can't believe that his mother won't leave her violent partner. So he constructs an imaginary tower – a place where he can escape the violence and fear pervading their home.

When things finally spin out of control, Jake and his mum wind up with a grandmother he's never known. As old resentments and bitterness froth to the surface of their lives, Jake discovers an entirely new world. It is here that previously accepted truths are shattered and his mythical father becomes a wonderful reality.

Subtle yet dramatic, it's a stark, painful novel at times, but it also stands as a beacon of hope – as powerful as Jake's tower itself.

**Jonny Zucker**

### Next?

Another Elizabeth Laird? Try *Kiss the Dust* (UTBG 227), about the trials of a Kurdish refugee family, or *The Garbage King* (UTBG 150), a powerful tale about street children, or maybe *The Witching Hour*, set in a 17th-century Scotland beset by fear of witchcraft.

Catherine Forde's *Fat Boy Swim* has a bullied hero empowered in a way he never expected. (UTBG 128)

*Freak the Mighty* by Rodman Philbrick contains protagonists who find the strength to overcome incredible adversity. (UTBG 147)

# JAMAICA INN Daphne Du Maurier

### Next?

You'll find more terrific historical romance in Georgette Heyer's *These Old Shades* (UTBG 392) *The Red Necklace* (UTBG 329) by Sally Gardner and Mary Hoffman's *The Falconer's Knot* (UTBG 127).

More Daphne Du Maurier? Try *My Cousin Rachel*, about love, doubt and murder, or *Rebecca* (UTBG 328).

Robert Goddard's *Set in Stone* is about grief and a mysterious old house.

Mary Yellen couldn't possibly have imagined the wild and twisted adventure she would embark on after she moved into Jamaica Inn. She quickly realises that it's no ordinary inn, since there are no guests staying there, and before long she starts to hear mysterious visitors who come and go in the dead of the night... Uncle Joss, a monstrous hulk and brute of a man, is not her real uncle, but rather her half-witted, terrified Aunt Patience's husband. But Mary isn't scared of Uncle Joss, and is not about to leave her aunt alone in his clutches, and so she chooses to stay at the Inn. In doing so, she is swept up in all its dark secrets.

Your hair may be on end before you finish *Jamaica Inn*; if you enjoy a good suspenseful romance, this one won't disappoint you.

**Candida Gray**

# The JAMES BOND books Ian Fleming

When I was about 12, and a pupil at a boys' boarding school in Berkshire, we all read the **Saint** books avidly.

But then one day a man named Ian Fleming wrote a book called *Casino Royale*, about a super-spy with a licence to kill. Almost overnight, every one of us dropped the Saint and picked up James Bond. The Fleming books weren't better written than the Charteris books and Bond's adventures weren't more exciting; but they contained a treasure trove of meticulous and rather grown-up detail – Walther PPK pistols and supercharged Bentleys, vodka martinis ('shaken, not stirred'), gambling dens and shadowy organisations which went in for really *horrible* torture. Lastly, but most importantly, Ian Fleming wrote about beautiful girls with wonderful names who did a whole lot more than just kiss the hero fleetingly on the lips. With that sort of competition, the poor Saint didn't stand a chance.

**Ian Ogilvy**

### Next?

If you like James Bond, try the detailed and realistic books by Tom Clancy. Start with *Patriot Games*.

Curious about Bond's back-story? Try the brilliant *SilverFin* (UTBG 362).

Or maybe try Bond after Fleming – Sebastian Faulks's *Devil May Care* is even written in Fleming's style!

For more spies, but a slightly tougher read, try John le Carré's classic, *A Perfect Spy*.

# JANE EYRE Charlotte Brontë

### Next?

Mr Rochester's early life is imagined in *Wide Sargasso Sea*. (UTBG 438)

Charlotte's sisters wrote of love and passion, too. Try *Wuthering Heights* (UTBG 447) (Emily) or *Agnes Grey* (Anne).

Elizabeth Gaskell knew Charlotte; her *Life of Charlotte Brontë* is a fascinating study. And while you're reading Gaskell, try her novel, *North and South*.

*Jane Eyre* caused a real stushie – a storm of protest – when it was first published. Politicians, press and churches wanted it pulped. It was too dangerous, too depressing, full of controversial 'issues' and revolutionary ideas that had no place in a novel read by impressionable young people. In fact, it was cutting-edge stuff, a roaring success with the young readership who were supposedly threatened by it.

Having survived a grim and loveless childhood, Jane ventures into the world on her own, still a teenager, and falls in love with her rich employer. But this man has a dark secret...

This story of a young character's ultimate survival in a brutal world has resonated with generation after generation – and it's still gripping stuff for readers today.

**Julie Bertagna**

# OFF THE RAILS
## by Kevin Brooks

The first book I read that really grabbed hold of me and took me away to another world was *The Catcher in the Rye* by J.D. Salinger. I read it when I was about 14. My English teacher just gave it to me one day and said: 'See what you think of that.' He was one of those crazy English teachers who actually encourage you to read stuff you don't have to read for school. He was also fond of throwing chairs at people, but that's by the by. Anyway, I read *The Catcher in the Rye* and I loved it, and I've never forgotten it.

You can read more about this classic story on p. 69, but basically it's about a teenage boy called Holden Caulfield who goes a bit crazy and runs away from school, and then his life starts spiralling out of control. *That* was the part that really grabbed me – the spiralling-out-of-control part – and ever since then I've always been drawn to reading (and writing) books about people whose lives go off the rails.

It's not a uniquely teenage experience – there are plenty of books about adults losing control of their lives – but in the teenage world the dividing line between order and chaos is so much more fragile than in the adult world, which makes it a perfect setting for journeys into chaos and confusion. When we're growing up, everything is unsettled – our lives, our emotions, our relationships – and so it doesn't take much to step over the line and become lost in the spiral.

That's how it was for me, anyway. In fact, that's *still* how it is for me!

---

### MORE OFF THE RAILS

*Junk* by Melvin Burgess

*The Outsiders* by S.E. Hinton

*Candy* by Kevin Brooks

*Disconnected* by Sherry Ashworth

*Trainspotting* by Irvine Welsh

*Go Ask Alice* by Anonymous

*Come Clean* by Terri Paddock

**Gossip Girl** series by Cecily von Ziegesar

Which is where the fascination comes from, I suppose. I like to read about stuff that *could* happen to me, but probably – and hopefully – won't, because it allows me to experience all the fears and the thrills and the confusion of going off the rails without actually doing it myself.

All books, of course, work on lots of different levels – which is part of what makes reading so great – and this kind of story is no different. Take *Peace Like a River* (UTBG 308) by Leif Enger, for example. Yes, it tells the story of a young boy whose life suddenly changes when his older brother kills a man and goes on the run, and, yes, it's all about that spiralling journey into an unknown world – but there's so much more to it than that. There's tragedy, poetry, mystery. There's stuff to make you think. There's beautiful language, unforgettable characters, a compulsive story... Basically, there's everything you could ever wish for in a book.

Another brilliant story about stepping over the line is *Skarrs* (UTBG 364) by Catherine Forde. Again, the book is chock-full of all sorts of other things, too, but one of the central themes is how the main character, Danny, struggles with his conscience as he gets drawn into a world which he knows is wrong for him, but he finds very hard to resist. It's this kind of struggle, this inner conflict, that takes us right inside the character's mind, and once we're in there, that's when the story becomes real. We're living it. We're there. It's happening to us. Great stuff.

Think **you** can **get away** with it? So did Jack.

A final example, this time an intriguing mixture of fiction and reality, is *Hole In My Life* (UTBG 183) by Jack Gantos. This book tells the true story of what happened to the writer Jack Gantos when he was convicted of smuggling drugs as a young man. We learn about his somewhat chaotic early life, his constant struggle to find himself, and his time in prison, where he finally began to do what he'd always wanted to do – write books. It's an amazing story, and I suppose one of the most fascinating things about it is that the wonderful books that Jack Gantos now writes are often about the kind of young people whose lives are prone to tumbling out of control, just like his did.

Is that a neat ending, or what?

# JEANNIE OF WHITE PEAK FARM
Berlie Doherty

I love this book. It tells the story of human beings in their own wide landscape of hills and sky. This same Derbyshire landscape has driven many of my own novels in the time I have lived here.

Jeannie lives on an isolated farm 'in the soft folding hills of Derbyshire... Nothing ever seemed to change there'. Yet over four years the life of each member of Jeannie's family does change – violently. Jeannie tells us in her truthful teenage way the stories of her gran, her sisters, her mother and brother, their triumphs and tragedies. Brooding over the family like the dark hillside is the character least willing to face change or the outside world: Jeannie's implacable father. Jeannie herself grows up during the time span of the story. She learns to recognise not only the warmth and beauty in her life, but also the cruelty and unhappiness.

**Caroline Pitcher**

> ### Next?
> Another by Berlie Doherty? Try *Deep Secret* or *The Children of Winter*, a time-slip novel also set in Derbyshire.
>
> Another lyrical book about rural life? Try Alan Garner's *The Stone Book Quartet*.
>
> If you hanker after the vivid landscape and passion, read the classic *Wuthering Heights*. (UTBG 447)

# The JEEVES stories  P.G. Wodehouse

P.G. Wodehouse wrote dozens of novels and short stories about Jeeves, and they almost all have the same basic plot. Likeable upper-class twit Bertie Wooster gets himself into some sort of pickle; his efforts to put things right only make it worse, and in the end his super-capable manservant Jeeves exerts his mighty brain to save the day. But in P.G. Wodehouse's hands the formula never grows stale, and the fact that the world of gentleman's clubs and country-house parties he writes about is so dated that it feels like fantasy doesn't matter, either. The writing is fresh and chatty, the jokes are funny and the plotting is brilliant. The short stories in particular are perfect little pieces of comic engineering, and wonderfully entertaining.

**Philip Reeve**

> ### Next?
> P.G. Wodehouse's many **Blandings** stories are every bit as good as the **Jeeves** ones. Try the *Life at Blandings Omnibus*.
>
> Or for something from the same era that is equally funny, try Stella Gibbons's *Cold Comfort Farm*. (UTBG 83)
>
> Margery Allingham's detective stories also have a delightful relationship between a rich man and his butler; start with *Mystery Mile*.

# JEMIMA J  Jane Green

**Next?**

Other books by Jane Green you may enjoy: *Mr Maybe*, *Girl Friday* and *Bookends*.

*Tales of the City* and its sequels by Armistead Maupin are unputdownable, quick to read and full of characters to fall in love with. (UTBG 387)

Something just as satisfying? Try Isabel Wolff's *A Vintage Affair* or Sophie Kinsella's *Twenties Girl*.

There's a whole world of must-read pink lit out there; see our feature on pp. 74–75.

Reading *Jemima J* is as satisfying as a Sunday afternoon on the sofa with a box of Maltesers. A deliciously compulsive read, it tells the story of Jemima Jones's transformation from overweight and lonely reporter for the *Kilburn Herald* to size ten, sought-after, glamorous feature writer and international jet-setter. This is a totally feel-good book that has you laughing, crying and falling in love along with Jemima. There are some positive messages too: about dieting, best friends, fashion and learning to love yourself. Plus some hints about surviving long-haul transatlantic flights that I have found invaluable!

**Abigail Anderson**

# JIMMY CORRIGAN, THE SMARTEST KID ON EARTH  Chris Ware

If you thought that comics were just about superheroes, think again. Chris Ware is probably the greatest comic artist working today and this novel about three generations of the Corrigan family is both moving and beautiful. Two men, grandfather and grandson, both named Jimmy Corrigan and living in Chicago a hundred years apart from each other, are abandoned by their fathers. Both lead lonely, difficult childhoods and spend their lives searching for love and family in a fumbling, sometimes tragic way. The story shuttles back and forth between them; in the past, one is abandoned as a child, while in the present, his adult grandson is contacted out of the blue by his father and makes a fateful journey to meet him.

**Ariel Kahn**

**Next?**

Chris Ware has also written *Quimby the Mouse*, about a love / hate relationship between a cat and mouse. Quimby also appears in *The Acme Novelty Library*: a collection of comic strips and articles.

*Jar of Fools* by Jason Lutes has a magician searching for his father.

*Postcards from No Man's Land* by Aidan Chambers interweaves the story of a boy with the shocking truth he discovers about his grandfather who fought in World War II. (UTBG 318)

# JOHNNIE'S BLITZ  Bernard Ashley

**Next?**

More Bernard Ashley? Try *The Trouble with Donovan Croft* (UTBG 405), or *A Kind of Wild Justice*, about another boy on his own, trying to deal with a violent gang.

Robert Westall's *The Kingdom by the Sea* is about a boy on the run in World War II. (UTBG 225)

*Creepers* by Keith Grey is an exciting, gritty thriller about what you'll do for your friends.

Other books set during the Blitz? Try Robert Westall's *Blitzcat* or *Blitz* by David Orme.

Johnnie thinks he's hard, grown-up and tough as they come. Running away from Approved School he heads home, only to find London torn apart by Hitler's bombing raids and everything he knew gone. Forced into going on the run, he meets up with his cousin, Tommy, and Tommy's simple-minded child-bride Bren, who's got a baby girl. A baby who isn't Tommy and Bren's. The three misfits skip London and head for a gypsy camp where they think they'll be safe. But when Bren starts to hurt the baby, Johnnie knows he has to do something, so he heads off again, trying to get the baby home.

Dark, unheroic, so real you can almost taste the fear and misery, this is a stunning recreation of a time too often glamorised in stories.

**Leonie Flynn**

# JONATHAN LIVINGSTON SEAGULL
## Richard Bach

This book was a massive bestseller on publication and has retained its iconic status. It is one of those rare, utterly simple stories that achieve the enduring quality of myth.

Dedicated to 'the real Jonathan Livingston Seagull who lives within us all', the book tells the tale of a bird who is expelled from his flock for trying to do so much more than fly. Outcast and alone, he learns that 'boredom and fear and anger are the reasons a gull's life is so short', and discovers the compassion he needs to return to the flock.

The book is enhanced by the close and detailed observations of nature and flight. Because Richard Bach was an aviator as well as an author, the aeronautical detail is exact. A powerful tale of freedom and transcendence that speaks to us all.

**Next?**

Try *Wind, Sand and Stars* by Antoine de Saint-Exupéry, who was also an aviator.

More Richard Bach? Try *Illusions: The Adventures of a Reluctant Messiah*.

Or Paulo Coelho's road trip of self-discovery, *The Alchemist*. (UTBG 15)

Or for a novel that explores what it is to be human, Hermann Hesse's *Siddhartha*.

**Livi Michael**

# JONATHAN STRANGE AND MR NORRELL ✱✱✱
## Susannah Clarke

**Next?**

Try Charles Dickens's vast and brilliant *Bleak House*.

Something more modern? Glen David Gold's *Carter Beats the Devil* relates the rivalry between two very different magicians... Or read about magicians, superheroes and more in Michael Chabon's *The Amazing Adventures of Kavalier and Clay* (UTBG 20).

Or for much more British myth and legend, introduce yourself to Merlin in *The Once and Future King*. (UTBG 292)

Strange by name and strange by nature, this huge book looks at first glance like a historical novel, complete with old-fashioned spellings and elaborate footnotes. But start reading and you find yourself drawn into a fantasy 19th century where magic works and lost roads lead into the wild and dangerous realms of the mysterious Raven King...

The complex story revolves around the rivalry between two magicians: the reclusive Mr Norris and his rebellious pupil Jonathan Strange. It has been compared to **Harry Potter**, but it is far better than that; Ms Clarke's magic seems rooted in a deep love of British landscape and folklore, and her intensely visual writing make this one of the most fully realised imaginary worlds since Tolkien's.

**Philip Reeve**

# JOURNEY TO THE RIVER SEA   Eva Ibbotson   ✱

This is classic storytelling! The heroine Maia has been tragically orphaned. Word comes that she has an uncle and aunt who are willing to adopt her; the only snag is that they live on the Amazon. But Maia is a plucky girl. While her schoolmates fear she could be eaten by crocodiles or poisoned by snakes, she sets off with excitement at the prospect of seeing the river and all the plants and animals which live in the forest. Best of all, she looks forward to meeting her cousins – the twins, Beatrice and Gwendolyn. But when she arrives, the family aren't nearly as welcoming as she'd hoped.

Underneath the fairy-tale atmosphere of bad people and hapless children is the power of the human spirit to overcome adversity. And there is such a sense of fun in the brilliant way Ibbotson allows her plot to twist and turn right to the bitter, and wonderful, end.

**Jamila Gavin**

**Next?**

Another Eva Ibbotson? Try *The Star of Kazan*, about an orphan girl in Vienna. Or *The Secret Countess*, a story of tragedy, romance and hope.

Read Karen Wallace's *Raspberries on the Yangtze* for a wonderful evocation of both a place and sibling rivalries / friendships. (UTBG 326)

Or try Jamila's own vivid story of growing up in India, *The Wheel of Surya*.

# JUNK   Melvin Burgess

This is the story of two young people, Gemma and Tar, who fall in love with each other, and with drugs. If you've ever wondered why anyone would be daft enough to stick a needle in their arm and inject heroin, this book will tell you. It charts the downward spiral of Gemma and Tar with a clinical, terrifying precision that lets you see the slide is easier than you'd think. This doesn't make for comfortable reading. The events seem very real. Many of them are highly unpleasant, and become more so as the book goes on ... but by then it's too late: you like and care about the main characters so much you have to keep reading.

**Andrew Norriss**

*winner of the Guardian Fiction Award and the Carnegie Medal*

## Next?

You'll probably enjoy *Doing It*, also by Melvin Burgess, which looks at sex with the same ruthless honesty. (UTBG 112)

And if gritty, real-life stories are to your taste, why not try *Stone Cold* by Robert Swindells? (UTBG 377)

K.L Going's *Fat Kid Rules the World* is about an unlikely friendship, drugs, music and life just as it is. (UTBG 129)

A real-life warning about the power of substance abuse is Carrie Fisher's *Postcards from the Edge*.

Gemma and Tar run away together, escaping from their unhappy, quarrelsome families. They fall in with people who live differently, dress differently and look at the world in a different way. Their new life is exhilarating, like flying – and part of the exhilaration comes from taking drugs.

But *Junk* isn't 'a book about drugs'. It's about *people*. People so real that you're right inside their heads, sharing their excitement and fears, the lies they tell themselves and the hard lessons they learn. The questions all the characters face are: What's real? What's solid enough to last a lifetime?

Finding out takes them through painful and difficult experiences and they don't all come up with the same answers. Not a book for the squeamish, but it's a terrific read.

**Gillian Cross**

# JURASSIC PARK  Michael Crichton

When I was about 12 I read *The Lost World* by Arthur Conan Doyle and was entranced by an adventure in which brave men found themselves having to cope with dinosaurs. After all, though dinosaurs have a prehistoric reality, they somehow contrive to be fabulous, too. *Jurassic Park* gets off to a scary beginning and is able to call on modern genetics to give a science-fiction credibility to the dinosaurs in this story, but at heart it has a lot in common with Conan Doyle's original fantasy. A park intended to display recreated dinosaurs has been scientifically contrived, but inevitably things go wrong and once again brave men have adventures as they confront prehistoric monsters.

**Margaret Mahy**

### Next?

Read *The Lost World* by Arthur Conan Doyle and see for yourself how Crichton was influenced.

Other Michael Crichtons to look out for include *The Andromeda Strain*, about the threat of alien bacteria capable of wiping out the human race, and *Sphere*, about a 300-year-old spaceship found on the Pacific Ocean floor.

Or for a fast-paced mystery story, try Dan Brown's *The Da Vinci Code*. (UTBG 97)

# JUST HENRY  Michelle Magorian

### Next?

If you haven't already read it, you must try Michelle Magorian's most famous book, *Goodnight Mister Tom*, the classic story of a boy evacuated to the countryside at the start of World War II.

For another story of growing up in the unsettled post-war years, try Nigel Hinton's *Time Bomb* (UTBG 396); or for something tougher, *The Hard Man of the Swings* (UTBG 171) by Jeanne Willis.

From film buffs to TV buffs – read Paul Magrs's *The Diary of a 'Dr Who' Addict*, his sequel to *Strange Boy* (UTBG 380). Or to see how another writer uses old films in his work in a quite different way, read Brian Selznick's *The Invention of Hugo Cabret* (UTBG 206).

Henry loves films, all sorts of films. He also loved his dad, but his dad died in World War II, or so Henry, his mother, stepfather and little half-sister thought... Now Henry suspects he is being followed, so when he is given a camera he starts taking lots of photos – and in them there is a mysterious man... Henry's mother takes one look at the photos and knows it is Henry's father. How will Henry react? Read the book and find out...

I loved the way the book is written. It keeps itself wrapped up in a veil of mystery, begging you to unravel it and find out more. The way the author describes Henry's reaction to meeting his dead father is mixed in with *The Third Man* (a 1949 film). Fabulous!

**Charlie Whiteside, age 11**

# JUST IN CASE
## Meg Rosoff

Like almost everyone else on the planet, I loved Meg Rosoff's *How I Live Now*. Her second book, *Just in Case*, is somewhat different, although still highly original and readable. One day, David Case saves his baby brother Charlie's life and realises, with a shock, just how arbitrary and cruel fate can be. In an attempt to thwart the unknown and thus keep himself safe, he alters his appearance and also changes his name, to Justin Case.

The book's prose is dreamy, almost poetic, but Rosoff's strength is that she manages to ground the teenage David / Justin's strange experiences in solid realism – his hopes and fears for the future, and his worries about sexuality and identity. Thoughtful, sensitive readers will warm to this book.

**Narinder Dhami**

**Next?**

More Meg of course. Read *How I Live Now* (UTBG 190) and *What I Was* (UTBG 431) next.

For another emotional book about life, death and the meaning of it all, try Sarah Dessen's *The Truth About Forever*. (UTBG 406)

Another boy who feels marked by death is in Geraldine McCaughrean's *The Death Defying Pepper Roux*.

# JUST LISTEN
## Sarah Dessen

**Next?**

For more by Sarah Dessen, try *Someone Like You* and *That Summer*: together they provided the inspiration for the movie *How to Deal*. Or maybe *Along for the Ride*, in which lonely Auden and Eli find a bond in their mutual insomnia.

Ibi Kaslik's *Skinny* deals with some of the same eating issues that appear in *Just Listen*.

Or for a teen who thinks she's really ordinary, try Joanna Nadin's *My So-Called Life: The Tragically Normal Diary of Rachel Riley*. (UTBG 274)

Have you ever needed someone to just sit down and listen to what you have to say? In Sarah Dessen's book *Just Listen*, the main character, Annabel Greene, needs just that. Annabel is going through the hardest year of her life, dealing with harsh friends, the pressure of modelling, and a family that is slowly falling apart. In the midst of all the turmoil, she is unexpectedly falling in love. As an ordinary teenage girl myself, I found that I am going through many of the same things that Annabel is. Sarah Dessen explores the reality of tough, controversial topics while still touching upon love and life. So take the time, and Just Listen.

**Sarah Whitson, age 17**

# The JUST WILLIAM series
## Richmal Crompton

**Next?**

If you like audio books, check out the **William** stories read by Martin Clunes – they're great.

William has a companion in crime – **Jennings** by Anthony Buckeridge.

For books that take a hilarious look at what school used to be like, read *Down with Skool!* and its sequels. (UTBG 113)

Probably the funniest boy you'll find in more recent books is Sue Townsend's Adrian Mole. (UTBG 347)

Has there ever been a funnier, messier, more anarchic, more exuberant, more moody, more golden-hearted, more human example of our species than William Brown? Has there ever been a more unlikely author to have created him than Richmal Crompton, genteel and sober Latin and Classics mistress at a posh London school for young ladies? Has there ever been a series of novels that gave us more fun as kids and that we're less likely to grow out of, no matter how sophisticated and worldly we become later in life?

If there has, please let me know because I've read all the **William** books about 20 times each.

*Just William* is a good one to start with, and if you like it there are 37 more.

**Morris Gleitzman**

# KATHERINE
## Anya Seton

This was the first historical novel I ever read, and it took me over completely, luring me into a medieval world of lust and intrigue. When I was at school, the only way you could get away with reading anything even a little bit sexy was to have it wrapped up in a historical package, and I'm sure my teachers must have thought I was more interested in the court of Edward III than Katherine's love affair with his son, Prince John, which is at the heart of the book. Having said that, this book did get me into reading about the past, and I ended up studying history at university, so perhaps the teachers knew what they were doing after all!

**Eleanor Updale**

**Next?**

There are some fabulous historical novels to read. Try *The Other Boleyn Girl* (UTBG 301) by Philippa Gregory, the 13th-century-set *Lords of the White Castle* by Elizabeth Chadwick, a book about Queen Elizabeth in *Innocent Traitor* by Alison Weir, the story of Henry VIII's wives in Jean Plaidy's *Murder Most Royal* and almost anything by Dorothy Dunnett, especially *The Game of Kings*.

Or look out for *The Lady in the Tower* by Marie-Louise Jensen. (UTBG 231)

# KEEPER  Mal Peet

Don't be put off this book if you don't like football – it will still captivate you. *Keeper* tells the life story of El Gato – the Cat – the world's greatest goalkeeper. During an interview with journalist Paul Faustino, El Gato reveals how he, an impoverished boy from the South American rainforest, became the iconic figure Faustino reveres. As the interview progresses, El Gato reveals how the mysterious figure he calls 'The Keeper' taught him almost everything about goalkeeping from a makeshift goalmouth in the heart of the rainforest. Peet's story is as original as it is gripping, building up tension as skilfully as any penalty shoot-out. Once you've read this book, I guarantee you will never watch a goalkeeper in the same way again.

**Helena Pielichaty**

CARNEGIE MEDAL-WINNING AUTHOR

**mal peet**

keeper

Haunted by the spirit of the game

## SPIES AND SOLDIERS

**Alex Rider** series by Anthony Horowitz

**Young Bond** series by Charlie Higson

*Boy Soldier* by Andy McNab

**CHERUB** series by Robert Muchamore

**Spy High** series by A.J. Butcher

**Nemesis** series by Catherine MacPhail

**Alpha Force** series by Chris Ryan

**Special Agents** series by Sam Hutton

**Henderson's Boys** series by Robert Muchamore

### Next?

There are two sort-of sequels: *The Penalty* (UTBG 309) and *Exposure* (UTBG 125). *Keeper* was Mal Peet's first novel; his second, very different, novel is *Tamar*. (UTBG 388)

In **Match of Death** by James Riordan, football becomes a sideline to much darker and more dangerous issues in World War II.

Bernard Ashley's **Down to the Wire** is about an African Premiership footballer caught up in the civil war.

# A KESTREL FOR A KNAVE  Barry Hines

Billy Casper is about to leave school with no job skills and no prospects. His life is hard and lean and he is in trouble with everyone, particularly his dangerous older brother, Jud. But there is another side to Billy, which emerges when he is with the hawk that he has nurtured and trained.

The author is so close to his character that we engage with everything that happens to Billy – we feel his pain and humiliation and rage at the frustrations of his life, and we soar with his spirit when he flies the wild and beautiful kestrel. This is a fast, gritty novel that raises important questions about the values of modern society. It was also made into a landmark British film, *Kes*.

**Kate Thompson**

### Next?

Chris d'Lacey's *Fly, Cherokee, Fly* is about a boy finding an injured racing pigeon and trying to heal her. Or the sequel, *Pawnee Warrior*, about a boy training racing pigeons.

Melvin Burgess is well known for hard-hitting social realism; *Kite* is less gritty than some, but is still a very real account of a boy raising a bird of prey – not a good idea when your father is a gamekeeper.

Or what about a boy whose life is turned upside down by some chickens? Try *Chicken Dance* by Jacques Couvillon. (UTBG 73)

# KIDNAPPED  Robert Louis Stevenson

### Next?

*The Three Musketeers* and *Twenty Years After* by Alexandre Dumas, for flawless 18th-century action adventure.

Another adventure set in Scotland? Try John Buchan's *The Thirty-Nine Steps*. (UTBG 394)

Or for more Jacobites, try *The Flight of the Heron* by D.K. Broster, the first in a trilogy about the Stuart uprisings.

Or more Stevenson – try *Treasure Island* (UTBG 402) or *The Master of Ballantrae*.

It's the year 1751, and orphaned David Balfour has set out to claim his inheritance from his uncle Ebenezer. But his uncle has other plans, and David finds himself a prisoner on the high seas – until he befriends exiled Jacobite Alan Breck Stewart. Together they escape, but before David can wreak his revenge on Ebenezer, he and Alan are pursued across Scotland by the English, who regard Alan as a dangerous rebel.

You can't get better historical fiction than this. Alan is wonderfully believable, full of flaws, but brave and shrewd and cocky. David is the perfect foil, with his even temper and dogged good sense. The language and attitudes take you straight back in time; you'll find yourself speaking with a Scottish accent after reading this book. A classic!

**Cathy Jinks**

# KIM  Rudyard Kipling

**Next?**

Kipling was a great writer of short stories, many of them set in India. Try the collections *Plain Tales from the Hills* and *Soldiers Three*.

More undercover (and underground) activities, this time in pre-war Europe, are to be found in Geoffrey Household's *Rogue Male*. Or try P.C. Wren's *Beau Geste* (UTBG 36).

If you want to know more about spies in the Hindu Kush, read *The Great Game: on Secret Service in High Asia* by Peter Hopkirk.

*Kim* reads like a fantasy quest through a fabulous landscape of sweltering plains, snowy passes among towering mountains, roads, trains and cities teeming with people – holy men, soldiers, pilgrims, thieves, spies. But it is not a fantasy; this is 19th-century India, before Partition, and the quest is two-fold: a Buddhist lama seeking a sacred river and a youth involved in 'The Great Game' of espionage between the British Raj and the expansionist Russian Empire across the North-West Frontier. This is old-style spying, with codes, passwords, disguises and secret agents. Some aspects of Kipling can be hard to like these days but in *Kim* he celebrates every race and religion; it's a story as much about tolerance and friendship as it is about adventure.

**Jan Mark**

# THE KIN  Peter Dickinson

This epic tale was originally published as four books, each told from the viewpoint of a youngster growing up in Africa at the dawn of humanity. Suth, Noli, Ko and Mana have to face bears, tigers, famine and human enemies on their long and hazardous journey towards adulthood.

The individual stories fit beautifully together, and I especially liked the invented myths between the chapters – such as 'How People Were Made' – which feel as though they have been transcribed from ancient cave walls, even though we have no written records from so long ago. Mixing myth and history with a moving and entertaining story, this is one of those books that lingers in the soul long after the final page has been turned.

**Katherine Roberts**

**Next?**

Another brilliant Peter Dickinson is the fantasy-based *The Ropemaker*. Or try his book about monsters and volcanoes, *Tears of the Salamander*. (UTBG 390)

You might also like *Wolf Brother*, which is set at the time of the first humans and is terrifically exciting. (UTBG 442)

If you like a bit of romance and are looking for a more adult read, you should enjoy Jean M. Auel's **Earth's Children** sequence, starting with *The Clan of the Cave Bear*.

# THE KINGDOM BY THE SEA   Robert Westall

**Next?**

Another Westall set during the war? *Blitzcat*. Don't let any prejudice against books with animals put you off – it's brilliant (and not cosy at all)!

For a very different setting and war, try *Across the Nightingale Floor* by Lian Hearn. (UTBG 11)

Felix makes a terrifying journey across Nazi-occupied Poland in Morris Gleitzman's *Once*. (UTBG 292)

It's World War II. Harry has got used to air raids, but this one's different: when he comes out of the shelter, his home and family are gone. Grief-stricken, he decides to make a new life on his own. He starts walking, following the coastline and adopting a stray dog along the way.

Away from the death and destruction on Tyneside, he quickly meets new dangers – but also finds beauty and kindness, often in the most unlikely places. He is starting to love and trust again, when a shocking turn of events threatens his hard-won peace and he must find a way of holding onto his hopes and dreams.

Both brutal and beautiful, *The Kingdom by the Sea* is the story of a boy journeying towards independence and finding his place in a new world. I defy any reader not to cry at least once.

**Graham Gardner**

# THE KING MUST DIE   Mary Renault

Plunged headlong into the colourful world of ancient Greece, you identify so strongly with the hero that you, too, would have sacrificed yourself rather than your honour, and sailed to Crete to dance the dance of death with the bulls. Theseus comes across as a real person: a womaniser and a warrior, thoughtful though not academic, ambitious but not ruthless. When he reaches Knossos and the Labyrinth, he must take part in the dangerous rite of bull-leaping. No one survives for long – but Theseus really *is* made of kingly stuff. This is one of the most exciting books I have ever read; I reread it every few years, and enjoy it just as much each time.

**Elizabeth Kay**

**Next?**

The good news is that there's a sequel: *The Bull from the Sea*. Mary Renault wrote many other books about the ancient world, and they're all worth looking out for, particularly *The Last of the Wine* and *Fire from Heaven* (UTBG 133).

Or try some detective stories set in ancient Rome with Stephen Saylor's **Gordianus the Finder** stories, starting with *The House of the Vestals*.

A very modern take on the same idea runs through *The Hunger Games* by Suzanne Collins, but instead of bull-leaping, the kids fight to the death. (UTBG 192)

# KING SOLOMON'S MINES   H. Rider Haggard

*King Solomon's Mines* is an old-fashioned, rollicking adventure story. Alan Quartermain, an elephant hunter by trade, is asked by Sir Henry Curtis and Captain Good to help find Sir Henry's brother, who has disappeared in search of the eponymous diamond mines. They are accompanied by the mysterious native, Umbopa. After almost dying of thirst and hunger, they reach the beautiful land of the Kukuana people, ruled over by a murderous tyrant, Twala. Umbopa is revealed as the rightful king and the travellers help him to overthrow Twala. They then discover a vast hoard of treasure hidden in the mountains, but are lucky to escape with a few diamonds each…

Progressive by the standards of its time, *King Solomon's Mines* is, nevertheless, riddled with a casual racism and brutality that can make it uncomfortable, if often gripping, reading.

**Anthony McGowan**

### Next?

More adventure set in colonial Africa? Read another Haggard first, *She*. Then *Tarzan of the Apes* by Edgar Rice Burroughs.

For a real look at Africa, read *Things Fall Apart* by Chinua Achebe.

Or try Alexander McCall Smith's series, **The No.1 Ladies' Detective Agency**. (UTBG 285)

Or for a coming-of-age story set in South Africa, read Bryce Courtenay's *The Power of One*.

# KISSING THE RAIN   Kevin Brooks

### Next?

If you enjoyed this, try some more Kevin Brooks – the gripping *Martyn Pig* (UTBG 256), the (relatively) gentler *Lucas* (UTBG 249) or the shocking *Candy* (UTBG 66).

For a story about weight, race and family, try Jennifer Choldenko's *If a Tree Falls at Lunchbreak*.

*Grass* by C.Z. Nightingale is the story of a girl who witnesses a racist attack, and the subsequent decisions she is forced to make.

'I shoulda kept my big mouth shut. I DIN'T SEE NOTHING, ALL RIGHT?'

Moo Nelson has it really tough. Bullied at school for being fat, his greatest pleasure is standing on a road bridge, staring, staring at the traffic and letting it shut him into a world of his own… Until the day he witnesses a murder from the bridge, and gets deeply involved in another, far more seedy and sinister world where he's forced to make some impossible choices.

Moo narrates his own story at breakneck speed, in a tone that's aggressive and defensive at the same time, so you can just feel what it's like to be inside his head. And it's not a comfortable place to be, I can tell you.

**Susan Reuben**

# KISS THE DUST  Elizabeth Laird

Tara's father is involved with the Kurdish rebels under the terrifying regime of Saddam Hussein. The family are forced to flee their home, and eventually they arrive in London as refugees. They have lost everything: their friends and neighbours, their possessions and the community who spoke their language and understood their ways.

Set in the time of the first Gulf War in the 1990s, this is the book to read if you want to understand what life must be like for refugee and asylum seekers in our country today.

**Yvonne Coppard**

**Next?**

Elizabeth Laird also wrote *Red Sky in the Morning*, about a girl living with the prejudices surrounding her family life with a disabled brother.

*Refugee Boy* describes what it's like to be a refugee in Britain today. (UTBG 330)

*Mud City* by Deborah Ellis is about an Afghan girl's life in a Pakistan refugee camp.

# THE KITE RIDER  Geraldine McCaughrean

**Next?**

All Geraldine McCaughrean's books are great. Try her stunning sequel to J.M. Barrie's *Peter Pan*: *Peter Pan in Scarlet*; or *The White Darkness* (UTBG 435) for a story of obsession and loneliness; or *Tamburlaine's Elephants*, about a Tartar boy fighting with the Mongol army.

*Lost Horizon* by James Hilton is about finding paradise hidden in the Himalayas.

*Tulku* by Peter Dickinson is an extraordinary adventure set in China and Tibet. (UTBG 408)

Haoyou's father flies up into the clouds and comes back without a soul, his heart having burst with fear 'like a sack of grain'. Now Di Chou, the man who sent his father to his death, wants to marry Haoyou's mother. While escaping from both his grasping uncle Bo and Di Chou, Haoyou is taken on by the Great Miao Je, owner of an exotic circus, and becomes a virtuoso kite rider, seeking his father's spirit in the sky. But Miao Je is on a dark quest of his own.

This is a stunning story of revenge and restoration that will keep you hooked to the final page.

**Livi Michael**

# THE KITE RUNNER
## Khaled Hosseini

I couldn't put this book down once I'd started reading it. There are three things I like in a book: 1) a good story that keeps me gripped; 2) that it's well written / a pleasure to read; and 3) that it gives an insight into another way of life. This book does all three. It is about the value of friendship and family with 1970s Afghanistan as the background and starting point. It is written with such warmth and I came away feeling that I knew more about what had happened over there than I could have gained from watching a hundred in-your-face documentaries. Everyone (and I mean everyone) I have recommended this to has loved it as much as I did!

**Cathy Hopkins**

> **Next?**
>
> More by Khaled Hosseini? Try *A Thousand Splendid Suns*, which follows the harrowing lives of two Afghani women and deals with victimisation, class and religion.
>
> *Memoirs of a Geisha* by Arthur Golden also gives a glimpse into another culture and time. (UTBG 260)
>
> *My Forbidden Face* by Latifa is a searing account of life under the Taliban.
>
> *The Bookseller of Kabul* is Asne Seierstad's story of her time living with a family in Kabul.

# KIT'S WILDERNESS   David Almond

> **Next?**
>
> Among David Almond's other books, *The Fire-Eaters* is my favourite. It has the same quality of looking at the real, everyday world and seeing something mysterious. (UTBG 133)
>
> *Red Shift* (UTBG 329) and *The Owl Service* (UTBG 306) by Alan Garner do this, too.
>
> If you like David Almond's ability to describe real places, linking past and present, you might enjoy *Sea Room* by Adam Nicolson. It's a non-fiction book about the little islands that his father gave him when he was 21, and I think it's magic.

*Kit's Wilderness* explores 'the desire we have to be terrified, to look into the darkness'. When Kit Watson makes friends with John Askew and Allie Keenan, they play the game called Death, and Kit finds himself drawn into a strange place where the darkness of the past links somehow with the darkness inside his own head and the dark tunnels of the disused mines.

There is danger and cruelty and, in the end, a real death, but the book is full of warmth, too. In Kit's stories and Askew's drawings, in the acting of Allie, 'the good-bad ice girl', and in the character of Kit's grandfather, the darkness becomes a source of strength and beauty. It's an extraordinary book. But don't take my word for it. Read it yourself.

**Gillian Cross**

# THE KNIFE OF NEVER LETTING GO
## Patrick Ness

**Next?**

Next in the **Chaos Walking** sequence is *The Ask and the Answer*.

Or try Tim Lott's *Fearless* for something else about power and resistance, difference and prejudice – and brilliantly written. (UTBG 129)

Stephen Baxter's *The H-Bomb Girl* is set in 1962, but actually encompasses time travel, the nuclear destruction of Liverpool and the Cuban missile crisis. It's brilliant and makes you think.

Todd's world is full of Noise. Not in the same way as ours. The Noise in Todd's world comes from men's thoughts. He lives in a place without women, an angry dystopia where there's no escaping what's in other people's heads. He can even hear what his dog is thinking.

And then Todd finds a patch of silence. It takes his breath away and he pursues it through the swamp and forest. The patch of silence is a girl. And once he finds her, they both have to run.

Unflinching, sometimes brutal, always gripping, this is also a book about the redemptive power of friendship and the triumph in never giving up. A wildly imaginative, thought-provoking, heart-quickening read.

**Jenny Valentine**

# THE KNIFE THAT KILLED ME
## Anthony McGowan

The great title of this novel is also its opening phrase, and the promise it holds makes this book very hard to put down. The 'me' is Paul Varderman, an average teenager in a rough school where everyone seems to be sorted into gangs. Accidentally, he attracts the attention of Roth, a clever and charismatic bully, and for Paul this could mean very bad news. Strangely, it looks like Roth is actually trying to befriend him. And he's not the only one. Shane, the cool leader of the 'freaks' also seems to take a shine to Paul, and with the attractive Maddy Bray being a member of Shane's gang, Paul is certainly tempted to join them. It's not long before Paul finds himself torn between the two gangs and events start to spiral out of his control. And all the time, the knife that killed him is coming closer and closer.

**Next?**

*Shattering Glass* by Gail Giles is also about a bully who befriends a freak – but with ulterior motives.

You have to read more Anthony McGowan, too – particularly the foul, hilarious *Henry Tumour*. (UTBG 175)

There's another knife crime in Gillian Philip's tough and gripping *Crossing the Line*.

**Noga Applebaum**

# KNIGHT CREW  Nicky Singer

The Knight Crew are at war with the Saxons. The violence escalates out of control and Knight Crew leader Art, inspired by the wise words of an old mystic, realises that revenge is futile. Seeking to find a new way, where talk, thought and governance are valued over impulse, pride and anger, Arthur gathers the Crew and asks them to swear allegiance to his new code of honour. With his sweetheart by his side, he can be a force for good. But the presence of a new Crew member threatens to bring down the new order.

*Knight Crew* updates the Arthurian myth, placing it in a contemporary urban setting. The narrative is fast-paced, the combat scenes are adrenalin-fuelled and the dialogue is lively. At the same time the universal themes of honour and respect, passion and betrayal have a weighty resonance, which makes this a compelling and affecting read.

**Nikki Gamble**

**Next?**

More Nicky Singer? Try *Feather Boy* (UTBG 130) or *Doll*.

For more on the Arthur story, try Philip Reeve's *Here Lies Arthur* (UTBG 175) or Kevin Crossley-Holland's *Arthur: The Seeing Stone* (UTBG 352).

Or try the original teen gang novel, *The Outsiders*. (UTBG 305)

# LADY CHATTERLEY'S LOVER  D.H. Lawrence

**Next?**

Another D.H. Lawrence? *Sons and Lovers* is probably the best known; I've always rather liked his short stories, too.

*A Clockwork Orange* is in no way like Lady Chatterley, except that it too was scandalous when it was first published. (UTBG 82)

For more tensions in the British class system, read *The Go-Between* (UTBG 159) or E.M. Forster's *Howard's End*.

*Chatterley* is arguably the most controversial novel of the 20th century. What shocked its readers (and those who didn't read it but followed the famous obscenity trial in the newspapers) wasn't the boundary-breaking story of a married aristocratic lady having an affair with a working-class man, a gamekeeper on her estate, but the way the book was written – or more particularly the way the sex scenes were written. The rough, honest, earthiness of the language was unlike anything any respectable person had ever read before. Or at least would admit to having read before. Such language! In print! Outrageous!

And it's great. The whole book – not just those few famous and controversial scenes – is energetic and rough and unfussy, and the characters live and breathe from the first page to the very last. Read it and see what all the fuss was about.

**Daniel Hahn**

# THE LADY IN THE TOWER Marie-Louise Jensen ☀

## Next?

More Marie-Louise Jensen? Try *Between Two Seas*, in which a girl searches for her absent father.

For more historical drama featuring feisty young women, try *Witch Child* by Celia Rees, set in the 17th century (UTBG 441), or *The Ruby in the Smoke* by Philip Pullman, which takes place in Victorian London (UTBG 341).

A dastardly murder plot, an imprisoned lady, an evil chaplain and a brave young girl – here are all the elements of a rollicking historical drama.

Set in the time of Henry VIII, the story tells of young Eleanor, who leads a happy life in the family castle until, suddenly and inexplicably, her father imprisons her mother in a tower and allows no one – not even Eleanor – to see her. Eleanor and her mother manage to communicate secretly by letter, but this is their only means of contact for the next four years. Then Eleanor discovers a plot to murder her mother and realises that she must find a way to free her before it's too late...

**Susan Reuben**

# LAST CHANCE TO SEE ☀ ☀
## Douglas Adams and Mark Carwardine

Douglas Adams takes the writing style that we all adored in *The Hitchhiker's Guide to the Galaxy* and applies it to a series of trips to see some of Earth's most endangered species. And it works! The descriptions of the creatures themselves are beautifully interwoven with tales of the people who devote their lives to trying to save them. In one part, Adams is going to an area with lots of poisonous snakes so he goes to see an expert on venom. He asks what he should do if he gets bitten by a deadly snake and is told: 'You die, of course. That's what deadly means'.

**Anthony Reuben**

## Next?

Read *The Hitchhiker's Guide to the Galaxy* (UTBG 182) if you haven't already. Or try *Dirk Gently's Holistic Detective Agency*, which starts with a missing cat and spins off into wild, wonderful Adams-ish fantasy.

Bill Bryson is another travel writer who is worried about snakes in Australia, in his book *Down Under*.

Mal Peet's *Keeper* is partially about the destruction of the rainforest. (UTBG 222)

# LAST SEEN WEARING TRAINERS
Rosie Rushton

**Next?**

More Rosie Rushton? Read *Just Don't Make a Scene, Mum!* or *What a Week to Get Real*, about four friends coping with boys and life.

In *The Illustrated Mum*, the children have to support a mother who's finding it hard to cope. (UTBG 200)

If you enjoy exploring different sides of a story through multiple narrators, try Steven Herrick's *The Simple Gift*. (UTBG 363)

This book is dedicated to 'Everyone who has been scared by someone they love; and all those with the courage to face their fears'. It presents differing points of view – the narrative is told by Katie, Lydia, Tom and Grace. A mum and her daughter have trouble coping, teenagers try to make sense of their worlds and a secret emerges. A complex web of family relationships unfolds. Lives intertwine and decisions taken years ago create terrifying consequences. The pace is fast, the plot twists and there is real tension. What will people do in the name of love? I know it is a cliché but this is one thriller you really can't put down. Do try it!

**Brenda Marshall**

# THE LAST SIEGE   Jonathan Stroud

The nearby ruined castle has never interested Emily and Simon – for them it's just a place for tourists. Then one snowy winter, when the castle is locked up, they meet Marcus. His vivid imagination and fascination with the castle's murderous past bring the ruin to life. He persuades them to break in and spend the night there. But the place starts to exert a more powerful grip than any of them could have imagined. And when they feel the castle is under siege, they are prepared to defend it.

Stroud has written a powerful psychological thriller. His depiction of the castle is especially vivid, and as it goes from being a place of refuge to a nightmarish trap, you really feel as though you're there.

**Katie Jennings**

**Next?**

*Silent Snow, Secret Snow* by Adèle Geras is about a family snowed in at a remote house and the secrets and lies that emerge. (UTBG 362)

More Stroud? Read *The Leap*, about a girl who won't believe that her brother is dead. Or try his altogether different fantasy sequence, the **Bartimaeus** trilogy which starts with *The Amulet of Samarkand* (UTBG 21).

Or read Robert Westall's *The Devil on the Road*, about a motorbike rider who takes refuge in a barn with strange symbols carved over the door, and inadvertently triggers a terrifying chain of events that could lead to a girl's death.

# LAST TRAIN FROM KUMMERSDORF
## Leslie Wilson

A superb World War II story told from the viewpoint of the defeated Germans. Hanno is one of Hitler's boy soldiers, sent to stop the inevitable Russian advance. After seeing his twin Wolfgang killed, Hanno joins a stream of refugees fleeing west to surrender to the Allies rather than the avenging Russians.

Hanno has never questioned the Nazi philosophy; it is all he has ever known. However, when he meets up with Effi, whose family has been in the Resistance, he starts to wonder what his dead father got up to in Russia and to doubt the morality of the Nazi cause. The reader can feel the hunger and fear of the refugees, and also the pain of having to make sense of a changing world without a leader and without the certainties that the defeated nation had been used to.

**Ann Jungman**

> ### Next?
> *The Ice Road* is about the Siege of Leningrad, and the struggle of ordinary people to survive. (UTBG 196)
>
> For a book about more recent refugees, try *The Other Side of Truth*, about escaping from war-torn Nigeria. (UTBG 302)
>
> How about a tense, fast-paced thriller that also looks at the Nazis in a thought-provoking way? Try *Ausländer* by Paul Dowswell. (UTBG 32)

# LBD: IT'S A GIRL THING   Grace Dent

> ### Next?
> The bambinos are back and still determined to go to the Astlebury Festival in *LBD: The Great Escape*. Find out if they do in *Live and Fabulous* and *Friends Forever*.
>
> There's more girl power in *Guitar Girl* by Sarra Manning, about a teenage girl's rise to rock stardom.
>
> For more about music, try Graham Marks's *Radio Radio* or Jonny Zucker's *One Girl, Two Decks, Three Degrees of Love* (UTBG 295) or K.L. Going's *Fat Kid Rules the World* (UTBG 129).

Fourteen-year-old Ronnie Ripperton and her best friends Claude and Fleur are the feisty trio who call themselves the LBD – *Les Bambinos Dangereuses*.They love boys and music and are all longing to go to a local music festival, which naturally offers great snogging opportunities, and where even the gorgeous Spike Saunders will be playing. When their parents forbid them from going, Claude comes up with the brilliant idea of staging their own charity concert at the school. They start organising auditions, but things start to go awry almost immediately and soon there's drama and excitement to be had all round. Very funny, and totally believable – it's a great summer read.

**John McLay**

# LEADER OF THE PACK  Kate Cann

**Next?**

Try other books by Kate Cann – especially the *Moving Out*, *Moving In* and *Moving On* trilogy that also has a male central character. Or check out her *Escape*. (UTBG 122)

*Rain* by Kate le Vann looks at growing up through the eyes of two generations of women. And yes, there are boys there, too...

Paul Magrs writes about boys and growing up. Try his *Exchange*, about a boy, a grandmother, a girl and a bookshop. (UTBG 124)

Fans of Kate Cann will not be disappointed by *Leader of the Pack*. The story focuses on the developing relationship between rugby-playing Jack and artistic Gem. As the book starts, they appear to have little in common, apart from a strong physical connection – but will this be enough to keep them together?

Cann always makes her characters feel real, and *Leader of the Pack* is full of her usual insights into the ups and downs of a strongly realised teenage relationship. However, the story also takes a fascinating and convincing look at what it means to grow up, from boy to man, in 21st-century Britain. It is fast-paced, deftly characterised and by turns funny, thought provoking and moving.

**Sophie McKenzie**

# LEAVING POPPY  Kate Cann

*Leaving Poppy* is a very modern ghost story that cleverly integrates the anxieties of teenagers leaving home for the first time with a genuinely creepy supernatural plot. Amber has fled to a ramshackle old house in a seaside town, escaping a cloying, hyper-critical mother and a borderline psychotic sister. Things look up when she makes friends with her student housemates and finds work in a local restaurant. However, everything begins to unravel when goth sister Poppy turns up. There is something evil in the house and Poppy is the perfect vessel for its malevolence. Amber's struggles, both to carve a new life for herself and to confront her supernatural foes, make her a vulnerable, sympathetic heroine. Although the book may be light on gore for horror lovers, it packs a serious psychological punch.

**Anthony McGowan**

**Next?**

There's more Kate. She writes fun, insightful, teen romances (*Footloose*, *Diving In*) and deeply scary, unsettling paranormal romances – try *Possessing Rayne*.

Michelle Zink's *The Prophecy of the Sisters* is about demons, spirts and very different twin girls.

Or for outright scary – and gory – look out Marcus Sedgwick's *My Swordhand Is Singing*. (UTBG 275)

# THE LEFT HAND OF DARKNESS
## Ursula Le Guin

**Next?**

If you liked this book, you'll enjoy *A Wizard of Earthsea* (UTBG 442) about the wizard Ged and the responsibilities of magic; also Le Guin's short stories in *The Wind's Twelve Quarters*, which are superbly imaginative.

Virginia Woolf's *Orlando* has a life that spans centuries and crosses the gender divide. (UTBG 299)

Another author who plays with gender is C.J. Cherry; try her **Foreigner** series.

On the glacial planet of Gethen it's always deepest winter. When an ambassador from the Ekumen (a federation of planets) visits, he discovers that the inhabitants live a feudal existence and that they have only one gender, becoming male or female at different times in their lives. In a wonderful story of love and danger and journeying through landscapes of ice, Le Guin plays havoc with our preconceptions of male and female, and imagines how it would be if a person could be both a mother and father. This isn't just an ideas book though – it's a rich, exciting story. Definitely one of the all-time classic fantasies.

**Catherine Fisher**

# LETTERS FROM THE INSIDE
## John Marsden

I can do no better than quote Robert Cormier, who described this book as 'absolutely shattering as it brings to vivid life two teenage girls and then strangles your heart over what happens to their relationship'.

The girls start as strangers writing letters to each other, pen pals with secrets and fears, which they slowly reveal. But what they reveal will change them in ways they could not have predicted, and their lives become tangled together. You have to concentrate while you are reading, because the whole story is in the letters and you don't quite know what to trust. But the effort will be rewarded, I promise, and you will not forget this book.

**Nicola Morgan**

**Next?**

For a book about secrets and lies and the harm they can do, try E.R. Franks's disturbing story of new girl Stacy, *Friction*.

You may well enjoy another book by John Marsden, such as *Tomorrow When the War Began*, in which a group of friends return from a camping trip to find their families dead and the world a changed place.

You might also like any of Robert Cormier's dark, edgy books. Start with **Heroes**. (UTBG 176)

# THE LIAR  Stephen Fry

It must be great to be as clever as Stephen Fry. Apart from the various other difficult things he's very good at, he's also managed to write this fantastically funny novel; and what's more he makes the writing and the humour – both light and elegant – seem altogether effortless.

It's the story of the brilliant and decadent Adrian Healey, student at St Matthew's College in Cambridge, who worships toast (pronounced 'taste') almost as much as he worships Hugo Alexander Timothy Cartwright, and who is, frankly, a bit of a tart. There's also a bit of light murder, some spying, and a scene involving lots of brand names that makes me laugh just thinking about it. What more could you want? It's a pleasure to read.

**Daniel Hahn**

> **Next?**
>
> Stephen Fry has written other novels including **The Stars' Tennis Balls** as well as an exceptional memoir, **Moab Is My Washpot** (UTBG 267).
>
> If you fancy trying a very different story of Cambridge life, read E.M. Forster's **Maurice**, or (for real life, not fiction) Clive James's **May Week Was in June**.
>
> I can't think of many books that have made me laugh as much as this one. But try something by the very funny (though otherwise quite different) Ben Elton. Start with **Popcorn**.

# LIFE, INTERRUPTED
## Damian Kelleher

> **Next?**
>
> There's more about living with illness in the poignant and moving **Before I Die** by Jenny Downham. (UTBG 37)
>
> In Kate Le Vann's **Things I Know About Love**, a girl, after years of illness, tries to rediscover her life.
>
> Or for another funny yet poignant journey through loss, try **Walk Two Moons** by Sharon Creech. (UTBG 422)

What happens when your mum collapses at work, your brother is in the hospital with yet another football injury, and your dad isn't around?

Luke is 14 when his mum is admitted to hospital and a beast of a child minder moves in, taking over the house. His accident-prone little brother keeps on playing football, apparently oblivious to the severity of the situation – does he not understand? Or is he just dealing in his own way?

Kelleher creates real and lovable characters, insightfully navigating their journey through the difficult terrain of family grief. It will leave you touched by the understanding, humour and emotion of each character as they find their own way through. Prepare to smile through sadness.

**Tessa Brechin**

# LIFE OF PI
## Yann Martel

After the tragic sinking of a cargo ship carrying his family and their zoo, 16-year-old Pi is left shipwrecked. Think things could not get any worse? Add the endless Pacific Ocean, a hyena, a zebra (with a broken leg), a female orang-utan … and a 450-pound Royal Bengal tiger. Well, it's not a normal story.

*Life of Pi* is a captivating novel written from Pi's own point of view as he bobs about in the middle of a never-ending expanse of ocean. It's a story of courage, survival and nerve, with a mixture of suspense, tension, surprise and cleverness. It takes a while to get going, but patience is a virtue as the story culminates in an interesting twist...

**Louise Manning, age 14**

### Next?

Did you like the tale of boy and tiger? Try Rudyard Kipling's *The Jungle Book*. He also wrote about another boy in India, *Kim* (UTBG 224).

If you liked the magical realism, there are many more wonderful books to look out for. Try Isabelle Allende's *House of the Spirits* (UTBG 189), or García Márquez's *Love in the Time of Cholera* (UTBG 248).

Or try some of Yann Martel's short stories – *The Facts Behind the Helsinki Roccamatios* – they're thought provoking, inventive and quite dazzling!

## The Ultimate Teen Book List

### LEONIE'S DESERT ISLAND SELECTION

**Across the Nightingale Floor (p. 11)**

**The Eagle of the Ninth (p. 117)**

**Good Omens (p. 162)**

**The Magic Toyshop (p. 251)**

**Regeneration (p. 330)**

**Rowan the Strange (p. 336)**

**The Shell House (p. 358)**

**Strange Boy (p. 380)**

**Strange Meeting (p. 380)**

**The Traitor Game (p. 402)**

**The Watch House (p. 426)**

**A Wizard of Earthsea (p. 442)**

# LOLA ROSE   Jacqueline Wilson

What would you do if you felt your life was a mess, and there was no way out – but then luck suddenly dealt you a winning card? When Jayni's mum wins the lottery they can finally escape the torture and torment that they face from Jayni's dad, so they move to London to start a new life. That's when Jayni decides to stop being plain old 'Jayni' and becomes 'Lola Rose' instead.

It's a high life, with rich clothes and posh hotels. Then, inevitably, the money runs out, forcing them to move into a grotty flat. Everything seems fine until Lola's mum becomes seriously ill, and Lola has to grow up far too quickly...

A fast-paced, heart-warming must-read; Lola's struggle to come through problem after problem is utterly inspirational.

**David Gardner, age 16**

**Next?**

Wilson has a wonderful way of seeing family living. *The Diamond Girls* (UTBG 104) looks at tough single-parent family life; *Dustbin Baby* stars an adopted child tracing her parents, and *The Kiss* is about the agonies of first love.

Diane Hendry's *You Can't Kiss It Better* takes another look at children trying to cope with being adults.

Sarah Dessen's *Dreamland* is about a girl whose boyfriend turns his violence against her.

# THE LONG WALK
## Stephen King / Richard Bachman

**Next?**

More Stephen King? Start with the horror story, *Carrie*, about a girl with psycho-kinetic powers who goes on the rampage in small-town America.

James Herbert writes psychologically adept horror; try *The Rats*.

Or try some other linked short stories: *Uncle Montague's Tales of Terror* by Chris Priestley. (UTBG 413)

Stephen King's the most commercially successful author in the world. But one fine day he got suspicious and wondered if he could repeat his success as an unknown author. To find out he wrote five Bachman books, and *The Long Walk* is the best of them.

The US government has started up a race. One hundred teenage boys are selected for it. But it's no ordinary race. It's a long walk, and once you start you can't stop. If you do, the penalties are terrifying. There can be only one winner. Will it be 15-year-old Ray Garrity, or will he be gunned down like all the others before he can reach the prize?

This is a vintage King. I can honestly say that every teenage boy over the age of 14 I have given *The Long Walk* to has loved this dark and brilliant tale.

**Cliff McNish**

# THE LONG WALK  Slavomir Rawicz

This is the most extraordinary escape story one could possibly imagine – and it's all true. The writer, Slavomir Rawicz, was a Polish cavalry officer who was taken prisoner by the Russians during World War II, tortured, and sentenced to 25 years' hard labour in one of the murderous gulags that Stalin set up in Siberia. From a guarded encampment in the middle of hundreds of miles of snowbound forest, he and six fellow captives scrambled under the wire and escaped. They set out on a journey of unimaginable hardship and endurance, crossing the icy wastes of Siberia, the Gobi desert, Inner Mongolia and Tibet before reaching safety and freedom in India. This book had me on the edge of my seat right the way through. Trust me. Your hair will stand on end.

**Elizabeth Laird**

> **Next?**
>
> *Seven Years in Tibet* by Heinrich Harrer is the story of a man's escape from a prisoner of war camp and his refuge in a monastery in Tibet.
>
> The story of another Siberian prisoner who endures terrible hardship in order to find freedom is told in *As Far as My Feet Will Carry Me* by Josef M. Bauer.
>
> Climbing trips that go horribly wrong are recounted in *Touching the Void* (UTBG 400) by Joe Simpson and *Into Thin Air* (UTBG 205) by Jon Krakauer.

# A LONG WAY FROM VERONA  Jane Gardam

If you want an account of what school was like during the war, if you are curious to see the way some writers become writers, if you like eccentric characters and an accurate depiction of relationships between girls, then this is the book for you. Jessica Vye is an honest and engaging narrator. Her first-person voice is strong and clear and what she has to tell us is fascinating. The book begins with a visiting writer (his appearance at school is most beautifully described), who manages to inspire Jessica to such an extent that she runs after him and thrusts her complete works into his hands as he's leaving for home on the train. He returns her work with a note that says: 'Jessica Vye, you are a writer beyond all possible doubt.' It's hard to tell how autobiographical this book is, but that judgement also applies to Jane Gardam, and it's a pleasure to be in such competent authorial hands.

> **Next?**
>
> A story that weaves books, friendship and rivalries together is *Old School* by Tobias Wolff, set in a US prep school.
>
> Another Jane Gardam? Try *Bilgewater* (UTBG 43), set in an English public school, or *The Flight of the Maidens*.
>
> Or for an account of a real writer's growing up, read Penelope Lively's *Oleander Jacaranda: A Childhood Perceived*.

**Adèle Geras**

# LOOKING FOR JJ   Anne Cassidy

Children who murder other children – cases like this make BIG headlines in newspapers. But what is the real story behind the headlines, and what is it like if you are the teenage girl who was convicted of murder, now newly released into the world? What I liked about this brave story is that it makes you really think about the issues, and see things from an unusual perspective.

'JJ' has been given a new identity on her release – she has a job, and a boyfriend and a new life to look forward to – but someone knows who she is, and is looking for her. She has to go on the run yet again. At the same time as these compelling and powerful events are happening, another story is unravelling, about the murder itself: why and how it happened. I found this novel compulsive reading!

**Julia Green**

> **Next?**
>
> More Anne Cassidy: *Missing Judy*, about how the loss of a sister affects a family, or *Tough Love*, about the blinkers love puts on truth.
>
> *Fade* by Robert Cormier takes a violent look at mass murder.
>
> Or for a really dark read about a boy who witnesses his father's murder and discovers a whole new life, try Graham Marks's *Zoo*. (UTBG 453)
>
> *As If* is Blake Morrison's response to the real-life case of two child killers.

# THE LOOKING GLASS WARS   Frank Beddor

Using Lewis Carroll's classic children's story *Alice's Adventures in Wonderland* as his inspiration, Beddor has created a storming, imaginative, bloody *tour de force* that deserves not to be overlooked.

The author imagines that Alice's Wonderland did indeed exist and that it was not fairy tale after all. Princess Alyss Heart was heir to the throne of Wonderland, but was cruelly usurped when her Aunt Redd stormed Wondertropolis and murdered her parents. Fleeing for her life, Alyss was transported to our world, the world of Charles Dodgson and literary Oxford in the late 19th century. Beddor has pulled off a wonderfully complicated twist of creativity and his ambitious novel is a visual feast that is begging to be made into a film.

**John McLay**

> **Next?**
>
> The second book in the trilogy is *Seeing Redd*.
>
> Where better to start than with Beddor's inspiration, *Alice's Adventures in Wonderland* and *Through the Looking Glass* by Lewis Carroll?
>
> Stuart Hill's *The Cry of the Icemark* involves another princess fighting for her rightful kingdom. (UTBG 90)
>
> *The Eyre Affair* takes characters from famous books and makes them do some strange things... (UTBG 125)

# LORD LOSS  Darren Shan

**Next?**

If you haven't read Darren's other books – and you like to be scared witless – do so! *Lord Loss* is the first book of the **Demonata** sequence, which continues with *Demon Thief*. Or try **The Saga of Darren Shan**, beginning with *Cirque du Freak*.

Other bloodthirsty accounts of werewolves can be found in *Wereling* by Stephen Cole or *Flesh and Blood* by Nick Gifford.

Or try one of Darren's own favourites, such as Charles Dickens's thrilling story of the French Revolution, *A Tale of Two Cities*. (UTBG 386)

Everything goes wrong for Grubbs Grady from the moment he plays a joke on his sister. Though why his family get so uptight about a few rotting rat guts is a mystery – one that gets solved pretty quickly when Lord Loss appears, along with his nightmare companions, Vein and Artery. Demons one and all, they literally tear Grubbs's family apart. Locked into a home for the mentally unstable, Grubbs is just about ready to give up, until one day his long-lost uncle comes to take him home. To peace and quiet? Not likely…

This book is not for the fainthearted! From the end of chapter one you step into a world of demons – a world that drips with gore, pain, magic, werewolves and bloodcurdling excitement.

**Leonie Flynn**

# LORD OF THE FLIES
## William Golding

*Lord of the Flies* tells the story of a group of young boys stranded without adults on a deserted island after a plane crash. After a promising beginning, the group fragments and very soon descends into savagery. It is brilliant because it gives an idea of what could happen when ordinary boys are left alone.

I could easily identify with the characters and I used to think about my own friends and what character from the book they would be. With such vivid descriptions of the setting it was easy to wonder what might have happened if it had been us left alone on that island…

**Andy McNab**

**Next?**

William Golding wrote complex books – try *The Spire*, about the building of a cathedral, or *The Inheritors*, about the first humans.

Sam Mills's *A Nicer Way to Die* is also about the darker side of humanity.

Conrad's *Heart of Darkness* is about another journey into violence and madness. (UTBG 174)

Or for a look at a world without responsible adults, try *Gone* (UTBG 160) by Michael Grant, *Slave Harvest* by Andrew Butcher, or *The Enemy* by Charlie Higson.

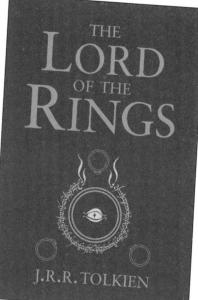

## Star Title

# THE LORD OF THE RINGS trilogy
## J.R.R. Tolkien

After reading *The Hobbit* and loving it, I thought I should try the trilogy that followed. So I did. For six days I spent my time reading, rereading and losing myself in Middle Earth, where the story is set. The trilogy begins with *The Fellowship of the Ring*, following the journey of one hobbit, Frodo Baggins, who must destroy the One Ring in order to save Middle Earth. Frodo starts off in a fellowship of nine, but by the end of the book the Fellowship has lost four members and the remaining group decide to go their separate ways. Frodo's quest to destroy the Ring is continued in the next two books – *The Two Towers* and *The Return of the King*.

**Florence Eastoe, age 13**

---

### Next?

If you are one of the many who devoured the appendices at the end of **The Lord of the Rings**, then try Tolkien's *The Silmarillion* and *Unfinished Tales*.

Gone are the days when the closest to a fantasy section that bookshops got was science fiction. Now there's almost too much to choose from. My personal favourites are: the novels of Robin Hobb – particularly the **Farseer** trilogy (UTBG 127), Philip Pullman's **His Dark Materials** trilogy (UTBG 181), and last, and perhaps best of all, Katherine Kurtz's **Deryni** novels. Start with *Deryni Rising*.

If you haven't read it already, try *The Hobbit* – the story of how the Ring was found. (UTBG 183)

---

Ask six different people why this book is important to them and you'll get six different answers.

For some it's the sheer scale of the story – the epic struggle between Good and Evil that will always be relevant to our own lives. For others it's the Fellowship, the friendship that binds nine disparate individuals and keeps them going through one perilous adventure after another. And then there's Tolkien's creation of an alternate world, complete with its own language and history.

For me, it's always been the realism. The characters may be hobbits and elves and walking trees but I know what they eat, when they sleep and how they feel. When I read this book, I believe in it utterly – and that's fantasy at its best.

**Laura Hutchings**

# The LORD PETER WIMSEY books
## Dorothy L. Sayers

Peter Wimsey is an intellectual, highly sensitive amateur detective with a taste for good wine. He appears in around a dozen books full of quirky characters and ingenious plots. The solutions often depend on his detailed knowledge of subjects like bell ringing and arsenic poisoning, and the author has a characteristic way of weaving obscure quotations into the dialogue.

Don't expect graphic details of sex and violence or serious discussion of current issues. The books are elegant puzzles, written to tantalise and entertain. But they don't trivialise life. Everything is underpinned by Wimsey's curiosity and enjoyment of the world around him, and his commitment to rigorous intellectual honesty.

**Gillian Cross**

### Next?

My favourite Wimsey books are *Strong Poison*, *Gaudy Night* and *Murder Must Advertise*.

You might also enjoy Margery Allingham's detective stories, and Agatha Christie's who-dunnits – try *The Body in the Library*. (UTBG 51)

Or for no detection but plenty of period detail, read the **Jeeves** stories. (UTBG 214)

# LOST AND FOUND   Valerie Mendes

### Next?

More Valerie Mendes? Try *The Girl in the Attic* (UTBG 155), or *The Drowning*, about a girl dealing with grief, love and her own ambitions.

For a beautiful tale of falling in love, read *Naked without a Hat*. (UTBG 275)

For a story of finding love, friendships and loss, try *Going for Stone*. (UTBG 159)

This book is described on the cover as a 'mystery', but I don't think that's really what it is. Sure, there's a secret waiting to be revealed, and a few gripping chapters of Missing Persons and calling the police and anxious waiting by the phone and chases down the canal bank. But the best bits of the story for me were watching the main character Daniel as he begins to form relationships – with Clare and Martin, his new foster parents; with his adopted 'grandmother' Laura; and with the lovely Jade, the new girl over the road with the entrancing singing voice and the rainbow-coloured dress.

Daniel is a wonderfully drawn and sympathetic character, and you can't help wanting things to work out for him; the story is enchanting, but never sentimental; and of course there's also all that 'mystery' excitement, too – what more could you want?

**Daniel Hahn**

# THE LOST ART OF KEEPING SECRETS
## Eva Rice

**Next?**

*I Capture the Castle* by Dodie Smith, another story of lost riches, wasted talent, growing up in a different era. (UTBG 195)

*Playing with the Grown-ups* by Sophie Dahl: though set in the 1980s, Dahl's full-length debut echoes both the style and faded upper-class setting of Rice's novel. Another beautifully written tale of a girl trying to find her way without a father, and play grown-up to a flaky mother.

Or *The Infinite Wisdom of Harriet Rose* by Diana Janney; this time set in the present, but still dealing with absent fathers, bohemian mothers, and a teenager at sea in an adults' world.

I have recommended this book to every one of my friends – from 14 to 94 – and they have fallen as deeply in love with it as I did.

Rice's adult bestseller chronicles the end of an era – the last days of debutantes, and the beginning of rock and roll, as Britain wakes from the war years to the possibility of American plenty.

Full of frocks and first kisses, it is the story of naïve Penelope, her Elvis-mad brother Inigo, and their heartbroken young mother Talitha, as they try to find a place in the new world order, and save their crumbling stately home, Milton Magna.

Like eating fairy cakes, it is a complete treat.

**Joanna Nadin**

# LOVE, FIFTEEN   Ros Asquith

This is a heartrending and hard-hitting story about the risks that go hand in hand with falling in love for the first time. Feisty and full of fun, Amy ends up pregnant after a drink too many to console herself over her boyfriend's move to the US. Knowing that a baby doesn't fit into her life plan to hit the big time as a rock star, she has some difficult decisions to make and confides many of her thoughts to her diary. Refreshingly, the focus is on her friends' and family's lives, too, and this carefully researched story strikes just the right balance between responsibility and froth. It's sure to hit home.

**Eileen Armstrong**

**Next?**

Ros Asquith is best known for *I Was a Teenage Worrier* (UTBG 209) and its sequels, featuring the irrepressible **Lettie Chubb**, a kind of female Adrian Mole with attitude.

Fans of these books will love Louise Rennison's crazy **Angus, Thongs and Full-Frontal Snogging** (UTBG 23) (think Bridget Jones as an angst-ridden, lovesick teenager), and devour Cathy Hopkins's **Mates, Dates...** series (UTBG 257).

Or try Sue Limb's books, starting with *Girl, 15, Charming But Insane*, starring Jess and her long-suffering mother. (UTBG 154)

# LOVE IN A COLD CLIMATE    Nancy Mitford

This English classic describes, hilariously, the doings of the Radletts, a large, titled family living in a chilly country house in the run-up to World War II. Fanny, the narrator, is a cousin who spends long holidays with the family. They hunt (and are hunted! – Fanny's fierce and eccentric Uncle Matthew delights in setting his bloodhounds on his children in 'child-hunts'), and discuss sex in the 'Hons' Cupboard' – the only warm place in the house. The girls dream of parties in heated mansions, and going to school (banned by Uncle Matthew), and running away, and not being bored any more. As they grow up, all this and much more comes to pass, with the emphasis on Fanny's favourite cousin, Linda, who, as someone truly remarks, 'is such an interest in one's life!' Never out of print in over 60 years, this is a must for anyone who wants insights into, and a good laugh at, the upper classes.

**Lynne Reid Banks**

# LOVE IN A PERIOD FROCK

*Arabella* by Georgette Heyer

*A Great and Terrible Beauty* by Libba Bray

*Luxe* by Anna Godberson

*These Old Shades* by Georgette Heyer

*Frenchman's Creek* by Daphne Du Maurier

*Jamaica Inn* by Daphne Du Maurier

*Katherine* by Anya Seton

*Gone with the Wind* by Margaret Mitchell

*The Ruby in the Smoke* by Philip Pullman

### Next?

*The Pursuit of Love* is the brilliant sequel. You could also try her hilarious novel about one of the most manipulative children ever, *The Blessing*.

Or for the story told by a different sister (and without the fictional cover story), read *Hons and Rebels* by Jessica Mitford.

Eva Rice's charming coming-of-age tale, *The Lost Art of Keeping Secrets*, is set in a crumbling country house in the 1950s. (UTBG 244)

# SCIENCE FICTION
## by Andrew Norriss

I grew up with a comic called *The Eagle*, which
had stories on the front page about a pilot in the
United Planets Spaceforce called Dan Dare. He
had his own spaceship, the *Anastasia*, that could
take him anywhere in the galaxy, and I so
wanted to go with him. His adventures were
set far in the future – about the year 2000 as I
remember – and I've been hooked on science
fiction ever since. They say the genre began
with people like Jules Verne and H.G. Wells, but
for my money science fiction really started in
the 1940s and 1950s, and the three big names
that launched it were Isaac Asimov, Robert
Heinlein and Arthur C. Clarke. These were the
guys, I later discovered, who had inspired the writers of
*Dan Dare*. Heinlein wrote stories about humanity colonising the planets and
spreading out across the galaxy, much as
Americans had conquered the West, but fighting
off aliens instead of Indians. Asimov's **Foundation**
trilogy (UTBG 140) went even further into the
future and described the fall of the first human,
stellar empire, while in *2001* Arthur C. Clarke
wondered if we hadn't already been visited by
aliens in the distant past who might yet return
and take humanity on to the next level.

Nobody took these guys seriously as
literature, but the ideas they were coming up
with were mindblowing – and they were just
the tip of the iceberg. I'll never forget the first
time I came across the idea of stargates, in
Murray Leinster's *The Wailing Asteroid*. Clifford
D. Simak's *The Way Station* was my favourite
reread for years, and I still have my dog-eared
copy of Theodore Sturgeon's *More Than
Human*, which suggested that humanity
might evolve into gestalts... The ideas went
on and on, and the possibilities and the
hope seemed endless.

I didn't much like it when science fiction grew up. I knew that writers like Ray Bradbury and Kurt Vonnegurt were seriously clever, but they used sci-fi – in books like *Fahrenheit 451* (UTBG 126) or *Slaughterhouse 5* (UTBG 368) – to show humanity screwing it up on a galactic scale. They were well written, but they weren't what I was looking for.

I wanted the fun stuff, and fortunately it's still around. A lot of it gets written for television these days – for *Star Trek*, *Babylon V* or *Farscape* – but there are still some authors producing ideas that will astound, and describing worlds you wish you could live in. Iain M. Banks would be top of my list. His **Culture** novels – *Consider Phlebas* (UTBG 86) or *Excession* – have the same mind-expanding power as the old days. I liked David Brin's **Uplift** novels, beginning with *Sundiver*, and Jerry Pournelle's **Falkenberg's Legion** stories are rip-roaring sagas where you know the right guys will always win through.

Some of these writers may not be quite what you're looking for, but the good news is that bookshops these days have whole shelves stuffed with sci-fi. All you need to do is dip and pick until you find the stuff that works for you. Good luck in the hunt! And may the Force be with you as you boldly go to infinity and beyond...

---

### SOME CLASSIC SCI-FI

*I, Robot* by Isaac Asimov

*Do Androids Dream of Electric Sheep?* by Philip K. Dick

*Starship Troopers* by Robert A. Heinlein

*The Left Hand of Darkness* by Ursula Le Guin

*Ender's Game* by Orson Scott Card

*The Hitchhiker's Guide to the Galaxy* by Douglas Adams

*Dune* by Frank Herbert

*The Day of the Triffids* by John Wyndham

*The War of the Worlds* by H.G. Wells

---

### CYBERPUNK AND STEAMPUNK

*Neuromancer* by William Gidson

*Mortal Engines* by Philip Reeve

*Snow Crash* by Neal Stephenson

*Mirrorshades: An Anthology of Cyberpunk* edited by Bruce Sterling

*Perdido Street Station* by China Miéville

'A marvellous and complex book, simply written but leaving all kinds of resonance in the mind'
BRIAN W. ALDISS

Philip K. Dick

Do Androids Dream of Electric Sheep?

# LOVE IN THE TIME OF CHOLERA
## Gabriel García Márquez

✹ ✹ ✹

If you long to escape from our everyday world, and would like to travel far away (to South America) and long ago (the start of the 20th century), this book will take you there. You are slowly drawn into a dazzling world of extraordinary detail, and begin to tune in to the life of two young people: Florentino and Fermina. Their love affair is drawn out over decades, and years must pass before it will reach some kind of dream-like resolution.

It's the kind of book you can only read very slowly, allowing one of the great writers of our age to hypnotise you with his evocation of a society that is beautiful and magical but also brutal and primitive. The book is hugely satisfying. I want to read it again NOW. Although, speaking as a hypochondriac, I felt there was maybe a *teeny* bit too much about love and not *quite* enough about cholera.

**Sue Limb**

### Next?

García Márquez has written some of the best-loved books of the past few decades. Try *One Hundred Years of Solitude* next. (UTBG 296)

Something similar, but not similar? A Greek story by an Englishman about an Italian? *Captain Corelli's Mandolin* by Louis de Bernières.

Isabelle Allende's usual colour is brought to the high adventure of *Zorro*.

# THE LOVELY BONES  Alice Sebold

✹ ✹

### Next?

*Lucky* by Alice Sebold is the account of a traumatic rape and its aftermath.

Sharon Dogar's *Waves* weaves two stories, one told by a girl in a coma.

Or Ali Smith's beautifully woven *Hotel World*, in which five people at the Global Hotel (one of them a lately dead girl) tell their stories.

Or try Neal Shusterman's *The Everlost*. After a fatal accident, Allie and Nick are trapped in a terrifying Limbo. As their memories fade, will they ever succeed in getting back the lives they lost?

This is a startling book. Within a few lines you learn that the narrator is Susie Salmon, a murdered 14-year-old girl. She describes her own grisly murder at the hands of a neighbour. She is in a kind of heaven, a frozen place where she can only watch the life she has left behind. We see the effects of the murder on her mother and father, how it destroys their life together. We also see, with horror, that the murderer is not caught – and there is evidence of other deaths.

There is life after death for Susie but she's in a lonely place. We often read about the loss felt by grieving relatives, but Susie's loss is greater: she has lost everything.

**Anne Cassidy**

# THE L-SHAPED ROOM  Lynne Reid Banks

**Next?**

*Two Is Lonely* and *The Backward Shadow* complete the trilogy.

*The Dud Avocado* (UTBG 116) and *The Greengage Summer* (UTBG 167) are both about girls coming of age in the mid-20th century.

*The Bell Jar* (UTBG 39) by Sylvia Plath is another first-person narrative about a young woman in crisis, as is Judy Blundell's *What I Saw and How I Lied* (UTBG 431).

The L-shaped room is at the top of a run-down boarding house in Fulham run by a tyrannical landlady and full of colourful characters – not to mention bedbugs! 27-year-old Jane runs here when her father throws her out after discovering she is pregnant. Jane feels numb, like her life has ended, but gradually she discovers that her life is just beginning. This is one of the most unflinchingly honest and self-aware books I have ever read: it tells you a lot about what it means to grow up, however old you are. Bear in mind that this book was written in 1960 and some of its attitudes towards race, religion, class and sexuality seem to come from another planet; but it's a fascinating look at London two generations ago: how much has changed, how little.

**Abigail Anderson**

# LUCAS  Kevin Brooks

Kevin Brooks writes powerful, original stories. *Lucas* is my favourite so far. The main character, Caitlin, tells the story of what happened to her one extraordinary summer, when a mysterious, beautiful boy called Lucas arrived at the island where she lives with her dad and brother in a close-knit but fearful community. Caitlin's friendship with Lucas helps her to be the person she really is, rather than going along with how most of the other teenagers behave, but that's a really difficult thing to do when you're 15. Lucas, the outsider, becomes a focus for all the fear and hatred the islanders feel about someone 'different' from them, with terrible and tragic consequences. I loved the island setting, the descriptions of the sea and the mudflats and dunes, and the way we are powerfully shown the danger of the 'crowd mentality'. You won't forget this story.

**Julia Green**

**Next?**

Other books by Kevin Brooks? *Kissing the Rain* (UTBG 226) and *Martyn Pig* (UTBG 256), both are about outsiders.

*The Fire-Eaters* by David Almond, because this is another powerful story about an outsider, and the nature of fear. (UTBG 133)

Or you could try the classic, *The Ox-Bow Incident*, by Walter Van Tilberg Clark, which is about how groups can be less tolerant than individuals, and how the innocent always suffer because of it.

# LUCKY STAR  Cathy Cassidy

Fans of Cathy Cassidy (and there are many) will enjoy the return of Mouse Kavanagh, who appeared in Cassidy's first novel, *Dizzy*. Now older, but not necessarily wiser, Mouse is annoying both his teacher and his social worker, but things seem to improve when he meets the gorgeous Cat, and a friendly stray dog he names Lucky. The first few chapters are surprisingly low-key, but tension starts to rise as Mouse discovers that his new pet actually belongs to one of the well-known villains on the notorious estate where he lives. And pretty, middle-class Cat is also not all she appears to be.

A story that takes a little while to get going but builds well, with some unexpected twists.

**Narinder Dhami**

### Next?

If you missed *Dizzy* (UTBG 110), read that. Or for more of Ms Cassidy, try *Ginger Snaps* (UTBG 154) or *Angel Cake*, about a Polish girl trying to start a new life in the UK and bad boy Dan, who makes everything more complicated.

Cathy Hopkins's **Cinnamon Girl** series begins with *This Way to Paradise*, about a girl who, thanks to her father, is always moving about the world.

Rachel Wing writes funny, sharp, blissfully good books – try *Love Struck* or *Star Struck*.

# The LYONESSE trilogy  Jack Vance

### Next?

Vance's most famous book is *The Dying Earth*; linked tales set in the far future, when the sun is feeble and science has corrupted into magic. More rewarding than a dozen epic fantasies.

Another great American fantasist was Fritz Leiber. Check out his tales of the roguish heroes Fafhrd and the Gray Mouser, collected in *The First Book of Lankhmar*.

**Lyonesse** is set in the days before King Arthur. If you like recreations of the Dark Ages, try Mary Stewart's books about Merlin, beginning with *The Crystal Cave*. (UTBG 90)

This fantasy blew me away when I first read it 20 years ago, and it's one of the few I still enjoy rereading now. Set on the Elder Isles, lands now submerged in the Atlantic, it features a staggering cast of interlinked characters: kings and princes vying for power, magicians working eerie tricks upon their rivals, a boy brought up in a fairy mound, a changeling girl masquerading as a princess in a court. The writing is rich, and the mix of politics and fantasy pungent and morally ambivalent: this is a world away from the simple patterns of good versus evil found in Tolkien and his imitators. It also features some of the best depictions of magic found anywhere. Read it and spread the word!

**Jonathan Stroud**

# THE MACHINE-GUNNERS
Robert Westall

Chas McGill is a boy living in England during World War II. For him, the war presents an opportunity to collect shrapnel and other military bits and pieces. It's an exciting adventure that he and his friends are all enjoying. But when a German plane crashes, they take its pilot 'hostage' and Chas gets his hands on a real, fully functioning machine gun...

A raw, powerful beast of a book, this features some of the most realistic and genuinely likeable characters in all children's fiction. Robert Westall wrote many fine books, but this is far and away his finest, and one of my all-time favourites when I was a teenager. *Nil carborundum*!

**Darren Shan**

### Next?

The sequel, *Fathom Five*. Chas is now 16, but still finding adventures, this one about a suspected spy. Or other Westall? Try the deeply scary *The Scarecrows* (UTBG 342).

Or what about a boy in a very different war? Try the **Pagan Chronicles** starting with *Pagan's Crusade*. (UTBG 307)

Martin Booth's *Music on the Bamboo Radio* is about a boy who escapes into China after the fall of Hong Kong.

# THE MAGIC TOYSHOP
Angela Carter

### Next?

If you like the poetry of the language and the sense of magic, try *Orlando* by Virginia Woolf. (UTBG 299)

If you like the way Angela Carter uses fairy tales, read her short stories, *The Bloody Chamber* – you'll never read the originals in the same way.

If you like the way Angela Carter describes the decisions Melanie faces as she grows older, try *The Last September* by Elizabeth Bowen.

Fifteen-year-old Melanie secretly slips into the night wearing her mother's wedding dress. The next day she learns that her parents have been killed in a plane crash. She is sent with her little brother and sister to live with their unknown uncle Philip, the toymaker. Burdened with guilt and responsibility, Melanie has to confront her approaching adulthood in the strange, surreal world she has entered. Surrounding her are an aunt struck dumb on her wedding day, magical mechanical birds, and puppets that are either dream or nightmare but are definitely not toys. Controlling everything is Uncle Philip. Does he see Melanie as a person, or as another puppet he can shape and control? A rich and disturbing novel with no easy answers.

**Antonia Honeywell**

# The MAIGRET books   Georges Simenon   ✹ ✹

### Next?

Simenon without Maigret?
Try *Stranger in the House*,
*The Mouse* or *The Man Who
Watched the Trains Go By*.

For something lighter, try other
famous detectives like Chandler's
Marlowe in *The Big Sleep* (UTBG
42), Conan Doyle's **Sherlock
Holmes** stories (UTBG 359) or
Christie's Poirot in *Death on the
Nile*. Or Colin Dexter's more
recent **Inspector Morse** books
(UTBG 204) or the **Inspector
Frost** books by R.D. Wingfield.

I love Maigret. Simenon wrote his **Maigret** detective books at breakneck speed, often in just a few days. Maybe that's why the stories feel so immediate and alive. I love Simenon's sparse and simple prose, his claustrophobic settings, where tensions simmer away and then explode – driving quite ordinary people to violence. I love the way Maigret bumbles about, often just as confused as we are, 'feeling' his way towards a solution. And how he struggles, as we often do, to understand the darker secrets of the human heart and why people behave as they do.

Where to start? Perhaps with *Maigret Goes to School* or *Maigret Goes Home* or *Inspector Cadaver*, and if you get hooked there are 73 more!

**Susan Gates**

# MAKE LEMONADE   Virginia Euwer Wolff   ✹ ✹

A beautifully written book about LaVaughn, a 14-year-old girl, who is determined to break out of the inner-city poverty of her upbringing and get to college. To raise funds she takes on a regular babysitting job for Jolly, a struggling single mother, but ends up getting drawn deeper and deeper into the seemingly hopeless situation in which Jolly has found herself.

It's a very sensitive, deeply moving but highly readable story, told in the first person without a single wasted word. It explores themes of friendship, family and self-respect; and of young people against all the odds aiming to make something of their lives. Although it deals with the most difficult of issues, this is a book brimming with warmth, humour and hope, and leaves the spirit soaring.

**Malachy Doyle**

### Next?

There are follow-ups, both of which are excellent, *True Believer* and *This Full House*.

The theme of being trapped by life, as an unloved and unwanted daughter, is explored in Adeline Yen Mah's autobiographical *Chinese Cinderella*. (UTBG 77)

Or try *Girl in Red* by Gaye Hicyilmaz, in which Frankie is captivated by a Romanian gypsy girl who comes to live close by, but has to deal with the fact that his own mother is leading the fight to get her and her family evicted.

# MALARKEY   Keith Gray

We've all had it: that feeling you get when you're the new kid at school. The feeling that your every move makes you stick out like a sore thumb, when all you want is to blend in.

It's like that for John Malarkey at Brook High, only worse. He's been there for two weeks and already the gang that runs the school has singled him out for special treatment. When somebody steals from a teacher and plants the stolen item in Malarkey's bag, the new boy finds himself on the run from both students and staff, and life becomes seriously hectic.

The situation and setting in *Malarkey* are instantly familiar to me, though it's a very long time since I was at school. It's still a mean old scene, and Keith Gray's got it absolutely spot-on.

**Robert Swindells**

**Next?**

Try another Keith Gray, such as *Warehouse* (UTBG 423), or *The Fearful*, about a boy trying to make sense of what his father wants him to be, or *Ostrich Boys* (UTBG 300).

In John Singleton's *Skinny B, Skaz and Me* the hero has to deal with gangs and friends who aren't what they seem. (UTBG 366)

There's more gritty realism in Catherine MacPhail's books – try *Grass*, about a boy who witnesses a murder.

# THE MALTESE FALCON   Dashiell Hammett

**Next?**

Dashiell Hammett's other great private eye is the Continental Op, a pudgy, indefatigable investigator who narrates the bloody, brutal *Red Harvest* and the short stories of *The Continental Op*.

Or try Raymond Chandler, also stylistically brilliant, but – beneath the wisecracks – softer and more sentimental. Try *The Big Sleep* (UTBG 42) or *Farewell, My Lovely*.

For a very different take on crime, and a compelling depiction of good and evil, try Margery Allingham's superb *The Tiger in the Smoke*.

Sam Spade is a private eye, laconic, weary, hard drinking, with an eye for beautiful, mysterious women and a nose for trouble… Yes, this is clichéd now – but it wasn't when Hammett wrote. He invented the genre, and his writing transcends it. The plot involves the murder of Spade's partner and the quest for the Falcon – a fabled treasure missing in San Francisco – and builds to Spade's battle of wits with a motley group of criminals. But the plot is not the point. If you want to know how to write gem-hard dialogue, create description that's both pithy and punchy, and invent characters (such as the delectable Brigid O'Shaughnessy, and the fat, purringly villainous Gutman) that truly live on the page, Hammett is your man.

**Jonathan Stroud**

# MAN AND BOY  Tony Parsons

**Next?**

If you want to find out what ultimately happens to Harry, why not read the sequel, *Man and Wife*? Or look out for Tony Parsons's novel about growing up during the Punk era – *The Stories We Could Tell*.

Nick Hornby's *About a Boy* is also about a man who's never really stopped being a teenager. (UTBG 10)

Blake Morrison's *And When Did You Last See Your Father?* is the author's memories of his father, told with both irritation and great affection.

Finally, a book about sex, love, and marriage from the man's perspective! Harry Silver would appear to have it all. There's the beautiful wife, the adorable son and the high-paid job. But Harry throws it all away in a moment of weakness. Now, quickly approaching 30, he must re-evaluate his life and learn how to be a single dad.

This book is about growing up, becoming a responsible adult and taking a hard look at yourself and your relationships. It is funny and endearing, but also sad at times. Harry's relationship with his own father is one of the highlights of the book and is tackled in a touching way. Tony Parsons manages to deliver a book filled with wonderful characters that is both stimulating and refreshing.

**Ileana Antonopoulou**

# THE MAN IN THE HIGH CASTLE
## Philip K. Dick

Philip K. Dick is deservedly a legend among sci-fi writers. Several of his books formed the basis of some great movies, *Blade Runner* among them. With *The Man in the High Castle* he gave an enormous boost to the 'alternative history' genre, in this case the idea that Germany and Japan actually won World War II and divided the defeated US between them.

The story is set in 1962 against a background of mounting tension between Japan and a Nazi Germany bent on total world domination, and the destinies of several characters become entangled as the plot is worked out. This strange, haunting book and its Zen-like approach to history and the clash of cultures will resonate in your mind for a very long time.

**Next?**

Other stories that use counterfactual histories are Robert Harris's *Fatherland* (UTBG 128) (Germany won the war and invaded the UK), and Ben Jeapes's *New World Order* (aliens alter the course of the English Civil War).

More Philip K. Dick? Try *We Can Remember It for You Wholesale*. (UTBG 430)

Or Harry Turtledove's *Ruled Britannia*. 16th-century London is under the Spanish.

**Tony Bradman**

# MANSFIELD PARK
## Jane Austen

**Next?**

*Pride and Prejudice* (UTBG 320) is probably Jane Austen's most famous novel. *Northanger Abbey* (UTBG 286) is wonderful, too. So is *Persuasion*... Come to think of it, they all are!

For another comedy of manners that's every bit as sharp and telling, read *Vanity Fair* by William Makepeace Thackeray.

Or try Karen Joy Fowler's modern story of five people who meet every month in *The Jane Austen Book Club*.

This is funny, really very funny, and has excellent dialogue and such honesty from Fanny the heroine that even the most solipsistic teenager could not help but learn something from her. At the beginning, the characters are assembled at a country house and planning to perform a play. This device is as brilliant as any psychological workshop for showing the reader a multitude of behaviours that intensify through the novel.

Jane Austen is my favourite English novelist, and although this book is not faultless – I find the ending a little frustrating – it is clever and perceptive. Read it and recognise your friends and yourself, and just hope you are not BB.

**Raffaella Barker**

# MARLEY AND ME John Grogan

When John Grogan first shared his memories of Marley with the readers of the newspaper he worked for, little did he know that he was starting a new trend in the book world. Go into any big bookshop now and amongst the bestsellers you'll find heart-warming tales of people adopting dogs from war zones and rescue shelters. There are dog biographies, dog 'autobiographies' and dog diaries. Many of these dogs are difficult and some are just downright bad, but none is Marley. Grogan's book is a wonderful account of a dog determined to do things his way. Marley can't help the fact that he's a thief, afraid of thunder, prone to demolishing buildings and possessed of some truly disgusting habits – he's a Labrador!

**Laura Hutchings**

**Next?**

There's more John Grogan – *Bad Dogs Have More Fun: Selected Writings on Animals, Family and Life*, a selection of his writings for the *Philadelphia Enquirer*.

For classic dog stories, read Jack London: *The Call of the Wild* (UTBG 65) or *White Fang*, both are realistic and moving.

Or how about something else very funny (with more animals)? Try *My Family and Other Animals* by Gerald Durrell. (UTBG 273)

# MARTYN PIG  Kevin Brooks

What do you do when you're in love with the girl across the street, a girl you think outclasses you in every department? *Martyn Pig* starts from this premise and then gets a good deal darker. Martyn's gloomy, self-deprecating nature makes him the ultimate angst-ridden teen, while his drunken father is the epitome of the boozed-up middle-aged lout.

The first-person narrative illustrates the claustrophobic nature of Martyn's loneliness, trapped inside his own head, yearning for something he believes to be out of his reach. This gritty thriller doesn't flinch away from some grim themes, but Martyn, for all his flaws, is a sympathetic character, and the twist in the tale is both moving and satisfying.

**Thomas Bloor**

### Next?

If you like tough, gritty reality, look out for Kevin Brooks's other books, too. Or there's depression and death in Chris Lynch's *Freewill*.

*Boy Kills Man* also sees young people driven to murder. (UTBG 56)

Raymond Chandler's *The Big Sleep* contains another poignant and lonely narrative voice, hidden behind the hard-boiled front. (UTBG 42)

Like *Martyn Pig*, P.D. James's English crime novels, such as *A Taste For Death* also have an air of chilly melancholy to them.

# MASSIVE  Julia Bell

This brilliant novel is simultaneously funny and utterly tragic. It's about an anorexic mother driving her daughter towards the same condition.

Carmen's mother is obsessed with making her daughter thin and beautiful, but Carmen finds comfort in food ... at first. The real awfulness begins when Carmen herself decides she *would* like to be thin – very thin. Then it's no longer funny.

Parents should read this book. It reveals how we often don't support or understand each other: there are teachers, girls and parents who are ignoring pain when they should be supporting and caring for those in trouble – in the book and in real life. I laughed and cried while reading this book. It is wise and witty and wincingly poignant.

**Nicola Morgan**

### Next?

Julia Bell pulls no punches. *Dirty Work* is about the trafficking of girls to sell as sex-slaves – it's dark, ferocious and deeply unsettling.

*The Opposite of Chocolate* by Julie Bertagna also shows girls at their most and least supportive of each other. (UTBG 298)

There are a lot of books dealing with negative body image. Some you could try include: *Second Star to the Right* (UTBG 346), *Speak* by Laurie Halse Anderson, *Pretty Face* by Mary Hogan and *Monkey Taming* by Judith Fathallah.

# MASTER AND COMMANDER  Patrick O'Brian

The first in a series of 20 superb novels chronicling the lives and adventures of two unforgettable characters: Jack Aubrey, the dashing sea captain in Nelson's navy – bluff, courageous, magnificently flawed; and his friend, the naval surgeon Stephen Maturin – moody, taciturn, fascinatingly complex. This is historical fiction of the very highest order. Don't worry about the nautical terms. You're in the safest of hands and, besides, these are not just stories about the sea. There are storms, shipwrecks and battles to be sure, but there are also intrigues, affairs, scandals, duels, the murky world of secret intelligence and much more. O'Brian's canvas is huge. These are stories of love and loyalty, humour and humanity, beautifully written and with a sense of the period so powerfully evoked you'll think that you're there.

**Tim Bowler**

### Next?

If you want more about life under sail, try the **Hornblower** books by C.S. Forester or the **Bolitho** books by Alexander Kent.

For warfare on land, you can't get much better than Bernard Cornwell: try the stand-alone *Azincourt*, his **Grail Quest** series, starting with *Harlequin*, his **Alfred the Great** books, starting with *The Lost Kingdom*, or his **Sharpe** books (UTBG 357).

# MATES, DATES... series  Cathy Hopkins

### Next?

The first in the series is *Mates, Dates and Inflatable Bras*. Or try another of Cathy's series – **Cinnamon Girl**.

Carolyn Mackler also tackles entertainingly what it's like being a teenager today. Try *The Earth, My Butt and Other Big Round Things* (UTBG 118) or *Vegan, Virgin, Valentine*.

Make sure you read Georgia Nicolson's diaries, starting with *Angus, Thongs and Full-Frontal Snogging*. (UTBG 23)

Ros Asquith is another writer who understands what teenage life is really like. Try *I Was a Teenage Worrier* for starters. (UTBG 209)

Lucy, Nesta, TJ and Izzie seem as real as the people you meet at school, in the mall, at the market and so on. These four girls come from very different backgrounds, but their mateship bonds them together for life – more so than with boys (although their friendship is strained on more than one occasion because of boys). Each book tells the story of a few weeks of change in one of the girls' lives, but we always know what the others are thinking and doing, and most importantly how they all help each other resolve their problems. Frank and funny, moving and thought provoking, the **Mates, Dates**... series makes for compelling reading about what it's like being a teen today.

**Jon Appleton**

# MAUS   Art Spiegelman

An extraordinary 'graphic' or comic-book novel about the Holocaust. In Poland, in the 1940s, Jews hide from the Nazis who are seeking to exterminate them. It's a game of cat and mouse, and Spiegelman makes that metaphor the basis of his drawings. The Polish Jews are mice, the Nazis are cats; *Maus* becomes a darkly fascinating version of Beatrix Potter's twee fantasies.

Two narratives run side by side: the story of Spiegelman's parents and their struggle to survive, and an account, set in contemporary America, of Spiegelman's thorny relationship with his ageing and difficult father, Vladek.

At the heart of the book is a painful question. To paraphrase Vladek, addressing his son, the author: 'I survived Hell so that you could be born; why aren't you what I wanted you to be?' It's a question that survivors of tyranny continue to ask and their children still struggle to answer. Maybe a book as good as this is the answer.

**Mal Peet**

THEY TOOK US TO A BUILDING IN A PART OF SRODULA SEPARATED BY WIRES— A GHETTO INSIDE THE GHETTO – AND THERE WE HAD TO SIT AND TO WAIT.

### Next?

*Persepolis* uses pictures to illuminate a dark story – better than any amount of text. (UTBG 310)

Someone who has taken sides and written about it is Joe Sacco with his graphic novel, *Palestine*.

Or for something else about the Holocaust, try *Daniel, Half Human* by David Chotjewitz (about how a friendship is torn apart when one boy is found to be half-Jewish), or *Friedrich* by Hans Richter (about the destruction of a Jewish family).

# MAXIMUM RIDE: THE ANGEL EXPERIMENT  James Patterson

### Next?

There are sequels: *Maximum Ride: School's Out Forever*, *MR: Saving the World*, *MR: The Final Warning*, *MR: Max* and *MR: Fang*.

Something with more horror and just as much excitement: Darren Shan's *Lord Loss*. (UTBG 241)

A boy who suffers bullying and yet has a priceless gift is the hero of Nigel Richardson's *Wrong Hands*. (UTBG 447)

Max is 14; she's a wise-cracking, quick-witted girl. Oh, and she has wings. With two-per-cent bird DNA, she and her group, or 'flock', are the result of genetic engineering. Light-boned, strong, fast, they live as outcasts from the 'school' that bred them, until the day the Erasers – half-wolf killing machines – steal away Max's youngest flock member, Angel, and the race to save her from being no more than a lab-rat is on.

This is a book where you dive straight into the action and keep on going. With love and friendship, great villains, and enough thought-provoking back-story to keep you thinking as well as frantically page turning, this is fast and furious fiction at its best.

**Leonie Flynn**

# ME AND MICKIE JAMES  Drew Gummerson

The nameless 'me' and his boyfriend Mickie are going to be huge in the pop world. Yep, they just know that their band, Down by Law, will be the next big thing. They need all that boundless optimism, as their story zips them through a hilarious, helter-skelter ride that takes in the seedier boundaries of pop, porn movies, fun fairs, the Iraq war, Tokyo, sex, Viet-Nam and rather a lot of masturbation. Always ready to seize the slightest opportunity, they live for music, write songs they know are as catchy as anything by Kylie, but have titles along the lines of 'Wacky Iraqi' – and slide through the world with the imperviousness of the truly innocent. And the truly in love.

Funny, warm, quirky and filled with deadpan humour, this is a screwball comedy of modern manners. It's not exactly a 'how to' guide to stardom, but it's the funniest book about not quite making it that you could wish for.

**Leonie Flynn**

### Next?

There's another innocent with a strange view of the world in Keith Waterhouse's *Billy Liar*.

Or for a classic take on someone who fails totally to see himself as others see him, try George and Weedon Grossmith's *Diary of a Nobody*. (UTBG 105)

*Me and Mickie James* reads like a comic. Try a comic that reads like a novel: *Bone* by Jeff Smith.

# THE MEDICI SEAL  Theresa Breslin

*The Medici Seal* tells the story of Matteo, a young gypsy boy who finds himself at the heart of a grand conspiracy involving the golden seal of the powerful Medici family in early 16th-century Italy.

The story begins terrifically, with Matteo pursued by the villainous Sandino, hit man for Cesare Borgia. He is rescued by Leonardo da Vinci, and becomes the artist's helper, gradually acquiring the learning to go with his keen intelligence. There are rapes and murders, and Breslin does a fine job of explaining the fiendishly complex politics of Northern Italy in the Renaissance. Matteo's relationship with the Maestro is nicely done, and we learn plenty about the art of fresco; and if the intense excitement of the opening is not quite sustained, the writing is never less than subtle and powerful.

**Anthony McGowan**

### Next?

More Theresa Breslin? Try something about the French court: *The Nostradamus Prophecy*.

There's more fiction based on history in Mary Hooper's *Newes from the Dead*, which concerns a girl hanged for a crime she didn't commit, who somehow doesn't actually die. (UTBG 282)

Libba Bray's **Gemma Doyle** books are set in a Victorian boarding school. The first is *A Great and Terrible Beauty*.

# MEMOIRS OF A GEISHA
## Arthur Golden

### Next?

If you want to read more about geishas, try Liza Dalby's *Geisha* or Lisa See's *Snow Flower and the Secret Fan*.

The real-life geisha Arthur Golden interviewed tells her own story in *Geisha of Gion* by Mineko Iwasaki.

To read of the wartime experiences of a Japanese community abroad, try *Snow Falling on Cedars*. (UTBG 370)

This has everything I want in a book. Beautifully written, it gives an insight into another time and culture – in this case from 1929 to the post-war years of Japan. It is told from the point of view of Sayuri, a geisha girl.

The closed world of geishas has always fascinated me, from the ritual that dominates every aspect of their days to the intimate details of their personal lives. Part of the appeal of this book was that the author claimed to have got his information from a real geisha who told him her life story. But it is what he has done with what she told him that makes this such a great read – he has woven fact and fiction into a heartbreaking and breathlessly lovely tale.

**Cathy Hopkins**

# MEMOIRS OF AN INFANTRY OFFICER
## Siegfried Sassoon

**Next?**

*Memoirs of a Fox-hunting Man* is the first in the trilogy and *Sherston's Progress* the last. Sassoon's poems are wonderful, too; they appear in *Anthem for Doomed Youth* (UTBG 26).

Sassoon appears as a character in Pat Barker's *Regeneration* (UTBG 330). He also appears in Robert Graves's memoir *Goodbye to All That*.

For years I resisted reading *Memoirs of an Infantry Officer*, knowing that it was a description of Sassoon's experiences of the First World War. I could hardly bear to read of the horrors that were to destroy the idyll he had grown up with. But, in due course, read it I did. It didn't disappoint. I should have known that, despite the brutality overwhelming him, despite the unbearable anguish of loss, and his growing realisation that a 'noble' war had become monstrously evil, the poet in him never ceased to identify beauty, humour and humanity. Amidst the carnage, he could find beauty in a sun setting over a ravaged landscape, or a bird trilling above the rattle of guns. It's a book you can get immersed and lost in, but finally emerge feeling that, just when the world seems completely irredeemable, 'Suddenly everyone burst out singing; and I was filled with such delight as 'prisoned birds must find in freedom…'.

**Jamila Gavin**

# THE MERRYBEGOT   Julie Hearn

Do people only see what they believe they can see? In this rollicking, rumbustious historical novel set in the superstitious West Country during the English Civil War, boundaries are blurred between delusion, illusion, magic and the everyday.

Nell is a Merrybegot, a child conceived on May morning and thus sacred to nature. She is gradually learning her craft so that she can follow her grandmother as cunning woman of the village. But if you are an unconventional, feisty girl in a period of witch-hunting, you are surrounded by malice and danger. Characters both human and supernatural romp through the story, which sparkles with audacious humour, yet is touching, too.

**Patricia Elliott**

**Next?**

Julie Hearn's first novel, *Follow Me Down*, is a time slip set in contemporary London and among the 'monsters' of old Bartholomew Fair. (UTBG 137)

Try also two other historical novels about witch hunting: Celia Rees's *Witch Child* (UTBG 441) and Melvin Burgess's *Burning Issy*.

Or Sarah Singleton's *Heretic*, which encompasses history, the hidden fairy world, religion and witches. There's a sequel, too: *Out of the Shadows*.

# THE MERSEY SOUND
## Adrian Henri, Roger McGough and Brian Patten

I was given this book in my early teens and it felt like I had been given a secret. So it's great to share the secret with you. All good books are like shared secrets. Maybe it's because of the way we huddle up and read them, or the way we put them in our bags and bring them out when we are on our own. I didn't know that this was one of the most successful books of poetry published by living poets. It made me realise that poets were exciting people who found vibrancy in the everyday. Alternatively, poets are vibrant people who make the everyday exciting. All the poets in this book have become very famous, but this book is where it all began. It's now a classic with a great title. It's called *The Mersey Sound*.

**Lemn Sissay**

> **Next?**
>
> All the Mersey poets went on to write more – try Adrian Henri's *Collected Poems*; Roger McGough's *That Awkward Age* and Brian Patten's *Selected Poems*.
>
> Or try a poet who writes accessible poems about now: Carol Ann Duffy.

# MIDNIGHT IN THE GARDEN OF GOOD AND EVIL  John Berendt

> **Next?**
>
> There isn't another book quite like this, though *Cannery Row* has some of the flavour. (UTBG 66)
>
> John Grisham's legal thrillers are set in a similar world. Try *The Runaway Jury*. (UTBG 338)
>
> Another book with murder at its heart is *The Girl with the Dragon Tattoo* by Stieg Larsson.

When this book first came out in America, readers thought it was a novel. But according to Berendt, he really did have the luck to meet this extraordinary cast of characters and to witness the bizarre plot. It all takes place in the Deep South, in Savannah, where Berendt, a New York journalist, finds himself captivated enough by the place to rent a home there for several months every year. He meets society belles and low-life characters, too, like the sleazy lawyer Joe Odom, whose life is one long travelling party. But the real stars are the Lady Chablis (the transvestite black cabaret artist) and the ambiguous millionaire Jim Williams, who is tried four times for the same murder.

Some of the subject matter is very 'adult', but not gratuitously so; the city of Savannah plays a central part in this book, and it's this subject matter that gives the city its decadent character.

**Mary Hoffman**

# THE MIDWICH CUCKOOS John Wyndham

This is the book that introduced me to science fiction. It is a strange, haunting tale of alien invasion and the human response to it.

Midwich is a small, nondescript village in England; the cuckoos, aliens who are born to all the women following the 'Dayout' – 24 hours when the village is cut off. As the golden-eyed children grow, their alien characteristics are revealed. They are more intelligent than their human counterparts, and have powers of telepathy and telekinesis, which become increasingly menacing, endangering the lives of those around them, and leading to the book's shocking climax.

Although science fiction, this classic can be read as an allegory of the generation gap between all children and their parents, and the moral issues it raises are as relevant today as when it was written, 50 years ago.

**Paul Stewart**

### Next?

More John Wyndham is a must; try *The Trouble with Lichen* or *The Day of the Triffids* (UTBG 98).

In the superhero comics **The New X-Men**, by Grant Morrison, there is a group of quintuplets calling themselves the Stepford Cuckoos.

Or for a more humane kind of science fiction, try Margaret Atwood's *The Handmaid's Tale*. (UTBG 170)

# MILKWEED Jerry Spinelli

### Next?

For the most famous true account of the Holocaust, read *The Diary of a Young Girl* (UTBG 106). Or for a 'based on a true story' account of the Warsaw Ghetto uprising, read *Mila 18* by Leon Uris.

*My Secret Camera: Life in the Lodz Ghetto* by Mendel Grossman and Frank Dabba Smith is full of photos taken in a Polish ghetto, showing what life was like there.

And more Spinelli? Try *Smiles to Go*.

*Milkweed* is an utterly compelling, moving and engrossing story with a main character whose life at the beginning is worse than most of us could imagine, and which deteriorates steadily throughout.

It is also a book about the Holocaust.

Misha Pilsudski is a wild little thief without family, home or education. Is he Jew, gypsy or neither? It makes little difference as he is herded into the Warsaw Ghetto with the rest of the boys in his gang and begins to live through the horrors of life there.

Jerry Spinelli has an uncanny ability to plunge right to the heart of a character. Misha is endlessly energetic with a spirit that is never crushed and he whirls you along with his story.

**Susan Reuben**

# MILLIONS Frank Cottrell Boyce

I like nothing better than being drawn into a story right from page one and *Millions* does just that. It's about a boy called Damian Cunningham who lives with his older brother Anthony and their widowed father.

Damian is obsessed by the saints and knows all there is to know about each and every one of them, much to the consternation of his teacher and classmates who can't shut him up. Fast-paced, multi-layered and humorous, the plot really takes off when the brothers find a bag of stolen money at the bottom of their garden, with mixed but hilarious consequences.

Read the book first, laugh, cry and enjoy, then go see the film and buy the T-shirt. Then read the book again.

**Helena Pielichaty**

**Next?**

*Joey Pigza Swallowed the Key* by Jack Gantos is about a boy with ADHD who has the same heart-tugging warmth as Damian.

*Holes* by Louis Sachar is another multi-layered, real-life adventure story with an edge. (UTBG 184)

*Ruby Holler* by Sharon Creech is a poignant story of a brother and sister using humour and cunning to overcome life's perils. (UTBG 337)

In *Hoot* by Carl Hiaasen, the new kid in town overcomes the bullies in an ingenious way. (UTBG 186)

# THE MILL ON THE FLOSS
## George Eliot

One of George Eliot's most famous and best-loved books, this is the tragic story of Maggie Tulliver and her brother Tom. An intelligent and passionate teenager, Maggie is bored by the stifling and judgmental villagers of St Ogg's. She longs for the love and approval of her brother, who is forced to study. Tom, embarrassed by his sister's passionate nature, ultimately rejects and humiliates her. This isn't an easy book to read, but the portrait of Maggie's conflicted and frustrated character is subtle and moving and gives the reader a real sense of how hard growing up must have been for girls in the 19th century who weren't allowed equal access to education.

**Julia Bell**

**Next?**

More Eliot – try *Silas Marner* (UTBG 361) next. Or the wonderful (wonderful!) *Middlemarch*.

If *Middlemarch* doesn't grab you, you could try a different novel of repressed passion – Wilkie Collins's *No Name*.

Or Woolf's *A Room of One's Own*, about the role of creative women in society. (UTBG 334)

Or something by another woman writing about her struggles to be completely herself – Charlotte Perkins Gilman's *Herland*.

# THE MILLSTONE  Margaret Drabble

I wasn't even born when this book was first published, and neither were you; and yet it's not hard to imagine the effect it must have had on its first readers. The early 1960s, when the story is set, was in many ways a quite different world to the one we know today. Rosamund lives in a society on the cusp between sexual restriction and permissiveness, and her own feelings are quite ambivalent. What she knows about sex and love comes from her reading of 'cheap fiction', and in truth she's more than happy to forego both in order to concentrate on researching her thesis. But then something happens to make her rethink her plans, and her whole life changes.

This was a boundary-breaking book in many ways; but really you can forget about all that now and just read it for Rosamund herself, for her voice, and some perfectly poised writing.

**Daniel Hahn**

### Next?

For more Margaret Drabble, try my favourite, the sequence of novels that begins with *The Radiant Way*.

Lynne Reid Banks's *The L-Shaped Room* is another story of the experience of a single mother in early 1960's London. (UTBG 249)

Ian McEwan's *On Chesil Beach* is another early 1960's story, about the damage done to a couple's life by their inability to speak frankly about sex.

---

# MINE  Caroline Pitcher

### Next?

For more Caroline Pitcher, try *11 o'clock Chocolate Cake* or *Cloud Cat*.

For another teen story of the supernatural, read Margaret Mahy's gripping *Alchemy*. (UTBG 16)

For a story of another girl who finds herself cut off from society, this time through pregnancy, try *Dear Nobody*. (UTBG 101)

Or for a girl who talks to ghosts, try Meg Cabot's **Mediator** series.

Shelley feels like nothing belongs to her. Her dad won't let her come to stay for Christmas with him and his new family; her mum loves her little brother best; and she's stuck in a remote village with no friends and no one she wants to talk to.

But there are people who want to talk to *her*, whether she likes it or not – two disembodied voices, one on the stairwell and one out by the old mine, who have stories of loneliness to tell that have strange echoes of her own. At first Shelley tries to ignore the voices, but she can't help getting slowly drawn into their increasingly shocking tales.

This is a bleak but compelling story of teenage isolation, with a supernatural element to give it a disturbing twist.

**Susan Reuben**

# M IS FOR MAGIC
## Neil Gaiman

**Next?**

More Neil Gaiman? Look out for *The Graveyard Book* (UTBG 165), as well as his wonderful graphic novel series, **The Sandman** (UTBG 342).

There's more mingling of faerie, myth and reality in Susanna Clarke's short story collection, *The Ladies of Grace Adieu*.

Or you could try Angela Carter's intense look at fairy tales, *The Bloody Chamber*.

Or for more scary short stories, *Uncle Montague's Tales of Terror* by Chris Priestley. (UTBG 413)

Sometimes you don't feel like a whole novel. You want a quick read – not necessarily an easy one, but something that will entertain you for a while without leaving you hanging off a cliff until you've got time to come back. You need a book of short stories – and *M Is for Magic* is just the ticket. The Holy Grail turns up in a charity shop. Gourmets sit down to feast upon phoenix. Aliens hold suburban parties. And Jack Horner's private investigation into the untimely death of Humpty Dumpty means you'll never look at nursery rhymes in the same way again. By turns funny, intriguing and downright sinister, this is a chocolate box of a book – full of bite-sized treats.

**Antonia Honeywell**

# MISS SMILLA'S FEELING FOR SNOW
## Peter Høeg

Peter Høeg's novel took the world by storm when it appeared in the early 1990s. It was a totally unexpected bestseller. It's the story of a Danish woman – by birth a Greenlander, an ice-dweller – who stumbles on a major conspiracy.

The delight is in the detail, and Høeg's minute description of a wintry world is as magical (to those of us from less extreme climates) as anything you'd find on top of the Christmas tree.

The book falls into two distinct halves and some may find the second – when Smilla leaves Copenhagen for the Arctic seas and the heart of the mystery – to be harder going. But the dazzling prose will propel you all the way.

**Sarah Gristwood**

**Next?**

More Peter Høeg? Try *Borderliners*, about a group of kids suffering at an experimental school or *The Quiet Girl*, a thriller set in a Copenhagen populated with strange and mystifying people.

Other surprise hits in a similar vein were David Guterson's *Snow Falling on Cedars* (UTBG 370) and Nicholas Evans's *The Horse Whisperer*.

Or try Rebecca Wells's wonderful *The Divine Secrets of the Ya Ya Sisterhood* – though this one is strictly for the girls.

# MISTER PIP  Lloyd Jones

### Next?

Once you've read *Mister Pip*, you really don't have any choice but to read *Great Expectations* by Charles Dickens. And you won't be disappointed. Crime, guilt, revenge, reward, love, hate and fate – it's got the lot! (UTBG 166)

Set in an unspecified future time in a lawless and rabidly anti-intellectual America, Ray Bradbury's *Fahrenheit 451* is all about the power of literature. (UTBG 126)

Or try *Inkheart*, which shows how blurred the boundary between books and reality can be… (UTBG 203)

Thirteen-year-old Matilda lives on an island in Papua New Guinea in the 1990s. Civil war has disrupted her safe, predictable life; the young men have left to fight, the village school has closed, and eccentric Mr Watts, a.k.a. Pop Eye, steps in to teach the children by reading aloud from *Great Expectations*. Gripped by the tale of Dickens's orphan hero, Pip, the children begin to imagine new possibilities for their own lives. But reading can be subversive as well as escapist, and Matilda's fascination with 'Mr Pip' leads to horror and tragedy that no one could anticipate.

This is an amazing novel, full of hope, humour and heartbreak; you'll be as swept away by it as Matilda is by *Great Expectations*.

**Kathryn Ross**

# MOAB IS MY WASHPOT  Stephen Fry

This autobiography covers Fry's first 20 years. If you are a fan of his brand of humour you will love this, but you will also be surprised by it. Stephen Fry is a very complex character and his story makes for fascinating reading. He was a disruptive and rebellious pupil but still managed to get to Cambridge University. He spent time in prison for forging credit-card signatures, but somehow comes across as straightforward and honest. He is a talented comedian and yet has battled with depression and suicidal tendencies. Fry writes frankly and with no holds barred about his life, his sexuality and his family, in a book that is by turns witty, poignant, perceptive, sad and very funny.

**Yvonne Coppard**

### Next?

If you haven't already, read Fry's *The Liar*. (UTBG 236)

There are a lot of showbiz autobiographies, but not many are worth reading for any more than gossip. But you could try Pamela Stephenson's very good biography of her husband Billy Connolly, *Billy*.

Like Fry, actor Dirk Bogarde wrote both novels and volumes of memoir, the first of which, *A Postillion Struck by Lightning*, is a wonderful evocation of growing up in the country.

# MONDAYS ARE RED   Nicola Morgan

Following a case of meningitis, Luke discovers that his senses have been strangely altered; he sees music, smells colours and can taste through his fingertips. He has developed a condition called synaesthesia, and the author's dexterity with language allows us to experience the world as richly as Luke does. 'Mondays are red. Sadness has an empty blue smell. And music can taste of anything from banana puree to bat's pee.' But there's a flip side to this sensation-drenched world, and it's Dreeg, a foul creature who has taken up residence in Luke's brain and who persuades him that he can do anything. Ugliness is heightened as well as beauty and in his fight to recover his full health, Luke grows ever more selfish and mean-minded, even putting his family at risk. This is a startlingly original novel and a sensory roller coaster that will leave you breathless.

**Kathryn Ross**

> **Next?**
>
> More Nicola Morgan? Try *Sleepwalking*, a chilling vision of a future world where individual thought is outlawed.
>
> The hero of Tim Bowler's *Starseeker* is a musical genius who also has synaesthesia. (UTBG 376)
>
> Two novels that explore the heightened senses of smell and taste are Patrick Süskind's *Perfume* (UTBG 310) and *Chocolat* (UTBG 77) by Joanne Harris.

# MONTMORENCY   Eleanor Updale

> **Next?**
>
> The sequels so far are: *Montmorency on the Rocks*, *Montmorency and the Assassins* and *Montmorency's Revenge*.
>
> There's more Victorian crime in *The Extraordinary and Unusual Adventures of Horatio Lyle* by Catherine Webb. Look out, too, for the glorious Cat in Julia Golding's 18th-century-set *The Diamond of Drury Lane*.
>
> Raffles was the first famous gentleman thief; track down his stories by E.W. Hornung, starting with *Raffles: The Amateur Cracksman*.

Although written for young people, there are no child characters in this witty tale of the rise of Montmorency. His life in Victorian London is a challenge after his body's been put back together by a surgeon and he's spent time in prison. He has a double persona – there's Montmorency the wealthy, upper-class gentleman, and the degenerate servant, Scarper, a thief who uses the sewers of London to get in and out of all sorts of places to rob the city's rich. The police are baffled by the wave of mysterious and seemingly unstoppable thefts but Montmorency must always remain on his guard – the smallest mistake could destroy both his lives... The book is full of intrigue and ingenious plots and is a real page-turner.

**Wendy Cooling**

# THE MOON RIDERS Theresa Tomlinson

## Next?

For another story about Amazons, you might like to try *The Amazon Temple Quest*, published as part of Katherine Roberts's **Seven Fabulous Wonders** series, or try *I Am the Great Horse*, the story of Bucephalus, Alexander the Great's beloved horse.

If you are interested in the story of Troy, then try Adèle Geras's *Troy*. (UTBG 405)

There's another tribe of women at the centre of Alice Hoffman's *The Foretelling*.

Or you could seek out a translation of *The Iliad* – the epic Greek poem about Achilles's adventures. Alexander the Great kept it under his pillow so he could read about his hero every night! (UTBG 199)

The legendary Amazon warriors were a tribe of women from what is now Turkey, who lived without men and fought their own battles on horseback. Their culture is seldom explored very deeply, but in this book they are called 'Moon Riders' and dance under the moon, as well as fighting when called upon to do so.

Myrina, a young Moon Rider, rides to the aid of Troy when the city is besieged by the Greeks, which gives us a familiar tale told from a different point of view. The dramatic black cover adds to the atmosphere, and by the end of the book I wanted to leap on a horse and join them!

**Katherine Roberts**

# THE MOONSTONE
## Wilkie Collins

The poet T.S. Eliot described this book as 'the first modern English detective fiction'.

When Rachel Verrinder inherits the Moonstone – a huge and cursed yellow diamond stolen generations ago from an Indian shrine – from her distant relation John Herncastle, she has no idea what havoc this gift is about to wreak. We discover that Herncastle, alienated from his family, has bequeathed the stone to Rachel as a form of revenge, and as the events of the novel unfold it becomes almost impossible to put it down. Both this novel and *The Woman in White* were Victorian equivalents of blockbuster bestsellers like *The Da Vinci Code* – hugely popular and read by almost anyone who could read.

**Julia Bell**

## Next?

Other Wilkie Collins to look for are *The Woman in White* (UTBG 443) and *No Name*.

*Beau Geste* is a mystery and adventure that hinges on the theft of the Blue Water sapphire. (UTBG 36)

Or for a mystery involving an ancient chalice and a curse, try Margery Allingham's *Look to the Lady*, involving her aristocratic sleuth Albert Campion. Or a modern mystery – *The Lost Symbol* by Dan Brown.

# MORTAL ENGINES
## Philip Reeve

*Mortal Engines* follows the fortunes of city boy Tom and a disfigured outcast girl, Hester. It's set in a world where gigantic motorised cities roam the earth; a future in which our civilisation is just a fragment of memory and technological advancement has proved flawed and fleeting. The story introduces a host of richly drawn characters as it rushes towards an apocalyptic conclusion.

This is adventure on a grand scale, but Tom and Hester never get lost in the sweep of it all. Reeve is also determined to keep the moral waters murky, challenging preconceptions at every turn.

**Thomas Bloor**

### Next?

The sequels: *Predator's Gold* and *Infernal Devices*, which is set 16 years on and centres on Tom and Hester's daughter, and the fourth, *A Darkling Plain*, which brings the sequence to a close. Luckily for us there's a prequel, too: *Fever Crumb*.

For more sprawling adventure, try the Brian Aldiss science-fantasy sequence, the **Helliconia** trilogy.

Different views of how the future might be are found in *Children of the Dust* and *Ender's Game* (UTBG 121).

Or what about flying, prison, escape and totally thrilling adventure? Try Eoin Colfer's *Airman*. (UTBG 13)

# THE MOTH DIARIES  Rachel Klein

### Next?

Well, as I said, there's nothing like it. But try *Mr Wroe's Virgins* by Jane Rogers, another fascinating look at young women together – written for adults.

And *Catalyst* brilliantly depicts the intensity of friendships and of life during adolescence. (UTBG 68)

Another series about intense emotion, passion and friendship set in a boarding school is Adèle Geras's **Happy Ever After** trilogy, starting with *The Tower Room*.

There is simply nothing else like this book. I could read it again and again. Set in a girls' boarding school in America, it delves deep into the intense world of female adolescence, through the extraordinary eyes of a girl with a 'borderline personality disorder, complicated by depression and psychosis'.

The book is Gothic, dangerous, oozing passion, paranoia and blood. Not to mention deaths – several. Is creepy Ernessa merely creepy, or is she a vampire? And is Lucy becoming weak through anorexia, or is her blood being sucked by Ernessa? The ironic tone is perfect, the voice utterly original. It is absolutely my favourite book in the world. Ever. Can you tell?

**Nicola Morgan**

# THE MOTORCYCLE DIARIES
## Ernesto 'Che' Guevara

You probably know something of the most romantic revolutionary of all time. This is the back-story, the man before he became the myth, in his own words...

Che Guevara was born in Argentina and fought alongside Fidel Castro in the three-year guerrilla war in Cuba. He became Minister for Industry following the victory of the Cuban revolution, but found 'ordinary' life unfulfilling, and went to fight for freedom in the jungles of Bolivia where he was caught and murdered under orders from the US. Written eight years before the Cuban Revolution, these are Che's diaries as he drives a 500cc Norton motorbike across Latin America, with his mate Alberto. Their adventures, written up by Che during and after the journey, make up this wonderful, beautiful and painful book.

**James Riordan**

### Next?

Read Alberto Granado's book: *Travelling with Che: The Making of a Revolutionary*; or the excellent biography by Jon Lee Anderson.

For something that explains his politics, try Che's *Guerilla Warfare*.

Jack Kerouac famously journeyed across the America of the 1950s in his classic *On the Road*. (UTBG 297)

# MR MIDSHIPMAN EASY  Captain Marryat

Don't be put off by the rather dated philosophising in this book. It was written in the middle of the 19th century, after all. The author was himself a midshipman in Nelson's navy and rose to be a captain. Many of the dashing escapades he describes are based on real events.

Reading the book, you can understand why the beginning of the 19th century was the heroic age of sail, when boys as young as 12 fought the great sea battles alongside hardened sailors, shinned up the masts in gales to haul in the sails, and stormed the forts on enemy shores to capture their guns. This book is especially dear to me because my great-great-great-grandfather was serving on this very ship. He was 15, and a third-class boy. Fred Marryat was 16 and a junior officer. They can't have been friends, but they must have known each other.

### Next?

If you like the idea of sea warfare, try Alexander Kent's books, starting with *Midshipman Bolitho*.

Another series of famous sea stories is the **Hornblower** series by C.S. Forester. *Mr Midshipman Hornblower* is first.

And don't forget the **Aubrey / Maturin** novels by Patrick O'Brian. (UTBG 257)

**Elizabeth Laird**

# MURKMERE  Patricia Elliott

Aggie comes to Murkmere Hall and Leah's story begins. Two teenagers of wildly differing character and background meet in turbulent times, setting in motion a chain of dark and richly mysterious events.

*Murkmere* is set in an alternative 18th-century England, ruled by a corrupt élite who lord it over a downtrodden people. There's an oppressive state religion that sees wild birds as objects both of veneration and of terror. This divided society is mirrored in Murkmere Hall, where the reclusive Master, crippled in a mysterious accident, broods in his library while his predatory butler exerts a sinister control over the household.

*Murkmere* blends Gothic fantasy with invented history, to create a world as convincing as it is enthralling.

**Thomas Bloor**

**Next?**

Garth Nix's *Sabriel* is another fantasy novel grounded in a re-imagined historical period, where trenches and barbed wire are little use against the walking dead. (UTBG 339)

*Jane Eyre* by Charlotte Brontë is the tale of a troubled master with a dark secret. (UTBG 211)

There are more Gothic secrets in Jane Eagland's *Wildthorn*. (UTBG 439)

# MY BRILLIANT CAREER  Miles Franklin

**Next?**

More Sybilla? Try *My Career Goes Bung*.

Jane Austen writes about another world where women escaped drudgery through the right marriage. Try *Pride and Prejudice* (UTBG 320) or the matchmaking *Emma*.

*The Yellow Wallpaper* by Charlotte Perkins Gilman is from the same period, and tells of a marriage and one woman's breakdown. (UTBG 451)

Written in 1895 when the author was 16, the language of *My Brilliant Career* is old-fashioned but vivid. 'Do not fear encountering such trash as descriptions of beautiful sunsets and whisperings of wind' writes heroine Sybilla, promising the reader stronger stuff. She longs to be a writer, but her life in the Australian bush is drudgery. She loathes and loves her resigned mother, drunken father, pretty younger sister and dirty little brothers. Escape looks unlikely, till rich handsome Harry Beecham offers marriage. Should she accept?

This book has realism, romance and humour, big feelings and big ideas. It captures the longings and conflicts of teenage life – and the even greater frustrations of a century ago – and you may well find it inspiring.

**Julia Jarman**

# MY DARLING, MY HAMBURGER
## Paul Zindel

**Next?**

Other books by Paul Zindel are a must: *The Pigman* (UTBG 312), *The Undertaker's Gone Bananas* and *I Never Loved Your Mind*. Nobody else writes quite like him, so you should read them all!

*Are You There, God? It's Me, Margaret*, *Just as Long as We're Together* and *Forever* (UTBG 139) by Judy Blume are great if you enjoy the American context and want to see the world from a girl's perspective.

This isn't *Dawson's Creek*, and it's certainly not *The OC*. It's a no-glamour look at American teen life – losing your virginity and parents / teachers totally missing the point. This book packs a real emotional punch and – I think I can say this – doesn't have a happy ending. Maggie, Liz, Sean and Dennis are all in their final year at High School, negotiating the world of dating, first love and sex. Just when is the right time to stop snogging and suggest going for a hamburger?

The story is told in a mixture of letters, short stories, notes passed in the cafeteria and the usual 'Liz got out of the car' type narrative. It's like having hidden cameras in each of the characters' homes, so you really get to know them.

**Abigail Anderson**

# MY FAMILY AND OTHER ANIMALS
## Gerald Durrell

First published in 1956, this is the autobiography of an English schoolboy whose family moved to the Greek island of Corfu.

Gerald Durrell loved animals, and in this laugh-out-loud yarn he recounts the astonished and often-horrified reaction of his mother, two brothers and sister as he ferries home a selection of strange and wonderful insects, birds and beasts (including the odd octopus, toad and glow-worm). Durrell paints a beguiling portrait of the Ionian landscape and a rural way of life that has since vanished. He explores the island with his dog Roger, gets into scrapes, has adventures and wonderfully conveys the sheer exuberance of life. A Natural History classic.

**Sara Wheeler**

**Next?**

The series continues with *Birds, Beasts and Relatives*, and there are loads more.

*All Creatures Great and Small* is the first of James Herriot's autobiographical tales about being a vet in Yorkshire.

Gerald Durrell's brother Lawrence also wrote a book about a Mediterranean island – a lyrical evocation of southern Cyprus, *Bitter Lemons*.

# MY SIDE OF THE MOUNTAIN   Jean George

## Next?

If you liked the wildlife aspect of this book, try *A Kestrel for a Knave* by Barry Hines. (UTBG 223)

Other great books about animals and the wilderness are *The Call of the Wild* (UTBG 65) and *White Fang*, both by Jack London.

*Woodsong* by Gary Paulsen is about growing up in northern Minnesota and training sledge dogs for a race.

Some books manage to capture your dreams, and for me this is one of them. It tells the story of a young boy called Sam Gribley who runs away from his cramped New York home to live off the land in the woods of the Catskill Mountains. With only himself and his tamed animals for company, Sam spends a lot of time thinking about things that he hasn't really thought about before – life, living, other people, his family – and gradually he begins to find out all about himself. This book's got it all – adventure, escapism, insights and feelings – and it's told in such a wonderfully simple way that you feel as if Sam is talking directly to you. If you read it, you'll never forget it.

**Kevin Brooks**

# MY SO-CALLED LIFE   Joanna Nadin

Fourteen-year-old Rachel Riley lives a nice, normal life with nice parents and nice friends at a nice school in a nice area. Her diary, then, can be nothing more than 'earthshatteringly, tragically normal', until this year, the year when she decides that she will have to take steps to inject some excitement and exoticism into her life and become both tragic and interesting. This is sharply observed writing that will leave young teenage girls wondering how the author knows so much about them. Rachel's snappy diary entries will soon turn even the most bookphobic girls into more enthusiastic readers. Die-hard Rennison, Hopkins, Manning and Limb fans should be tempted by Teen-of-Queen-nominated Nadin and, happily, there are sequels.

**Eileen Armstrong**

## Next?

More teen diaries? Try *Big Woo* by Susie Day, *My Desperate Love Diary* by Liz Rettig or *Cathy's Book* by Jordan Weisman and Sean Stewart.

Or more Rachel? Joanna Nadin continues her story in *The Life of Riley*, *The Meaning of Life* and *My (Not So) Simple Life*.

Or try Sue Limb's **Zoe and Chloe** series: *On the Prowl*, *Out to Lunch* and *Girls to Total Goddesses in Seven Days*.

The most famous teen diary ever has to be Sue Townsend's *The Secret Diary of Adrian Mole aged 13¾*. (UTBG 347)

# MY SWORDHAND IS SINGING
## Marcus Sedgwick

Infused with folklore of Eastern Europe, this vampire story breathes new life into the tale of the living dead.

Peter and his father Tomas arrive in the isolated village of Chust. Peter is perplexed by his father's behaviour. Why does he carry a battered wooden box with him? Why does he secretly guard its contents? And why has he created a moat-like channel around their hut? A brooding presentiment hangs over the village, where murder and abduction are commonplace. All seems grey and miserable in Peter's life until he encounters a band of travelling gypsies. They are the vampire slayers. With the help of the beautiful gypsy girl Sofia, Peter determines to rid the village of its curse.

Set deep in the Transylvanian forest, with its long winter, greying light and unyielding snow, this is a story of fear and hope, of loss and redemption. A perfect winter read for those who like their horror served with a thoughtful twist.

**Nikki Gamble**

### Next?

Though not a direct sequel, Marcus has written a follow-up with *Kiss of Death*. It's another tense, dark read, this time set in Venice.

For other Marcus, try *Revolver*. And yes, it really is about a gun… (UTBG 331)

Anne Fine is another novelist who writes so well you feel you're living the story; try her cold, bleak and intriguing *The Road of Bones*. (UTBG 332)

# NAKED WITHOUT A HAT   Jeanne Willis

### Next?

Other Jeanne Willis? Try *Rocket Science*, in which a boy finds an alien creature that apparently feels neither fear nor pain. Or *The Hard Man of the Swings*, set in post-war Britain. (UTBG 171)

*The Shell House* is an atmospheric novel about trying to fit in and first love. (UTBG 358)

*Naked without a Hat* is a story about love and acceptance. Throughout the book an underlying secret waits to be discovered. The story is highly original and the twist at the end is unpredictable. The book touches on modern subjects that have previously been taboo. It exposes people's judgements. It is interesting to see, once you have learnt the secret of the book, if you can reread it without prejudice. I found it to be a highly enjoyable read, and was eager to discover the secret. It was interesting to see the world through the eyes of a young man in love and this story made me, a self-confessed cynic, believe that young love could exist.

**Anna Posner, age 16**

# THE NAME OF THIS BOOK IS SECRET
## Pseudonymous Bosch

The joke that runs through this book, starting from its title and its author's name, and permeating every page from then on, is that the adventures it contains are so secret and so dangerous that the author should not really be telling you about them.

The trick works – it adds a whole layer of entertainment to an already fun story. The book only starts properly in chapter two: chapter one is left blank because the information it contains is too high-risk to divulge. When the plot does get going, you'll discover that it features three lonely children, a magician with a long-lost brother, a symphony of smells and a highly exclusive holiday resort for the rich and famous. But perhaps I have already revealed too much?

**Susan Reuben**

### Next?

Move on to the quirky and dark sequels, *If You're Reading This, It's Too Late* and *This Book Is Not Good for You*.

Or try **A Series of Unfortunate Events** by Lemony Snicket, which issues dire warnings to its readers in a very similar way. (UTBG 353)

There's more mysteries to decipher in Rick Riordan's series, **The 39 Clues**. The first book is *Maze of Bones*.

Or more magic and hilarity? Try *Magyk* by Angie Sage.

# NARZISS AND GOLDMUND   Hermann Hesse

A book for 'seekers'! I read this when I was a teenager and loved it. I was going through my 'looking for the answers to the Universe' phase (actually still am, come to think of it...) and I found Hermann Hesse's books a joy as he seemed to be asking similar questions to my own. What is the way to happiness? The pleasure of the flesh or its denial?

In *Narziss and Goldmund*, Hesse creates two very different characters to represent the flesh versus the spirit: Narziss the aesthete, who lives a life of serenity in a monastery, and Goldmund the artist, restless and discontented, who seeks answers through pleasure, art and beauty. Different roads but with the same destination in mind. Reading what they both have learnt at the end is a revelation.

**Cathy Hopkins**

### Next?

More Hermann Hesse? *Siddhartha* is also about a seeker and his path to find knowledge and happiness.

*The Prophet* by Kahlil Gibran is a collection of beautifully written passages about life.

*Illusions* by Richard Bach is another cult exploration of why we exist, as is his *Jonathan Livingston Seagull*. (UTBG 216)

Or try *The Alchemist* by Paolo Coelho. (UTBG 15)

# NATION  Terry Pratchett

Terry Pratchett's *Nation* is a dazzler, fizzing with fresh ideas and jokes so funny, you'll barely realise you're also being made to think about quite big themes. Mau is going through a manhood ritual on an island in the South Pacific in the 19th century. While he's facing the ritual alone, a huge tsunami wipes out his entire island, leaving him as the sole survivor. The same tsunami has also washed up the extremely proper Daphne, young daughter of a diplomat travelling to meet her father. Their cultural misunderstandings are so much deeper and funnier than the usual run of things, and Pratchett slyly asks hard questions about faith, tradition, and science. Moving, hilarious and extraordinary, a classic in the making.

**Patrick Ness**

> ## Next?
>
> More theology? Well, Big Questions anyway, along with dry wit and a great anti-hero… Try C.S. Lewis's *The Screwtape Letters*. (UTBG 344)
>
> More adventure on an island? Try *The Lost Island of Tamarind* by Nadia Aguiar, or the classic by Daniel Defoe, **Robinson Crusoe**.
>
> Or more Pratchett? Read all of his books really. The **Discworld** series (UTBG 107) begins with *The Colour of Magic*, or you could head for the riotous fun of *Only You Can Save Mankind*.

# THE NATURE OF THE BEAST  Janni Howker

> ## Next?
>
> Janni has written two other powerful novels: *Isaac Campion*, which tells the story of a boy's bitter relationship with his father, and *Martin Farrell*, about plunder, robbery and vengeance. There is also a short-story collection, *Badger on the Barge*.
>
> *Billy Elliot* by Melvin Burgess is set in a northern town during the miners' strike, about a boy who wants to dance but is up against prejudice.
>
> Ally Kennen's aptly named *Beast* is about a fostered, troubled boy and the secret he hides in the reservoir. (UTBG 35)

A terrifically powerful novel by one of Britain's finest authors. It's set in a northern English mill town and superbly conveys the effects of unemployment, in terms of the pain and the anger it brings on the entire community.

Meanwhile, out on the moors, there's a sheep-killer on the loose and to young Bill Coward, desperate to do something to help, it becomes a symbol of the turmoil in his own life. He decides to track down the creature and kill it, and the tension builds and builds to a truly heart-stopping finale.

This is one of those rare books where the people feel totally real and we're right there with them – in their loss of work, dignity and hope.

**Malachy Doyle**

# NEMESIS series   Catherine MacPhail

*Into the Shadows* is the first book in the **Nemesis** quartet, a blade-sharp crime thriller series by the brilliant Catherine MacPhail, who puts the 'grrr' into gritty writing! Trapped in a lift with a dying man, Ram has no memory of who he is or where he's come from; but he knows he's in trouble as he fights to stay one step ahead of the police who suspect Ram of murder, and others who seem determined to kill *him*. Ram isn't super-fit or loaded with gadgets and his very ordinariness adds to the depth, realism and humour of this high-octane ride. The pace and tension increase as Ram discovers more about his past and his identity with each book.

**Kathryn Ross**

## Next?

The **Nemesis** series consists of:
*Into the Shadows, The Beast Within, Sinister Intent* and *Ride of Death*

Read more by Catherine MacPhail. Try *Worse Than Boys* about rival girl gangs or go for laughs with her hilarious **Granny Nothing** series.

Some say the **Nemesis** series is like a junior **Bourne** trilogy, Robert Ludlum's spy thriller series. Start with *The Bourne Identity*.

And if you're still hungry for rip-roaring action, Joe Craig's **Jimmy Coates** series will satisfy your appetite for thrills and spills.

# THE NEVERENDING STORY
## Michael Ende

Bastian Balthazar Bux loves stories – they're a way for him to escape from the school he hates, and the other boys who bully him. So when he finds *The Neverending Story*, he just has to take it away to read.

But *The Neverending Story* is no ordinary book – it's a gateway to Fantasia, where Atreyu the Hunter is on a quest to save the Childlike Empress. As the story unfolds, Bastian realises that he is what Atreyu is searching for, and to save the Empress he will have to enter Fantasia. In Fantasia, Bastian can have everything he's ever wished for, but there's a hidden danger waiting to trap him: while entering Fantasia was hard, leaving it will be all but impossible…

**Benedict Jacka**

## Next?

*The Princess Bride* by William Goldman is the only other book I know of with the same 'feel'. (I can't put it any more specifically than that!) (UTBG 322)

Cornelia Funke's *Inkheart* is another book in which books come to life. (UTBG 203)

For another book that blurs the lines between fantasy and reality, try Alan Garner's *Elidor*, in which a group of children must save a dying land.

# NEVERMORE  Linda Newbery

An imposing and isolated country estate, eccentric characters, shady secrets and a spirited heroine who will stop at nothing to get answers to her constant questions, are all key ingredients in some of the best and most timeless children's fiction. Here, they are given a new and contemporary twist.

Twelve-year-old Tizzie arrives at the mysterious Roven Mere expecting to make friends with the strangely absent Lord Rupert's daughter Greta, while her mother takes up a position as cook. Greta is nowhere to be found, however, and as Tizzie starts to gather clues to her whereabouts, she finds herself dragged into an intriguing mystery in which she plays a vital part.

This is perfect winter's night reading to lose yourself in for a few hours, with deliciously slow-building suspense and a satisfying but unguessable ending.

**Eileen Armstrong**

### Next?

Linda Newbery's other books; try *Flightsend*, about a girl moving to a remote cottage, or *The Shell House* (UTBG 358) next, but all of them are wonderful.

Mysterious houses are catnip for authors; try *Flora Segunda of Crackpot Hall* (UTBG 135); *The Treasures of Weatherby* by Zilpha Keatley Snyder or *Larklight* by Philip Reeve.

# NEW BOY  William Sutcliffe

Hysterically funny, deeply cynical and absolutely filthy, this book is every mother's nightmare. Mark makes friends with Barry, the handsome new boy in his class. Actually, first of all he checks him out in the showers, and proceeds to fancy him madly for the course of their friendship. Of course, this doesn't make him gay. Not at all. He even gets to lose his virginity to a girl – who happens to be Barry's sister and looks just like him. Then Mark's brother comes home from university and things start to really get complicated...

As well as being about sex, *New Boy* is also about the horrors of school, the homoerotic undercurrents of rugby, the terror of choosing a university and how seriously mad most teachers are.

**Leonie Flynn**

### Next?

Mark thinks that *Le Grand Meaulnes* is juvenile and boring – but I think it's amazing. (UTBG 164)

Mark adores *Portnoy's Complaint* (more sex!) and reckons it should replace the school hymn book. It's by Philip Roth, and very funny indeed.

William Sutcliffe has also written a brilliant, funny and touching novel about mothers and sons: *Whatever Makes You Happy*. Or read his feature on cult books on pp. 280–281

# CULT BOOKS
## by William Sutcliffe

What is a cult book? Is it more than just a book that your granny would hate?

To qualify as a cult book, you have to be popular, but only with the right people. You mustn't be too popular, and your readers must absolutely not be grannies or golfers; they should be tattoo artists or rock stars. *Pride and Prejudice* (UTBG 320) is not a cult book. *The Da Vinci Code* (UTBG 97) certainly isn't a cult book.

Even though it has sold at least a million copies, *Trainspotting* (UTBG 401) is still a cult book, but only because those million readers are mostly under 30, and because the book is exclusively populated by drug addicts, weirdos and psychopaths. *The Beach* (UTBG 35) was once a cult book, but since the Leonardo di Caprio film, it probably doesn't qualify any more. It's hard to define a cult book, but you know one when you see one.

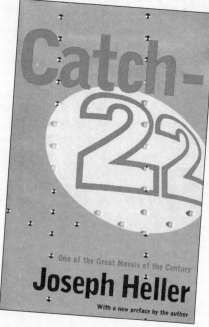

I had always wanted to write one, and first began to think I might have done it when I saw a heap of pirated photocopy editions of *Are You Experienced?* (UTBG 28) for sale near an Indian beach. Although the bookseller was, in effect, robbing me, the strange thing was, I felt more flattered than annoyed. It felt, in some way, like an induction into an exclusive gang.

One of the most important things about cult books is that they don't go away. When I was 18, you just had to read *On The Road* (UTBG 297), *Catch-22* (UTBG 68), *Steppenwolf* and *A Clockwork Orange* (UTBG 82), and that's just as true today. When my son hits that age in another 17 years, I expect he'll probably want to turn to them, too.

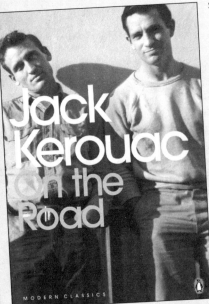

You could say that it's something to do with sex, drugs, travelling or adventure, and there's an element of truth in all those things. These books are all about forbidden or dangerous ways of life. They are culty because they give you intimate contact with people you'd be a little afraid to sit next to on the bus. The characters in these books are bigger, louder, crazier and more reckless than anyone your parents will ever introduce you to.

And that's exactly why these books are so important to read as you enter adulthood. As you begin to chafe at the restrictions of your life in the parental home, these are the books that take you out of your safe little nest and show you all the best, worst, riskiest, brightest and stupidest things that you could possibly do with your life.

At 18, anything is possible, and you have to read these books to find out what 'anything' really means. You'd be dumb to set about emulating the characters in these novels, but if you're intelligent and curious about the world, this is where you turn to find out what the limits are, and what happens if you reach them.

## MORE CULT BOOKS TO ENJOY

*Jonathan Livingston Seagull* by Richard Bach

*Narziss and Goldmund* by Hermann Hesse

*Generation X* by Douglas Coupland

*Interview with the Vampire* by Anne Rice

*The Buddha of Suburbia* by Hanif Kureishi

*The Alchemist* by Paolo Coelho

*The Fountainhead* by Ayn Rand

*The Celestine Prophecy* by James Redfield

*The Dice Man* by Luke Rhinehart

*Chariots of the Gods* by Erich Von Däniken

'Welsh writes with a skill, wit and compassion that amounts to genius. He is the best thing that has happened to British writing for decades' SUNDAY TIMES

# Trainspotting

## IRVINE WELSH

the dice man

'Novelist of the century'
*Loaded*

## LUKE RHINEHART

# NEWES FROM THE DEAD Mary Hooper

*Newes from the Dead* is the true story of Anne Green, a servant girl sent to the gallows accused of murdering her own baby. Hooper skilfully interweaves Anne Green's reflections on the black emptiness she finds herself in and the story of how she came to be there, alongside the viewpoint of Robert, a young medical scholar in the room with her body, waiting to witness his first dissection.

When Robert observes her eyelid twitch, the doctors are presented with a difficult dilemma: should they attempt to revive her?

An evocative account of 17th-century life and how easily a young servant girl can face injustice at the hands of her master – disturbing and captivating, I could not put this book down.

**Tessa Brechin**

> **Next?**
>
> For another novel based on real historic characters, try *Fleshmarket* by Nicola Morgan. (UTBG 134)
>
> Or for other historical fiction, try Celia Rees's *Witch Child* (UTBG 441) or *Coram Boy* by Jamila Gavin (UTBG 87).
>
> Of for more by Mary Hooper, try *At the Sign of the Sugared Plum* (UTBG 31), the first in a historical fiction series set in Elizabethan England. Or try the **Haunted** series of ghost stories, starting with *Haunted House*.

# THE NEW POLICEMAN Kate Thompson

> **Next?**
>
> This is the first in a triology. JJ Liddy also appears in *The Last of the High Kings* and *The White Horse Trick*. Mind you, the rest of Kate's books are all great; try *Creature of the Night*, a mysterious, scary thriller set deep in the Irish coutryside.
>
> *Fire and Hemlock* by Diana Wynne Jones features a set of mysterious events which, as one girl suspects, have much to do with Scottish myth and the dangerous Queen of the Fairies. (UTBG 132)
>
> Dark, scary and full of mystery, try Frances Hardinge's *Verdigris Deep*.

There's a new policeman in Kinvara, but he doesn't seem to do his job very well. He certainly finds it difficult to stop the musicians down at the pub from playing late into the night. JJ Liddy is a young fiddle player, and he finds the policeman plain odd. Other things JJ finds odd are the growing number of missing socks, the way there never seems to be enough time, and the rumour that his grandfather was a murderer. Can all these be connected somehow? JJ sets out to investigate, and finds the answers are out of this world. Myth, traditional musical tunes, Celtic gods and fairies make this an exciting Irish mystery that is waiting to be solved.

**Noga Applebaum**

# THE NIGHT COUNTRY  Stewart O'Nan

This is an adult novel, but its perfectly pitched teen voice, setting and subject matter make it a book that many teen readers will enjoy.

The story is based in familiar territory: a Hallowe'en tragedy in small-town America; three teens are killed in a car accident; one of the passengers lives on severely brain damaged; and one escapes unharmed. A year on and the dead have returned to visit the living...

Sad, funny and chilling by turns, this is a highly unusual ghost story. O'Nan takes you through the quiet streets, the hopes, fears, and dreams of suburban America. The story is told from the point of view of the ghosts, who have been summoned by the living and whose bitter longing helps to shape the tragedy unfolding before them.

**Celia Rees**

> **Next?**
>
> Both Stephen King and Peter Straub love this book – maybe you should try one of theirs next? Start with King's *The Long Walk* (UTBG 238) or Straub's *Koko*.
>
> For another American writer who finds the distinctly odd inside the ordinary, try Ray Bradbury's collection of short stories, *The Golden Apples of the Sun*. Or Lois Duncan's *I Know What You Did Last Summer*, about a group of teenagers with a secret.

# NIGHT WORLD: SECRET VAMPIRE
## L.J. Smith

> **Next?**
>
> The **Night World** series is now available bound together in three volumes, with three books in each.
>
> Cassandra Clare's fantasy series, **Mortal Instruments**, begins with *City of Bones*, which introduces Clary to a shadow-world of demons.
>
> Melissa de la Cruz has a delicious vampire series that starts with *Blue Blood*. Or you might like Rachel Caine's **Morganville Vampires** series.

Sixteen-year-old Poppy is dying of cancer – it's inoperable and she has only weeks to live. Her best friend James is devastated. He knows that he can save Poppy – but in order to do so he will have to break the most fundamental rules of the Night World and, by so doing, place his own life in danger.

*Secret Vampire* is the first in the incredibly popular **Night World** series and if you liked *Twilight* and *True Blood* then these are the books for you. Well written, fast-paced and smart, they take the ordinary world of American teenagers and mix it up with the supernatural.

So beware of that good-looking boy in your class – he could be a vampire in search of his next meal!

**Laura Hutchings**

# NINETEEN EIGHTY-FOUR  George Orwell ✳ ✳

It is the future. Britain is ruled by a totalitarian government. The Party demands total obedience; dissent is a crime punished by imprisonment, torture or death. There is no freedom: whoever you are, wherever you are, somebody could be watching you. Winston Smith works for the Ministry of Truth, fabricating the present and rewriting the past. He does his best to conform – to love The Party and all that it stands for – but dreams of rebellion, revolution and liberation. Captured by the dreaded Thought Police, he is imprisoned and subjected to terrifying interrogation and indoctrination. Can he maintain his freedom of mind and spirit – particularly after he finds out what is inside Room 101?

First published in 1949, George Orwell's novel is as powerful and relevant today as it was 60 years ago. Utterly convincing, utterly terrifying, it will change the way you look at the world.

**Graham Gardner**

---

**Next?**

For another view of a totalitarian future where hope is at a premium, try *Fahrenheit 451*. (UTBG 126)

For a world where slavery is legal, where to be Jewish is a crime, try *The Man in the High Castle* by Philip K. Dick. (UTBG 254)

Something quite different by Orwell? Try *Keep the Aspidistra Flying*.

---

## The Ultimate Teen Book List

## COSTA CHILDREN'S BOOK AWARD WINNERS

# THE No.1 LADIES' DETECTIVE AGENCY
## Alexander McCall Smith

This is a humorous first novel in a series of books set in Botswana, Africa. The story follows the doings of the colourfully named Precious Ramotswe as she founds a detective agency.

The book is great fun to read and the author describes the scenes so vividly that it is easy to imagine the landscape, the people and of course the cattle – a subject which everyone refers to regularly during conversation.

So open the cover and pack your Factor 99 sun cream and before you know it you'll be driving along a dusty road called Zebra Drive in a rickety old white van, before passing such landmarks as Tlokweng Road Speedy Motors, The Botswana Secretarial College and, of course, The No. 1 Ladies' Detective Agency.

**Alexander Carn, age 12**

> **Next?**
>
> The rest of the **No. 1 Ladies' Detective Agency** books – there are lots in the series. *Tears of the Giraffe* comes next.
>
> *The Eyre Affair* (UTBG 125) by Jasper Fforde is a harder read, but if you know anything about books it's brilliant. Or why not a series where the detective is Jane Austen? Read *This Pen for Hire* by Laura Levine.
>
> *Brat Farrar* by Josephine Tey is a very English and very good detective story. (UTBG 58)
>
> *West with the Night* by Beryl Markham tells of the author's youth in Kenya.

# NOODLEHEAD   Jonathan Kebbe

> **Next?**
>
> There's another terrible prison in *Furnace: Lockdown* by Alexander Gordan Smith. Or try a classic story of juvenile rehabilitation – with a twist – Louis Sachar's *Holes* (UTBG 184).
>
> K.K. Beck writes a mean adventure story – try *Fake*, in which two boys are about to get locked up, but escape...
>
> Or *Zoo* by Graham Marks, in which a boy is kidnapped, kills a man while escaping, but then finds he might not be running in the right direction after all. (UTBG 453)

Marcus hates being cooped up in school, so he runs away. No doors, no rules – perfect. Except they keep dragging him home. But, after one run too many when they haul him back from France, it's not to his home but to Dovedale Young Offenders' Institute.

Sharing a room with three no-hopers, his head stuffed with drugs so he can't even think, he finds it worse than school, worse than his nightmares. But Marcus is made of strong stuff, and the day they lock him up is the day the real battle begins as he struggles against drugs, sadists and do-gooders, all in an effort to prove his worth – and his sanity.

**Leonie Flynn**

# NORTHANGER ABBEY  Jane Austen

Catherine leaves her dull village to visit the city of Bath, with its parties and fashionable people. She is daunted at first – but she is not a complete innocent, for she has read all about such exciting places in novels. So she knows very well that, whilst everyday people are kind, honest and respectable, there are also villains in the world who commit dark deeds. Distinguishing one from the other, however, proves strangely difficult, and this leads Catherine into all sorts of embarrassments, troubles and dangers.

*Northanger Abbey*, like all Austen's novels, is a comedy about a girl testing her beliefs about the world and finding love on the way. It's full of marvellous characters and jokes, but at the same time it's very subtle. It's a bit like a whodunnit (it contains what is very nearly a murder mystery), for everyone has their own agenda, and no one is quite as they appear. Or not to the poor heroine, in any case!

**Sally Prue**

> ### Next?
> More Jane Austen? Try *Sense and Sensibility* or *Pride and Prejudice* (UTBG 320) first.
>
> If you're interested in Gothic novels, try the one Catherine is hooked on: *The Mysteries of Udolpho* by Mrs Radcliffe.
>
> For a more modern Gothic novel, read *The Woman in Black*. (UTBG 443)

# NO SHAME, NO FEAR  Ann Turnbull

> ### Next?
> For another story that brings the past vividly back to life, try Nicola Morgan's *Fleshmarket*. (UTBG 134)
>
> For more about Quakers, read the World War II novel *Slap Your Sides* by M.E. Kerr.
>
> There's more religious intolerance in the 17th century in Shona MacLean's thriller debut, *The Redemption of Alexander Seaton*.

During the 17th century, the Quakers were persecuted for their beliefs and were not allowed to assemble in groups of more than five. Susannah, a Quaker girl whose father is in prison at the start of this novel, falls in love with Will. His father is alderman of a town opposed to this new breed of believer.

Susannah and Will narrate the story in turn, chapter by chapter, and so we have a fascinating overview of the time. Turnbull writes most beautifully and the daily details of life, work, prison and so on are brilliantly depicted. Susannah and Will's emotions could be those of any of us living today and the book will appeal to readers with a taste for a love story that is about much more than just two teenagers falling in love. Boys as well as girls will enjoy it and learn from it in equal measure.

**Adèle Geras**

# NOT A PENNY MORE, NOT A PENNY LESS   Jeffrey Archer

### Next?

Jeffrey Archer has written many fast-paced novels including *Kane and Abel*, and several volumes telling of his own experience in prison – *The Prison Diaries* by FF 8282.

Robert Harris writes exciting page-turners; try *Fatherland*, which speculates about what might have happened had Germany won the war. (UTBG 128)

*House of Cards* by Michael Dobbs and *The Client* (or indeed anything) by John Grisham are also exciting thrillers.

Four men from very different backgrounds – an aristocrat, a doctor, an art dealer and an academic – are conned into buying shares in Prospecta Oil, which turns out to be a dud company. But agent Harvey Metcalfe picked the wrong victims this time. The four men band together and form elaborate plans to swindle Metcalfe back until they have regained the exact sum of money he took from them – not a penny more, not a penny less.

Jeffrey Archer is not a popular man, having spent time in prison himself for perjury, but he knows how to plot a good story and this is his best.

**Yvonne Coppard**

# NOT DRESSED LIKE THAT YOU DON'T
Yvonne Coppard

If Jennifer thinks one thing it can be guaranteed her mum will think the opposite. While Jennifer is worried about fashion, friends, parties and boyfriends, her mum worries about Jennifer's GCSEs and if she'll get good grades. Jennifer writes about her feelings in a diary. What sets this apart from other teen-angst books is that her mum is writing a diary, too, and by reading their cleverly alternating diary entries we are allowed into their relationship, privileged to see both sides of the all-too-familiar arguments! Everyone who's ever had or been a teenager should read this laugh-out-loud-funny book. Spiky cartoon drawings enhance the humour.

**Eileen Armstrong**

### Next?

*Everybody Else Does, Why Can't I?* continues the mother-daughter conflict, as Jennifer gets a boyfriend...

Jeff Kinney's *The Diary of a Wimpy Kid* is a hilarious story, of, well, just what its title says... Oh, and it has pictures too – stick-figure ones!

Pete Johnson's *Faking It* is the diary of a boy who invents himself a girlfriend for want of a real one and how that one fib spins out of control. (UTBG 126)

# A NOTE OF MADNESS  Tabitha Suzuma

**Next?**

Tabitha Suzuma's books all challenge you to think, and to feel. Read the sequel *A Voice in the Distance*. Or try *From Where I Stand*, about a grief-stricken young man called Raven.

Meg Rosoff's *Just in Case* is about a boy trying to come to terms with himself. (UTBG 220)

A deeply troubled girl is at the centre of Joanna Kenrick's *Red Tears*.

Flynn, an outstanding young pianist studying at the Royal College of Music, has been chosen to perform a concert at the Albert Hall. However his mood swings, obsessive practice and bouts of lethargic misery are due to more than pre-performance jitters. Flynn's brilliant mind has mysteriously started to work against itself.

*A Note of Madness* is a gripping portrayal of manic depression, as experienced from within. We are submerged in Flynn's mind as it slips across the invisible line into mental illness, and we see his bewildered friends from the outside, their kindness, concern and common sense irrelevant to a growing nightmare they cannot understand. A necessary reminder that 'madness' is often far more terrible and frightening for those who suffer from it than for the people around them.

**Frances Hardinge**

# NOTES FROM A SMALL ISLAND  Bill Bryson

This book should come with a health warning: *Do Not Read on Public Transport or You'll Laugh Out Loud and People Will Think You're a Loony.*

Bryson is journeying around Britain on a farewell tour before moving back to the US; on the way he manages to take a wry sideways swipe at the British and their eccentricities both endearing and baffling (he lists Sooty, HP sauce, steam trains and making sandwiches from bread you've sliced yourself among the things he doesn't really get), without ever making you think he holds anything other than great fondness for us all. He's that apparently rare creature, an American who understands irony – just don't get him started on 1960s and 70s UK town planners or you'll regret it…!

**Catherine Robinson**

**Next?**

Bill Bryson's *Notes from a Big Country* repeats the same funny formula, this time in the USA, as does *Down Under*, about Australia.

*Round Ireland with a Fridge* by Tony Hawks isn't serious travel writing but it is seriously funny! (UTBG 335)

The classic round-Britain travelogue is Paul Theroux's *The Kingdom by the Sea*.

*Queenan Country* by Joe Queenan features another American laughing at Britain, but – like Bryson – loving it really.

# NOTES ON A SCANDAL Zoë Heller

**Next?**

Zoë Heller's *Everything You Know* is another exploration of people's weaknesses and strengths. Or try *The Believers*, about a Jewish family in New York.

*Friction* by E.R. Franks is a tense story also based in a school, and about falling in love with a teacher, but this time there's bullying, too.

*Doing It* by Melvin Burgess is about a group of boys and their sex lives (including an affair with a teacher). (UTBG 112)

Sheba is having an affair with a male pupil at her school. The only problem with this is that she's a teacher. Sheba confides in trusted colleague Barbara, who is flattered by being party to this secretive tryst.

Barbara starts a journal – tracking the development of Sheba's teacher-pupil relationship along with insights about her own friendship with Sheba. It is through Barbara's eyes that we see Sheba's increasingly complex entanglement with the student.

But as petty rivalry and jealousy ignite Barbara's insecurities, her loyalty and devotion to Sheba slither into acts of spite and revenge. The tale unfolds darkly, with cruel twists that make you wince.

I literally could not put this book down – it's sharp, menacing and totally outstanding.

**Jonny Zucker**

# NOT THE END OF THE WORLD
## Geraldine McCaughrean

This is, quite simply, a fantastic book. A retelling of the story of Noah that asks the most profound questions about faith, the relationship of man to animals, and what it might actually be like to be plunged into the 'dark reeking paradise' that is Noah's Ark.

What is it like to leave behind neighbours, your best friend, the rest of your family, to certain death? What is it like when you have to butcher the last of a species that a future world will never know? As everything degenerates into madness, sickness and squalor, it is up to the overlooked member of the family, Timna, the one whose name will not be remembered when the Old Testament version is told, to find a new way in a wholly new world. This is a small book with many dimensions – an epic, thundering read.

**Livi Michael**

**Next?**

John Rowe Townsend's *Noah's Castle* has a different take on the Noah story, or Julie Bertagna's *Exodus* (UTBG 124), also about escaping from a flood – one in the future.

Or try Anne Provoost's *In the Shadow of the Ark*, which focuses on the workmen building the ark and the girl who will become part of the plan to repopulate the world.

# NOUGHTS AND CROSSES
## Malorie Blackman

Once in a while you discover a mind-blowing, thought-provoking, gut-wrenchingly emotional book that changes your life. Not often, but it does happen, and *Noughts and Crosses* is one such book. If you don't read another book all year, read this and you will never look at issues such as bullying or racism in the same way again.

Malorie Blackman is such a master at creating believable characters, you feel you've known them all for years. This means, of course, that when they face pain, danger or tragedy, you share it with them; so grab a box of tissues and a slab of chocolate before you start reading.

The two main characters are Sephy, a Cross (and you'll understand what that means within the first few pages) and Callum, a Nought, who has been Sephy's best mate since childhood. The problem is that in their world Noughts and Crosses don't mix, never mind profess eternal friendship to one another. Their parents, locked in their own worlds of prejudice, tunnel vision and fear, battle to make their children understand the rules they live by.

The wonderful thing about this book is that it shows us all that, in the end, you can and must live by your own conscience and follow your own star. There is no other way.

**Rosie Rushton**

---

### Next?

The sequence in order is: *Noughts and Crosses*, *An Eye for an Eye* (a short World Book Day book that is included in later editions of *Noughts and Crosses*), *Knife Edge*, *Checkmate* and *Double Cross*.

Or for slavery and prejudice in the recent American past, read Mildred D. Taylor's *Roll of Thunder, Hear My Cry*. (UTBG 333)

For a story of a poor 'white trash' girl and her rich black friend, try Jacqueline Woodson's *I Hadn't Meant to Tell You This*.

---

This powerful, hard-hitting book is a stunning story of friendship over difference, of love over racism.

In this make-believe world, society is divided between the rich, righteous, pompous and perfect Crosses, and the 'second-class, second-hand' Noughts who, while being treated like dirt, still fight back, though their desire for equality (and revenge) only spurs on further hatred. But the story shows how two people can love each other and want to be with each other, even if their races are so different that mixing them would be against the law.

The message at the heart of this novel is truly inspiring. Yes, there are lessons to be learned, but mainly it's such a good book that you won't want to put it down for a second.

**Sam Lowenstein, age 13**

# OF MICE AND MEN   John Steinbeck

Two migrant workers, Lennie and George, travel from farm to farm. Lennie thinks that they look after each other, but really all the looking after is done by George: Lennie has the mind of a four-year-old. Trusting, affectionate, he understands nothing of what goes on around him: the hopes and disappointments of adulthood, sexuality or racial prejudice. He does not know that he is a man, dangerously strong, unaware of how he seems to women and to other men. George's whole life is dedicated to caring for his childhood friend who is still a child, until the day comes when something happens that George has always dreaded...

Not a love story, this is one of the greatest stories ever written about love.

**Jan Mark**

### Next?

*Cannery Row* and *Sweet Thursday* (UTBG 66), also by Steinbeck, are tragi-comic stories about the people who live in a poor area of Monterey on the California coast.

Another strange friendship is movingly explored in Rodman Philbrick's *Freak the Mighty*. (UTBG 147)

Or try Harper Lee's classic tale about prejudice, set in small-town America, *To Kill a Mockingbird*. (UTBG 398)

---

# THE OLD MAN AND THE SEA
Ernest Hemingway

### Next?

If you liked this Hemingway, you could try his novel based around his experiences in the Spanish Civil War, *For Whom the Bell Tolls*, or his account of life as a poor writer in Paris in the twenties in *A Moveable Feast*.

Another epic battle between a man and a fish? *Moby Dick* by Herman Melville (OK, not technically a fish, but a whale does live in the sea...).

F. Scott Fitzgerald was a friend of Hemingway's; try his masterpiece set in 1920's Long Island, *The Great Gatsby*. (UTBG 166)

*The Old Man and the Sea* is really just a long short story, but part of Hemingway's attraction is his ability to convey an emotional world with spare and simple prose. Santiago is an old fisherman down on his luck. He hasn't caught a fish for 84 days and the other fishermen think he's all washed up. But far out to sea he finally hooks a huge marlin – the largest he has ever hooked – and so ensues a battle between the old man and the fish that lasts not hours, but days.

It may not sound much to build a story on, but this is a powerful book about the hopes and fears that life is founded on, played out through the tired but noble figure of the old man.

**Marcus Sedgwick**

# ONCE  Morris Gleitzman

Once there was a boy called Felix who escaped from the Nazis and saved a little girl called Zelda. And once you start reading, you won't be able to stop. With a child's innocence, Felix does not understand the horror that surrounds him and makes up stories to keep the reality at bay. But as his journey unfolds, he realises the brutal events that threaten their safety and uses his storytelling to protect other children.

This excellent book avoids the stark realism of its subject matter, but creates empathy for the children's terrifying escape and I couldn't put it down. The journey across Poland is frightening but poignant, and the suspense of whether the children will be captured filters through every page. By the end of the book I was desperate to know what happened to Felix and Zelda, and now, two years later, the sequel has arrived.

**David Gilman**

> **Next?**
>
> *Then* picks up where *Once* finished, and is just as wonderful.
>
> Or try *I Am David* by Anne Holm. A boy escapes from a prison camp and, knowing only his first name, sets off across Europe to look for his mother. (UTBG 193)
>
> For another story about children escaping the horror of war, read *When Hitler Stole Pink Rabbit* by Judith Kerr.

# THE ONCE AND FUTURE KING  T.H. White

> **Next?**
>
> Interested in King Arthur? Try the more historically accurate *Sword at Sunset* by Rosemary Sutcliff
>
> Marion Zimmer Bradley's *Mists of Avalon* tells the Arthur story through the eyes of the women involved. As does the extraordinary *Here Lies Arthur* by Philip Reeve (UTBG 175).
>
> Rick Yancey's *The Extraordinary Adventures of Alfred Kropp* is about a plot to steal Excalibur.

From the magic-infused good humour of the opening chapters, this vivid retelling of the Arthurian legends gradually moves into darker territory. The plot sweeps from the Welsh borders to the Orkneys and to Cornwall, covering the length of the land.

But the drama is painfully human in scale. Witness the Orkney brothers, desperately seeking their mother's attention through a horrifying unicorn hunt, or Lancelot running mad in the forest, or Arthur, alone in his pavilion before the final battle, contemplating the collapse of all his hopes.

This is less a story of good versus evil, more a depiction of idealism set against mankind's innate destructiveness. Though grounded in an alternative medieval Britain, this is still very much a parable for our times.

**Thomas Bloor**

# ONCE IN A HOUSE ON FIRE

Andrea Ashworth

**Next?**

If you like memoirs and confessional literature, try *Bad Blood* by Lorna Sage, about her childhood.

Or *The Bell Jar* by Sylvia Plath, one of the most important books written by a woman in the 20th century. (UTBG 39)

Another evocation of 1970's schooldays is *The Rotters' Club* by Jonathan Coe.

Author Andrea Ashworth's father drowned when she was five. Her sister was three, her mother Lorraine 25. They lived in Manchester and money was tight. Lorraine's film-star looks soon attracted a new man and she fell pregnant with a third daughter. But the girls' new father beat Lorraine and she wore sunglasses all year round to hide her bruises.

Ashworth's memoir recounts her childhood in a house ablaze with violence. She survived and excelled, escaping the heat by winning a place at Oxford. Her memoir is a love story of sorts, and her bright passion for words eclipses the darkness of her subject matter.

**Francesca Lewis**

# ONE DAY IN THE LIFE OF IVAN DENISOVICH   Alexander Solzhenitsyn

In Stalin's USSR, five million people were locked up in prison camps (called gulags). Most were innocent. You could find yourself imprisoned for a 'wrong' opinion or for being a Baptist. At a whim, sentences were increased by ten years. Countless numbers died.

This novel is an account of a single day in the life of Ivan Denisovich Sukov, imprisoned for escaping from the Germans in World War II. Life in the gulag is harsh: ice four-cm thick inside the dormitory windows, filthy soup, inadequate clothes, cruelty. Stupidity, too: attempting to build a power station when the earth is as hard as granite and concrete freezes in the bucket before it can be used.

Solzhenitsyn, a Nobel Prize winner, was such a prisoner. This short, readable and explosive novel brought the gulag system to the attention of the world.

**Next?**

*Papillon* by Henri Charrière is a thrilling account of life on and escape from Devil's Island.

*The Wooden Horse* by Eric Williams is the story of one of the most famous escapes from a German prisoner of war camp in World War II.

*An Evil Cradling* by Brian Keenan is the true story of his kidnapping and survival against the odds. (UTBG 123)

**Alan Temperley**

# ONE FLEW OVER THE CUCKOO'S NEST ✳✳✳
## Ken Kesey

**Next?**

Tom Wolfe's *The Electric Kool-Aid Acid Test* is the account of Ken Kesey and his friends' road trip across the USA.

*On the Road* by Jack Kerouac is another essential read from this period and uncovers the soul of the Beat movement. (UTBG 297)

For another trippy road-trip chronicle, **Fear and Loathing in Las Vegas** by Hunter S. Thompson.

Set on a mental ward run by the iron-fisted Nurse Ratched, *One Flew Over the Cuckoo's Nest* is a classic. When Randell McMurphy, a free-spirited, fun-loving inmate, joins the ward, the rest of the patients are amazed by his antagonistic behaviour toward the hospital staff. As his antics inspire other patients to act up, Nurse Ratched's hold over the ward is threatened. A battle of wills ensues, capturing the spirit of individuality and rebellion against the conformity of the time.

The dated approach to mental health will be a bit shocking, and it is surprising to read about the extensive electro-shock therapy and debilitating frontal lobotomies. Once readers become familiar with the many characters on the ward and with Kesey's language, the plot will quickly move through to one of the most unforgettable endings ever.

**Mary Kate Castellani**

# ONE FOR THE MONEY Janet Evanovich ✳✳

When Stephanie Plum loses her job in a lingerie store, she decides to become a bounty hunter. I guess that's what you do if you're born in New Jersey – a place where houses are neat, cars are all-American, guns are big and little girls all want to be Barbie. The hunt for sadistic prize-fighter Benito Ramirez takes her into some dark (and quite gruesome) territory. But things aren't all doom and gloom – the love of Stephanie's life so far has been Rex the hamster, but soon she's torn between cool cop Joe Morelli and Ranger the macho mercenary.

The **Stephanie Plum** series has run to 14 books already, and every one of Evanovich's fans wait for another with bated breath.

**Sarah Gristwood**

**Next?**

Sue Grafton writes great classic detective stories with a female private investigator; the first is *A Is for Alibi*.

For a historical slant, try Elizabeth Peters's **Crocodile on the Sandbank**, about Egyptologist Amelia Peabody.

Another detective series that's funny and fast-paced? Try Lindsey Davis's **Falco** books, starting with *The Silver Pigs*, or the **Lily Bard Mysteries** by Charlaine Harris.

# ONE GIRL, TWO DECKS, THREE DEGREES OF LOVE  Jonny Zucker

**Next?**

Try *Saffy's Angel*, about the wonderful, sassy Casson family. (UTBG 340)

And for a teenager who doesn't fit in at all, try Jerry Spinelli's *Stargirl*. (UTBG 375)

For a grittier take on getting into the music industry, read Benjamin Zephaniah's *Gangsta Rap*.

Zoe Wynch is determined to become a DJ. She spends every spare moment in her room practising on her decks, but everything and everyone seem to be against her dream: her architect mum thinks she should be devoting loads more time to her homework; Rix, the patronising creep at the record store, keeps telling her that girls can't possibly be DJs; and at the music station where she works on Saturdays she has to spend her whole time glued to the photocopier. But worst of all, despite calling herself 'DJ Zed' Zoe's never actually had her own gig, and it doesn't look like there's much prospect of her getting one.

This is one sassy heroine whose life, loves and hopes make for great reading, whether or not you're into the music scene.

**Susan Reuben**

# ONE HUNDRED SHADES OF WHITE
## Preethi Nair

This is a bleak story told in such lush, sensuous prose that the reality of what is happening only hits you when you stop and think about it. Race, immigration, lies, truth, motherhood, trust, fidelity and betrayal all feature strongly – with food the binding force that pulls the whole together.

Alternately the story is told through Nalini's and her daughter, Maya's, eyes. Two other women are hugely important to the story, too: the grandmother whose voice we never hear, but whose influence permeates the lives of her children and grandchildren, and Maggie, the Irish woman Nalini ends up lodging with. Twisting back and forth with truth as it is perceived by different people, this is a sometimes funny, but far more often thoughtful look at how women live, and how culture is something that goes far deeper than skin colour.

**Next?**

Chitra Banerjee Divakaruni's *Mistress of Spices*, another book in which spices act as food, medicine and therapy.

Or try Joanne Harris's wonderful *Chocolat*. (UTBG 77)

For more Preethi Nair, try *Gypsy Masala*, a book she self-published and turned into an international success.

**Leonie Flynn**

# ONE HUNDRED YEARS OF SOLITUDE
## Gabriel García Márquez

Often prize-winning books aren't as brilliant as we are led to believe they are. This novel is. By the winner of the 1982 Nobel Prize for Literature, this is a journey into South America, following the fortunes of generations of the Buendia family as they found and then strive to retain the town of Macondo. With its wonderful writing, often-insane characters and a charm that many so-called classics lack, you fall into this story and start to question what is real and what isn't, as flying carpets, women who give birth to iguanas and clouds of yellow flowers escape from the pages. A magical, fantastical book. A real triumph of the imagination. Novels do not come much better than this.

**Bali Rai**

### Next?

Gabriel García Márquez has written many wonderful books. Try *Love in the Time of Cholera* (UTBG 248) for starters, or the haunting *Of Love and Other Demons*.

If you found the South American setting interesting, try Isabel Allende's *House of the Spirits* (UTBG 189), or for something else strange and fairy-tale-like, *The Alchemist* by Paulo Coelho (UTBG 15).

# ONLY FORWARD Michael Marshall Smith

### Next?

*Only Forward* was Michael Marshall Smith's first novel; he followed it with *Spares*, a sci-fi / comedy / thriller all wrapped up in one, with just as many weird thrills.

Or try anything by Douglas Adams, who must have been a huge inspiration for Michael Marshall Smith.

And don't forget Raymond Chandler's original wise-cracking detective, Philip Marlowe. *The Big Sleep* (UTBG 42) is the first time we meet him, or try *Farewell My Lovely*.

Stark is our gun-toting, cat-loving hero – a detective with a special talent that no one else alive possesses. He travels within the strange, future city of a thousand neighbourhoods on a seemingly impossible rescue mission, beset at every twist and turn by ever more bizarre and life-threatening challenges.

This wholly original adventure will linger in the minds of readers not simply because of the whirlwind blur of genres, jokes and violent thrills, but because of its powerful emotional core. You not only want Stark to win, you actually care for him, too.

More poignant than Terry Pratchett, more bloodthirsty than Douglas Adams: get ready for a bumpy ride. I guarantee you will not have read anything like this before.

**Keith Gray**

# ON THE ROAD   Jack Kerouac

**Next?**

Other cult books? Try *Heart of Darkness* by Joseph Conrad, a quest into the heart of the African jungle and the human heart. (UTBG 174)

Or *One Flew Over the Cuckoo's Nest* by Ken Kesey, about an outsider who takes on the authorities in a mental institution. (UTBG 294)

There's other famous road trips in *The Motorcycle Diaries* (UTBG 271) by Che Guevara and *Huckleberry Finn* (UTBG 191), the original, thrilling road trip, following Huck's adventures with escaped slave, Jim.

Join Sal Paradise for the journey of a lifetime across the US in search of love, music, and inspiration. In *On the Road*, Kerouac recasts his own experiences in the company of madman, prophet and con-man Neal Cassady (Dean Moriarty in the novel). They don't know where they're going, only that they have to go, and the faster, the better, in search of the ultimate high, until they cross the border into magical Mexico. Kerouac captures the intense joys and sorrows along the way, in a book that opens the wide spaces of America on the page until you can almost smell them. Once you've read this book, no journey you make will ever be the same.

**Ariel Kahn**

# OPERATION RED JERICHO   Joshua Mowll

Mowll takes that cheesy old device, the hidden archive of a secret society, and fills it with zing. The plot is preposterous, the narrative action so incessant that it makes an **Indiana Jones** adventure look half-asleep, and the book itself is a thing of beauty.

The setting is Shanghai and the South China Seas in 1920. Becca and Douglas McKenzie get involved with the activities of the Honourable Guild of Specialists (founded 1533) in their search for a lost gravitational device of awesome power. They get more than they bargained for: tons of violence and an awful lot of cod science.

Beautifully designed, the book features maps, period photos, cut-away diagrams, pencil sketches and ephemera of all sorts. A must for nerdy swashbucklers and swashbuckling nerds.

**Mal Peet**

**Next?**

The rest of the trilogy: *Operation Typhoon Shore* and *Operation Storm City*.

For a pirate story that is more than it seems, read Tanith Lee's *Piratica*. Or you could try the exciting adventures that make up Justin Somper's **Vampirates** series starting with *Demons of the Ocean* (UTBG 418).

And definitely try Philip Pullman's *The Ruby in the Smoke* and the rest of his **Sally Lockhart** books. (UTBG 341)

# THE OPPOSITE OF CHOCOLATE
## Julie Bertagna

It's a long hot summer and Sapphire's relationship with her boyfriend Jay ends on the same night that she finds out she's pregnant. Someone is starting fires on the estate where she lives and she watches them burn night after night as her own family implodes with news of her pregnancy.

There are lots of books about teen pregnancy, but this tackles the issue in a fresh way. Sapphire's mother wants her to have an abortion. Her father wants her to keep the baby. Her sister wants her to sell it. Sapphire shakes them all off and makes an unusual bond with a lad who is a loner. Together they find out things about each other, taking the novel towards a tragic and unexpected end. Riveting stuff!

**Anne Cassidy**

> ### Next?
>
> Other books about relationships and pregnancy: the **Megan** trilogy by Mary Hooper, *Roxy's Baby* (UTBG 336) by Catherine MacPhail or *Dear Nobody* (UTBG 101) by Berlie Doherty.
>
> More Julie Bertagna? Try *Exodus* (UTBG 124), set after a drowning from global warming, and its sequel, *Zenith*.

# THE ORACLE  Catherine Fisher

This, the first in a compelling trilogy set in an invented yet highly believable Graeco-Egyptian world, drew me immediately into a parched Mediterranean landscape.

Mirany has become the new Bearer of the terrifying scorpion bowl in rituals that serve their god, who inhabits a chosen man called 'The Archon'. But the old one has died and Mirany must search for the new god in secrecy, surrounded by treachery and danger. For a girl who has always privately questioned the actual existence of the god, her quest is especially fraught. This is powerful writing, as vivid and full of colour as a painting, yet with concise, intense sentences conveying an almost unbearable sense of danger.

The second book, *The Archon*, is just as gripping, but there are deeper truths to be found, too – about faith, choice and loyalty. These extraordinary, original novels culminate in the breathtaking *The Scarab*.

**Patricia Elliott**

> ### Next?
>
> Try Catherine Fisher's next trilogy – it starts with *Incarceron* and is set in a world divided between the rich and those in prison.
>
> For more absorbing, believable otherworlds try the **Pellinor** quartet by Alison Crogan, starting with *The Gift*.
>
> In Susan Price's *The Sterkarm Handshake*, the future clashes with the past in an original time-slip novel. (UTBG 376)

# ORANGES ARE NOT THE ONLY FRUIT
## Jeanette Winterson

Jeanette doesn't have an easy time of things. Adopted, growing up in a fiercely religious Pentecostal family, she has to endure endless church meetings, and her 'Mam's' conviction that she is actually God's Chosen One. Jeanette is not even sure she believes in God.

As if that weren't enough, she falls in love with a fiery-haired girl from the fishmonger's, and starts having visions of her very own personal orange demon. She has to decide if she is to live up to the expectations of her community, or follow her heart and her visions.

Threaded through this funny, moving, semi-autobiographical story of first love and big ideas are brilliant retellings of fairy tales that comment on the unique, entrancing story.

**Ariel Kahn**

> ### Next?
>
> *Blankets* also describes a boy's struggle to break away from his religious community. (UTBG 47)
>
> *Sugar Rush* explores what happens when Kim falls for her best friend Maria. (UTBG 384)
>
> Another lesbian classic? Try *Rubyfruit Jungle* by Rita Mae Brown. A young girl moves from small-town America and discovers the delights of city life.

# ORLANDO
## Virginia Woolf

> ### Next?
>
> More Virginia Woolf? Try the slim, satisfying and thought-provoking *A Room of One's Own*. (UTBG 334)
>
> Other historical novels which are also great classics include Walter Scott's *Ivanhoe* (UTBG 208) and Charles Dickens's *A Tale of Two Cities* (UTBG 386).
>
> For more recent takes on past times, try a Philippa Gregory such as *A Respectable Trade* or, come to that, historical detective stories like Lindsay Davis's *The Silver Pigs* or *Shadows in Bronze*.

Virginia Woolf jokingly called *Orlando* 'a biography' – and also 'a writer's holiday'. The title character was based on her own lover Vita Sackville-West, and the book is set in Vita's family home of Knole. The novel follows him / her through a magically long, ever-youthful life, with a sex change from man to woman along the way.

It may sound too bizarre, but Woolf's sheer exuberance and pleasure sweep you along, from the Elizabethans through the Victorians to Woolf's own day. Racy, rushing prose, so lush you could drown in it, informed by a loving, intimate knowledge of 400 years of English history.

**Sarah Gristwood**

# OSTRICH BOYS Keith Gray

Blake, Kenny and Sim are angry and sad. Sad because their friend Ross has died, and angry because they reckon he had a lousy funeral and a few scores left to settle. What can they do? Settle the scores for a start, but then they have a better idea: Ross always wanted to go to Ross, in Scotland, so they decide to steal his ashes and take him there, to give him a proper send-off. The ensuing mishaps are both hilarious and moving. The story is emotionally raw while written with the light touch and perfect control for which Keith Gray is known. A really important book – seemingly about death but offering much more to say about life, living and loving.

**Nicola Morgan**

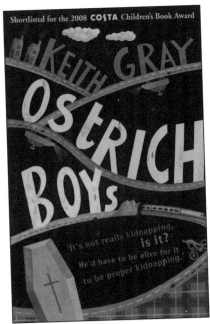

Shortlisted for the 2008 **COSTA** Children's Book Award

KEITH GRAY

OSTRICH BOYS

It's not really kidnapping, is it?
He'd have to be alive for it to be proper kidnapping.

## KIDS RUN WILD

**Jimmy Coates** series by Joe Craig

**Alpha Force** series by Chris Ryan

**H.I.V.E.** series by Mark Walden

**Special Agents** series by Sam Hutton

**The New Heroes** series by Michael Carroll

**Traces: Luke Harding, Forensic Investigator** series by Malcolm Rose

*Thieves Like Us* by Steve Cole

*Sure Fire* by Jack Higgins and Justin Richards

**The Power of Five** series by Anthony Horowitz

### Next?

More Keith Gray. Start with *Warehouse* (UTBG 423) or *Hoodlum*, another book that tells exactly what it's like to be young, male and pressurised by parental expectation, friends and, above all, loyalties.

There's another person's ashes in Jenny Valentine's wonderful *Finding Violet Park*. (UTBG 132)

Or for a book about how friendship can go wrong, try B.R. Collins's *The Traitor Game*. (UTBG 402)

# THE OTHER BOLEYN GIRL  Philippa Gregory  ✷✷✷

The riveting story of Anne Boleyn's sister, Mary, who at the age of 13 was first introduced to Henry VIII by her family to further their ambitions at court, and was gradually replaced in Henry's affections by Anne.

Gregory creates cold and calculating characters so completely nasty and manipulating that we cannot help but empathise with Mary and enjoy the comeuppance Anne receives after her rise to greatness. The equally fascinating historical detail of daily life at court creates a stunning backdrop to the drama of the characters' relationships, really bringing the history books to life.

**Eileen Armstrong**

## Next?

Gregory's *The Queen's Fool* charts the power struggle between Mary Tudor and her sister Elizabeth, as both try to become Queen of England. *The Virgin's Lover* focuses on the impossible love triangle involving Elizabeth and her married lover Robert Dudley. *The Constant Princess* tells the story of Catherine of Aragon.

In *Mary, Bloody Mary* by Caroline Meyer, Mary Tudor, daughter of Henry VIII, tells the story of her childhood.

Anya Seton's *Katharine* is about the real-life mistress, and later wife, of John of Gaunt. (UTBG 221)

---

# OTHER ECHOES  Adèle Geras  ✷✷

## Next?

More books about growing up abroad are *Oleander, Jacaranda: A Childhood Perceived* by Penelope Lively and *The Flame Trees of Thika* by Elspeth Huxley.

You can learn about the events that provide the background to Flora's story in J.G. Ballard's *Empire of the Sun*. (UTBG 120)

For books about going to boarding school, as the older Flora does, read Adèle Geras's wonderful **Happy Ever After** series, beginning with *The Tower Room*.

Flora is a thoughtful sixth-former convalescing after fainting dramatically at her boarding school. Unsettled by a dream of her childhood in Borneo, Flora makes a record of that long-ago time, painstakingly sorting and arranging vivid, sometimes half-remembered memories into a coherent story. *Other Echoes* is a jewel of a book about a teenager looking back at a pivotal time in her life. What could have happened then that makes her feel so compelled to write it down now? The answer is partly young Flora's discovery of who lives in the haunted house on the hill, but mostly it concerns ghostly memories, loss, and the realisation of how cruel life can be even in the midst of beauty.

**Gill Vickery**

# THE OTHER SIDE OF TRUTH Beverley Naidoo

When Sade and Femi's mother is shot in front of them as punishment for their journalist father's controversial newspaper articles, they see no choice but to trust a female contact to take them to safety in Britain where their uncle lives. The woman, however, takes their money and abandons the children in London. The rest of the book follows Sade and Femi in their increasingly desperate attempts to find their uncle and stay in Britain. Help comes in the unlikely form of a very familiar newsreader.

If you have ever heard other people make negative comments about refugees and secretly agreed with them, then this is a book that you really need to read. I guarantee that it will make you think differently.

**Laura Hutchings**

### Next?

You can see how Sade and Femi get on in the sequel, *Web of Lies*.

Another very powerful book by Beverley Naidoo is *Journey to Jo'burg*, which deals with what life was like under apartheid rule in South Africa.

If you like books that make you think about real-life issues, then try *Noughts and Crosses* (UTBG 290) and its sequels by Malorie Blackman, *Stone Cold* by Robert Swindells (UTBG 377), or *Private Peaceful* (UTBG 324) by Michael Morpurgo.

# OUR MAN IN HAVANA Graham Greene

### Next?

In Graham Greene's *The Comedians*, a hotelier (Mr Brown), a confidence trickster (Mr Jones) and an innocent American (Mr Smith) pass time in Papa Doc's Haiti.

Ernest Hemingway was also fascinated by Cuba. Try *The Old Man and the Sea*. (UTBG 291)

Another exciting novel set in Cuba? Read Elmore Leonard's *Cuba Libre*.

Or why not try a novel by a Cuban writer? The dense, eccentric, playful *Three Trapped Tigers* by G. Cabrera Infante is written in a style as unlike Greene as you can imagine.

Graham Greene specialised in creating and perfecting his own vivid world, inhabited by lonely men, spies and assassins. His heroes are ordinary men who find themselves out of their depth in James-Bond-style adventures.

In *Our Man in Havana*, Jim Wormald has a humdrum job selling vacuum cleaners in 1950's Cuba. But he needs more money. So he accepts an offer to become an agent of the British Secret Service, which asks him to recruit his own network of agents in Cuba, something Wormald has no idea how to do. So he decides, simply, to make it all up. But his lies soon develop a life of their own. The more Wormald invents, the more dangerous his life becomes.

**James Reynolds**

# OUT OF BOUNDS  Beverley Naidoo

**Next?**

Other books by Beverley Naidoo about South Africa under apartheid include *Journey to Jo'burg*, *Chain of Fire* and *No Turning Back*.

*Cry the Beloved Country* by Alan Paton gives another view of the same times.

*To Kill a Mockingbird* is a story of growing up in the racially segregated southern United States. (UTBG 398)

Or try Linzi Glass's tale of 1970's Johannesburg, apartheid and first love, *Ruby Red*.

For 50 years South Africa was ruled by the system of apartheid, the white minority making sure they remained in control by colour coding the rest of the population and making it progressively harder for them to live, work and get an education. These stories show how the lives of ordinary harmless people were destroyed: families were forced to leave their homes because the neighbourhood was reserved for lighter skins; people were beaten and jailed for having friends of a different colour; a father was separated from his children for being a different shade of brown. First they endured, then they began to fight back, and finally Nelson Mandela was set free to lead them to a new start. Likely to leave you seething in furious disbelief, but it's all true.

**Jan Mark**

# OUT OF THE BLUE  Sue Welford

Kegan thinks his life couldn't get any worse – his father is an abusive drunk, his mother barely knows he exists, at school he doesn't have any friends (at least, not any he wants) and everybody calls him Rat Boy.

Then it does get worse! A family tragedy, and a threat to the family of foxes he has come to love – the only things that made his life liveable. But matters improve when he befriends odd new-girl, Zoë. She makes him take control of his life, fight for what he wants and pursue his dreams.

So much is packed into this slim book – a fine central character, a thought-provoking plot and a lot of emotional punch. It's about things that happen, those moments that surprise and change you – good things and bad things, things that just happen, out of the blue...

**Next?**

Carl Hiaasen's *Hoot* (UTBG 186) is another story that mixes human lives with a plan to rescue endangered animals, or try his fast-moving, humorous eco-thriller, *Scat*.

Read Matthew Sweeney's touching *Fox*, about an unlikely friendship between a boy and a fox.

Try more Sue Welford – how about *Waiting for Mermaids*, or *Nowhere to Run*?

**Daniel Hahn**

# OUT OF THE DUST  Karen Hesse

**Next?**

Something by Berlie Doherty herself? Try *Granny Was a Buffer Girl*.

Or Steven Herrick's *The Simple Gift* (UTBG 363), about running away from an alcoholic father, or *Locomotion* by Jacqueline Woodson. Both are told in verse form.

Another Karen Hesse – *Brooklyn Bridge*, set in New York.

Deservedly, Hesse won the 1997 Newbery Medal with this tight, spare novel. It is written as a series of free-verse poems that depict a year in the Oklahoma Dust Bowl in the 1930s.

The narrator is 14-year-old Billy-Jo, and through her eyes we watch the land giving itself up to the dust storms; dust invades her family's fields, their home, their food, their minds. It is like another character, mercilessly wearing down all hope as the weeks and months progress.

Then a terrible disaster strikes the family: Billy-Jo's mother dies. She and her father blame themselves and each other and can't find a way of talking about it and healing the grief. But there's another character, too – music. Like her mother, Billy-Jo is a brilliant pianist. The accident that killed her mother scarred Billy-Jo's hands, and she despairs that she will ever play again. And if she can't, what's left for her?

This is a story about tremendous courage and strength, and the personality of the narrator sings through every line.

**Berlie Doherty**

# THE OUTSIDER  Albert Camus

Written in the first person, *The Outsider* opens with the death of the narrator Meursault's mother. Meursault is a young bachelor in Algiers. Shortly after his mother's funeral, he gets involved in some violence with Arabs in the town, which results in him shooting one of them on the beach later that day. He goes to court, but the court seems to be more interested in his apparent lack of grief for his mother than his killing of the Arab.

Camus was an interesting man – a French Algerian, a philosopher, and a pretty good goalkeeper, too. *The Outsider* is a product of the existentialist philosophy that Camus explored – the nature of what it is 'to be', whether life has meaning or not, and by implication questions of how we should exist within the rules of society.

**Marcus Sedgwick**

**Next?**

Try *The Catcher in the Rye*, a very different novel that shares some of the same themes. (UTBG 69)

More Camus? Try his gripping account of an outbreak of the Black Death in a modern-day French town, *The Plague*.

For something equally bleak, try Franz Kafka's *Metamorphosis*. It is surreal, yet somehow deeply real.

# THE OUTSIDERS S.E. Hinton

**Next?**

More S.E. Hinton? Try *Rumblefish*, which has a similar theme. (UTBG 337)

*Bloodtide* (UTBG 49) by Melvin Burgess is set in a future London ravaged by warring gangs, or try Bernard Ashley's thrilling and uncompromising *No Way to Go*.

*The Brave* by David Klass is about a moral dilemma: join a gang and fit in, or don't and be bullied.

Hinton was 17 when she wrote this great novel and it is her most popular book to this day. Set in late 1960's America, it's a story about social divisions and gangs.

According to Ponyboy Curtis there are only two types of people in this world – Greasers and Socs (short for 'socials'). The Socs have it all and they flaunt it to Ponyboy and his mates who come from the wrong side of town. Life is tough if you're a Greaser but the long nights are often livened up when the Socs and the Greasers have a rumble. The problems start when Ponyboy's friend Johnny kills a Soc during yet another fight. Ponyboy feels the death more than he thought he would and begins to question all the things he's ever taken for granted.

**Bali Rai**

# OVER A THOUSAND HILLS, I WALK WITH YOU Hanna Jansen

Rwanda, 1994. At the start of this harrowing novel, Jeanne d'Arc Umubyeyi is living an unexceptional life. She argues with her parents, is annoyed by her sister and teases her brother. That normality is fractured with the outbreak of violence: the mass killing of Rwanda's Tutsis by Hutu militia.

Hanna Jansen's compelling narrative tells the real-life story of her adopted daughter who, like so many others, lost her entire family in the Rwandan genocide. It is a personal and painful story that captures the terror, the horror and the suffering of the Rwandan people. Jansen makes it clear that this was not tribal warfare perpetrated by primitive people, but an act of the most shocking brutality orchestrated by an educated and civilised society. In spite of the bleak subject, this is an inspiring read. If you care about the world in which you live, you will most certainly want to read this unforgettable and important story.

**Next?**

There's more brutality and a look at how humans behave to each other in Anna Perera's *Guantanamo Boy*.

For another story of a girl facing hardships in Africa, Berlie Doherty's *Abela*.

Or try *Noughts and Crosses*. (UTBG 290)

**Nikki Gamble**

## Star Title

# THE OWL SERVICE   Alan Garner

When they find a stack of old plates in the attic, Gwyn and Roger see an abstract, floral pattern, but Alison sees something else. Owls. Strange and sinister things start to happen in the Welsh valley. Gwyn discovers the beginnings of the story in an ancient legend of magic and murder, but its end, it seems, is still to come. Only the gardener, old Huw Halfbacon, will talk about it. But he, surely, is mad...

On its opening page, the book draws the reader into its eerie atmosphere, and from then on the tension never lets up. It has its lighter moments as well, though, and the characters are complex, engaging and often funny. A powerful, unforgettable book, well worthy of its classic status.

**Kate Thompson**

A teenage girl becomes obsessed by the owl patterns on an old dinner service found in a disused attic. At the same time, her stepbrother and the son of their housekeeper become rivals for her affections. What none of them realise is that they are replaying a tragedy that occurred centuries before. As ancient jealousies are translated into fresh hatred, it seems inevitable that they will destroy each other unless they can find a way to overcome terrifying forces they barely comprehend.

*The Owl Service* is a rare and special book that combines mythology and fantasy with social realism. Its real strength comes from the way it shows how good and evil stem from the passions of individual human beings, and how the battle between them takes place in all of us.

**Graham Gardner**

### Next?

Alan Garner has written some of the most amazing books ever! Try the strange and haunting *Red Shift* (UTBG 329), the vivid excitement of *Elidor* or his book of folklore, *A Bag of Moonshine*.

Margaret Mahy writes complex, dark and scary books, too; try *The Haunting* or *Alchemy* (UTBG 16).

Someone else who mixes the very real and the altogether unworldly is David Almond; try *Skellig* first. (UTBG 365)

Catherine Fisher often weaves Welsh legends into her stories. *Corbenic* is a wonderfully atmospheric mystery. (UTBG 87)

# PADDY CLARKE HA HA HA  Roddy Doyle

Paddy Clarke is a ten-year-old boy growing up on a council estate in Dublin in the late 1960s. His world revolves around his gang, his school and thinking of ways to torture his younger brother Sinbad. In Paddy's world, parents argue, teachers whack you and everything is a sin. It's more cutting edge than **Just William** – these kids are one step ahead of the law.

The book is narrated as a diary, and we really feel sympathy for Paddy. He's worried his parents are about to split up. His world is cruel and yet loving – he's confused. The book is funny, and also sad. But beware – it's full of Dublin slang that you may have to work at to understand at first!

**Anne Flaherty**

> ### Next?
>
> Roddy Doyle's **Barrytown** trilogy, about the life of the Rabbitte family in Dublin, starts with **The Commitments** and continues with **The Snapper** and **The Van**.
>
> For a look at life in Ireland before the war, read Frank McCourt's memoir, **Angela's Ashes**. (UTBG 22)
>
> Jamie O'Neill's **At Swim, Two Boys** is a story of two Dublin boys at the time of the First World War.
>
> Or for something rather more brutal, read Patrick McCabe's disturbing **Butcher Boy**.

# PAGAN'S CRUSADE  Catherine Jinks

This book is set in the 12th century, but don't expect to find any antiquated language – the hero thinks and speaks as if he's around today. Sixteen-year-old Pagan Kidrouk (born in Bethlehem, but not in a stable) is a streetwise, foul-mouthed monastery brat who sees life as a series of opportunities. Usually opportunities that aren't altogether legal. Employed as squire to a Templar knight, Lord Roland, he thinks he'll be escorting pilgrims to the Holy Land, which sounds cushy, but instead of the easy life he ends up in Jerusalem fighting Saladin.

Pagan is a great character, with a sharp wit and sharper tongue. The books chart his relationship with Lord Roland, who eventually becomes both friend and mentor, and his own journey into adulthood. Full of huge battles, brutal violence, and fascinating historical detail, these books are brilliant and should be read by everyone!

**Leonie Flynn**

> ### Next?
>
> The Pagan books continue with **Pagan in Exile**, **Pagan's Vows** and **Pagan's Scribe**.
>
> For another orphan who is befriended by a knight, try Lian Hearn's brilliant **Across the Nightingale Floor**, though the Japanese setting makes it very different. (UTBG 11)
>
> Or for something else set during the same period of history, try Elizabeth Laird's **Crusade**.

# PAPER FACES  Rachel Anderson

**Next?**

Read the famous *The Diary of a Young Girl* by Anne Frank for a true account from a young Jewish girl during World War II. (UTBG 106)

An excellent story about an evacuee is *Goodnight Mister Tom* by Michelle Magorian. Or try the same author's look at post-war British life: *Just Henry* (UTBG 219).

For an adventurous, thoughtful and moving tale about a boy's experience in a time of conflict, read *I Am David* by Anne Holm, in which a boy sets off across Europe in search of his mother. (UTBG 193)

The war is over, but Dot isn't happy – if anything, she's more afraid than before. The end of the war means the looming threat of her father's return – a man who's just a paper face to her from the snapshot in her mother's handbag – and a new life that she can't predict.

This is the tale of one child's life in post-war Britain. The whole story is seen through Dot's young, inexperienced eyes, and you have to deduce for yourself the poverty and semi-neglect in which she lives, with a mother who loves her but is too young and dizzy to try to make a good life for her. It's so beautifully written that I read it slowly, to savour every word.

**Susan Reuben**

# PEACE LIKE A RIVER
## Lief Enger

Eleven-year-old Reuben Hand begins life by not breathing for 12 minutes. But by a miracle he survives 'in order to be a witness' to other miracles. Reuben has a poetic younger sister, a brave older brother and a wise father. He suffers from terrible asthma but survives to become the narrator of this funny, tragic and ultimately uplifting story. *Peace Like a River* has elements of *To Kill a Mockingbird*, *Cold Mountain* and Cormac McCarthy's modern Westerns, but it is a masterpiece in its own right. Every sentence is a joy, every thought is fresh, every character believable. Without being preachy or moralising, it does what stories are meant to do: it inspires you to live a better life.

**Caroline Lawrence**

**Next?**

More Lief Enger? Try the tougher *So Brave, Young and Handsome*, which is also set in the West of cowboys, outlaws and strange friendships.

Or try some of Cormac McCarthy's stories – start with *All the Pretty Horses* or *The Road*.

Other classic Western novels include *Hombre* (UTBG 185) by Elmore Leonard, *Lonesome Dove* by Larry McMurty and *Shane* by Jack Schaefer.

# PEACE WEAVERS   Julia Jarman

Forced to live with her father on a US airbase while her mother protests against the outbreak of war in Iraq, 16-year-old Hilde gets involved with an archaeological dig. Unearthing a gold brooch she wonders about its owner Maethilde, a 16th-century peace weaver, and ponders the parallels in their lives. Drawing strength from Maethilde's heroic efforts and determination, Hilde begins to speak out about the futility of war and the need for peace, trying to influence the political decision-makers around her.

This is an intricately woven story for our time that asks big questions about war, morality, politics, responsibility and whether fighting is ever justified. It offers no easy answers but nevertheless radiates hope that through open communication, honesty and more-visionary young people like Hilde, peace is possible.

**Eileen Armstrong**

**Next?**

Jarman's *Hangman* wraps up cruel school bullying in a haunting time-slip story about World War II, while the spooky *Ghostwriter* is a suspenseful thriller.

Hanna Jansen's *Over a Thousand Hills, I Walk with You* is a horrifying story about the Rwandan genocide. (UTBG 305)

*The Shell House* skilfully straddles two time periods. (UTBG 358)

# THE PENALTY   Mal Peet

**Next?**

Mal Peet's *Keeper* (UTBG 222), and the third **Faustino** book: *Exposure* (UTBG 125).

There are spirit guides, South America and a dangerous journey in Isabelle Allende's *City of Beasts*.

Or for someone learning something important from a ghost, read Dickens's *A Christmas Carol*.

This is the second book featuring the laconic South American sports reporter cum detective, Paul Faustino. *Keeper*, Faustino's first outing, used football as a jumping-off point from which Peet could discuss the rape of the rainforest. Likewise in *The Penalty*, the real subject is slavery.

Faustino is drawn into the mysterious disappearance of El Brujito, the 'Little Magician', who has just fluffed a penalty in a key game. Faustino is kidnapped and taken to the poverty-stricken area where El Brujito grew up. The story of Faustino's investigations alternate with the gripping, mysterious account of the life and voodoo-deification of Paracleto, an African slave taken to South America in the 18th century. The two storylines come together in a climax that is unsettling, uncanny and, it has to be said, a little obscure. Throughout, Peet's prose is as nimble-footed and skilful as the doomed El Brujito himself.

**Anthony McGowan**

# PERFUME Patrick Süskind

**Next?**

*Under the Skin* by Michel Faber – hard to say why this came to mind, except that it's also brilliantly bizarre, macabre and sinister, and it's a book I love.

*Dan Leno and the Limehouse Golem* by Peter Ackroyd is another historical murder story, and also fast-moving and gripping.

There's murder and perfume in Sarah Singleton's deliciously Gothic *The Poison Garden*, a mystery set in the 1850s. (UTBG 317)

I lent my copy of *Perfume* to my daughter when she was 14. I never got it back. A murder story steeped in sensuality, utterly original and often shocking, it's set in stinking 18th-century Paris and is about a man called Grenouille who has 'the finest nose in Paris and no personal odour'. His ambition is to make the most wonderful perfume in the world – distilled from the scent of murdered girls.

This is a richly written book that will open your eyes (and nose) wide, and you will learn and think and wonder. It's the sort of adult book that teenagers often love – it reaches deep inside you and changes you.

**Nicola Morgan**

# PERSEPOLIS Marjane Satrapi

Quite unique! Marjane Satrapi draws in powerful black-and-white comic-strip images. *Persepolis* is her own story about growing up in Iran as the outspoken child of wonderfully open-minded parents. When the Shah is overthrown by the Islamic revolution, a beloved Marxist uncle and friends return from the Shah's barbaric jails. But joy is short-lived. A new religious tyranny takes over. War follows with Iraq. To have a rebel spirit is dangerous, so for her own safety 14-year-old Marjane is sent away to school in Austria.

*Persepolis 2* follows the lonely story of this witty, sharply honest teenager into young adulthood as 'a Westerner in Iran and an Iranian in the West'. It's powerfully personal, opening our eyes to the politics and human beings behind black veils. I laughed, gasped and cried.

**Beverley Naidoo**

**Next?**

*Maus* (UTBG 258), about the Holocaust, and *In the Shadow of No Towers*, from the graphic artist Art Spiegelman.

Look out, too, for more Satrapi: *Embroideries* is about the women in her Iranian family, particularly their relationship with men. *Chicken with Plums* is about her great-uncle, who after his favourite musical instrument was smashed, took to his bed to die.

Or try *The Breadwinner*, about an Afghan girl trying to save her family from starving. (UTBG 59)

Or you could watch the film version of *Persepolis*. It's great!

# PICNIC AT HANGING ROCK Joan Lindsay ✹ ✹

**Next?**

For more in an Australian setting, try Miles Franklin's *My Brilliant Career*, about a girl hungering for life and love while coping with the outback. (UTBG 272)

For something spooky and atmospheric, Daphne Du Maurier's *Rebecca*. (UTBG 328)

An Australian author who writes lyrically about the most unsettling things is Sonya Hartnett; try *Surrender*. (UTBG 385)

A short and strange novel that purports to recount a genuine mystery from St Valentine's Day 1900 in the Australian bush. The book is so convincing that many people quickly believed it to be true. In fact it is a work of fiction, but a rather surreal and excellent film version by Peter Weir in 1975 helped to establish this story as an enduring modern myth.

Set in and around a girls' school in rural Australia, the darkness of the book quickly establishes itself as a day trip by the girls and their teachers to the local picnic site at Hanging Rock turns into a nightmare when four of them go missing. By nightfall the girls still cannot be found, though the alarm has been raised and seemingly every inch of the eerie cliffs has been searched. And what happened on the rock is never explained, which adds to the claustrophobic and sinister atmosphere that the book creates. A timeless gem.

**Marcus Sedgwick**

# THE PICTURE OF DORIAN GRAY ✹ ✹
## Oscar Wilde

You will find some of the attitudes in this book – taken for granted in Wilde's time – unacceptable today. The style is also overblown and more florid than you might be used to. But if you can accept these limitations, you will be fascinated by the story of Dorian Gray, who sacrifices his soul for eternal youth and good looks. The corrupting effects of Dorian's lifestyle, however, have to show up somewhere and they are mirrored in his portrait; the more violent and decadent Dorian's actions, the more warped and ugly the painting becomes. Eventually it degenerates into such a hideous parody of Dorian that he destroys it, thus bringing about an unpredictable and terrifying climax to the novel.

**Gill Vickery**

**Next?**

*Dr Jekyll and Mr Hyde* is also about someone whose hideous alter ego personifies the evil in his soul. (UTBG 115)

Alyson Noël's **The Immortals** series is an up-to-date look at immortality.

For books about swapping bodies, read the terrifying ghost story *The Victorian Chaise Longue* by Marghanita Laski.

# PIED PIPER  Nevil Shute

Sometimes you dream of finding a treasure trove: jewels or money or a map of a secret island. I found treasure when I rented a furnished flat and found a whole trunk full of novels by Nevil Shute.

*Pied Piper* is about an old man who goes on a fishing trip to France during the first months of the war against Hitler. As the Germans advance he has to try and make his way back to the coast, and safety in Britain – but on the journey he meets more and more people who beg him to take along their children. He ends up with a whole collection of them – French ones, English ones, Dutch ones...

The way the children interact to help each other, and the adventures they encounter on the way, are both touching and exciting. It's a book that breaks down barriers between nationalities and between the old and the young, and I've read it about seven times!

**Eva Ibbotson**

> **Next?**
>
> Everything by Nevil Shute is good but *A Town Like Alice* is particularly rich and colourful. (UTBG 401)
>
> *A Little Boy Lost* by Marghanita Laski is about a man's search for his son who has been lost in the war.
>
> Or *The Machine-Gunners* – a boy finds a gun from a crashed bomber and sets up a fortress to defend his town. (UTBG 251)

# THE PIGMAN  Paul Zindel

> **Next?**
>
> *The Pigman* is a bit of a one-off, but *Boy Kills Man* (UTBG 56) by Matt Whyman and *Friction* by E.R. Frank both portray situations where someone gets in too deep and everything spirals out of control.
>
> There is a sequel: *The Pigman's Legacy*. Or try Paul Zindel's *My Darling, My Hamburger* (UTBG 273).
>
> *Girl in a Garden* by Lesley Chamberlain also has a similar theme, though a different and less in-your-face feel.

John and Lorraine are ordinary kids with ordinary names and ordinary lives. The Pigman, or Mr Pignati, is a sad and lonely old man who is somewhere between ordinary and extraordinary. Their friendship with him becomes the catalyst for extraordinarily awful events. On page four you learn that the Pigman eventually dies, but this knowledge does not lessen the impact of the way in which John and Lorraine each tell their stories of the shockingly realistic and ultimately heartrending events leading up to his death.

This is a story of what happens when simple events spiral out of control. It's also a story of taking responsibility – even if it's too late.

**Nicola Morgan**

# PIRATES! Celia Rees

Boys have had juicy adventure stories for ever, while girls have had to make do with much tamer stuff. But not now. *Pirates!* is set on the docks of 18th-century Bristol, in the turquoise bays and emerald mountains of pirate-haunted Jamaica, and in the jungles of Madagascar. The heroine finds life as a merchant's daughter unsatisfying; especially when her stepmother decides to make a young lady of her. After her father's death, she's shipped off to Jamaica, and is shocked to learn how her family made its money – slavery. She learns that the law tolerates injustice and cruelty; and she has to join an outlawed pirate crew to find a sort of democracy, and also friendship, loyalty and love.

It's all so exciting and well told that you won't even notice the solid knowledge and research that underpins it all. You simply believe that Celia Rees could captain a fast Yankee schooner from the Indies to Africa's shore. A wonderful read!

**Susan Price**

> ### Next?
>
> For another girl pirate, *Piratica* by Tanith Lee is about a girl whose life is not quite what she thinks it is. Julia Golding's **The Ship Between Worlds** has a boy press-ganged onto a pirate ship. Or try a classic pirate adventure: *The Sea-Hawk* by Raphael Sabatini. And pirates in icy waters? *Sea of Trolls* by Nancy Farmer. (UTBG 345)
>
> For a different Celia Rees, try her acclaimed *Witch Child*. (UTBG 441)

# PLAGUE Malcolm Rose

> ### Next?
>
> Of course there was a real plague in London back in 1665, and you can read about that in *At the Sign of the Sugared Plum* by Mary Hooper. (UTBG 31)
>
> Malcolm Rose's excellent **Traces** series is about Luke Harding, who at 16 is the youngest person ever to qualify as a Forensic Investigator. Start with *Framed*.
>
> In John Wyndham's *The Day of the Triffids*, the world goes blind – but why? (UTBG 98)

*Plague* is one of the most exciting – and gruesome – scientific thrillers you'll ever read. It's set in ordinary, everyday Milton Keynes. There, one by one, the inhabitants fall victim to a new strain of a virus that results in a haemorrhagic fever – which means you bleed uncontrollably until you die. As yet there is no cure. It's a race against time to find one, and caught up in the drama are three teenagers – Rev, from the good side of town, Lucy, his girlfriend from the council estate, and Scott, son of one of the doctors at the hospital.

*Plague* is pacy, nerve-wracking and not for those of a delicate disposition!

**Sherry Ashworth**

# COMING OF AGE
## by Matt Whyman

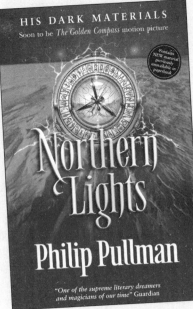

Becoming an adult doesn't require an entry exam. There's no need to go on a training course, or do anything that involves pass or fail. It's just something that happens to everyone at some stage, whether they like it or not.

So how do you graduate to the grown-up world? Is it something to do with your developing body, the way you see your place in the world, or how people relate to you? The truth is everyone has a different experience. For some it can be a slow and subtle transformation, while others might encounter a single event that changes their life for ever...

Ultimately, there is no right or wrong way to go through it. What matters is that you're able to make sense of things, so you can get on with making the most of your life. Which is where books can work wonders...

Whether you're into action, adventure, romance, gritty realism or faraway fantasies, a book works best when it stirs up your heart and mind. A really good one won't end with the full stop either. If a story strikes a chord, it can leave a question mark hanging over your head. You're left to think about what you've just read, and how it relates to your growing sense of identity. It doesn't have to be exclusively about characters on the cusp of adulthood, like the hormone-crazed lads in *Doing It* (UTBG 112) by Melvin Burgess, or the girls in Julie Burchill's *Sugar Rush* (UTBG 384). You might connect with big ideas, like those explored across Philip Pullman's **His Dark Materials** trilogy (UTBG 181) or simply admire the attitude that shines from any tale that grips you.

It's all about stirring up emotions, and making you feel alive.

James Herbert wrote my coming-of-age novels of choice. I was addicted to being scared witless as an endless chain of inescapable horror confronted the hero. It might've stopped me from sleeping at night, but the fact that these guys always managed to survive showed me the value of determination. The lovemaking scenes were an added bonus, and frankly I learned more about how to do it from *The Rats*, *The Fog* and *The Survivor* than I did when we covered human reproduction in biology. It may have led me to believe that 'unsafe sex' meant getting under the covers together without first checking the room for zombies and bloodthirsty rodents, but then I learned about life wherever I could get the information.

Nowadays, there are non-fiction books that cover all the subjects I so desperately wanted to know about. They can be a great source of information and advice, especially when it comes to issues we find hard to talk about with friends and family. You might be concerned by personal stuff that's just too embarrassing for words, and so it can come as a revelation when you find what you're looking for on the page. Knowledge, after all, is power.

With clear, balanced information to hand, you can reach decisions with confidence about how to make the most of your life. It beats just hoping for the best and then lying awake worrying at night. Besides, you need that time to enjoy the books that make your world go round.

## MORE COMING-OF-AGE STORIES

*This Boy's Life* by Tobias Wolff

*A Boy's Own Story* by Edmund White

*The Secret Life of Bees* by Sue Monk Kidd

*Gigi* by Colette

*The Dud Avocado* by Elaine Dundy

*Empire of the Sun* by J.G. Ballard

*The Rachel Papers* by Martin Amis

*Le Grand Meaulnes* by Alain-Fournier

*The Cement Garden* by Ian McEwan

*The Go-Between* by L.P. Hartley

*A Separate Peace* by John Knowles

*Goodbye, Columbus* by Philip Roth

MEG ROSOFF

How I Live Now

'Magical and utterly faultless'
– Mark Haddon

Shortlisted
ORANGE AWARD
for new writers

# POBBY AND DINGAN  Ben Rice

Are you a fruit-loop if you talk to people who don't exist? Ashmole thinks his sister Kellyanne definitely is, because of her devotion to her invisible friends Pobby and Dingan. But when these friends go missing at their father's opal mine and Kellyanne sinks into a decline, Ashmole has to face the fact that they are utterly real, at least to her – and also that he loves her enough to risk humiliation and even violence to make the folks of Lightning Ridge take Pobby and Dingan seriously.

This short novel paints a memorable word-picture of a small mining community in Australia, and of a family riven by struggles and differences. With Ashmole as catalyst, they all rally round in the crisis of Kellyanne's illness.

Ashmole is a true hero, not least because he is torn between disbelief and belief in his little sister's friends, who in the end can only be seen as the intangible soul, not only of Kellyanne, but of Lightning Ridge itself.

**Lynne Reid Banks**

'Intensely moving and brilliantly realised...a pocket masterpiece'
*Observer*

Pobby
and
Dingan

**Ben Rice**

Winner of the 2001 Somerset Maugham Award

## Next?

More Australian novels? Try the romantic suspense of Marianne Curley's *Old Magic*, the funny *Feeling Sorry for Celia* by Jaclyn Moriarty, or the eerie *The Ghost's Child* by Sonya Hartnett.

Another slim but moving book is Paul Gallico's *The Snow Goose*. (UTBG 370)

For another book about believing in people, try *The Storm Catchers* by Tim Bowler.

# A FINE LINE – MADNESS AND DEPRESSION

*A Note of Madness* by Tabitha Suzuma

*Red Tears* by Joanna Kenrick

*Prozac Nation: Young and Depressed in America* by Elizabeth Wurtzel

*The Bell Jar* by Sylvia Plath

*Cut* by Patricia McCormick

*It's Kind of a Funny Story* by Ned Vizzini

*One Flew Over the Cuckoo's Nest* by Ken Kesey

# THE POISON GARDEN   Sarah Singleton

**Next?**

If you enjoy Sarah Singleton's unique blend of beautiful description and true horror, try her **Century** (UTBG 72), about two sisters imprisoned in a house that is trapped in time, or **The Island**, about a gap-year trip that turns into a nightmare.

For a younger fantasy with a story that involves a magical box, try John Masefield's **The Box of Delights**.

And for detective stories set in approximately the same time period as **The Poison Garden**, try any of Arthur Conan Doyle's **Sherlock Holmes** stories. (UTBG 359)

All of us, at some point in our lives, dream of having a place of our own – somewhere that we can stamp with our own identity. In *The Poison Garden*, Sarah Singleton creates a world where seven people do precisely that. When an ancient secret comes into their hands, the members of the Guild of Medical Herbalists each create their own magical gardens. Unbeknown to them, however, an enemy is stalking them and gradually, one by one, they begin to die. It falls to Thomas, the 14-year-old grandson of one of the guild, to try and solve the mystery. Part detective story, part fantasy, this is a book that takes its time as it builds to an unforgettable revelation.

**Laura Hutchings**

# A PORTRAIT OF THE ARTIST AS A YOUNG MAN   James Joyce

James Joyce is considered by many to be the greatest writer of the 20th century. This, his first novel, is closely based on his own life, and is an amazingly convincing portrayal of the thoughts and actions of a highly sensitive young man.

The book takes us from the early childhood of Stephen Dedalus, our hero, through to university and a decision to leave Dublin, Ireland, faith and family. Stephen is tormented by religious and sexual guilt, but also changed for ever by the idea and experience of beauty. It's not always an easy read, this, but the writing is superb and you may well find it a truly inspirational book, as I did.

**Malachy Doyle**

**Next?**

Some other powerful stories of young men growing up are to be found in **Cider with Rosie** (UTBG 80) and **Le Grand Meaulnes** (UTBG 164).

**Counting Stars** by David Almond tells stories of his own youth. (UTBG 88)

**The Toll Bridge** (UTBG 399) by Aidan Chambers and Robert Westall's **Falling into Glory** are both about the complexities of love.

# POSTCARDS FROM NO MAN'S LAND
## Aidan Chambers

**Next?**

More Aidan Chambers? Try *Dance on My Grave* (UTBG 94).

At the start of *Postcards...*, Jacob has just visited Anne Frank's House; read *The Diary of a Young Girl*. (UTBG 106)

Sarah Dessen's *The Truth About Forever* deals with growing up. (UTBG 406)

As compelling as all Chambers's novels, this deserves more than one reading. Jacob is in Amsterdam to visit relatives of the family who saved his grandfather, wounded in the Arnhem fighting. His experiences in the present alternate with the memoirs of Geertrui, who rescued and loved his grandfather. Readers will be equally gripped by both stories, and by Jacob's questioning of his identity as he meets the novel's other characters: Daan, Geertrui's angry, charismatic grandson; the fascinating Ton, whom Jacob attempts to pick up; Hille, an engaging possible girlfriend; and Geertrui herself, now dying of cancer and awaiting euthanasia.

All their stories weave together into a gripping, thought-provoking story.

**Linda Newbery**

# A PRAYER FOR OWEN MEANY  John Irving

This is definitely my favourite novel by John Irving, and I've read them all. It's dead funny, totally unpredictable (as all good writing is) and ultimately, gut-wrenchingly tragic. It's about a boy called Owen Meany who SHOUTS ALL THE TIME and is physically quite little, even when he 'grows up'. Fairly early on in the story, Owen accidentally deprives the narrator of his mum during a baseball game, when he clobbers the ball which hits and kills her.

After reading this book I was completely convinced I had knocked around with Owen Meany during my own childhood and teenage years but couldn't quite remember where he lived or what school he'd gone to. All I did know was that we'd had some great times together and that he'd been my best pal ever. However, I suspect that most people feel the same once they've read this fantastic book.

**Michael Cox**

**Next?**

More John Irving? *The World According to Garp* is another tragic, hilarious book that will make you think. (UTBG 444)

Garrison Keillor is another author who writes about weird characters in rural America. Start with *Lake Wobegon Days*.

Another American youth, but this time a powerful true story – Tobias Wolff's *This Boy's Life*. (UTBG 394)

# THE PRETENDER David Belbin

Teenager Mark Trace is a very talented writer. The only problem is that he hasn't discovered his own 'voice' yet, and his talents lie only in mimicking the styles of other writers – some of the real greats, in fact. Or perhaps it's not a problem after all? Surely there's good money to be made by someone who can 'discover' new works by Graham Greene, or Roald Dahl, or Ernest Hemingway? Mark gets work on a small, struggling literary magazine, and finds that his unusual talent might just be able to keep it afloat… But will he be found out?

Literary forgery is a pet subject of mine (to read about, not to perpetrate, you understand), and it's great to find a novel that uses it thoughtfully as the basis for such an exciting, entertaining, and surprisingly plausible story!

**Daniel Hahn**

### Next?

Want to try another David Belbin? *Festival* is different, but very good, as is *Love Lessons*, about an affair between a teacher and his student.

For real-life tales of forgers and forgeries, read Magnus Magnusson's delightful *Fakes, Forgers and Phonies*.

Or try some of the writers that Mark reads and copies – Ernest Hemingway (UTBG 291), Roald Dahl (UTBG 388) or Graham Greene (UTBG 62), for starters.

# PREY
## Michael Crichton

### Next?

If you like the movie *Die Hard*, you'll love Philip Kerr's *Gridiron*, a techno-thriller set in a state-of-the-art skyscraper (with a mind of its own).

*The Big Picture* by Douglas Kennedy, about a stressed out Wall Street lawyer, who is disillusioned with his life, is another movie for the mind, and a hugely addictive page-turner.

Or try *A Simple Plan* by Scott Smith, in which two brothers find a million bucks, but at what price? So much better than the film adaptation.

People often dismiss books that 'read like a movie'. I have never understood why. I was raised on films, and the hours I spent in front of the silver screen inform my novels today. Michael Crichton knew how to write thrillers that truly play out in your mind's eye. That his novels tend to become major films speaks volumes. *Jurassic Park* may be his most celebrated work, but I think *Prey* is better. There are no dinosaurs in this cautionary tale of technology run wild. The bad guys here are nanobots – microscopic flying machines with an instinct to swarm, that turn on their scientist creators. Read the book now, before the film comes to a cinema near you!

**Matt Whyman**

# PRIDE AND PREJUDICE Jane Austen

When I was 13, I found *Pride and Prejudice* and was hooked from the moment I read the opening sentence: 'It is a truth universally acknowledged, that a single man in possession of a good fortune, must be in want of a wife.' The novel, set in the late 18th century, concerns Mr and Mrs Bennet and their five daughters, all of whom, in their mother's eyes, are in need of a good husband, especially one with a fortune.

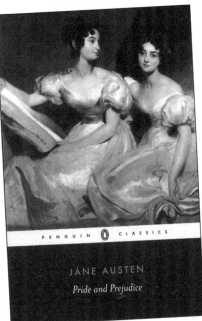

Jane is pretty and sweet-tempered, Kitty and Lydia are frivolous and flirtatious, and poor stolid Mary is dull. Then there is Elizabeth, the heroine at the centre of the story, a spirited young woman well able to stand up to the rather arrogant Darcy when he comes wooing her. The characters are all convincingly and wittily drawn and live on in the memory long after one finishes the book.

**Joan Lingard**

## Next?

More Jane Austen, of course. To compare, try **Persuasion**, which has another cracking hero, Captain Wentworth.

The marriage problem is still around; read about it in Bali Rai's **(Un)arranged Marriage**. (UTBG 413)

A woman who sees marriage entirely as a means to her own ends (getting very rich) is Becky Sharp in William Makepeace Thackeray's **Vanity Fair**.

For more Regency romance you can't beat Georgette Heyer; try **Arabella**.

Or for something completely different? **Pride and Prejudice and Zombies** by Jane Austin and Seth Grahame-Smith.

I love books that you can read over and over and still find something new to enjoy in them. *Pride and Prejudice* is that kind of a book. The very first time I read it, it was as a romance. I wanted the spirited Elizabeth to marry Darcy. I found his aloofness really sexy. And she turned him down! I could never understand how she could prefer the smarmy Wickham! The next time I read it, I laughed out loud at Mr Collins, cringed at Mrs Bennet and enjoyed the dry wit of her husband.

It is a totally compelling story. There are no surprises for me now. I know exactly what is going to happen, but I never tire of reading this book.

**Catherine MacPhail**

# THE PRIME OF MISS JEAN BRODIE
## Muriel Spark

This is an immensely readable and funny book about a group of girls in a select Edinburgh school and their unconventional teacher, Miss Brodie. Set in the 1930s just before the outbreak of World War II, it charts the girls' development from the ages of 11 to 18, at Marcia Blaine School where students wear lilac uniforms and hatlessness is an offence. Miss Brodie – who cultivates a small group of students as her elite 'set' – is charismatic and inspirational but ultimately dangerous – not least because of her admiration of fascism and her dubious sexual motives. There is an excellent play based on the novel by Jay Prissori (which I was in, aged 17!) and also a great film starring Maggie Smith.

**Sue Mayfield**

### Next?

Joan Lindsay's *Picnic at Hanging Rock* is about a girls' school where things go very wrong during a walk in the country. (UTBG 311)

More by the great Muriel Spark? Try *The Girls of Slender Means* and *The Ballard of Peckham Rye*.

Iris Murdoch was another writer who wrote exquisitely about relationships. All her books are brilliant, but try *The Bell* (UTBG 39) or *The Sandcastle* first.

For another book about girls in the 1930s, try *The Pursuit of Love* by Nancy Mitford.

## The Ultimate Teen Book List

### SUSAN'S DESERT ISLAND SELECTION

**84 Charing Cross Road**
**(p. 9)**

**The Beach**
**(p. 35)**

**Candy**
**(p. 66)**

**Counting Stars**
**(p. 88)**

**Journey to the River Sea**
**(p. 217)**

**The L-Shaped Room**
**(p. 249)**

**Nineteen Eighty-Four**
**(p. 284)**

**Notes on a Scandal**
**(p. 289)**

**A Room with a View**
**(p. 335)**

**Saffy's Angel**
**(p. 340)**

**The Snow Goose**
**(p. 370)**

**The Truth About Forever**
**(p. 406)**

# THE PRINCESS BRIDE William Goldman

You know a book is really good when you remember certain details about reading it: what the weather was like, what colour socks you were wearing. When I plopped myself down on my green vinyl beanbag chair and opened *The Princess Bride*, it was raining and my socks were red. And I don't think I moved for the next six hours because Westley, the handsome farm boy, was risking death (and much worse) for Buttercup, his one true love.

This book is an amazingly fun ride – a cut-to-the-chase story of love, adventure, really good guys and wickedly bad guys. It's also smart, funny and hard to put down – and not just for fantasy lovers.

**Sara Nickerson**

Now, I know what you young males are thinking. You're thinking *there's no way I am going into a bookstore and asking for a novel with the words 'princess' and 'bride' in the title*. I know this, because that's what I thought myself many years ago. Some of my more enlightened classmates had read the book and were urging me to get it, but for a while I couldn't get past my machismo. Finally the glowing reviews became too much to ignore, so I asked a friend if I could borrow it. And he said *No, you have to buy this yourself. You have to walk up to the counter and say the words. It's like a badge of courage*.

So I did. I walked in there and said the words. Then I went home and did not eat for eight hours. Instead I devoured Mr Goldman's masterpiece. This is simply the funniest book you will ever read, packed with hilarious one-liners, riotous characters and side-splitting situations. It is also jammed with swordfights, giants, riddles, revenge, magic and torture chambers. The plot is clever, the style is hypnotic and the conclusion is satisfying. William Goldman should be paying me for all the nice things I'm saying. But they're true, all true. Take my word for it, break open the piggy bank, go down to the store and say the words. You will not be disappointed.

**Eoin Colfer**

'Brilliant and funny' OBSERVER

THE PRINCESS BRIDE

THE ORIGINAL BOOK OF THE CULT CLASSIC FILM

WILLIAM GOLDMAN

## Next?

A very funny book that satirises all the stories of wizards, elves and poor boys who end up saving the world is Paul Stewart and Chris Riddell's *Muddle Earth*.

*Good Omens* is a totally loopy look at the battle between good and evil. (UTBG 162)

More funny fantasy? Try Robert Rankin's anarchic *Waiting for Godalming* or *Blart* by Dominic Barker, about a pig-boy reluctantly dragged into a quest.

# THE PRINCESS DIARIES  Meg Cabot

### Next?

There are ten volumes in this series – look out for them all. And of course all the other Meg Cabot books, including *Avalon High* and *Airhead*.

Gail Carson Levine writes modern fairy stories; try *Ella Enchanted*, about a princess who at birth is given the gift of obedience.

*The Sisterhood of the Travelling Pants* is about a group of girls like Mia. (UTBG 364)

Mia's your average American teenager until her dad arrives with a secret that's been hidden since she was born: she's really a princess! But how? Enter 'Grandmère', to turn the 5'9" 'freak' into a beautiful, graceful princess. Soon Mia is being plucked, styled and tutored to within an inch of her life, yet she still can't understand boys. Mia's life is changing, and not necessarily for the better!

I love this book. Any girl will sympathise with Mia's problems and understand her worries. Meg Cabot's way of telling the story through diary entries really works, and you end up knowing Mia, and hoping that she gets her happy ending.

**Issie Darcy, age 13**

# THE PRISONER OF ZENDA  Anthony Hope

Rudolf Rassendyll, a rather idle English gentleman, decides to journey to Ruritania to see a distant cousin, whom he's never met, be crowned king. In Ruritania, Rassendyll dozes against a tree before continuing on to the castle. He wakes to voices discussing his striking likeness to the future king (also called Rudolf). That night the two cousins – Rudolf Rassendyll and Rudolf the soon-to-be King of Ruritania – dine together. Early next morning, Rassendyll is woken and told that the future king is out cold – he drank too much the night before – and that he, Rassendyll, must stand in for him at the coronation. But this is only the beginning of the adventure. When the king is abducted by his jealous brother Michael and his ruthless henchman Rupert of Hentzau, Rassendyll is forced to keep up the pretence that he is the king – in the course of which he falls for Princess Flavia, the king's betrothed.

The young reader who loves tales of intrigue, adventure, heroism and villainy (and doesn't mind a spot of love) need look no further…

**Michael Lawrence**

### Next?

…except perhaps afterwards, to the sequel, *Rupert of Hentzau*.

Then move on to *The Count of Monte Cristo* by Alexandre Dumas which has more impersonated nobles, heroism and romance.

Or John Buchan's classic thriller set just before World War II: *The Thirty-Nine Steps*. (UTBG 394)

# PRIVATE PEACEFUL   Michael Morpurgo

Nobody has written more classic children's books than Michael Morpurgo – but for me this is his best book yet.

Set against the background of the First World War and the shocking fact that over 290 soldiers were unjustly executed for cowardice, it tells the story of two brothers, Charlie and Thomas Peaceful, their life in the English countryside before the war, their recruitment and subsequent fate.

It's a book with an angry heart, but the mood is often gentle, even elegiac. In one chapter, an aeroplane flies over the two brothers. It's a moment of wonder. A defining moment in an English summer. And yet also a harbinger of the horrors to come.

*Private Peaceful* is brilliantly structured, with a twist that took me completely by surprise. It should be read by anyone studying the First World War... In fact, by anyone wanting to read a great writer at the top of his form.

**Anthony Horowitz**

'We hear the shell coming and know from the shriek of it that it will be close, and it is.'

Life in the battlefields of the First World War was ghastly and left men with the most horrific memories. Old and young men fought and spent long hours together in the squalid conditions of the trenches.

For young Private Thomas Peaceful it is no different. Patriotic and naïve, he joins up to follow his older brother into war. He soon finds out that war is not what the posters back home said it would be like. Spending many an hour in the trenches, he reflects on his childhood and fond countryside memories.

Michael Morpurgo's writing style is amazing and brings the story to life. It leaves you shocked, stunned and sad all at once. A mixture of reflection, romance and a poignant climax make this book a definite must-read.

**Louise Manning, age 14**

**Next?**

For a book that deals with the same war, and some of the same issues, try Sonia Hartnett's *The Silver Donkey*.

Or for a slightly harder read about the First World War, read *When the Guns Fall Silent*. (UTBG 433)

Michael Morpurgo writing about a different war? Try *Waiting for Anya*. Or you might like a book he edited of short stories about war: *War: Stories About Conflict*.

# THE RACHEL PAPERS  Martin Amis

Charles Highway is turning 20 tomorrow and is making the most of the occasion to put his teenage years into order – to reflect on his romantic conquests (and other rather less important things) and file away his collection of notes...

Charles is implausibly clever and well read, and a methodical planner of every amorous encounter he has (his *Conquests and Techniques: A Synthesis* is particularly handy for this). But when he meets Rachel, well... OK, so Charles' seduction techniques may work, maybe he will be able to get her to sleep with him – but what then? He soon discovers there are certain things you can't plan...

This dazzling novel was Martin Amis's first, published when he was just 25. It's funny and filthy, the writing is electric, and it boasts a captivating main character you cannot stop listening to. You may not approve of him, but those characters are often the most interesting, aren't they?

**Daniel Hahn**

> **Next?**
> *The Cement Garden* is nothing like this – except, I suppose, that it's about teenagers and sex and is pretty shocking – but it was Ian McEwan's first novel, too. (UTBG 71)
>
> For another narrative voice with seriously powerful energy, read D.B.C. Pierre's *Vernon God Little*. (UTBG 419)

---

# RACHEL'S HOLIDAY  Marian Keyes

> **Next?**
> All Keyes's books have equally sharp insights into love, marriage, divorce, babies, perfect partners (or not!) and female friendship; try *Lucy Sullivan Is Getting Married* next.
>
> For another unsorted heroine, read *The Secret Dreamworld of a Shopaholic*. (UTBG 350)
>
> Cecelia Aherne is another Irish writer. Try her *P.S. I Love You*.

One of the funniest so-called 'chick-lit' authors you'll ever find, but she's so much better than that. Keyes's tongue-in-cheek humour, witty one-liners and sparkling dialogue is so real you'll almost hear it, and watch her characters spring out from the pages as you read.

Although the Rachel of the title swears to herself and those around her that she only uses recreational drugs for purely recreational reasons, she nevertheless finds herself at the Cloisters Rehab Clinic 'just in case'. She quickly consoles herself that she's not at all like any of the other mad, bad and loser residents (some of whom are truly hilarious) but soon finds her salvation – and soulmate – in Chris, definitely a 'man with a past'.

Like the purple-wrapped toffee in a box of chocolates, Keyes's fiction always hides something important at the centre. And it's as moreish as those chocolates, too.

**Eileen Armstrong**

# RANI AND SUKH  Bali Rai

**Next?**

Another Bali Rai? Try *The Angel Collector* (UTBG 22), about an Indian boy who finds that his girlfriend has become involved with a racist cult, or *The Last Taboo*, in which an Indian girl falls for a black boy, much to her family's horror.

Or to read about India, try Jamila Gavin's *Out of India*, a memoir of her childhood.

Or look for *Does My Head Look Big in This?*, about a Muslim girl's struggles with her identity. (UTBG 112)

Two kids in the same year at school: fit lad, fanciable girl. There's a mutual attraction and they get together, but there's a problem. 'Well, isn't there always?' I hear you ask. Yes, but this one's different.

Rani's and Sukh's parents are from the Punjab, and something happened there, years ago, that neither youngster knows about. It means that to this day, the Sandhu and Bains families – to which the two kids belong – will have nothing to do with each other. No exceptions, even in the face of true love. If the families meet by chance, there's bloodshed.

I found Bali Rai's novel absorbing because the conflicts in it arise from both a clash of cultures and a clash *within* a culture. Exciting stuff.

**Robert Swindells**

# RASPBERRIES ON THE YANGTZE
## Karen Wallace

The brilliant first sentence of this book cannot fail to draw you in. The story seems simple and slow to begin with, but builds up quickly as secrets unfold one by one. Nancy, the narrator, is a nosy young girl growing up in a small town in Quebec, Canada, some decades ago. She spends most of the time horsing around with her brother and friends. A piece of gossip she overhears leads Nancy to investigate the goings-on at the home of the prim and proper Wilkins family, where things are clearly amiss. The story is told in a very funny, but also honest and touching, manner. This short gem of a book is bound to charm your socks off.

**Next?**

The sequel takes Nancy to an English boarding school in *Climbing a Monkey Puzzle Tree*. Or try another book by Karen Wallace, *Wendy*, which reimagines the story of Peter Pan's Wendy Darling.

*To Kill a Mockingbird* is a novel told from the point of view of a girl growing up in a small American town during the 1950s. (UTBG 398)

*Huckleberry Finn* is the quintessential novel about growing up in northern America (even if it isn't quite Canada). (UTBG 191)

**Noga Applebaum**

# RAVEN'S GATE  Anthony Horowitz

## Next?

**The Power of Five** series continues with *Evil Star*, *Night Rise* and *Necropolis*, with one more to come.

If the idea of battling it out with sinister villagers appeals, try *Yaxley's Cat* by Robert Westall.

Or if you enjoy the idea of a group of people coming together to fight the powers of darkness, try **The Dark Is Rising** series by Susan Cooper. (UTBG 96)

There's more gripping adventure in N.M. Browne's *Shadow Web*, about a girl entering a dark, alternate reality when she meets someone identical.

What I want to know is how Anthony Horowitz does it?! Does he ever sleep? Not only do we have the excellent **Alex Rider** books, but now there's **The Power of Five** series, too!

*Raven's Gate* is the first book and it introduces Matt Freeman, a 14-year-old boy with powers that even he doesn't fully understand. There's a little incident involving robbing a warehouse and Matt finds himself an unwilling part of a new government scheme for young offenders, forced to go and live with a sinister stranger, Mrs Deverill, in a remote village in Yorkshire.

Obviously, nothing is as it seems and soon Matt finds himself up against the powers of darkness, fighting for his life.

**Laura Hutchings**

# THE READER  Bernhard Schlink

This extraordinarily original novel bears the stamp of lived experience on every page. A young German man studying in his native city shortly after World War II gets deeply involved with an older woman neighbour. She's a simple bus conductor without social graces, and he's embarrassed to introduce her to his friends and family. This, and not their love affair, makes him deeply guilty, and when she disappears he feels sure it's because of him.

Years later he learns the shattering truth about her wartime past, and a secret even deeper than that which has blighted and deformed her whole life. A profoundly moving story about love, shame and expiation, strongly recommended for serious readers.

**Lynne Reid Banks**

## Next?

*Sophie's Choice* by William Styron – a heartbreaking story of decisions about love, loss and the Holocaust.

Or *Schindler's Ark* by Thomas Keneally (based on a real person and real events), about Jews saved from the Nazis by the heroism of seemingly ordinary people.

Another book about how secrets change our worlds is Alan Gibbons's *Blood Pressure*, in which a boy discovers his father's dirty secret.

For another novel that looks at the effects of war, read Pat Barker's *Regeneration*. (UTBG 330)

# REBECCA  Daphne Du Maurier

**Next?**

Du Maurier's classic Cornish spine-tingling mystery, *Jamaica Inn*. (UTBG 210)

Sally Beauman's *Rebecca's Tale* sets out to fill in some of the gaps, as does *Mrs de Winter* by Susan Hill.

The original tale of inexperienced-young-girl-meets-and-falls-in-love-with-older-man-with-a-secret, Charlotte Brontë's *Jane Eyre* is a must! (UTBG 211)

Some people find the narrator of this classic romantic mystery, set in 1930's Cornwall, to be wimpy and insipid. And yes, perhaps, compared to today's out-there, kick-butt-style heroines she might seem a touch passive. But I think anyone who's ever felt socially ill at ease, or that they don't really deserve a particular chunk of happiness, or even but-why-does-he/she-love-*me*? – and let's face it, that's pretty much all of us – will readily identify with her.

This haunting, magical, gripping Gothic tale starts as an account of how the narrator meets the handsome, brooding and irresistible Maxim de Winter. And it soon becomes apparent that his past holds a dark mystery...

Du Maurier's wonderfully descriptive writing makes this page-turner one of my fave books ever – and if the ending doesn't leave you open-mouthed with disbelief, turning the pages to see if some are missing, I'll eat my PC!

**Catherine Robinson**

# The REBUS books  Ian Rankin

Ian Rankin's **Rebus** books are a masterful example of the best of crime fiction, centred around a truly memorable hero. Detective John Rebus is a shameless user of cigarettes and alcohol with a difficult personal life. Rankin uses a dry, cynical humour mixed with cultural references and a carefully constructed cast of supporting characters on both sides to depict an unseen Edinburgh in which no one is incorruptible.

Rankin always keeps us guessing; these are no formulaic open-shut murder cases, but brilliant character studies on the righteous, the greedy, the zealous and the misled, offering a powerful discourse on justice, rights and morality. It's hard to pick a particular single book to recommend within the series – once you've read one, you'll want to read them all.

**Next?**

Start with *Knots and Crosses*, then go on to *Hide and Seek*...

One of the joys of the **Rebus** books is Rebus himself. Other detectives who fascinate (though English rather than Scottish) include Colin Dexter's Morse; start with *Last Bus to Woodstock* (UTBG 204); and Lord Peter Wimsey by Dorothy L. Sayers (UTBG 243).

**Colum Fraser**

# THE RED NECKLACE  Sally Gardner

Paris, 1789. Using their magical gifts to earn a living as entertainers, three friends stumble across the path of the evil Count Kalliovski and into his sinister web of blackmail and murder. One is killed and the gypsy, Yann, only escapes with his life thanks to Sido, the daughter of the vain and stupid Marquis de Villeduval. But the French Revolution is barely a heartbeat away, and Sido, as an aristocrat, faces almost certain death. To save her, Yann must learn to harness the magic powers of his gypsy blood, but with the Count on his heels and Revolution raging, the odds are stacked against him.

*The Red Necklace* is part historical novel, part fantasy, and will satisfy fans of both.

**Antonia Honeywell**

> ### Next?
>
> Find out what happens next to Yann and Sido in the sequel to *The Red Necklace*, *The Silver Blade*. Or try more Sally Gardner. *I, Coriander* (UTBG 196) mixes the real world with the fairy world.
>
> *A Tale of Two Cities* by Charles Dickens is the all-time classic story of the French Revolution.
>
> Joan Aiken writes historical fiction with her own twist; try *Midnight Is a Place*.

# RED SHIFT  Alan Garner

*Red Shift* is neither a teen novel with pretensions, nor an adult novel in disguise, but one of the very few genuine crossover novels. It was written before such a term was even invented, and was one of the books that made me want to write for teenagers.

Garner writes with spare energy and a narrative mastery that allows him to challenge and question our assumptions as readers. The story moves backwards and forwards in time, and between different characters all linked by their presence in one particular place, Mow Cop in Cheshire. The location has witnessed dark, powerful human emotions that resonate still.

*Red Shift* takes in myth, history, philosophy and astrophysics, and can move seamlessly from bitter love story to a meditation upon the space-time continuum. This one slim volume manages to say far more that is profound than much longer, more ponderous works.

**Celia Rees**

> ### Next?
>
> Other novels written by Alan Garner for younger readers are *Elidor*, *The Weirdstone of Brisingamen* (UTBG 430) and *The Owl Service* (UTBG 306). His adult novels include *Sandloper* and *Thursbitch*.
>
> Other books that I would consider to be crossovers are William Golding's *Lord of the Flies* (UTBG 241) and the novels of Robert Cormier.

# REFUGEE BOY Benjamin Zephaniah

Where can you go when nobody wants you? This is the dilemma that Alem Kelo faces. His father is Ethiopian, his mother Eritrean, and when these neighbouring countries plunge into a bloody war, Alem and his family are persecuted wherever they go. When Alem's father suggests a short vacation in England, Alem is happy to leave the strife behind. However, he soon discovers his father's true intention. Fearing for their son's life, Alem's parents have decided to leave him behind in England to seek asylum. Through Alem's personal story, Zephaniah uncovers the trials and tribulations that refugees go through in England. The heartlessness of the law is powerfully contrasted with the kindness of the local community that reaches out to Alem to offer him a new home.

**Noga Applebaum**

> **Next?**
> Zephaniah's other fiction is all worth reading; try *Face* and *Teacher's Dead* (UTBG 389).
>
> *The Frozen Waterfall* by Gaye Hicyilmaz is also about immigrants, this time a Turkish family in Sweden. And *Voyage* by Adèle Geras takes place in the early 20th century, on a ship filled with Eastern refugees hoping to start a new life in America.

# REGENERATION
## Pat Barker

> **Next?**
> *Regeneration* is part of a trilogy. It continues with *The Eye in the Door* and *The Ghost Road*.
>
> The poems themselves: *Collected Poems of Wilfred Owen* and *War Poems of Siegfried Sassoon*, or the anthology, *Anthem for Doomed Youth* (UTBG 26).
>
> *Testament of Youth* by Vera Brittain is based on her own diaries written while working as a nurse at the battlefront in the First World War.
>
> The brilliant *Birdsong* by Sebastian Faulks brings First World War trench warfare to terrifying life. (UTBG 44)

Anyone interested in the First World War will love this book. It's set in a mental hospital – at Craiglockhart near Edinburgh – where the poet Siegfried Sassoon is sent for treatment after criticising the war. There, Sassoon meets Wilfred Owen (another young poet) and William Rivers, a psychiatrist charged with 'curing' the mentally disturbed so that they can be sent back to fight again.

It's a great story, and you'll want to keep reading just for that, but along the way it deals with poetry, bravery, friendship, and the central question of whether it is sane to fight. If you're struggling with the War Poets at school, reading this book will make everything fall into place.

**Eleanor Updale**

# REVOLVER  Marcus Sedgwick

**Next?**

All Marcus's books are exciting reads; first of all try the brutal *My Swordhand Is Singing* (UTBG 275) and its sequel, *Kiss of Death*.

For snow and adventure at the other end of the world, try Geraldine McCaughrean's *The White Darkness*. (UTBG 435)

Never one to shy away from complex issues, Robert Cormier often dealt with violence; *After the First Death* looks at a terrorist attack on a bus from various standpoints. (UTBG 12)

Marcus Sedgwick's *Revolver* is so pure and fresh, it's like cleansing your palate after a heavy meal. Brief but action-packed, there are riches aplenty. It's 1910 in the Arctic Circle. Fourteen-year-old Sig Andersson discovers his father frozen to death on the ice. But what secrets is he hiding in his papers, and who is the dangerous stranger arriving at the family's hut, threatening them all with the title weapon?

*Revolver* is daring (and deceptive) in its simplicity, and Sedgwick weaves in themes of family and growing up on the cold, snowbound plains. There's menace, too, and ingenuity and bravery. The opposite of the baroquely plotted teenage novel, this is a breath of fresh air to an eager reader.

**Patrick Ness**

# THE RIDDLE OF THE SANDS  Erskine Childers

I'm not one for sea stories, but simply can't resist this one. Carruthers, a young Edwardian dandy, is cooped up in London all August by work. Then he's invited by his friend Davies to join him yachting and duck shooting in the Baltic. Carruthers goes; but nothing is as expected. The *Dulcibella* is a 'scrubby little craft', not for pleasure; and there are no ducks. Instead, Davies reveals his suspicions that Germany is secretly preparing for an invasion of England (this is some ten years before the outbreak of the First World War in 1914). The springboard would be the Frisian islands that fringe the North Sea coastline. The two friends sail the *Dulcibella* through treacherous tides, shifting sandbanks and blinding fogs to outwit a prospective enemy. There are even maps and charts. A breathless read.

**Next?**

A natural follow-up is *The Thirty-Nine Steps*, an adventure novel that in 1935 was made into a classic Hitchcock film. (UTBG 394)

*Brat Farrar* by Josephine Tey involves a mystery about identity. (UTBG 58)

Or for navigating a way through a different war, try Jill Paton Walsh's *The Dolphin Crossing*, about the evacuation from Dunkirk.

**Philippa Pearce**

# RIVER BOY Tim Bowler

This book – which made me cry – is the story of Jess and her relationship with her unusual and cantankerous grandfather, a painter in the last stage of his life. Jess, her mother and father and gravely ill Grandpa go on holiday to a remote cottage beside a river in the place where Grandpa lived until he was 15. Here, Grandpa struggles to complete a strange painting while Jess, a long-distance swimmer, has a series of mysterious encounters while swimming in the river.

This is a beautiful, moving, mystical novel that uses the metaphor of rivers and swimming to explore themes of death and fulfilment. Tim Bowler manages to capture deep truths without being sentimental or didactic.

**Sue Mayfield**

> ### Next?
>
> More Tim Bowler? Try the haunting *Apocalypse* (UTBG 27) and *Frozen Fire* (UTBG 149), or *Shadows*, about a squash-playing boy and his bullying father.
>
> Another book about grandfathers is Sharon Creech's *Walk Two Moons* (UTBG 422). Or try David Almond's haunting *Kit's Wilderness* (UTBG 228).
>
> Another book that uses a river journey in a symbolic way is Mark Twain's *Huckleberry Finn* (UTBG 191). The writing is nothing like *River Boy*, though!

# THE ROAD OF BONES Anne Fine

> ### Next?
>
> Try *The Tulip Touch* (UTBG 407), about an appalling girl, or *Round Behind the Ice-House*, about a brother and sister slowly being pulled apart.
>
> Society – and people – are quite often wrong. Try Linzi Glass's *The Year the Gypsies Came* for a different take on that idea. (UTBG 451)
>
> What can you do if you think our own society is going that bit too far in watching us? Try Graham Marks's page-turning *Omega Place* and find out.

How does it feel to live in a country ruled by a totalitarian regime, where people disappear and are never seen again, and where a careless word can earn its speaker a sentence of death? Yuri lives with his grandmother and parents in just such a grim post-revolutionary world. Life is hard, cold, bleak and comfortless. As Yuri journeys from boyhood to manhood, compassion and kindness are squeezed out of him until, with a relentless, dreadful inevitability, victim is transformed into persecutor.

It's a brilliant book: a starkly honest portrayal of the brutalising effects of a terrifying regime. Reading it is a bit like jumping into an icy lake: shocking and chilling, but ultimately an extraordinarily invigorating experience.

**Tanya Landman**

# ROLL OF THUNDER, HEAR MY CRY
## Mildred D. Taylor

Set in the violent and aggressively racist American Deep South of the 1930s, *Roll of Thunder...* became an instant classic. The Logans, a black family, are struggling not just to survive, but to make a better life for themselves in a world that is hell-bent on keeping them down in the dirt.

Told from the point of view of Cassie, the Logan's fiercely defiant daughter, this vivid fictional account records the relentless everyday injustices and vicious brutalities that real people suffered in that part of America at the time.

Cassie's stubborn refusal to be cowed by the racists, and the inventiveness and cunning with which she outwits them time and again, are testimony to the brave struggles that helped bring about the Civil Rights movement and transformed that region of the US. *Roll of Thunder...* is unforgettable, deeply moving and, above all, uplifting.

**Neil Arksey**

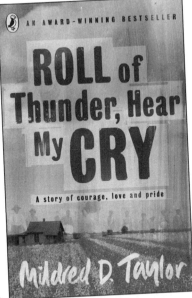

## Next?

More Mildred D. Taylor? Try others about the Logan family: **Let the Circle Be Unbroken** and **The Land**, which is a prequel to *Roll of Thunder...*

**A Gathering Light** is a story of what life was like for black communities in early 20th-century America. (UTBG 151)

Or look for Paula Fox's **Slave Dancer**, about a boy kidnapped so he can play his flute on board a ship carrying a cargo of slaves.

## GRITTY AND REAL

*Teacher's Dead* by Benjamin Zephaniah

*The Dirty South* by Alex Wheatle

*Black Rabbit Summer* by Kevin Brooks

*The Chocolate War* by Robert Cormier

*Soldier Boy* by Danny Rhodes

*The Knife That Killed Me* by Anthony McGowan

*Boy Kills Man* by Matt Whyman

*Slam* by Nick Hornby

*Asboville* by Danny Rhodes

*Refugee Boy* by Benjamin Zephaniah

# THE ROMANCE OF TRISTAN AND ISEULT
## Retold by Joseph Bédier

'My lords, if you would hear a high tale of love and death...' is how this short, great masterpiece begins. It's one of the most famous stories in the world, and what's striking about the way it's retold by Joseph Bédier is the sense of fatality that hangs over the lovers. The language is simple, forceful and beautiful. (Chapter headings include, for example: The Philtre, Ogrin the Hermit, The Quest for the Lady with the Hair of Gold, Iseult of the White Hands, and The Ordeal by Iron.) Only a stone could read it without a sickening sense of rising doom and, towards the end, make sure you keep the tissue box handy.

**Anne Fine**

### Next?

If you fancy another great epic romance, try a version of Thomas Malory's *Morte d'Arthur*, or Shakespeare's *Romeo and Juliet*.

For a more modern (more modern, but still pretty old) doomed love story, you can do no better than *Wuthering Heights*. (UTBG 447)

For more fate and passion, read Audrey Niffenegger's *The Time-Traveler's Wife*, Bali Rai's *Rani and Sukh* (UTBG 326) Stephenie Meyer's *Twilight* (UTBG 411), or watch the movie, *West Side Story*!

# A ROOM OF ONE'S OWN  Virginia Woolf

### Next?

Fay Weldon's *Letters to Alice; on First Reading Jane Austen* is another skilled and funny take on women and writing.

Or, for more first-hand experience of the problems to be faced by women who want to write, try some of their journals – Sylvia Plath's, or Katherine Mansfield's maybe.

Virginia Woolf features in the wonderful *The Hours*. (UTBG 187). Jeanette Winterson has cited Woolf as a major influence; try her *The Passion*.

OK, so it's one of the building blocks of feminism. But the real point about Virginia Woolf's essay is the delicately lush writing, the angry imagination, that make reading it a pleasure every inch of the way.

Why – she asked, back in the 1920s – had women been able to tell so little of their own story? Was it because of the stumbling blocks in their way? Imagine that William Shakespeare had had a sister, just as talented as him ... what might her fate have been? Some of the conditions Woolf describes may be different now. (In order to write, she said, a woman needs a room of her own 'and five hundred pounds a year'.) But some may feel that the fundamentals have not altered greatly.

**Sarah Gristwood**

# A ROOM WITH A VIEW E.M. Forster

**Next?**

For more comedies of manners, try Jane Austen's *Pride and Prejudice* (UTBG 320) or *Sense and Sensibility*.

E.M. Forster's *Collected Short Stories* will introduce you to more of his preoccupations; several, including 'The Machine Stops', have a fantasy element.

Another wonderful, colourful book set in Italy is *Miss Garnet's Angel* by Sally Vickers.

Or try *The Remains of the Day* by Kazuo Ishiguro for more love restrained by class convention.

With its bright social comedy and its cast of distinctive characters, *A Room with a View* (first published in 1908) is the most accessible of E.M. Forster's novels – and is also an excellent film starring Helena Bonham-Carter as the young, impressionable Lucy Honeychurch.

On the Grand Tour in Italy, Lucy meets passionate George who claims to love her for her very essence – but back at home in Surrey she becomes engaged to the pompous, buttoned-up Cecil. Lucy must defy convention if she's to follow her instincts rather than class expectations. Stuffy Aunt Charlotte, liberated novelist Eleanor Lavish and the kindly Reverend Beebe attempt to guide her – although several of the characters are not what they seem.

**Linda Newbery**

# ROUND IRELAND WITH A FRIDGE
## Tony Hawks

This was the first of a crop of books in which somebody makes a drunken bet, does something ridiculous and then writes a book about it. In this case, Tony Hawks is bet £100 that he cannot hitchhike around the circumference of Ireland with a fridge within one calendar month. The premise is clearly very silly. Fortunately, Hawks is an excellent writer and a very funny man, so the fridge just becomes an icebreaker (if that's possible) in conversations with the many entertaining people he meets on his quest. Highlights include his entry into the Ballyduff Bachelor Festival and his bizarre decision to take the fridge surfing in Sligo.

**Anthony Reuben**

**Next?**

There's a sequel! Well, more of a meditation: *The Fridge-Hiker's Guide to Life: How to Stay Cool When You're Feeling the Heat*. Or look for *A Piano in the Pyrenees*, in which, well, you can guess…

*McCarthy's Bar* by Pete McCarthy is an Irish travelogue based on a less silly premise.

*Are You Dave Gorman?* by Dave Gorman and Danny Wallace is another highlight of the 'making stupid bets while drunk' genre. (UTBG 28)

# ROWAN THE STRANGE   Julie Hearn

I read a lot of books. Sometimes I like them, sometimes I don't. Sometimes, though, I adore a book. I consume the pages passionately, I live with the characters and feel their joy and their despair. These are the books I never want to end. This is one of those books.

Rowan is schizophrenic. Voices in his head tell him to do appalling things; he smashes his sister's fingers, he almost knifes a policeman. At a loss, and with the world on the brink of all-out war, his family send him to an asylum where the latest therapies are promised, but not explained. There he meets a fellow inmate who sees angels, and a doctor who has his own demons. But after the 'therapy' Rowan forgets who he is, as now he is Superboy from the planet Krypton. This is Rowan's story, as both himself and 'Superboy'. It's also the most uplifting book about tragedy I've ever read.

**Leonie Flynn**

### Next?

More Julie Hearn! *Ivy* and *Hazel* are closest to *Rowan* in tone, but they are all wonderful.

Mental health problems are tackled in other books too; try Tabitha Suzuma's *A Note of Madness* (UTBG 288) or *Black Jack* by Leon Garfield.

Or for something about what it was like to live during World War II, try Michelle Magorian's *Goodnight Mister Tom*.

# ROXY'S BABY   Catherine MacPhail

### Next?

Read more Catherine MacPhail – *Run, Zan, Run*, about bullying, or *Bad Company*, in which a friendship turns toxic.

Or for another thrilling chiller, *Girl, Missing* by Sophie McKenzie is about a girl who finds she might have been kidnapped at birth. (UTBG 156)

For a rather less alarming book (but still a powerful one) about a young mother-to-be, read Julia Green's *Blue Moon* (UTBG 50) and its sequel, *Baby Blue*.

I made the mistake of starting this brilliant book late one night – a mistake because I then had to stay up to read it all, but also because it then gave me the most appalling nightmares. It's that sort of book...

Roxy is going to have a baby. She won't tell her mum or stepdad or her goody-two-shoes sister – they won't understand. Instead, she runs away. Before long she meets the kindly Mr and Mrs Dyce, who offer to take her to a home they have set up to look after girls in just her predicament. When she arrives it's beautiful, friendly, safe – it's perfect. Except it's really none of those things. Roxy has a terrible suspicion there's something sinister going on. She's right. And it's worse than the worst thing you can possibly imagine...

**Daniel Hahn**

# RUBY HOLLER  Sharon Creech

The Boxton Creek Home for Children is run by the unpleasant Trepids. Twins Florida and Dallas won't toe the Trepids's line and are consequently on the receiving end of multiple punishments. So they spend their days dreaming of escaping. The Trepids would love to rid themselves of Florida and Dallas, but every family they've been placed with has returned them to Boxton Creek like an unwanted package.

So when they're sent to spend time with the elderly Tiller and Sairy in Ruby Holler, the twins await their inevitable return to the home. But Tiller and Sairy aren't your average couple and Ruby Holler is a truly wondrous place.

As Florida and Dallas finally enjoy the sweet taste of freedom, their hopes and dreams change radically. It's a very moving, well-paced and clever tale.

**Jonny Zucker**

### Next?

More Sharon Creech? Try *Love That Dog*, a brilliant book told in verse, or *The Wanderer* (UTBG 422), a sea-bound adventure.

*Children of the Oregon Trail* by A. Rutgers van der Loeff focuses on another orphan – John Sager – and his epic journey to the wild west.

Gary Paulsen's *The Beet Fields* has a rural setting – a 16-year-old boy leaves home to forge a new life. (UTBG 37)

Or for another boy whose life is changed by an elderly person, try Louis Sachar's *The Boy Who Lost His Face*.

# RUMBLEFISH  S.E. Hinton

### Next?

More S.E. Hinton? Try *That Was Then, This Is Now*, her classic *The Outsiders* (UTBG 305), or her adult novel, *Hawkes Harbour*.

Bali Rai has also written convincingly about gangs; try his hard-hitting *The Crew*.

For a girl gang in the 1950s, read Joyce Carol Oates's *Foxfire*.

A rare example of a classic novel becoming a cult film, *Rumblefish* is in my opinion Hinton's greatest work. It centres on Rusty James, a disillusioned tough guy who longs to emulate his absent brother Motorcycle Boy and become a gang-fight legend. But when Motorcycle Boy returns, he's changed and Rusty James doesn't understand him any more. Then Rusty's world begins to fall apart and things take a tragic turn.

This is a hard-hitting, no-nonsense read that takes you right into the heart of Rusty's world. Read the book and try and see the film, too, directed by Francis Ford Coppola and starring Mickey Rourke and Matt Dillon. Neither will disappoint you. Brilliant.

**Bali Rai**

# THE RUNAWAY JURY John Grisham

**Next?**

More Grisham? Try *The Partner* next.

For another legal thriller, a little denser, try Scott Turow's *Presumed Innocent*.

Or José Latour's gripping Miami-based thriller, *Outcast*.

Or what about some detective stories? Try Ian Rankin's **Rebus** books, starting with *Knots and Crosses*; they're tough, grim and totally gripping. (UTBG 328)

You know what you're going to get when you open a John Grisham book: a great, clear plot, plenty of suspense, a sympathetic hero and a fair bit of courtroom drama. If you want poetry, go somewhere else; for irresistible, page-turning, must-find-out-what-happens-next narrative, Grisham's your man. And as an ex-lawyer himself, he knows his legal stuff, but never lets the details get in the way of a thrilling story.

*The Runaway Jury* is vintage Grisham and, I think, my favourite. This time the court case in question is a suit against a massive tobacco corporation. It seems that someone is tampering with the jury selection to try and guarantee the sort of verdict Big Tobacco will like. But one of the jurors, Nicholas Easter, has an agenda of his own, too. Complications ensue. Great stuff.

**Daniel Hahn**

# RUNEMARKS Joanne Harris

*Runemarks* is a brilliant teen fantasy debut for Joanne Harris, better known for her adult fiction. Old Norse myths are wonderfully interwoven with the story of Maddie Smith, who lives in a world that's 500 years on from some apocalyptic event, known as The Tribulation. Maddy's world is governed by a strict religious group – The Order – but remnants of the old ways linger on, in the birthmarks that some bear, including Maddie. The marks, in the shape of Norse runes, signify that the bearer can wield the old gods' magic.

In a story that brings in the myths of Ragnarok and the end of the world, Maddie's story is a brilliantly told quest that's fast-paced and utterly enthralling.

**Elizabeth Reid**

**Next?**

The Norse myths are a treasure trove for authors; try Catherine Fisher's the **Snow-walker** trilogy, Nancy Farmer's *The Sea of Trolls* (UTBG 345), *The Black Book of Secrets* by F.E. Higgins, Katherine Langrish's **Troll** trilogy (UTBG 404) and *Feasting the Wolf* by Susan Price.

Read Joanne's adult books; start with *Chocolat*. (UTBG 77)

Look out too for Jonathan Stroud's *Heroes of the Valley*, a terrific, fast-paced tale of an ancient blood feud. (UTBG 177)

# SABRIEL   Garth Nix

**Next?**

Of course you'll want to read the sequels: *Lirael* and *Abhorsen*.

Garth Nix has also written the **Keys to the Kingdom** series, which starts with *Mister Monday*, about a boy who is supposed to die but instead becomes involved in a battle against evil.

Or try the dark, claustrophobic mystery of *Tunnels* by Roderick Gordon and Brian Williams. (UTBG 408)

The sun is shining in Ancelstierre. A few yards away, across the border in the Old Kingdom, it's snowing. But that's not surprising because everything is different there. Machinery doesn't work, the dead won't stay in their graves and the magic of the Great Charter, intended to keep the kingdom safe for ever, is faltering as blood is shed on ancient stones. Dreadful creatures from beyond the Seventh Gate of Death have been waiting for this moment for centuries. Now their chance has come, and only one person stands against them: Sabriel, a 16-year-old schoolgirl with a terrible destiny.

This is an utterly compelling book, and one that will make you remember why you first enjoyed reading.

**Brian Keaney**

# SABRINA FLUDDE   Pauline Fisk

*Sabrina Fludde* is a strange and lyrical story that transforms the everyday into the mythological. A girl is washed up on the banks of a river, with no memory of how she got there or who she is. She discovers she is in the ancient market town of Pengwern, but as she wanders its streets nothing is familiar. As she searches for clues to her identity, she finds that her past is entwined with a local legend. But with this knowledge comes danger.

What has stayed with me is the vivid and magical atmosphere of the setting, which is both contemporary – with its shopping malls and graffiti – and steeped in history and legend. The eccentric, misfit characters the free-spirited heroine encounters on her quest are equally memorable – from Phaze II, a homeless boy who lives high in the eaves of a railway bridge, to a boatsman descended from Barbary pirates.

**Katie Jennings**

**Next?**

Try David Almond's *Jackdaw Summer* for more lyrical magical realism. (UTBG 209)

Alan Garner's *The Owl Service* has Welsh legends and magic combined with darkly atmospheric writing. (UTBG 306)

*Fire and Hemlock* by Diana Wynne Jones has a brilliant opening chapter in which a girl gatecrashes a funeral... (UTBG 132)

# SAFFY'S ANGEL   Hilary McKay

**Next?**

The doings of the Casson family are continued in *Indigo's Star*, *Permanent Rose*, *Caddy Ever After* and *Forever Rose*.

Or you might want something just as real, yet just as warm? Try *Threads* by Sophia Bennett, about fashion and friendship.

You might also enjoy E. Nesbit's books about the Bastable family – *The Treasure Seekers* is first.

And don't miss Dodie Smith's *I Capture the Castle*, another funny / sad novel about a wholly eccentric family falling in and out of love. (UTBG 195)

Cadmium, Saffron, Indigo and Rose Casson were named by their eccentric artist parents after paint colours. But Saffy discovers that the colour saffron isn't on the paint chart and this leads to a shocking discovery about her place in the family. Suddenly, she no longer belongs. Only a haunting dream of a heat-filled garden and a mysterious angel link her to her past, and thus begins her quest – for the angel and for some deep part of herself.

I love the way McKay balances the sheer ordinariness of family life with its moments of emotional intensity: she perfectly captures why certain things just matter. *Saffy's Angel* is wonderfully funny: this slightly mad but wholly believable family really stay with you. You'll laugh – but also ponder.

**Helen Simmons**

# SALEM'S LOT   Stephen King

This book changed my life. A modern-day riff on *Dracula*, it follows the downfall of a town besieged by vampires. The beauty of this book is in watching King build up a totally convincing cast and town, then subject them to the horrors of a vampire attack. In the book, vampirism is like a plague, and King details the fallout of such a disaster. I LOVED this. It opened up a whole new world of nightmares to me and, as all horror fans know, nightmares are cool! Like most of King's books, there's stuff in here which isn't suitable for younger readers – so if your parents catch you reading this and kick up a fuss, don't tell them *I* recommended it to you!

**Darren Shan**

**Next?**

*Dracula* by Bram Stoker – the original. (UTBG 113)

*Weaveworld* by Clive Barker is another complex and involving horror story. (UTBG 429)

How would it feel to be the last human on a planet inhabited by ravenous vampires? Try *I Am Legend* by Richard Matheson to find out... (UTBG 194)

Edgar Allen Poe's stories have frightened readers for over 100 years. Try his *Tales of Mystery and Imagination*. (UTBG 387)

# The SALLY LOCKHART books   Philip Pullman ✱ ✱

The first three novels in this series are exciting mystery-adventures set in Victorian London, starring Sally Lockhart and her friends. Sally is 16 when *The Ruby in the Smoke* begins, desperate to widen the limited horizon before her as an orphaned middle-class Victorian girl of slender means, and to find out who killed her father in the South China Sea.

Her final confrontation with her enemy takes three books to arrive, and on the way in *The Shadow in the North* and *The Tiger in the Well*, Philip Pullman leads us everywhere shunned by polite Victorian society: opium dens, music halls, East End missions and socialist gatherings. In *The Tin Princess*, the focus shifts to Central Europe and the perils of a small kingdom hemmed in by rival powers but it still manages to bring the sequence to a satisfying conclusion.

**Geraldine Brennan**

> **Next?**
>
> Anthony Hope's *The Prisoner of Zenda* has strange happenings in a Central European country. (UTBG 323)
>
> There's more historical detection in Karen Wallace's **Lady Violet Mysteries**, starting with *The Secret of the Crocodiles*.
>
> Or try Y.S. Lee's **The Agency** series, about Mary Quinn, orphan, thief and spy!

# SAMMY AND JULIANA IN HOLLYWOOD ✱ ✱ ✱
## Benjamin Alire Saenz

> **Next?**
>
> *CrashBoomLove: A Novel in Verse* by Juan Felipe Herrera is about a boy growing up as a migrant worker.
>
> *Fallen Angels* by Walter Dean Myers is about a Harlem teenager who enlists to fight in Vietnam, and his struggle to survive.
>
> Or try Anthony McGowan's look at contemporary school life, complete with knives, bullies and angst: *The Knife That Killed Me*. (UTBG 229)

*Sammy and Juliana in Hollywood* tells the bleak and beautiful story of Sammy Santos, a Mexican-American teenager growing up not in California's city of dreams, but in a bleak neighbourhood in Las Cruces, New Mexico, in the late 1960s. A loner, Sammy finds all-too-brief happiness with the damaged Juliana, as he struggles to come of age in a time and place riven by racism, poverty and the violence of the Vietnam War.

In language that's sometimes stark, sometimes poetic and always strikingly authentic, Alire Saenz shows us a young man's journey from innocence to experience, and how for Sammy, as for so many others in the summer of '69, love walked hand-in-hand with loss.

**Jennifer Donnelly**

# THE SANDMAN series  Neil Gaiman

Imagine if death were a goth punk and she had three strange sisters: Delirium, Despair and Desire; and three brothers: Destiny, Destruction and the mysterious Dream. Blending myth, fantasy and horror with powerful stories of the real world, this 12-volume series changed the face of comics.

Morpheus, the Lord of the Dreaming, is the key to the whole series. At its opening he is the prisoner of a crazy sect who wants the secret of immortality. When he frees himself, he must relearn his powers and reshape his kingdom, discovering new allies – and new enemies. His magical journey will keep you riveted, with narrow escapes, retellings of famous legends that blaze with life, and a shocking, surprising ending.

**Ariel Kahn**

### Next?

Death, one of the best characters in **The Sandman** series, gets two of her own books: *The High Cost of Living* and *The Time of Your Life*.

Alan Moore's **Swamp Thing** series is a modern retelling of 'Beauty and the Beast' with added villains.

Philip Pullman's **His Dark Materials** trilogy explores similar themes. (UTBG 181)

Or try Neil Gaiman and Terry Pratchett's *Good Omens*. (UTBG 162)

# THE SCARECROWS  Robert Westall

### Next?

Robert Westall has written some of the scariest books around. Read *The Watch House*, about a battle between two ghosts – one benign, the other really not! (UTBG 426)

Or what about a collection of macabre short stories by great writers? Try *Gothic!*, edited by Deborah Noyes.

Or for more skin-crawling fear, try Malcom Rose's *The Tortured Wood* or *The Kiss of Death*.

Simon hates his stepfather, who is unlike his real, dead father in every way imaginable. Angry and lonely, he distances himself from his family at every opportunity. Then he discovers the old water mill. Somehow, it seems to welcome him. Simon spends more and more time there, brooding. But the mill has a violent past, and his rage awakens murderous ghosts. Three scarecrows appear in the field next to his home. No one will admit to putting them there. Every day they get a little closer – until Simon realises that only he has the power to fight off the evil threatening his family.

*The Scarecrows* is a rare book: both scary supernatural thriller and moving family drama. Almost every page taut with menace, it shows how ordinary people can bring evil into being and give it terrifying life.

**Graham Gardner**

# THE SCARLET PIMPERNEL  Baroness Orczy

Forget any film versions you've seen of this book and read the real thing. You'll find that the hero Sir Percy Blakeney is younger than he's shown on screen, and built like Arnold Schwarzenegger. Although some of the attitudes and beliefs of the time in which it was written are surprising and even distasteful to us today, the story of dandified young Englishmen forming a secret league dedicated to spiriting away French aristocrats from the shadow of the guillotine during the Reign of Terror is still an exciting one. If you can disregard the unpleasant attitudes, you'll enjoy the novel for its plot and historical background, showing a time when fear and brutality stalked the streets of Paris.

**Gill Vickery**

### Next?

For a more realistic and brutal account of the French Revolution, read Leon Garfield's *Revolution*. Or look for Sally Gardner's *The Red Necklace* (UTBG 329) and its sequel.

A classic novel set in this period is Charles Dickens's *A Tale of Two Cities*. (UTBG 386)

Or look for the series **Pimpernelles** by Patricia Elliott, about a rich aristocratic girl who defies the Revolution. Start with *The Pale Assassin*.

---

# SCATTERHEART  Lili Wilkinson

'Once upon a time…' begins *Scatterheart*, but any illusions that this is a fairy tale are quickly shattered.

Hannah Cheshire is beautiful, rich and snobbish, and thinks herself above ordinary people, until it transpires that her debonair father is a criminal. From this moment, things go very badly wrong and Hannah finds herself on a ship, being transported to Australia in appalling conditions.

Each chapter begins with a snippet of another tale about a girl called Scatterheart, who is not unlike Hannah. Hannah's story is full of gritty detail: there is blood, sex, dirt, deformity, illness; Scatterheart's, on the other hand, has an ethereal, folksy feel to it. But as the book goes on, the similarities between the two become more and more apparent.

This is a gripping, colourful adventure, with the two parallel stories giving it an extra, thought-provoking edge.

**Susan Reuben**

### Next?

*Newes from the Dead* by Mary Hooper, is another historical story, also about a miscarriage of justice. (UTBG 282)

Another feisty heroine in an historic setting? Try *The Ruby in the Smoke* by Philip Pullman. (UTBG 341)

Or read *Witch Child* by Celia Rees. Mary tries to avoid her grandmother's fate. (UTBG 441)

# SCOOP Evelyn Waugh

John Boot, a fashionable novelist, is desperate to be a war reporter. His distant cousin William Boot is blissfully happy writing about badgers on his impoverished country estate. John's famous – William's not. John can write – William can't. John's streetwise – William's scared of London. And because, in Evelyn Waugh's comic novel, everyone knows they're right and no one listens to anyone else, it's William who ends up in a war no one knows is happening, to invent news stories he doesn't understand, to satisfy a media which is only interested in profit. Scoop's a bit dated, but the central cynicism about the way the media manipulates world events is, if anything, more relevant now than it was in 1938 when the novel was published.

**Antonia Honeywell**

### Next?

If you liked the satire – the way Evelyn Waugh shows how corrupt the world is by making you laugh – try reading Christopher Brookmyre's *Quite Ugly One Morning*.

If you liked the political comment, try reading Orwell's *Nineteen Eighty-Four*. (UTBG 284) or his classic allegory, *Animal Farm*.

If you liked Mrs Stitch, the ridiculous society hostess, try Anita Loos's *Gentlemen Prefer Blondes*.

# THE SCREWTAPE LETTERS C.S. Lewis

### Next?

For another C.S. Lewis, try *The Great Divorce*, where the inhabitants of Hell take a holiday in Heaven.

*The Alchemist* is another tale of finding a spiritual path. (UTBG 15)

Or try Jonathan Swift's *Gulliver's Travels*. It shows human nature at its most absurd.

My teacher commended this to me – woeful handicap for any book – but I loved it anyway. Wormwood, a raw recruit in the Infernal Civil Service, is assigned to win a young man's soul by tempting him to stray from the straight and narrow and damn himself. Since the young man is in love, the task shouldn't prove too hard...

The pressures on both are intensified by the setting: wartime London. (Indeed, I'm guessing the book was some kind of spiritual bomb shelter C.S. Lewis built for himself as World War II raged around him.) Wormwood is answerable to his high-ranking uncle, Screwtape – an affectionate and patient teacher. The book takes the form of correspondence, and it is their relationship which sticks in the mind, even more than the will-he-won't-he? progress of the poor sinner. The end is a real gut-wrencher. Think you know C.S. Lewis? Narnia this ain't.

**Geraldine McCaughrean**

# SEA OF TROLLS  Nancy Farmer

## Next?

Move straight on to the sequels – *The Land of the Silver Apples* and *The Island of the Blessed*.

*Beowulf* (try Seamus Heaney's translation) is another story of a brave and daring quest.

Or for more stories based on the same legends, try Catherine Fisher's **Snowwalker** trilogy, *Runemarks* (UTBG 338) by Joanne Harris or *Troll Fell* (UTBG 404) by Katherine Langrish.

Jack is an apprentice bard. He has a hard life, but things go from bad to worse when his village is raided by Vikings and he and his spoiled baby sister are taken as slaves by Olaf One-Brow. He is taken far into the North to the court of Ivar the Boneless and his half-troll queen. After accidentally causing the queen's hair to fall out, Jack finds himself sent on a quest to find Mimir's Well and on his journey finds trolls, dragons, sea monsters, berserkers, battles, a troll-boar called Golden Bristles and a shield maiden who wants to die.

Weaving Norse myth into spellbinding adventure, this is storytelling on a grand scale. I really couldn't put it down, devouring it in one (very long!) sitting, totally unable to do anything but read and read until I knew exactly what was going to happen to Jack.

**Leonie Flynn**

# SEASON OF SECRETS  Sally Nicholls

Told in a deceptively naïve way, this is the story of Molly who, one dark and stormy autumn night, tries to run away from home. Instead, she finds an injured man by the side of the road; a hunted man, desperate, bleeding and exhausted. But when she tries to bring others to help him, he's gone. Is he real? Is anything that happened real? Molly certainly believes so.

Myth and magic are here, as are legends from Britain's dark past. But the story that grounds all the mystery is a very real one. One of love turning to madness in the wake of a terrible death; of a family who love each other, but can't find a way to show it. As the days shorten and winter takes hold, Molly cares for the man she rescued, hiding him away from the creatures that hunt him. But his story is an old one, and sometimes fate cannot be escaped.

**Leonie Flynn**

## Next?

Alan Garner's books delve into legends from the British Isles; try *The Weirdstone of Brisingamen*, in which two children find adventure involving 140 knights sleeping underground, waiting for the moment to rise and fight. Or try his British stories: *A Bag of Moonshine*.

There's another stranger in David Almond's *Skellig*. (UTBG 365)

# SECOND FROM LAST IN THE SACK RACE ✷✷✷
David Nobbs

**Next?**

There are two sequels: *Pratt of the Argus* and *The Cucumber Man*.

Tom Sharpe has written some hilarious satirical novels – try the classic *Porterhouse Blue*, about university life.

Or try *The Rotters' Club*, also about 1970's youth, by Jonathan Coe himself. He has a very good line in bittersweet humour.

There are plenty of famous coming-of-age stories. This one is less famous; Nobbs was a well-known TV writer in the 1970s and 80s, and British cultural snobbery has probably stopped him from being taken as seriously as his novels deserve. This is perhaps his funniest and saddest book, about a lonely youngster called Henry Pratt who has an unsettled upbringing in Yorkshire before being sent off to a posh boarding school, where he finds himself hopelessly out of his depth and surrounded by characters with names like Tosser Pilkington-Brick. The novel's insights into childhood are heartbreakingly truthful, but are also cushioned by warm irony and brilliant comic set-pieces.

**Jonathan Coe**

# SECOND STAR TO THE RIGHT ✷✷
Deborah Hautzig

Leslie has the kind of life anyone would like. She has a brilliant best friend, does well at school and gets on great with her mum. But Leslie's not happy. If only she were thin, then life would be perfect, wouldn't it?

She loses her first few pounds by accident, during a spell of flu. It's the break she needs and Leslie starts to diet, seriously, egged on by the 'dictator' inside her. The pounds start dropping off, but getting thinner doesn't make things perfect. What Leslie eats, or doesn't eat, becomes an obsession; it takes over her life and in the end she risks losing everything she cares for most.

This harrowing insight into the mind of a girl with anorexia nervosa is brilliantly observed and utterly compelling.

**Susila Baybars**

**Next?**

In Sarah Dessen's *Just Listen* (UTBG 220) Annabel's sister is anorexic. Or hunt down *Perfect* by Natasha Friend, about a girl with bulimia.

*Massive* by Julia Bell is about three generations of one family, all with eating disorders. (UTBG 256)

Or read *Last Seen Wearing Trainers*, about a girl running away from her alcoholic mother. (UTBG 232)

# THE SECRET DIARY OF ADRIAN MOLE AGED 13¾  Sue Townsend

I am very fond of Adrian Mole. In this, his first diary, our hero from Ashby de la Zouch talks frankly and candidly about his life. His days are spent pawing over *Big and Bouncy*, despairing at the behaviour of his wayward parents, trying to control ancient Bert Baxter, agonising about his spots, writing (dreadful) poetry and measuring his 'thing'. Life is difficult for an intellectual such as Adrian.

Sue Townsend

the secret diary of

adrian mole aged 13¾

'The funniest book of the year' – Daily Mail

Adrian's diaries have been essential reading for all our family over the years. The humour is subversive, laugh-out-loud, and sometimes bittersweet. Adrian's distinct voice flows easily on and on … and on. His diaries provide a delightful social history and I look forward to Adrian becoming a pensioner and behaving as unpredictably as ever.

**Caroline Pitcher**

## Next?

If you also grow fond of Adrian, then read the further diaries; next is *The Growing Pains of Adrian Mole*.

If you like Sue Townsend's humour, you will love her *The Queen and I*, in which the Queen (and, more troublesomely, the Duke of Edinburgh) move to a council estate.

Or try a girl's version; *My So-Called Life: The Tragically Normal Diary of Rachel Riley*. It's laugh-out-loud funny and very perceptive, too. (UTBG 274)

Adrian is an average teenager. He has typical problems: acne, bullies and a troublesome love life. His parents don't care what he does (while his gran cares too much – worse luck!) and his dog's always getting ill. He looks after a beetroot-sandwich-obsessed senior citizen called Bert Baxter, who doesn't appreciate him at all.

*Adrian Mole...* is hilarious. It's well written and I found it very true to life. And this is only the first book in a whole series, during which we watch him grow up – he's in his mid-30s in the latest instalment, and still hopeless!

**Max Arevuo, age 13**

# HISTORICAL FICTION

## by Nicola Morgan

So you think history is boring? Just useless facts about dead people? Not relevant to our lives? I admit I probably thought that, too. My memories of history lessons at school are not exactly inspirational. Mainly, I remember one teacher making us do press-ups if we got a date wrong and another teacher punctuating her terrifying lessons with cries of 'Henry VIII *never* fiddled with his pencil!' The only thing this taught us was how to clench our stomach muscles so hard that the laughter did not explode. And I can still do press-ups.

All that changed when I found myself writing a historical novel, *Fleshmarket* (UTBG 134). It came about by accident, after I heard a story – a true story – so powerful that the woman in it began to haunt me. The trouble was, I didn't know the history of the time. OK, I knew some dates and facts – that's the easy bit (and the boring bit, to be honest) but I didn't really *know* the past. When I began the research, reading history books, I found I still didn't *know*, not really. Then I found primary sources, original newspapers, the actual paper touched by actual people from the time, and I began to have the inklings of connection. My heart began to beat faster. But I was still outside, looking through a doorway. Only when I began to know my own fictional characters, the characters I pushed through that door, did I properly understand. Only then did I *feel* the past.

That is why historical fiction is very different from a history lesson and why it should never feel like one (especially not like the ones I remember). Non fiction tells you a type of truth – it can tell you the freezing point of water and even how the molecules behave as they freeze, but only fiction can make you feel the cold. The task for a novelist is to make you feel the cold without lecturing you about the behaviour of molecules, without appearing to teach anything.

Historical fiction *is* relevant to us today: it gives us a reflection of our own times, something we can compare our lives with; sometimes showing how much the world has changed, often showing how little anything changes. The one thing that remains the same is human nature, in all its richness and its potential for good and for evil. And really, a historical novel is exactly like any other, just with a different setting. It shows humans behaving like humans, behaving as we always have done and always will.

## DIP INTO THESE PASTS...

*Girl with a Pearl Earring*
by Tracy Chevalier

*At the Sign of the Sugared Plum*
by Mary Hooper

*Blood Red Horse* by K.M. Grant

*Pagan's Crusade* by Catherine Jinks

*The Bride's Farewell* by Meg Rosoff

## (GREAT) WAR STORIES

*All Quiet on the Western Front*
by Erich Maria Remarque

*Goodbye to All That*
by Robert Graves

*Birdsong* by Sebastian Faulks

*Strange Meeting* by Susan Hill

*Regeneration* by Pat Barker

*Remembrance* by Theresa Breslin

*Private Peaceful*
by Michael Morpurgo

*Memoirs of an Infantry Officer*
by Siegfried Sassoon

# THE SECRET DREAMWORLD OF A SHOPAHOLIC   Sophie Kinsella

OK, listen up: if there is one book you read this year, it has to be this. It will tell you everything you should NOT do when it comes to money. You see, Becky loves to go shopping. All she has to do is enter a shop and she suddenly finds that she MUST have at least one or two items off the shelves. This would be fine if she were unbelievably rich, but she isn't, and nasty little unpaid credit card bills and bank letters start to pile up...

Becky remains unbelievably lovable every step of the way, even when you desperately want to stop her from doing the next unthinkable thing. For money problems lead to lies, and lies to bigger lies... What will happen when Becky lands a job advising people what to do with their money? Or worse, when she falls in love?

**Candida Gray**

### Next?

There are sequels; *Shopaholic Abroad*, *Shopaholic Ties the Knot*, *Shopaholic and Sister* and *Shopaholic and Baby*.

*Does My Bum Look Big in This?* is a funny look at single life. (UTBG 111)

Jane Green also writes very warm, funny books about being female and single. Try *Bookends*.

# THE SECRET HISTORY   Donna Tartt

### Next?

More Donna Tartt? Try *The Little Friend*. It took her ten years to write it.

Another tale of a crime and its consequences, Fyodor Dostoyevsky's *Crime and Punishment*. (UTBG 89)

Evelyn Waugh wrote tellingly about the decadent lives of the rich in *Brideshead Revisited*. (UTBG 61)

Richard sees Hampden College as the chance to leave behind his unglamorous past and fashion a new identity. Drawn to an elite group of students, centred around their charismatic classics professor, Richard is captivated by their sophistication, eccentricity, casual affluence and the way they seem to live in a world set apart from the everyday. But as he sets about working his way into their confidence, he discovers they have a secret history far darker than his own: one involving blackmail and murder.

This psychological thriller is far more than a whodunnit (we find out the facts on almost the first page). It's not even about whether the murderers are going to get caught. The book's skill lies in the way it makes murder appear rational and justifiable before the event and then hits you with the true horror of its consequences. It may sound grim, but Tartt injects black humour into even the bleakest situations.

**Katie Jennings**

# THE SECRET LIFE OF BEES Sue Monk Kidd

Lily lives with guilt caused by her belief that, when she was four, she killed her mother. Her only friend is her servant, Rosaleen. But Rosaleen is black, and this is South Carolina in 1964 when being black meant at best you were a second-class citizen. Lily saves Rosaleen from some racists, and together they run away. Guided only by the few things Lily owns that were her mother's, they end up staying with three black sisters.

Lily is just 14. At the beginning of the story she's a little broken by life, but her journey takes her through a search for love and forgiveness into a place where she finally begins to live. On the way she meets the most amazing people, people she (and the reader) learn to care for and love. This book made me cry – and not always from sadness.

**Leonie Flynn**

### Next?

There's more racism and learning how to grow up in the classic *To Kill a Mockingbird* by Harper Lee. (UTBG 398)

Sadie Jones's *The Outcast* is another brilliant story in which a child and a murder are violently linked.

*A World without Bees* by Alison Benjamin and Brian McCallum is about the threat to our bee population – something you might care about even more after reading *The Secret Life of Bees*.

# SECRETS IN THE FIRE / PLAYING WITH FIRE Henning Mankell

### Next?

Aubrey Flegg's *The Cinnamon Tree* begins with a landmine explosion. Shifting between Africa and Ireland, it is a thriller involving the arms trade.

Peter Dickinson's *AK* is a dramatic story about a boy soldier and the terror of war.

For more about AIDS in Africa, read *Chanda's Secret* by Allan Stratton.

Can you imagine losing your legs? That's war. In *Secrets in the Fire*, Sofia steps on a landmine beside the path in a remote region of Mozambique. Henning Mankell has based Sofia on a real girl: a young friend with no legs but an indomitable spirit.

In the sequel, *Playing with Fire*, Sofia is envious that her older sister Rosa can laugh and dance with the boys after her hard day's work in the fields. Sofia is too embarrassed by her plastic legs and crutches to join them. But when Rosa falls ill (she has AIDS), it is Sofia who helps both Rosa and her mother to face the harsh truth.

Mankell writes beautifully. Both stories are deeply moving. They might also leave you very angry.

**Beverley Naidoo**

# THE SEEING STONE  Kevin Crossley-Holland

**Next?**

There's more: *Arthur: At the Crossing Places*, *Arthur: King of the Middle March* and a book all about Arthur's friend, *Gatty's Tale*.

For a completely different take on Arthurian legend, try T.H. White's *The Once and Future King*. (UTBG 292)

Philip Reeve has re-imagined Arthur, too – read his *Here Lies Arthur*. (UTBG 175)

Or try the Arthur story relocated to contemporary gangland in Nicky Singer's *Knight Crew*. (UTBG 230)

Set in the Welsh Marches in 1199, this is the tale of Arthur de Caldicot who discovers his namesake, the legendary boy-king Arthur, in his 'seeing stone'. In a time of transition between one century and another, one king and another, between childhood and manhood, the 'between places … tremble like far horizons' and all certainties and loyalties are brought into question.

Bullied by his older brother Serle and supported by his friend Gatty, Arthur increasingly identifies with the boy-king as he unravels the true nature of his quest, while the enigmatic figure of Merlin moves effortlessly between one dimension and another. A dense, absorbing tale told in a beautiful, spare style.

**Livi Michael**

# SEEKER  William Nicholson

For as long as he can remember, Seeker has wanted to join the Nomana, the mysterious group of powerful 'warriors'. Morning Star and the Wildman want to, too. They all think they understand the Nomana, and ought to be allowed to join. But it's not quite that simple. The Nomana won't accept just anyone...

Will the three of them ever be let in? What's the terrible 'secret weapon' the Nomana are muttering about that's set to destroy them? What happened to Seeker's brother, the heroic Blaze? Where's Morning Star's mother? And what is the source of the Nomana's power?

Many of your questions will be answered in this wonderful book, and for the rest, well, thankfully there are sequels! William Nicholson has another classic series on his hands.

**Daniel Hahn**

**Next?**

Those sequels are *Jango* and *Noman*.

For power struggles and mysterious tribes, try Marcus Sedgwick's *The Dark Horse*.

Or read one of my favourites, Susan Cooper's **The Dark Is Rising** series. (UTBG 96)

There's more tribal warfare in the terrific time-slip books by N.M Browne, starting with *Warriors of Alavana*.

# A SEPARATE PEACE   John Knowles

It's hard to imagine now what it's like growing up in a world truly at war, where you and many of your peers may well be dead within a year. That's the situation in which Gene, Phineas and their friends – the class of 1943 at an expensive boys' boarding school in New England – find themselves. But while World War II looms large, and the weight of duty to their country weighs heavily for this 'draft bait', the key battle recounted in *A Separate Peace* is fought closer to home.

Gene, the narrator, is an introverted intellectual. His roommate Finny is a popular athlete and a natural leader, who is crippled by an accident that may be Gene's fault. Knowles beautifully captures Gene's tortured brooding and the destructive jealousy that can turn even the closest friends into enemies.

**Terri Paddock**

> **Next?**
>
> *Peace Breaks Out* – although not a sequel, John Knowles's later book is set at the same school, where war hero Pete has returned to teach after World War II.
>
> J.D. Salinger's *The Catcher in the Rye* portrays another memorable protagonist. (UTBG 69)
>
> William Golding's *Lord of the Flies* – shipwrecked schoolboys explore their baser instincts. (UTBG 241)

# A SERIES OF UNFORTUNATE EVENTS
## Lemony Snicket

> **Next?**
>
> *The Bad Beginning* is the first in the series.
>
> Or try Neil Gaiman's Gothic *The Graveyard Book*. (UTBG 165)
>
> For children treated awfully, try anything by Charles Dickens. *Oliver Twist* will start you off.
>
> Or for more elaborate prose, try *Flora Segunda of Crackpot Hall* by Ysabeau S. Wilce. (UTBG 135)

Become part of the Baudelaire orphans' grim epic as they are pursued by the dastardly and stunningly inept Count Olaf, who wants to get his hands on the Baudelaire family fortune. But these are orphans with many talents: Violet is an inventor who can fashion a solution to almost any problem; Klaus is a bookworm who has read innumerable books on every subject imaginable; and Sunny ... well, Sunny likes biting things.

**A Series of Unfortunate Events** is written for younger children, but older readers will still find plenty to enjoy here, whether it is the wonderfully Gothic and drear atmosphere of the books, the novelty of reading a children's story that flatly refuses to give you a happy ending, or simply the ghoulish glee of watching the Baudelaire orphans suffer.

**Chris Wooding**

# THE SERIOUS KISS Mary Hogan

Whether drunk or sober, Libby's dad is a pig. He's also a waster who loses all the family money, meaning they have to move away from everything she knows, out of the city and into a trailer park on the edge of a shabby desert town. White-trash lifestyle? Thank you, Dad.

Libby hates it all. Even her old best friend drops her, and the only person prepared to befriend her now is the fat school misfit. In fact, life looks like it might be just about over. But then she meets a boy, and makes friends with some of the weirdest (but coolest) people. So, will her dad stop being a loser? Will her mum stop feeding them take-outs and actually start cooking? And what about that kiss?

**Leonie Flynn**

> ### Next?
>
> More Mary Hogan; *Pretty Face* is about overweight Hayley and how she goes to Italy and learns how to like her own skin, or look for *Susanna Sees Stars* about a girl who really wants to be a journalist.
>
> *My So-Called Life: The Tragically Normal Diary of Rachel Riley* is the hilarious account of a really very ordinary girl. (UTBG 274)
>
> Or look out for Louisa Plaja's books; *Extreme Kissing*, about two friends and their secrets, or *Split by a Kiss*, which takes one girl and shows two paths her life could take.

# SET IN STONE Linda Newbery

> ### Next?
>
> Now try Linda's other books, particularly *The Shell House* (UTBG 358) and *The Sandfather*, about troubled Hal and how he is affected by his new life by the sea.
>
> For more secrets and mysteries try *The Woman in White* (UTBG 443) or *The Woman in Black* (UTBG 443).
>
> Another book set amongst a strange family is Mervyn Peake's *Titus Groan*, the first of the **Gormenghast** trilogy. (UTBG 163)

*Set in Stone* begins in 1920, with successful artist Samuel Godwin looking back to his youth and his employment as tutor to the daughters of recent widower, Ernest Farrow. Samuel is intrigued by the ménage he finds at Fourwinds, which includes the enigmatic Charlotte Agnew, companion to the girls. He senses a mystery involving Gideon Waring, sculptor of the magnificent carvings that give the house its name.

Linda Newbery characteristically refuses to compromise, either in narrative complexity, or in subject matter. A shocking secret lies at the heart of the family; no one is quite as Samuel sees them, and nothing is quite as it seems. His shifting perspectives make *Set in Stone* a powerful page-turner, gripping to the end.

**Celia Rees**

# SEVENTH HEAVEN   Alice Hoffman

It is 1959. The oldest member of a small community on Long Island suddenly dies. His wife leaves town, and their empty house on Hemlock Street gradually falls apart. A terrible smell invades the street and a flock of vicious birds arrives to terrorise the neighbourhood. The people wonder if they are being punished. But for what? It has always been a happy and peaceful community.

This sounds like the opening to a horror story, but *Seventh Heaven* is nothing like that. It is the story of ordinary people whose lives, gently explored, become strange and remarkable. So when 17-year-old Ace begins to fall in love with a ghost, we are not at all surprised, just incredibly moved.

**Jenny Nimmo**

## Next?

Try some of Alice Hoffman's other novels; *Turtle Moon*, *The River King* and *Illumination Night* have the same blend of ordinary lives touched by enchantment.

Or read Sonia Hartnett's *The Ghost's Child*. It encompasses a whole life – and a death.

Or you could try Anne Tyler's novels; *The Accidental Tourist* and *Dinner at the Homesick Restaurant* are not only touching, but also enthralling and, sometimes, very funny.

Or how about Carol Shields's *The Stone Diaries*, the story of one woman's life from birth to death.

# SEVENTH TIDE   Joan Lennon

## Next?

If you enjoyed Joan Lennon's imaginative fiction, why not try her first novel, *Questors*?

Like the idea of a tear in the fabric of the universe opening the door to another world? Look to Philip Pullman's fantastic **His Dark Materials** trilogy. (UTBG 181)

Eo is a 15-year-old shapeshifter not yet able to change shape. Prone to distraction, he drives his teacher Professor Pinkerton Hurple, a talking ferret, to despair.

When Eo absentmindedly causes a tear between worlds and agrees to the Seventh Tide challenge, both he and Hurple are catapulted through time with every tide. Desperately they search for gifts to help them rescue their world from the beautiful soul-sucking Kelpies.

Hurple's book in progress intersperses the prose with helpful facts; like why spring tide doesn't only occur in the spring and how a ferret can write despite its lack of opposable thumbs.

Mythology, dinosaurs, an underwater city, a 24th-century chick, a 6th-century monk, and demons thirsty to destroy the world of the G – what more does a fantasy novel need?

**Tessa Brechin**

# SHADOWMANCER G.P. Taylor

**Next?**

Another G.P. Taylor? Try *Wormwood*, about an astronomer, a prophecy and an angel whose feathers are cruelly plucked, one by one.

For a different slant on God and religion, you have to try Philip Pullman's **His Dark Materials** trilogy (UTBG 181). And also C.S. Lewis's *The Screwtape Letters* (UTBG 344).

Or for more mystery and magic, try Trudi Canavan's the **Black Magician** trilogy. (UTBG 45)

'It is the song of the deep. They are calling the dead to feast. The Seloth will not stop until the ship is broken on the rocks. They want sacrifice not mercy.'

It is the 1700s. Thomas, Kate and Raphah are brought together in mysterious ways, and are sent on a mission from God to retake a golden statue (the Keruvim) from the cruel, power-hungry priest Demurral, before he can use it to kill God and control the universe. But there are many complications...

This is a fast-moving tale of magic, evil, superstition and witchcraft that never fails to keep you in suspense. If you want to be transported into a time where not even life can be taken for granted, you will enjoy this book.

**Samuel Mortimer, age 11**

# THE SHADOW OF THE WIND
## Carlos Ruiz Zafón

This is a beguiling tale full of intrigue and heartbreak. Daniel, the son of a widowed bookseller, who lives with his father above their shop in post-war Barcelona, sets out on a quest to discover the truth about Julian Carax, a mysterious writer whose novel is at the centre of the mystery. Along the way, there are stories within stories, and different narrators take up the tale. Although books and writing are central to this novel, ultimately it is infatuation, young love and heartbreak that hold the complex plot together.

With a host of fabulous characters and a back-story that unfolds through the dark times of the Spanish Civil War, *The Shadow of the Wind* captures the old-world charm of an almost-forgotten Barcelona. One minute you're on the edge of your seat, the next you're reaching for the tissues. An enormously readable book.

**Next?**

Zafón has also written a sort of prequel, *The Angel's Game*.

For other books set during the same war, try Ernest Hemingway's *For Whom the Bell Tolls* or Laurie Lee's *As I Walked Out One Midsummer Morning*.

Another book about books and the power of words is Marcus Zusak's *The Book Thief*. (UTBG 52)

**Neil Arksey**

# THE SHAMER'S DAUGHTER Lene Kaaberbol

**Next?**

Lene Kaaberbol has written a further three books about Dina and her journey to understanding the role of the Shamer: *The Shamer's Signet*, *The Serpent Gift* and *The Shamer's War*.

You might also like *The Giver* and *Gathering Blue* by Lois Lowry, set in a world where everyone is engineered to be the same.

For another exhilarating fantasy, try Clive Barker's *Abarat*. (UTBG 10)

Dina's mother, the Shamer, is haughtily summoned by Lord Drakan to prove a murderer's guilt. But the man is innocent. So she refuses to testify against him and finds herself, Dina and the 'murderer' caught up in a deadly power game. Dina struggles desperately to save her mother and the accused man from death, and in doing so she begins to come to terms with inheriting her mother's Shamer power.

I'm not a regular fantasy reader, but I loved this: filled with tension, the story whips along at a cracking pace and – scary dragons apart – it's set in a very real and tangible world. Dina certainly has guts, and will make you see that the role of the Shamer – teller of truth – isn't for fantasy worlds alone. Exciting and thought provoking.

**Helen Simmons**

# SHARPE'S COMPANY Bernard Cornwell

Sharpe is a soldier in the Peninsular wars – the wars Britain fought in Spain and Portugal against Napoleon in the early 1800s. These were times of great cruelty and great heroism, and Bernard Cornwell describes them better than anyone. His hero is a rough, tough lieutenant of the 95th Rifles, and the events in which he is involved actually happened. When you read in the book about the 'forlorn hope' and the attack on the great fortress of Badajoz, you will be blown away – as were most of the men in the first advance...

*Sharpe's Company* is the third of a wonderful series and possibly my favourite. Cornwell makes you wonder how anyone could think history was boring.

**Andrew Norriss**

**Next?**

You will certainly want to read other **Sharpe** books – I've got 18 on my shelf and Cornwell is still writing them. Chronologically, they start with *Sharpe's Tiger*, but the first one he wrote – and one of the best – is *Sharpe's Rifles*.

C.S. Forester's **Hornblower** series is set at sea during the Napoleonic wars, as is Paul Dowswell's fast and action-packed *Powder Monkey*; or try his very different *Ausländer* (UTBG 32).

# SHARP NORTH   Patrick Cave

An isolated spot in the Highlands, an unknown woman pursued by grey-clad men, red blood spills on white snow as a young girl accidentally witnesses a murder. This is the atmospheric opening of Cave's gripping sci-fi thriller. Mira's simple existence is shattered by the violent scene, sending her on a long journey to find her true identity.

The book is set in a futuristic Britain: a half-drowned country governed by powerful families who would do just about anything to retain their control – including some very unethical experiments. A web of lies and political corruption is slowly closing in on Mira, who must use every resource she has to survive.

**Noga Applebaum**

> **Next?**
>
> The sequel, *Blown Away*; or *House of the Scorpion* (UTBG 189) by Nancy Farmer, another fantastic sci-fi thriller.
>
> *Exodus* by Julie Bertagna also takes place in a futuristic, flooded Britain. (UTBG 124)
>
> Or how about the different but equally thrilling **The Oracle** trilogy by Catherine Fisher, for another brilliantly imagined other world? (UTBG 298)

# THE SHELL HOUSE   Linda Newbery

> **Next?**
>
> More books that set the troubles of sexuality against a backdrop of the First World War: Jennifer Johnston's *How Many Miles to Babylon?* and Susan Hill's *Strange Meeting*. (UTBG 380)
>
> For more Linda Newbery, read *Sisterland*, which weaves a compelling story around Alzheimer's, sexuality and racism.
>
> Like many of his books, Aidan Chambers's *Dance on My Grave* also deals with complex issues of sexuality. (UTBG 94)

This is a big and complex novel that explores in some depth, and with great honesty and tenderness, the emotional awakening of two young men from different periods of history. One is Greg, a modern teenager, drawn into the past by his involvement in the restoration of a stately home. The other is Edmund, a young soldier, who fought and loved – and subsequently disappeared – during the First World War.

Sexual identity, as revealed through Edmund's sufferings, is one strand of this many-layered novel. Another is the nature of religious belief, as Greg's girlfriend, the aptly named Faith, struggles with her Christianity. Still another is the need for Greg to discover what he really feels and thinks, and to remain true to his ideals.

An astonishingly wide canvas is covered, ranging across both time and the conflicting emotional landscapes of the two main characters. All in all, a deeply satisfying read.

**Jean Ure**

# The SHERLOCK HOLMES stories
## Arthur Conan Doyle

It's impossible to imagine a world without Sherlock Holmes. Arthur Conan Doyle's creation is more famous than many historical figures. The actor / director Orson Welles once described Holmes as 'the greatest man who never lived and who will never die'.

I'd start with the very first story, *A Study in Scarlet*, and then read the first half-dozen or so short stories in order. That way you'll get to know Holmes, his faithful companion Doctor John Watson and the Victorian world they inhabit. After that, you can pick and choose. There are 56 short stories and four short novels, offering an extraordinary mix of pure deduction, adventure and intrigue. Like them, and they will stay with you for ever.

**Philip Ardagh**

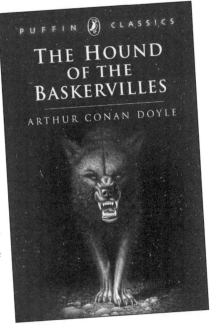

### Next?

There are heaps more Holmes stories: *The Adventures of Sherlock Holmes*; *The Memoirs of Sherlock Holmes*; *The Return of Sherlock Holmes*; *The Casebook of Sherlock Holmes*.

For something more modern, go to P.D. James (UTBG 204, 415), Colin Dexter (UTBG 204), or Ruth Rendell (UTBG 361). They all write books where the same detective returns to solve new mysteries.

Or try Dorothy L. Sayers' **Lord Peter Wimsey** stories, like *Clouds of Witness*. (UTBG 243)

I can remember how my heart sank when I opened a big present and found this heavy volume inside. I must have been about 14, and I couldn't imagine anything less enticing. Sometimes that's the best way to approach a book. The thrill of being surprised is wonderful. These four stories: *A Study in Scarlet*, *The Sign of Four*, *The Hound of the Baskervilles* and *The Valley of Fear* are all you need to get hooked on Holmes and Watson, and their world of crime and mystery. The stories were first published in the late 19th century, and these days there may even be an extra thrill: Holmes is wonderfully politically incorrect. A modern publisher would insist on cleaning up his habits and attitudes before allowing you anywhere near these compelling stories.

**Eleanor Updale**

# SHORT STORIES H.G. Wells

H.G. Wells is the founding father of British science fiction – a brilliant storyteller whose books are full of speculations about the future. Of the short stories, the most famous is 'The Time Machine', in which the hero travels through untold millennia to the very end of the world. Then there's 'The Country of the Blind', where the sighted man is at no advantage, and 'The Man Who Could Work Miracles', who ends up dearly wishing he couldn't. Wells imagines what would happen if the Earth stopped revolving, if diamonds could be grown, if a man could see two periods of time at once, if tentacled invaders were to crawl from the sea. Through stories, he explores his theories and beliefs, mixing terrifying fantasy with the world of Edwardian Britain.

**Catherine Fisher**

### Next?

Try Wells's novels. *The War of the Worlds* (UTBG 424) is a classic of alien invasion, and *The Invisible Man* takes the idea of invisibility to its logical limits.

Wells's work inspired William Hope Hodgson's bizarre and brilliant *The Night Land*.

Or try some rather more recent science fiction, such as Arthur C. Clarke's *Childhood's End*, or Isaac Asimov's *I, Robot* (UTBG 207). And look at our sci-fi feature on pp.246–247.

# THE SHORT STORIES OF SAKI H.H. Munro

### Next?

Rudyard Kipling was writing many of his short stories at about the same time as Munro. Try *Debits and Credits* or *Limits and Renewals*.

Once you get a taste for short stories, it's hard to get enough. Sylvia Townsend Warner wrote some very entertaining and rather strange tales, often tinged with the supernatural, such as those in *One Thing Leading to Another*.

Or try G.K. Chesterton's thrilling *The Man Who Was Thursday: A Nightmare*, about an anarchist and a policeman.

Tobermory the cat is taught human speech and starts repeating in public everything he has overheard in private. A stray child turns out to be a werewolf. Conradin makes a god of his pet ferret and prays for vengeance on his hateful guardian – successfully. Through these very short stories rampage fiendishly inventive children, dictatorial aunts, liars, bored young men who make life hell for other people just to pass the time, and every species of animal from chickens to wolves, usually wreaking havoc of some kind. Often savage, sometimes sad, always witty, these portraits of Edwardian society are like snapshots taken with a camera that has a crack in the lens.

**Jan Mark**

# A SIGHT FOR SORE EYES  Ruth Rendell

Rendell is my all-time favourite author and this thriller is one of her best. Teddy Brex is born a beautiful, lovable child into a family lacking in love. After her mother's violent murder, Francine Hill is encaged in a strict family setting that permits no emotion and encourages a desperate desire for escape. When the two young adults meet, there's an instant attraction. But can a man who's never been loved learn to love? And is it inevitable that ugliness is so corrosive that it can taint even the most beautiful subject? These are two questions asked in Ruth Rendell's compulsively readable thriller, which as always spins several threads at once and culminates in a devastating, brilliant end.

**Jon Appleton**

### Next?

Although now in her 70s, Rendell knows what it's like to be young. Some of her best evocations of youth are found in *Going Wrong* and *The Crocodile Bird*.

P.D. James writes mainly about Inspector Dalgliesh, like in *Original Sin*, but why not try one of her books about Cordelia Gray instead? *The Skull Beneath the Skin* is my favourite.

And of course you can turn to our feature on detective stories on pp. 108–109 for more recommendations.

# SILAS MARNER  George Eliot

This was the first 'posh' book I read outside school. I had heard of George Eliot, and how she was a woman hiding behind a man's name, but I was put off by the size of her books on the library shelves. So I chose the thinnest: *Silas Marner*. It's a great story, set in the early 19th century.

Silas Marner, a weaver, is turned into a reclusive, miserly outsider when falsely accused of theft. Then he is transformed again when he finds and adopts a young girl. This book has everything: tragedy, mystery, and a dissolute, sexy, aristocratic villain. At school, we read Eliot's *The Mill on the Floss* out loud in class. It took weeks. I thought I was going to die of boredom. But *Silas Marner* was fab.

**Eleanor Updale**

### Next?

I went on from this to *Tess of the d'Urbervilles* (UTBG 391) by Thomas Hardy (more rural England and dastardly men), and *Jane Eyre* (UTBG 211), the ultimate book of unjust suffering and longing.

One of the themes of *Silas Marner* (though I don't think I realised it at the time) is the dignity of labour. You can get more of that from *Sons and Lovers* by D.H. Lawrence.

Some people do like *The Mill on the Floss* (UTBG 264), of course. Try it and see if you are one of them. Look out for *Middlemarch*, too.

# SILENT SNOW, SECRET SNOW    Adèle Geras

**Next?**

You can't go wrong with Adèle Geras. Try *Troy* (UTBG 405) next, or *The Tower Room*, part of the **Happy Ever After** series.

For a light look at family Christmases, try Anne Fine's *The More the Merrier* and its sequel, *Eating Things on Sticks*.

The ideal read for a cold winter's day. Curl up on the sofa with a box of your favourite chocolates within a hand's snatch and ENJOY! All human life is here, with its fancies and foibles and its deep, dark secrets.

Snowed in at the Big House, cut off from the outside world, the Golden Family spend their Christmas loving, hating – laughing, crying – pining for what might have been, planning for what will be. And we as the readers become privy to it all, as we see through the eyes of each character. Soft is the snow, and silent are the secrets, in this hidden world of the emotions.

**Jean Ure**

# SILVERFIN    Charlie Higson

James Bond is 13, and a new boy at Eton. School is bad enough, but then he makes enemies and his holiday in Scotland becomes something less than relaxing. With the help of a beautiful girl and a tough, streetwise kid, Bond survives the attentions of an obsessed millionaire, imprisonment, experimental drugs, torture, perilous escape and coming to terms with the death of seemingly everyone he loves.

This is brilliantly researched and perfectly in keeping with the other Bond stories. From the gruesome opening chapter to the final scenes, this is a rip-roaring adventure, and one that Ian Fleming would surely have approved of.

**Leonie Flynn**

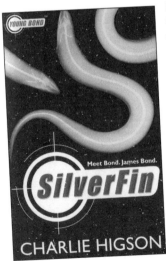

**Next?**

The sequels so far: *Blood Fever*, *Double or Die*, *Hurricane Gold* and *By Royal Command*. SilverFin is now available as a graphic novel, too. Or for something quite different, tyr Higson's zombie thriller, *The Enemy*.

Robert Muchamore writes brilliant adventures for his teen heroes. Try *The Recruit*, the first in the **CHERUB** series first. (UTBG 73)

Or for another story set in the wilds of Scotland, try John Buchan's *The Thirty-Nine Steps*. (UTBG 394)

# THE SIMPLE GIFT
## Steven Herrick

Written in free verse, this story is told through short, stand-alone poems, each a little masterpiece in its own right. A most unusual novel, it opens with 16-year-old Billy abandoning his loveless home and cruel father to hit the road and live rough. But if you think you're in for a grim, downbeat read, you'll be surprised.

Basically, *The Simple Gift* explores goodness and kindness. Despite his background, Billy is a character of fundamental dignity and integrity. He might be down and out, living in an old railway carriage, but his decency enriches the lives of others. And ultimately in this gritty, uplifting fairy tale for our times, Billy himself trades his past for true friendship and love.

**Catherine Forde**

### Next?

*The Simple Gift* reminds me – weirdly, I know – of Bunyan's *Pilgrim's Progress*.

And the father-son relationship has echoes of Kevin Brooks's *Martyn Pig*, although with a happier outcome. (UTBG 256)

*The Lost Boys' Appreciation Society* is also about finding a home in a harsh world.

Or try a futuristic version of the theme, in the page-turning *As Good as Dead in Downtown* by Neil Arksey.

# THE SIRENS OF TITAN   Kurt Vonnegut

Everyone knows Vonnegut wrote *Slaughterhouse 5*. And yes, it's a brilliant book that must be read. But he wrote a lot of other classics, too. This, one of his earliest, is also one of his best. A wickedly funny satire about the meaning (and meaninglessness) of life, it features many of his trademarks – time travel, knowledge of the future, questions about man's role in the universe and his ultimate end.

Vonnegut is a great writer. His books can be bleak as well as hilarious – but they'll always make you think. Don't let phrases like 'chrono-synclastic infundibulum' put you off. Vonnegut's books come dressed as sci-fi, but they're always about humans and our struggles to make sense of the world and of life. But be warned: if you read this book, you might never look at *The Bible* in the same light again!

**Darren Shan**

### Next?

*Slaughterhouse 5* (UTBG 368) and *Cat's Cradle* (UTBG 70) both by Kurt Vonnegut.

*Childhood's End* by Arthur C. Clarke is about what humanity might become, with encouragement from outside.

Douglas Adams's *The Hitchhiker's Guide to the Galaxy* must be the funniest sci-fi novel ever. (UTBG 182)

# THE SISTERHOOD OF THE TRAVELLING PANTS   Ann Brashares

This is the story of one pair of trousers, four very different girls and one very special friendship. Carmen, Lena, Bridget and Tibby are destined to go their own separate ways in the summer but resolve to share their lives by passing the pants (a rather stylish pair of jeans that somehow fits each of them perfectly) from one to the other in turn. The four girls' summer experiences, with all their highs and lows, are woven skilfully together into a satisfying story of friendship and self-discovery.

**Philippa Milnes-Smith**

**Next?**

The series continues with; *The Second Summer of the Sisterhood*; *Girls in Pants: The Third Summer of the Sisterhood*; *Forever in Blue: The Fourth Summer of the Sisterhood*; *3 Willows: The Sisterhood Grows*. There's also *Keep in Touch: Letters, Notes, and More from the Sisterhood of the Travelling Pants*.

Try *Feeling Sorry for Celia* by Jaclyn Moriarty; wry, hilarious and written in the form of letters. Or Carolyn Mackler's *Love and Other Four Letter Words*, about moving to New York, parents separating, and love.

# SKARRS   Catherine Forde

**Next?**

Liked the way Catherine Forde writes? Then try her first book, *Fat Boy Swim* (UTBG 128), or her tense and disturbing *Sugarcoated*.

Want to know more about what happened to prisoners in Japan during the war? Read James Clavell's *King Rat* or J.G. Ballard's semi-autobiographical *Empire of the Sun* (UTBG 120).

More books with music? Benjamin Zephaniah's *Gangsta Rap* or *Just Listen* (UTBG 220) by Sarah Dessen.

This is a story in two parts; with two voices, two tales to tell. First there's Danny, who's in trouble – all attitude and bravado and paper-thin front, ready to take on anyone, especially when he's with Jakey, the bad boy gone worse who's befriended him.

And then there's Grampa Dan, who's just died and whom we learn about through the diary he wrote while a prisoner of the Japanese in Burma during World War II.

The two stories dovetail together beautifully in a book which is set in Forde's native Scotland and uses a lot of dialect, but is so well written you won't need subtitles. *Skarrs* is edgy, page-turning and full of great characters, and I loved it.

**Graham Marks**

# SKELLIG David Almond

This is one of my favourite books of all time! It's about a boy called Michael, who has just moved to a rather derelict house and whose baby sister is so seriously ill we don't know whether she's going to survive. It's about fear, and sadness, and loss, but also about healing and recovery and love, and tenderness. At the heart of the story is the extraordinary figure of Skellig, whom Michael discovers in the tumbledown garage. At first he seems like a disgusting old man, covered in cobwebs, but bit by bit Michael's (and the reader's) view is transformed.

Michael, his friends Leaky and Coot, Mina (a home-educated girl with a special way of seeing things) and Michael's family are all real and totally believable, but this story is also magical and extraordinary. Reading it felt to me like going on an intense, moving journey. I couldn't put it down!

**Julia Green**

### Next?

*Coraline* (UTBG 86) is a magic / reality mix with a far darker and more sinister edge, not unlike a creepier version of Lewis Carroll's *Alice's Adventures in Wonderland*.

More David Almond? Try his disturbing look at good and evil, *Clay*. (UTBG 81)

Another slightly surreal story about a 'reality' not quite being what it seems is Alan Garner's *Elidor*.

With a new house and a new school, Michael has a lot to cope with even without his baby sister falling dangerously ill. With his parents preoccupied with the baby and the doctor always in the house, Michael is left to his own devices, and one day finds a mysterious man – or is it a bird? – or maybe an angel? – in the ramshackle garage at the bottom of the garden. Together with his new friend Mina they take the strange being, with wings and a peculiar liking for flies and Chinese takeaways, to her grandfather's house, and Michael's life changes for ever...

Words aren't enough to describe the magic of this book. It's a story about faith and hope, life, love and death – big serious issues – but there's humour, too, and it's so well written you feel you're there with them. Imaginative, inspired, original, full of poetry and emotion: you'll not be able to put it down when you're reading it or put it out of your head when you've finished.

**David Gardner, age 16**

# SKIM   Mariko Tamaki and Jillian Tamaki

Skim is the nickname of Kimberly Keiko Cameron, would-be Wiccan, Goth and depressed Japanese-Canadian schoolgirl. A little lost, a little lonely, a little confused by life, Skim confides everything to her diary – all her hopes, her dreams and her feelings. Everything from what happens when one of her peers kills himself, to how she falls shatteringly in love with one of her teachers. A female teacher.

Dreamlike in places, heartbreakingly real in others, this is a story told with truth. Truth about being a teenager, about family, culture, race, self-belief and friendship. There's a thousand-page novel hidden in these few pages. Reading this lets you completely inhabit another life – and possibly understand your own a little more afterwards.

**Leonie Flynn**

> **Next?**
>
> Another life is encapsulated in Marjane Satrapi's *Persepolis*. (UTBG 310)
>
> *Epileptic* by David B. tells the heartbreaking true story of David's life with an epileptic brother and the lengths his parents go to in trying to cure him – from faith healers to voodoo and macrobiotics.
>
> *Fun Home* by Alison Bechdel is another coming-of-age story, in which the heroine also likes other women.

# SKINNY B, SKAZ AND ME   John Singleton

> **Next?**
>
> More John Singleton? Read *Angel Blood*, about four children condemned to live in an appalling sanatorium. It's thought-provoking, compelling reading.
>
> Funny and real? Try *Noodlehead* (UTBG 285) by Jonathan Kebbe, *Rules of the Road* by Joan Bauer or *Girls in Love* (UTBG 157) by Jacqueline Wilson.
>
> There's illness, too, in Damian Keller's *Life Interrupted*, but don't let that put you off. (UTBG 236)
>
> Another author who makes the everyday world special is David Almond. Try *Kit's Wilderness*. (UTBG 228)

Fourteen-year-old Lee doesn't like his sister, Skinny. After all, in their house the first rule is: what Skinny wants, Skinny gets. But then Skinny gets sick, and whilst Lee is trying to show that he does care (after all, nothing says I love you so much as hair glitter, right?) life takes a turn for the worse.

Just how Lee gets on the wrong side of the Hoodz5 boys, ends up climbing a death-trap water tower with his best 'friend' Skaz – who literally leaves him hanging – and finds out that the girl he fancies is the daughter of the local crime boss, makes a fast-paced, enjoyable read.

This is a book that tells it how it is and leaves you wishing for more.

**Laura Hutchings**

# SLAKE'S LIMBO  Felice Holman

A great American novel that deserves far greater fame in Britain. Artemis Slake is 'born an orphan at the age of 13, small, near-sighted, dreaming, bruised, an outlander in the city of his birth'. Fleeing from constant bullying, he goes underground, literally. He finds a cave in New York's subway system and doesn't go home again. From his hideout, cautiously, he builds a new, almost-independent life, forming delicate relationships with subterranean people who, to his surprise, do not want to hurt him.

The story is free of sentimentality, even of pity, and Holman's writing is wonderful. Somehow it manages to be dense and rich but laid-back at the same time; sometimes it jolts and sparks like a speeding underground train. And it's miraculously compact – a mere 90 pages. An unmissable masterpiece.

**Mal Peet**

### Next?

More books about running away and the problems it brings? Try Keith Gray's *Runner* and *Warehouse* (UTBG 423) or Steven Herrick's *The Simple Gift* (UTBG 363). In *Fake* by K.K. Beck, two boys run away from a centre for juvenile rehabilitation.

*Underworld* by Catherine MacPhail is about a group of kids trapped underground, and how they survive.

# SLAM  Nick Hornby

### Next?

Nick Hornby's books are all about men, boys, and men who are still boys. Try the football-fixated *Fever Pitch* next. (UTBG 131)

There are some brilliant books in which having a baby feature; try Siobhan Dowd's *A Swift Pure Cry* (UTBG 385), *Blue Moon* (UTBG 50) by Julia Green, or *Dear Nobody* (UTBG 101) by Berlie Doherty.

Sixteen-year-old Sam's life is just taking off; first serious girlfriend, plans for college, and newly free of his mum's latest 'rubbish boyfriend'. However, life has other plans for Sam when his girlfriend announces that she's expecting his baby, a slam worse than any hard fall he's had while skateboarding, his other passion. Don't expect this to be just another issues book though. Sam seeks advice from the poster of his skater hero, Tony Hawk, and through their imagined conversations and weird glimpses into the future, Sam starts to grow up and shoulder his responsibilities. The strength of this story is in the telling. Sam is a typical, honest, straight-talking, endearing and very funny teenager you can't help rooting for. And this being Hornby, there's a very definite soundtrack linking the characters and events. Gripping stuff for girls and boys, skaters or not.

**Eileen Armstrong**

# SLAUGHTERHOUSE 5  Kurt Vonnegut

**Next?**

For another war book – that makes you see just how horrible it is – try *Catch-22* by Joseph Heller, one of the funniest books written about this subject – and the scariest. (UTBG 68)

Or for a vision of the future that'll chill you, where knowledge and ideas are forbidden and books are burned, try Ray Bradbury's *Fahrenheit 451*. (UTBG 126)

Or maybe you fancy something else by Mr Vonnegut? Try *Breakfast of Champions*, a hilarious, cynical roller coaster of a novel.

Kurt Vonnegut lived through the firebombing of Dresden in World War II and then spent 20 years trying to find a way to write about it. He finally came up with this – one of the most famous anti-war novels of all time. Billy Pilgrim, with his blue and ivory feet, stumbles through time and space. Billy becomes an optometrist, a private in the US army, a specimen on show in an alien zoo, an innocent, a father, a son, a husband – quite often all at once. People die. A lot of people die. So it goes.

Absurd, tragic and very funny, this is Vonnegut's masterpiece. As a plea for less butchery and less blind obedience to authority, it sears.

**Leonie Flynn**

# THE SLIGHTLY TRUE STORY OF CEDAR B. HARTLEY  Martine Murray

What can I say about this book, other than that it's extraordinary? It reads like an Australian Margaret Atwood with an added layer of quirkiness. For starters, Cedar B. Hartley's real name isn't Cedar B. Hartley at all, but Lana Monroe, who as well as telling the story draws weird little pictures with captions such as 'terrapin inside a sock' and 'Oscar in cone shape'. This is a story about being an outsider, growing up and growing friendships with a big dose of acrobatics thrown in for good measure. And then there's Oscar with his brain injury, Kite (who's a bird person) and Stinky the dog. If there's only one book you read from this guide, make it this one!

**Philip Ardagh**

**Next?**

You'll want to read the sequels; *Cedar B. Hartley: Flying High*, and *Cedar B. Hartley: Upside Down*.

Martine Murray is also an illustrator. Check out her drawings in *Henrietta* or *A Moose Called Mouse*?

More quirky characters? Try *Stargirl* (UTBG 375), *Artemis Fowl* (UTBG 29) by Eoin Colfer, or *Up on Cloud Nine* (UTBG 415) by Anne Fine.

# SNAKEHEAD   Ann Halam

Ann Halam's retelling of the Perseus and Andromeda story will entrance readers who thrive on the drama of myth and legend. When Perseus meets a mysterious girl amidst the bustle of the market, he is captivated by her beauty and intelligence. But the path of true love does not run smoothly: the girl is Andromeda and her destiny decrees that she must, in a pact to save her people, sacrifice herself to the Kraken. A powerful secret will perish with her, unless Perseus fulfils the Medusa quest and brings back the head of the Gorgon – and that will come at a personal cost.

Halam's Perseus and Andromeda are real flesh-and-blood characters, and their love story is convincing. No passive princess miserably awaiting her fate, this Andromeda strides purposefully toward her destiny. Meanwhile, the capricious gods, capable of unthinking cruelty and tolerated rather than revered, are as much a part of daily life as the hustle and bustle of the market place. This is a beautifully rendered tale of hope and survival, which combines a fast-moving plot with wit and intelligence.

**Nikki Gamble**

## Next?

Anne Halam writes witty, complex, intriguing stories; her other books to try include *Taylor Five* (UTBG 389) and the chilling dystopian world of *Siberia*.

There are more star-crossed Greek lovers in *The Penelopiad: The Myth of Penelope and Odysseus* by Margaret Atwood. It'll make you rethink what you think you know about *The Odyssey*!

Holly Black mixes up the myth of Faerie in her books; try *Tithe*. (UTBG 397)

## EPIC FANTASY

The **Earthsea** quartet by Ursula le Guin

The **Dragons of Pern** series by Anne McCaffrey

The **Black Magician** trilogy by Trudi Canavan

The **Inheritance Cycle** by Christopher Paolini

The **Farseer** trilogy by Robin Hobb

**The Belgariad** by David Eddings

**The Lord of the Rings** by J.R.R. Tolkein

# SNOW FALLING ON CEDARS   David Guterson ✹ ✹ ✹

**Next?**

More Guterson? Try *Our Lady of the Forest*, about a girl who has visions or his collection of stories, *The Country Ahead of Us, the Country Behind*.

For another portrait of a small fishing town, try Annie Proulx's *The Shipping News*.

A book about Japan just after the war is Arthur Golden's *Memoirs of a Geisha*. It reads like a true story, but it's not. (UTBG 260)

This book is set in 1954 on the island of San Piedro off the coast of Washington. The death of a local white fisherman in suspicious circumstances leads to the arrest of Japanese-American Kabuo Miyamoto, who is charged with his murder. The narration is by the local newspaper editor and one-time boyfriend of the accused's wife. The story then twists and turns and we're treated to flashbacks to the 1940s, following the bombing of Pearl Harbour, when the island's Japanese-Americans were sent to internment camps. The imagery is beautiful and vivid, and the characters rich. The book becomes a courtroom drama, a romance, a murder mystery and an account of the war seen from the side of the 'enemy'. If you've seen the movie don't be put off. This book is priceless.

**Ileana Antonopoulou**

# THE SNOW GOOSE   Paul Gallico ✹

This moving and haunting little story was first published in 1940. It's about the relationship that develops between a lonely older man (Philip Rhyader) and a young girl, Frith, who brings him a wounded snow goose to be healed. Philip, an artist, feels a special connection with the wild birds on the marshes near his home on the east coast: 'His heart was filled with love for wild and hunted things'. It's this same feeling that drives him to take his boat to help rescue the soldiers stranded at Dunkirk, joining many other 'little ships'.

The story is simply and beautifully told. It captures perfectly the remote setting, and the birds, and the feelings of the girl who comes to love the lonely and isolated man.

**Next?**

The stories in Michael Morpurgo's collection *The White Horse of Zennor* also have a haunting quality and a strong sense of place. (Incidentally, Michael is a *Snow Goose* fan, too.)

William Fiennes's *The Snow Geese* is a blend of travel and autobiography, as the author follows migrating geese from Canada to the Gulf of Mexico.

Most of Paul Gallico's novels are now out of print, but do try and hunt out *Thomasina*, about a girl and a cat.

**Julia Green**

# SOLACE OF THE ROAD  Siobhan Dowd

**Next?**

*Junk* is a tough-talking, addictive book about runaways, drugs and prostitution. (UTBG 218)

*Girl, Missing* is about another runaway, but this time she's thinks she may have been kidnapped as a baby. (UTBG 156)

Joan Bauer's *Rules of the Road* features another girl with a difficult home life, who takes to the road and learns a lot along the way.

Or try another of Siobhan Dowd's acclaimed novels, such as *A Swift, Pure Cry* (UTBG 385) *or Bog Child* (UTBG 51).

Holly Hogan puts on a glamorous blonde wig, steals herself a dress that shows off her slim-slam hips, and turns herself into Solace the Unstoppable – running away from her miserable life, and off to Ireland to find her mammy.

Holly meets a whole lot of people on her journey, who help her find out where she really belongs – a vegan truck driver with God inside him; a girl who gives her a free sandwich; a small, earnest boy in a museum. And she looks deeper and deeper into her past as she goes.

You live inside Holly's head the whole time you're reading, travelling with her and feeling her pain, her defiance, her sassiness and yearning need for love. It's an absorbing place to be.

**Susan Reuben**

# THE SONG OF AN INNOCENT BYSTANDER
## Ian Bone

Imagine that when you are nine years old you are one of the hostages in a siege – a man with a gun holds you and a load of adults who don't know you in a fast-food restaurant, because he HATES the company that owns it. Imagine that you survive, and ten years later a journalist wants to interview you. But imagine, too, that you have worse memories – and guilt – from that horrible event than anyone knows or imagines. Except the strangers who were with you.

This book examines terrible memories, and the reader experiences them with the young girl. Has she been damaged? Can she be healed? It's gripping, sometimes horribly so, but exceptionally real and moving.

**Next?**

*Looking for JJ* is another great book that examines how a terrible event in childhood can have resonances in later life. (UTBG 240)

*Noughts and Crosses* by Malorie Blackman also vividly portrays young people dealing with guilt and remorse within a traumatic setting. (UTBG 290)

*Z for Zachariah* by Robert C. O'Brien is about a girl's disturbing encounter with an older man. (UTBG 452)

**Nicola Morgan**

# SOPHIE'S WORLD
## Jostein Gaarder

### Next?

If you want to read more about philosophy, watch out! Many books tend to be a bit stodgy. But anything with the word 'beginner' in the title is usually a safe bet.

*The Bluffer's Guide to Philosophy* is glib, quite rude, very funny and very useful!

*Illusions: Adventures of a Reluctant Messiah* by Richard Bach helps, too.

Jostein Gaarder has written many books for children. Try *The Solitaire Mystery*, a philosophical novel with a dwarf.

This amazing book starts with two simple questions: Who are you? and Where does the world come from? When 14-year-old Sophie finds these questions written on pieces of paper in her mailbox one day, her extraordinary journey into the history and mystery of philosophy is only just beginning.

If you thought philosophy was dull and boring, or only for large-brained geniuses – think again! It really is astonishing and fascinating stuff, and it's so fundamental that it relates to everything we do. The story itself is full of suspense and excitement, with plenty of twists and turns, and it'll keep you thinking and guessing right to the end.

**Kevin Brooks**

# SPIGGOT'S QUEST
## Garry Kilworth

A college boy called Jack crashes his motorbike and finds himself trapped in a world where all of mankind's myths, legends and fairy tales are frighteningly real. He meets a boggart called Spiggot who has been sent by his father to deliver a suit of golden armour to the King of the Fairies. He is accompanied by Kling, a giant water rat. Spiggot is tempted into wearing the armour himself to do battle with a foe. His quest through Liofwende involves encounters with trolls, goblins, ogres, gnomes and fairies. The fantasy world is vividly brought to life and there is also humour, particularly where the reader shares Jack's perspective on the mythical world.

**Brenda Marshall**

### Next?

This is the first book in the **Knights of Liofwende** trilogy; next is *Mallmoc's Castle*, then *Boggart and Fen*. Or try more Garry Kilworth with *The Hundred Towered City*, which mixes magic, Prague and a search for lost parents.

*Faerie Wars* by Herbie Brennan is another book where the human and fairy worlds meet.

In *Sabriel*, the first of a trilogy by Garth Nix, a girl has to make a terrifying journey in the hope of rescuing her father. (UTBG 339)

# SPINDLE'S END  Robin McKinley

**Next?**

Robin McKinley has also retold the story of 'Beauty and the Beast' in *Beauty*. (UTBG 36)

And if you like complex retellings of traditional tales, try Adèle Geras's *The Tower Room*, or Angela Carter's *The Bloody Chamber*, a collection of short stories based on fairy tales.

For more magic with a twist, read *Wicked: The Life and Times of the Wicked Witch of the West* by Gregory Maguire – it challenges our notions of good and evil.

You might think you know the story of 'Sleeping Beauty' but you don't, not as Robin McKinley tells it. The country in which it takes place so drips with magic that every ordinary household tries to have a fairy on hand to control it.

Katriona's aunt is a fairy, but it is Kat herself who has the adventure, which involves rescuing a certain bewitched baby princess and keeping her in hiding till she comes of age. The last part of the book involves a cunning plan to outwit the wicked witch and becomes very surreal indeed.

Don't be put off by the slow pace by which the story unfolds: you'll find complex magic, romance and masses of atmosphere.

**Mary Hoffman**

# SPUD  John van de Ruit

John Milton – known as 'Spud' – is 13 and the time has come for him to start boarding school. It doesn't bode well. He will be forced to share a dormitory with a set of oddballs and misfits (Rambo, Gecko, Rain Man, Mad Dog…); together they make up the 'Crazy Eight'. To their new dorm-mate they seem peculiar, infuriating and impossible; but to us, reading Spud's diary, they are very, very funny. Poor Spud's home life is much the same – his parents and his grandmother (Wombat) are every bit as mad as his school friends, and a joy to read about.

With all the usual boarding-school exploits you'd expect, plus a very beautiful girl (Mermaid), a possible ghost (Mango), some bullying, some politics, a school play and lots of missing underpants, *Spud* is a delightful chronicle of a boy's struggles to grow up in a crazy world – sometimes moving, but more often hilarious, full of memorable characters and brilliant set-piece moments.

**Next?**

The follow-up, *Spud – the Madness Continues…* takes Spud into his second year at boarding school.

Spud's closest literary forebear is Adrian Mole – read his diary! (UTBG 347)

Why not sample some of Spud's own reading? There's a lot to try – the classics *Catch-22* (UTBG 68) and *Catcher in the Rye* (UTBG 69) for starters.

**Daniel Hahn**

# SPY HIGH series A.J. Butcher

**Next?**

Move on to the rest of the series: *The Chaos Connection*; *The Serpent Scenario*; *The Paranoia Plot*; *The Soul Stealer* and *The Annihilation Agenda*.

Or Chris Ryan's **Alpha Force** series: try *Rat-Catcher*. (UTBG 19)

Or read Sam Hutton's equally gripping *Deep End*; it's the first in the **Special Agents** series.

Deveraux College is an exclusive boarding school for teenagers with great potential. But not just academic potential – these teens are training to be secret agents. To those enrolled at Deveraux, it's known as Spy High.

Book one of the series, *The Frankenstein Factory*, introduces six new recruits – Bond Team – and we watch them face the demands of Spy High training, including battles against Stromfeld, a virtual reality megalomaniac villain.

This isn't a book to read if you're looking for beautifully turned passages of descriptive prose, nor indeed for detailed and sophisticated characterisation; but if you want a gripping story, an easy read with breathless pace, they don't come any better.

**Daniel Hahn**

# THE SPY WHO CAME IN FROM THE COLD John le Carré

A classic spy story. It's a story of secrets and schemes, betrayals, double agents and triple agents, barbed-wire checkpoints, interrogations. The story twists and turns back on itself, as we try to work out whose side everyone is really on.

British secret agent Leamas is on one final mission to eliminate East German head of counter-espionage Mundt; but it seems that Mundt may really be a double agent for the British. Except he isn't really. Except he is. Is he?

This is a world where you can't trust anyone, can't believe anything they say; Leamas can trust only himself, his girl Liz and his boss Control. And yet can he? As he gets closer and closer to the nail-biting finale, the question of who his real friends are will take on the greatest importance imaginable. Gripping stuff.

**Next?**

For more spies and complicated plots, try Len Deighton's **Hook, Line and Sinker** series.

Or for another classic le Carré, look no further than *A Perfect Spy*.

For the opposite take on spies, try Ian Fleming's **James Bond** books. (UTBG 211)

A wartime story about boys who take their spying a little too seriously is Michael Frayn's *Spies*.

**Daniel Hahn**

# STARGIRL   Jerry Spinelli

I recommend *Stargirl*, unreservedly, wherever I go. It's a fabulous, lyrical, magical book about individuality and being different; about being yourself and having the maturity to allow everyone else to be themselves, too. It's also about being one of the herd, peer pressure, and the cautionary tale of what happens when you give in to that force and don't follow your own heart and your own star. Furthermore, it's a joyous story of first love, bittersweet and poignant, full of tension and emotion, beauty and tragedy, thrilling, inspiring, and a homage to non-conformity.

If ever there was a book that should be compulsory 'rites-of-passage' reading for everyone, male and female, this is the one. Unforgettable.

**Chris d'Lacey**

### Next?

The next book is *Love, Stargirl*, and in it Stargirl writes to Leo, and slowly comes to terms with losing him.

Quirky reads are my favourites. I thoroughly recommend *Holes* (UTBG 184) by Louis Sachar, *Joey Pigza Swallowed the Key* by Jack Gantos, and *Saffy's Angel* (UTBG 340) by Hilary McKay.

Another Jerry Spinelli? Try *Eggs*, in which two troubled and damaged children find hope with each other.

# STAR OF THE SEA   Joseph O'Connor

### Next?

There's a sequel (of sorts), *Redemption Falls*, which takes up the story 18 years later; a big, bold, breathtaking read.

Another Joseph O'Connor? Try the very different *Inishowen*, a black comedy about relationships.

If you like a story of murder at sea, why not try *The False Inspector Dew* by Peter Lovesey?

Herman Melville also wrote about life at sea in *Billy Budd* and the classic (and immense!) *Moby Dick*.

This book tells the stories of the captain and passengers of the *Star of the Sea*, a ship sailing to New York in 1847. Through them, the author examines the misery caused by the Irish potato famine, one of the greatest disasters of the 19th century, which killed as many as one million people and forced another two million to emigrate. We see the issues through the eyes of all levels of society, from the fallen aristocrat eating fine food in first class to the peasants eating gruel below deck, who have had to sell everything they own to pay for their passage. In the background is a deeply political story of social upheaval, but the narrative is strong enough to make it feel like more of a murder-mystery than a historical document.

**Anthony Reuben**

# STARSEEKER Tim Bowler

Luke has exceptionally sensitive hearing. He is also, like his dead father, musically talented. Sounds dominate his world: playing the piano, the music in his head, hearing other sounds and being captivated or fascinated by them. One part of what Bowler does so well in this book is to give us an insight into what it might be like to be 'gifted'. But it's also the story of a boy trying to come to terms with his mother's new partner. Both these elements are cleverly bound together by a gripping thriller plot about Luke's struggle to break free of Skin and Daz, bad boys whose spell he has fallen under. And Bowler evokes so well the awful dilemma of someone who is being intimidated by bullies into carrying out their dirty work for them. Luke is supposed to break into an old lady's house and steal a jewellery box, but the house holds far more treasure than mere jewellery...

**Neil Arksey**

**Next?**

More Tim Bowler? Try *Apocalypse* (UTBG 27) or *River Boy* (UTBG 332).

*You Don't Know Me* is also about a boy trying to deal with his mother's new partner. (UTBG 452)

A different book about being 'gifted' is John Wyndham's *Chocky*. Matthew starts counting in binary code, which is odd; and odder still, who's that living inside his head?

# THE STERKARM HANDSHAKE Susan Price

**Next?**

Find out what happened next in *The Sterkarm Kiss*. Or for more Susan Price, read *Ghost Drum*, a fantasy set in a frozen country.

Caleb is on a tourist trip from the future when he gets caught up in a murderous plan in Ian Beck's *Pastworld*.

Will Peterson's *Triskellion* features centuries-old evil and secrets. (UTBG 404)

Like all great fantasies, *The Sterkarm Handshake* is simple. Every part clicks into place, making exact sense.

A multinational corporation develops the technology to travel into the past to exploit untapped resources, but fails to take into account the people they will encounter. The time tunnel is situated in the Borders. 21st-century scientists meet 16th-century Sterkarms: a fierce, amoral clan of border raiders who live by stealing and fighting. The Sterkarms think the scientists are elves, so that's all right then...

Susan Price makes use of history, language and myth, setting past and present at angles to act as mirrors, each world illuminating the other. The cultural differences can be very funny, but the implications are ominous and the consequences potentially tragic, not least for lovers Per and Andrea, caught between worlds.

**Celia Rees**

# STONE COLD
## Robert Swindells

Driven from home by a drunken, abusive stepfather, teenage Link is forced to live on the streets. In the hands of a less skilful writer this might have just been an 'issues' book about homelessness. And Swindells does indeed detail the grinding misery of sleeping rough, but he is also a master storyteller. The inclusion of a chilling and predatory serial killer adds an extra dimension to the novel. Though passionate, the book isn't in any way preachy. The plot and sub-plot sweep along, drawing the reader towards the satisfyingly unsettling conclusion. This is the novel for which Robert Swindells deservedly won the 1994 Carnegie Medal. It's a terrific read.

**Alan Gibbons**

### Next?

For a different take on killing, try Nick Gifford's *Incubus*, in which a boy's father is found guilty of multiple murders.

For gangs, sex, poverty and racism, read Bali Rai's *The Crew*.

All Robert Swindells's books are brilliant. Try the terrifying *Brother in the Land* or *Shrapnel*, set in the confused world of bomb-ravaged England.

---

# STONE HEART  Charlie Fletcher

### Next?

You have to find out what happens next, so look for *Iron Hand* and *Silver Tongue*.

London-based adventures abound; try *Darkside* by Tom Becker, about a London under London; *Un Lun Dun* by China Miéville (UTBG 414), about, amazingly, what happens to all the things Londoners throw away; and Sam Enthoven's *The Black Tattoo*.

Or for another series that's just as thrilling and terrifying; try Joseph Delaney's **Wardstone Chronicles** starting with *The Spook's Apprentice*.

After breaking a dragon statue in a fit of rage, George finds himself fleeing through a hidden London where two tribes of statues, spits and taints, are sliding from hostility into outright war. The only human who is not blind to his plight is a girl named Edie, a 'glint' with the power to see the past and 'make stones weep'.

This is one of those books that show us a mysterious and magical world, and then make us realise that we are already living in it. The author uses real locations, and they continue to *feel* real even when terrifying stone pterodactyls drag themselves from walls, or metal Minotaurs battle on double-deckers. Exciting, macabre and cinematically vivid.

**Frances Hardinge**

# THE STONES OF MUNCASTER CATHEDRAL
## Robert Westall

There are actually two long short stories in this book, and while 'Brangwyn Gardens' is a creepy enough tale of the supernatural, it is the title piece, 'The Stones of Muncaster Cathedral', that shines.

Joe Clarke is a steeplejack who has been hired to restore the stonework on the tower of Muncaster Cathedral. Like all steeplejacks he knows that some jobs are unlucky, but there's something different about this one. Right from the start he senses something present in the claustrophobic stones around him; something that turns out to be full of evil intent towards the young boys of the town. A truly shocking ending awaits as Joe finally discovers the secrets of the tower and its hideous gargoyle.

**Marcus Sedgwick**

**Next?**

This story by Robert Westall is a bit older than some of his others, but you could try **Urn Burial** or **The Scarecrows** (UTBG 342), both of which are deeply scary and unsettling.

Or read **The Dark Tower** sequence by Stephen King, starting with **The Gunslinger**.

For more sophisticated horror, try H.P. Lovecraft. Read any of his extremely bizarre tales and enjoy!

# STORM  Suzanne Fisher Staples

**Next?**

Something else by the same author? Try **Shiva's Fire**, about a girl in India born with strange abilities and a gift for dance.

Rosa Guy's **The Friends** is about prejudice of all sorts.

For another powerful story of racism in America during the Depression, read Harper Lee's classic **To Kill a Mockingbird**. (UTBG 398)

Or try Mary Ann Rodman's **Yankee Girl**, about a white girl moving to the Deep South in 1964.

This is a beautifully written and deeply moving account of two teenagers – a black girl, Tunes, and a white boy, Buck. Tunes's father works for Buck's family and they have grown up together. But friendship and loyalty are tested when Tunes becomes the suspect in a local murder.

You never doubt for one minute that Tunes has been falsely accused and that the threatened injustice is a result of racism. And any momentary doubts that Buck has are quickly brushed aside. But as the story progresses, with Tunes's young life in the balance, the teenagers' desperate struggle against the blinkered attitudes of local white adults is painful to follow – all the way to its sad and courageously truthful end.

**Neil Arksey**

# STRAIT IS THE GATE André Gide

I read this book in my late teens and just picking it off the shelf again gave me a jolt of almost physical pain. The story concerns Jerome's fierce love for his cousin Alissa, a lofty meeting of souls where Alissa's devotion to 'something higher than herself' allows God, in Jerome's view, to tear off his lover's wings. But in the battle between holy virtue and personal happiness, Jerome himself is, in fact, not without blame. With a similarly sacrificial devotion he allows himself to believe that 'any path, provided it climbed upwards' will lead to his dearest one. And so in just over 128 stark pages the doomed lovers ascend inexorably to a climax that is as bleak as it is compelling.

**Nicky Singer**

> **Next?**
>
> If you're now yearning for a rather more instinctual sexual awakening, try D.H. Lawrence's *The Virgin and the Gipsy*.
>
> Or for other French views of love and passion, try Gustave Flaubert's *Madame Bovary* and *A Sentimental Education*, or Françoise Sagan's *Bonjour Tristesse* (UTBG 52).
>
> Or the different, comic-strip *Gemma Bovary* by Posy Simmonds.
>
> Gide is not an easy writer, but he makes you think. Try *La Symphonie Pastorale*, about a blind girl learning bitter truths about the world.

# THE STRANGE AFFAIR OF ADELAIDE HARRIS Leon Garfield

> **Next?**
>
> More Garfield; he was a brilliant storyteller. Look out for *Smith*, *John Diamond* or *Devil-in-the-Fog*.
>
> For more funny historical fiction, try Mark Twain's *A Connecticut Yankee at King Arthur's Court*; or to find out what happened to unwanted babies in another time, *Coram Boy* (UTBG 87).
>
> Joan Aiken wrote great historical adventure – read her *Midnight Is a Place*.

This is one of the funniest school stories ever written. We're in the past – the 18th century. Bostock and Harris, two schoolboy friends, commit a dreadful deed: having been taught the history of ancient Sparta, they decide that they, too, would like to expose a baby to be either eaten, or else rescued by a wild animal. They start a huge hue and cry among the masters and boys of the school, and the whole thing attracts the attention of a sinister detective, a Mr Raven, whose mind is still not black enough to plumb the depths of Bostock and Harris. This book has an amazing ending – the cheekiest and most appalling you will ever meet.

**Jill Paton Walsh**

# STRANGE BOY  Paul Magrs

Growing up is never easy, but for ten-year-old David it's more difficult than for most. His parents' marriage breaks up and he has a bunch of awkward relations to deal with. But luckily David has superpowers – or so he thinks. He also finds he's attracted to John, the older boy down the road.

*Strange Boy* is a delightfully tender, funny and honest account of a childhood spent in the north east of England in the 1970s – and immensely readable. All the characters are sympathetically drawn and you may discover that, as original a creation as David is, you find lots in him to identify with – especially if you've ever felt slightly on the outside of things.

**Sherry Ashworth**

> **Next?**
>
> There'a a sequel: *The Diary of a 'Dr Who' Addict*. And don't forget to look out for Paul's *Hands Up!*, about a puppet, a boy and great deal of whacky humour.
>
> *Brothers* also treats the subject of a boy discovering his true sexuality with delicacy and understanding. (UTBG 64)
>
> *The Wrong Boy* is a funny and recognisable book about angsty adolescence. (UTBG 446)

# STRANGE MEETING  Susan Hill

> **Next?**
>
> One of the most famous books about the First World War is *All Quiet on the Western Front* by Erich Maria Remarque. (UTBG 19)
>
> Susan Hill wrote a clutch of short, brilliant novels and then stopped, in favour of other kinds of books. Seek out her early books, especially *I'm the King of the Castle* (UTBG 201) and the terrifying *The Woman in Black* (UTBG 443).
>
> Or if you like crime, read her later books, starting with *The Various Haunts of Men*.
>
> Or try *How Many Miles to Babylon?* by Jennifer Johnston, another bleak book about the First World War.

It's 1916, in the midst of the First World War (which will be over by Christmas, so they're told). After three months' active service, John Hilliard returns to his family, wounded. Back at the frontline, he finds that his battalion has altered drastically – fatally. More changes occur, of which the most significant is meeting David Barton. Barton seems able to articulate a wealth of feeling that Hilliard never thought possible. He writes endless letters back home, describes heartfelt emotions about the brutality of war, and becomes close to Hilliard. Yet Hilliard still feels he does not understand him. Their bond intensifies as death looms ever closer. Compelling and devastating.

**Jon Appleton**

# STRANGERS ON A TRAIN   Patricia Highsmith ✺✺✺

## Next?

Almost everything Patricia Highsmith has written is worth reading, particularly *The Tremor Of Forgery* and *The Talented Mr Ripley* (UTBG 386) and its sequels.

How about another book that was filmed by the great Alfred Hitchcock? Try Robert Bloch's *Psycho*.

Another great crime novel is Dashiell Hammett's *The Glass Key*, with its TB-ridden, gambling, hard-drinking hero.

Two men get talking on a train. Both want somebody murdered. Each needs a perfect alibi. So they agree to swap murders. Or at least one of them – an alcoholic called Bruno who turns out to be a psychopath – thinks they've agreed. So he carries out the murder. Complications arise…

Highsmith's a great suspense novelist, rather than a crime writer, and this novel became a fine Hitchcock film with a script by Raymond Chandler. I can't easily explain why I'm so drawn to her work, which shows remarkable sympathy for sociopaths, yet little for her own sex. Although American, she was only greatly appreciated in Europe. Her work is dark, laconic, unsettling and almost always gripping.

**David Belbin**

# STRAVAGANZA: CITY OF MASKS
## Mary Hoffman

Is there any city more magical than Venice? Yes – but one must travel to another, parallel world, where it is known as Belleza, in the land of Talia, to find it. This is what happens to Lucien, a young cancer patient, when he inadvertently comes into possession of an item from Belleza, which was brought to his world by a Stravagante, or traveller between the worlds. This object turns Lucien into a Stravagante, too, and somehow he has to learn how to cope in both worlds; one where he is recovering from chemotherapy, and another where the dangers are different, but just as terrible.

This is a thrilling story, with both the gritty, modern normality of Islington and the lush, Renaissance beauty of Belleza exquisitely described. Lucien's adventures are breathtakingly exciting and, in the end, deeply poignant.

## Next?

The sequels: *City of Stars*, *City of Flowers*, *City of Secrets* and *City of Ships*. Though each book has a different boy or girl as the focus, all the characters weave in and out of the books. Or try the different *The Falconer's Knot* (UTBG 127).

*The Undrowned Child* by Michelle Lovric is set in the real Venice of 100 years ago. Real, but with added magic and mystery!

**Elizabeth Reid**

# HORROR AND GHOST STORIES –
## spooks, crooks and mystery books
### by Hugh Scott

Listen. Weird things happen. I was sitting alone and a pen rose up off the arm of an armchair, then it dropped to the floor. When I was in primary school, my best friend passed me on the stairs, and when I got to the playground, he was walking along the pavement.

Other strange events have stirred my imagination; but the main fascination for me is this: if such things can happen, then there is more to life than being born, doing things, and then dying. So I write spooky stories. I love to be involved in puzzles that gradually reveal solutions.

When I wrote *The Place Between*, I was creating a ghost story where somebody walked through walls, and somebody else disappeared before the eyes of startled witnesses. These things happen. But when you write them as a story, you must explain how it all works, and I was astonished to discover, when the book was finished, that I had come up with an explanation for ghosts.

And this is what writing (and reading) are about: *discovery*! Finding out what is possible, and occasionally revealing an answer to a great mystery. Aren't we all fascinated by mystery? Isn't every child and adult at least slightly curious about the Loch Ness monster? And flying saucers?

We are always asking questions, and sometimes we find answers. Then we dig into the next mystery, swiftly and keenly, because we love the unknown. If there is no mystery in our lives, we make one by writing or reading the next book, and send the hairs on the back of our necks rising in terror.

---

### BOOKS TO MAKE YOU WANT TO KEEP THE LIGHT ON...

*Lord Loss* by Darren Shan

*The Watch House* by Robert Westall

*The Rats* by James Herbert

*Alchemy* by Margaret Mahy

*Frankenstein* by Mary Shelley

*The Spook's Apprentice* by Joseph Delaney

*The Fourth Horseman* by Kate Thompson

*Breathe* by Cliff McNish

*Scared to Death* by Alan Gibbons

*The Summoning* by E.E. Richardson

Let me tell you this: if you love weird stories, go to your local charity shop and look for volumes of ghost stories. Most of these stories will be old-fashioned, like 'The Upper Berth' by F. Marion Crawford, where the storyteller books his passage to sail to America, and finds that his companion in the upper berth is a drowned man, and he himself will be next to go overboard – unless he can find a way of escaping!

Or find perhaps 'The Whistling Room', which is a scream-making tale of a room with a past – and also a horrifying present. My heart almost stopped beating when I was reading this amazing story. It was written by William Hope Hodgson. Some of the scariest stories of ghosts and the macabre were written a while ago – try E.F. Benson's 'The Tale of an Empty House'; the *Ghost Stories* of M.R. James (UTBG 153); Edgar Allan Poe's *The Fall of the House of Usher*, and his *Tales of Mystery and Imagination* (UTBG 387); or Algernon Blackwood's *Ancient Sorceries and Other Weird Tales*. H.P. Lovecraft wrote short stories and novellas that take you into other dimensions, leaving you gasping with relief when you remember you are merely reading.

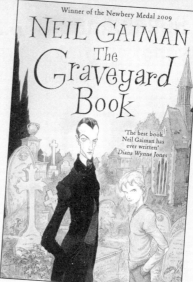

Winner of the Newbery Medal 2009

NEIL GAIMAN
The Graveyard Book

'The best book Neil Gaiman has ever written'
*Diana Wynne Jones*

Tithe
A Modern Faerie Tale
HOLLY BLACK

### ROMANCING THE SUPERNATURAL

*Twilight* by Stephenie Meyer

*Wicked Lovely* by Melissa Marr

*Tithe* by Holly Black

**The Morganville Vampires** series by Rachel Caine

*City of Bones* by Cassandra Clare

*The Book of Shadows* by Cate Tiernan

*Night World: The Secret Vampire* by L.J. Smith

**Blue Bloods** series by Melissa de la Cruz

**House of Night** series by Kristen Cast

*Generation Dead* by Daniel Waters

**Mortal Instruments** series by Cassandra Clare

# SUGAR RUSH  Julie Burchill

*Sugar Rush* does exactly what it says on the cover. It's a high-speed, toxic slice of teen life, an emotional melting pot, a story that's so evocative you can smell the perfume, taste the vodka, hear the soundtrack. This is Julie Burchill's first teen novel, although she's been writing (mostly journalism) since punk rock upset the music-biz apple-cart back in the 1970s. Her debut follows Kim who, having had to move schools, meets, falls for, and has a full-on relationship with Maria, a.k.a. Sugar. The book, which has no pretensions to be anything but as entertaining as possible, is set in Brighton and holds up a very honest mirror to what it's like to be young and in lust.

**Graham Marks**

## Next?

Read the equally outrageous sequel: *Sweet*.

Another book set in Brighton and just as outrageous is by one of Julie Burchill's friends, Sara Lawrence: *High Jinx*. Or try Julie's *Made in Brighton*, which charts the state of the nation via one seaside town.

*Weetzie Bat*, part of the **Dangerous Angels** series, is about a group of friends / lovers living in LA.

You'll find a more intense look at falling for another girl in *Oranges Are Not the Only Fruit*. (UTBG 299)

## BREAKING BOUNDARIES

*Doing It* by Melvin Burgess

*Killing God* by Kevin Brooks

*Junk* by Melvin Burgess

*Forever* by Judy Blume

*Inexcusable* by Chris Lynch

*The Cement Garden* by Ian McEwan

*Tender Morsels* by Margo Lanagan

# SURRENDER  Sonya Hartnett

### Next?

All of Sonya Hartnett's novels are worth reading. Both **Thursday's Child** (UTBG 396) and **Stripes of the Sidestep Wolf** have won major book prizes and **The Silver Donkey** is a very different book about the First World War.

**Surrender** is in a category of its own, but elements of it made me think of Anne Fine's **Up On Cloud Nine** (UTBG 415) and **The Tulip Touch** (UTBG 407).

Another book that turns everything on its head in the final pages is Meg Rosoff's coming-of-age story, **What I Was**. (UTBG 431)

This is possibly the best book that I've read since the first edition of the *UTBG* was published. *Surrender* tells the story of Gabriel and his best (and only) friend Finnigan. Gabriel is 20 and he's dying. Looking back on his short life, he reflects on a childhood of loneliness and abuse – made tolerable only by the presence of the mysterious Finnigan. The book is beautifully written but it is its dénouement that makes it stand head and shoulders above its peers. Sonya Hartnett does something so audacious in the final pages that I got to the end and had to go straight back to the beginning and start it again. I can't recommend *Surrender* highly enough.

**Laura Hutchings**

# A SWIFT PURE CRY  Siobhan Dowd

After the death of her Mam, 15-year-old Michelle 'Shell' Talent looks after her two younger siblings, hindered by her father's alcoholic mood swings and wild displays of religious fervour. When a new young priest arrives in their Irish village, Shell's shattered faith revives, and she feels that her mam's spirit has returned to protect her … just in time for Shell's world to collapse around her.

Although it looks fearlessly at teenage pregnancy, cot death, poverty, alcoholism, bereavement and scandal, this book is never bleak. Instead it is vividly poetic, warm, and finally uplifting. Shell is a likeable innocent, but one with enough inner strength to emerge from her ordeals triumphant and without bitterness.

This beautiful book won the Branford Boase Award, and was short-listed for the Carnegie and the Guardian Children's Prize. After the first page, you will see why.

### Next?

Try another Siobhan Dowd; they're all worth reading. Start with **Bog Child** (UTBG 51) or **Solace of the Road** (UTBG 371).

Chris Lynch's **Inexcusable** is about a boy dealing with the aftermath of a girl's rape. (UTBG 202)

Or try Suzanne Phillips devastating look at a girl whose past is destroying her so much that she wants to self-destruct; **Miss America**.

**Frances Hardinge**

# THE TALENTED MR RIPLEY  Patricia Highsmith ✷✷

In 1950's Italy a penniless young American named Tom Ripley charms his way into a group of rich, arty expatriates. Tom's envy of his host's carefree life and beautiful possessions propels him into murder, several changes of identity and a tense game of cat and mouse as he tries to evade the Italian police and his victim's family. Tom Ripley is a fascinating character: nervy, audacious, imaginative and almost completely amoral. But despite his tendency to bludgeon people to death with blunt instruments, he never becomes a mere monster; this brilliant and unsettling book is written in such a way that you sympathise with Tom entirely in both his crimes and his panicky, improvised attempts to cover them up, and the short chapters and constant twists will keep you turning the pages right to the end.

**Philip Reeve**

> **Next?**
>
> Patricia Highsmith wrote four sequels to *The Talented Mr Ripley*; they are all good, but the first two, *Ripley Under Ground* and *Ripley's Game*, are the best.
>
> A different Highsmith? Read *Strangers on a Train*, about planning a perfect murder. (UTBG 381)
>
> For another story with an anti-hero, try the difficult but amazing classic, *Crime and Punishment* by Fyodor Dostoyevsky. (UTBG 89)

# A TALE OF TWO CITIES  Charles Dickens ✷✷

> **Next?**
>
> More Dickens? Try the very different *Nicholas Nickleby*.
>
> *Fleshmarket* by Nicola Morgan brings a cruel, gory and brutal 19th-century Edinburgh to life. (UTBG 134)
>
> Or for another classic about the French Revolution, read Baroness Orczy's *The Scarlet Pimpernel*. (UTBG 343)
>
> *The Red Necklace* by Sally Gardner is set at the time of the French Revolution – though the style is very different from Dickens, it's just as readable.

I'd read a few Dickens books, and enjoyed them, but hadn't been blown away. Then I read this and my opinion of him changed completely. This is a masterful, suspenseful novel with more twists than any modern thriller. Set at the time of the French Revolution, the two cities are Paris and London, and the story centres on a few unfortunate individuals who get caught up in the madness of the time. Both epic and personal, this is a book that will take your breath away. Plus, it has maybe the strongest opening and closing lines in all literature! Brooding and incisive, it also boasts some wickedly sly scenes – the revelation of why one character always has dirt under his nails had me howling out loud with laughter! Even if you think you don't like Dickens, read this book!

**Darren Shan**

# TALES OF MYSTERY AND IMAGINATION

## Edgar Allan Poe

My aunt Nancy had a spooky bookcase in a dark corner of the hall, and among the books there was this one. Now I loved language when I was a boy; I loved the way words fitted themselves together in my mouth, and I loved finding words I didn't recognise; and in that volume, Poe fitted words together with such precision that I was delighted; and as for words I didn't know – well, the stories were stacked with them and made reading his tales not only a journey into mystery, terror and imagination, but it also revealed a new language.

Edgar Allan Poe's stories are still published, even though he lived in the early 19th century, and they are still as terrifying! Stories like 'The Black Cat', 'The Gold Bug', 'Hop-Frog' and, oh, so many more. Treat yourself to a good scare. I dare you...

**Hugh Scott**

> **Next?**
>
> Anything by Algernon Blackwood. Or M.R. James's *Ghost Stories* (UTBG 153).
>
> How about scary stories in pictures? Start with the first volume of Neil Gaiman's fabulous **The Sandman** series and see how far you dare go... (UTBG 342)
>
> Or try something of Hugh's: *Why Weeps the Brogan?*. (UTBG 437)

# TALES OF THE CITY  Armistead Maupin

> **Next?**
>
> You'll want to read them all! The series is best read in order: *Tales of the City, More Tales of the City, Further Tales of the City, Babycakes, Significant Others, Sure of You*. There's one volume that tells of Michael's later life: *Michael Tolliver Lives*.
>
> Maupin's *Maybe the Moon* and *The Night Listener* are good, too.
>
> Edmund White's trilogy of fictionalised memoirs about growing up gay will be too explicit for some and loved by others; it starts with *A Boy's Own Story*.

I devoured Armistead Maupin's *Tales of the City* on a three-hour bus journey across Crete, then had to wait until I got home before I could read the next in the series. These novels, originally written as a newspaper serial, are compulsive reading: a soap opera about a San Francisco full of promise (and secrets) for gay and straight characters alike. They're insightful and enormous fun, with lots of mysterious twists and aspects that will challenge some readers' prejudices.

The mood gets darker and the writing even better as the series progresses. Maupin only comes a cropper when he sets one novel in the UK – *Babycakes*. (Think of *Friends* set in London and you'll know what I mean.)

**David Belbin**

# TALES OF THE UNEXPECTED  Roald Dahl

**Next?**

Roald Dahl's children's stories can be enjoyed by anyone. Read *The BFG*, *The Witches* and *Danny, the Champion of the World*. Or try his autobiography, *Boy*.

H.H. Munro and O. Henry are two other fine writers of short stories. I am also a fan of the **Rumpole** stories by John Mortimer.

Or if you fancy something more macabre, try Edgar Allan Poe's *Tales of Mystery and Imagination*. (UTBG 387)

As well as his famous children's books, Roald Dahl wrote a series of brilliant short stories for adults, many grotesque and with a twist in the tale.

After the death of a crabbed old professor, his brain is kept alive in a laboratory basin. It has one floating eye. His wife, whose life he has made a misery, wishes to take him home...

Mary Maloney, six months pregnant, kills her husband with a frozen leg of lamb then pops it in the oven. Detectives searching for the murder weapon eat it with relish...

Would you risk a bet with a smart, old gentleman? If you win, you get his gorgeous Cadillac; if you lose he gets to chop off one of your fingers...

Great fun.

**Alan Temperley**

# TAMAR  Mal Peet

1944: two young Dutchmen code-named Tamar and Dart, trained in England by the Special Operations Executive, are parachuted into the Occupied Netherlands to organise local resistance groups who are by no means united in their struggle against the invaders. The liberation of Europe is imminent but conditions are desperate, bringing out the worst as well as the best in people.

50 years later, the suicide of Tamar sends his granddaughter in pursuit of her inheritance – not the money he has left her, but a secret of identity enclosed in the events of that last terrible winter of the war. This is not a testosterone-fuelled actioner but a quiet, remorseless account of civilian heroism, of men and women living in continuous fear, driven to unthinkable acts.

**Next?**

*Between Silk and Cyanide* by Leo Marks (who appears in *Tamar* very briefly), is the true story of World War II secret agents and their wireless codes.

Set in the same period, *Fair Stood the Wind for France* by H.E. Bates tells of a wounded RAF bomber pilot escaping through occupied France.

*Keeper*, also by Mal Peet, is completely different but no less absorbing. (UTBG 222)

**Jan Mark**

# TAYLOR FIVE: THE STORY OF A CLONE GIRL  Ann Halam

Is a clone a whole human being or just a photocopy of one? Taylor asks herself this question as she grows up at a remote jungle refuge for orang-utans. From an early age she is aware that she was cloned so that her body tissues could be used to develop a cure for a terrible disease. Taylor finds this hard to take and refuses to meet her gene mother, an extraordinary scientist. However, Taylor's world is about to collapse as terrorists invade the refuge and she escapes into the jungle with Uncle, an intelligent orang-utan. This is the start of a treacherous journey, and Taylor experiences fear and loss on the way to discovering her true self. Pain and violence are powerfully described in this action-packed sci-fi novel.

**Noga Applebaum**

> ### Next?
> Try Ann Halam's *Siberia* or *Snakehead* (UTBG 369).
>
> Many books discuss the ethical dilemma presented by human cloning. Try *House of the Scorpion* (UTBG 189), *Unique* (UTBG 414) or *Sharp North* (UTBG 358).
>
> *How I Live Now* by Meg Rosoff is about a girl living in a country under violent occupation. (UTBG 190)

# TEACHER'S DEAD  Benjamin Zephaniah

> ### Next?
> More Benjamin Zephaniah? Try both *Face* and *Refugee Boy* (UTBG 330).
>
> For another story of a teenager investigating a murder (this time it's his sister) try the excellent *Road of the Dead* by Kevin Brooks.
>
> Robert Cormier's *Tenderness* is also about a teenage killer; or how about Anne Cassidy's brilliant story of a child murderer, *Looking for JJ* (UTBG 240)?
>
> Or what about a boy who works as a mortician and has an obsession with serial killers? Try the dark world of Dan Wells's *I Am Not a Serial Killer*.

Two boys murder their history teacher in front of a class of their peers. Of course they're guilty and they are duly sentenced and sent to jail. Their classmates are offered counselling, but one boy decides that, in order to come to terms with what he witnessed, he needs to understand exactly *why* the boys killed. Jackson's investigation brings together the widow and the mother of one of the murderers, and gradually he begins to realise that all is not as it seems.

This is a gripping story that grabs your attention from the word go. It manages to be humorous despite the subject matter and, in a world where far too many teenagers carry knives in order to feel safe, it has real relevance.

**Laura Hutchings**

# TEARS OF THE SALAMANDER  Peter Dickinson

**Next?**

More Dickinson?
Look out for *The Kin*.
(UTBG 224)

There's another unusual
fantasy in Janice Hardy's
**The Pain Merchants**
series, in which a girl
must hide her unusual
abilities, starting with
*The Healing Wars:
Book One*.

And for something
magical and zany – Terry
Pratchett's **Discworld**
series. (UTBG 107)

Peter Dickinson is a master storyteller I discovered late in life, but this is a favourite. When 12-year-old Alfredo is sent a talisman by his mysterious uncle Giorgio, tragedy strikes his family. From an ordinary life in his Italian village, the boy is taken by his uncle into the mountain of fire, where family secrets unfold.

This book weaves an enchanting fantasy, where a complex turn of events brings Alfredo to the mystical salamanders, whose tears are turned into gold by his alchemist uncle. But is Uncle Giorgio a force of good or evil? As the boy's grief softens, he realises that his uncle knew about his family's tragedy before it happened, escape seems impossible and, as danger and magic await him, the salamanders talk to him through their music. This mysterious story opens doors into the reader's imagination and is unpredictable to the end.

**David Gilman**

# TERRA INCOGNITA  Sara Wheeler

This travel book has everything: eye-opening descriptions (Antarctica – the Terra Incognita of the title – is 'intact, complete and larger than my imagination could grasp'); very funny characters, including José who married his Harley Davidson, and the penguin experts who can tell individual penguins apart; and there's even a recipe for Antarctic bread-and-butter pudding. The author spent months with polar scientists who are as much a part of her story as are the famous explorers whose lives she recounts. Incidents range from the funny – the seal that unexpectedly pops up through the ice-hole latrine – to the sublime – playing Beethoven's Fifth in the virgin landscape. A warning: you might not think you're interested in Antarctica now, but after this book you will be.

**Jane Darcy**

**Next?**

More classic travel writing?
Try Robyn Davidson's
*Tracks* (about crossing
Australia on a camel),
Bruce Chatwin's **Songlines**
or Patrick Leigh Fermor's
*A Time of Gifts*, about
walking across Europe
in the 1930s.

The best account of the
Scott expedition, by a
man who was on it, is
*The Worst Journey
in the World* by Apsley
Cherry-Garrard. (UTBG 445)

# TESS OF THE D'URBERVILLES Thomas Hardy

**Next?**

If you liked this novel by Hardy, then there are many more to choose from – *Under the Greenwood Tree* and *Far from the Madding Crowd* are many people's favourites.

Another dark love story set against the backdrop of a wild landscape is Emily Brontë's *Wuthering Heights*. (UTBG 447)

Or try the bleak world of Ross Raisin's *God's Own Country*. It's told in dialect and set amongst the isolated Yorkshire moors.

Maybe the best known of Hardy's novels set in his semi-fictional county of Wessex, *Tess of the D'Urbervilles* is both beautiful and sad. The story draws the reader quickly into the life of Tess Durbeyfield, an unassuming servant girl who comes to discover that her true heritage lies with the powerful D'Urberville family. But this is no joyous rags-to-riches story. Tess is a tragic figure, manipulated and misled, and makes a striking heroine for this classic novel of suffering.

The greatest strength of the book is the poetry of Hardy's writing, with which he creates wonderfully dark and mysterious atmospheres. Tess was Hardy's favourite heroine and this is a good place to start reading his work. But be warned – there are no happy endings!

**Marcus Sedgwick**

# THERE'S A BOY IN THE GIRLS' BATHROOM Louis Sachar

No one likes Bradley Chalkers, so when new fifth-grader Jeff offers to sit next to him, you hope this will be the start of a friendship. But life isn't that simple with Bradley. His opening words to Jeff are 'Give me a dollar or I'll spit at you'. Bradley is so out of control he's sent to the school guidance counsellor, Carla. To his surprise she doesn't criticise him, even when he's discovered in the girls' bathroom. Bradley's big moment comes when one of the girls invites him to her birthday party – his first invitation since that time he sat on someone's birthday cake...

This is a very funny book that might help you to understand why some people behave as they do...

**Jane Darcy**

**Next?**

Another funny and thoughtful book about troublesome boys is Louis Sachar's *Holes* (UTBG 184) and the follow up, *Small Steps*.

Or try something by Jerry Spinelli. *The Mighty Crashman*, *Loser* and *Miles to Go* are all well worth a read.

A sadder (and harder) book is Cynthia Voigt's *A Solitary Blue*, about a boy torn between his parents. It's one of the *Tillerman* series. (UTBG 185)

# THÉRÈSE RAQUIN Émile Zola

Passion, murder, ghosts and guilt – what more can a teenage girl ask for in a novel? Thérèse lives with her sickly husband Camille and his adoring mother. Then Laurent comes into her life, and Thérèse throws herself into adultery, and ultimately the murder of her husband, with complete abandon.

But even Camille's death can't bring them happiness. His drowned ghost haunts them, standing in the shadows of their room night after night, turning their life into a constant nightmare, until in the end their passion turns to hatred. This is a claustrophobic story steeped in atmosphere. I loved it when I was 15, and I love it now.

**Catherine MacPhail**

## Next?

If you like stories of murder, love and obsession, why not try *The Postman Always Rings Twice* by James M. Cain?

Shakespeare's *Macbeth* has some similarities, too.

Guy de Maupassant is another 19th-century French fiction writer of exceptional skill; read *Boule de Suif* or any collection of his short stories.

Or look for more French doom in Gustave Flaubert's classic *Madame Bovary*.

# THESE OLD SHADES Georgette Heyer

Justin, the Duke of Avon, is the epitome of 18th-century elegance. But he's also a very dangerous man. When he comes across Leon, the illegitimate teenage son of his greatest enemy, living a rough life in Paris, he takes the boy on as his page, hoping to devise a plan with which to humiliate the boy's father. Soon, however, he discovers that Leon is really a Leonie, and that she may not be illegitimate after all.

Beneath his suave and chilly exterior, Justin is really a street fighter, just like Leonie. But unlike Leonie, who's hot-tempered, he believes that revenge is a dish best served cold. This historical romance matches up two intense and enormously colourful characters in a totally satisfying way.

**Cathy Jinks**

## Next?

*Devil's Cub* is the sequel to *These Old Shades*, but anything by Georgette Heyer is worth a read, especially *Frederica* and *Arabella*, which are both Regency romances.

Another girl who dresses as a boy in order to get what she wants is Alanna in Tamora Pierce's **Song of the Lioness** quartet. (UTBG 14)

Meg Cabot also writes Regency romances; try *Victoria and the Rogue*. It's a frothy romp that will make you smile. Or for more historical romance, look out for Jean Plaidy – try *Madame Serpent* first.

# THE THIEF LORD
## Cornelia Funke

**Next?**

For more by Cornelia Funke, try *Inkheart* and its sequels, *Inkspell* and *Inkdeath*. (UTBG 203)

Another fantasy set in Italy, Mary Hoffman's **Stravaganza** series takes readers on a similarly fast-paced journey to a fantastic new world. Start with *City of Masks*. (UTBG 381)

Jonathan Stroud's **Bartimaeus** trilogy, starting with *The Amulet of Samarkand*, won't disappoint fantasy lovers. (UTBG 21)

I was in desperate need of a good book to stop the line of mediocre ones I had been reading when a friend suggested *The Thief Lord*. I was immediately enthralled. This story wraps you up and doesn't let you go until the last page.

The story follows the characters of Prospero and his younger brother Bo, who run away together when they find out that their nasty aunt wants to adopt Bo but not his brother. The boys escape to Venice, where they are taken under the wing of the Thief Lord, Scipio, and his gang of street children. Race along with the intense action scenes, and fall in love with all of the endearing characters. The plot twists will keep you guessing!

**Allison Hawthorne, age 16**

# THINGS FALL APART
## Chinua Achebe

'Okonkwo was well known throughout the nine villages and even beyond.' Thus begins *Things Fall Apart*. Okonkwo is a member of the Ibo tribe in an area of Africa known as Biafra. The story of Okonkwo is in many ways the story of black Africa and its confrontation with white colonialism and Christianity.

When the story opens, Okonkwo has been a champion wrestler for over 20 years. He is famous. He is feared. He is respected by all. His is the world of the rainforest: spirits and drums and unflinching tradition. Into this world comes the white man with his religion and guns and civilised ways. Okonkwo has met the match of his life.

**Jerry Spinelli**

**Next?**

*The Song of Solomon* by Toni Morrison begins with an African folk tale and transforms it into a quest for identity. Or try her **Beloved** (UTBG 42), about a slave who escapes but never finds real freedom.

For an anti-colonial view, read Joseph Conrad's masterpiece **Heart of Darkness**. (UTBG 174)

More Achebe? Try **The Arrow of God**, about an Ibo village priest in conflict with the British in 1920's Nigeria.

# THE THIRTY-NINE STEPS John Buchan

This is a classic thriller – a story of pursuit and escape. The hero, Richard Hannay, bored with his return to life in Britain, finds himself unexpectedly involved in an adventure in which he is hunted not only by the police for a murder he did not commit, but also by a rather more sinister group bent on destroying Britain and anxious (since he has clues to their identity) to eliminate him. He evades his pursuers with a variety of innovative disguises and hair's-breadth escapes, enriching his story with an account of his moods and responses, and with descriptions of the varying landscapes (especially those of Scotland) that themselves become part of the adventure. Despite certain racist elements (it was written a long time ago), this is a great story told at breakneck pace.

**Margaret Mahy**

> **Next?**
>
> There are more Richard Hannay adventures. Try the famous *Greenmantle*.
>
> Another classic, gripping story is *Rogue Male* by Geoffrey Household, about a plot to assassinate Hitler.
>
> Another adventure that starts with a mistaken identity is *The Prisoner of Zenda*. (UTBG 323)
>
> *Tamar* by Mal Peet is about spies and espionage in World War II, and it is a thrilling read. (UTBG 388)

# THIS BOY'S LIFE Tobias Wolff

> **Next?**
>
> There's a sequel – *In Pharaoh's Army* – but go on to read Wolff's short stories instead.
>
> Jack's brother Geoffrey has also written a memoir – *The Duke of Deception*; read it to find out about the other half of the family...
>
> *The Sea-Wolf* by Jack London is about a literate, civilised man up against a brutal ship's captain.

This story begins with ten-year-old Toby and his mother driving from Florida to Utah 'to get away from a man my mother was afraid of and to get rich on uranium'. In Utah it'll all be different – and to prove it Toby changes his name. From now on, we are to call him Jack. He's borrowing the name from Jack London.

Of course, Utah isn't what Jack expected. There's no fortune to be made, and his mother just ends up with another man Jack can't stand, the violent car mechanic Dwight. We watch Jack face those same challenges that we all have to deal with – how to find out who he is, to learn to understand other people, to find his way in the world. In short, we watch him grow up.

Wolff's writing is simple and effective – and it's a true story, too. Ten-year-old Toby grew up to be a very fine writer.

**Daniel Hahn**

# THREE MEN IN A BOAT
## Jerome K. Jerome

This is a comic classic. Three young Victorian men – the unnamed narrator, George and Harris, together with Montmorency the dog, set off on a leisurely boat trip up the Thames. They've dreamed of picnics on riverbanks, evenings beneath the stars and some comfortable nights at country inns. The reality is somewhat different, as the narrator finds when he accidentally takes an early-morning plunge in the river, or when Harris claims he's been attacked by 32 swans. Along the way are memories of other mishaps, including the time when Harris said he knew how to get round the maze at Hampton Court (he didn't) and when he tried to sing a funny song without knowing the words. Priceless.

**Jane Darcy**

## GOTHIC (OLD AND NEW)

*Pact of Wolves* by Nina Blazon

*Set in Stone* by Linda Newbery

*Tales of Mystery and Imagination* by Edgar Allen Poe

*Uncle Montague's Tales of Terror* by Chris Priestley

*The Poison Garden* by Sarah Singleton

*Possessing Rayne* by Kate Cann

*The Foreshadowing* by Marcus Sedgwick

*The Haunting of Alaizabel Cray* by Chris Wooding

### Next?

Other hilarious travel books include Pete McCarthy's *McCarthy's Bar* and Bill Bryson's *Neither Here Nor There*.

Or try some other very funny classics – *Diary of a Nobody* (UTBG 105), *The Diary of a Provincial Lady* by E.M. Delafield, *1066 and All That* (UTBG 8), *Right Ho, Jeeves* (UTBG 214) by P.G. Wodehouse or *Mapp and Lucia* by E.F. Benson.

Or try one of the great American humourists – James Thurber. Anything he wrote. Anything.

# THURSDAY'S CHILD   Sonya Hartnett   ✸✸

**Next?**

Read about a boy who uses fire as a way of dealing with the pressures in his life in Chris Wooding's *Kerosene*.

*Of Mice and Men* by John Steinbeck is a novel of the American Depression. (UTBG 291)

For a tale of staying alive in the Australian outback, try James Vance Marshall's *Walkabout*. (UTBG 420)

More Hartnett? Try *Butterfly*, about peer pressure and body image.

From the very first sentence: 'Now I would like to tell you about my brother, Tin...' this remarkable book grabs you by the throat

The narrator is Harper Flute, telling of her childhood in rural Australia between the two World Wars when her father, a scarred survivor of the First World War, brings his family to live on an almost unsustainable parcel of land during the Great Depression. Tin, Harper's young brother, becomes obsessed with tunnelling beneath the earth, and he is the pivot on which the story turns... Born on a Thursday and so fated to his wanderings...

This book has an immensely powerful realisation of place; compelling characters; soul-tearing moments; and atmosphere that seeps into your life.

**Theresa Breslin**

# TIME BOMB   Nigel Hinton   ✸

Four friends experience one final summer of freedom before beginning secondary school. But this is post-war Britain and the bombsite where they play hides a terrible danger. When Eddie is betrayed by one adult after another, he swears his friends to secrecy and takes his revenge.

You'll find yourself thinking about this story long after you've put the book down. Not only does Nigel Hinton manage to conjure up the ghost of the long, hot summer of August 1949, but he lets you into the lives of Andy and his friends to such an extent that the epilogue comes almost as a body blow. Unforgettable!

**Laura Hutchings**

**Next?**

Robert Westall's *The Machine-Gunners* is also about a group of friends in the 1940s who hide a wartime secret. But Britain is still at war and their secret can talk! (UTBG 251)

Other highly recommended Robert Westall titles (all of them set during World War II) include *Blitz* (short stories), *The Kingdom by the Sea* (UTBG 225) and *Blitzcat*.

Another Nigel Hinton? He is probably best known for *Buddy*, but try the excellent *Collision Course*, about a boy who accidentally kills an old lady when he's out joyriding.

# TIN GRIN   Catherine Robinson

After the misery of a big city and a violent father, Mattie, her sister and her mum are quite happy living in the country on their own. But then Mum gets herself a new husband, one who comes complete with a son – Geoffrey, an uber-nerd with bad dress sense, spots and braces. Mattie hates him on sight.

Add to the mix the god-like Sam Barker, sex, having to share a room with her messy sister, everyone else pretending that life is great, and Mattie's life becomes a nightmare. Or does it? It's not often you read stories centred on people you don't like? And in this, you grow to like Mattie, you want her to be happy, to get the boy and banish Tin Grin for ever.

Then, slowly, you start to see the world from other people's point of view…

**Leonie Flynn**

**Next?**

More Catherine Robinson? Try *Celia*, about a girl trying to find her real mother, or *Mr Perfect*, about a girl pursued by an older man.

In *Phosphorescence* by Raffaella Barker, Lola moves from the country into the city. Will she survive – especially when the school plans a camping trip back to her old village?

Or for more suggestions, read our feature about love and relationships on pp. 178–179.

# TITHE   Holly Black

**Next?**

For the next two books from the world of Faerie, try *Valiant* and *Ironside*.

The **Mortal Instruments** series by Cassandra Clare is a wild tale of hidden identity, love, vampires and a secret world. Read *City of Bones* first.

For a different kind of eerie tale, and a love story between two ghosts, try Laura Whitcomb's *A Certain Slant of Light*.

There's more Faerie in Melissa Marr's *Wicked Lovely*. There's also sex, violence and real-world issues, but don't let that put you off!

Or read *Twilight* by Stephanie Meyer, if you haven't already. (UTBG 411)

*Tithe* is a fresh approach to the traditional world of fairies. Holly Black captures not only the cunning and cheekiness of the fairy folk, but also their magic and mystery. It is refreshing to find out that our heroine is not an angelic, two-dimensional character, but a spunky and delightfully frayed creature from another world.

I really enjoyed reading this book. A fantasy novel is only enjoyable if the characters and the fantastical world are able to rise out from the confines of the book and play out like reality. The fantasy world of *Tithe* manages to do this elegantly and convincingly.

**May Aung, age 17**

# TO KILL A MOCKINGBIRD
## Harper Lee

Scout was in grammar school when it happened – the thing that rocked her family and divided her sleepy Southern town. She is a patient storyteller, telling of the odd neighbours down the block with their dark history; her life in a single-parent household; and the angst of a southern girl who doesn't have it in her to be a lady. And then there's her father, Atticus. If you're looking for father figures, like I was as a teenager, he's your man. This book changed my life and continues to challenge me as a writer and a reader. It introduced me to characters of honour who stood for their ideals despite raging injustice. This is a stunning story about childhood colliding with ignorance and prejudice, and the grace people need to build a better world.

**Joan Bauer**

TO KILL A MOCKING-BIRD

*Pulitzer Prize Winner*
*over 30,000,000 sold*

HARPER LEE

### Next?

*A Separate Peace* by John Knowles brilliantly brings to life the world of a wartime boarding school. (UTBG 353)

John Steinbeck's *Of Mice and Men* is also set in the American South and is about difference and acceptance. (UTBG 291)

You'll find a more recent look at false accusation and prejudice in Rosa Guy's *The Disappearance* or David Guterson's *Snow Falling on Cedars* (UTBG 370).

This is one of those astonishing books that stay with you for ever. Set in the Deep South of America during the Great Depression of the 1930s, it tells the story of Scout and Jem Finch and their father, Atticus, a lawyer who defends a black man wrongly accused of raping a white girl.

On one level, it's an apparently simple tale about the fears and prejudices of a small-town community, and how one man stands up for what he thinks is right; but within that simplicity there's so much more. It's a story about innocence and growing up, about conscience and courage, about seeing the world for what it is. Wonderfully told by nine-year-old Scout, *To Kill a Mockingbird* has everything you could ever want in a book: a gripping story, strong emotions, engaging characters and – best of all – that very special feeling of being alive.

**Kevin Brooks**

# THE TOLL BRIDGE  Aidan Chambers

**Next?**

Try *Breaktime* (UTBG 60), *Dance on My Grave* (UTBG 94), *Now I Know*, or *Postcards from No Man's Land* (UTBG 318) – Aidan Chambers's **Dance** sequence.

Or *You Don't Know Me*, about a boy and his violent stepfather. (UTBG 452)

Another boy, another bridge? Try the equally thought provoking *Kissing the Rain* by Kevin Brooks. (UTBG 226)

A light-hearted look at what it means to be gay can be found in Paul Magrs's *Strange Boy*. (UTBG 380)

Aidan Chambers is a wonderful writer – intelligent, provocative, profound. His novels exert a grip that may have you turning the pages too quickly, yet they're always worth rereading and re-rereading. *The Toll Bridge* is probably my favourite. 'Jan' (not his real name) is at a transitional period of his life, symbolised by his taking up residence in a toll-house by a river bridge. Seeking isolation, he finds his privacy invaded by the deeply disturbed Adam, by forthright Tess, and by Gill, the devoted girlfriend who loves him oppressively. There's an utterly compelling intensity to this novel of adolescents in search of purpose, identity and escape.

**Linda Newbery**

# TOMMY GLOVER'S SKETCH OF HEAVEN
## Jane Bailey

Kitty returns as a student teacher to the Gloucestershire village where she was evacuated during World War II and fostered by a couple who, although not actively unkind, showed her little affection. Undaunted, Kitty found companionship elsewhere, forming a devoted bond with Tommy, a boy from the local orphanage. In those days Kitty knew little but learned fast and, sensing the strained relationship between her 'uncle and aunt', asked questions that no one else dared to utter. Her forthright curiosity cut through adult prudery and nasty-mindedness to uncover secrets both sad and dreadful – and almost everyone in that small community had something to hide, including Tommy. Kitty realised too late that she might have exposed one secret too many, and that she and Tommy could have sabotaged their own chances of a happy ending.

**Next?**

More Jane Bailey; *Mad Joy* is about a feral girl, secrets and being in love with a fighter pilot.

For memories of a real Gloucestershire childhood, read Laurie Lee's *Cider with Rosie*. (UTBG 80)

*The Go-Between* is another story of an adult returning to visit the scene of traumatic childhood experiences. (UTBG 159)

**Jan Mark**

# TOUCHING THE VOID Joe Simpson

An astounding adventure story, with the extra-special ingredient of being true. Author Joe Simpson and fellow mountaineer Simon Yates tackle one of the highest unclimbed peaks in the Peruvian Andes. They get to the top, but on the way down Joe falls and breaks his leg. Simon, in an astonishing feat of bravery, somehow manages to lower him down, until Joe topples over an edge and is left hanging in space. Simon, tied to him, is being slowly pulled off the mountain and is eventually forced to break the last rule of mountaineering – he cuts the rope. Convinced Joe's dead, Simon descends, but meanwhile Joe, showing quite incredible courage and determination, tries to crawl to safety.

This is a riveting and inspiring read, even if you've never climbed higher than the top of a stepladder.

**Malachy Doyle**

> **Next?**
>
> More mountaineering? Try *Facing Up* by Bear Grylls, the youngest Briton at the time to have climbed Everest.
>
> Or Joe Simpson's *Dark Shadows Falling*, about recent mountaineering tragedies.
>
> For more snow (but with fewer peaks), read Sara Wheeler's *Terra Incognita* – about Antarctica and the people who have had to understand its wilderness. (UTBG 390)

# TOURIST SEASON Carl Hiaasen

> **Next?**
>
> *Native Tongue* by Carl Hiaasen – more low-life hi-jinks from the Sunshine State. He also writes for younger readers; try *Flush*, *Hoot* (UTBG 186) or his latest, *Scat*.
>
> *Me Talk Pretty One Day* by David Sedaris – everyday confessions of an ordinary American who happens to be hugely funny.
>
> Or try an Elmore Leonard – more Florida, more guns. Start with *Rum Punch*.

A critic once wrote that Carl Hiaasen's comedy thrillers are 'better than literature' and I agree wholeheartedly. I read *Tourist Season* after a weighty Russian classic about long winters and thin gruel. To find myself in the sweltering heat of Florida was refreshing, and the anarchy and savage exuberance packed into the story came as a revelation. A native son of the state itself, Hiaasen's novels rage against the destruction and corruption of his beloved environment. In this, his first novel, it's Florida's tourist industry that he picks apart with glee.

Just don't read it in company. You'll laugh and snort and hoot so much that everyone will want you to explain what's so funny.

**Matt Whyman**

# A TOWN LIKE ALICE  Nevil Shute

**Next?**

You'll probably enjoy other Nevil Shute books. *Trustee from the Toolroom* is one of my favourites; or you could try *On the Beach*, about life after a nuclear war.

If you're interested in World War II in the Far East, read *Quartered Safe Out Here* by George MacDonald Fraser, *The Seed and the Sower* by Laurens van der Post or *Empire of the Sun* (UTBG 120) by J.G. Ballard.

Or for the true story of life in a Japanese prisoner of war camp, try *The Railway Man* by Eric Lomax.

This story begins with a solicitor trying to trace a woman who is due to inherit a fortune. When he finds her, Jean Paget turns out to be a simple typist – but like all Shute's 'ordinary' people, Jean is not really ordinary at all. As a prisoner of the Japanese during the war, she saw and did some extraordinary things, and how she decides to spend her money is even more extraordinary.

This is a war story and a love story combined. It moves at a slow and gentle pace, but be patient. It is a brilliant yarn about a woman determined to use all her resources to heal and create, after a period in history that had seen so much hatred and destruction.

**Andrew Norriss**

# TRAINSPOTTING  Irvine Welsh

*Trainspotting* is about a group of drug addicts, the levels to which they'll stoop to get drugs and how drugs dominate their lives. It doesn't glamorise drug taking; in fact quite the reverse, it tell the story of life under the influence – exciting, dangerous, ruinously destructive, all-consuming and ultimately soul-destroying. But it's told in such a gripping way you're carried along without stopping to make judgements as you go.

This is a roller-coaster, hair-raising, unputdownable read – its energy, vitality and rawness make it so fresh and new. The language, once you've got a handle on it, is so evocative of the lifestyle. It gives you such an immediate sensation of the world the characters inhabit, you really feel as if you're right in there with them – which, thankfully, you're not. It's daring, thrilling, frightening and very funny.

**Arabella Weir**

**Next?**

More dark Scottish writing? Alan Warner's *Morvern Callar* begins with a girl waking up next to her dead boyfriend (and a great deal of money).

Moving south, Jonathan Coe's *The Rotters' Club* is a bitter-sweet story of adolescence.

Cult novels usually change from generation to generation. Try J.D. Salinger's enduring *The Catcher in the Rye* to see why this one hasn't. (UTBG 69)

# THE TRAITOR GAME B.R. Collins

Michael has survived years of bullying at one school, but found friendship at his new one. Or so he thinks. Then one day all his trust, all his faith, everything that's held him together, is shattered by an act of betrayal – and the damage inflicted upon him in the past determines how he reacts, and that reaction changes everything.

This book consists of two strands: Michael's and Argent's. Argent lives in Evgard, the fantasy world that Michael and his friend Francis created, a world that is – for all its beauty – deeply corrupt and oppressive. The two strands make absolute sense, as Michael uses Evgard as his escape; a place in which someone suffers even more than he does.

This is a brilliant debut, and despite the fact that there are 'issues' involved, they never lead the story. I'd suggest that anyone who has ever been bullied reads it – and anyone who is a bully is made to read it!

**Leonie Flynn**

**Next?**

The next B.R. Collins: *A Trick of the Dark*.

A more complicated fantasy world is that of Robin Hobb's the **Farseer** trilogy. (UTBG 127)

*Inventing Elliot* by Graham Gardner is also about trying to fit in. (UTBG 206)

Another claustrophobic school story? Try Anthony McGowan's *The Knife That Killed Me*. (UTBG 229)

# TREASURE ISLAND Robert Louis Stevenson

**Next?**

If the character of Long John Silver fascinates you, try *Dr Jekyll and Mr Hyde*, a chilling story of good and evil. (UTBG 115)

More pirates? For girl pirates, try *Piratica* by Tanith Lee, about a girl who accidentally becomes a pirate, or *Pirates!* (UTBG 313) by Celia Rees. Or for the more traditional male pirates, try Brian Jacques' *Castaways of the Flying Dutchman*.

*Treasure Island* is a perfect story of exotic adventure. It starts on homely dry land – but coastal – at the Admiral Benbow pub. The innkeeper's young son, Jim Hawkins, tells the tale and is its daring hero. Mystery, dread and tension build up with the arrival of Blind Pew, tap-tapping his way to deliver 'the black spot', a doom of execution, to a double-crossing old shipmate. We realise that these are pirates on the track of treasure. But it's Jim who lays hands on the essential treasure map and, with the local squire and doctor, sets sail. Chief among their rascally crew is one-legged, parrot-on-the-shoulder Long John Silver: he conceals black treachery under geniality and seeming honesty and helpfulness. No wonder there is bloodcurdling action on Treasure Island...

**Philippa Pearce**

# A TREE GROWS IN BROOKLYN Betty Smith

I don't remember how I came across *A Tree Grows in Brooklyn* but I do remember the deep pleasure of reading it and how the story stayed with me a long time afterwards. The book is set in Brooklyn, New York, at the turn of the 20th century. It focuses on Francie Nolan and her younger brother Neeley, taking us through their poverty-stricken but never dull childhood. Guided by their hardworking, determined mother Katie, their handsome but drunkard father Johnny and their wonderful but wanton Aunt Sissy, the children, like the hardy Trees of Heaven growing through the Brooklyn gutters, struggle to reach the sky. Problems are overcome with tough love, tenderness, humour and, in one powerful incident, carbolic acid and a bullet.

**Helena Pielichaty**

**Next?**

*My Childhood* by Maxim Gorky – a Russian account of childhood poverty, beautifully and movingly told.

*Angela's Ashes* is the story of a poor Irish family. (UTBG 22)

Or, for a more up-to-date version of the above, try Roddy Doyle's *The Snapper*, in which a modern working-class Irish family get to grips with their teenage daughter's unexpected pregnancy.

Or more Betty Smith? Try *Joy in the Morning*.

# THE TRICKSTERS Margaret Mahy

**Next?**

Margaret Mahy's *The Changeover* (UTBG 72) and *Alien in the Family* have a similar mix of beautifully realised characters and magical events.

Alice Hoffman's *Illumination Night* and *The River King* are novels about young people caught in strange situations.

Or try *Night Maze* by Annie Dalton, about an orphan boy battling a family curse.

For a different take on love, try Sonia Hartnett's *The Ghost's Child*.

Harry (or Ariadne) is 17, shy, self-conscious (she wears glasses) and a budding writer. She and her large, noisy family are spending the summer by the sea, in a place where a boy was drowned almost 90 years ago. His body was never found.

One hot afternoon, Harry dives under the sea and a hand touches hers. Whose hand? She immediately surfaces and sees a figure on a rock, 'water streaming from every part of him'. And then he is gone. Eventually the ghostly drowned boy becomes real, but in a surprisingly and completely unexpected form. Harry's relationship with this unique character makes for an enchanting and spine-tingling story.

**Jenny Nimmo**

# TRISKELLION   Will Peterson

Life for twins Rachel and Adam is getting tough. Their parents are splitting up. Their mother has sent them away to live with their gran. They travel from America to England by plane and then by train through England to the small village of Triskellion. They find Triskellion an unwelcoming village – but then they meet Gabriel, a strange boy who seems to know a lot about them…

*Triskellion* is an enthralling page-turner. Brilliantly written – especially the part where they discover two dead bodies and the first blade of the Triskellion, a three-bladed symbol that lies in the centre of Triskellion's town square. This is one of the best books I have ever read!

**Charlie Whiteside, age 11**

> ### Next?
>
> There are sequels! The first is *The Burning* and the final volume is *The Gathering*.
>
> Another complex, exciting, thought-provoking read can be found in Michael Scott's series, **The Secrets of the Immortal Nicholas Flamel**. The first book is *The Alchemyst*. (UTBG 16)
>
> For other stories about what can lie beneath the seemingly ordinary surface of life, try Catherine Fisher's collection, *The Glass Tower: Three Doors to the Otherworld*.

# TROLL FELL   Katherine Langrish

In an unspecified Nordic landscape of fjords and extreme weather, Peer's life has suddenly been turned upside down. Before the ashes of his father's funeral pyre have even cooled, up turns one of his mean uncles who then drags him off to be kept as a virtual slave in a dilapidated mill. Peer's only solace is in the company of Hilde, a neighbour from a nearby farm – together they uncover Peer's uncles' devilish plot to steal troll treasure from the dark and magical Troll Fell – a course not recommended if one values one's life.

This is a novel that is atmospheric, dramatic, stylish and intensely engaging. It is by turns gritty and bleak, but also magical and uplifting.

**John McLay**

> ### Next?
>
> Look out for *Troll Mill* and *Troll Blood*, Katherine Langrish's sequels to her first Scandinavian troll-fest. They have more chilly drama and fantasy.
>
> *Sea of Trolls* by Nancy Farmer is a blockbuster of a troll novel, with more dragons and Vikings (and, yes, trolls) than you can shake a stick at. (And have you ever tried shaking a stick at a troll?) It's the first in a page-turning trilogy. (UTBG 345)
>
> Or read Catherine Fisher's **Snow-walker** trilogy, which blends Norse myth with adventure.

# THE TROUBLE WITH DONOVAN CROFT   Bernard Ashley

When Keith Chapman's parents tell him that he is to have a foster brother his own age, Keith holds out high hopes of having someone to play football with and share his games. When his foster brother arrives, however, things don't work out quite as Keith had planned. Donovan turns out to be a deeply troubled boy of West Indian origin, whose way of dealing with the trauma of leaving his parents is to remain silent.

Despite Keith's best efforts to look after him and make him happy, Donovan's misery is deepened by encounters with bullying and racism, often by people who should know better.

This is a deeply moving story that deals with issues that are always relevant in our society.

**Elizabeth McManus**

**Next?**

Try Bernard Ashley's *A Kind of Wild Justice*; or his *Little Soldier*, about a boy transplanted from war-torn Africa to England.

Other powerful books dealing with clashes of cultures include *Out of Bounds* (UTBG 303) by Beverley Naidoo and *The Burning City* by Ariel and Joaquín Dorfman.

# TROY   Adèle Geras

**Next?**

Geras continues her retellings in *Ithaka* and *Dido*. Or try something else by her in *Silent Snow, Secret Snow* (UTBG 362), about a family full of secrets and betrayals.

Christopher Logue's *War Music* is a marvellous retelling of Homer's *The Iliad* in modern verse.

Or for a prose version, read Rosemary Sutcliff's classic *Black Ships Before Troy*.

*No Shame, No Fear* by Ann Turnbull is also about forbidden love, this time between a Quaker girl and a rich young man. (UTBG 286)

You probably know the famous story of Helen of Troy, whose face launched a thousand ships and inspired a bloody battle that lasted for ten long years. If you don't it doesn't matter. Geras tells you what you need to know and more: the inside story, the woman's-eye view, the best bits. Seen for the most part by two sisters, Xanthe and Marpessa, it shows the war affecting the lives of ordinary folk as well as the famous. Fittingly it begins in the Blood Room, where Xanthe awaits the wounded from the latest battle – for blood runs through the story. But so does humour, friendship and love. Stories within the great story, all vividly told, will keep you gripped to the end.

**Julia Jarman**

# THE TRUTH ABOUT FOREVER Sarah Dessen

Forever cool, calm and collected, Macy claims everything in her life is fine; she's a model student, perfect daughter and devoted girlfriend. But underneath it all, Macy is in pieces, struggling silently to come to terms with the death of her father years ago. A new group of friends help Macy take steps into the unknown, move on, accept her emotions, discover that who she is isn't so bad after all and that her life is for living to the full.

Sarah Dessen is a sensitive, subtly humorous and powerful writer who helps you think about the important things in life through some of the most believable and inspiring characters you'll ever meet in the pages of a book. She's Jacqueline Wilson meets Jodi Picoult for the teenage market and deserves much wider acclaim.

**Eileen Armstrong**

The Truth about Forever
Sarah Dessen

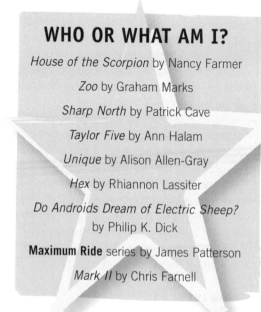

## WHO OR WHAT AM I?

*House of the Scorpion* by Nancy Farmer

*Zoo* by Graham Marks

*Sharp North* by Patrick Cave

*Taylor Five* by Ann Halam

*Unique* by Alison Allen-Gray

*Hex* by Rhiannon Lassiter

*Do Androids Dream of Electric Sheep?* by Philip K. Dick

**Maximum Ride** series by James Patterson

*Mark II* by Chris Farnell

**Next?**

More Sarah Dessen. Try *Lock and Key*, about a girl moving from poverty to live with her older sister. Or maybe *Someone Like You*, about friendship, a pregnancy and one long summer.

*Sloppy Firsts* by Megan McCafferty is another book about teen life as it is.

Or try Sophie McKenzie's *Six Steps to a Girl*, about a boy determined to go out with one girl – even though she's already got a boyfriend.

# TRUTH OR DARE   Celia Rees

This engrossing book is essentially a detective novel, but not in the traditional sense. Josh reluctantly accompanies his mother when she goes to care for his ill grandmother. It's a bleak experience, separated from his friends and holed up in a house in which the chill wind of illness seems compounded by an atmosphere of secrets and lies. Gradually, almost unintentionally, Josh begins to ask questions about his surroundings, and about the splinters of family stories which don't quite match up to make sense. He begins to uncover the story of an uncle he believed had died in his teens. The real story is revealed by evidence from the present, and stories of the past – and it is just as tragic, in its way.

**Lindsey Fraser**

> ## Next?
>
> Family secrets often provide the heart of great novels. I'd recommend *The Opposite of Chocolate* by Julie Bertagna (UTBG 298), *The Secret Line* by William Corlett and *Tell Me No Lies* by Malorie Blackman as compelling follow-ups to this.
>
> *The Curious Incident of the Dog in the Night-Time* by Mark Haddon centres around a character with Asperger's. (UTBG 92)
>
> *Worm in the Blood* by Thomas Bloor is about a family tainted by an ancient curse. (UTBG 445)

# THE TULIP TOUCH   Anne Fine

Natalie is a good girl. Tulip is not. But when their paths cross, the relationship is almost magnetic – Natalie simply can't resist her mesmerising friend. As their story gradually unfolds, we watch, horrified, as Tulip pushes Natalie further towards the point of no return.

Anne Fine doesn't resort to histrionics or drama to tell her stories. The language of each sentence is as clear as a bell. Yet this story, like so many of her others, keeps us wondering long after we've closed the book. That's largely because we become so engrossed in the characters that their realness extends beyond the last page. But it's also because we wonder what we might have done, and how we would have reacted in the same situation.

**Lindsey Fraser**

> ## Next?
>
> I'd recommend anything by Anne Fine, especially *Goggle Eyes* and *Step by Wicked Step*.
>
> *Big Mouth and Ugly Girl* by Joyce Carol Oates and *Noughts and Crosses* (UTBG 290) and its sequels by Malorie Blackman look in very different ways at the role prejudice can play in people's judgements about other people.
>
> *Kamo's Escape* by Daniel Pennac is another take on the impact one person's life can have on another's.

# TULKU  Peter Dickinson

**Next?**

*She* and *Ayesha* by H. Rider Haggard, for more tales of exotic adventure; or *Greenmantle* by John Buchan, about adventures in Arabia.

Or for more-adult books about spiritual journeys, try *Siddhartha* or *Narziss and Goldmund* (UTBG 276), both by Hermann Hesse.

Peter Dickinson wrote other amazing books; try *The Kin*. (UTBG 224)

Very occasionally a book comes along that is too big for the pages it is written on, so that it spills right off the edges into a larger-than-life reality of its own. *Tulku* is one such book.

During the Boxer Rebellion, the Christian mission where Theo has been brought up is destroyed and his father killed. While escaping, he meets an intrepid plant collector called Mrs Jones, and her guide, Lung. Their journey is at once a breathtaking adventure story and a spiritual rite of passage. All Theo's rigid beliefs unravel as they penetrate the mysteries of Tibet, and Mrs Jones is transformed from eccentric adventurer to spiritual warrior and mother of the Tulku, or Dalai Lama.

There are so many things to love about this vivid novel that I cannot possibly do them all justice. You will have to read it!

**Livi Michael**

# TUNNELS  Roderick Gordon and Brian Williams

Will and his father share a passion for digging and making tunnels. Between them, they dig all sorts of tunnels beneath London, discovering a whole manner of things. But while working on a secret tunnel, Will's father suddenly goes missing and it is down to Will and his friend Chester to try and find him. As the boys descend into Will's father's tunnel, they start to discover a world unknown to most people. Heavily guarded by 'Styx', an over-zealous police force, it's a world in which they are both trespassing. Then the boys find themselves trapped underground, where they make discoveries that will have a massive impact on both their lives.

**Next?**

The next book in the series is *Deeper*, in which the boys delve deeper into the hidden world and make more discoveries. Follow that with *Freefall*.

For other stories of hidden worlds underground, try either *City of Ember* by Jeanne DuPrau or Jules Verne's classic *Journey to the Centre of the Earth*.

Other brilliantly imaginative and thrilling London adventures include Charlie Fletcher's *Stone Heart* (UTBG 377), China Miéville's *Un Lun Dun* (UTBG 414), and Eleanor Updale's *Montmorency* and its sequels.

**Adam Lancaster**

# TURBULENCE  Jan Mark

**Next?**

Clay makes a passing reference to the superb *The Great Gatsby* by F. Scott Fitzgerald, and it's worth reading it to see exactly why. (UTBG 166)

There's no one who wrote quite like Jan Mark, so if you like this, seek out more of hers – try *Useful Idiots* (UTBG 418) and *They Do Things Differently There*.

In *The Tricksters*, Margaret Mahy writes brilliantly about people whose sudden presence undermines other people's lives for good. (UTBG 403)

Jan Mark has written some brilliant books and this is one of her best. Clay (Clare) Winchester narrates what happens when her parents bring home Sandor Harker and his wife Ali for dinner one evening. It's Sandor who shines that night, making everyone feel that they're the most important person in the room. Clay is flattered, but soon everyone she knows falls under Sandor's spell, and their own solid relationships show signs of foundering as a result. Sandor's exhibitionism and his insidious pervasion of Clay's close circle of family and friends make gripping and at times disturbing reading, but the book is infused with Jan Mark's uniquely dark, sometimes laugh-out-loud, humour.

**Jon Appleton**

# THE TURN OF THE SCREW  Henry James

This must be one of the most terrifying ghost stories ever written. A young governess, appointed to an Essex country house, becomes instantly devoted to Flora, her young charge. When Flora's brother Miles is sent home from school in disgrace, the two children develop an oddly knowing behaviour that makes the governess deeply uneasy. They are apparently under the malevolent influence of Peter Quint and Miss Jessop, former employees at Bly, both now dead. All the young woman's courage is needed to protect her charges from the silent, watchful pair. Uncertainty about whether the manifestations are real, or only imagined by the children or by the disturbed governess herself, adds to the chilling ambiguity of this unforgettable tale.

**Next?**

Try the *Ghost Stories* of M.R. James (UTBG 153), Edgar Allen Poe's *Tales of Mystery and Imagination* (UTBG 387), or *The Oxford Book of Victorian Ghost Stories* edited by Michael Cox.

Or read the story of that other famous governess, *Jane Eyre* by Charlotte Brontë. (UTBG 211)

Or read Daphne Du Maurier's captivating *Rebecca*, about a young girl who finds herself haunted by her husband's first wife. (UTBG 328)

**Linda Newbery**

# TURTLE DIARY  Russell Hoban

William G. works in a bookshop and Neaera H. is a children's writer seeking inspiration for her next book. They lead careful, reserved English lives, but the large sea turtles confined in the aquarium at the London Zoo independently haunt them both. Through their diaries their stories unfold, revealing tragedy, self-doubt and strange parallels. Keen observers, sensitive and honest, they wonder at the way we humans treat nature, and they stand in awe of the turtles' instinct to navigate vast oceans when it seems so hard to navigate their own lives. Then, despite themselves, William G. and Neaera H. become jointly part of 'an event that seemed to want to happen'. This intimate, funny-sad book is quite wonderful. Russell Hoban is an original and a poet.

**Elizabeth Honey**

### Next?

Douglas Adams and Mark Carwardine's *Last Chance to See* is a serious book about endangered animals, but it's also extremely funny. (UTBG 231)

*Hoot* manages the tricky task of being both about saving wildlife and a wild adventure story. (UTBG 186)

Another Hoban? Try the complex and wonderful *The Mouse and His Child*. It's not just a book for kids, so don't be put off by the title!

---

# THE TWELFTH DAY OF JULY  Joan Lingard

### Next?

Kevin and Sadie's story continues with *Across the Barricades, Into Exile, A Proper Place* and *Hostage to Fortune*.

Other Joan Lingard books include *Tell the Moon to Come Out*, about a boy travelling illegally into Franco's Spain to try and find his missing father; and *Natasha's Will*, which weaves together two stories, one an escape from war-torn Russia, the other a search for the escapee's will many years later.

Theresa Breslin's *Divided City* is about conflict between Protestants and Catholics in Scotland. (UTBG 107)

Belfast in the run up to the 12th of July is a time for parades and celebration for the Protestant community, and a time of fear and resentment among the Catholics. A dare carried out by Kevin, a Catholic, involving entering a Protestant 'no-go' area, triggers a chain reaction of events, both exciting and very dangerous. It leads to an unlikely and somewhat risky friendship between Kevin and Sadie, an attractive, feisty Protestant.

As the action escalates, tempers fly, and something happens that causes both sides to examine their prejudices and bigotry. The issue of the Troubles is dealt with in a clear and balanced way in this exciting, fast-moving book.

**Elizabeth McManus**

# TWILIGHT Stephenie Meyer

You don't have to be a vampire fan to love *Twilight*. I know I'm certainly not, but this extraordinary book makes my top five favourites, hands down.

Stephenie Meyer has breathed life into her characters – even the undead ones – like no other author has before. Shy and awkward teenager Bella, the beautiful vampire Edward and the rest of the Cullen family are all so easy to relate to that Meyer has half her readers desperately hoping – and often convinced – there are actual vampires wandering around the country somewhere.

Bella, a reluctant newcomer to rainy Forks, Washington, (literally) stumbles upon a family of 'vegetarian' vampires, and is instantly charmed by the magnetic Edward Cullen, who puts most teenage boys to shame. As the two face emotional and physical challenges, and toy with the seductive lure of dangerous love, readers will find themselves equally seduced by the world Meyer has created.

**Claire Easton, age 16**

## Next?

Definitely don't miss the next three books about Edward and Bella, *New Moon*, *Eclipse* and *Breaking Dawn*.

For more high school vampires, try *Secret Vampire*, the first of the **Night World** books by L.J. Smith. (UTBG 283)

But if you like your bloodsuckers to have a little more bite then it's high time you met Lestat, anti-hero of Anne Rice's vampire novels. Start with *Interview with a Vampire*. (UTBG 205)

In many respects this book is a sheep in wolf's clothing. It may well have given the vampire genre a much needed injection of fresh blood but reading it is like snuggling up with a mug of hot chocolate on a snowy winter's day. From the moment Bella nobly volunteers to go and live with her father, swopping the dry desert heat that she loves for the perpetually rainy days of Washington State, you know that this is going to be one of those feel-good novels that you devour rather than read. And when you've finished it, there's always the remarkably faithful film version to enjoy. Best bit for me? When geeky Bella arrives at school with the gorgeous Edward Cullen and everyone turns to stare. Now that's fantasy!

**Laura Hutchings**

# UGLIES Scott Westerfeld

The first in an ongoing series of novels, *Uglies* is set in a terrifyingly plausible future of happy-drugs, extreme sports, body modification and State-imposed mind control. Tally is an Ugly, a normal girl awaiting her 16th birthday, when she will be surgically remade, to emerge as a newborn Pretty. After that, she can rejoin her friends in New Pretty Town, a place where young people, their flaws corrected by surgery, are perfect, happy, bubble-headed, and ready to party all day long.

But there is a dark side to being Pretty, as Tally very soon discovers. And outside New Pretty Town, in the rebel camp, the truth is gradually spreading. But torn between two sets of loyalties, can Tally ever find her place?

**Joanne Harris**

**Next?**

The quartet continues with *Pretties*, *Specials* and *Extras*. There's also a guide to the Uglies' world: *Bogus to Bubbly*.

More of Scott Westerfeld's books? Try *Parasite Positive*, a breathtakingly different take on the whole vampire myth, or the **Midnighters** trilogy starting with *The Secret Hour*.

Melvyn Burgess takes a sardonic look at the whole cult of youth and celebrity in *Sara's Face*.

# ULTRAVIOLET Lesley Howarth

**Next?**

More Lesley Howarth? *Carwash* (UTBG 67) takes place in a small town, while *Maphead* is the story of an alien trying to make sense of our world.

*Breaktime* by Aidan Chambers is another novel that plays around with narrative and blurs the boundary between fact and fiction. (UTBG 60)

*Sharp North* by Patrick Cave also tells the story of a resourceful girl in a world affected by environmental changes. (UTBG 358)

Vi lives with her father in a futuristic, damaged world in which the sun's radiation makes it impossible to venture out for most of the year and people live in underground cities. To compensate for the lost outdoors, Vi and her peers play virtual-reality games. Some of these are so sophisticated that players can paste elements from their own lives into the game. Vi becomes restless and 'leaks' outside, dressed in protective fabric that her father invented. Her outdoor adventure seems straightforward at first, but watch out for the twists as this book borrows the narrative structure of a computer game – in other words, there is more than one way for it to be played out! A great book from an unusually imaginative author.

**Noga Applebaum**

# (UN)ARRANGED MARRIAGE Bali Rai

Manny is a typically rebellious teenager, rejecting the authority of his violent, drunken 'old man', beaten by his brothers, frustrated by his mother's subservience. Destined for an arranged marriage he hasn't asked for, to a girl he doesn't know or want, he deliberately sets out to make himself the most unmarriageable husband material possible. He's determined to follow his own path through life, but reckons without being tricked into a trip to India by his tradition-bound Punjabi family, that threatens to put an end to his dreams...

Culture clashes, family loyalty, honour, traditional values, taking chances, alienation and identity are all brought sharply into focus through the eyes of a 17-year-old boy. With a sharp ear for contemporary dialogue, a stunning eye for detail and perfect pace, Rai is truly one of the strongest writers around for young people.

**Eileen Armstrong**

> **Next?**
>
> *Rani and Sukh* is Bali Rai's take on *Romeo and Juliet*. (UTBG 326)
>
> In Sharon Dogar's *Falling*, nightmare-haunted Neesha is saved by Sammy, but something is forcing them to replay a love affair that ended in violence and death.
>
> *Anita and Me* is about growing up in the only Punjabi family in a British town. (UTBG 24)

# UNCLE MONTAGUE'S TALES OF TERROR
## Chris Priestley

> **Next?**
>
> There's more horror in Chris's *Tales of Terror from the Black Ship*. Or try one of his novels; *Death and the Arrow* is a dark look at 18th-century London, or *The New World*, which takes a boy from Elizabethan London to the danger and violence of newly colonised America.
>
> For another book of brilliant short stories, try Neil Gaiman's *M Is for Magic*. (UTBG 266)
>
> Or try the master of scary – Edgar Allen Poe and his *Tales of Mystery and Imagination*. (UTBG 387)

Short stories have become rather unfashionable since the heyday of Ray Bradbury, but if anyone can put this right then it's Chris Priestley. Uncle Montague is a bachelor who lives in a house packed with intriguing objects that he uses to tell his nephew Edward spine-tingling stories. These are satisfyingly dark and end unhappily, with nods towards the great writers of ghost and horror stories such as M.R. James and Edgar Allan Poe. Just like with *The Illustrated Man* (my other choice for the *UTBG*) I was propelled through the book by wonderfully inventive storytelling that reminded me why I love short-story collections like these.

**Chris Riddell**

# UNIQUE  Alison Allen-Gray

### Next?

There's more by the same author in *Lifegame*.

*Truth or Dare* by Celia Rees is another exciting book about dark family secrets. (UTBG 407)

If you like fast-paced adventure stories, why not try *The Burning City* by Ariel and Joaquín Dorfman? Its plot lunges forward like the main character's hurtling courier bike.

*House of the Scorpion* (UTBG 189) by Nancy Farmer also deals with the subject of cloning, as does *Clone* by Malcolm Rose.

What might happen if a person were cloned from a sibling who'd died? Dominic is one such boy, but he's nowhere near as clever or talented as his dead brother was. The unbearable weight of expectations now heaped on him by his parents pushes him to the edge. So he sets out to answer a myriad of questions...

It's a journey beset with hazards and dangers, as Dominic must make vital decisions in his quest to uncover the truth at the heart of his family's dark secrets.

*Unique* is a perfect mix of sci-fi and science. It's powerful and scary because in the near future it could well be a description of a new reality.

**Jonny Zucker**

# UN LUN DUN  China Miéville

Zanna and Deeba's ordinary life has turned distinctly strange. It all started when the respectful fox bowed before them; now the postman's acting weirdly, and someone's painting 'Zanna For Ever!' on London bridges...

Yet nothing's prepared them for stumbling into UnLondon – an impossible city of scavenger trashpacks, ghosts, and broken umbrellas. A city populated by all the unwanted rubbish and people of London. An urban wasteland gripped by war. Can Zanna and Deeba find their way home? And why does everyone seem to expect them to save the whole city?

China Miéville will dazzle and enthral you with this imaginative and entertaining book. Between the illustrations, unique characters, and clever wordplay, you won't be able to put it down.

### Next?

For other tales of an alternate London, read *Neverwhere* by Neil Gaiman, *Mortal Engines* (UTBG 270) by Philip Reeve, *Stone Heart* (UTBG 377) by Charlie Fletcher, *Black Hearts in Battersea* by Joan Aiken and *The Amulet of Samarkand* (UTBG 21) by Jonathan Stroud.

Alternatively, try *The Looking Glass Wars* by Frank Beddor. (UTBG 240)

**Matthew Humpage**

# AN UNSUITABLE JOB FOR A WOMAN
## P.D. James

I read this book in one go on the night before my daughter Catherine was born. She has turned out to be a great fan of detective fiction, and I often wonder whether that last experience in the womb is to blame!

This is the story of Cordelia Gray, tackling the mystery of two apparent suicides: of her partner in a detective agency, and of a 21-year-old Cambridge student. It's a good introduction to the work of P.D. James, one of my favourite murder-mystery writers. Her books always have more to them than just the solution to a puzzle. Stick with them, and her main character, the sleuth and poet Adam Dalgliesh, will become one of your best friends.

**Eleanor Updale**

### Next?

There are plenty more P.D. James books to choose from. Try *Cover Her Face* and *The Skull Beneath the Skin*.

James can be a little gory. If you want something more gentle, go for Dorothy L. Sayers **Peter Wimsey** books. *The Nine Tailors* is a good place to start. (UTBG 243)

If you want something even more bloody than P.D. James, try Ian Rankin's **Rebus** series, starting with the violent *Knots and Crosses*. (UTBG 328)

# UP ON CLOUD NINE
## Anne Fine

### Next?

Sadly, you won't find anything else quite like this book! I suppose the closest you'll come are the novels of Sharon Creech, in which mysteries are slowly unravelled. Try *Walk Two Moons* or *The Wanderer* (UTBG 422), about a sea journey that helps a girl remember the truth about her past.

The theme of friendship is explored in very different ways in *The Tulip Touch* (UTBG 407) by Anne Fine and *Vicky Angel* by Jacqueline Wilson.

Or you could try *Freak the Mighty* by Rodman Philbrick. (UTBG 147)

When Stolly falls out of a top floor window it's only the jasmine bush that saves him from certain death. His best friend Ian, spending the day at Stolly's hospital bedside, thinks back over their childhood and gradually begins to understand what Stolly has tried to do and why.

If you've ever wondered what a 'life-affirming' book is then read this one. It's about life (and death) and why some people seem to manage better in this world than others. As far as I'm concerned books don't get any 'Finer' than this!

**Laura Hutchings**

# RACE IN YOUNG-ADULT FICTION

## by Bali Rai

When I was at school, finding books about ethnic minority characters was like a treasure hunt. I'd start at one end of the school library and search every shelf, scanning the titles for any hint of ethnicity. I'd take the promising novels off the shelf and read the blurb on the back, looking for tell-tale signs, such as Asian names or Caribbean settings. I'd study the covers, too, hoping to see an ethnic face. Like most treasure hunts, most of the time I was doomed to failure. All the books seemed to me to be about middle-class white kids from posh families who never swore or worried about money. And mostly they never had non-white friends.

Someone gave me *A Little Princess* by Frances Hodgson Burnett, which did have an Indian character in it, but I didn't like it. And I wasn't Indian. I was British and Asian. Where were all the characters that reflected my life, at home and at school? Finally I found books by Farrukh Dhondy and Bernard Ashley and I was satisfied for a while. But I read those quickly and when they were gone, there were no more.

### RACE AND RACISM

*Refugee Boy* by Benjamin Zephaniah

*Jupiter Williams* by S.I. Martin

*Noughts and Crosses* by Malorie Blackman

*Rani and Sukh* by Bali Rai

*(Un)arranged Marriage* by Bali Rai

*One Hundred Shades of White* by Preethi Nair

*Run!* by Farrukh Dhondy

*Does My Head Look Big in This?* By Randa Abdel-Fattah

*Falling* by Sharon Dogar

Today there are more books about British Asians and blacks but not as many as there should be. Reading rates amongst young men of Afro-Caribbean and Pakistani / Bengali descent in particular are very low. One of the reasons is that they don't find books that relate to them and their lives. Too often the characters that they do find are like those mobile phone snap-on covers. The colours are different but the underlying component is universal. That's one of the reasons that I write about characters from different backgrounds to the literary norm. To try and represent the 'real' voice of multi-ethnic Britain. As do authors such as Benjamin Zephaniah, Malorie Blackman, Narinder Dhami and Preethi Nair.

That is not to say that Asian youngsters, for example, should only read about Asian lives. That would be wrong. But they must feel as though their lives are a part of the literary tradition. And many of them do not. That is why race and writing about race is so important. To get non-readers from ethnic minority backgrounds to start reading you need to pull them in. One of the best ways is to give them novels about characters that they can relate to. Real characters whose lives reflect Britain today.

Not the middle-class utopia of boating lakes, boarding schools and wizards, but the streets of inner-city Britain, which is where the vast majority of ethnic minority kids live. Once books about such young people become a norm and not a speciality, only then can we start to say that race in Britain is truly represented in fiction. Things are changing from when I did my treasure hunts but I still get young ethnic minority people asking me if I know of other books, like mine, which deal with their lives, their hopes and their dreams. I'll only be happy when they stop asking me that question. And that is still a long way off.

From the best-selling author of FACE

A modern tale of love and vengeance

RANI & SUKH

bali rai

## URBAN WARS

*The Dirty South* by Alex Wheatle

*The Outsiders* by S.E. Hinton

*Gangsta Rap* by Benjamin Zephaniah

*Caught in the Crossfire* by Alan Gibbons

*The Crew* by Bali Rai

*Malarkey* by Keith Gray

*Scorpions* by Walter Dean Myers

*Angel Boy* by Bernard Ashley

# USEFUL IDIOTS  Jan Mark

The year is 2255. Climate change has altered the shape of the world; whole countries and great cities are under water. What's left of Britain is now The Rhine Delta Islands, part of the United States of Europe. Jan Mark's wonderfully imagined new world order depends upon homogeneity; genetically engineered humans lead long and blandly pleasant lives. Anything that encourages non-conformity and individualism is deeply distrusted. Digging up the past to discover one's 'primitive' roots is therefore a dangerous activity, and when a group of archaeologists unearth a rare intact skeleton on 'Aboriginal' land they find themselves in deep trouble.

Part sci-fi, part crime thriller, *Useful Idiots* asks thorny and absorbing questions about what it takes to be an individual in a world submerged in historical and political amnesia.

**Mal Peet**

### Next?

Jan Mark's books often look to the future to make us think about the present. Try *Riding Tycho* next, about a girl who discovers that there is more to life than misery and tyranny.

Or read Arthur C. Clarke's *2001: A Space Odyssey*, which makes us question everything we know about our origins.

*A Rag, a Bone and a Hank of Hair* by Nicholas Fisk is also about cloning.

# VAMPIRATES  Justin Somper

### Next?

In order, the series so far, runs: *Demons of the Ocean* (and in here fits the World Book Day mini, *Dead Deep*), *Tide of Terror*, *Blood Captain* and *Black Heart*.

More pirates? Try Rafael Sabatini's wonderful *Captain Blood* – and hunt out the movie, too – it's great.

There are few series that grip from page one and keep you eagerly awaiting more. **Vampirates** is one. And why not, when even the name itself is intriguing – vampire pirates? Bring them on! After all, who isn't fascinated by the other-worldliness of vampires, or by the brutal, free-spirited life of the pirate? In books and movies, pirates and vampires are often misunderstood, lonely outcasts in need of something or someone to save them from their own baser natures. And with so much shared background, it's surprising no one thought to bring the two genres together before!

Pick up one and dive into the shimmering other world. Be enthralled, wince at the gore and gasp at the huge set-piece fights. Yet along with all that, you'll come to think of all these characters as real, you'll feel for some and want them to succeed and you'll hate others – after all, this is a world where even the monsters are very human.

**Leonie Flynn**

# THE VANISHING OF KATHARINA LINDEN
## Helen Grant

*The Vanishing of Katharina Linden* is that rare pleasure these days: a book that doesn't try to be like anything else out there. Written with maturity and without condescension, the story of Katharina's disappearance from Bad Münstereifel, the provincial German town where she lives, is related by Pia, a young half-English, half-German girl, determined to investigate. With only her reluctant comrade Stefan for support, they begin to uncover the truth, but then the next girl goes missing and the situation starts to escalate. Particularly enjoyable is the way in which fairy tale and reality, and the way that these two can become confused in a young child's mind, are depicted. An elegant tale.

**Marcus Sedgwick**

### Next?

In Kevin Brooks's *Black Rabbit Summer* the main character's best friend goes missing, and the book is partly about trying to unravel why. (UTBG 46)

Or look out for Celia Rees's *The Vanished*, which is also about children going missing.

Or for a different twist, try Michael Grant's *Gone* (UTBG 160), in which all the adults have disappeared, or Lucy Christopher's *Stolen*, the story of a kidnapping told by the missing girl.

# VERNON GOD LITTLE   D.B.C. Pierre

### Next?

For another distinctive and off-centre American hero, try John Irving's brilliant *A Prayer for Owen Meany*. (UTBG 318)

For a narrative voice that's energetic and captivating (and a little odd), read Patrick McCabe's dark and dazzling *Butcher Boy*, though for some of it you'll need a strong stomach.

And if you've not read J.D. Salinger's *The Catcher in the Rye*, now's your chance. I'd have thought Vernon and Holden would have got along. (UTBG 69)

Just when I start complaining that books don't surprise me any more, along comes one like *Vernon God Little*. And *Vernon God Little* didn't just surprise me – it pretty much knocked me over. I don't know when I've last read a book with the energy, the freshness and fearlessness, the relish, the sheer hurtling momentum of this one.

It's the story of a teenager in a small Texan town, in the wake of a terrible school shooting. The town is Martirio, the barbecue-sauce capital of Texas. The narrator's voice belongs to Vernon Little – and what a voice it is. Angry and sharp and smart and witty and profane, and with the power to blow away a stolid, cynical seen-it-all-before reader like me. It's a great feeling.

**Daniel Hahn**

# V FOR VENDETTA
## Alan Moore, illustrated by David Lloyd

**Next?**

More Alan Moore? Try the stunning **Watchmen** graphic novel and see why it's so revered. (UTBG 426)

**Hero** by Perry Moore tells the story of a world where superheroes are the norm, and anyone could grow up with special powers. (UTBG 176)

Comics can tell real stories, too. Look out for Art Spiegelman's retelling of the Holocaust in **Maus** (UTBG 258), or **Persepolis** (UTBG 310) by Marjane Satrapi.

What if Guy Fawkes had succeeded? This dark, gripping graphic novel blends George Orwell's *Nineteen Eighty-Four* with *Robin Hood*. The mysterious 'V' is a mask-wearing, Shakespeare-spouting terrorist, committed to bringing down the government in a 21st-century fascist Britain. On the very first page, he succeeds in blowing up the Houses of Parliament; but this is just the beginning of his plans. Evie, a young woman he rescues from a vicious police attack, gradually uncovers more about his extraordinary past. For he is a man betrayed, and he will stop at nothing to bring down those responsible. Evie herself is to play a key role in his schemes, one that no one could have predicted.

**Ariel Kahn**

# WALKABOUT  James Vance Marshall

As a teenager, I loved this for the descriptions of the Australian landscape – wild and remote, beautiful but also dangerous – as well as for the powerful story of what happens when two children crash-land in the middle of the Australian desert. They have no chance of survival: it's thousands of miles to Adelaide, where they are going, in intense heat with no food and hardly any water. And then they meet an Aboriginal boy, who knows everything about survival in this place. Their meeting is also the meeting of two very different cultures and, without giving too much away, what happens is a tragic mirror of what has happened so often when people misunderstand and fear each other.

*Walkabout* was written back in 1959, and some of the language about race is totally inappropriate today, but don't let that put you off this moving story.

**Next?**

Gillian Cross's **The Dark Ground** is about a boy alone in a strange jungle. (UTBG 95)

Sonya Hartnett is a great Australian writer; try **Stripes of the Sidestep Wolf**.

Or what about a riches-to-rags story of a girl sentenced to be transported to the penal colonies in Australia? Read **Scatterheart** by Lili Wilkinson. (UTBG 343)

**Julia Green**

# WALKING NAKED  Alyssa Brugman

Suicide isn't an easy subject, but *Walking Naked* tackles it head-on with starkly elegant, wry humour. Megan is one of the beautiful people; Perdita is the school outcast. Thrown together in detention, Megan is drawn to Perdita, who is unexpectedly funny, intelligent, uncompromising – and desperate. But when her friends force Megan to take sides, she shuns Perdita – and then must live with the consequences.

Megan's honesty about her own behaviour – of which she's not proud – is painful, but this isn't a grim book. Perdita introduces Megan to poetry, a connection which underpins their unorthodox friendship, and helps to reveal Perdita's personality and Megan's growing understanding of herself – and of someone utterly different.

**Helen Simmons**

## DEATH AND BEYOND

*Before I Die* by Jenny Downham

*Ways to Live Forever* by Sally Nicholls

*Bitter Fruit* by Brian Keaney

*The Ostrich Boys* by Keith Gray

*Brothers* by Ted van Lieshout

*From Where I Stand* by Tabitha Suzuma

*Elsewhere* by Gabrielle Zevin

*The Great Blue Yonder* by Alex Shearer

*The Lovely Bones* by Alice Sebold

*Bog Child* by Siobhan O'Dowd

*If I Stay* by Gayle Forman

### Next?

*Lucas* is about a mysterious, beautiful outsider who arrives on an island, but for some reason everyone hates him. (UTBG 249)

*Girl, Interrupted* by Susanna Kaysen deals with the feeling that you don't want to go on with your life. Not as gloomy as it sounds, as it is full of raw humour and hope.

Nick Hornby's funny and sad *A Long Way Down* tackles the theme of suicide, and is about four very different people who become each other's support group.

# WALK TWO MOONS  Sharon Creech

**Next?**

Other books by Sharon Creech:
try *The Wanderer* (UTBG 422); or
*Chasing Redbird*, about growing up
and facing death, or *Absolutely
Normal Chaos*, in which a girl
diarizes her summer of first love.

*To Kill a Mockingbird* is a wise,
wonderful, moving story, which is
also about seeing from someone
else's point of view, and has a strong
female narrator. (UTBG 398)

Joan Bauer is another great
American writer; try *Hope Was
Here*, about a girl constantly moving
from place to place.

Sal (short for Salamanca) and her father moved a year ago, after her mother left 'in order to clear her heart of all the bad things' and never returned. In this wonderful novel, Sal travels back with her gram and gramps to find her mother, and over the long journey across America to Idaho she tells them the story of her friend Phoebe; while at the same time she is revealing another story, about herself. The ending of this story moves me to tears each time I read it.

There are great characters, funny bits, wise sayings: 'Don't judge a man until you've walked two moons in his moccasins'; and most importantly of all, Sal's utterly convincing voice telling the story. I loved this book!

**Julia Green**

# THE WANDERER  Sharon Creech

Sophie has persuaded her three uncles and two cousins to let her join them on a trip of a lifetime aboard *The Wanderer* – a 45-foot sailboat which they plan to sail north up the coast from Connecticut, then east across the ocean towards England where Sophie's grandfather is looking forward to a visit from his three sons. Thirteen-year-old Sophie is an orphan, daydreamer and headstrong tomboy, and an absorbing and intriguing main character. During several windswept weeks at sea, Sophie manages to inspire everyone around her despite being on the very brink of coming to terms with her own fractured and half-remembered family history. The author's descriptions of the sea and of Sophie's emotional and physical journeys are first class.

**John McLay**

**Next?**

*Ruby Holler* is also about
family and loyalty, but is more
quirky and magical. (UTBG
337)

Michael Morpurgo writes
movingly of identity, the past
and the sea in his *Alone on
a Wide, Wide Sea*.

Something different? If you
like swashbuckling adventure
on the high seas, with some
pirates who are also vampires
thrown in, try Justin Somper's
*Vampirates* series. (UTBG
418)

# WAR AND PEACE  Leo Tolstoy  ✷ ✷ ✷

Count Tolstoy served as a military officer in the Crimea, but turned against war and began the pacifist movement of which Gandhi was his most eminent disciple. He is also Russia's greatest novelist. He spent ten years creating his masterpiece, *War and Peace*, an epic (i.e. whopping great) novel about Napoleon's invasion of Russia, seen through the lives of three aristocratic families. Tolstoy himself appears in the novel as the gentle, peaceable, bumbling Pierre Bezukhov.

Don't be put off by the length of the book, or by Uncle Reg's comment that he 'started reading it once, but never finished it'. This is one of the greatest books ever written, so it merits perseverance.

**James Riordan**

### Next?

After this massive book you may find yourself hooked on Russian classics. Move on to Tolstoy's *Anna Karenina* (UTBG 25) (tragic love story), Dostoyevsky's *Crime and Punishment* (UTBG 89) (tragic, thought-provoking thriller), or Mikhail Lermontov's *A Hero of Our Time* (psychological tragedy).

Or for something epic and *not tragic at all*, Vikram Seth's *A Suitable Boy*, set in India – many families and many classes and many generations (and many pages) – a great and glorious read.

# WAREHOUSE  Keith Gray  ✷ ✷

### Next?

*Stone Cold* (UTBG 377) by Robert Swindells is about homelessness, while *The Simple Gift* (UTBG 363) by Steven Herrick and *Paper Towns* by John Green are about running away from home and how bleak an experience that can be.

Other Keith Gray? Try *The Fearful*, about a father and son trying to come to terms with each other and the past, or *Ostrich Boys* (UTBG 300).

*The Lost Boys' Appreciation Society* by Alan Gibbons is about trying to cope with grief.

The Warehouse is a place where kids go when everything in their lives has fallen apart. Robbie's brother beats him up. Amy has had everything stolen from her. Independently they end up with Canner, the Can Man, the fixer, who helps them to the sanctuary of the Warehouse. Once there, we find a twilight society in which the young people try to pull the broken bits of their lives together. We find out about Canner, and then there's King Lem, the boss man who has problems of his own.

The freshness of this story comes in the way it is shaped. Parallel tales are told from the perspective of different characters. It reminds the reader that the Warehouse is a place of many potential stories, not just one.

**Anne Cassidy**

# THE WAR OF THE WORLDS H.G. Wells

Imagine invaders from Mars arriving at the end of your street! H.G. Wells's science-fiction adventure will have you on the edge of your seat as sinister cylinders rain down from space on South London and slowly unscrew to reveal Martians brandishing heat-rays...

The narrator of this story is one of the first to witness the Martians' war machines – huge tripods – stalking across the scorched heathland near his former home. Meeting up with a fellow survivor, he hides in a house that is hit by a second wave of cylinders. What are the Martians making in their crater? Will our hero be reunited with his wife? Will the Martians and their tripods take over the world? Can humanity – and the Earth – hope to survive? H.G. Wells studied biology, and his answer may take you by surprise!

**Lesley Howarth**

**Next?**

For something a bit more guns 'n' battles, try *Starship Troopers* by Robert Heinlein.

Or more H.G. Wells? Try *The Time Machine*.

Fancy some more recent classic sci-fi? Try Kim Stanley Robinson's **Mars** trilogy, starting with *Red Mars*.

Or check out our sci-fi feature on pp. 246–247 for more suggestions.

# WARRIOR GIRL Pauline Chandler

**Next?**

*Dark Thread* by Pauline Chandler tells the time-travelling life story of Kate, a young weaver girl.

Or try her *Viking Girl*. And don't forget *The Mark of Edain*, about a Celtic slave-girl trying to outwit an emperor.

Period detail as authentic and engrossing as in *Warrior Girl*, this time of Elizabethan everyday life, can be found in *Tread Softly* by Kate Pennington.

Or try Mary Hooper's *Newes from the Dead*, about a hanged scullery maid who is revived just before her autopsy begins. (UTBG 282)

A sweeping and dramatic historical epic, which tells the story of Mariane, Joan of Arc's brave and trustworthy friend whose parents have been brutally murdered by the occupying English army. Persuaded to rally to Joan's cause, Mariane had reckoned without those wanting to have an English ruler on the throne, including her scheming and corrupt uncle, Sir Gaston. Mariane is forced to choose between saving herself and saving her country fighting at Joan's side.

Meticulous research, larger-than-life characters from every social class, a fiery heroine, fast pace and a nifty ending make this an unforgettable evocation of 15th-century France, which really pulls readers into the heart of the action.

**Eileen Armstrong**

# THE WASP FACTORY  Iain Banks

*The Wasp Factory* is not for the squeamish. Banks piles on the horror in graphic detail, BUT it is also extremely well written, compulsively readable and studded with the author's trademark dark humour. The narrator is Frank Cauldhame, a disturbed and disturbing 16-year-old who lives on a small island with his reclusive father. He lives his life according to a series of bizarre and unpleasant rituals, which usually involve killing something and which bring some kind of twisted order to his troubled world.

Frank is obsessed with death; indeed he tells us that he has killed three children. But can we believe anything Frank says when he himself is so clearly deranged? Banks's skill as a writer lies in making the monstrous Frank human and in making us care about him.

**Kathryn Ross**

---

### Next?

More Iain Banks? My favourite is *The Crow Road*, which follows young Prentice McHoan as he attempts to make sense of his complex, wildly eccentric Scottish family.

*O Caledonia* by Elspeth Barker is another surreal and hilarious tale of a dark and troubled adolescent.

And if you've got the taste for well-crafted horror, read Melvin Burgess's *Bloodtide*, a terrifying epic of love, betrayal and revenge. (UTBG 49)

---

## The Ultimate Teen Book List

### BOOKTRUST TEENAGE PRIZE WINNERS

| 2009 | The Graveyard Book (p. 165) |
|------|------------------------------|
| 2008 | The Knife of Never Letting Go (p. 229) |
| 2007 | My Swordhand Is Singing (p. 275) |
| 2006 | Henry Tumour (p. 175) |
| 2005 | Century (p. 72) |
| 2004 | Looking for JJ (p. 240) |
| 2003 | The Curious Incident of the Dog in the Night-Time (p. 92) |

MY SWORDHAND IS SINGING
*Marcus Sedgwick*
In the dead heart of winter evil stirs . . .

# THE WATCH HOUSE  Robert Westall

**Next?**

Oscar Wilde's *The Canterville Ghost* is also about a ghost and a little girl – a mix of humour and horror.

Another very spooky haunted house can be found in Susan Hill's chiller *The Woman in Black*. (UTBG 443)

More Westall? Many of the books he writes are unsettling. Try *The Scarecrows* for starters. (UTBG 342)

*The Turn of the Screw* by Henry James is one of the scariest stories ever written. (UTBG 409)

Or try *Breathe* by Cliff McNish for more ghosts and the supernatural. (UTBG 60)

My favourite ghost story of all time: not just because it's very spooky, but because it's long enough for you to discover the full history behind the ghost (or ghosts) and the building they haunt. The story centres on the Watch House on top of a cliff, from where the lifeboat men used to look out for ships in distress. Anne comes to live in the cottage next door for the summer as her parents' marriage is in trouble. This unhappy girl becomes a channel for the unhappy ghost; she gets drawn into the world of Victorian Garmouth and discovers a grisly secret. Full of great comic characters as well as scary bits, this book presents interesting theories on what ghosts are and how they work.

**Abigail Anderson**

# WATCHMEN
## Alan Moore and Dave Gibbons

Don't ever let anyone tell you that comics are just for kids. *Watchmen* puts that idea well and truly to rest. Alan Moore is a superb writer, Dave Gibbons a startlingly good artist, and together they serve up one hell of a story, which first came out in 1986 as an award-winning 12-issue mini-series, and then later as a graphic novel. OK, so it's more than 20 years old, but the paranoia, the multiple plot-lines, the tension and the unique mix of sci-fi, philosophy and conspiracy theories still ring true. Moore writes as densely plotted a storyline as you could wish for, while Gibbons packs more detail, thought and design into a single page than you'll find in most complete comic books.

**Next?**

Check out Moore's *The League of Extraordinary Gentlemen*, which is drawn by Kevin O'Neill, and his collaboration with Eddie Campbell, *From Hell*, about Jack the Ripper; both are far better than the movies made from them.

And look out for Frank Miller's great Batman story, *The Dark Knight Returns*.

For something non-graphic, why not try Joseph Heller's mind-boggling *Catch-22*? (UTBG 68)

**Graham Marks**

# WATERSHIP DOWN
## Richard Adams

**Next?**

*The Incredible Journey* by Sheila Burnford is another story about a group of animals travelling a long way.

Or try *Urchin of the Riding Stars*, part of the **Mismantle Chronicles** by M.I. McAllister, about a world where animals are in charge.

If you want something as epic as *Watership Down*, though, your best bet is **The Lord of the Rings** trilogy (UTBG 242), though **The Duncton Chronicles** by William Horwood are pretty good, too!

Something terrible is going to happen to Hazel's home warren. His brother Fiver has foreseen disaster, and Fiver's sixth sense is never wrong. So, along with a handful of companions, Hazel and Fiver set off into the unknown. And so begins a great adventure, in which the small band of rabbits will face every danger imaginable in their search for a new home.

There's no other book like *Watership Down*. It's an animal story, an adventure and an epic all rolled into one. I've read it more than ten times, and each time I find something new.

**Benedict Jacka**

# WAVING, NOT DROWNING  Rosie Rushton

There's Jay, trying to look after his forgetful nan while keeping his own troublesome life under control. Fee, whose boyfriend has stopped calling her, whose parents' marriage is falling apart and who might – just perhaps – be pregnant. And there's Lyall – angry and hurting and unable to cope with the memories of his sister's death, the guilt and the rage at himself and the world. Three 16 year olds, whose stories wind in and out of each other in clever and often surprising ways; I read it gripped in a single sitting, and no doubt you will, too.

*Waving, Not Drowning* is a book about teenagers struggling as their lives spiral out of control, but it's not maudlin or grim – really it's a story of growing confidence, learning to trust and love, finding answers and finding happiness.

**Next?**

For a story with echoes of Lyall's, read Sue Welford's *Out of the Blue*. (UTBG 303)

For a story more like Fee's, try Julia Green's **Blue Moon** and the sequel **Baby Blue**. (UTBG 50)

Or if Jay was the one you found most interesting, try Valerie Mendes's **Lost and Found**. (UTBG 243)

Or more Rosie Rushton? There's her series that updates the stories of Jane Austen, starting with **The Secrets of Love**, the *Sense and Sensibility* retelling.

**Daniel Hahn**

# WAYLANDER   David Gemmell

### Next?

If you enjoyed *Waylander*, why not read another of Gemmell's **Drenai** novels, such as the equally excellent *Winter Warriors*. Or you could try his **Trojan War Trilogy**.

How about some dragons with your sword-and-sorcery? Try Anne McCaffrey's **Dragons of Pern** series, starting with *Dragonflight* (UTBG 114) or Robin Hobbs's **Farseer** trilogy.

Or for a doorstop read that will keep you enthralled, try *Magician* by Raymond E. Feist.

The Drenai king is dead – murdered by a ruthless assassin. Enemy troops invade the Drenai lands. Their orders are simple – kill every man, woman and child. Stalked by beast-like men, the great warrior Waylander has to journey alone to the shadow-haunted lands of the Nadir to find the legendary Armour of Bronze to save the kingdom. But can he be trusted? For he is Waylander the Slayer: the traitor who killed the king.

David Gemmell is a British writer who has been writing great sword-and-sorcery fantasy novels for over 20 years, and now has a huge adult and teenage readership. If you like your heroes tough, with frequent explosive action, with war or the threat of it always in the air, then Gemmell's for you.

**Cliff McNish**

# WAYS TO LIVE FOREVER
## Sally Nicholls

Sam is eleven and likes to collect facts. Sam is also dying from leukaemia.

Sally Nicholls's story is about what it is like for a child to know that they are dying. Sam is a brave boy, and in the way that only children can, he asks those questions throughout the book that no one else will. Questions such as 'How do you know that you've died?' and 'Why does God make children ill?'

Sam's humour throughout the book makes his illness more poignant, and as he creates a list of ways to live forever, his struggle to accept what's happening and to maintain a brave face for his loving family is clear.

**Adam Lancaster**

### Next?

For more fiction celebrating life and dealing with teenage illness, try Jenny Downham's *Before I Die* (UTBG 37). Or try Damian Kelleher's story of a boy whose mother falls ill, *Life, Interrupted* (UTBG 236).

For beyond-the-grave fiction try *Elsewhere* (UTBG 120) by Gabrielle Zevin, an excellent, uplifting book about life and death, or Alice Sebold's *The Lovely Bones* (UTBG 248).

Sally Nicholls's *Season of Secrets* is very different, but equally moving. (UTBG 345)

# WAYWALKERS   Catherine Webb

Catherine Webb was only 16 when she wrote this novel, but it doesn't feel as if it was written by a novice.

The hero, Sam, is a son of Time who harbours an unsuspected alter ego. He leads us through time from First World War horror scenes to the present day, where Scandinavian gods are threatening to unleash Hell. Embarking on a hunt for the keys to stop Armageddon, Sam begins to discover the full extent of his powers...

The narrative moves fast, incorporating enough red herrings to engage the brain – though too many complications and characters if you like your adventures simple. The style is colourful and often funny. The battles, which crop up on a regular basis, are well done. And the climax whets your appetite, supplying just enough to satisfy but leaving you hungry for more – which is where the sequel, *Timekeepers*, comes in...

**Geraldine McCaughrean**

> **Next?**
>
> Catherine Webb writes about the power of dreams in *Mirror Dreams*.
>
> S.E. Hinton also started writing very early indeed – *The Outsiders* is another astonishing debut. (UTBG 305)
>
> More Norse myth? Try Catherine Fisher's *The Snow-walker's Son* and its sequels.
>
> Christopher Paolini began writing *Eragon* when he was 15! (UTBG 121)

# WEAVEWORLD   Clive Barker

> **Next?**
>
> You might like Clive Barker's other stories, such as *Imajica*. Or, for an easier read, look for his beautifully illustrated *Abarat* quartet (UTBG 10).
>
> Try James Herbert's *The Rats* and its follow up, *Lair* – and never look at journeys on the Underground the same way again...
>
> In Ray Bradbury's *The Illustrated Man*, a fairground worker's tattoos come alive and tell their stories. (UTBG 200)

When one of his father's racing pigeons escapes, Cal chases it to a strange gathering of birds over what looks to be an old carpet thrown out in a back yard. This carpet belongs to Suzanna, who has just inherited it from her grandmother. But in this story of magic and nightmares, nothing is quite what it seems. For the carpet contains another world – Weaveworld – inhabited by people with terrifying powers, who call us 'Cuckoos'.

Stalked by a sinister salesman called Shadwell and by Weaveworld refugee Immocolata, Cal and Suzanna are sucked into terrifying adventures a million miles away from Harry Potter and his tame wizard school. This book weaves fantasy with horror into a story that amazed me when I first read it and has continued to delight me ever since.

**Katherine Roberts**

# WE CAN REMEMBER IT FOR YOU WHOLESALE  Philip K. Dick

✶ ✶ ✶

A marvellous collection of sci-fi short stories with surreal titles like 'The Electric Ant', 'Your Appointment Will Be Yesterday' and 'Cadbury, the Beaver Who Lacked'. The title story was made into the film *Total Recall*. Apart from other films directly based on his stories (*Blade Runner*, *Minority Report*, etc.) you will see Philip K. Dick's influence in films such as *The Matrix*, *Twelve Monkeys* and *Eternal Sunshine of the Spotless Mind*.

Dick loved to toy with concepts like time travel, memory and identity. For example: a Gulliver-like time traveller finds people are tiny in the past and huge in the future. Why? Because the universe is expanding. Simple, but brilliant.

**Caroline Lawrence**

> **Next?**
>
> More Philip K. Dick? Try *Do Androids Dream of Electric Sheep?* (UTBG 111) or *The Man in the High Castle* (UTBG 254).
>
> Or what about **Neuromancer** by William Gibson, the book that spawned the whole cyberpunk genre?
>
> Or try a short story collection – *The Ascent of Wonder: The Evolution of Hard Sci-fi*, edited by David G. Hartwell.

# THE WEIRDSTONE OF BRISINGAMEN
## Alan Garner

✶

> **Next?**
>
> You won't want to miss the sequel, *The Moon of Gomrath*.
>
> If you like stories that make your spine tingle, try Alan Garner's *The Owl Service*. (UTBG 306)
>
> In Kate Thompson's *The New Policeman*, time, music and the world of Fairie all blend in an exciting adventure. (UTBG 282)
>
> Or read Susan Cooper's **The Dark Is Rising** sequence – five books that bring together Arthurian legend and a magnificent battle between good and evil. (UTBG 96)

Deep underground, a wizard watches over 140 magical knights. But the stone that binds them – the Weirdstone of Brisingamen, 'Firefrost' by name – is lost. Two seemingly ordinary children, Colin and Susan, are the key to finding it again. But they know nothing about their destiny until they are chased across Alderley Edge by dark creatures seeking to pursue and destroy them. The wizard rescues Colin and Susan from the dark creatures, and the fight between good and evil is on!

Long before we first heard of Harry Potter, this story was gripping its readers. It's wonderfully eerie, with great characters.

**Yvonne Coppard**

# WHAT I SAW AND HOW I LIED
## Judy Blundell

An excellent title for an excellent first novel. Set in the US in the early 1950s, this teenage girl's rites-of-passage tale primarily takes place in an out-of-season Palm Beach hotel. The narrator, Evie, looks back at her life, aged 16, to the time when she tries to step out of her blonde-bombshell mother's shadow. She soon discovers that all is not what it seems, with a heady mix of half-truths, outright lies, deceit, violence and anti-Semitism bubbling just below the surface. Everything from her family to society as a whole is rotten to the core.

Blundell combines convincing characters with a spot-on period backdrop to create an atmospheric page-turner. This is a must-read.

**Philip Ardagh**

> **Next?**
>
> There's more coming-of-age angst in the classic French novel, *Bonjour Tristesse* by Françoise Sagan. (UTBG 52)
>
> There's a love triangle with a lot of bite in Stephenie Meyer's vampire saga, beginning with *Twilight*. (UTBG 411)
>
> Or try Robert Cormier's *Heroes*, in which an 18-year-old soldier returning from World War II goes back to his home town with vengeance in mind. (UTBG 176)

# WHAT I WAS
## Meg Rosoff

> **Next?**
>
> Meg Rosoff's debut novel, *How I Live Now* (UTBG 190), is already a classic. Read it. Or try her very different Gothic adventure, *The Bride's Farewell*.
>
> There's more about boarding-school life in Joanne Harris's *Gentlemen and Players*, set in the north of England.
>
> Libba Bray's *A Great and Terrible Beauty* is set in a Victorian girls' boarding school.

The narrator of this book lives a lonely existence at a grim boarding school on the East Anglian coast. His life changes when one day he glimpses Finn, a teenager who lives alone in a hut by the sea. Quickly, the narrator becomes infatuated by the beautiful Finn and the freedom and romance that Finn's lifestyle represents. He is drawn frequently to the hut by the sea, despite Finn's seeming indifference to his presence. Then, one stormy night, events take a dangerous turn and his relationship with Finn is shaken to its core.

This unusual love story will gradually draw you in with its slow, languid prose, which builds up to a shocking and thought-provoking ending.

**Rebecca Wilkie**

# WHAT THE BIRDS SEE  Sonya Hartnett

Stories about children are not necessarily for children. Nine-year-old Adrian, taken from his unstable mother, abandoned by his father, is raised by his gran, who looks after him but never troubles to conceal the fact that she finds him a burden; her own adult children are enough of a headache. But she would be very sorry if something happened to him, especially as the neighbourhood, a quiet Australian suburb, is haunted by the fate of three young children who went missing and were never found. This beautifully written, desperately sad story about a lost child and the unhappy adults who fail him, is also haunted by a sense of unspoken horror that becomes only too real at the end.

**Jan Mark**

### Next?

Another novel by Sonya Hartnett is **Thursday's Child**, about a family surviving during the Depression of the 1930s. (UTBG 396)

There are many books around by Australian writers. Look for **Wolf on the Fold** by Judith Clarke, about different generations of one family; and **Jinx** by Margaret Wild, a novel told entirely in short poems.

Or read about another lost person in Meg Rosoff's **What I Was**. (UTBG 431)

# WHEELS  Catherine MacPhail

### Next?

Other Catherine MacPhail books include **Underworld**, **Roxy's Baby** (UTBG 336), set in a refuge for young pregnant girls, and **Another Me**, a thriller about a girl coming face to face with her double.

**Unique** by Alison Allen-Gray is another thriller, this time about cloning. (UTBG 414)

**Saffy's Angel** (UTBG 340) by Hilary McKay and **Paralysed** by Sherry Ashworth take very different looks at life in wheels of steel.

How would you feel if your dad was killed in a car accident one night and that same accident left you faced with spending the rest of your life in a wheelchair? That's exactly what happens to James. But when he is still in hospital recovering, something weird happens. He's sure he sees the other man who was supposedly killed, the man who was driving the car... So how come he's still alive?

MacPhail keeps us in suspense, with a surprise on every page. *Wheels* forces us to think again about how the disabled are treated in society. It shows us that wheels aren't everything and friendship and determination are stronger than metal. An edge-of-the-seat thriller, which really hooks you from the start.

**David Gardner, age 16**

# WHEN ISLA MEETS LUKE MEETS ISLA ✳ ✳
## Rhian Tracey

**Next?**

The sequel: *Isla and Luke: Make or Break*. Rhian Tracey has also written *True Colours* and *The Bad Girls' Club*, another lively story with multiple narrators.

Other great books with multiple narrators include *Lost and Found* (UTBG 243) and *Waving, Not Drowning* (UTBG 427).

Isla meets Luke – girl meets boy (and vice versa). Just like any old fairy tale. But you'll soon see, this is no fairy tale.

There aren't many love / relationship stories I'd recommend equally readily to readers of both sexes, but *When Isla Meets Luke...* is one of them. The fact that the chapters alternate between the two characters' points of view certainly helps; but what really makes it special is a strong and believable story that's sometimes touching but never soppy, and its two altogether lifelike lead characters.

You'll get attached to both Isla and Luke – you'll get frustrated by them, as with real people, but they'll make you laugh, too. You may well find yourself hoping that Rhian Tracey will take the easy road and let them have a fairy-tale ending. Wouldn't that be nice? But Tracey is a far better writer than that.

**Daniel Hahn**

# WHEN THE GUNS FALL SILENT ✳ ✳
## James Riordan

Rats nesting in corpses, the firing squad for deserters, filth, noise – and the constant danger of death. Welcome to the Western Front in 1914.

Jack lies about his age to enlist – after all, why waste time when everyone says the war'll be over by Christmas? He doesn't want to miss any of the fun. But Jack learns that war isn't anything like he imagines, and instead of fun it's just about as awful as anything can possibly be.

There's no real way for us to know what it was like to be human cannon-fodder, but this book has a good try. Sparsely told, with letters and diary entries alongside the narrative, it simply tells the story of one boy's war, complete with terror, love, friendship and loss. Oh, and football, too.

**Next?**

James Riordan writes brilliantly about war. Try *Match of Death*, in which a young team literally have to play for their lives, or *The Prisoner*, where two kids find a wounded German pilot and then have to decide what to do with him.

For one of the best war books of recent years, try Michael Morpurgo's stunning *Private Peaceful*. It looks a simple read, but try it and see what you think. (UTBG 324)

**Leonie Flynn**

# WHEN THE WIND BLOWS   Raymond Briggs

### Next?

For another graphic novel dealing with grim themes, move on to **Maus**. (UTBG 258)

**Z for Zachariah** is a powerful story set in a post-nuclear holocaust. (UTBG 452)

More Raymond Briggs? Try the wonderfully disgusting **Fungus the Bogeyman**! Meanwhile **Ethel and Ernest** (UTBG 123) also has a strong, moving story...

James arrives home, his wife greets him. 'Hullo dear.' 'Hullo love.' 'Did you have a nice morning, dear?' Peaceful, domestic, altogether unthrilling; gentle, no urgency, no alarm. But soon we see that this tranquillity and this routine are about to be broken. It is 1982, the height of the Cold War, and the Russians are about to drop The Bomb. James and Hilda remember World War II; but the Third will be the ultimate; it'll mean complete devastation, and thanks to the madness of Mutually Assured Destruction, absolutely everyone will die.

And in this stunning graphic novel, Briggs doesn't pretend otherwise; there's no last-minute salvation (An antidote! In the nick of time!). Though his story is simple and witty, you should prepare to have your heart broken. And this half-hour read will stay with you for ever – I don't know anything like it.

**Daniel Hahn**

# WHIP HAND   Dick Francis

This thriller is set in and around the world of horse racing. Sid Halley was a champion steeplechase jockey until a fall and then a sadistic crook robbed him of half his left arm. Surgeons have fitted him with an electrically operated plastic hand which is rather clumsy. As a consequence he has had to renounce the thrill of riding and has become a private investigator, specialising in the racing world. With his friend Chico, a cheery young judo teacher, Sid is enquiring into a series of mysterious events, principally the poor performance and death of several promising young racehorses. This brings him to the attention of some very nasty criminals. Sid values his courage above all things, and it's sorely tested when a villain threatens to blow off his remaining hand with a shotgun...

**Alan Temperley**

### Next?

The first Sid Halley story is **Odds Against** – it tells how he lost his hand.

John Francome, another ex-jockey, also writes thrillers: start with **Dead Ringer** or **High Flyer**. There's also Graeme Roe – try **Odds On Death**, and Lyndon Stacey – try **Blindfold**.

Or try Robert Harris; **Fatherland** (UTBG 128) supposes Germany won World War II and **Enigma** is about code breaking during the war.

# THE WHISPERING ROAD  Livi Michael

**Next?**

Another Livi Michael? Try *The Angel Stone* next. It's set in two different times, with a girl in Manchester now and a boy back in 1604 linked by a cathedral's Angel stone.

No one wrote better historical adventure series than Joan Aiken. Read *Go Saddle the Sea*.

*The Cup of the World* is an epic adventure set in a fantasy Middle Ages. (UTBG 91)

'There's always been Annie,' says Joe; but many times he is tempted to abandon her and, for a desperate period, he does give in to that temptation. She is his little sister and they are on the run together from the cruel masters that they have been farmed out to by the workhouse. Their bid for freedom takes them to dangerous places, and they have to live on their wits to survive.

It is a picaresque story in which one extraordinary situation follows another and characters as strange as the people of dreams or nightmares weave in and out of their lives. The incidents that the children are involved in are as wild and fascinating as the stories Joe tells, and as the visions his sister has.

This is a great, pacy adventure story that works on many levels; it's both a disturbing and a heart-warming read.

**Berlie Doherty**

# THE WHITE DARKNESS  Geraldine McCaughrean

After her father's death, 14-year-old Sym – shy, awkward and out of step with her classmates – is whisked away on a dream holiday by her eccentric 'Uncle' Victor. Soon she's stranded in the chillingly beautiful Antarctic with a man whose plans seem increasingly sinister…

I loved this book so much that when I'd finished I went straight back to page one and started reading it again. It's haunting, lyrical, painful, funny and peopled by characters who escape the confines of the page and live and breathe in the room alongside you. It's also a gripping page-turner with a captivating heroine and one of the most appealing heroes I've ever had the pleasure of falling for.

**Tanya Landman**

**Next?**

There's more by Geraldine McCaughrean, of course. Try *The Kite Rider* (UTBG 227) or the *Death-Defying Pepper Roux*, about exactly what the title says!

Malorie Blackman's *Tell Me No Lies* is another completely gripping, taut psychological thriller.

Tanya Landman's own *Apache* looks deeply into another culture, and finds reflections of our own there. (UTBG 26)

# WHITE TEETH Zadie Smith

**Next?**

*Brick Lane* by Monica Ali also tells a story of multicultural London.

More Zadie Smith? Try *The Autograph Man*, *On Beauty* or *Changing My Mind*.

*The Buddha of Suburbia* by Hanif Kureishi is a fabulous book about London, sex and being half-Indian. (UTBG 64)

*White Teeth* is about two unlikely friends, Archibald Jones and Samad Iqbal, who meet in a tank during World War II. The novel then fast-forwards to 1970's London, where the friends meet again. They both get married, Archie to Clara – the daughter of a Jamaican Jehovah's Witness, and Samad to Alsana. Both men have children and the story twists and winds though seminal years in their lives. Their friendship grows and strengthens as they struggle to adapt to a world neither of them belongs to. This may sound sad, but it isn't. The book is hilarious and tackles the issues of multiculturalism and religion in a touching way. Zadie Smith has produced a novel that is always funny and poignant, but at the same time wise. I loved it and so will you!

**Ileana Antonopoulou**

# WHO IS JESSE FLOOD? Malachy Doyle

Jesse Flood is different from other kids – he's hopeless at school, sports and talking to girls (though he's a whizz at ping-pong). Jesse lives in his head to shut out

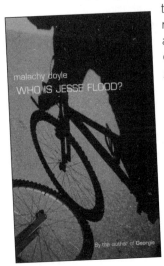

the world, and his diary reveals his thoughts on life and love, as well as his embarrassing failures with girls. He describes teenage life in a small town like being in a long tunnel, waiting for the light to shine through. Malachy Doyle shows great sympathy for the pain of being a teenager and the boredom of small-town life, and creates a distinctive character in Jesse Flood.

**Anne Flaherty**

**Next?**

Try *Feather Boy* (UTBG 130) by Nicky Singer and *Snow Spider* by Jenny Nimmo, both of which feature boys who feel different and who struggle to find their identity.

*Fat Boy Swim* by Catherine Forde is about a boy who finds a most original way of making a difficult life bearable. (UTBG 128)

Or Linda Newbery's *Lost Boy*, about a boy and a secret from the past.

# WHY WEEPS THE BROGAN? Hugh Scott

There are some books that you just can't say a lot about, for fear of spoiling the plot. *Why Weeps the Brogan?* is just such a book. Gilbert and Saxon are brother and sister and they live in a museum. Daily life is a battle against the poisonous spiders that have started to infest the building and there's a monster on the upper levels that they have to feed. And that's about all I can tell you.

This is a novel where everything hinges upon what is revealed in the final page (don't read it first!) and when you've reached that final page you will want to turn around and start at the beginning all over again. Very clever and totally unforgettable.

**Laura Hutchings**

### Next?

It's a little difficult to suggest read-ons for this book without giving too much away! *Z for Zachariah* (UTBG 452) by Robert O'Brien, *Brother in the Land* by Robert Swindells and *Children of the Dust* by Louise Lawrence have similar survival themes.

You might also enjoy the science-fiction novels of John Wyndham. *The Day of the Triffids* is the place to start with these. (UTBG 98)

Or for something that mixes time travel, horror, demons and action? The **Hell's Underground** series by Alan Gibbons, starting with *Scared to Death*.

# WICCA: BOOK OF SHADOWS Cate Tiernan

### Next?

The **Wicca** series continues with *The Coven*, *Blood Witch* and *Dark Magyk*. There are ten books in total, and the stories are also available in omnibus editions.

Holly Black's *Tithe* (UTBG 397) is a powerful drama woven with magic and supernatural excitement, or try Maite Carranza's *War of the Witches*.

*Witch Child* by Celia Rees is a historical story featuring a teenager accused of being a witch. (UTBG 441)

*The Merrybegot* delves into a period of history when it was unsafe to be different. (UTBG 261)

This is the first in a long teen series that is both addictive and very spooky. Sixteen-year-old Morgan is smitten when Cal Blaire, who is a real hottie, transfers to her school and throws a party in a huge field to which everybody goes. Around the campfire, he asks them to join him in a Wiccan thanksgiving ritual. Reactions range from curiosity to fear. Most leave but others, including Morgan and best friend Bree, stay. Some are curious about Wicca. Some are attracted to others present and want to stay near them. And some, like Morgan, have more complex motivations. She's an orphan and curious about her origins, and it turns out Wicca might hold all the answers.

**John McLay**

# WIDE SARGASSO SEA  Jean Rhys

The Sargasso Sea, mysterious and sluggish, swirls between Europe and the West Indies, its waters choked with seaweed, its floor strewn with shipwrecks. This image of the sea mirrors the confused and dangerous relationship between Britain and the West Indies during the 19th century. Edward Rochester marries Antoinette Cosway, a Creole (white West Indian) for her money, only to find she has none. Once in England Antoinette finds herself renamed Bertha and locked away in a secret annexe. Mad with grief, Bertha burns the house to the ground. This is *Jane Eyre* from the point of view of the Creole woman, sidelined and despised in the original book; the 'madwoman in the attic' has been given a voice at last.

**Gill Vickery**

### Next?

*The Awakening* by Kate Chopin is another account of a woman desperate to escape from the stifling life that's imposed on her.

*The Yellow Wallpaper* by Charlotte Perkins Gilman is a brilliant, absolutely terrifying, 'madwoman in the attic' story. (UTBG 451)

You may also enjoy Andrea Levy's *Small Island*, a modern novel about the Windrush generation arriving in Britain from the West Indies.

Or try Jean Rhys's collection of bitter-sweet short stories: *Tigers Are Better Looking*.

# A WILD SHEEP CHASE  Haruki Murakami

### Next?

Read the **Sherlock Holmes** stories for more mysteries within mysteries. (UTBG 359)

Another Murakami? Read the fabulous *Norwegian Wood*, which became a national obsession in Japan; or the wonderfully surreal *The Wind-Up Bird Chronicle*.

Or how about surrealism without the humour? Try Kafka's dark and disturbing *The Trial*, or the short stories that start with *Metamorphosis*.

Murakami is one of those authors you just have to trust. In his books the strange runs parallel to the mundane. Sometimes the two blur, until it's hard to tell the difference. His books read like dreams, and this one is no exception. The hero is quiet and ordinary, but his life, with its endless circular journeys, its despair, is changed when he's hired by Mr Big to find the sheep that changed *his* life. Yes, the title is almost literal! On his quest he meets a girl with the most beautiful ears in the world, talks with the dead, meets a Sheep Man and reads *Sherlock Holmes*.

Surreal, darkly comic, utterly engrossing, this is a wonderfully written book that just might change *your* life.

**Leonie Flynn**

# WILD SWANS  Jung Chang

A mind-opening and mindblowing account of three generations of Chinese women living in Maoist China. From the painful practice of binding women's feet so that they could only take dainty steps, to the struggles of the Long March, it is the fascinating and often shocking details that make this true story so gripping.

It reads like a novel, and you have to keep reminding yourself that it's not. The way the Communist authorities imposed control and turned friend against friend and relative against relative is vividly brought to life – but what shines through most of all is the sheer power and determination of the human spirit. It's an inspirational book.

**Nicola Morgan**

### Next?

For another true and moving story about the Chinese way of life, try Adeline Yen Mah's *Falling Leaves*.

Jung Chang has followed this up with a biography of the tyrannical Chinese leader – *Mao: the Unknown Story* (which she has written with her husband Jon Halliday).

Or if you want to read another story of surviving traumatic early years, try *A Child Called 'It'* by Dave Pelzer. (UTBG 76)

# WILDTHORN  Jane Eagland

### Next?

A boy who also ends up in the 'loony-bin' is the hero of Julie Hearn's wonderful *Rowan the Strange*. (UTBG 336)

Libba Bray writes sensuously about growing up in Victorian times – try *A Great and Terrible Beauty*.

A book set much further back in time – it's Tudor England and Henry VIII is on the throne – but just as complex and intriguing is Marie-Louise Jensen's *The Lady in the Tower*. (UTBG 231)

Set in Victorian times, this book is about a girl, Louise Cosgrove, who gets tricked into being locked up in a asylum – a 'hospital' for people with mental illness. Wildthorn Hall is a terrible place, one where they mentally abuse the patients; Louisa has her clothes and jewellery – and even her name – taken from her. Stripped of everything, she is forced to do nothing but sit still all day. Bewildered and frightened, she is frantic to escape – and to try and work out why her family were so desperate to have her locked away.

Told in flashbacks, you only gradually find out the secrets of Wildthorn Hall, and of Louisa herself. The story is about her journey of understanding, and of growing up. Sex, abuse and love all feature in this amazing story, which is one I'll never forget.

**Jake Curtis, age 12**

# WIND ON FIRE trilogy William Nicholson

This is a fantasy trilogy as full of human truth as it is of adventure, and you may well love it even if fantasy's not usually your thing. In *The Wind Singer*, the Hath family live in the city of Aramanth, where the whole of life is controlled by exams. Even two year olds have to play their part, taking tests that will help decide on their family's future. When Kestrel Hath dares to rebel against the system, she starts off a chain of events that launches her on an epic journey.

*Slaves of the Mastery* and *Firesong* are set five years later: the peace of Aramanth is shattered when the entire population is taken as slaves by warrior invaders. The Hath family emerge as true leaders as they struggle to set their people free and to lead them to their homeland.

**Susan Reuben**

> **Next?**
>
> William Nicholson's other fantasy series, beginning with *Seeker*. (UTBG 352)
>
> Philip Pullman's **His Dark Materials** trilogy is also loved by fantasy lovers and haters alike. (UTBG 181)
>
> Or try the wild adventure that is **The Fourth Horseman**, in which Kate Thompson mixes fantasy, genetic experimentation, fundamentalism, cricket and the end of the world. (UTBG 141)

# THE WISH HOUSE Celia Rees

> **Next?**
>
> Celia Rees has written many books ranging from **Witch Child** (opposite) to thrillers such as **Truth or Dare** (UTBG 407), and exciting adventures like **Pirates!** (UTBG 313)
>
> Linda Newbery's **Set in Stone** also features a country house and an impressionable young man who falls under its spell. (UTBG 354)
>
> Or try Theresa Breslin's story of a boy who gets mixed up with Leonardo da Vinci: **The Medici Seal**. (UTBG 260)

Readers who know Celia Rees through her best-selling *Witch Child* or *Sorceress* are likely to be surprised by this more recent coming-of-age novel, set in the 1970s. On holiday in South Wales with his exceedingly dull parents, Richard is captivated by The Wish House and its unconventional inhabitants, in particular Clio, the beautiful, troubled girl who befriends him, and with whom he has his first sexual experience. Her father, the egotistical artist Jethro Dalton, exerts an autocratic rule over the household; as secrets emerge, Richard realises how thoroughly he has been manipulated.

An enticing feature of this novel is the art-show catalogue preface to each chapter, which Celia Rees has written so skilfully that the reader almost sees the exhibits.

**Linda Newbery**

# WITCH CHILD  Celia Rees

Forget boring historical novels about long-dead people; *Witch Child* is so 'now' and so vivid that you sometimes forget that the heroine Mary lived in the 17th century. Celia Rees is one of those writers with the magical gift of drawing the reader into a relationship with her characters by the end of page one, with the result that homework goes undone, sleep is set aside and a vast amount of chocolate is munched until the adventure comes to an end. Except that in *Witch Child*, it doesn't. So gripping is the writing and so believable the plot that when you reach the final page – and no, I'm not going to tell you just how cleverly executed it is – you simply have to rush out and buy the sequel, *Sorceress*.

This is a book for readers who want believable characters, loads of emotion and a vivid insight into how prejudice and bullying have affected lives for centuries. Without doubt, an unforgettable read.

'A powerful, absorbing and unusual novel' *The Bookseller*

**Rosie Rushton**

### Next?

*Pirates!* is another Celia Rees book set in the past, this time a swashbuckling romance. (UTBG 313)

Or for another book about outsiders, try Elizabeth G. Speare's **The Witch of Blackbird Pond**, about a girl forced to move from Barbados to her Puritan family in Connecticut.

**The Merrybegot** (UTBG 261) by Julie Hearn is a story of superstition and witchcraft, as is Elizabeth Laird's **The Witching Hour**.

## FOR THE LOVE OF A MERMAID (OR MERMAN)

*Ingo* by Helen Dunmore

**Goddess of the Sea** series by P.C. Cast

*Aquamarine* by Alice Hoffman

*The Flowing Queen* by Kai Meyer

*The Undrowned Child* by Michelle Lovric

*Sleeping with the Fishes* by Mary Janice Davidson

*The Tail of Emily Windsnap* by Liz Kessler

*Sirena* by Donna Jo Napoli

# A WIZARD OF EARTHSEA Ursula Le Guin

Ursula Le Guin's books sink their claws into you and don't let go. Written in simple yet powerful prose, they deal with classic themes of good and evil, and what it means to grow up. Her world of Earthsea is one of the great creations in fantasy: a place of many peoples, with a wild surging ocean, dragons, ancient magic and wizards both wise and foolish. This book, the first in her **Earthsea Quartet**, taught me the power of words. To me, *A Wizard of Earthsea* feels like a myth or legend, a half-remembered song. If you are looking for a grand saga, I cannot recommend it highly enough.

**Christopher Paolini**

### Next?

If you love *A Wizard of Earthsea*, there's good news for you – there are sequels: *The Tombs of Atuan*, *The Farthest Shore*, *Tehanu* and *The Other Wind*. There is also a collection of stories in *Tales from Earthsea*.

Frank Herbert's *Dune* and its sequels – *Dune Messiah*, *Children of Dune*, *God Emperor of Dune* and *Road to Dune* – mix science fiction and fantasy in an epic adventure about a young man who fulfils an ancient prophecy about his birth. (UTBG 116)

# WOLF BROTHER Michelle Paver

### Next?

More Michelle Paver? There are five more books in the **Chronicles of Ancient Darkness**: *Spirit Walker*, *Soul Eater*, *Outcast*, *Oath Breaker* and *Ghost Hunter*.

Jenny Nimmo's **Red King** sequence, starting with *Midnight for Charlie Bone*, is a magical thriller.

John Flanagan's **Ranger's Apprentice** series is about a boy learning to live off the land, and the skills of silent, unseen movement, tracking and concealment. The first book is *The Ruins of Gorlan*.

*Wolf Brother* brilliantly recreates the world of 6,000 years ago and follows a young boy, Torak, as he learns to survive in a vast and dangerous forest following the violent death of his father. There are raging rivers, hostile tribes, fever, starvation and, most frightening of all, a demon that has taken the shape of a giant bear.

Michelle Paver certainly knows her stuff – and she doesn't pull any punches. Torak is totally convincing as a primitive hero. When he kills a roe buck and cuts it up to use every bit of it either as food, clothes or weapons (he turns the stomach into a waterskin) you begin to see just how difficult it's going to be for him to survive. Paver is also a great storyteller. Just about every chapter ends on a cliffhanger, although personally I could have done without the slightly old-fashioned illustrations.

**Anthony Horowitz**

# THE WOMAN IN BLACK  Susan Hill

### Next?

Not as well known as *The Woman in Black*, *The Mist in the Mirror* is another atmospheric ghost story by Susan Hill.

The classic *Ghost Stories* (UTBG 153) of M.R. James haven't dated in their power to scare. Look out, too, for collections by E.F. Benson, Algernon Blackwood, Edith Wharton and Elizabeth Gaskell.

For contemporary ghost stories, try *Yaxley's Cat* by Robert Westall or *Breathe* (UTBG 60) by Cliff McNish.

The whole idea of ghosts is turned on its head in Neil Gaiman's wonderful *The Graveyard Book*. (UTBG 165)

There was a point in this chilling ghost story when I actually felt afraid to turn the page, so powerfully and convincingly does the author evoke the haunted atmosphere of Eel Marsh House and the bleak marshland in which it stands. This is where Arthur Kipps, a young solicitor, comes to sort out the papers left by the late Mrs Drablow.

Arthur himself narrates the story – at first confident, carefree, slightly arrogant, then gradually more and more fearful. His changing voice gives the story its terrifying immediacy so that you shudder with him. And just when you think it's all over…

Compulsive and truly frightening, this is in the tradition of the very best ghost stories.

**Patricia Elliott**

# THE WOMAN IN WHITE  Wilkie Collins

You must read *The Woman in White* when you're a teenager – you'll love it, for ever. This is a Gothic story of love, good times and bad, and there is nothing conditional about Walter Hartright's feelings for Laura Fairlie. It has an ethereal quality, a ghostliness and a sense of place that is both eerie and satisfying, and it gives a rich and fascinating insight into how different and difficult mid-Victorian life could be for girls. The strangeness, the madness, the ghostliness resonated for me long after I finished this book, and sent me on a journey through many other Wilkie Collins novels.

**Raffaella Barker**

### Next?

More Wilkie Collins? My favourites to go on to are *The Moonstone* (UTBG 269) (another thriller) and *No Name*.

Try some other great Gothic romances: *The Mysteries of Udolpho* by Ann Radcliffe or *Lady Audley's Secret* by Mary Elizabeth Braddon.

Then there's the parody of such things, Jane Austen's *Northanger Abbey* (UTBG 286).

Or read *The Warden* by Anthony Trollope, the first of the **Chronicles of Barsetshire**, which tell the complex stories of a cathedral town.

# THE WONDERFUL STORY OF HENRY SUGAR  Roald Dahl

**Next?**

**The Sandman** series by Neil Gaiman has a similar mixture of myth and reality. (UTBG 342)

Robert Cormier's *I Am the Cheese* tells the strange story of Adam, who is being interrogated by a psychiatrist with an ulterior motive. (UTBG 194)

*Breaktime* by Aidan Chambers explores similar themes – crime, friendship, first love – and it has teasing multiple layers. (UTBG 60)

Or look out for Dahl's astonishing autobiography, *Boy*.

Roald Dahl isn't just the author of wickedly funny, brilliantly imagined children's books. He also wrote these surreal and disturbing stories, creating a host of different worlds, each one compelling, moving and terrifying. There's a modern-day *Peter Pan*, who travels the seas on the back of a giant turtle; there's a bullied boy who has a swan's wings strapped to his arms. In a third tale, the discovery of buried treasure corrupts everyone who touches it. The title story is the best of the lot, as Henry Sugar learns to stare into a flame, see through a blindfold and become a real magician. There's even the story of how Dahl himself became a writer. This is Roald Dahl as you've never read him before.

**Ariel Kahn**

# THE WORLD ACCORDING TO GARP
## John Irving

This is a great, big, wonderful book, and while the movie has a good stab at getting John Irving's extraordinary story up on screen (it has Robin Williams in one of his first non-comic roles), this is one you *have* to read. It'll make you laugh, possibly out loud, it'll make you sad and it will definitely stay with you long after you've put it down.

What's it about? It may sound like a big cop-out to say it's beyond description, but that's the truth, although I can tell you it has a lot to do with wrestling (with other people as well as with consciences), and that this man is one of the best writers ever. Really.

**Graham Marks**

**Next?**

More John Irving – *The Hotel New Hampshire*, *A Prayer for Owen Meany* (UTBG 318), *The Cider House Rules* – you can't go wrong.

For an odd, all-encompassing American novel with the most bizarre characters, read Tom Robbins's *Another Roadside Attraction*.

Or how about a weird and sprawling mass of a novel set in a Scottish family – Iain Banks's *The Crow Road*?

# WORM IN THE BLOOD   Thomas Bloor

## Next?

The trilogy continues with *Beast Beneath the Skin* and *Heart of the Serpent*.

Jonathan Stroud's *Buried Fire* also has change at its crackling core, but in a very different setting.

N.M. Browne's *Hunted* is about a girl who becomes a fox in an ancient world.

For spine-tingling horror, try Ann Halam's *Don't Open Your Eyes* and *The Fear Man*, which really will make you wary of the dark.

'Sam's skin has started to itch...' I've always been fascinated by the theme of metamorphosis. This is an exciting and ambitious contemporary urban horror story about transformation and the power of love, inspired by Chinese and Welsh mythology. Brief, tense episodes, like pieces of a jigsaw, finally form a picture in which past and present come together. There is a large cast of characters and enjoyable macabre humour in the scenes with the small, vulnerable Father David Lee and his formidable 'protector', Mrs Hare. Sam's transformation is convincingly described, and the atmospheric setting – the brackish canal and marshland beyond the city streets – is suitably nasty.

**Patricia Elliott**

# THE WORST JOURNEY IN THE WORLD
## Apsley Cherry-Garrard

Killer whales, deadly blizzards, temperatures of minus 70 degrees – this is without a doubt the greatest adventure story ever written.

Author Cherry-Garrard was 24 when he was chosen by Scott to be part of the South Polar expedition, and this is his account of the two years that the men spent in Antarctica. The book is a mixture of personal reminiscences and extracts from diaries and letters, and it covers far more than just Scott's doomed walk to the Pole.

The account is written by the one man who could have saved Scott, if only he'd known it – and I for one will be forever grateful that Cherry-Garrard had the courage to publish this account. Without it, men such as Captain Oates and Birdie Bowers would have remained nothing but names in a history book.

## Next?

Read a fictional account of Scott's journey in Beryl Bainbridge's brilliant *The Birthday Boys*.

Or try Geraldine McCaughrean's *The White Darkness*, about a girl obsessed with the Antarctic explorer, Captain Oates. (UTBG 435)

One of the best books about the perils of modern mountaineering is Joe Simpson's *Touching the Void*. (UTBG 400)

**Laura Hutchings**

# A WRINKLE IN TIME  Madeleine L'Engle

**Next?**

This is part of the **Time** quartet; the others are: *A Swiftly Tilting Planet*, *A Wind in the Door* and *Many Waters*.

There's more time travelling that's part of a deadly game in Joan Lennon's *Seventh Tide*. (UTBG 355)

*From the Mixed-Up Files of Mrs Basil E. Frankweiler* by E.L. Konigsburg has another great brother-sister relationship. This time, the siblings run away from their boring suburban life to live in the Metropolitan Museum in New York.

Written in 1963, this award-winning book still manages to hover in the top 500 of Amazon.com – and though only slightly known in the UK, it has a fanatical American following.

It's the story of Meg Murry and her genius baby brother, children of two brilliant scientists, and their quest to rescue their father from a faraway planet overtaken by the dark shadow of evil. It's not really science fiction (phew!), though there are enough challenging scientific ideas about time travel to keep you on your toes. Instead, it's about the triumph of Meg's difficult, unruly, passionate personality where intellect alone has failed. And it's the perfect book for those of us with messy, stubborn characters, who don't always feel appreciated by the rest of the world.

**Meg Rosoff**

# THE WRONG BOY  Willy Russell

Raymond Marks is a nice, normal boy from a normal, northern town, until the new headmaster at his primary school makes a scapegoat of him and Raymond becomes the Wrong Boy – a social outcast. Raymond soon discovers that being accused of one crime leads to being accused of another, and he becomes the unwitting prey of a chain of apparently well-meaning but self-seeking adults who are trying to 'help' him: Psycho The Rapist, a Lert, and the So Shall Worker. *The Wrong Boy* is both a heartrending tale of the effects of victimisation and a laugh-out-loud funny book of startling originality. It will both shock and delight you – and you won't be able to put it down.

**Sherry Ashworth**

**Next?**

Try *Strange Boy* by Paul Magrs, another funny-but-moving tale of an outsider growing up in the north of England. (UTBG 380)

For a more adult read than Magrs, try the classic *The Catcher in the Rye* by J.D. Salinger, about a boy who flunks schools and drops out, spending three days alone in Manhattan. (UTBG 69)

Try one of Willy Russell's brilliant plays – *Educating Rita* and *Shirley Valentine* are the best known.

# THE WRONG HANDS   Nigel Richardson

Graham Sinclair is a 14-year-old with huge, freaky hands and a big secret. But surely he's not a terrible criminal, is he?

Graham moves down to London to spend some time with his uncle George ('Mr Porky') and sort himself out, but when a dreadful plane crash happens, Graham suddenly finds himself a national hero. The press all want to know him, and even beautiful Jennifer Slater has started taking an interest. But it's all too good to be true... And now maybe he should tell someone his big secret, but when he tried that back home, that's when things all started going wrong for him, and whom can he trust with it now?

Nigel Richardson has created an engaging and distinctive voice for his wonderful hero; an extraordinary, unique young man, but one we can all identify with.

**Daniel Hahn**

**Next?**

There's another unique hero to be found in Richardson's *The Rope Ladder*.

Or, for a change, try something about kids who can turn into animals at will; Ali Sparkes's **Shapeshifter** series begins with *Finding the Fox*.

And more secrets (and heroes) abound in Perry Moore's *Hero*. (UTBG 176)

# WUTHERING HEIGHTS   Emily Brontë

**Next?**

OK, fair cop: if you prefer better mannered lovers and happier endings, then check out *Pride and Prejudice* by Jane Austen. (UTBG 320)

Or if you like your love more cerebral, try *Strait is the Gate* by André Gide. (UTBG 379)

If casual amorality is your thing, try 17-year-old Cécile's view of love in *Bonjour Tristesse* by Françoise Sagan. (UTBG 52)

Or for a different Brontë? From Anne, *The Tenant of Wildfell Hall* or from Charlotte, *Jane Eyre* (UTBG 211).

Forget Mr Darcy – Heathcliff is the sexiest man in English literature. I first read this book when I was 13 and reread it pretty much every year for the next decade. It's a monumental love story carved of passion and brutality. In a dilemma that has resonated with women down the centuries, Cathy Earnshaw must choose between the 'good' and civilised man, Edgar Linton, and the 'bad' wild foundling of nature, Heathcliff. Linton's soul is as different from Heathcliff's as 'moonbeam from lightning, or frost from fire'. Cathy's final decision, and the revenge that follows, exact a terrible penalty on two generations of Earnshaws and Lintons. A beautiful and savage book that makes you grateful to be alive.

**Nicky Singer**

# SHORT AND GRIPPING BOOKS

## by Pete Johnson

Sometimes you want to read a story that doesn't hang about. You'd like to find a tale that grips you from the very first line, with strong characters and lively, realistic dialogue.

And you don't fancy a very long book, either. For life becomes extremely busy, especially in your teens. And by the time you've read all that boring stuff for school there's only a tiny bit of time – say 20 minutes before you go to sleep – to read anything for pleasure.

Well, 20 minutes is all you need to savour a short story by Paul Jennings, who's brilliant at

**Reluctant to read? Not with these you won't be:**

*Diary of a Wimpy Kid* by Jeff Kinney

*You're a Bad Man, Mr Gum*
by Andy Stanton

*Dr Who: Made of Steel* by Terrence Dicks

*Dr Who: I Am a Dalek* by Gareth Roberts

*Simone's Letters* by Helena Pielichaty

*Christina's Face* by Penny Kendal

**Glory Gardens** series by Bob Cattell

*There's a Boy in the Girl's Bathroom*
by Louis Sacher

*Toad Rage* by Morris Gleitzman

**Blade** series by Tim Bowler

**Diamond Brothers** series
by Anthony Horowitz

**The Princess Diaries** by Meg Cabot

*The Outsiders* by S.E. Hinton

*Stone Cold* by Robert Swindells

grabbing your attention with a fantastic situation that's written in a totally believable way.

Diaries can also be great to dip into last thing at night. And if you want to fall asleep laughing, then I would strongly recommend Sue Townsend's *The Secret Diary of Adrian Mole Aged 13 ¾* (UTBG 347) (and the numerous sequels). And if you're looking for a 'fabbity fab' diary with a teenage girl at the centre, then check out *Angus, Thongs and Full-Frontal Snogging* (UTBG 23) by Louise Rennison.

If you prefer a novel, how about something by Robert Swindells or Morris Gleitzman? With short chapters and tight plotting, their books are impossible to put down.

And if you would like to read a shorter novel (say about 8,000 words) there's a publisher who specialises in books like that: Barrington Stoke. They even have teenagers acting as editors on their books, highlighting any words or phrases which tripped them up, or scenes which slowed the pace down too much. (Check out their website – www.barringtonstoke.co.uk – if you'd be interested in helping out!)

There's certainly not a wasted moment in *The Cold Heart of Summer* by Alan Gibbons, a heart-pounding horror tale about sightings of a girl killed 50 years ago; or Theresa Breslin's richly atmospheric *Prisoner of Alcatraz*; or Kevin Brooks's roller-coaster read *Bloodline*.

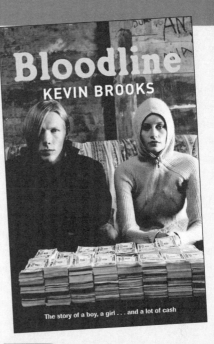

The story of a boy, a girl . . . and a lot of cash

### Some easier Barrington Stoke books to try:

*Bicycle Blues* by Anthony Masters. Jamie has just got a new bike for his birthday, and someone has nicked it! Jamie is determined to find out who has taken it, but the only person helping him is Greg Dawson, and Jamie doesn't trust him.

*Sticks and Stones* by Catherine MacPhail. Greg thinks he's hilarious. He's great at making up nicknames for people, and doesn't understand why they don't find it funny, too. So he's really surprised when he's accused of something he didn't do, and realises he's been set up. Surely he doesn't have any enemies? Does he?

*To Be a Millionaire* by Yvonne Coppard. Josh would do anything for fame and fortune (and to get a gorgeous girlfriend, of course). And now he thinks he's come up with a brilliant plan to get just what he wants. But it's not that simple...

Another book that sweeps you along is *Text Game* by Kate Cann, a love story which turns into a thriller when vicious text messages start being sent. I've written three books for Barrington Stoke myself: *Runaway Teacher* about an over-friendly teacher; *The Best Holiday Ever* about that first holiday without parents; and *Diary of an (Un)teenager*, which is undoubtedly the most personal of the three. It concerns Spencer, who is about to hit 13 and absolutely dreading it, especially all the fuss about becoming a teenager. I've had so many letters from readers saying they felt exactly the same – but thought they were the only one.

That's another great thing about stories: they help us realise we're not on our own. So it's worth finding the time – even if it's just a few minutes at night – to read. And if you want to speed off into a pacy tale… Well, now you can. But don't just take my word for it. Check out any of the books I've mentioned. Just read the first two sentences and you'll be totally hooked…

"...you got used to the everyday abuse once it's been happening for long enough. It becomes part of your life. Your routine..."

### Some harder Barrington Stoke books to try:

*I See You, Baby...* by Kevin Brooks and Catherine Forde. A surprising turn of events takes Keith and Sally to Rock Out, a music festival where they meet. But each of them is pretending to be someone else, which makes it all rather more complicated!

*No Stone Unturned* by Brian Keaney. Lisa Foster leaves her brutish husband for another man. This is the story of the furious husband's revenge – and a chilling read. Keaney maintains the momentum brilliantly – you'll be hooked from the first intriguing page to the terrifying ending.

*What's Your Problem?* by Bali Rai. Jaspal and his family move from Leicester to a small village where they are the only non-white family. Immediately the racist attacks start – first it's just muttered abuse, but it soon develops into something worse; much worse… An unsettling story about a very real problem.

# THE YEAR THE GYPSIES CAME
Linzi Glass

This eloquent book is a microcosm of the ills of 1960's South Africa; the ugliness is disguised by a beautiful landscape and a child's innocence. Twelve-year-old Emily lives in a cocoon of privledge, but her life is made vulnerable by the harshness of apartheid. But her wealthy veneer is slowly stripped away by an engaging story that never fails to surprise.

Emily's dysfunctional parents invite strangers to be their house guests – a temporary distraction that offers a solution to ease their own fractious relationship. But when rough-and-ready Peg and Jock's itinerant Australian family arrive, Emily's world is altered for ever. As friendship blossoms, a frightening act of violence shatters Emily's life.

This book's tenderness shines through the pain of a young girl's harsh exposure to the reality of life.

**David Gilman**

> **Next?**
>
> *No Turning Back* and *Road to Nowhere* by Beverley Naidoo capture the agony and beauty of South Africa and are classics that should not be missed.
>
> There's a terrific adventure set in the Rift Valley, *Rift* by Beverley Birch.
>
> Or for a book set in a post-apartheid South Africa, try *Spud* by John van de Ruit. (UTBG 373)

# THE YELLOW WALLPAPER
## Charlotte Perkins Gilman

> **Next?**
>
> *The Awakening* by Kate Chopin was considered shocking on publication.
>
> Virginia Woolf's *A Room of One's Own* set out her ideas about the role of women. (UTBG 334)
>
> Henry James's *Daisy Miller* is another story of a young woman. (UTBG 93)
>
> Or for how insanity used to be perceived, try *Wide Sargasso Sea* by Jean Rhys. (UTBG 438)

Written in the first person, this short story reads like a diary. The protagonist, a married woman with a young child, has just been relocated to the country. Her husband thinks she is tired and in need of a good long rest. Essentially he wants her to do nothing at all, and is even opposed to her writing in her diary. But she continues to write, and thus we have a story. Desperate for something to do, but not allowed to do anything, she begins to obsess about the wallpaper in her bedroom.

*The Yellow Wallpaper* was written in a time where women who were artistic, creative, or just a little different were often shunned by society. Their desire to be actively engaged was considered strange and unnatural, and they were often deemed insane; and sometimes they did, quite literally, lose their minds.

**Candida Gray**

# YOU DON'T KNOW ME David Klass

### Next?

The lead character in Kevin Brooks's *Martyn Pig* accidentally kills his useless dad. (UTBG 256)

Another David Klass? Try *The Braves*, about (amongst other things) gangs, football and fitting in.

Or try the tense and terrifying *Dark Angel*, and find out what it means to your life, family and friends when your brother comes home after serving five years in prison for murder.

Another boy who wants to be left alone is Bobby in Kate Thompson's *Creature of the Night*.

The voice of John, the narrator of this novel, is one of the best ever achieved in fiction for teen readers. By turns incredibly funny, and then uncomfortably violent, the book tells the story of 14-year-old John and the images in his head, his life inside a life, as he tries to escape the crushing reality of his mother's abusive new boyfriend. At school he feels isolated, despite being liked by his teachers and peers. And John is a likeable character; ordinary in many ways, but his views on the absurdities of modern life make him very special indeed. In trying to make himself unknowable, he inadvertently reveals everything that he is. A powerful and moving novel.

**John McLay**

# Z FOR ZACHARIAH Robert C. O'Brien

Every time I read this book I can't help but wonder what the author would make of its ending! Robert C. O'Brien died before he could finish the story and so his wife and daughter completed it, working from his notes.

Sixteen-year-old Ann Burden is trying to survive after a nuclear war. She lives alone but safe in a remote valley that has escaped the fallout. Then Loomis, a government scientist, arrives.

The sheer unfairness of what happens next will have you gnashing your teeth, but ultimately what stays with you is the ending. Long after you've finished the book you will find yourself wondering about Ann and her final decision. Intrigued? Read the book!

**Laura Hutchings**

### Next?

The science-fiction novels of John Wyndham, particularly *The Day of the Triffids* (UTBG 98) and *The Kraken Wakes* offer glimpses of the end of the world as we know it.

For other post-apocalyptic novels, try the harrowing *Brother in the Land* by Robert Swindells, *The War of the Worlds* (UTBG 424) by H.G. Wells, *The Postman* by David Brin or *On the Beach* by Nevil Shute.

Or John Christopher's haunting *Empty World*.

# THE ZIGZAG KID  David Grossman

**Next?**

There's another David Grossman you're bound to love: *Someone to Run with* about life in modern Jerusalem.

For a story about stories, try Salman Rushdie's beautiful *Haroun and the Sea of Stories*.

For something else funny and thoughtful, try John Irving's *A Prayer for Owen Meany*. (UTBG 318)

Nonny is about to turn 13. And what a birthday it's going to be... You see, he thinks he's getting on a train to visit his Uncle Samuel, The Great Educator, who will give him an unbearable lecture on responsible behaviour. But Nonny wasn't counting on meeting Felix Glick, and he wasn't expecting what happens next...

Nonny's father and stepmother have cooked up a magical birthday surprise, a mystery adventure tour of discovery and self-discovery. And author David Grossman has done just the same for us. His little miracle of a book is funny, thought provoking and touching (the three most important things in a book, I reckon). It may seem like an odd thing to say, but I'm just glad this book exists; I hope you will be, too.

**Daniel Hahn**

## ZOO  Graham Marks

Cam Stewart's comfortable, laid-back American lifestyle is shattered when he is kidnapped and held for ransom. Escaping and killing a man on the way, Cam relies on the kindness of strangers to pick him up physically and mentally as he desperately tries to run away from the past, and starts to discover the unexpected and shocking truth of who he really is.

Edgy, hard-hitting and high-octane, Cam's disaster-ridden narrative unfolds like an episode of *24*. Cleverly timed chapters accelerate the action and maintain the momentum in this edge-of-the-seat action adventure.

**Eileen Armstrong**

**Next?**

More Graham Marks? Try *Tokyo*, about a boy searching for his sister in the seedy backstreets of Tokyo, *Kai-ro*, set in the year 2499, or *I Spy – The Constantinople Caper*.

*Unique* by Alison Allen-Gray also looks at the issue of cloning through the medium of a nationwide chase. (UTBG 414)

A similar psychological thriller is Kevin Brooks's *Kissing the Rain*. (UTBG 226)

# About the Contributors

**DAVID ALMOND** was born in Newcastle and grew up in a big Catholic family. He has been a teacher and is now a writer, best known for the remarkable *Skellig*. He lives with his family in Northumberland, just beyond Hadrian's Wall, which for centuries marked the place where civilisation ended and the wastelands began.

**ABIGAIL ANDERSON** is a theatre director who works all over the place, but especially in the beautiful Theatre Royal, Bury St Edmunds. She likes characters to become her friends, whether they're stepping out of the page or onto the stage.

**ALICIA ANDERSON** is a teen services librarian for Hennepin County Library, Minneapolis. She frequently and enthusiastically reads below her age level. Her reviews and general book-related ranting can be found at http://bookbarker.blogspot.com

**ILEANA ANTONOPOLOU** was born in Greece, where she first got addicted to books. Since leaving school she has lived in England where (in between books) she has studied medicine at Oxford and occasionally gone scuba diving, looking for old things.

**NOGA APPLEBAUM** has a PhD in Children's Literature and currently teaches creative writing at the Hampstead Garden Suburb Institute. She regularly interviews children's authors for the Write Away website.

**JON APPLETON** has worked widely in children's books as a reviewer, a book club buyer, but mostly as an editor – at Orion Children's Books, Piccadilly Press, Hodder, Scholastic and A & C Black, where he commissioned the very first *UBG* way back in 2002.

**PHILIP ARDAGH** is probably best known for his **Eddie Dickens** adventures and his impressive beard. He regularly reviews for the *Guardian*.

**MAX AREVUO** is 13 years old. He lives in Golders Green with his parents and sister. An enthusiastic reader, he prefers autobiographies, but enjoys most books that are put in front of him. As his favourite sport is cricket, he really likes cricket-based books.

**NEIL ARKSEY** writes for TV when he's not being an author. His books for teens include *Brooksie*, *MacB*, *Playing on the Edge* and *As Good as Dead in Downtown*.

**OLIVIA ARMES** is 15 and lives in London. She enjoys relaxing with friends, photography and surfing. She has two cats called Coco Darling and Wooster. She has a brother, who she also likes to think of as a pet.

**EILEEN ARMSTRONG** is a school librarian in Northumberland, a reviewer and feature writer for a variety of professional journals and author of *Fully Booked!: Reader Development and the Secondary School LRC*. She is currently chair of the national School Library Association.

**SHERRY ASHWORTH** has written many novels for teenagers, including *Close-Up*, *Paralysed* and *The Dream Travellers*. Her own books are reality- and character-based, but she enjoys reading everything and anything. She lives in Manchester and has a husband, two grown-up daughters and two very lazy cats.

**MAY AUNG** attends Eleanor Roosevelt High School in New York City. She enjoys reading, writing and watching television in her spare time.

**LYNNE REID BANKS** has written many books, but is best known for *The L-Shaped Room* for adults and *The Indian in the Cupboard* for children. She also has the distinction of being one of the UK's first-ever woman TV news reporters!

**ANDREW BARAKAT** was born in New York City and moved to London in 2002. He attends Arnold House School and enjoys visiting the library and reading. Academic work is a priority, though he loves sport and music, too.

**DAVID BARD** is an inquisitive, sporty and enthusiastic 13 year old, who attends Arnold House School. Always up for a challenge, often willing to try new things and always ready for a good chat, David is great company, whatever the circumstances. Occasionally, he even reads a book.

**RAFFAELLA BARKER** lives in Norfolk. She has written seven adult novels, and one for teens called *Phosphorescence*. She was paid by her father to read as a nine-year-old and the investment yielded huge dividends: it taught her that no price is too high to get children to read. Her sons have cost a fortune but it has been worth it.

**FELICITY-ROSE BARROW** is an aspiring writer and illustrator who left school at 15. She lives in a small colourful bubble in Warwickshire with her books and plants and is now studying art at college.

In her nine novels, **JOAN BAUER** explores difficult issues with humour and hope. A *New York Times* best-selling author, her books have won numerous awards. She lives in Brooklyn, NY with her husband.

**NINA BAWDEN** has written over 40 novels. Her best-known books for children are the award-winning *Carrie's War* and *The Peppermint Pig*.

**SUSILA BAYBARS** has spent the last 17 years immersed in children's books. After a short spell at Waterstone's, she has worked for many of the leading publishers, and has loved every minute of it.

**K.K. BECK** is the author of 21 crime thrillers. Her novels for young-adult readers are *Fake* and *Snitch*.

**DAVID BELBIN** is the author of *Love Lessons*, **The Beat** series, *Denial* and many other novels for young adults. He has also written a book about ebay.co.uk and numerous short stories for both adult and younger readers.

**JULIA BELL** is a novelist whose publications include the novels *Massive* and *Dirty Work* and the *Creative Writing Coursebook*.

**JULIE BERTAGNA**'s first-published work was a glowing review of her brother's appalling rock band for the local paper when she was a teenager, and she has been writing ever since. Her novels include *Exodus* and *The Opposite of Chocolate*.

**THOMAS BLOOR**'s novels include *Worm in the Blood*, *The Memory Prisoner* and *Factory of Shadows*. He is married and has two children.

**TIM BOWLER**'s novel *River Boy* won the Carnegie Medal. His recent books include *Frozen Fire*, the **Blade** series and *Bloodchild*.

**TONY BRADMAN** decided at the age of 13 that he wanted to be a writer. He published his first children's book in 1984, and since then has written or edited nearly 200 further titles.

**TESSA BRECHIN** is a Brighton-based obsessive reader. Having recently completed her Masters in Creative and Professional Writing, she is back to trying to balance paid work with continuing to write her first book for young adults, a hybrid prose / graphic novel.

**GERALDINE BRENNAN** is a children's literature consultant and former books editor of the *Times Educational Supplement*.

**HERBIE BRENNAN** is the author of 108 published books, including the *New York Times* best-seller *Faerie Wars* and the multi-million international super-selling gamebook series *GrailQuest*. He lives with his wife and too many cats in an 18th-century rectory in Ireland.

**THERESA BRESLIN** loves reading and writing books for young people, and is prepared to talk about this to anyone who will listen! Her novel *Whispers in the Graveyard*, about a boy who struggles to read and write, won her the Carnegie Medal.

**KEVIN BROOKS** has had loads of horrible jobs and also spent many years involved in music (writing and recording) and art (painting and sculpture). He's been a full-time writer for the last five years and his novels include *Martyn Pig*, *Lucas* and *Candy*.

**MELVIN BURGESS** was born in Twickenham. He did poorly at school, which he didn't much enjoy. Writing was his ambition since the age of 14, and after many rejections, his first book was published in 1990. Since then his work has been published around the world and it has won several prizes.

**MEG CABOT** is the best-selling author of several series for young adults, including **The Princess Diaries**, **Airhead** and **Missing**, as well as *All American Girl*, *Teen Idol*, *Nicola and the Viscount* and many books for older readers.

**STACY CANTOR** has been working in the publishing industry since 2004. She enjoys swimming, knitting and, of course, reading. She lives in New York City on an island even smaller than Manhattan.

**ALEXANDER CARN** is 13 years old and lives in London with his mother, father and sister. He prefers academic work to sport, but enjoys clay-pigeon shooting.

**ROSEMARY CASS-BEGGS**, after a degree in psychology, specialised in focus groups for consumer research and tutored in the Open University. She re-discovered literature for children in the 1960s and has read it ever since.

**ANNE CASSIDY** worked as a bank clerk and a teacher before she became a writer. She has written many crime novels for teenagers including *Looking for JJ* and, most recently, *The Dead*

*House*. When she's not writing, she is shopping or watching junk TV.

**MARY KATE CASTELLANI** has worked in the publishing industry since 2005. She lives in New York City, where she likes to take long walks through new neighbourhoods, and can usually be found sitting in a coffee shop with a book.

**GARY CHOW** is a 17-year-old Hong Konger living in Rugby. He has many hobbies, such as reading, reading and more reading.

**JONATHAN COE** is the author of eight novels, including *What a Carve Up!*, *The House of Sleep* and *The Rain Before It Falls*.

**EOIN COLFER** was born and still lives in Ireland. He is the author of many books including the best-selling **Artemis Fowl** series, which grew from his love of Irish history and legend. His *And Another Thing…*, the sixth title in Douglas Adams's **Hitchhiker's Guide to the Galaxy** series, was published in 2009.

**CLIO CONTOGENIS**, 14, lives in uptown Manhattan in a little-known neighbourhood called Hudson Heights. She occupies herself by ruthlessly devouring books, writing her own stories and singing. She also enjoys acting and is usually involved in some sort of play.

**WENDY COOLING** is the creator of Bookstart, which gives free books to every baby in the UK, for which she was awarded the MBE in 2008.

**YVONNE COPPARD** was a teacher and then a child protection adviser before taking up writing full time. She writes serious and humorous novels for children

and teenagers, and some books for teachers.

**MICHAEL COX** has written over 35 children's books and is published in more than a dozen countries, including Russia, Brazil and Korea (although he says that translating 'knock-knock' jokes into Korean always gives him a headache).

**MICHAEL CRONIN** is an actor and writer. He has worked throughout the world on stage, in film and on TV. He has written a trilogy for children, starting with *Against the Day*.

**GILLIAN CROSS** has been writing for young people for over 30 years. She is perhaps best known for her **Demon Headmaster** books and she has won the Smarties Prize, the Whitbread Children's Book Award and the Carnegie Medal.

**BENJAMIN CUFFIN-MUNDAY** is a pupil at the King's School, Chester. He plays clarinet and piano (with a special interest in jazz), and his other hobbies include rocks and fossils, pencil collecting, and of course All Things Books! In 2004, he was a judge for the Blue Peter Book Awards.

**JAKE CURTIS** is a rock-hard guitarist with as yet unsigned band 'Small Man Complex'. He likes eating, reading and reating (eating whilst reading). He likes sport, but has realised he'll never get more than the 'good effort' prize.

**KAREN CUSHMAN**'s first book, *Catherine, Called Birdy*, was named a 1995 Newbery Honor Book. *The Midwife's Apprentice* won the Newbery Medal for 1996 and changed her life. She is also the author of *The Ballad of Lucy Whipple*, *Matilda Bone*

and *Rodzina*.

**ISSIE DARCY** is 13 and likes singing, dancing and drama. She loves reading everything from **Harry Potter** to *Lord of the Flies*. She has two dogs and seven chickens.

**JANE DARCY** taught English for years before giving it all up to go back to university, where she is now studying English again and can read books all day. Sadly, not all of these are children's books.

**NARINDER DHAMI**'s many books include *Bhangra Babes*, *Bollywood Babes*, *Bindi Babes* and *Bend It Like Beckham*, which was made into a film. Her new series about friends and football is called **The Beautiful Game**.

**CHRIS D'LACEY** has written books for children of all ages, including the dragon series starting with *The Fire Within*. He is a regular visitor to schools, libraries and book festivals throughout the land.

**BERLIE DOHERTY**'s books and plays have won many awards. Her titles include *Dear Nobody*, winner of the Carnegie Medal, *Deep Secret*, *The Starburster* and, most recently, *A Calf Called Valentine*, the first in the **Peak Dale Farm** series.

**JENNIFER DONNELLY** lives in Brooklyn, NY with her husband, daughter and two greyhounds. As a child, she loved to write and often inflicted dreadful poems and stories on her family and friends. She loved to read, too, and the high point of her week was a Saturday trip to the library. It still is.

**JENNY DOWNHAM** worked in community theatre for many

years before concentrating on her writing full time. Her debut novel, *Before I Die,* won several awards and is currently being made into a film.

**MALACHY DOYLE** writes picture books, young fiction and teenage novels. His work as a special needs teacher inspired his extraordinary first novel, *Georgie.*

**FLORENCE EASTOE** is 13 and lives in East Kent with her parents and younger brother. Her pastimes include reading, shopping and caring for the menagerie of household pets – mainly the cats and chickens.

**CLAIRE EASTON** is 16 and lives in New Jersey, which must be why she has an extreme fondness for diners and malls. She also enjoys books, good music and eating Chinese food at Man Hing with her friends.

**PATRICIA ELLIOTT**'s novels include *The Ice Boy, The Night Walker* and *Murkmere.* Her most recent novel is *The Pale Assassin,* the first in the **Pimpernelles** trilogy. Patricia lives in London and Suffolk with her husband and a labrador.

**ANNE FINE** was Children's Laureate from 2001–3 and has won numerous awards for her novels, including the Whitbread and the Carnegie (both twice) and the Guardian Children's Fiction Prize. Her most recent book is *Eating Things on Sticks.*

**CATHERINE FISHER** is a poet and novelist. Her best-known works include *Corbenic, Darkwater Hall,* the acclaimed **Book of the Crow** series, *Incarceron* and its sequel, *Sapphique.* She lives in Wales with her two cats, Jess and Tam.

**KEN FISHER** is an artist and historical researcher. He is married and lives in Kent. There he collects odd facts, curious history books, academic degrees and children – five of his own and six grandchildren (so far!).

**ANNE FLAHERTY** worked as a news journalist in Ireland, South Africa and Hong Kong before studying for an MA in Children's Literature. She now lives in London and is a freelance writer, in between looking after her two children, Daniel and Holly Mei.

**HALEY FLETCHER** is 17 and attends Hudson High School in Hudson, Wisconsin. She loves reading because it is the most relaxing thing to do. It allows her to create images and stories she wouldn't be able to do otherwise.

**CATHERINE FORDE** writes stories with young adults as her central characters. Her novels include *Fat Boy Swim, Skarrs* and, most recently, *Dead Men Don't Talk* and *Bad Wedding.*

**COLUM FRASER** grew up in Glasgow, Inverness and Edinburgh. He is currently studying maths and politics at the University of Glasgow.

**LINDSEY FRASER** was a children's bookseller in Cambridge before she became Executive Director of Scottish Book Trust. She is now a partner in Fraser Ross Associates, the Edinburgh-based literary agency and consultancy.

**EDDIE FRY** (aka Haggis Basher) is a small, scruffy-haired boy. He is 12, and is fanatical about rugby, Jaffa Cakes and Scotland. Although he is a

mature head boy at his school, he still can't wait for the new *Beano* annual.

**NIKKI GAMBLE** is the director of Write Away, a consultancy which trains teachers, libraries and parents in reader development, creative writing and drama.

**DAVID GARDNER** is a Y11 student and National Literacy Trust accredited Reading Champion. Anyone who says teenagers don't read any more has obviously never met David. He's made it his mission to ensure no one leaves the school library empty-handed.

**GRAHAM GARDNER** wanted to be a writer from age eight. He went through at least 30 jobs before he saw his first novel published. When he can find the time, he plays classical, rock and ragtime piano and listens to all kinds of music. Graham is the second-eldest of ten children and lives in West Wales.

**SUSAN GATES** lives in the north of England. She has taught in schools in Malawi and County Durham. She likes, among other things: the north of England, playing guitar and her husband's cooking. Her teenage novels include *Dusk* and *Firebird* and *Beyond the Billboard.*

**JAMILA GAVIN** is well known for her books reflecting her Anglo-Indian background, such as the **Surya** trilogy. Her Whitbread Children's Book Award-winner *Coram Boy* has been turned into a major play.

**ADÈLE GERAS** has written more than 90 books for children. Her books for young adults include *Troy, Ithaka, Dido* and the **Happy Ever After** trilogy.

**ALAN GIBBONS**'s early love of reading led to a career in teaching. After 18 years at the chalkface, Alan took the gamble to become a full-time writer. His books include the Blue Peter Award-winning *Shadow of the Minotaur*, and the **Hell's Underground** series. He is also a prominent library campaigner.

**DAVID GILMAN** created teen-hero Max Gordon in **The Danger Zone** series. He has been all over the world, but when he's not travelling, he lives in Devon with his wife and three cats.

**MORRIS GLEITZMAN** was born in England but grew up in Australia. He always wanted to write, and after many TV comedy scripts, started writing for children. His recent titles include *Once*, *Then*, *Grace* and *Toad Surprise*.

**CANDIDA GRAY** has degrees in Theatre, Art History and History, but she has always wanted to have one in Literature, too! Candida works in education and claims that she would never have survived adolescence without books.

**KEITH GRAY**'s first book, *Creepers*, was published when he was only 24. He has written several award-winning novels including *The Runner* and *The Fearful*. His most recent novel is *Ostrich Boys*. Keith lives in Edinburgh with his girlfriend and their parrot.

**JOHN GREEN** is the Michael L. Printz Award-winning author of *Looking for Alaska* and *An Abundance of Katherines*. When he was little, he made a list of things he was good at. The list included 'telling lies' and 'sitting'. So he became a writer. You can visit him at www.sparksflyup.com

**JULIA GREEN** writes mainly for young adults, and lectures in Creative Writing at Bath Spa University. She is programme leader for the MA in Writing for Young People. Her titles include *Breathing Underwater*, *Blue Moon* and *Baby Blue*.

**ELENA GREGORIOU** is a teacher in a London prep school. She believes the best thing about the summer holidays is being able to read all day in the sun (and eating ice cream!).

**SARAH GRISTWOOD** is a former journalist, specialising in the cinema and writing for the *Guardian*, the *Telegraph* and the *London Evening Standard*. She is the author of three historical biographies – *Arbella*, *Bird of Paradise* and *Elizabeth and Leicester*.

**HATTIE GRYLLS** is 13. She lives in Islington with her mum, dad, younger brother, and the newest member of her household, a rescue dog called Lolly. When not playing with Lolly she reads, swims and listens to her iPod.

**FRANCES HARDINGE** is the author of *Fly by Night*, *Verdigris Deep* and *Gullstruck Island*, and confuses everyone by living in both London and Oxford at once. She is seldom seen without her hat, and is addicted to volcanoes.

**JOANNE HARRIS** is the author of a dozen books, including *Chocolat*, which was made into a film starring Juliette Binoche and Johnny Depp. Her fantasy novel, *Runemarks*, came out in 2007. She lives in Yorkshire with her husband and daughter.

**ALLISON HAWTHORNE** is your average literature-loving 16 year old from Hudson, Wisconsin. She has been reading since

she was a toddler and has only gained speed and interest since.

**SARAH HILARY** writes fiction and non fiction, sometimes winning awards. She is the mother of an eight-year-old bookworm but has not as yet won any awards for this. She lives in hope.

**MARY HOFFMAN** is the author of over 90 books for children and teenagers. Her two most famous series are **Amazing Grace** and its sequels, and the **Stravaganza** fantasy series. From 1999 to 2008 she edited the online book-review magazine *Armadillo*. She now blogs at bookmavenmary.blogspot.com

**ELIZABETH HONEY** illustrated books by other people for years, then she tried writing and illustrating her own. Now there's no stopping her. Her most recent title is *To the Boy in Berlin*. Elizabeth and her family live in Melbourne.

**ANTONIA HONEYWELL** is a writer, teacher and award-winning barbershop singer. She is a prolific producer of small children and unpublished novels, and is hoping to achieve publication before the former outnumber the latter.

**MARY HOOPER** has been writing for young adults for an awfully long time and enjoys the variety of being able to write historical fiction one day and funny stuff the next. She has two grown-up children and lives in Hampshire. Her hobbies are pottering about and being nosy.

**CATHY HOPKINS** lives in North London with her husband and three mad cats. She writes for teenagers and children, and is the author of the **Mates, Dates...**

series, the **Truth, Dare** series and the **Cinnamon Girl** series.

**ANTHONY HOROWITZ** is the author of the best-selling **Alex Rider** series – the first of which, *Stormbreaker*, has been made into a film – and the **Power of Five** series. He lives in Crouch End with his wife, children and his dog, Loony.

**LESLEY HOWARTH** has written over 20 books for children and teenagers and she has always had a special interest in science fiction. Her novel *MapHead* won the Guardian Children's Fiction Prize. Her latest novel is *Bodyswap: The Boy Who Was 84.*

**MATTHEW HUMPAGE** has just finished his MRes in Creative and Professional Writing and is planning for his PhD. His interests lie mainly in innovative fiction, identity studies and ecocriticism.

**LAURA HUTCHINGS** is head of English at a boys' prep school in North London. One of the things she enjoys most about her job is the fact that it gives her an excuse to read all the children's books that she'd be reading anyway!

**EVA IBBOTSON** writes for both adults and children. Her novels *Journey to the River Sea*, *The Star of Kazan* and *The Dragonfly Pool* are about journeys to exotic places.

**BENEDICT JACKA** is half-Australian, half-Armenian, and grew up in London. Before becoming a full-time writer, he worked as a bouncer, held a job in the Civil Service and went to Cambridge University. He now divides his time between writing, reading, martial arts and playing games.

**JUDI JAMES** has 30 years' experience as a teacher in Primary and Secondary education. She was chair of judges for the 2009 Booktrust Teenage Prize. Having written her *UTBG* entry, she is now about to start work sculpting a clay orang-utan.

**JULIA JARMAN** was born talking, or so her mum says. In fact she only stops talking in order to read and write. Writing, she thinks, is another way of talking, and she has written over 100 books. Her books for teenagers include *Peace Weavers*, *Hangman*, and *Crow Haunting.*

**KATIE JENNINGS** is a children's book editor, working for Stripes Publishing. She lives in London and, like most people in children's books, she owns two cats.

**CATHERINE JINKS** was born in Brisbane, Australia in 1963. She is the author of many children's books and also writes for adults. Her books for young adults include *The Reformed Vampire Support Group* and *Genius Squad.*

**PETE JOHNSON** has worked as a film critic for Radio One and as a teacher. He now writes books, some of which are funny and some of which are scary, but all of which (in the editors' opinion) are great. They include *How to Train Your Parents* and *Diary of an (Un)teenager.*

**ANN JUNGMAN** was born in London of refugee parents. She has published over a hundred books for children, including *Vlad the Drac* and the **Romans** series. In addition to writing, Ann runs Barn Owl Books, which reprints out-of-print quality children's books.

**ARIEL KAHN** lectures in Literature and Creative Writing at Roehampton University (which currently involves reading a great deal of comics), watches films for his job at Ealing studios, and generally suffers for his art when he is not working on his first novel.

**ELIZABETH KAY** is half-Polish and half-English, and she went to art school. She has written the **Divide** trilogy, and researches her fantasy settings in places as diverse as the jungles of Borneo, the deserts of Egypt, the volcanoes of Costa Rica and the glaciers of Iceland.

**BRIAN KEANEY**'s parents were Irish and he grew up listening to his mother telling stories. He made up his mind at an early age that he wanted to be a writer, and considers it the best job in the world. His novels include *Jacob's Ladder* and the **Nathaniel Wolfe** stories.

**ALLY KENNEN**'s first novel, *Beast*, was short-listed for the Carnegie Medal. She lives in Somerset where she writes books and looks after her small, crazy children.

**ELIZABETH LAIRD** has always been a traveller. Born in New Zealand, she has lived in Malaysia, Ethiopia, Iraq, Lebanon and Austria, and those feet still keep itching. Some of her books reflect her travels, but others are set right here in Britain.

**ADAM LANCASTER** is the Chair of the Federation of Children's Book Groups, a book consultant, and secondary school librarian at Monk's Walk School in Hertfordshire.

**TANYA LANDMAN** is the author of several books for teenagers and younger readers. Her latest novel, *The Goldsmith's Daughter*, was long-listed for the Guardian Children's Fiction prize. *Apache* was short-listed for the Carnegie Medal and the Booktrust Teenage Prize.

**CAROLINE LAWRENCE** is a Californian whose obsession with ancient history and languages brought her to England to study Classics at Cambridge and Hebrew at London. In 1999 she began writing the **Roman Mysteries**, which in 2009 won the Classical Assocation prize. The 17-book series was concluded in 2009 with *The Man from Pomegranate Street*.

**MICHAEL LAWRENCE** became a writer for young people with the publication of *When the Snow Falls* in 1995. Since then he has published the best-selling **Jiggy McCue** series, the acclaimed trilogy about alternative realities, **The Aldous Lexicon** and the **Withern Rise** series.

**GAIL CARSON LEVINE** grew up in New York City and has been writing all her life. Her first book for children, *Ella Enchanted*, was a 1998 Newbery Honor Book. With her husband David, and their Airedale Baxter, she lives in a 200-year-old farmhouse in the Hudson River Valley.

**FRANCESCA LEWIS** read English at Cambridge. She graduated in 1995 and has worked in publishing and public relations. She has two children.

**SUE LIMB** is a writer and broadcaster specialising in comedy. She is the writer of the bestselling **Girl, 15** series. She lives in Gloucestershire in a slightly haunted cottage with

her daughter Betsy, who is an ex-teenager. Sue is a very bad cook. Her favourite animal is the toad.

**JOAN LINGARD** has written many books for young people, the best-known being the **Kevin and Sadie** series, her Ulster quintet about Catholic Kevin and Protestant Sadie in war-torn Belfast, beginning with *The Twelfth Day of July*. Her latest novel is *What to Do About Holly*.

**SAM LOWENSTEIN** likes literature, sport and music and, having passed his C.E. exams in style, is currently en route to St Paul's on a music scholarship. He lives in Hampstead with his mum, two younger brothers and a frisky black spaniel, Murphy.

**CATHERINE MACPHAIL** lives in Scotland. She always wanted to be a writer, but it was only after her children were born that she had the courage to send off her first short story. Since then she has had major success with her novels for young people. Her latest is a ghost story, *Hide and Seek*.

**MARGARET MAHY** has lived in New Zealand all her life. A hugely acclaimed author, she has won many awards, including the Carnegie Medal, twice. Her books for young adults include *The Changeover*, *Alchemy* and *Memory*.

**LOUISE MANNING** lives in London. She loves to read (obviously), anything from **Harry Potter** to *Pride and Prejudice*. She says she doesn't have a favourite book – she just loves all of them. In her free time she likes going out with her friends or going swimming at her local pool.

**JAN MARK** lived in Oxford with four cats and a houseful of books, and wrote many novels for all ages. She gave up teaching to become a full-time writer, twice winning the Carnegie Medal. Jan died at the beginning of 2006.

**GRAHAM MARKS** is an ex-graphic designer turned author. His novels include *Radio Radio*, *Zoo*, *How it Works* and, most recently, *I Spy – The Constantinople Caper*.

**BRENDA MARSHALL** is head of English and librarian at Port Regis, a prep school in Dorset. She is also the English co-ordinator for IAPS, an editor of *4–11*, the magazine of The English Association, and an independent schools' inspector.

**ROSA MATEO**, 17, was born in the Dominican Republic and is looking forward to graduating from the In-tech Academy 368. She's been a volunteer for the New York Public Library for five years and loves books.

**SUE MAYFIELD** was originally a teacher. Sue often leads workshops in schools and has been a youth worker and writing therapist. Born near Newcastle, she now lives in Cheltenham with her husband and three teenage sons.

**MEGAN MCCAFFERTY** is the *New York Times* best-selling author of *Sloppy Firsts*, *Second Helpings*, *Charmed Thirds* and *Fourth Comings*, and the editor of the short-story collection *Sixteen*. Her books have won awards from the ALA and and New York Public Library and have been translated into ten languages. For more, go to www.meganmccafferty.com

**GERALDINE MCCAUGHREAN** writes for all ages. She has won the Carnegie Medal, Guardian Children's Fiction Prize, Blue Peter Book Award, four Smarties Bronze Awards, and three Whitbread Children's Book Awards. Perhaps because she has one teenage daughter, Ailsa, she most enjoys writing for the category '12 to adult'. Her books include *A Little Lower Than the Angels*, *The White Darkness*, *The Kite Rider* and *Peter Pan in Scarlet*.

**ANTHONY MCGOWAN** is the author of two adult thrillers, *Stag Hunt* and *Mortal Coil*, and three young-adult novels, *Hellbent*, *Henry Tumour* and *The Knife That Killed Me*. He has also written **The Bare Bum Gang** series for 7–11 year olds.

**SOPHIE MCKENZIE** writes teen thrillers. Her award-winning novels include *Girl, Missing*, *Blood Ties* and *Six Steps to a Girl*. Her new book, *The Set-Up*, is about a group of teens with psychic powers – and the first in **The Medusa Project** series.

**JOHN MCLAY** is director of the Bath Festival of Children's literature and a children's books literary scout. He is also a lecturer, an anthologist and a book reviewer. He has previously worked for Puffin Books, been a children's bookseller and sold translation rights internationally.

**LIZ MCMANUS** was born in Wales, came to London to do a degree, and whilst a student secured a job as a chauffeuse during Wimbledon fortnight, driving the tennis stars around London. She stayed to teach in secondary schools around the Wimbledon area.

**ANDY MCNAB**, DCM MM, joined the army as a boy soldier and is a former member of the SAS, one of the world's elite special forces commando units. His book *Bravo Two Zero* is the best-selling war memoir of all time and launched his career as a writer. His titles for young adults include *Boy Soldier* and *Avenger*.

**CLIFF MCNISH** is a fantasy writer whose series, the **Doomspell** trilogy, won him an instant and avid readership. He has followed up this success with his **Silver** sequence and novels *Angel* and *Breathe*.

**VALERIE MENDES** knew she wanted to be a writer when she was six and her first short story was published in her school magazine. Her books include *Girl in the Attic*, *The Drowning* and *Coming of Age*.

**LIVI MICHAEL** began writing for children in 2000 when she wanted to amuse her seven-year-old son over the holidays. Among her books are the **Frank** series, *The Whispering Road*, *Sky Wolves* and, most recently, *Faerie Heart*.

**ELEANOR MILNES-SMITH** has often been described by her friends – at least the human ones – as completely insane. She has always been an avid reader of fantasy and now, aged 13, is a fan of Terry Pratchett and Christopher Paolini.

**PHILIPPA MILNES-SMITH** is a literary agent and children's specialist at the agency LAW (Lucas Alexander Whitley). She has worked for many years in children's publishing and was previously the managing director of Puffin Books.

**NICOLA MORGAN's** first novel was *Mondays Are Red*. She now writes non fiction and fiction, and has a busy schedule of school talks, festivals and conferences. Her most recent title is a thriller called *Deathwatch*.

**SAMUEL MORTIMER** lives in Devon. His hobbies include playing guitar (he's really into rock music), judo and reading.

**JOANNA NADIN** is the author of the best-selling **Rachel Riley** series, as well as several award-winning books for younger readers. She lives in Bath with her daughter.

**BEVERLEY NAIDOO** grew up in Johannesburg. As a student she joined the resistance to apartheid, ending up exiled in England. Her first book *Journey to Jo'burg* was banned in South Africa. That spurred her to keep writing! She won the Carnegie Medal for *The Other Side of Truth*.

**PATRICK NESS** was born and raised in America. He is the author of two critically acclaimed works of fiction for adults, *The Crash of Hennington* and *Topics About Which I Know Nothing*. He has also written for radio and is a literary critic for the *Guardian*. His first novel for young adults was the multi-award winning *The Knife of Never Letting Go*.

**LINDA NEWBERY** writes fiction for all ages. Her young-adult novels, *The Shell House* and *Sisterland*, were both short-listed for the Carnegie Medal. She also writes short stories and poems, and teaches writing courses for children, teenagers and adults.

**SALLY NICHOLLS** was born in Stockton, in a thunderstorm. She is the author of *Ways to Live Forever*, which won the Waterstone's Children's Book Prize 2008, and *Season of Secrets*. She now lives in a little flat in London, writing stories and trying to believe her luck.

**SARA NICKERSON** wrote for TV and film before publishing her first novel *How To Disappear Completely and Never Be Found*. When not writing, she's anxiously waiting for her two tadpoles to sprout legs.

**JENNY NIMMO** worked in the theatre before joining the BBC where she became a writer / director in children's TV. As a novelist, she has twice won the Smarties Gold Award and has written the popular **Children of the Red King** series, starting with *Midnight for Charlie Bone*.

**ANDREW NORRISS** has written and co-written some 150 episodes of sit-coms and children's drama for television. His children's books include *Aquila*, which won the Whitbread Children's Book Award. He lives in a village in Hampshire with his wife and two children.

**IAN OGILVY** is best known as an actor – in particular for the role of The Saint. He has also made a number of films and starred on the London stage. His series of popular books about Measle Stubbs begins with *Measle and the Wrathmonk*. He lives in southern California with his wife Kitty and two stepsons.

**KENNETH OPPEL** is the author of the **Airborn** series, as well as the **Silverwing** trilogy, which has sold over a million copies worldwide. He published his first novel at 17, after receiving

encouragement from Roald Dahl.

**CHARLI OSBORNE** is the head of teen services at the Oxford Public Library in Oxford, Michigan. She reviews regularly for *School Library Journal* and *Library Journal*. A former Michael L. Printz Committee Member, she is now serving her second term on the Alex Awards Committee.

**TERRI PADDOCK** is the author of one teen novel, *Come Clean*, and one adult novel, *Beware the Dwarfs*. Formerly a freelance journalist, she is now the editor of the monthly *Theatregoer Magazine* and www.whatsonstage.com.

**MELANIE PALMER** works as an editor of children's books, makes occasional appearances in furry mouse or spotted leopard outfits, and lives in North London with seven other vagabonds.

**CHRISTOPHER PAOLINI** was born in 1983, and was home-schooled by his parents in Montana. He began writing *Eragon* as a hobby, and it was originally self-published. Carl Hiaasen brought *Eragon* to his publisher's attention, and it became the first title in the **Inheritance Cycle** and was subsequently made into a film.

**PHILIPPA PEARCE** was a highly acclaimed and much-loved children's writer, whose most famous title *Tom's Midnight Garden* won the Carnegie Medal. She died in 2006.

**MAL PEET** grew up in Norfolk and escaped to read English and American Literature at Warwick University, which threw him out a year later. He spent many years drawing cartoons

while avoiding proper jobs, then settled down to write and illustrate books for children – his first novel was *Keeper*. He won the Carnegie Medal with his novel *Tamar*.

**HELENA PIELICHATY** won a bar of chocolate for writing a story when she was ten. She can't remember the story but she does remember the chocolate. Later, in Y9, she read *Jackie* magazine and was engrossed by 'Cathy and Clare's Problem Page'. Her books for young adults include *Accidental Friends* and *Saturday Girl*.

**CAROLINE PITCHER** writes stories for all ages. Her books for young adults include *Silkscreen*, *Mine* and *On the Wire*.

**ANNA POSNER** is now a university student who got to contribute to this book as she is the niece of one of the editors.

**SUSAN PRICE** was born and still lives in Dudley in the Midlands. She had her first book published when she was 16. Her novel *The Ghost Drum* won the Carnegie Medal and she won the Guardian Children's Fiction Prize for *The Sterkarm Handshake*.

**SALLY PRUE** was rubbish at writing stories at school, but as she grew up she gradually realised she couldn't do anything else, much, either. So, as writing didn't require money or qualifications, she had a go; and, after only 15 years of toil, had her first novel, *Cold Tom*, published. She lives in Hertfordshire with her husband and elder daughter.

**BALI RAI** is a fairly young and occasionally exciting author. He has written over ten books that deal with the realities of life in modern Britain for young adults / teens. He is also on a mission to convert all young people to his own religion – Liverpool FC. If you read his books backwards and upside down you will find that every sentence reads: You WILL support LFC.

**CELIA REES** writes for teenagers. Her novels include *Witch Child*, *Sorceress*, *Sovay*, and the vampire novel, *Blood Sinister*. She divides her time between writing, talking to readers in schools and libraries, acting as a tutor on creative writing courses and reviewing.

**PHILIP REEVE**'s first book for children, *Mortal Engines*, created one of the most intriguing worlds in fantasy fiction. It forms part of a series of five titles, including, most recently, a prequel called *Fever Crumb*. Other books include *Here Lies Arthur*, which won him the Carnegie Medal.

**ELIZABETH REID** has a lifelong book habit, which is becoming increasingly hard to control. Not only has she a vast knowledge of children's books from her own childhood, but now has three boys who require constant advice as to what to read next, which has introduced a whole new set of authors over whose books she can obsess.

**ANTHONY REUBEN** is a BBC business journalist and television producer. He only got to contribute to this book because he is married to one of the editors.

**JAMES REYNOLDS** is a BBC news correspondent. He has been based in South America, the Middle East, and China. In his spare time, he enjoys floating in the Dead Sea, and studying the effects of galactic trash.

**CHRIS RIDDELL** is the hugely popular and award-winning creator of **The Edge Chronicles** and the **Ottoline** books, among lots of others. He is also a political cartoonist for the *Observer*. He has a Hungarian Butler and an invisible dog.

**JAMES RIORDAN** is Emeritus Professor at the University of Surrey and a Fellow of the Royal Society for the Arts. To keep sane in the world of academia, he also writes both picture books and novels for young people of his own writing-age ability – 11–15. His books include *The Sniper* and *Sweet Clarinet*.

**KATHERINE ROBERTS** graduated from Bath University with first-class honours in mathematics, but always wanted to be a fantasy writer. Her debut novel was *Song Quest*, and ten years of working as a racehorse groom led to her Alexander epic *I Am the Great Horse*. She lives in a workhouse in Stroud.

**CATHERINE ROBINSON** has been writing books for children of all ages, from pre-school to teens, for over 20 years. Her books for teenagers include *Tin Grin*, *Fat Chance* and *Soul Sisters*.

**KATHRYN ROSS** is a former English teacher, independent bookseller and deputy director of Scottish Book Trust. She is now a partner in Fraser Ross Associates, the Edinburgh-based literary agency.

**MEG ROSOFF** won great acclaim for her first novel, *How I Live Now*, which was published in 2004. Her second book, *Just in Case*, won her the 2007 Carnegie Medal. She is also the author of *What I Was* and, most recently, *The Bride's Farewell*. An American, she lives in London with her husband and daughter.

**ALYSON RUDD** is a sports writer for *The Times* and since running *The Times* Books Group has become addicted to judging literary awards. She has published two non-fiction titles and is working on a novel.

**ROSIE RUSHTON** has had over 30 books published worldwide. From light-hearted series to more serious novels, her focus is always on the issues and conflicts facing young people today. Her titles include *Last Seen Wearing Trainers* and *Waving, Not Drowning*.

**HUGH SCOTT** is me and time past gone I found words fun like blank jigsaws for together putting with love and meanings way beyond usual; so write I did and rot a Book called *The Plant That Ate the World*, and chum book called *Freddie and the Enormouse*, and bigger tough chum book called *Why Weeps the Brogan?*, and three chums wow! publishers entered for Whitbread Prize thrill, and *Brogan* won, wow again.

**MARCUS SEDGWICK** is an award-winning author of children's books. He has worked in publishing for nearly 20 years, as bookseller, editor, publisher and in sales. His titles include *The Dark Horse*, *The Book of Dead Days* and, most recently, *Revolver*.

**DARREN SHAN** always wanted to be a writer and is now a publishing phenomenon! His **Saga of Darren Shan** and **Demonata** series are hugely popular, if not for the fainthearted…

**NICK SHARRATT** is the illustrator of Jacqueline Wilson's multi-million selling novels. He also illustrates picture books for writers like Julia Donaldson and Giles Andreae, as well as writing and illustrating his own, which include *Muddlewitch* and *Ketchup on Your Cornflakes*.

**RACHEL SHAW** is in Y9. She enjoys spending time with her friends. These are her first book reviews – and she enjoyed doing them!

**HELEN SIMMONS** works in a small independent bookshop in Bath and has specialised in children's books for most of her career. She also has a job as a school librarian and is a reviewer for Booktrust.

**NICKY SINGER**'s first novel for children, *Feather Boy*, won the Blue Peter Book Award and was made into a TV drama. Her second, *Doll*, was short-listed for the Booktrust Teenage Prize. Her other books include *The Innocent's Story* and *GemX*.

**LEMN SISSAY** is a poet whose books include *Listener*, *Rebel without Applause*, and the children's collection, *The Emperor's Watchmaker*. The *Independent* says about him, 'His name is magic, his poems are songs of the street'.

**GARETH SMITH** lives in South Wales. Like most contributors to this book, Gareth loves reading, in both English and Welsh. He was a judge for the 2004 Blue Peter Book Awards.

**JERRY SPINELLI** is especially happy when readers do more than read his books. Readers of *Stargirl*, for instance, have organised Stargirl Societies. They follow Stargirl's example in performing random acts of kindness. 'They make me proud,' says Jerry.

**PAUL STEWART** has written everything from picture books to football stories, fantasy and horror, and his collaboration with Chris Riddell on **The Edge Chronicles** has taken him to bestseller lists in both the UK and USA. Paul lives in Brighton with his wife and two children.

**JONATHAN STROUD**, the author of the best-selling **Bartimaeus** trilogy, lives in Hertfordshire with his wife, his children and two guinea pigs. His latest novel is *Heroes of the Valley*.

**WILLIAM SUTCLIFFE** was born in 1971 in London. He is the author of five novels, *New Boy*, *Are You Experienced?*, *The Love Hexagon*, *Bad Influence* and *Whatever Makes You Happy*.

**REBECCA SWIFT** is an editor, writer and director of The Literary Consultancy. Her publications include a correspondence between Bernard Shaw and Margaret Wheeler, *Letters from Margaret*. She has also published poems and has written the libretto for the opera, *Spirit Child*, with composer Jenni Roditi.

**ROBERT SWINDELLS** was born in West Yorkshire and has lived there all his life. He has been a proofreader, a clerk, an airman, a factory worker, a security guard, a bingo checker and a teacher. He has written full time since 1980. His titles include *Stone Cold*, *Room 13* and *Blitzed*.

**MARIANNE TAYLOR** lives in North London. She is the sub-editor for *Birdwatch* magazine, and also a freelance writer, artist and cartoonist. In her free time she enjoys running the occasional marathon and falling over at her Aikido club.

**ALAN TEMPERLEY** lives in Scotland and can often be found on speaking tours of Scottish schools. He has written many books including *Harry and the Wrinklies*, which was made into a TV series, and *The Magician of Samarkand*.

**KATE THOMPSON** was born in Yorkshire but lives in Ireland. She plays Irish traditional music and renovates old fiddles in her spare time. In 2005 she won the Guardian Children's Fiction Prize and the Whitbread Children's Book Award for *The New Policeman*.

**MATT THORNE** is the author of the **39 Castles** series, and six novels for adults, including *Eight Minutes Idle* and *Cherry*, which was long-listed for the Booker Prize.

**JEREMY TRAMER**, 17, lives in Santa Monica, California. He is the author of the literary works *What I Did Over Summer Vacation*, *Why Soda Should Be Allowed in the Vending Machines* and *What I Did Over Spring Break*.

**ELEANOR UPDALE**'s historical novel, *Montmorency*, won the Blue Peter Book Award for 'The Book I Couldn't Put Down'. It has three sequels. Eleanor is a patron of the Prince of Wales Arts and Kids Foundation.

**JEAN URE** had her first book published while she was still at school, and she has been writing ever since. Her many titles include the **Girlfriends** series, *Love and Kisses* and *Fortune Cookie*. She lives with her husband in a 300-year-old house in South London, with their family of four cats and seven dogs, all from rescue centres.

**JENNY VALENTINE** worked in a wholefood shop in Primrose Hill for 15 years where she met many extraordinary people and sold more organic loaves than there are words in her first novel (the award-winning *Finding Violet Park*). Jenny is married to a singer / songwriter and has two children.

**GILL VICKERY** studied fine art and painting at college, and since then has worked as a children's librarian and English teacher. She has written the novel, *The Ivy Crown*.

**JILL PATON WALSH** has been a professional writer most of her working life. She has written for children and for adults. Her award-winning titles include *The Emperor's Winding Sheet* and *Gaffer Samson's Luck*. Jill has three children and three grandchildren and lives in Cambridge.

**ARABELLA WEIR** is a comedy writer / performer. She wrote the bestseller *Does My Bum Look Big in This?* and starred in the BBC's hit comedy series, *The Fast Show*.

**SARA WHEELER** writes non-fiction books, sometimes travel narratives and sometimes biographies. She has written a travel book about the Antarctic called *Terra Incognita*, and a biography of Denys Finch Hatton, *Too Close to the Sun*.

**CHARLIE WHITESIDE** is an 11-year-old boy who likes reading, writing stories, eating cauliflower cheese and playing the guitar. He lives in London, and was

lying about the cauliflower cheese.

**SARAH ILEEN WHITSON**, 17, is from a small town in Kansas – El Dorado. She loves reading because there is so much to discover in a book. It's so different from a movie and television because you, as the reader, get to create how the characters look.

**MATT WHYMAN** is the author of several acclaimed novels, including *Boy Kills Man*, *Goldstrike* and *Inside the Cage*. He is also the editor of the Red House *Young Writers' Yearbook* and an agony uncle for numerous teen magazines.

**REBECCA WILKIE** has worked with children's books for several years – first as a bookseller, then for a literary agent and now for Booktrust, where she edits their children's book website www.booktrustchildrensbooks.org.uk.

**JEANNE WILLIS** is married with two children and lives in North London. Since 1980 she has had over 100 books published including novelty books, picture books and novels. She has won several awards and was short-listed for the Whitbread Children's Book Award for her novel, *Naked without a Hat*.

**CHRIS WOODING** travels a lot, writes a lot, and drinks enough coffee to stun a full-grown bison every day. He writes screenplays, books for children and adults, cartoon series, graphic novels, TV shows and just about anything else he can. He lives in London, beneath an ever-increasing pile of manuscripts.

**SARA ZARR** is the author of *Story of a Girl* and *Sweethearts*. *Story of a Girl* has been named a NYPL Book for the Teen Age and won the Utah Arts Council Original Writing Competition before it was published. Sara lives in Salt Lake City, Utah, with her husband.

**JONNY ZUCKER** writes for children and teenagers. His work includes the **Venus Spring – Stunt Girl** series and the **Max Flash** series. Along the way he has worked as a stand-up comedian and a primary school teacher.

# Acknowledgements

## For the first edition

We thought that the second book would be easier, and that we wouldn't need to depend on quite as much help from other people this time around. We were really very wrong indeed. The list of people to whom we owe a debt for helping to bring this book out is enormous. And still we're bound to have forgotten people – if we have, our apologies.

To begin with, we must give thanks to all those who made the first book a success – in particular to Jill Coleman who commissioned it, and to Jon Appleton who turned our chaotic manuscript into an exciting and special book; and then to Nicky Potter, Tabitha Pelly and Rebecca Caine, who made sure everyone in the press knew just how exciting and special it was…

We were lucky enough to receive awards for the first book from Blue Peter and the National Literacy Association, for which, too, we are grateful; they helped to enhance the success of the first book, but more importantly worked wonders for our morale as we trudged through the assembling of volume two.

And so to this, the UTBG. Our most important thanks must be to our contributors, whose words make up the bulk of the book. From those who wrote single exquisite entries to those who heroically took on a dozen or more (special round of applause for Eileen Armstrong here, please): your work is – of course – what makes this book what it is. We are especially pleased that our contributors to this volume include a number of teenagers; the quality of their work, their enthusiasm, their professionalism were admirable – the rest of us could learn a great deal from them. As last time, many of our contributors have generously waived their fees, which are being donated to our chosen charity, Hope and Homes for Children (www.hopeandhomes.org) – we are delighted to have been able to raise well over £2,000 from this book to help them to continue their vital and inspiring work.

Support from publishers' publicists and authors' agents has allowed us to get hold of new titles to review and contributors to review them, without which this really wouldn't have been much of a book; so thanks to them, too.

All three of us have friends and family who have helped in any number of ways with the UTBG-ing process – some of them by writing entries or making useful suggestions, others by taking us out for drinks to take our minds off the uglier aspects of our proofreading obsessions.

To Jenny Hicks for her encouragement; to Simon and Sarah and all at the Kilburn Bookshop; to Nicholas Allen and all at Arnold House School; to Noga Applebaum; to Miranda Duffy for another day spent sifting through hundreds and hundreds and hundreds of reviews sent to us by teenagers from around the country; to Sarah and David for keeping Leonie sane (not the easiest of tasks) – thanks to you all. In particular, Laura Hutchings and Anthony Reuben have shown extraordinary patience as the UTBG invaded every room of their homes and every moment of their lives – their work on the UTBG has been tireless, as has their work on other matters that have freed up the editors to get on with UTBG work when it was really their turn to do the washing-up. Laura moved house almost single-handedly on Leonie's behalf. If Anthony could possibly have carried Susan's pregnancy on her behalf, to allow her to get on with drafting her read-on suggestions, we have no doubt that he wouldn't have hesitated.

Which brings us to the latest member of the UBG team, Isaac, who very thoughtfully resisted the temptation to be born too early and throw our schedules out of kilter. His patience is more appreciated than he yet knows. In fact he turned up very efficiently a matter of hours before our deadline – before the deadline, mind, but at the last possible moment. His mother's dominant publishing gene is clearly in evidence here. And thanks, too, to David Almond who kindly agreed to write an introduction to this book, though we did all have some doubts about whether we should invite him to write it, as on the whole we don't want him to do anything with the hours in his day but write more and more books for us to be enchanted by. Leonie and Susan disagree vigorously about the merits of almost every book they discuss – David is possibly unique in earning the highest praise from both. Not forgetting the designers of the book, Helen Taylor for the insides and Terry Woodley for the cover, a massive thanks for making it all look so fantastic.

In the UBG we described our agent Philippa Milnes-Smith as the book's godmother, and we're delighted to say that as we graduated to book two she hasn't shirked that important rôle one bit. She and her assistants Helen Mulligan (last book) and Helen Norris (this book) have been more than generous with their time and thoughts, more than efficient in their work and – of course – a delight always. We do know how lucky we are to have them.

Finally to Susila Baybars and Katie Jennings at A & C Black, who bravely took on this project. Thanks so much for the huge amount of work you've put in. We three have enjoyed working with you on the *UTBG* tremendously – and just hope you have enjoyed it, too.

## For this edition

The contributions of all those mentioned above still stand, so we continue to be grateful to them all. More thanks all round. The usual 'especially' is of course our agent Philippa, for everything; and our editor Susila (this time with the valuable collaboration of Ruth Dix), who makes it all happen. Also to the designers of the book, Helen McTeer, for the insides, and Terry Woodley, for the cover, and finally to Helen Boyd for all her checking and double-checking.

For permission to reproduce copyright material in *The Ultimate Teen Book Guide*, the publisher thanks:

**Barrington Stoke** for permission to reproduce the following covers: *Bloodline* by Kevin Brooks, which appears on p. 449; *Prisoner in Alcatraz* by Theresa Breslin, which appears on p. 449; *Text Game* by Kate Cann, which appears on p. 450; *What's Your Problem?* by Bali Rai, which appears on p. 450.

**Bloomsbury Publishing Plc** for permission to reproduce the following covers: *Al Capone Does My Shirts* by Gennifer Choldenko, which appears on p. 14; *At the Sign of the Sugared Plum*, which appears on p. 349; *Girl, 15, Charming But Insane* by Sue Limb, which appears on p. 74; *The Graveyard Book* by Neil Gaiman, which appears on p. 383; *Holes* by Louis Sachar, which appears on p. 184; *The Princess Bride* by William Goldman, which appears on p. 322; *Refugee Boy* by Benjamin Zephaniah, which appears on p. 417; *Who Is Jesse Flood?* by Malachy Doyle, which appears on p. 436; *Witch Child* by Celia Rees, which appears on p. 441; *Zoo* by Graham Marks, which appears on p. 453.

**Faber and Faber Ltd** for permission to reproduce the following cover: *Walking Naked* by Alyssa Brugman, which appears on p. 421.

**HarperCollins Publishers Ltd** for permission to reproduce the following covers: *Angus, Thongs and Full-Frontal Snogging* by Louise Rennison, which appears on p. 75; *The Dice Man* by Luke Rhinehart, which appears on p. 281; *Feather Boy* by Nicky Singer, which appears on p. 130; *Homecoming* by Cynthia Voigt, which appears on p. 185; *The Lord of the Rings* by J.R.R. Tolkien, which appears on p. 242; *The Owl Service* by Alan Garner, which appears on p. 306; *Private Peaceful* by Michael Morpurgo, which appears on p. 324; *The Silmarillion* by J.R.R. Tolkien, which appears on p. 40.

**Hodder Children's Books** for permission to reproduce the following covers: *Bad Alice* by Jean Ure, which appears on p. 33; *Counting Stars* by David Almond, which appears on p. 88; *Fleshmarket* by Nicola Morgan, which appears on p. 348; *Skellig* by David Almond, which appears on p. 365.

**Little, Brown Book Group** for permission to reproduce the following covers: *I Know Why the Caged Bird Sings* by Maya Angelou, published by Virago, an imprint of Little, Brown Book Group, which appears on p. 198; *Twilight* by Stephenie Meyer, published by Atom, an imprint of Little, Brown Book Group, which appears on p. 411.

**Macmillan Children's Books** for permission to reproduce the following covers: *All American Girl* by Meg Cabot, which appears on p. 18; *Forever* by Judy Blume, which appears on p. 139; *Sugar Rush* by Julie Burchill, which appears on p. 384.

**Oni Press** for permission to reproduce the following cover: *Queen and Country Definitive Edition Vol. 1*, which appears on p. 144.

**Orion Books** for permission to reproduce the following covers: *Do Androids Dream of Electric Sheep?* by Philip K. Dick, copyright © Philip K. Dick 1968, published by Gollancz, which appears on p. 247; *Knots and Crosses* by Ian Rankin, Copyright © Ian Rankin 1987, which appears on p. 108; *My Swordhand Is Singing* by Marcus Sedgwick © Marcus Sedgwick 2006, which appears on p. 425; *Snakehead* by Ann Halam, which appears on p. 369.

**Oxford University Press** for permission to reproduce the

following covers: *The Kite Rider* by Geraldine McCaughrean, which appears on p. 227; *The Lady in the Tower* by Marie-Louise Jensen, which appears on p. 231.

**Penguin Books Ltd** for permission to reproduce the following covers: *The Big Sleep* by Raymond Chandler, which appears on p. 109; *Blue Moon* by Julia Green, which appears on p. 50; *Bridge to Terabithia* by Katherine Paterson, which appears on p. 62; *Bumface* by Morris Gleitzman, which appears on p. 448; *The Catcher in the Rye* by J.D. Salinger, which appears on p. 69; *The Chocolate War* by Robert Cormier, which appears on p. 78; *A Clockwork Orange* by Anthony Burgess, which appears on p. 82; *Deadkidsongs* by Toby Litt, which appears on p. 100; *Dizzy* by Cathy Cassidy, which appears on p. 110; *Doing It* by Melvin Burgess, which appears on p. 179; *The Great Railway Bazaar* by Paul Theroux, which appears on p. 167; *Hamlet* by William Shakespeare, which appears on p. 169; *The Hound of the Baskervilles* by Arthur Conan Doyle, which appears on p. 359; *How I Live Now* by Meg Rosoff, which appears on p. 315; *If You Come Softly* by Jacqueline Woodson, which appears on p. 197; *The Illiad* by Homer, which appears on p. 199; *Junk* by Melvin Burgess, which appears on p. 218; *Love in a Cold Climate* by Nancy Mitford, which appears on p. 245; *Maus* by Art Spiegelman, which appears on p. 258; *The Odyssey* by Homer, which appears on p. 199; *On the Road* by Jack Kerouac, which appears on p. 280; *The Outsiders* by S.E. Hinton, which appears on p. 212; *Pride and Prejudice* by Jane Austen,

which appears on p. 320; *Regeneration* by Pat Barker, which appears on p. 349; *Roll of Thunder, Hear My Cry* by Mildred D. Taylor, which appears on p. 333; *The Secret Diary of Adrian Mole Aged 13¾* by Sue Townsend, which appears on p. 347; *SilverFin* by Charlie Higson, which appears on p. 362; *The Truth About Forever* by Sarah Dessen, which appears on p. 406; *The War of the Worlds* by H.G. Wells, which appears on p. 246; *When the Wind Blows* by Raymond Briggs, which appears on p. 143; *Wuthering Heights* by Emily Brontë, which appears on p. 178.

**Piccadilly Press Ltd** for permission to reproduce the following cover: *Mates, Dates and Pulling Power* by Cathy Hopkins, Text copyright © Cathy Hopkins 2003, 2007, cover copyright © Sue Hellard, 2007, first published 2003, which appears on p. 75.

**The Random House Group Ltd** for permission to reproduce the following covers: *Birdsong* by Sebastian Faulks, which appears on p. 44; *The Boy in the Striped Pyjamas* by John Boyne, which appears on p. 55; *Catch-22* by Joseph Heller, which appears on p. 280; *The Cement Garden* by Ian McEwan, which appears on p. 314; *The Curious Incident of the Dog in the Night-Time* by Mark Haddon, which appears on p. 92; *Girls in Love* by Jacqueline Wilson, which appears on p. 74; *Good Omens* by Terry Pratchett and Neil Gaiman, which appears on p. 162; *The Gorgmenghast Trilogy* by Mervyn Peake, which appears on p. 163; *Heroes of the Valley* by Jonathan Stroud, which appears on p. 177; *Hole in My Life* by Jack Gantos, which appears on p. 213;

*I Capture the Castle* by Dodie Smith, which appears on p. 195; *Jimmy Corrigan, the Smartest Kid on Earth* by Chris Ware, which appears on p. 142; *The New Policeman* by Kate Thompson, which appears on p. 41; *Ostrich Boys* by Keith Gray, which appears on p. 300; *Pobby and Dingan* by Ben Rice, which appears on p. 316; *Rani and Sukh* by Bali Rai, which appears on p. 417; *Slaughterhouse 5* by Kurt Vonnegut, which appears on p. 246; *The Spook's Apprentice* by Joseph Delaney, which appears on p. 382; *Three Men in a Boat* by Jerome K. Jerome, which appears on p. 395; *To Kill a Mockingbird* by Harper Lee, which appears on p. 398; *Trainspotting* by Irvine Welsh, which appears on p. 281.

**Scholastic Ltd** for permission to reproduce the following covers: *Does My Head Look Big in This?* by Randa Abdel-Fattah, which appears on p. 416; *Northern Lights* by Philip Pullman, which appears on p. 314.

**Simon and Schuster Ltd** for permission to reproduce the following covers: *Gideon the Cutpurse* by Linda Buckley-Archer, which appears on p. 40; *Girl, Missing* by Sophie McKenzie, which appears on p. 156; *Tithe* by Holly Black, which appears on p. 383.

**Walker Books Ltd, London SE11 5HJ** for permission to reproduce the following covers: *The Earth, My Butt and Other Big Round Things* by Carolyn Mackler, Cover Photo © Yoshiyuki Itoh / Getty Images, which appears on p. 118; *Keeper* by Mal Peet, Cover Illustration © 2006 Phil Schramm, which appears on p. 222; *Skim* by Mariko Tamaki and illustrated by Jillian Tamaki, which appears on p. 145.

# Index